2d Edition

Essentials of
MANAGEMENT

Andrew J. DuBrin

Professor of Management
College of Business
Rochester Institute of Technology

GC63BA
PUBLISHED BY
SOUTH-WESTERN PUBLISHING CO.
CINCINNATI, OH   WEST CHICAGO, IL   DALLAS, TX   LIVERMORE, CA

COVER PHOTO: © Mitchell Funk/The Image Bank

Library of Congress Cataloging-in-Publication Data

DuBrin, Andrew J.
    Essentials of management / Andrew J. DuBrin. — 2nd ed.
      p. cm.
    Includes index.
    ISBN 0-538-80495-5
    1. Management. I. Title.
HD31.D793 1990   88-63606
658.4—dc20   CIP

4 5 6 7 8 9 D 7 6 5 4 3 2 1
Printed in the United States of America

PREFACE

Today's present and future managers place heavy demands on business schools and their instructors to provide usable knowledge. A few years back, the former president of the Academy of Management stated that these demands are increasing because "The problems out there are becoming more and more complex, unpredictable, uncertain, and sloppy." *Essentials of Management* is an attempt to meet this demand for usable knowledge by providing a comprehensive description of a select number of relevant topics relating to the practice of management.

This book is written for newcomers to the field of management and also for experienced managers seeking updated knowledge and a review of fundamentals. Based on extensive research about curriculum needs, *Essentials of Management* is designed to be used in introductory management courses, continuing education seminars, and supervision courses offered in educational and work settings. The first edition of the text was used in the study of management in such diverse programs as business schools, nursing schools, retailing programs, and hotel administration. The book can also be used as a reader for management courses that rely more heavily on lecture notes and handouts than on a formal text.

ASSUMPTIONS UNDERLYING THE BOOK

The approach to synthesizing knowledge for this book is based on five assumptions:

- A strong demand exists for practical and valid information about solutions to managerial problems. The information found in this text reflects the author's career-long orientation toward translating research findings, theory, and experience into a form both the student and the practitioner can use.

- Managers need both human relations and analytical skills to meet their day-to-day responsibilities. Although this book concentrates on the management of people, it also provides ample information about such topics as decision making, job design for high performance, and effective inventory managment.

- The study of management should emphasize a diversity of work settings including large, medium, and small and profit and not-for-profit organizations. Many students of management, for example, intend to become small-business owners. Examples and cases in this book therefore reflect a diversity of work settings.

- Effective managers and staff specialists are heavily concerned with productivity, quality, and job satisfaction. Therefore, productivity, performance, and job satisfaction are mentioned frequently throughout the text; a separate chapter on managing for quality is placed toward the end of the text.

- Introductory studies to management have become unrealistically comprehensive. Many introductory texts today are over 750 pages long, and they overwhelm the student who attempts to assimilate this knowledge in one quarter or one semester. Although the information may be valuable, students learn more when they approach a surmountable task. Toward this end, I have developed a text that I think represents the basis for a realistically sized introduction to the study of management.

FEATURES OF THE BOOK

Essentials of Management is designed to aid both student and instructor in expanding interest in and knowledge of management. The book contains the following features:

- A full page *photograph* opens each chapter to capture interest.

- Each chapter begins with *learning objectives,* which preview material to be covered.

- *"Key Terms and Phrases"* highlights the management vocabulary introduced in each chapter.

- *"Manager in Action"* and *"Organization in Action"* inserts present a portrait of how specific individuals or organizations practice an aspect of management covered in the chapter.

- Concrete, real-world *examples*, readily identified with by the reader, are found throughout the text.

- *Figures, tables, and self-examination quizzes* aid in the comprehension of textual material.

- Based on a narrative outline of the text, the *"Summary of Key Points"* pulls together the central ideas of each chapter.

- *Questions* at the end of each chapter may be used for classroom discussion and reader review.

- *Activities* at the end of each chapter will allow the reader to gain first-hand knowledge of a concept presented in the chapter.

- Two *case problems* at the end of each chapter can be used to synthesize the concepts contained in the chapter. In several instances where they are appropriate, analytical problems or self-examination quizzes are substituted for case problems.

- A list of *references* indicates the sources used by the author in developing each chapter.

- A *glossary* at the end of the book defines all key terms and key phrases (those printed in bold) as a ready reference for the reader.

CHANGES IN THE SECOND EDITION

Several changes have been incorporated into the new edition, based on our own thinking and on the suggestions of adopters, outside reviewers, and students.

- Chapter 2, "The Manager's External Environment," is new. The chapter deals with the external environment that exerts an influence on the manager's work, including social responsibility and ethics, the internationalization of business, and the movement toward lean and efficient organizations.

- The previous Chapter 2, "Managing Yourself," is now the last chapter in the text; it can therefore be readily incorporated into or excluded from the course.

- The chapter contents have been tightened. As a result, the chapters are shorter and even more manageable to beginning students.

- All chapters have been thoroughly updated. Topical subjects such as just-in-time (JIT) inventory management, robust quality, and gainsharing have been added. One-half of the cases are new.

SUPPLEMENTS

Essentials of Management is accompanied by comprehensive instructional support materials.

- *Instructor's Manual.* The instructor's manual provides resources to increase the teaching and learning value of *Essentials of Management*. An important new feature of the manual is the detailed section, "Chapter Outline and Lecture Notes." The outline and notes will be of particular value to instructors whose time budget does not allow for extensive class preparation.

  For each text chapter, the manual provides a statement of purpose and scope, outline and lecture notes, lecture topics, comments on the end-of-chapter questions and activities, responses to case questions, an experiential activity, and an examination. The examination contains twenty-five Multiple Choice questions, twenty-five True/False questions, and three Essay questions.

The manual contains answers to the comprehensive cases in the text. In addition, instructions are provided for the use of Computer-Aided Scenario Analysis (CASA). CASA is a user-friendly technique that can be used with any word-processing software. It allows the student to insert a new scenario into the case and to then re-answer the questions based on the new scenario. CASA helps to develop creative thinking and an awareness of contingencies or situational factors in making managerial decisions.

A set of transparency masters that duplicates key figures in the text is included in the manual.

● *Computer Test Package.* The examinations presented in the instructor's manual are also available on disk with the test generator program, MicroSWAT II. This versatile software package allows instructors to create new questions and edit and delete existing questions from the test bank.

● *Study Guide.* The study guide to accompany the second edition of *Essentials of Management* has been expanded and will be a real asset for your students. It was prepared by Ilona Motsiff of Trinity College in Vermont. She has included useful learning materials based on her experience in teaching introductory management to students of varied backgrounds.

For each text chapter, the *Study Guide* includes an overview; the objectives and key terms; an expanded study outline; review questions—Matching, Multiple Choice, True/False, and Fill in; short exercises and problems; and a longer exercise or case.

FRAMEWORK OF THE BOOK

This book is a blend of current and traditional topics organized around the functional (or process) approach to the study of management. The book is divided into six parts:

● Part One, "Introduction to Management," contains two chapters. Chapter 1, "The Manager's Job," explains the nature of managerial work with a particular emphasis on managing for productivity. Chapter 2, "The Manager's External Environment," describes how the external environment influences the manager's job.

● Part Two, "Planning and Decision Making," contains three chapters. Chapter 3, "Essentials of Planning," presents a general framework for planning—the activity underlying almost any purposive action taken by a manager. Chapter 4, "Problem Solving and Decision Making," explains the basics of decision making with a particular emphasis on the human element. Chapter 5, "Specialized Techniques for Planning and Decision

Making," describes several adjuncts to planning and decision making, such as break-even analysis, PERT, and production scheduling methods used in both manufacturing organizations and service organizations.

- Part Three, "Organizing," contains three chapters. Chapter 6, "Job Design and Organization Structure," explains how work is organized both from the standpoint of the individual employee and the larger organization. Chapter 7, "Delegation and Decentralization," describes the process of passing work down to subordinates and from a higher to a lower organizational unit. Chapter 8, "Staffing the Organization," explains the methods by which people are brought into the organization, trained, and evaluated. The emphasis is placed on the line manager's role in staffing, rather than on the human-resource specialist's contribution.

- Part Four, "Leading," deals directly with the manager's role in influencing subordinates. Chapter 9, "Leadership of Employees," focuses on different approaches to leadership that a manager can take and on the personal characteristics associated with leadership effectiveness. Chapter 10, "Motivating for Results," describes what managers can do to increase or sustain employee effort toward achieving work goals. Chapter 11, "Communicating with Other People," deals with the complex problem of accurately sending and receiving messages.

- Part Five, "Controlling," contains three chapters, each dealing with an important aspect of trying to keep performance in line with expectations. Chapter 12, "Essentials of Control," presents an overview of measuring and controlling performance. Chapter 13, "Managing Ineffective Performers," describes current approaches to handling substandard employees. Chapter 14, "Managing for Quality," is a capstone for the topic of managing others. It surveys the most significant measures a manager can take to enhance and sustain the quality of the goods and services offered by the firm.

- Part Six, "Managing for Personal Effectiveness," is comprised of Chapter 15, "Managing Yourself." The chapter describes how managers can make optimum use of their personal resources; it includes such topics as career-advancement techniques, improving personal productivity, and managing stress and burnout.

ACKNOWLEDGMENTS

Any project as complex as this requires a team of dedicated and talented people to see that it gets completed. I am grateful to those people. In particular, I would like to thank the following people for their helpful comments: Thelma Anderson, Northern Montana College; Brenda Britt, Fayetteville Tech Community College; B.R. Kirkland, Tarleton State University; Thomas Fiock, Southern Illinois University at Carbondale; Randall Greenwell, John Wood

Community College; Paul Hegele, Elgin Community College; Nathan Himelstein, Essex Community College; Peter Hess, Western New England College; Noel Matthews, Front Range Community College; Ilona Motsiff, Trinity College of Vermont; Joseph Platts, Miami-Dade Community College; Thomas Quirk, Webster University; and Bill Searle, Asnuntuck Community College.

I especially wish to acknowledge the contribution of Ilona Motsiff who prepared the *Study Guide* to accompany the second edition of the text. Also deserving special mention is Bernard Weinrich, St. Louis Community College, who reviewed the entire manuscript for the first edition and made a substantial number of useful suggestions.

Andrew J. DuBrin

ABOUT THE AUTHOR

Andrew J. DuBrin is Professor of Management in the College of Business at Rochester Institute of Technology, where he teaches courses and conducts research in management, organizational behavior, and career management. He received his Ph.D. in Industrial Psychology from Michigan State University.

Dr. DuBrin has prior business experience in personnel and human-resource management and is a member of a management consulting firm. As president of the Andrew J. DuBrin Group, he does consulting for organizations and individuals. His specialities include career counseling and management development.

Dr. DuBrin is also a well-known author of both textbooks and trade publications. He has written textbooks in management, organizational behavior, and human relations. His trade books cover many current issues including office politics and coping with adversity.

CONTENTS

PART THREE
Organizing

PART FIVE
Controlling

PART SIX
Managing for Personal Effectiveness

PART ONE
Introduction to Management

Chapter 1
The Manager's Job

Chapter 2
The Manager's External Environment

A logical starting point in studying management is a comprehensive look at the nature of a manager's job. Hundreds of studies have attempted to understand the nature of managerial work. Fortunately, the results from these studies are reasonably consistent. We know what competent managers do, or what they are supposed to be doing. In Chapter 1, and at various places in the book, you will be alerted to the manager's goal of maintaining high productivity and high morale. Virtually all managerial activity should be geared toward attaining these ends.

Chapter 2 deals with a topic of increasing relevance to modern managers: the external environment that influences the manager's work. Among these important environmental influences are social responsibility, ethical codes of conduct, the internationalization of business, and the quest of interested parties for lean and efficient organizations. Not all managers have the responsibility for directly dealing with these forces, yet these forces indirectly affect the jobs of most managers.

1
The Manager's Job

After studying the material in this chapter, you should be able to accomplish the following tasks:

1. Explain the meaning of the terms *manager, management,* and *organization.*
2. Describe the basic management functions and the many managerial roles.
3. Identify the basic managerial skills and understand how they can be developed.
4. Discuss management's role in enhancing productivity and morale.
5. Describe the primary schools of management thought and their approaches to studying management.

Key Terms and Phrases

Manager
Management
Operative
Specialist
Individual contributor
Executive
Middle manager
First-level manager
Line manager
Staff manager
Functional manager

General manager
Administrator
Entrepreneur
Small-business owner
Organization
Classical school of management
Behavioral school of management
Management science school
Systems approach to management
Contingency approach to
   management

Asked how she enjoyed her recent sight-seeing trip, office manager Judy Bannerstone replied, "Good and bad. On the good side, my family and I needed a vacation. Right now I feel recharged. But on the bad side, I worried a lot about the office. Nothing seems to happen when I'm away. We've got a lot of catching up to do back at work."

Bannerstone's comments point to the importance of management. Management is the force that makes things happen. It pulls together resources to get important things accomplished. A manager's job is therefore inherently exciting: a good manager makes things happen. In an address to a group of management-development specialists, Professor Leonard R. Sayles emphasized the importance of management:

> We must find ways of convincing society as a whole, and those who train managers in particular, that the real leadership problems of our institutions—the getting things done, the implementation, the evolving of a consensus, the making of the right decisions at the right time with the right people—is where the action is. Although we as a society haven't learned to give much credit to managers, I hope we can move toward recognizing that managerial and leadership jobs are among the most critical tasks of our society. As such, they deserve the professional status that we give to more traditional fields of knowledge.[1]

The importance of management to society also has been cited by Peter F. Drucker, a noted management authority. Almost twenty-five years ago, he proclaimed that effective management was becoming the main resource of developed nations, and that it was the most needed resource of developing nations.[2] His comments are still valid.

Effective managers are needed by all types of organizations. Not just business firms, but also governmental and nonprofit firms, need effective management. Consider the challenges presently facing the U.S. government. To help balance the budget, government managers will be forced to accomplish the same amount of work with smaller staffs. Hospitals, too, face the challenge of trying to maintain high-quality services while working with fewer dollars. Health maintenance organizations (HMOs) require talented health-care administrators to help them offer high-quality, but low-priced, health care.

The alternative to placing effective managers in charge of an operation is chaos. A major reason that so many small businesses fail is because they lack good management—people in charge who can get important things accomplished and tie together loose ends. Imagine planning a wedding with 200 guests, yet not placing a competent person in charge of managing the effort.

WHO IS A MANAGER AND WHAT IS MANAGEMENT?

If we accept the proposition that managerial work is relevant to society, it makes sense to define more precisely who a manager is and then to define the terms *management* and *organization*. The latter term refers to the setting in which management is practiced.

Who Is a Manager?

A manager is a person responsible for the work performance of subordinates. People who are given the job title "manager" sometimes have no subordinates reporting to them; theirs are not true management positions.

A manager has the formal authority to commit organizational resources, even if the approval of others is required. For instance, the manager of an H & R Block income-tax service outlet has the authority to order the repainting of the reception area. The income-tax specialists reporting to that manager, however, do not have the authority to have the area repainted.

⬤ Operatives are bottom-ranking employees who report to first-level supervisors. They perform the basic work of the organization. Production and clerical workers are operatives, but so are accountants.

Specialists are highly skilled workers who perform specific tasks. A specialist is an operative who has a high level of expertise, developed through education and experience. The term individual contributor sometimes is used to refer to all employees who are not managers.

What Is Management?

The concepts of manager and managing are intertwined. From Drucker's viewpoint, **management** is the specific practice that converts a mob into an effective, goal-directed, and productive group.[3] The term *management* in this book refers to the process of using organizational resources to achieve organizational objectives through the functions of planning and decision making, organizing, leading, and controlling.[4] These functions represent the broad framework for this book and will be described later. Management has three other meanings you will encounter frequently.[5]

Management as a Discipline or Field of Study.   You may be reading this book for a course in management. Management is thus a discipline with an organized body of knowledge, akin to the disciplines of journalism, criminal law, psychology, and dietetics. Note that about 25 percent of top business executives majored in management. Studying management can thus have an enormous return on investment.

Management as People.   "The thing I like most about working for IBM is management. They are all so helpful and kind." These comments indicate that "management" also refers collectively to the managers of a firm, the individuals who carry out the process of management.

Management as a Career.   Many organizations recruit graduates of business and hotel-administration programs by offering them the opportunity for a career in management. Successful candidates for management-training programs look forward to a career in management—a long series of related jobs progressively leading to more responsibility as the candidates exhibit more managerial competence.

Levels of Management

Another way of understanding the nature of a manager's job is to examine the three levels of management, as shown in Figure 1-1. The pyramid shape of this

Figure 1-1   Managerial Levels and Sample Job Titles

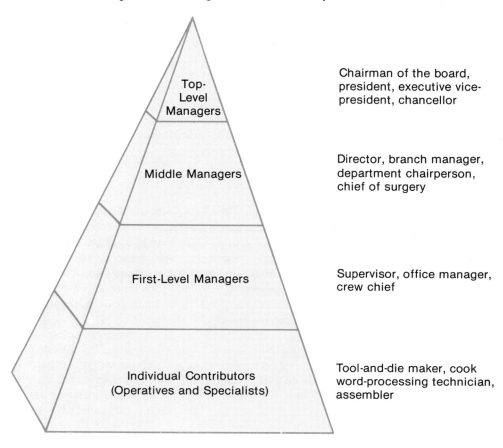

Top-Level Managers	Chairman of the board, president, executive vice-president, chancellor
Middle Managers	Director, branch manager, department chairperson, chief of surgery
First-Level Managers	Supervisor, office manager, crew chief
Individual Contributors (Operatives and Specialists)	Tool-and-die maker, cook word-processing technician, assembler

Note: Some individual contributors, such as financial analysts and administrative assistants, report directly to top-level managers or middle managers.

figure indicates that there are progressively fewer employees at each higher managerial level. The largest number of people is found at the bottom organizational level. (Note that the term *organizational level* is sometimes more precise than the term *managerial level*, particularly at the bottom level, which has no managers.)

Top-Level Managers. Most people who enter the field of management aspire to become executives—managers at the top one or two levels in an organization who are empowered to make major decisions affecting the present and future of the firm. Only an executive, for example, would have the authority to purchase another company, initiate a new product line, or hire hundreds of employees. **Top level managers** are the people who give the organization its general direction; they decide where it is going and how it will get there.

In popular terminology, a wide range of managers are referred to as executives. From the standpoint of the formal study of management, however, only the highest managers in any organization are truly executives. This is bad news for many highly ambitious people, because less than 1 percent of people in an organization make it to the highest level of decision making.[6]

Those 1 percent of employees who do make it to the top are well paid in both large and small organizations. The average total compensation for presidents of companies of all sizes is approximately $140,000 per year (in 1990 U.S. dollars). Here are four illustrative compensation figures (1987 salary, plus bonus, plus long-term compensation) for the 25 highest-paid executives of major business corporations:[7]

- Lee A. Iacocca, Chairman, Chrysler Corp.—$17,896,000

- Paul Fireman, Chairman, Reebok International Ltd.—$15,424,000

- John H. Bryan, Jr., Chairman, Sara Lee Corp.—$5,788,000

- August A. Busch III, Chairman, Anheuser-Busch Inc.—$7,980,000

Middle Managers. **Middle managers** are those managers who are neither executives nor first-level supervisors. They conduct most of the coordination activities within the firm, and they disseminate information to upper and lower levels. Middle managers vary substantially in responsibility and income. A branch manager in a large firm might be responsible for over 100 subordinates and be paid more than $140,000 per year. In contrast, a general supervisor in a small manufacturing firm might have 20 subordinates and earn $40,000 per year. A typical salary for a middle manager in business is approximately $60,000 per year (in 1990 U.S. dollars).

Theoretically, all middle managers have first-level managers reporting to them, because middle managers are situated in the second organizational level. In practice, organizations are not laid out in a consistent design. A middle manager, for example, may have the job title Manager of Human Resources. Although the people reporting to this manager are individual contributors (such as employment interviewers), the person is classified as a middle manager because of his or her pay level and professional status.

A traditional task of the middle manager is to process and disseminate information. For instance, the middle manager might speak to supervisors and clerks about inventory problems, prepare a report, and then pass this information up to top-level management. The widespread computerization of information has lessened the need for middle managers to perform this type of task, leading to a decrease in the number of middle-management positions available. We will discuss this topic later in the chapter.

First-Level Managers. Managers who supervise operatives are referred to as **first-level managers,** or first-line managers. We choose the term *first-level manager* because it is generic, whereas the term *first-line manager* has the connotation of supervising an assembly line. Traditionally, first-level managers were promoted from production or clerical positions into supervisory positions, and they rarely had formal education beyond high school. A dramatic shift has taken place in recent years. Many of today's supervisors are business-school graduates who are familiar with modern management techniques. The current emphasis on productivity and quality has elevated the status of many supervisors.

Management experts agree that the first-level supervisor's role will change radically in the future. The president of a consulting firm observes: "Supervisors aren't going to control people anymore. They [will] have to coach them, help them do the planning, approve their organizational direction, and make sure their directions are clear. It will be an enabling function rather than a control function." [8]

To understand the work performed by first-level supervisors, reflect back on your first organizational job. The majority of entry-level positions report to a first-level supervisor, among whom would be the following: supervisor of newspaper carriers, dining room manager, service station manager, maintenance supervisor, accounts payable supervisor, and department manager in a retail store. First-level supervisors help shape the attitudes of new employees toward the firm. Newcomers to the firm who like and respect their supervisors tend to stay with the firm longer. Conversely, new workers who dislike and disrespect their first supervisor tend to leave the firm early.

The salaries (in 1990 U.S. dollars) of first-level supervisors range from about $19,000 (for example, the supervisor of a produce department in a supermarket) to $49,000 (for example, a veteran production supervisor in an automotive plant). A typical starting salary for a supervisor with a business degree would be $25,000 per year. Starting salaries are influenced substantially by such factors as the specific industry, the particular firm in that industry, and the local cost of living. For example, a library supervisor in Jacksonville, Florida can anticipate a much lower starting salary than that of a canning supervisor at a food-processing company in Honolulu, Hawaii.

TYPES OF MANAGERS

Our discussion has focused on managerial jobs at different levels in the organization. Another way of understanding the manager's function is to describe different types of management jobs. One logical and convenient classification of management jobs is: line and staff managers, functional and general managers, administrators, entrepreneurs, and small-business owners.

Line and Staff Managers

Managers who are responsible for people involved with the primary purpose (or output) of the firm are referred to as **line managers.** In a bank, people who supervise work related to borrowing and lending money are line managers. In a municipal government, people who supervise the work of welfare departments are line managers, as are the people who supervise the work of highway construction departments.

Staff managers are responsible for the activity of employees who give advice or provide services to other departments within the firm. Staff managers in a manufacturing company include the managers of human resource (personnel), legal services, and information system departments. Note that managers are designated as line managers or staff managers on the basis of how closely their activities are tied to the primary purpose of the organization. The activity itself is not the reason why a job is classified as line versus staff.

Figure 1-2 presents another perspective on the relationship between the line and staff organizations. Together they account for the total organization—the entire rectangle in Figure 1-2. The fundamental difference between the line and staff organizations relates to output. The line organization delivers its output, such as goods and services, to clients and customers. Staff organizations, however, deliver their output, such as ideas and advice, to the line organization. Another important difference depicted in Figure 1-2 is that the line organization is almost always larger than the staff organization.

An example is in order. Assume that Shirley Levin is the manager of the information systems department in a manufacturing company. She is responsible for seeing that managers and individual contributors throughout the firm receive timely and relevant information. One service provided by her department, for example, is keeping the marketing department informed of the prices of competitive products. Levin decides she would enjoy the challenge of working as a line manager, yet she does not wish to leave the information-systems field. By the simple expedient of joining a consulting firm that provides information-systems services to small businesses, Levin becomes a line manager. Her new job title is Manager, Small-Business Systems. Levin is performing similar work, but she is now involved with the primary output of her new firm—consulting services to small firms. Information systems were not

Figure 1-2   The Line and Staff Organizations

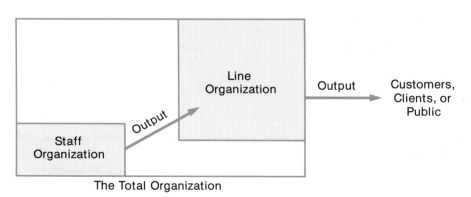

The Total Organization

the primary output of her previous firm, which manufactures industrial pumps.

The distinction between line and staff managers and between line and staff groups is sometimes blurred. Occasionally, staff managers have so much power that they function almost as line managers. For example, the top financial manager in a manufacturing company could be considered a staff manager because he or she is not engaged in manufacturing. Because so many manufacturing decisions are tied to money, however, the financial manager may be able to overrule some suggestions of line managers.

Functional Managers and General Managers

Another way of classifying managers is to distinguish between those who manage people engaged primarily in one type of specialized work and those who supervise the work of people engaged in different specialties. Functional managers supervise the work of employees engaged in specialized activities, such as accounting, engineering, quality control, food preparation, marketing, sales, and telephone installation. A functional manager is a manager of specialists and of their administrative and clerical support. Students who aspire to a career in management, yet acquire specific training—such as robotics technology—usually assume that they eventually will become functional managers. A logical goal would be to become the manager of robotics or of manufacturing technical services.

General managers are responsible for the work of several different groups performing a variety of functions. The frequently used job title Plant General Manager offers insight into the meaning of general management. Reporting to the Plant General Manager are a number of departments engaged in both specialized and generalized work, such as plant manufacturing, plant engineering, labor relations, quality control, safety, and warehousing. Company presidents are general managers. Branch managers also are general managers if they have different disciplines reporting to them.

Figure 1-3 portrays a segment of the organization chart of a typical large hotel. The management positions are classified by whether they are line or staff, or functional or general. The banquets manager and the guest rooms manager are classified as general managers because a wide mixture of operatives and specialists report to them. To illustrate, the banquet manager's subordinates include chefs, dishwashers, waiters, bartenders, and sales representatives.

Administrators

An administrator is a manager who works in public (government) or nonprofit organizations rather than in business firms. Among these managerial positions are hospital administrator, city administrator, and housing administrator. Managers in all types of educational institutions are referred to as administrators. One point of confusion is that some individual contributors in

Figure 1-3 A Segment of the Organization Chart for a Large Hotel

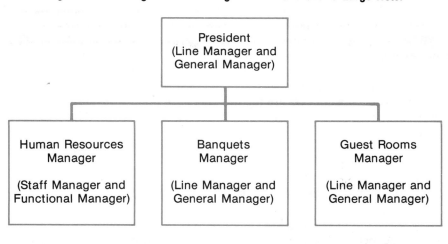

nonprofit organizations are referred to as administrators even though they supervise no one.

Entrepreneurs

The dream of many students and employees is to turn an exciting idea into a successful business. Many people think, "If Tom Monaghan started Domino's Pizza from scratch and is a multimillionaire today, why can't I think of a useful business idea?" Success stories such as Monaghan's kindle the entrepreneurial spirit of many people. Once the founder of an innovative business launches and develops the business into something bigger than he or she can handle alone, that person becomes a general manager.

Successful entrepreneurs usually are highly enthusiastic people who take sensible risks and devote extraordinary energy to launching and managing their enterprise.[9] We will say more about entrepreneurs in Chapter 9, "Leadership of Employees." For now, note that entrepreneurs contribute innovative thinking to society; they do not merely start small businesses.

The hotel depicted in Figure 1-3 uses the services of at least one entrepreneur as an adjunct to its formal organization structure. A small firm, Hotel Marketing, founded by Jeff Weinstein, was hired to help the hotel develop a plan for obtaining a bigger share of the banquet business in its area. One reason a firm uses consulting services is so it can hire expert help only as needed. If Weinstein and his employees all worked exclusively for one hotel, the result would be permanent expense for the hotel and not enough work for Weinstein. As consultants, Weinstein and his coworkers provide specialized services to a number of hotels.

Small-Business Owner

Similar to an entrepreneur, the owner and operator of a small business becomes a manager when the firm grows beyond several employees. **Small-business owners** typically invest considerable emotional and physical energy in their firms. The hotel in Figure 1-3 is served by a number of small businesses. One of them is Garcia Restaurant Suppliers, a firm founded by Carla Garcia, an enterprising woman who entered the work force after raising four children.

Note that entrepreneurs are (or started as) small-business owners, but that the reverse is not necessarily true. You need an innovative idea to be an entrepreneur.

WHAT IS AN ORGANIZATION?

Every society is dependent on organizations to accomplish its goals. Even prehistoric people banded together to hunt, fish, and defend themselves against alien groups. Almost every product you consume and every service you use is available because of the collective effort of two or more people. Organizations accomplish things, and they have a purpose. An organization is a group of two or more people working together as agreed to attain a set of goals. A major justification for hiring managers is that they help members of the organization achieve collective effort. The organization is the setting in which a manager practices management; there is no opportunity to practice management when the efforts of only one person are involved.

One point of confusion about the use of the term *organization* relates to the size of the entity involved. Most people who study management think of an organization as the total firm or as a sizeable unit of that firm. We refer to the giant publishing firm of McGraw-Hill as the organization and to one of its major units, *Business Week,* as a division or subunit. However, an editor at the magazine probably would be referring to *Business Week* when she said "my organization."

As you have probably already observed, our discussion of organizations is not restricted to large business firms, or "Fortune 500" companies. Throughout the text, we will provide examples and cases drawn from large and small private, public, and nonprofit organizations.

THE PROCESS OF MANAGEMENT

A helpful approach to understanding what managers do is to regard their work as a process, or a series of actions, that brings about something such as making a profit or providing a service. To achieve that objective, the manager uses resources and carries out four major managerial functions, as depicted in Figure 1-4: planning and decision making, organizing, leading, and controlling.

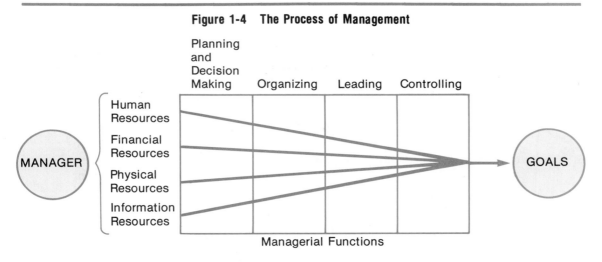

Figure 1-4   The Process of Management

Source: Griffen, Ricky W. *Management*, Second Edition. Copyright © 1987 by Houghton Mifflin Company.
Used with permission.

Resources Used by Managers

Managers use resources to accomplish their purposes, just as a carpenter uses resources to build a porch. These resources can be divided into four types: human, financial, physical, and informational.

Human Resources.   Human resources are the employees needed to get the job done. Managers' goals influence which employees they choose. Carla Garcia has the goal of delivering quality food to her hotel customers. Among the human resources she chooses are order clerks, truck drivers, and a part-time bookkeeper. The human resources chosen by the Secretary of Health and Human Services, to achieve the mission of that huge federal government agency, are much more varied.

Financial Resources.   The money that the manager and the organization use to reach organizational goals is a financial resource. A business organization relies on profits and investments from stockholders. Occasionally, a business must borrow cash to meet payroll or to pay for supplies. For instance, when Jeff Weinstein began his hotel-consulting business, he had to borrow money from his father-in-law to pay his first three months' rent. Community agencies fund the path to their goals through tax revenues, charitable contributions, and government grants.

Physical Resources.   Physical resources are a firm's tangible goods and real estate, including raw materials, office space, production facilities, office equipment, and vehicles. Most large organizations use hundreds of vendors to supply them with the physical resources they need to achieve organizational goals.

Information Resources.   The data that the manager and the organization use to get the job done are information resources. For example, in order to supply leads to the firm's sales representatives, the sales manager of an office-supply company might read local business newspapers to learn which new firms are coming to town. The manager of a successful consulting firm was asked how his firm developed so much new business. His response illustrates the effective use of information resources: "Each month I read a free government bulletin that describes what studies the government would like conducted. We bid on anything we think we can handle. We've gotten so good at writing government proposals that we have all the business we need."

The Four Major Managerial Functions

The central theme of Figure 1-4 is to use the four major resources in a way that goals are reached. To accomplish this feat, the manager relies on the functions of planning and decision making, organizing, leading, and controlling.[10]

Planning and Decision Making.   Planning and decision making involve setting goals and figuring out ways of reaching them. Planning is considered to be the central function of management, and it pervades everything a manager does. Planning looks to the future, saying, "Here is what we want to achieve, and here is how we are going to do it." Decision making enters the picture because choices have to be made along the way to reaching plans. For example, Carla Garcia at one time set up a goal of selling $20,000 of food to hotels each month. As the end of one month approached, she was $2,000 short of reaching her goal. A small hotel called in a $2,000 order, but asked for credit because they had no cash available. Garcia had an important decision to make. If she extended the credit and the hotel did pay, she would achieve her financial objective for the month. If she extended credit and the hotel did not pay, she would lose all her profit for the month. Garcia did extend the credit, and the small hotel was only one week late in making the payment. Garcia made the right decision!

Organizing.   Organizing is the process of making sure there are available the human and physical resources necessary to carry out a plan, thereby achieving organizational goals. Organizing also involves assigning activities, dividing the work into specific jobs and tasks, and specifying authority relationships among groups and among individuals. Another major aspect of organizing is to group activities into departments or some other logical subdivisions. The activities of a firm often are divided into departments, such as production and marketing, or territories, such as north and south.

Leading.   Leading is the managerial function of influencing others to achieve organizational objectives. It involves dozens of interpersonal processes, which we will describe in this text, such as motivating, communicating, coaching, and showing subordinates how they can reach their goals. Leadership is such an important part of management that management is sometimes defined as "accomplishing results through people."

Leading involves influencing people, and it requires many different actions by the manager.[11] A typical act of leadership would be for a middle manager to praise a subordinate who has done an exceptional job. "Chewing out" a subordinate also is an example of leadership behavior.

Controlling.   Controlling is the managerial function of ensuring that performance conforms to plans. It is the comparing of actual performance to a predetermined standard. If there is a significant difference between actual and desired performance, the manager takes some corrective action. An example would be increasing advertising to boost below-anticipated sales.

The large-scale use of computerized information has contributed to the complexity of the control process. There is now much more information available to help measure deviations from performance. The vice-president of the human resources department at a pharmaceutical firm explains how she uses one form of computerized control: "Each week my office receives a company-wide report that includes absenteeism figures from all our plants. If the rate is too high or too low at one plant, we investigate the situation. Too high an absenteeism rate could mean that management is leaning too heavily on employees. When the absenteeism rate is too low, it could mean that work at the plant is too easy. The employees could be under so little pressure that they hardly ever need to escape the work setting."

Managerial Functions at the Three Levels of Management

One important way in which the jobs of managers differ is in the relative amount of time they spend on planning and decision making, organizing, leading, and controlling. The influence of management level on the amount of time invested in the four major managerial functions is shown in Figure 1-5.

Top-level managers spend the most time in various forms of planning and the least time in leading subordinates. The highest level of planning involves preparing a mission statement, a description of the unique purpose of a firm and it products and services.[12] Person-to-person leadership is not so critical for executives because their immediate subordinates tend to be well paid and well motivated. However, top-level managers should be able to influence people from a distance by such means as making speeches and walking around the organization.

First-level managers spend the most time in leading subordinates and the least time in planning activities because they have to deal with the problems of employees on a daily basis, which includes listening to personal problems, giving technical advice, and resolving disputes. First-level managers usually are not required to do much planning, and much of their planning is short-range, perhaps for the day, the week, or the month.

Another important point illustrated in Figure 1-5 is that managers at all three levels spend about the same amount of time organizing. The type of organizing carried out by the different levels of managers, however, is not necessarily the same. For example, a top executive might decide whether the company should buy an existing plant or build a new one. In contrast, a middle manager might help a subordinate design a job for improved efficiency.

A model such as the one in Figure 1-5 is a stereotype that does not take into account individual differences. For example, a cautious manager at any level would tend to emphasize controlling more than the other managerial functions. A warm, people-oriented manager at any level would look for opportunities to lead.

THE 17 MANAGERIAL ROLES

To further understand the manager's job, it is worthwhile to examine the various roles fulfilled by managers. A role in this sense is an expected set of activities or behaviors stemming from one's job. Mintzberg has conducted several landmark studies of managerial roles.[13] His findings have been included in and extended by the research of Graham and Mihal.[14] We have grouped the roles delineated by these researchers under the major leadership functions they most nearly fit. Roles and functions are quite close; they are both activities carried out by people. Our description of these 17 roles should help you appreciate the richness and complexity of managerial work.

Planning

The researchers identified two managerial roles that fit in the planning function, the strategic planner and the operational planner.

Figure 1-5   The Relative Amount of Time Spent on the Four Management Functions by the Three Different Levels of Manager

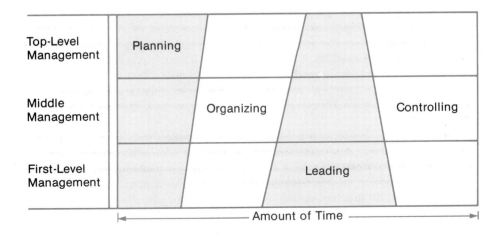

1. *Strategic Planner.* Top-level managers engage in strategic planning. Specific activities in this role include *(a)* developing long-range plans and priorities for one's department; *(b)* contributing to long-range plans for the total organization; and *(c)* helping to develop corporate policies.

2. *Operational Planner.* Operational plans relate to the day-by-day operation of the company or unit. Two such activities are *(a)* formulating operating budgets and *(b)* developing work schedules for the unit supervised by the manager. Middle managers are heavily involved in operational planning; lower-level managers are involved to a lesser extent.

Organizing

Five roles fit well under the organizing function.

3. *Organizer.* As a pure organizer, the manager engages in activities such as *(a)* designing jobs of subordinates; *(b)* clarifying assignments to subordinates; *(c)* explaining organizational policies, rules, and procedures to subordinates; and *(d)* establishing policies, rules, and procedures to coordinate the flow of work and information within the unit.

4. *Liaison.* The purpose of the liaison role is to develop and maintain a network of work-related contacts with people. To achieve this end, the manager does such things as *(a)* cultivating relationships with clients or customers; *(b)* maintaining relationships with suppliers, customers and other persons or groups important to the unit or organization; *(c)* joining boards, organizations, or clubs or doing public-service work that might provide useful, work-related contacts; and *(d)* cultivating and maintaining a personal network of in-house contacts through visits, telephone calls, and participation in company-sponsored events.

5. *Staffing.* In the staffing role, the manager tries to make sure that positions are filled with competent people. Also referred to as the employer role, its specific activities include *(a)* recruiting and hiring staff; *(b)* explaining to subordinates how their work performance will be evaluated; *(c)* formally evaluating subordinates' overall job performance; *(d)* compensating subordinates within the limits of organizational policy; *(e)* ensuring that subordinates are properly trained; *(f)* promoting subordinates or recommending them for promotion; and *(g)* terminating or demoting subordinates.

6. *Resource Allocator.* An important part of a manager's job is to divide resources in a manner that best helps the organization. Specific activities here include *(a)* authorizing the use of physical resources (facilities, furnishings, and equipment); *(b)* authorizing the expenditure of financial resources; and *(c)* discontinuing the use of unnecessary, inappropriate, or ineffective equipment or services.

7. *Task Delegator.* A standard part of any manager's job is to pass down assignments to subordinates. Among these task-delegation activities are *(a)* assigning subordinates projects or tasks; *(b)* clarifying priorities and performance standards for task completion; and *(c)* ensuring that subordinates are properly committed to effective task performance. (The task delegator role could be considered a part of the organizer role.)

Leading

Leading is a complex activity, so it is not surprising that the researchers identified eight roles that can be classified as part of the leadership function.

8. *Figurehead.* Managers, particularly high-ranking ones, spend some part of their time engaging in ceremonial activities, or acting as a figurehead. Four specific behaviors are *(a)* entertaining clients or customers as an official representative of the organization; *(b)* making oneself available to outsiders as a representative person in charge of the organization; *(c)* serving as an official representative of the organization at gatherings outside the organization; and *(d)* escorting official visitors.

9. *Spokesperson.* When a manager acts as a spokesperson, the emphasis is on answering letters or inquiries and formally reporting to individuals and groups outside the manager's direct organizational unit. As a spokesperson, the manager keeps five groups of people informed about the unit's activities, plans, and capabilities. These groups are *(a)* upper-level management; *(b)* clients or customers; *(c)* other important outsiders (such as labor unions); *(d)* professional colleagues; and *(e)* the general public. It is usually top-level managers who keep outside groups informed.

10. *Negotiator.* Part of almost any manager's job is trying to make deals with others for needed resources. Three specific negotiating activities are *(a)* bargaining with superiors for funds, facilities, equipment, or other forms of support; *(b)* bargaining with other units in the organization for the use of staff, facilities, equipment, or other forms of support; and *(c)* bargaining with suppliers and vendors for services, schedules, and delivery times.

11. *Coach.* An effective leader takes the time to coach subordinates. Specific behaviors in this role include *(a)* informally recognizing subordinates' achievements; *(b)* providing subordinates with feedback concerning ineffective performance; and *(c)* ensuring that subordinates know about steps that can improve their performance.

12. *Team Builder.* Today, much emphasis is placed on the leader building an effective team. Activities contributing to this role include *(a)* ensuring that subordinates are recognized for their accomplishments, such as through letters of appreciation; *(b)* initiating activities that contribute to group morale, such as giving parties and sponsoring sports teams; and

(c) holding periodic staff meetings to encourage subordinates to talk about their accomplishments, problems, and concerns.

13. *Team Player*. Related to the team-builder role is that of the team player. Three such behaviors are (a) displaying appropriate personal conduct (or decorum); (b) cooperating with other units in the organization; and (c) displaying loyalty to superiors by fully supporting their plans and decisions.

14. *Technical Problem Solver*. It is particularly important for first-level and middle managers to help subordinates solve technical problems. Two such specific activities are (a) serving as a technical expert or advisor and (b) performing individual contributor tasks on a regular basis, such as making sales calls or repairing machinery.

15. *Entrepreneur*. Although not self-employed, managers who work in large organizations have some responsibility for suggesting innovative ideas or furthering the business aspects of the firm. Three entrepreneurial role activities are (a) reading trade publications and professional journals to keep up with what is happening in the industry and the profession; (b) talking with customers or others in the organization to keep aware of changing needs and requirements; and (c) getting involved in situations outside the unit that could suggest ways of improving the unit's performance, such as visiting other firms, attending professional meetings or trade shows, and participating in educational programs. The accompanying "Manager In Action" illustrates the entrepreneurial function of corporate executive.

MANAGER IN ACTION:

Ellen Marram, Margarine Warrior

Ellen Marram, president of the Grocery Division of Nabisco Brands, Inc., holds a bachelor's degree from Wellesley and an MBA from Harvard. Several years ago she was named president of her division, which manufactures a group of eight product categories from cereal to margarine. Her major assignment was to lead eight vice-presidents (Marketing, Business Development, Finance, Manufacturing, Information Systems, Quality Assurance, Personnel, and Research and Development). Marram faced a challenge from Lever Brothers Co.—Promise margarine posed a threat to her company's Fleischmann's margarine, a 28-year-old, no-cholesterol product.

Marram was assigned the task of launching a counterattack which would need a multimillion-dollar budget. To obtain this money, she would have to divert money from other products. Marram said, "It was a big risk because we didn't know if our investment would pay off." To increase sales, she conceived a new ad campaign. "We wanted to talk about heart disease," she said. "But do you go all the way to someone who's had a heart attack or to someone who's worried about having one?"

Marram made a decision and the result was a powerful commercial: "I'm not an actor. I'm just a guy, 30 years old, who had a heart attack.... Fleischmann's margarine, ask your doctor." She also shared Nabisco's sales analysis of margarine brands with supermarkets, winning the goodwill of their management. They used the information to stock margarine more efficiently. In addition, Marram calibrated Fleischmann's promotional programs to regional markets. The result of Marram's strategies was a 15 percent growth in Fleischmann's sales, thus holding onto its lead.

Source: As reported in Laurie Baum, "Corporate Women: They're About to Break Through to the Top," *Business Week* (22 June 1987): 72–75.

Controlling

One role identified by the researchers fits the controlling function precisely. It is called *monitoring,* a term often used as a synonym for controlling. The *disturbance handler* role is placed under controlling because it involves bringing an unacceptable condition back to a stable condition.

16.   *Monitor.* The activities in the monitor role are *(a)* developing systems that measure or monitor the unit's overall performance; *(b)* monitoring the output of management information systems, such as productivity and cost measures; *(c)* talking with subordinates about progress on assigned tasks; and *(d)* monitoring the use of equipment and facilities assigned to the unit (for example, telephones and office space) to ensure that they are properly used and maintained.

17.   *Disturbance Handler.* Although we have placed the disturbance-handler role under the controlling function, it could be part of the leadership function. (Any method of classifying managerial activities results in some overlap because managers usually carry out more than one function simultaneously.) Four such activities are *(a)* participating in resolving formal grievances with the unit, such as working out a problem with a representative of a labor union; *(b)* resolving complaints from customers, other units, subordinates, and superiors; *(c)* resolving conflicts among subordinates; and *(d)* resolving work-flow and information-exchange problems with other units.

   To help you visualize an executive carrying out some of these roles, the accompanying "Manager in Action" presents a description of John Roach, the president of the company that operates Radio Shack stores. As you read the excerpt, try to identify Roach's various managerial roles.

MANAGER IN ACTION:

John V. Roach, Computer-Age Trail Boss

John Vinson Roach hates that familiar, frustrating game of "telephone tag": call, leave a message, wait for an answer, and miss the return call. So the president, chairman, and chief executive officer of Tandy Corp. has implemented his own solution; he answers the telephone himself.

"If you're going to have an open-door policy, you can't inhibit it by not answering the telephone," Roach says. "The employees know I'm always there." Then he grins and adds, "You find out things in different ways. Customers may just let you in on something your management people aren't exactly eager to tell you."

One day Roach took a call from a man seeking to market a new electronic device he had designed. Roach listened to the proposal with interest and made plans to follow up. "You get an occasional person who has a unique concept or has done some outstanding engineering," he explains. "And that's the business we're in—distributing the products of technology."

Roach works literally above the store, on the nineteenth floor of Tandy Center in downtown Fort Worth. There is no campus-think-tank-style headquarters for this $2 billion outfit. Roach stresses that the Tandy Radio Shack retailer "brings technology from the lab to the living room." He and his management team take the pulse of their business from the company's store downstairs.

Tandy does generate a wealth of computerized data for its own use. Ten thousand profit-and-loss statements appear each month and, according to Roach, nearly all that information is designed to reflect the performance of individual Tandy managers. No trend—a hot new product, a faltering outlet, or least of all the person responsible—goes unnoticed for long in the chairman's office.

Thousands of monthly profit-and-loss statements flowing into Tandy Center are disseminated throughout the company. They offer employees the opportunity to compile their own records of achievement, which will be noticed. Radio Shack store managers depend on the profit-and-loss statements to set their income levels; store managers are compensated in direct relation to store profits. For example, when a new regional manager must be chosen from among several hundred district managers, the company first runs a computer sort of each district manager's profit-and-loss results.

Roach may speak about a team spirit at the top of Tandy Center, but there's no doubt about the identity of the head coach. He says, "We have common goals and a game plan, and we've got a tradition of being winners. That's the way we think. That's the way we tackle problems."

Talking about his career with the company, Roach says, "I went into manufacturing without any experience in that sort of thing." What he did have, though, was a scientific background gained as a mathematics and physics major at Texas Christian University and an ability to hold the line on costs. He claims a lifelong instinct to guard the budget. "I'm so tight I could hardly bear to put a nickel in a jukebox when I was young," he admits.

Roach explains his angle: "It was hard for traditional computer manufacturers and their development people, who are so driven from a technological standpoint, to conceive that people would buy a no-frills machine. Radio Shack people are good at translating from what technology does to what a customer wants to buy, and to what that customer will pay for it."

Source: Adapted and excerpted with permission from Warren Kalbacker, "Computer-Age Trail Boss," *Success* (September 1983): 15–80, 50.

The Influence of Management Level on Managerial Roles

As mentioned at various places in our description of 17 managerial roles, a manager's level of responsibility influences which roles he or she is likely to engage in most frequently. This is illustrated in Figure 1-5, which indicates that managers' levels of responsibility influence which functions they emphasize. Recall that roles are really subsets of functions; therefore, your level of management responsibility (top, middle, bottom) helps determine which roles you emphasize.

Documentation about the influence of level on roles comes from research conducted with 228 managers in a wide variety of private-sector service firms (such as a bank or an insurance company) and manufacturing firms.[15] The roles studied were basically those described. One clear-cut finding was that, at the higher levels of management, four roles were the most important: liaison, spokesperson, figurehead, and strategic planner. Another finding was that the leader role is very important at the first level of management.

MANAGERIAL SKILLS

To be effective, managers need to possess technical, human, conceptual, diagnostic, and political skills. The first three skills have long been accepted as important for management; the last two have received more recent attention.[16]

The Five Skills

We will first define these skills and look at their relative importance at the three management levels, then we will comment on how they are developed.

Technical Skill.   As used here, technical skill involves an understanding of and proficiency in a specific activity that involves methods, processes, procedures, or techniques. Possible technical skills of a manager include the ability to prepare a budget, use a video-tape machine, lay out a production schedule, or program a computer. To rise into management positions, individual contributors usually must have some well-developed technical skill. For example, Lee Iacocca launched his career by being a competent engineer.

Human Skill.   In this context, human skill is the manager's ability to work effectively as a team member and to build cooperative effort in the unit. Technical skill deals primarily with things; human skill deals primarily with people. Many chapters in this book discuss human skills. The vast overwhelming majority of managers and individual contributors perceive themselves to possess superior skills in dealing with people. What is your self-evaluation?

Communication skills are an important component of human skills. They form the basis for sending and receiving messages on the job. Four different types of communication skills are important for managers. Speaking and writing skills are of obvious importance. A listening skill is also important. The fourth communication skill involves sending messages to people without using language, this is referred to as nonverbal communication.

Conceptual Skill.   Conceptual skill is the ability to see the organization as a total entity. "It includes recognizing how the various functions of the organization depend on one another, and how changes in any one part affect all the others; and it extends to visualizing the relationship of the individual business to the industry, the community, and the political, social, and economic forces of the nation as a whole."[17] Conceptual skill is particularly needed at top-level management because executive managers have the most contact with the outside world.

Diagnostic Skill.   Managers frequently are called on to investigate a problem and then to decide on and implement a remedial course of action. Diagnostic skills overlap with other skills because the managers need to use technical, human, conceptual, or political skills to solve the problems they diagnose. Much of the potential excitement in a manager's job centers on getting to the root of problems and recommending solutions. An illustration of the importance of diagnostic skill for managers took place at a newly opened restaurant. An embarrassingly low number of customers arrived, despite a beautiful decor, good food, and moderate prices. After studying the inside of the restaurant for the possible cause of the failure, the manager finally started to investigate the exterior. She reported:

> It finally dawned on me that our place did not look like a restaurant from the outside. If anything, it looked like a hair salon or an exclusive women's dress shop. My hunch was verified. I simply had the sign painter add the word "restaurant" to the logo on the window. Business picked up in no time.

Political Skill.   An important part of being effective in a large organization is being able to get your share of power and to prevent others from taking power away from you. Political skill primarily is the ability to acquire the power necessary to reach your objectives. Other political skills include establishing the right connections and impressing the right people. Middle managers generally need the most political skill because they often are intent on rising to top-level management positions.

Political skill can be used for the good of the organization and for self-interest. Assume that Tod Reuben, the plant safety and health manager, sees a potential health hazard. He believes that underground toxins are seeping up through the plant floor. To document this health hazard, he needs a larger budget for the department. He obtains this budget by making an effort to establish a good relationship with the plant manager, which includes complimenting her about the plant safety record. Reuben "plays politics" to get the money he needs. Toxic seepage is discovered later, and Reuben and his staff cure the problem before anyone is hurt. Without political skill, Reuben would not have had the budget to carry out his good deed.

Political skills are necessary on the job because the extent of each manager's authority often is uncertain, which leads to ambiguity and uncertainty. Political skills help clear up this ambiguity and get the job done. One assistant manager said, "I seize whatever authority I need to get my assignments done."

Relative Amounts of Skills Required at the Three Management Levels

Several tentative conclusions can be drawn about the relative amounts of managerial skills required at each level of management, as shown in Figure 1-6. Note that the relative lengths of the bars are more valid in comparing one management level to another than in making comparisons within the same level of management. For example, technical skill is more important for first-level managers than for top-level managers. However, the bar-graph lengths should not be interpreted to mean that technical skill is about three times more important than diagnostic skills for first-level managers. The most reliable conclusions to be drawn from Figure 1-6 are as follows:

1. Technical skill becomes less important as you move up the management hierarchy. However, even chief executive officers need some technical skills. For example, a troubled company will often hire as president a person who, as president in another company, showed great skill in reorganizing and returning some other ailing firm to profitability.

2. Conceptual skill becomes increasingly important as you move up the management hierarchy. "Seeing the big picture" is of obvious importance when you are placed on top of the organization.

3. Human skills are important at each management level, but they are of highest priority for first-level managers because of the heavy leadership demands of supervisory positions.

4. Diagnostic skill is important at each level of management, but it is most important at middle-level and top-level management.

5. Political skill is most important at the middle level because these managers are caught between two forces trying to grab some of their power. Not depicted in Figure 1-6 is the fact that politics takes different forms at the first and top levels. Political behavior at the supervisory level is aimed mostly at winning favor from people. At the top, the political tactics are focused on grabbing or holding onto large amounts of power. Middle managers use both sets of political tactics—winning favor and acquiring and retaining power.

Development of Management Skills

This text is based on the assumption that the management skills we described can be learned. Knowledge about management has been organized to be of practical value to future and present managers. In the words of Leonard R.

Figure 1-6   Relative Amounts of Managerial Skills Required at Each Level of Management

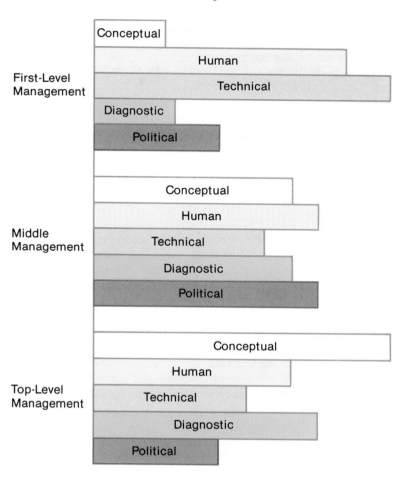

Sayles: "Managerial and leadership skill can be developed. There is, in fact, a conceptual field of knowledge that describes organizations and explains the role of managers and leaders. This knowledge is learnable, professional, and profoundly important."[18]

Sayles is referring to the formal study of management and its related fields of human relations and organizational behavior (basically applied psychology). Education for management begins in school and continues through one's career in the form of training and development programs, such as in seminars on how to be an effective leader or how to use database-management software.

Studying this text and doing the exercises should help you improve your management skills. The general approach would be first to study an idea or method (such as how to use goals to increase motivation and productivity), and next, to try out the skill in a work, a community, or a recreational setting. The idea or method may lead quickly to improved results, or it may require some fine tuning. Without practicing the ideas and methods described in this text, skill development is unlikely.

Experience is as important as formal education in forming effective managers. The issue is not whether education or experience is the best teacher. It is what combination of the two is the most beneficial for a particular individual in a particular situation. People who climb the organizational ladder usually have both education and experience in management techniques. One difference between the new and old breed managers is that the former integrate the computer into their work smoothly.

SCHOOLS OF MANAGEMENT THOUGHT

Management is such a complex subject that it can be approached from different perspectives, or schools of thought. Although these schools of thought are different, they do not compete with each other to discover the truth about practicing management. Instead, they complement and support each other. Well-trained managers take an eclectic viewpoint; they select the management ideas that seem to best fit the problem at hand. Correspondingly, this text borrows ideas from all schools of management thought.

The classical, behavioral, and management science schools are the major perspectives. They are supplemented by the contingency and systems approaches, both of which attempt to integrate the three basic schools. The systems and contingency approaches do not stand alone as schools of management thought. .

The Classical School

The **classical school of management** is the original formal approach to studying management.[19] Its students search for solid principles and concepts that can be used to manage work and people productively. The core of management knowledge is based on the classical school. One of its key contributions has been to study management from the framework of planning and decision making, organizing, leading, and controlling. Much of the information in this chapter stems from the classical school. Among the classical-school topics already discussed are line and staff managers, the nature of an organization, and the process of management.

The major strength of the classical school is that it has provided a systematic way of managing people and work that has proved useful over a long period. Its major limitation is that it sometimes ignores differences among people and situations. For example, some of the classical principles for designing an organization are not well suited to fast-changing situations.

The Behavioral School

Concerns that the classical school did not pay enough attention to the human element led to the **behavioral school of management.** Its primary emphasis is on improving management through understanding the psychological makeup of people.[20] The behavioral school has had a profound influence on management, and much of this book is based on behavioral theory. Typical behavioral school topics include leadership, motivation, communication, organizational politics, and employee counseling. Through its insistence that effective leadership depends on understanding the situation, the behavioral school initiated the contingency approach to management.

The primary strength of the behavioral school is that it encourages managers to take into account the human element. Many valuable methods of motivating employees are based on behavioral research. The primary weakness of the behavioral approach is that it sometimes leads to an oversimplified view of managing people. Managers sometimes adopt one simple behavioral theory and ignore other relevant information. For example, several well-known psychological theories of motivation pay too little attention to the importance of money in peoples' thinking.

The Management Science School

The **management science school** provides managers with a scientific basis for solving problems and making decisions. It uses a wide array of mathematical and statistical techniques. To many people, the use of computers in management is synonymous with management science.

Chapter 5, "Specialized Techniques for Planning and Decision Making," describes several important applications of management science. The primary strength of management science is that it enables managers to solve problems so complex that they cannot be solved by common sense alone. For example, management science techniques are used to make forecasts that take into account hundreds of factors simultaneously. A weakness of management science is that the answers it produces often are less precise than they seem. Although management science uses precise methods, much of the data are based on human estimates, which can be unreliable.

The Systems Approach

The **systems approach to management** is more a perspective for viewing problems than a school of thought.[21] It is based on the concept that an organization is a system, or an entity of interrelated parts. If you adjust one part of the system, other parts will be affected automatically. For example, if you offer low compensation to job candidates, it will influence product quality; the "low-quality" employees who are willing to accept low wages will produce low-quality goods. Figure 1-4, which depicts the process of management, reflects a systems viewpoint, as does Chapter 14, "Managing for Quality."

One major contribution of the systems approach is that it helps managers realize that every action they take has consequences somewhere inside or outside the organization. One potential problem is that it encourages lofty thinking. Sometimes, the manager is better off concentrating on the here-and-now problem. Systems theory offers few specific guidelines for dealing with everyday problems.

The Contingency Approach

The **contingency approach to management** emphasizes that there is no one best way to manage people or work. A method that leads to high productivity or morale in one situation may not achieve the same results in another. The contingency approach is derived from the leadership aspects of the behavioral school and from common sense. Experienced managers know that not all people and situations should be handled identically. The contingency approach is used throughout this book.

The strength of the contingency approach is that it encourages managers to examine individual and situational differences before deciding on a course of action. Its major problem is that it often is used as an excuse for not acquiring formal knowledge about management. If management depends on the situation, why study management theory? Because a formal study of management helps you decide which factors are relevant in what situations.

THE MANAGER'S RESPONSIBILITY FOR PRODUCTIVITY

The manager's responsibility for maintaining satisfactory levels of productivity cuts across many managerial functions and roles. Almost every action taken by a manager should directly or indirectly improve productivity, especially if productivity is regarded as the amount of useful work accomplished in relation to the amount of resources consumed.

What can managers do about maintaining or increasing productivity? Information on this topic is woven into every chapter of this book. Here it is sufficient to point out that managers are responsible for ensuring that the employees reporting to them are working productively. One set of strategies for this is for managers to do what they can to provide the best equipment, processes, and techniques for accomplishing the job. An office manager might recommend that the department acquire a second copying machine because employees are wasting too much time waiting for photocopies. Or, a manufacturing executive might recommend the use of industrial robots to get more high-quality work with fewer employees.

Another broad set of management strategies for achieving satisfactory levels of productivity is to encourage subordinates to want to be productive members of the team. Some management experts and executives think the proper management of people contributes more to productivity than does improved machinery and processes.

SUMMARY OF KEY POINTS

A manager is a person responsible for the work performance of other people. Management is the process of using organizational resources to achieve specific objectives through the functions of planning and decision making, organizing, leading, and controlling. However, the term *management* also refers to a field of study, a group of people running a firm, or a career field.

Organizational levels are divided into top-level managers, middle managers, first-level managers and individual contributors (operatives and specialists). Individual contributors also may hold higher-level positions. There are several useful ways of classifying managerial jobs: line managers versus staff managers; functional managers (for specialities within the firm) versus general managers; and administrators (managers in nonprofit firms), entrepreneurs (those who start an innovative business), and small-business owners.

Managers conduct their work in an organization, which is a group of two or more people working together as agreed to attain a set of goals. To accomplish organizational goals, managers use resources and carry out certain functions. Resources are divided into four categories: human, financial, physical, and informational. Top-level managers emphasize planning and decision making, whereas first-level managers concentrate on person-to-person leadership.

The work of a manager can be divided into seventeen roles that fit under the four major functions. Planning roles include the strategic planner and operational planner. Organizing includes the roles of organizer, liaison, staffing, resource allocator, and task delegator. Leading includes the roles of figurehead, spokesperson, negotiator, coach, team builder, team player, technical problem solver, and entrepreneur. Controlling includes the monitor and disturbance-handler roles. Top-level executives play more external roles than do lower-ranking managers.

Managers need technical, human, conceptual, diagnostic, and political skill to accomplish their jobs. The level of management influences which skills are the most important. For example, technical skills are the most important for first-level managers. Management skills are best acquired through a combination of education and experience.

The three major perspectives in management thought are the classical, behavioral, and management-science schools. Each complements and supports the others. They are supplemented by the systems and contingency approaches to management, which attempt to integrate the three schools.

QUESTIONS

1. Define the term *manager* in your own words.
2. How much prestige do you believe is associated with the occupation of manager?
3. Being a middle manager may be more stressful than being a first-level or top-level manager. Why might this be true?
4. Give examples of a line-manager position and a staff-manager position in a college or other post-secondary school.
5. Are the president of the United States and the prime minister of Canada general managers or functional managers? Are they even managers? Explain your reasoning.

6. Why is being an entrepreneur or small-business owner so attractive to so many people?
7. Identify several managerial roles that an entrepreneur should emphasize particularly.
8. How do students use the four major management functions to accomplish their goal of graduating?

ACTIVITIES

1. Interview a manager at any level in any organization. Determine which of the seventeen managerial roles that manager thinks apply to his or her job and which one or two roles are the most important. Be ready to discuss your findings in class.
2. Interview a small-business owner and find out from that person what he or she thinks are the most important managerial skills for successfully running a small business.

CASE PROBLEM 1–A: THE PROUD DUDE RANCH MANAGER

Bob Foster's workday usually begins at 6:30 A.M. at the Lost Valley Ranch, a four-star guest ranch, about ninety miles from Denver. The rest of his family is asleep, but Foster has already scheduled activities that will keep him busy until the next morning: payroll, payments, meals with guests, horseback riding with guests, telephone calls to suppliers, correspondence, and guest reservations.

"If we were large enough, I would hire someone else to take care of some of this," he said during a 10 P.M. break one Saturday night. "Because we're small, I wear many hats." (The Lost Valley Ranch has a 100-guest capacity.)

Thirty-nine-year-old Foster is the general manager at Lost Valley, a horse and cattle ranch nestled on 26,000 acres of national forest. Foster interacts with his guests frequently.

"In this business you really have to be a people person. Someone will usually come up to me at dinner and invite me back to the cabin to talk after the square dance. Before you know it you look at your watch and it's 12:30 A.M."

According to a magazine editor who interviewed him, Foster is highly qualified to run one of the few luxury dude ranches in Colorado. She observes, "Not only does he have the personality to endure people contact at sometimes excessive levels, but he's an expert horseperson and a solid business man. He's also an expert who'll take on any job at the resort, despite his title."

He says that he enjoys taking reservations. For one thing it helps keep his finger on the pulse of the business. He learns what "people want and where they heard about us." Taking reservations by himself also allows him to screen out guests that have an unrealistic expectation of the services provided at a dude ranch.

Foster joined the dude ranch, a family business, after graduating from a program in hotel administration. He believes he has overcome most of the problems that ordinarily plague a family business. He says, "The best thing that I've learned is that as long as my dad is around, I put my personal taste aside and don't get eaten up by small, petty issues. As long as he's active, if he feels strongly about something, then that's it. You don't have to turn everything into World War III.''

Foster's objective when he returned to the ranch at age twenty-eight was to convert Lost Valley from a six-month-a-year business (mid-April through mid-October) into a year-round business. Basing some of his ideas on a project he worked on in a hotel course, he added a new wing to the main lodge. The expansion enabled the ranch to enlarge its capacity from 60 to 100 guests and to provide housing for more staff. Foster also started cultivating off-season business by appealing to small corporations, associations, and city councils that wanted subdued settings for their meetings.

One challenge Foster is facing today is maintaining the ranch's homeyness while his parents are contemplating phasing out of the business. The ranch now is a domicile for 5 dogs, over 100 head of cattle, 150 horses, and 55 staffers during the summer. The operation is too big for Foster to run without his parents. Nevertheless, he wants to continue to offer a family-style atmosphere and personal service. One alternative solution to the problem is to bring his sister and brother-in-law back to the ranch to run food and maintenance. "What's going to keep me interested," he says, "is the people."

Case Questions

1.   What managerial roles does Bob Foster emphasize in his work?
2.   Explain whether you think Foster is an executive.
3.   What kind of entrepreneurial thinking has Foster displayed?
4.   What managerial roles might Foster be neglecting?

Source: As reported in Nancy Josephson, "What I Do on the Job: Hotel Manager," *Business Week Careers* (October 1986): 74–80.

CASE PROBLEM 1–B: THE UNMANAGED COMPANY

A few weeks before graduating from business school, Pablo Cervantes began his job search in the San Diego, California area. While he was reading through the classified advertisements, his eye caught one ad in particular:

Energetic, go-getter wanted to join newly formed firm in the waste-disposal field. We anticipate 500 percent growth in the first few years. Person joining our team must forget about constraints and roles imposed by most firms. Write us about yourself, Box 7654, this newspaper.

Thinking "What can I lose?" Cervantes sent in his letter and resume. Much to his surprise, he received a telephone call about one week later. Marty Berg, the caller, said he represented Solar Waste and would like to meet Cervantes. The two men arranged a convenient time. Cervantes followed the directions to a cinder-block building in a fringe area of the city.

Berg escorted Cervantes to a corner of a virtually empty building. They sat on two battered chairs adjacent to a work table. "Don't let appearances deceive you," said Berg. "We're into something big around here. We have a one-million dollar contract up front to experiment with a new sun-driven solid-waste disposal system. It's the wave of the future. The ad said we expect a 500 percent growth in the first few years, but that's a conservative estimate. The cofounder of the firm is a scientific genius. She thinks she has the right idea to cure the waste-disposal problems in any sunny climate."

"Sounds great to me," said Cervantes. "But what job do you have in mind? I have a business background. I can sell. I can solve problems. I can help you manage the company. What skills are you looking for? What would be my job title?"

With a smile, Berg looked at Cervantes and said, "Pablo, that's the point we were trying to make in the ad. Solar Waste will have no job titles, no job descriptions, and no levels of management. We will all pitch in and do whatever is needed to get the job done. You have to get rid of your hang-ups about classical organization theory to work here."

"You mean to say, you're going to try to fulfill a one-million dollar contract without doing any planning, organizing, leading, or controlling?"

"Now you're catching on. Around here, the traditional organization is dead. We'll work together as a group and do what needs to be done."

"But could you at least tell me what my job title would be?" asked Cervantes. "Would I be a manager? A sales rep? A specialist?"

"There you go again," said Berg. "Those titles will have no relevance in our pioneering little firm. We are looking for talent and ambition. We have an unconventional product to offer society, so we want an unconventional firm to carry out our mission. There will be no fixed roles for anybody."

"Okay, I get the point. But what about my starting salary if I joined Solar Waste. What would that be?"

"A lot would depend on what you think you are worth and how much money we have available to share among ourselves. We don't want to pay people fixed wages every month. So much depends on how much they contribute and how much work we get in."

At this point, Berg's telephone rang. After chatting for a minute, Berg said, "I have to take care of an emergency right now. Could you come back in twenty minutes? Then you can meet the cofounder of Solar Waste. I think I see some possibilities here. I know she would like to meet you."

Cervantes walked across the street to get a soft drink from a service-station vending machine. He thought to himself, "Should I jump in my car and make a U-turn? Or should I look further into this potentially great opportunity?"

Case Questions

1. What do you think of the management philosophy of Solar Waste?
2. Will the organizational structure Marty Berg has in mind work? Why or why not?
3. From your standpoint, is Marty Berg describing a utopia or a snake pit? Explain your reasoning.
4. What should Pablo Cervantes do after he finishes his soft drink?

REFERENCES

1. Quote adapted from Leonard Sayles, "The Unsung Profession," *Issues & Observations* (May 1984): 4.

2.   Peter F. Drucker, "Management's New Role," *Harvard Business Review* (November-December 1969): 54.

3.   Peter F. Drucker, *The Frontiers of Management* (New York: Truman Talley Books, E. P. Dutton, 1986), 1.

4.   Andrew J. DuBrin, R. Duane Ireland, and J. Clifton Williams, *Management and Organization,* (Cincinnati: South-Western Publishing Co., 1989), 4.

5.   John M. Ivancevich, James H. Donnelly, Jr., and James L. Gibson, *Managing for Performance: An Introduction to the Process of Managing,* rev. ed. (Plano, TX: Business Pubs., Inc., 1983), 8. 10.

6.   Judith M. Bardwick, "When Ambition Is No Asset," *New Management* 1, no. 4 (1984): 23.

7.   John A. Byrne, "Who Made the Most—and Why," *Business Week* (2 May 1988): 51.

8.   "The Old Foreman Is on the Way Out, and the New One Will Be More Important," *Business Week* (25 April 1983): 74.

9.   Joseph R. Mancuso, "Entrepreneur's Quiz," *New Accountant* (January 1988): 12.

10. Stephen J. Carroll and Dennis J. Gillen, "Are the Classical Management Functions Useful in Describing Managerial Work?" *Academy of Management Review* (January 1987): 48.

11. Lars-Erik Wilberg, "Should You Change Your Leadership Style?" *Management Review* (January 1988): 5.

12. John A. Pearce II, and Fred David, "Corporate Mission Statements: The Bottom Line," *Academy of Management Executive* (May 1987): 109.

13. This research is reported in Henry Mintzberg, *The Nature of Managerial Work* (New York: Harper & Row, 1973).

14. Our presentation of the roles themselves, but not the functional groupings, is adapted with permission from J. Kenneth Graham, Jr., and William L. Mihal, *The CMD Managerial Job Analysis Inventory* (Rochester, NY: Rochester Institute of Technology, Center for Management Development, rev. 1987), 2–6.

15. Cynthia M. Pavett and Alan W. Lau, "Managerial Work: The Influence of Hierarchical Level and Functional Specialty," *Academy of Management Journal* (March 1983): 170–177.

16. The first three skills are from Robert L. Katz, "Skills of an Effective Administrator," *Harvard Business Review* (September–October 1974): 90–102. The diagnostic skill is from Ricky W. Griffin, *Management* (Boston: Houghton Mifflin Co., 1984), 6. The political skill is from Pavett and Lau, "Managerial Work," 171.

17. Katz, "Skills of an Effective Administrator," 93.

18. Sayles, "The Unsung Profession," 4.

19. Allen C. Bluedorn, "Special Book Review Section on the Classics of Management," *The Academy of Management Review* (April 1986): 442–464.

20. Elton Mayo, *The Human Problems of an Industrial Civilization,* 2d ed. (New York: Macmillan, 1946).

21. James H. Donnelly, Jr., James L. Gibson, and John M. Ivancevich, *Fundamentals of Management,* 6th ed. (Plano, TX: Business Pubs., Inc., 1987), 7.

2

The Manager's External Environment

After studying the material in this chapter, you should be able to accomplish the following tasks:

1. Identify the major environmental forces influencing the manager's work.
2. Explain how managers and organizations can behave in socially responsible ways.
3. Describe how ethical codes of conduct influence the manager.
4. Recognize how business has become internationalized.
5. Pinpoint how organizational restructuring and consolidations have influenced the manager's work.
6. Specify how labor unions influence the manager's job.
7. Describe the increased legal power of employees.

Key Terms and Phrases

Indirect environmental force
Direct environmental force
Technology
Social responsibility
Stockholder viewpoint
Stakeholder viewpoint
Organizational social performance
Social audit
Trailing spouse
Family Leave
Ethics
Moral laxity
Organizational culture

Whistle blowing
Multinational corporation (MNC)
Global sourcing
Cultural sensitivity
Downsizing
Restructuring
Lean and mean
Production work teams
Labor agreement
Employment at will
Wrongful discharge
Right-to-know law

Chapter 1 described how the manager's job is influenced by such factors as the task at hand. For example, the manager might carry out a negotiator role if he or she needed a larger travel and entertainment budget. The manager's job is also profoundly influenced by forces and pressures in the outside environ-

Credit: ©Vince Streano, 1985; STREANO/HAVENS

ment, such as the availability of workers, government legislation, ethical codes of behavior, and the internationalization of business. In this chapter we examine some of these environmental factors and societal trends.

COMPONENTS OF THE EXTERNAL ENVIRONMENT

Large numbers of factors in the world outside the organization can and do influence the work of managers. Particularly challenging is that the list of influential factors keeps changing. At one time, for example, imported goods represented a competitive threat only to certain manufacturers. Today foreign competition is a serious challenge to many manufacturing *and* service industries. Similarly, the large number of employees and job candidates infected with the AIDS virus creates a potential financial threat to many employers.[1] No other disease presented a similar threat in the past.

Robert Albanese has summarized the multitude of environmental forces influencing organizations and their managers. His findings are presented in Figure 2-1. Each one of these components will be described briefly in the following paragraphs. The balance of the chapter highlights six of the environmental factors mentioned directly or indirectly in Figure 2-1.

Indirect Environmental Forces

Albanese divides the organization's external environment into indirect and direct environmental forces. An **indirect environmental force** influences the organization's goals, strategies, and tasks in a general way. A **direct environmental force** influences the organization in a regular and specific way.[2] The six major, indirect environmental forces are economic, social/cultural, political/legal, technological, and international.

Economic Forces.   Public and private organizations are profoundly influenced by general economic conditions. During prosperous times, for example, managers have more latitude in spending money and hiring personnel. In today's competitive work environment, even the forecast of bad times will influence some managers to reduce expenses or delay moving ahead with a proposed new program.

Social/Cultural Forces.   Changes in social values and demographics can exert important influences on management practices. Today many workers desire to participate in decisions about their work. In response, many managers now solicit the input of group members before making important decisions. Society's demand for equal employment opportunities for women and minorities has influenced organizations to guard against discriminatory employment practices. The desire of many workers to satisfy a full range of needs on the job has prompted some organizations to improve the quality of working life. Can you think of another change in value that has influenced management practices?

Figure 2-1   Major Forces in an Organization's External Environment

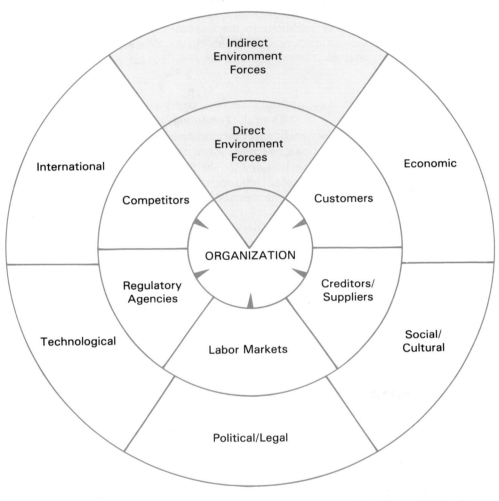

Source: Adapted with permission from Robert Albanese, *Management* (Cincinnati: South-Western Publishing Co., 1988), 147.

An important demographic change influencing organizations and managers is the decrease in the number of young people and the increase in the number of older people. Many service businesses, such as fast-food restaurants and supermarkets, now actively recruit senior citizens to perform the work typically performed by young adults.

Political/Legal Forces.   Some managers believe that business conditions can be influenced by the people elected to office and the party in power. Consequently, many executives are willing to engage in business expansion when the party of their choice retains or gains power. Legislation exerts a major influence on the work activities of managers. Laws and executive orders influence such activities as hiring practices, investment practices, safety regulations, the construction of buildings to meet the demands of the physically challenged, and the entertainment of business clients. Some of this legislation will be discussed later in this chapter and also in Chapter 8, "Staffing the Organization."

Technological Forces.   Organizations and managers are forced to adapt to the technology that exists in the world. **Technology,** in this context, is the systematic application of scientific or other organized knowledge to practical tasks. This means that technology includes ideas and new knowledge in addition to equipment.[3] Relevant technology for the firm includes methods of performing technical and human tasks. Desktop publishing (printing and graphics accomplished through a small computer and laser printer instead of typesetting equipment) influences how in-company print shops prepare brochures. Also, advances in the treatment of alcoholism might influence where managers refer employees with drinking problems.

Changing technology is one of the most critical issues facing executives today, especially in high-technology industries. The introduction of lasers is a case in point. Manufacturing and hospital executives alike ponder how they will incorporate laser devices into operations in order to remain competitive. Manufacturers might use lasers for shaping parts while physicians might use them for surgical procedures. An example of a thought technology is that advances in ergonomics (designing equipment to fit human characteristics) influences the choice and layout of equipment.

International Forces.   As described later in this chapter, business has become internationalized. All major corporations and most smaller ones engage in some trade with other countries. The internationalization of business affects the manager in such ways as competing on cost and quality with foreign-made goods and visiting operations and customers in other countries.

Direct Environmental Forces

Direct environmental forces exert a more specific impact on the organization and manager than the forces described above. The direct environmental forces, as shown in Figure 2-1, are customers, creditors/suppliers, labor markets, regulatory agencies, and competitors.

Customers.   As most small-business owners contend, "The real boss is the customer." Changes in customer or client preferences exert direct pressure on companies to satisfy these preferences. Changing demands often create a flurry of activity for organizations and managers, such as a sudden demand for energy-conserving products, followed by a decrease in such demand. Educational and medical institutions also are forced to respond to changes in consumer preferences such as the up-and-down demand for teacher training programs or the sudden growth in demand for cosmetic surgery among career-oriented people.

Creditors/Suppliers.   Organizations are also influenced by the people to whom they owe money (creditors) and the firms that provide them with the goods and services they need to operate (suppliers). It is common practice for the officer of a company's bank to serve on its board of directors. An important influence exerted by a supplier is to help its customer maintain high quality by providing the customer with high-quality components. The supplier thus influences the quality of the customer's product.

Labor Markets.   The labor market refers to the supply of workers available to the firm. The labor market influences the firm because without the right mix of workers, a firm cannot prosper. One of the selling points of many communities in attracting companies is its pool of potential employees.

Regulatory Agencies.   Government agencies regulate the activities of organizations and managers in five principal areas: consumer protection, investor protection, environmental law, preservation of competition, and labor-management relations.

Consumers are protected by such agencies as the Consumer Product Safety Commission (CPSC) and the Food and Drug Administration (FDA). The Securities and Exchange Commission (SEC) seeks to protect investors from illegal securities activities. The Environmental Protection Agency (EPA) attempts to prevent the environment from being damaged by business and other organizations.

Various antitrust laws attempt to prevent any one business from restricting the rights of other companies to compete successfully in the market place. Labor-management relations laws include those designed to allow employees to join labor unions and to work in a relatively safe and healthful environment. Many production managers therefore devote time to ensuring that their company is in compliance with Occupational Safety and Health Administration (OSHA) regulations.

Competitors.   Competition exerts a major influence on the actions of organizations and their managers. As a frustrated citizen said, "If the Department of Motor Vehicles had any competition, its employees would treat the public with more courtesy." Profit and nonprofit organizations must respond to competition. Colleges and vocational schools compete for students, and health-maintenance organizations (HMOs) compete for patients. At its best, competition forces organizations to be more innovative and productive. At its worst, competition encourages organizations to overwork its employees and to falsely disparage its rivals.

SOCIAL RESPONSIBILITY

Organizations do not exist in isolation, and managers do not work in isolation. As just described, there are many groups in society affected by the activities of organizations and their managers. Many people believe that organizations have an obligation to be concerned about these outside groups. **Social responsibility** is the idea that organizations have obligations to groups in society other than owners or stockholders and beyond that prescribed by law or contract.[4] To behave in a socially responsible way, managers must therefore be aware of how their actions influence the outside environment.

An important perspective to keep in mind is that many socially responsible actions are the by-product of sensible business decisions. For example, it is both socially responsible and profitable for a company to improve the literacy of entry-level workers. Literate entry-level workers for some jobs may be in short supply, and employees who cannot read instructions may be unproductive.

Three aspects of social responsibility examined here are *(a)* the two viewpoints of social responsibility, *(b)* the organizational social performance, and *(c)* the costs of social responsibility.

Stockholder Viewpoint versus Stakeholder Viewpoint

The **stockholder viewpoint** of social responsibility is the traditional perspective. It holds that business organizations are only responsible to their owners and stockholders. The job of managers is therefore to satisfy the financial interests of the stockholders. By so doing, the interests of society will be served in the long run. Socially irresponsible acts ultimately result in poor sales. According to the stockholder viewpoint, corporate social responsibility is therefore a by-product of profit seeking. A counterargument is that socially irresponsible acts sometimes do produce profits. An illustration of this point of view is presented in the accompanying "Organization in Action."

ORGANIZATION IN ACTION:

The Socially Irresponsible Hotels

Four young children died in a fire in a welfare hotel in Brooklyn. The parents were charged with endangering them and leaving them for hours locked in the family's single room, where the children apparently started the fire in a mattress. In the aftermath, the press focused not only on the parents' behavior but also on the conditions in the hotel. New York City officials noted that, although the hotel, like all welfare hotels, has many building and safety violations, none of these violations contributed to the fire and the deaths of the little children.

The four children who died in the fire, ages one through seven, lived with their parents in a 144 square foot room. For this the city pays the landlord $49 a night, or $1,500 a month. Some of the owners of these hotels charge $100 a room per night, more than $36,000 per year. New York City pays approximately $5 million per year rental fees for rooms in the hotel under discussion.

The owner of the hotel said his family had purchased the hotel in 1950 but had been leasing it to the present managers. The owner said, "I cannot tell the managers what to do." The owner has hired former New York City Mayor Robert Wagner as his lawyer to oppose the city's plan to have the hotel condemned.

Until quite recently, the city used fifty-five welfare hotels as a refuge for families priced out of New York City's high-priced housing market. Years of pressure by housing activists and advocates for the homeless have led the city administrators to pursue alternatives to these hotels—permanent low-income housing that will also cost the city considerably less. Nevertheless, such housing is still mostly a promise, and 3,400 welfare families continue to live in the hotels.

Living conditions are a more frequent killer than fire in these hotels. The infant mortality rate in the welfare hotels is 25 deaths per 1,000 births, a figure that is higher than the mortality rate in New York's poorest neighborhoods, and higher even than the rate in some of the world's developing countries.

Source: As reported in Sydney Schanberg, "New York's Profitable Welfare Hotels Endanger Children," *Newsday* (23 July 1986).

The **stakeholder viewpoint** of social responsibility contends that organizations must hold themselves responsible for the quality of life of the many groups affected by the organization's actions. These interested parties (stakeholders) include those groups composing the firm's indirect environment, described previously. Two categories of stakeholders exist. Internal stakeholders include owners, employees, and stockholders; external stakeholders include customers, labor unions, consumer groups, and financial institutions. Figure 2-2 depicts the stakeholder viewpoint of social responsibility.

Organizational Social Performance

Organizational social performance is the extent to which an organization responds to the demands of its stakeholders for behaving in a socially responsible manner. Such performance can be measured by a formal audit of the organization's activities or by a less formal assessment of how the organization responds to social issues.

Social Audit. A **social audit** is a systematic measure of an organization's social impact. The purpose of the audit is to measure, monitor, and evaluate the organization's performance with respect to its social programs and social objectives.[5] The results of the audit may be used to increase management's awareness of the social impact of the organization's actions. Social audits are difficult to conduct because they cover so much ground and require considerable subjective interpretation. For example, the auditor would have to speak to a generous sampling of the organization's stakeholders and then interpret a number of conflicting opinions. To make the social audit more objective, some firms have outside experts conduct part of the audit.

The results of the audit are communicated to shareholders and other interested parties. Atlantic Richfield Co. is one company that published several

Figure 2-2   The Stakeholder Viewpoint of Social Responsibility

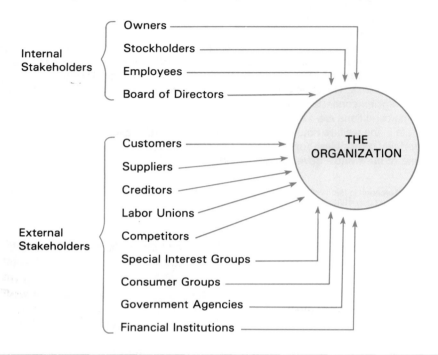

corporate social reports based partially on critiques from outsiders. One report, "Participation III," summarizes the company's activities in consumer affairs, human-resource management, environmental protection, energy conservation, philanthropy, and the advocacy of public policy. A specific company action taken in response to the audit was to appoint a woman to its board of directors.[6]

Response to Social Issues.   A more widely used method of assessing social performance is to observe the organization's response to selected social issues. Among these important issues are plant and office closings, child care, helping employees meet other family demands, and coping with AIDS in the workplace. We are discussing these issues from the standpoint of social responsibility. They can also be regarded as ways of attracting and keeping capable people that offer social benefits simultaneously. To repeat, social responsibility is often the by-product of good business practices.

Plant and Office Closings.   Business conditions often dictate that a company close a plant, office, or other facility. Plant and office closings occur frequently to increase organizational efficiency. During one five-year period, over twelve million Americans and Canadians lost their jobs to closings.[7] Some business firms have taken steps to reduce the human suffering and inconvenience associated with laying off all the workers at a given facility. For example, Electrolux Corp. gave employees six months advance notice of a layoff. State and local agencies were involved in an outplacement program; retirement planning was provided; transfers and moving assistance were offered; and employees were given paid time off for job interviewing.[8]

Child Care. A growing number of employers offer child-care programs on company premises or in nearby facilities. The number of these employer-sponsored child-care programs has grown in approximate proportion to the number of women in the work force. One motive for implementing child-care programs is to meet the needs of employees and to retain essential workers. Many employers also receive such benefits as lower absenteeism and turnover, improved productivity, higher morale, and improved recruitment.[9]

Other Family Demands. Many companies have taken the initiative to help their employees meet complex family demands. One program rapidly gaining in popularity is helping an employee's spouse find a new position when the employee is relocated. The **trailing spouse** (the spouse who accompanies the relocated partner) benefit is important because there are close to thirty million two-income couples in the work force. Hewlett-Packard offers in-house job counseling and up to five hundred dollars in job search costs.[10] In rare cases, a company will find a place on the payroll for both marital partners.

Another example of a corporate initiative to help employees meet family demands is **family leave**—a leave of absence to meet responsibilities at home. For example, Eastman Kodak Co. employees are granted the right to four months' unpaid leave to care for newborns, sick children, spouses, or parents. One reason family leaves are considered important is that more than one-half of women with children under one-year old are now in the labor force, up from about one-third in 1979.[11]

In addition to being socially responsible actions, the trailing spouse and family leave programs provide an important benefit to the employer. Some employees would not relocate unless their spouse could find a new position, while others would be forced to quit if not for the family leave program.

Coping with AIDS in the Workplace. By 1991 in the United States, an estimated 270,000 people will have had AIDS and close to 2 million people will be infected with the AIDS virus. Ninety percent of AIDS victims are working-age adults between the ages of twenty and forty-nine.

Dealing with AIDS in the workplace has therefore become a challenge for many employers. The Supreme Court has ruled that employees with AIDS must be treated as handicapped, and they are thus protected from sanctions because of their disease.[12] Although their numbers are relatively small, some employers have developed policies and programs to lessen the suffering associated with AIDS. An exemplary policy has been developed by the largest unit of local government in Minnesota, employing over 8,000 workers. The policy states

No employee, applicant, or client shall be subjected to testing, removed from normal and customary status, or deprived of any rights, privileges, or freedoms because of his or her AIDS status except for clearly stated, specific, and compelling medical and/or public health reasons.[13]

This message implies that the organization intends to handle the AIDS issue cautiously, yet it also says that a safe work environment will be maintained. Employee concerns about contracting AIDS from casual contact with AIDS victims must be dealt with openly because of the intensity of emotion surrounding the issue. Some employers have voluntarily provided latex gloves for any employees are who concerned about catching AIDS from clients, patients, or customers. (The occupations included here are ambulance drivers, undertakers, and dental hygienists.) It is possible that the same courtesy could be extended to employees worried about catching AIDS from coworkers.

Do you think providing concerned workers with latex gloves is an act of social responsibility? Or is it merely a response to the risk of lawsuits, strikes, or walkouts?

The Costs of Social Responsibility

Socially responsible actions by employers are not free. Specific costs of social responsibility include such matters as antipollution devices, safety air bags in automobiles, child-care centers for the children of employees, stress management programs for employees, and the retaining of nonproductive employees. Some of these costs are recovered through lower rates of illness and absenteeism. Other costs, such as retaining nonproductive employees, are not recoverable and are eventually paid by higher prices, higher taxes, and lower dividends to stockholders.

Another cost relates to the issue of competitive disadvantage. A company may stay even with its competitors if all the companies invest in social projects. A company that supports such projects alone, however, may lose business if its competitors invest surplus cash into strengthening their competitive positions.[14]

ETHICAL BEHAVIOR OF MANAGERS

Social responsibility is closely tied to ethics, because one consequence of ethical behavior is to be socially responsible. **Ethics** is the study of moral obligation, or separating right from wrong, and is therefore a broader concept than social responsibility.[15] Although many unethical acts are illegal, others are legal. An example of an illegal unethical act is giving a government official a *kickback* (rebate) for placing a contract with one's firm. An example of a legal, yet unethical, practice is hiring an employee away from a competitor, "picking her brains" for competitive ideas, then eliminating her job.

Data about the prevalence of unethical behavior are presented in Table 2-1. Observe that the first three behaviors on the list are unethical but legal, while the last four are both unethical and illegal.

Table 2-1   A Sampling of Unethical Behavior

Unethical Behavior	Percent Who Claim to Have Engaged in the Behavior	
	Business Executives	General Public
Taken home work supplies	74	40
Called in sick to work when not ill	14	71
Used company telephones for personal long-distance calls	78	15
Overstated income tax deductions	35	13
Driven while drunk	80	33
Smoked marijuana	17	25
Used cocaine	2	8

Source: Adapted with permission from Roger Ricklefs, "Executives and General Public Say Ethical Behavior Is Declining In U.S.," *The Wall Street Journal* (31 October 1983): 1.

The study of ethics in management is popular today because of the publicity surrounding such events as insider trading scandals and former government officials using their influence to obtain favors for clients. Here we discuss the causes and prevention of unethical behavior in business.

Causes of Unethical Behavior

Individuals, organizations, and society itself must share some of the blame for the prevalence of unethical behavior in the workplace. A major contributor to unethical behavior is individual greed and gluttony or simply maximizing gain for self at the expense of others. The same phenomenon has been referred to as "me-first management." As *Business Week* commented about the central figure in a major conviction of trading on the basis of information not available to the public (insider trading): "It was Ivan F. Boesky's consuming passion and his fatal flaw. He wanted to be the biggest arbitrageur on Wall Street, and when he achieved that, he wanted to be bigger."[16] (An *arbitrageur* is a person who endeavors to profit from the disparity in prices on something in different markets, such as buying silver in one country to sell it at a higher price in another.)

Another major contributor to unethical behavior in the workplace is an organizational atmosphere or climate that condones such behavior. According to a study conducted by William Frederick, even employees with high ethical standards may stray in a climate that promotes unethical behavior. Moreover, the organization's official code of ethics may not coincide with its actual culture. Instead, it is the organization's top executives who set the company's true moral tone.[17]

A third cause of unethical behavior is **moral laxity**, a slippage in moral behavior because other issues seem more important at the time. The implication is that the business person who behaves unethically has not carefully planned the immoral behavior, but lets it occur by not exercising good judgment. Many workplace deaths fit into this category. Three people died in an explosion in a restaurant when a furnace exploded. The owner did not plan to kill the workers, but nevertheless he tried to save money by not having a malfunctioning furnace repaired. The accompanying ''Organization in Action'' illustrates how moral laxity or negligence can result in workplace deaths.

ORGANIZATION IN ACTION:

The Lethal Silver-Recycling Plant

Three former executives of a silver-recycling plant in Maywood, Illinois, were sentenced to twenty-five years in prison and fined $10,000 each for their murder convictions in the job-related cyanide death of an employee. Cook County Circuit Court Judge Ronald J. P. Banks compared the actions of the three officials of the defunct Film Recovery Systems to someone who would leave a time bomb ticking in an airplane.

The murder convictions were the first in the nation of corporate officials in a job-related death. The convictions were based on the death of a 61-year old employee who died after inhaling cyanide fumes at the company plant. The cyanide was used to recover silver from used X-ray film.

The managers sentenced were the former president of Film Recovery Systems, the plant manager, and a supervisor. Banks revoked their bonds of $2,500 each and ordered the three managers into custody. Judge Banks said at the sentencing that the defendants were clearly aware of hazardous plant conditions and didn't have appropriate warning signs for the workers, many of whom were illegal aliens and couldn't speak English.

The convictions have been appealed, and the outcome of these appeals is still pending.

Source: As reported in ''3 Former Executives Sentenced in Job-Related Death of Worker,'' Associated Press (2 July 1985); Jonathan Tasini, ''A Death at Work Can Put the Boss in Jail,'' *Business Week* (2 March 1987): 38.

Unethical behavior also stems from four questionable rationalizations often made by businesspeople. As described by Saul Gellerman, these four rationalizations are as follows:

1. A belief that the activity is within ethical and legal limits—such as offering an employee a small bribe for not reporting a workplace accident.

2. A belief that because the activity is in the individual's or organization's best interest that the individual would be expected to undertake the activity. An example would be accepting a substantial gift from a vendor because the buyer felt that he or she is underpaid and therefore the gift can be regarded as a form of compensation.

3. A belief that the activity is "safe" because it will never be uncovered. Several years ago management at a food-processor substituted sugar water for apple juice in baby-food jars, reasoning that the infant consumers would never complain.

4. A belief that because the unethical activity helps the company, the company will condone the activity and protect the person. For example, the managers in the counterfeit apple-juice incident believed that saving the company money would exempt them from punishment.[18]

Steps Management Can Take to Minimize Unethical Behavior

Top management is not entirely at the mercy of unethical organizational members. Many constructive actions can be taken to prevent unethical behavior; a sampling of them is described next.

Create an Ethical Organizational Culture.   The strategic approach to prevent unethical behavior is to create an organizational culture that guides people toward ethical behavior. An **organizational culture** is a system of shared values and beliefs that guide behavior. If people throughout the organization believe that behaving ethically is "in" while behaving unethically is "out," ethical behavior will prevail. Specific actions that foster a high-ethics culture include the following:

• Top management behaving ethically in all its business dealings.

• Top management behaving ethically in its dealings with organization insiders and outsiders.

• Policies that encourage ethical behavior. For example, many companies and pension funds have established policies calling for the divestiture of funds in South Africa because they believe *apartheid* (the segregation of people by race) to be unethical.[19]

• Sanctions against unethical behavior including fining, demoting, suspending, and firing employees who behave unethically.

Publicize the Benefits of Ethical Behavior.   Another way of promoting ethical behavior is to publicize the financial advantages of behaving ethically. As Tad Tuleja reports: "The studies I looked at indicated that over the 20–30 year period measured, companies with an interest in public service did five to ten times as well as the national average of the American economy at large or [companies included in the] Dow Jones industrial average." Also, companies that treat their people ethically also seem to achieve good financial performance.[20]

Encourage Whistle Blowing.   An important way for unethical behavior to be exposed is through **whistle blowing**, the disclosure of organizational wrongdoing to parties who can take action. Wrongful deeds brought to outsiders' attention include expense account chiseling, toxic substances in the work environment, overcharging the buyer, and the government exceeding budget on projects. If top management encourages whistle blowing by lower-ranking organizational members, many unethical acts will be exposed.

Despite the contribution of whistle blowing, whistle blowers are at risk. Whistle blowers typically enter into conflict with their employer. Although many forms of retaliation by the employer are illegal, the whistle blower usually fares poorly in the firm. Whistle blowers are often passed over from promotion, receive below-average salary increases, and are given undesirable assignments.[21] Such treatment discourages employees from exposing unethical behavior.

INTERNATIONALIZATION OF BUSINESS AND MANAGEMENT

An important environmental influence on the manager's job is the internationalization of business and management. Approximately 10 percent of all jobs in the United States and Canada are dependent upon trade with other countries. Figure 2-3 provides details about the magnitude of U.S. trade with other countries. In general, as business has become more global the manager must adapt to the challenges of working with organizations and people from other countries. It is therefore important to understand something about multinational corporations and about being sensitive to cultural differences.

The Multinational Corporation

The heart of international trade is the **multinational corporation (MNC)**, a firm that has units in two or more countries. Here we describe the various stages of international trade and the practice of having components made in other countries.

Stages of International Business.   There are six methods of entering the international market, with each successive stage representing fuller involvement until true MNC status is reached:

Stage 1: Licensing.   Companies operating in foreign countries are authorized to produce and market products or services with specific territories on a fee basis.

Stage 2: Exporting.   Goods produced in one country are then sold for direct use or resale to one or more companies in foreign countries. Many small firms specialize in helping companies gain entry to foreign markets through exporting.

Stage 3: Local Warehousing and Selling.   Goods that are produced in one country are shipped directly to the parent company's or a subsidiary's storage and marketing facilities in one or more foreign countries.

Stage 4: Local Assembly and Packaging.   In this arrangement, components rather than finished products are shipped to company-owned facilities in other

Figure 2-3   Top United States Trading Partners

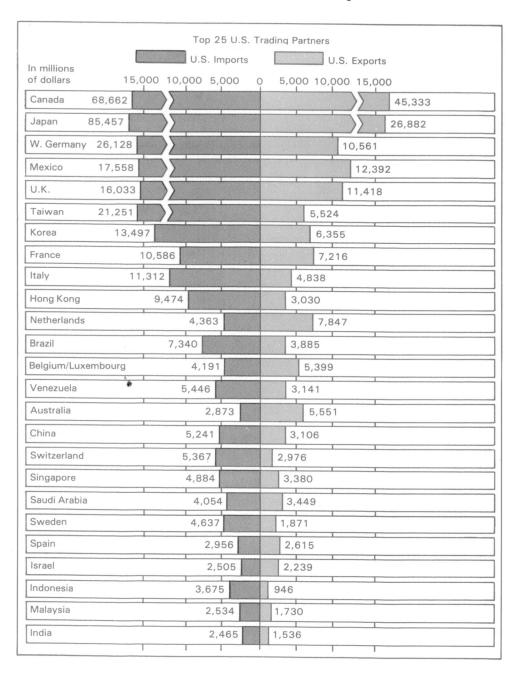

Source: *Democrat and Chronicle* (19 November 1987): 12D.

countries for final assembly and marketing. Trade regulations sometimes require that a large product, such as a mainframe computer, be assembled locally rather than shipped from the exporting country as a finished product.

Stage 5: Joint Venture.   Instead of merging formally with a firm of mutual interest, a company in one country pools resources with those of one or more foreign companies. Jointly they produce, warehouse, transport, and market products. Profits or losses from these operations are shared in some predetermined proportion.

Stage 6: Direct Foreign Investment.   The most advanced stage of multinational business activity takes place when a company in one country produces and markets products through wholly owned facilities in foreign countries. American Honda Motor Co. and Ford Motor Co. are two well-known MNCs that make direct foreign investments.[22]

Stage 1 offers the least protection for the company doing business in another country. Each successive stage offers more protection against political and economic risks. One major risk is that the firm in the other country may drop its affiliation with the multinational firm and sell the product on its own. The affiliate thus becomes a competitor.[23] Direct foreign investment is therefore recommended as the best way to protect the company's competitive advantage. The advantage is protected because the manager of the foreign subsidiary can control its operation.

International business is also subject to many other risks. One continuing challenge is adjusting to changes in currency exchange rates. When a country's currency is high in relation to foreign currencies, it makes the country's products more expensive in those foreign markets. In turn, the increased price creates a decreased demand. For example, when the value of the American dollar is low in relation to other currencies, exports into the United States become more expensive.

In 1988, the drop in the U.S. dollar contributed to a major surge in U.S. exports. Manufacturers of traditional products, often considered to be on a irreversible decline, were selling products that many thought could not be profitably made in the United States any longer. For example, American machine tools were being sold to West Germany and American shoes to Italy.[24] The accompanying ''Organization in Action'' describes how a well-known Irish company has been affected by the falling U.S. dollar.

ORGANIZATION IN ACTION:

Waterford Crystal in Trouble

The fall of the American dollar has dealt a shattering blow to the port city of Waterford, Ireland, whose reputation for fine crystal is known around the world. The steep drop in the currency makes high-priced imports from overseas even more expensive in the United States. As a result, the Waterford Glass Group PLC has been forced to lay off

1000 workers (one-third of its work force) in its crystal division. J. Patrick Hayes, chairman of the Waterford Group, labels the dollar's slide, "traumatic." David Daniels, the city's mayor, calls it a "body blow."

Waterford Glass's crystal sales fell 27 percent to £33.8 million in Irish currency ($55.1 million in U.S. currency) in the first six months of 1987 from a year earlier. Operating profits for the division plummeted 73 percent in the most recently reported period. Fifty percent of the company's crystal is exported directly to the United States and another 35 percent is bought by American visitors to other countries. Therefore 85 percent of all the crystal production depends on the U.S. dollar-Irish pound exchange rate. It now takes about $1.63 in U.S. currency to buy 1£ in Irish currency versus $1.37 to £1 a year ago.

Source: As reported in Cotten Timberlake, "Dollar Devaluation Cuts Crystal Firm's Employment," Associated Press (4 January 1988).

Global Sourcing.   As most consumers realize, products themselves or their components are frequently made in foreign countries. Relying on workers in other countries to manufacture goods is done either to save money on wages or to capitalize upon the special skills of these workers. The process is now referred to as **global sourcing,** the international division of labor in its most basic sense. For most multinational corporations, global sourcing represents a financially sound alternative.[25] Suggestions for making global sourcing effective include the following:

1.   Global sourcing should be a logical extension of the company's make-or-buy decisions. For example, should we make the part in our Charlotte, North Carolina plant, or should we buy it from an outfit in Hong Kong?

2.   Carefully assess the cost of shipping the product from the overseas manufacturing company. Shipping costs of some large components, such as a pump for a ship, can be prohibitive.

3.   Determine if external sourcing can contribute to sales. To illustrate, one Japanese manufacturer of electronic control devices has arranged for several of its products to be produced in the People's Republic of China. The net effect has been to freeze out competitive products from this country

  Consumers in the People's Republic of China now purchase the Japanese control devices because they are manufactured in their own country and are of higher quality than the Chinese companies can produce themselves.

4.   Be aware of the cost benefits of sourcing, but recognize that it has some costs of its own. Import agencies may be needed, a contract administrator familiar with the sourcing country must be hired, and travel costs will be high initially.

5.   Start small and grow gradually. Ample time should be allowed to explain carefully to foreign suppliers the company's product requirements.[26]

A general principle underlying outsourcing is that some products, components, or services (such as data entry) can be produced or performed anywhere. Outsourcing is most likely to be conducted when the product or service is labor intensive, thus elevating the importance of relatively low wages in inexpensive production. Special skills possessed by workers in another country are also important. For example, it is generally acknowledged that Asian workers are methodical and precise. Many American insurance companies are therefore having data-entry work performed in Hong Kong and Taiwan. Can you think of any products or services that are good candidates for outsourcing?

In the current era, many American firms are deemphasizing global sourcing; they have started to bring overseas operations home or to switch from foreign to domestic suppliers. A representative example of this trend is the RCA Division of General Electric Co. RCA now relies on its Bloomington, Indiana plant to assemble color televisions formerly purchased from Matsushita of Japan. The homeward move has been augmented by the fall of the American dollar against foreign currencies.[27]

Sensitivity to Cultural Differences

The guiding principle for people involved in international enterprise is sensitivity to cultural differences. **Cultural sensitivity** is awareness of local and national customs and their importance in effective interpersonal relationships. Ignoring the customs of other people creates a communications block that can impede business and create ill will. A recurring problem is that some Americans are impatient to close a deal while business people in many other cultures prefer to slowly build a relationship before consummating a deal. A sampling of cultural differences that can effect how business is conducted is presented in Table 2-2.

Candidates for foreign assignments generally receive training in the language and customs of the country in question. Intercultural training exercises include playing the roles of businesspeople from a different culture. The importance of such training was revealed by a study that found 30 percent of placements in foreign countries were mistakes. These mistakes were primarily due to the employees' failures to adjust properly to a new culture.[28]

ORGANIZATIONAL RESTRUCTURINGS AND CONSOLIDATIONS

Another current trend shaping the manager's environment is the movement toward more streamlined, efficient organizations. In order to remain competitive and provide shareholders with a suitable return on investment, many firms have undergone **restructuring**, the slimming down of operations in order to focus resources and boost profits or decrease expenses.

Restructuring can involve billions of dollars' worth of assets in mergers and acquisitions, sales of subsidiaries, layoffs of workers, plant closings and consolidations, write-offs of unprofitable operations, heavy borrowing, and stock buybacks.[29] (Layoffs are now commonly referred to as **downsizing**.) Here we present several examples of restructuring and consolidations, and we examine the impact of restructuring on the manager's environment.

Table 2-2   Cultural Mistakes to Avoid in Selected Countries

Insisting on getting down to business quickly in most countries outside the United States. (In most countries, building a social relationship precedes closing a deal.)

Licking postage stamps in India. (Indians regard this practice as offensive.)

Telling Indians you prefer not to eat with your hands. (If the Indians are not using cutlery when eating, they expect their guest to do likewise.)

Not interpreting "We'll consider it" as a "No" when spoken by a Japanese businessperson. (Japanese negotiators mean "No" when they say "We'll consider it.")

Giving small gifts to Chinese when conducting business. (Chinese people are offended by these gifts.)

Not giving small gifts to Japanese when conducting business. (Japanese people are offended by not receiving these gifts.)

A manager appearing in shirtsleeves at a business meeting in West Germany. (Germans believe that a person is not exercising proper authority when he or she appears at a meeting in shirtsleeves.)

Acting overly rank-conscious in Scandinavian countries. (Scandinavians pay relatively little attention to a person's place in the hierarchy.)

Appearing perturbed when somebody shows up late for a meeting in most countries outside the United States. (Time is much less valued outside the United States.)

Source: Several of the above errors are based on "International Business Tips," *The Pryor Report* (August 1987): 11; "American Manager/Foreign Employee," *Research Institute Personal Report for the Executive* (21 January 1986): 2.3.

Examples of Restructuring

Many small businesses are in a perpetual state of restructuring because they operate on such slim margins of profits. Often the owner will take on two jobs in order to save money. The restructuring of large organizations and government agencies receives more publicity. A representative example of a large-scale restructuring took place several years ago at the Kroger Co., a retail company with $17 billion in annual sales. Kroger closed 100 of its 1,100 grocery stores, pared corporate operating expenses and staff by 25 percent, and contemplated selling all of its 900 drug stores. A major reason for Kroger's restructuring may have been management's realization that the company had been operating inefficiently for many years.

The revamping of Kroger has continued. The new Kroger focuses on areas where it dominates and from which it yields good results, such as in hometown Cincinnati. By 1988, its president had shucked marginal operations and improved short-term results.[30]

In order to increase profitability, Exxon Corp. cut employment by 48,000, or one-third of its work force, over a seven-year period. Refinery capacity was reduced by 30 percent, and 19,800 service stations were eliminated. Exxon automated its refineries and focused its efforts on high-volume service stations, which it refurbished and modernized.[31]

Other substantial downsizings include AT&T cutting its workforce from 375,000 to 330,300; Eastman Kodak decreasing employment by 10 percent; General Motors reducing its white-collar work force by 25 percent; and Eastern Airlines reducing employment by 1,500 people. Despite these dramatic figures, a survey of 1,134 companies revealed that the average number of employees reduced in a downsizing was 362.[32]

Impact on the Manager's Job

The atmosphere created by restructuring affects the manager's job in several ways. Of major impact, managers in a downsized organization put much of their energy into surviving the economic downturn. As one manager noted, "We've become a 'triple-S firm': slash costs, save money, and salvage your hide." Many managers and nonmanagers alike weaken their bonds of loyalty to the firm because they believe they can no longer trust the company. The manager may thus have to operate with less loyal employees who are also suffering from a lowered work ethic. Cost reduction becomes the highest priority, while people management becomes significantly less important.[33]

Managers placed in a restructured environment must learn to make do without substantial support and backup personnel. A restructured organization is often referred to as **lean and mean**, because all the excess, or corporate "fat," has been removed. Frequently, the manager has to perform tasks that would have been performed by subordinates prior to downsizing.

Dealing with the survivors of a downsizing represents a challenge for the manager. Some employees who were not laid off in a major downsizing begin to feel that they are a burden to the company and that they may be laid off next. Shawn Murphy, an industrial psychologist, contends that employees who stay on after a company's downsizing sometimes experience "survivor guilt." They do not understand why they were so fortunate and therefore feel guilty.[34]

Another impact on the manager's job is that during and after a period of restructuring, employees become more cautious about making suggestions for improvement. They reason that if the suggestion backfires, they may lose their job. Similarly, employees are hesitant to make even justified complaints about working conditions for fear of retaliation by management. As a consequence of this low-risk-taking attitude, the manager has fewer useful suggestions at his or her disposal.

RELATIONSHIPS WITH LABOR UNIONS

Labor unions can be considered part of the manager's external environment because unions are formed outside of the firm. Nevertheless, unions can also exert a substantial influence on the manager's everyday work. Approximately 17 percent of the nonagricultural American work force is unionized, including both manufacturing and service workers. Thirty years ago, the comparable figure was about 34 percent. Part of this decline has been attributed to a loss of many manufacturing jobs in heavily unionized industries, and an increase in nonunion jobs (such as data processing workers).[35] Two factors, however, may create an upsurge in union membership in the upcoming decade. One is the revitalization of manufacturing, with its heavy concentration of union jobs. Second, it has been predicted that many low-paid service workers will look toward unionization to improve their plight.[36] Two topics will be described to illustrate how unions influence a manager's work: the new era of labor-management relations and working under a labor agreement.

The New Era of Labor-Management Relations

In the current era, relationships between management and unions are much more harmonious than in previous eras. The core contributor to this harmony is a recognition by both management and labor that an adversarial relationship places U.S. firms at a disadvantage in worldwide competition. As Daniel D. Luria notes, pay cuts, two-tier wage plans (lower pay scales for newly hired workers), and less stringent application of seniority rules have become commonplace in the auto, steel, and farm equipment industries. Industry-wide compensation agreements are also becoming less frequent, making it easier for managers to adjust to local circumstances.[37]

An illustration of the new era of cooperation is joint labor-management committees at many automotive plants. These committees, composed of members of both management and labor, have devised plans for boosting productivity and quality through such methods as **production work teams**. These teams are groups of individuals who work somewhat independently to perform a large task, with each team member being a generalist rather than a specialist. The implementation of production work teams requires reducing strict union work rules that limit the particular tasks performed by one worker.[38]

The U.S. Department of Labor has reported the result of more than two hundred successful labor-management efforts in a wide variety of industries. Following are several examples of this new era of cooperation resulting in productivity improvements:

- The Bethlehem Steel Corp./United Steelworkers joint effort involved 8,900 employees in labor-management participation teams, resulting in substantial improvements in product quality, production costs, scrap, and equipment downtime.

- A Beech Aircraft Corp. suggestion program operated by a labor-management productivity council resulted in several million dollars in cost savings over a period of years.

- The Fiber Products Division of Diamond International Corp. reported a 16 percent boost in productivity, a 40 percent reduction in quality problems, and a 55 percent reduction in grievances (formal complaints) through its cooperative project with the United Paperworkers Union.

Managing Under a Labor Agreement

The key document in labor–management relations is the **labor agreement,** a written contract between management and the union specifying a wide range of work issues. Among these issues are union membership requirements, wage rates, job security, management rights, and the grievance procedure. First-level managers, in particular, are affected by the labor agreement. Upper-level managers, however, sometimes become directly involved in interpreting the labor agreement, and they often consult with supervisors about disputes between supervisors and operative workers.

In general, working under a labor agreement can simplify some aspects of the manager's job. For example, if operative employees know that wages have already been negotiated for the life of the contract, managers do not have to get involved in salary discussions with employees. The many clauses of the agreement must serve as a specific guideline to supervisory practice; they are not to be violated unless under unusual circumstances such as a fire or power outage. Supervisors must study the labor agreement, and upper-level managers should also be familiar with the provisions. The labor-management agreement should be consulted whenever a dispute arises.

Consistency is important when interpreting provisions of the agreement. Suppose you tell one union member in your department that she can have one extra day of vacation because she was ill during one of her vacation days. The next request has to be treated in a similar manner.

Managers must also be cautious about making difficult interpretations of the labor agreement. Because a misinterpretation can result in a grievance and in many hours of haggling, the manager should seek help with difficult interpretations. For example, a recent United Autoworkers (UAW) contract with the Ford Motor Co. and General Motors Corp. guarantees the jobs of current workers under all circumstances except for falling sales.[39] A plant manager might have to consult a higher-level executive before declaring that sales had fallen sufficiently to justify laying off some workers at his or her plant.

A key role for the manager in working under a labor agreement is to protect the rights and interests of management. Although the agreement may restrict the latitude of managers, management still has many prerogatives remaining. Managers do not have to concede to every demand made by a union member out of fear that refusing the demand will create labor-management problems. As an official of a civil service workers union said, "We want to be proud of all our workers. If a few bad apples get out of line, we expect management to get on their case."

INCREASED LEGAL POWER OF EMPLOYEES

Another external environmental influence on the manager's job is the increased amount of legal power held by employees. Two manifestations of this increased legal power are the decline of management's authority to dismiss employees and the court-mandated protection of workers' rights.

Decline of the Employment-at-Will Doctrine

A key challenge facing all managers is that workers have developed a sense of entitlement to their jobs. When workers believe they have been dismissed unjustly, they have often sought retribution through the courts and won. Many years ago, the **employment-at-will** doctrine prevailed. Employers were allowed to dismiss employees for good cause or for no good cause, without being guilty of legal wrong.[40] Over the years, legislation has moved in the direction of employee rights. The employer who dismisses an employee may have to prove to a court that he or she deserved to be terminated. If this is not the case, the employee can sue for **wrongful discharge**, the firing of an employee for arbitrary or unfair reasons. Many employees—acting alone, or assisted by their unions—have been awarded damages in these cases,[41] as illustrated by the following incident:

> An office manager in a financial services firm was fired with the excuse that she had "a poor attitude that was rubbing off on other employees." Her superior mentioned that during staff meetings she maintained a disdainful smirk and that she had no interest in the profitability of the firm. The office manager, assisted by her attorney, sued the firm to win back her job. She won the case, with the judge ruling that the company presented no tangible evidence of poor job performance.

Laws and Court Rulings Favoring Employees

Numerous laws and court rulings protect the rights of workers in matters such as discipline, pay, discrimination, retirement age, and employee privacy. (Laws and rulings that relate to various forms of discrimination are described in Chapter 8, "Staffing the Organization.") One consequence of these many laws and rulings is that it is difficult for managers to control workers through the threat of job loss or negative employment reference. The following paragraphs describe a sampling of legislation and judicial decisions that have increased the legal power of employees.

Right-to-Know Laws.   A **right-to-know** law is one that requires the manufacturers, sellers, and users of hazardous chemicals and drugs to inform their employees and the public of the nature of their products and the dangers involved.[42] An employee who is harmed by a toxic agent on the job might readily sue an employer.

Judicial sentiment in favor of right-to-know laws has been positively influenced by such events as the disaster that took place at Bhopal, India late in 1984. A chemical leak at a Union Carbide Corp. plant resulted in the deaths of more than 2,200 persons. Allegedly thousands of others have suffered permanent damage to their nervous and reproductive systems from the same accident. Another incident favoring right-to-know legislation took place at a chemical plant in Metuchen, New Jersey, which forced the evacuation of 1,000 plant workers and residents.[43]

Protection of Whistle Blowers.   Over twenty states have passed laws protecting whistle blowers. The protection includes workers who report legal violations by their employer and those who refuse to carry out orders that violate a public policy, such as an environmental law.[44] One consequence of these laws is that managers cannot retaliate against an employee who, for example, informs the local government about a toxic spill committed by the company.

Employee Privacy.   Employee privacy is protected by a series of laws. The Federal Privacy Act of 1974 and ten state laws set limits on the data about individuals that the government can disclose to employers. For example, an employer cannot demand to see an employee's income tax statements or prison record.

A new federal law severely limits the use of polygraph (lie detector) tests for job applicants. Nine states grant employees access to their personnel files, making employers cautious about placing derogatory information in employee files. And twelve states restrict the use of arrest records in the hiring process.[45]

SUMMARY OF KEY POINTS

A large number of forces or factors in the external environment influence the work of managers. The major indirect environmental forces are economic, social/cultural, political/legal, technological, and international. The major direct environmental forces are customers, creditors/suppliers, labor markets, regulatory agencies, and competitors.

Many people believe that organizations should be socially responsible; they should have an obligation to groups in society other than owners or stockholders and beyond that prescribed by law or union contract. The traditional view of social responsibility holds that business organizations are only responsible to their owners and stockholders. By so doing, the interests of society will be served in the long run. The stakeholder viewpoint of social responsibility contends that organizations must hold themselves responsible for the many groups affected by the organization's actions.

An important aspect of social responsibility is organizational social performance. Such performance can be measured by a formal audit of the organization's activities or by an assessment of the firm's response to social issues. Current social concerns in business include socially responsible plant and office closings, child care, helping employees to meet other family demands, and coping with AIDS in the workplace. Many socially responsible acts are costly, including the use of antipollution devices and the establishing of day care centers for the children of employees. Some of the costs of performing socially responsible acts are recovered through increased productivity and decreased illness and absenteeism.

Business ethics is a topic of current concern. Major contributors to unethical behavior are the individual values of greed and gluttony. An organizational culture condoning unethical behavior also leads to poor ethics, as does moral laxity. Unethical behavior also stems from faulty rationalizations such as the belief that the unethical act will benefit the company.

Unethical behavior can be minimized by such steps as creating an ethical organizational culture, publicizing the benefits of ethical behavior, and encouraging whistle blowing.

The internationalization of business makes it necessary for managers to adapt to working with people from other countries. The heart of international business is the multinational corporation (MNC), a firm that has units in two or more countries. International business proceeds in six stages from licensing agreements to direct foreign investments (wholly owned subsidiaries). An important part of international business is global sourcing, or having some or all manufacturing carried out in other countries. Many factors have to be considered in global sourcing, including the cost of shipping and slowly evaluating the supplier. A countertrend to global sourcing is that many U.S. companies are now bringing overseas operations back home and relying on domestic suppliers.

The guiding principle for people involved in international enterprise is to develop sensitivity to cultural differences. Candidates for foreign assignments generally receive training in the language and customs of the country in question.

Another current trend shaping the manager's environment is the movement toward more streamlined, efficient organizations. To improve their return on investment, many firms have engaged in some form of restructuring, the slimming down of operations in order to focus resources and to boost profits or decrease expenses. A restructured organization is considered *"lean and mean,"* because all the excess has been removed. As a result, the manager is frequently understaffed.

Labor unions can exert a substantial influence on the managers' everyday work. Currently, labor unions and management are engaging in many joint activities to improve productivity and preserve job security. The key document in labor-management relations is the labor agreement, a written contract between the management and the union specifying a wide range of work issues. A key role for the manager in working under a labor agreement is to protect the rights and interests of management.

Workers have substantially increased their legal power despite a relative decline in union membership. A major source of power has been management's lessened authority to dismiss workers without just cause. Worker's rights have also been increased through a variety of laws and court rulings relating to right-to-know laws about harmful substances in the workplace, protection of whistle blowers, and right to privacy.

QUESTIONS

1. What force in the outside world is probably influencing the work of the plant manager in an asbestos factory?
2. What are two cultural values that exert an influence on work organizations?
3. Which interested parties have to be satisfied in order for a small-business owner to keep his or her company operating?
4. How can the following position be defended? "A company that focuses on profits will ultimately be forced to act in socially responsible ways."
5. How ethical is it for managers to lie to customers about delivery dates and quality problems?
6. How true do you think it is that most companies will overlook unethical behavior by employees so long as that behavior increases profits or reduces costs?
7. What steps can you take now to prepare for a career in international business?

8. What is the rationalization given for the positive aspects of corporate restructuring?
9. What is your prediction about the future growth of labor unions? Explain your reasoning.
10. What legal power can employees exert against their employers?

ACTIVITIES

1. Develop a list of acceptable lies for an employer to tell employees and customers, and also develop a list of unacceptable lies. Compare your lists with those of classmates.
2. Interview several people from cultures other than your own in order to develop a list of five "cultural bloopers" committed by Americans and Canadians.

CASE PROBLEM 2-A: THE ENTREPRENEURIAL SOVIETS

Peti Mirzoyan, a native of Yerevan, USSR, received an injury that prevented him from resuming construction work. To cope with the situation, he collected twenty-two friends and began producing plastic shoes from industrial scraps. Working for Mirzoyan, the workers doubled their previous salaries. Arabyat Garnikyan, also of Yerevan, and his extended family organized a cooperative to sew children's jackets from defective parachutes and other second-hand materials. The fifteen workers sew late into the night to keep up with orders. Both cooperatives are part of the tentative private enterprise agreement that the Soviet government sanctioned in an effort to close the huge gap between state-produced supplies and consumer demand.

Reforms outlined recently by the Kremlin took another step forward toward market economics when a new, individual labor law took effect. The program encourages citizens with discretionary time to supply goods and services that state enterprises have been unable to fill. Soviet officials are hesitant to characterize the cooperatives and individual labor as "free enterprise" or "capitalism," and they argue that the concepts are consistent with socialism and therefore permitted by the constitution. The private ventures are expected to retain only a small place in the national economy for the next several years. Nevertheless, the public has expressed enthusiasm for the small number of private cafes and businesses begun as experiments.

In Armenia, more than 2,500 applications for private business have been submitted since the market law was passed. Sabir Stepanyan, Armenia's procurement minister, said ten cooperatives are already in business. Four more are planned for the near future, but the earthquake of 1988 was not factored into the planning.

Cooperatives have fewer restrictions and lower taxes than the private businesses. Co-op output, however, is sold to the government under contract for fixed prices. At Mirzoyan's plastic cooperative and Garnikyan's sewing shop, workers' earnings are determined by their output. Each member of Mirzoyan's cooperative earns 250 rubles ($400 U.S.) per month, plus about 200 rubles ($320 U.S.) bonus for extra production. The average Soviet industrial worker earns about 190 rubles per month, or about $300 U.S. at the official exchange rate.

Black-market shop owners have expressed concern about the new cooperative system. "Why should I pay hundreds of rubles and high taxes to knit and sew for my friends?" a Moscow woman said when asked if she anticipated making her underground tailoring business legal. Officials have threatened stricter enforcement of laws banning black marketing, once the private work has begun. Details about the enforcement procedures have not yet been released.

Soviet citizens have high expectations of the new private labor. "He'll be sorry after the first of May," (the date for passage of the new individual labor law) a Moscow woman shouted after a state taxi whizzed past without stopping. "All of these hooligans will have to start earning their salaries."

Case Questions

1. What adjustments will Soviet managers accustomed to working under the state-owned enterprises have to make to manage under the new market system?
2. Do you think the new business system will provide more abundant goods for the Soviet consumer?
3. Should Soviet managers train in a western country before managing the new Soviet enterprises? Explain your answer.

Source: As reported in Carol J. Williams, "Soviet Consumers Liking Taste of Private Enterprise," Associated Press (6 May 1987).

CASE PROBLEM 2-B: THE TRUTH STRETCHERS

Bonita Chavez was excited about her new position as assistant to the vice president of administration at Long Haul Express, an interstate trucking firm. Chavez's responsibilities included preparing financial statements for her boss, investigating customer complaints, and writing speeches and presentations for company executives. In addition, she was assigned the task of updating the company policies and procedures manual.

Before updating the policies and procedure manual, Chavez carefully read its contents. She came upon a paragraph on the first page stating the company's philosophy. It read in part, "The cornerstone of our business is total honesty in dealing with customers, employees, and regulatory agencies. Nothing less than complete candor will be tolerated." Chavez thought to herself, "If this philosophy is meant to be followed, Long Haul is in trouble."

Several days later Chavez was still disturbed by what she perceived as a discrepancy between company philosophy and company practice. Unable to concentrate on revamping the manual, she requested a meeting with her boss, Roy Coleman.

"How can I help you, Bonita?" asked Coleman.

"I need to talk to you about a big gap between the written philosophy of Long Haul and the reality of what we do," said Chavez.

"What aspect of the philosophy are you talking about?" said Coleman. "I'm not familiar with every little detail contained in the manual."

"I'm referring to the statement that says Long Haul believes in total honesty in dealing with customers, employees, and government regulators. I've been working here thirteen months and, quite frankly, I think dishonesty is widely practiced by our managers."

"What are you specifically talking about? Can you give me some examples of dishonesty?" asked Coleman.

"Yes, Roy I can. I came prepared for the meeting. I wrote down four outright lies that I recall our managers have made, you excluded."

"Go ahead, I'm interested," said Coleman.

"Okay, here's my list:

"Last December management told the drivers and office workers that Long Haul would have to skip the employee bonus this year because profits were so slim. Yet, managers received an average bonus of $6,000.

"One of our customers was told that their shipment of china was damaged because a boulder rolled down onto the highway. In reality the driver in question was speeding and lost control on a slippery pavement.

"A state inspector was told that we purchase only top-quality, premium tires for our trucks. Yet, I know for a fact that we almost always purchase the lowest-priced tires that meet specifications.

"We tell many customers that we have given them our 'preferred customer rate' when all customers receive the same rate."

With a smile, Coleman said to Bonita, "The examples you have given me all fit into sensible business practice. You have to color the truth a little to stay in business. I think the corporate philosophy refers to lies that actually harm people. I'll go over these so-called lies one by one.

"It's true we didn't have enough profits to pay everybody a bonus. Because our managers have a bigger stake in the company, we give them bonuses first.

"How can you expect us to tell a customer that one of our drivers lost control because of speeding? That would be a sure way to lose a customer in the competitive world of trucking.

"Of course we tell the regulators we purchase top-quality tires only. When we do buy low-priced tires, we make sure they are top quality despite the low price. I see no problem there.

"You're right that we tell each customer they are receiving a preferred rate. It makes them happy, and they are not paying a *higher* rate. The number one principle in this business or any other business is to keep the customer happy."

"I understand what you are saying Roy, but I'm still perplexed. I am being asked to update a manual with a philosophy that isn't being taken seriously."

Case Questions

1. What is your opinion of Roy Coleman's position that you have to bend the truth a little to stay in business?
2. Is Chavez acting appropriately in bringing her concern about lying to her boss?
3. What should Chavez do next?

REFERENCES

1. "The Workplace & AIDS: A Guide to Services & Information," *Personnel Journal* (October 1987): 65–80.
2. Robert Albanese, *Management* (Cincinnati: South-Western Publishing Co., 1988), 145–160.
3. Albanese, *Management*, 150.
4. Robert Kreitner, *Management*, 3d ed. (Boston: Houghton Mifflin Co., 1986), 657.
5. James A. F. Stoner and Charles Wankel, *Management*, 3rd ed. (Englewood Cliffs, NJ: Prentice Hall, 1986), 68.
6. Ramon J. Aldag and Timothy M. Stearns, *Management* (Cincinnati: South-Western Publishing Co., 1987), 877.
7. Angelo Kinicki and associates, "Socially Responsible Plant Closings," *Personnel Administrator* (June 1987): 116.
8. Kinicki and associates, "Socially Responsible Plant Closings," 118.

9. Donald J. Petersen and Douglas Massengill, "Childcare Programs Benefit Employers, Too," *Personnel* (May 1988): 58.
10. John A. Byrne, "A Job for the 'Trailing Spouse' Too," *Business Week* (16 November 1987): 239.
11. Phil Ebersole, "Family Leave Comes of Age," *Democrat and Chronicle* (10 January 1988).
12. Lorraine Lutgen, "AIDS in the Workplace: Fighting Fear with Facts and Policy," *Personnel* (November 1987): 54.
13. Lutgen, "AIDS in the Workplace," 58.
14. Aldag and Stearns, *Management*, 872.
15. Kreitner, *Management*, G2.
16. Chris Welles, "Ivan Boesky's Secret 'Parking Lots'," *Business Week* (22 June 1987): 130.
17. "Lax Moral Climate Breeds White-Collar Crime Wave," *Personnel* (January 1988): 7.
18. Saul W. Gellerman, "Why 'Good' Managers Make Bad Ethical Choices," *Harvard Business Review* (July-August 1986): 88.
19. "Out of South Africa: Divestment Hits a Snag," *Business Week* (6 July 1987): 53.
20. Priscilla Petty, "Ethical Policies Pay Off in Employee Loyalty, Productivity, and Profits," *Democrat and Chronicle* (25 February 1986).
21. Clyde H. Farnsworth, "New Survey of Whistle Blowers Finds Retaliation, Few Regrets," *New York Times*, 2 March 1987; Janet P. Near and Marcia P. Miceli, "Retaliation Against Whistle Blowers: Predictors and Effects," *Journal of Applied Psychology* (February 1986): 137.
22. Kreitner, *Management*, 694–697.
23. Robert B. Reich and Eric D. Mankin, "Joint Ventures with Japan Give Away the Future," *Harvard Business Review* (March-April 1986): 78–86.
24. "Made in the U.S.A.," *Business Week* (29 February 1988): 60.
25. John E. McGrath and Charles E. Lucier, "Winning Against Low-Cost Rivals," *Management Review* (August 1987): 47; Gary Hamel and C. K. Prahalad, "Do You Really Have a Global Strategy?" *Harvard Business Review* (July-August 1985): 139.
26. McGrath and Lucier, "Winning," 48–49.
27. "Some U.S. Manufacturers Moving Home," *New York Times*, 19 February 1987.
28. P. Christopher Earley, "Intercultural Training for Managers: A Comparison of Documentary and Interpersonal Methods," *Academy of Management Journal* (December 1987): 685.
29. "Restructuring Alters Corporate Landscape," Associated Press, 14 February 1987.
30. Thomas Peters, "Hostile Bids Stir Business from Apathy," syndicated column, 24 August 1986; Zachary Schiller, "Kroger's White Knight Puts on a Black Hat," *Business Week* (3 October 1988): 38.
31. "America's Leanest and Meanest," *Business Week* (5 October 1987): 79.
32. Eric Rolfe Greenberg, "Downsizing: Results of a Survey by the American Management Association," *Personnel* (October 1987): 35.
33. W. Norman Smallwood and Eliot Jacobsen, "Is There Life After Downsizing?" *Personnel* (December 1987): 42.
34. Quoted in Smallwood and Jacobsen, "Is There Life After Downsizing?" 43.
35. "Organized Labor Loses 62,000 members in 1987," *Democrat and Chronicle* (23 February 1988).
36. Mark McColloch, "Labor Unions in U.S. Will Come Back Stronger than Ever," *Democrat and Chronicle* (1 September 1986).
37. Daniel D. Luria, "New Labor-Management Models from Detroit," *Harvard Business Review* (September–October 1986): 22.

38. Aaron Bernstein, "A Demanding Year for Labor," *Business Week* (11 January 1988): 34.
39. Bernstein, "Demanding Year," 34.
40. "Beyond Unions: A Revolution in Employee Rights Is in the Making," *Business Week* (8 July 1985): 72.
41. David A. Bradshaw and Linda Van Winkle Deacon, "Wrongful Discharge: The Tip of the Iceberg?" *Personnel Administrator* (November 1985): 74–76.
42. James O. Castagnera, "Right-to-Know Issues at State and Local Levels," *Personnel* (May 1986): 9.
43. Castagnera, "Right-to-Know," 10.
44. "Beyond Unions," 73.
45. "Beyond Unions," 73.

PART TWO
Planning and Decision Making

Chapter 3
Essentials Of Planning

Chapter 4
Problem Solving and Decision Making

Chapter 5
Specialized Techniques for Planning and Decision Making

Part Two describes the management function that underlies all others—the function of planning and decision making. No matter what actions managers take, they engage in planning and decision making. Chapter 3 presents a general framework for planning and describes that framework in depth. Chapter 4 explains how managers and professionals go about solving problems and making decisions. Emphasis is placed on the human element involved in these processes.

Chapter 5 deals with quantitative tools and techniques used by managers to assist them in making decisions based on hard data. The information presented in Chapter 5 serves as a brief introduction to management science or production and operations management.

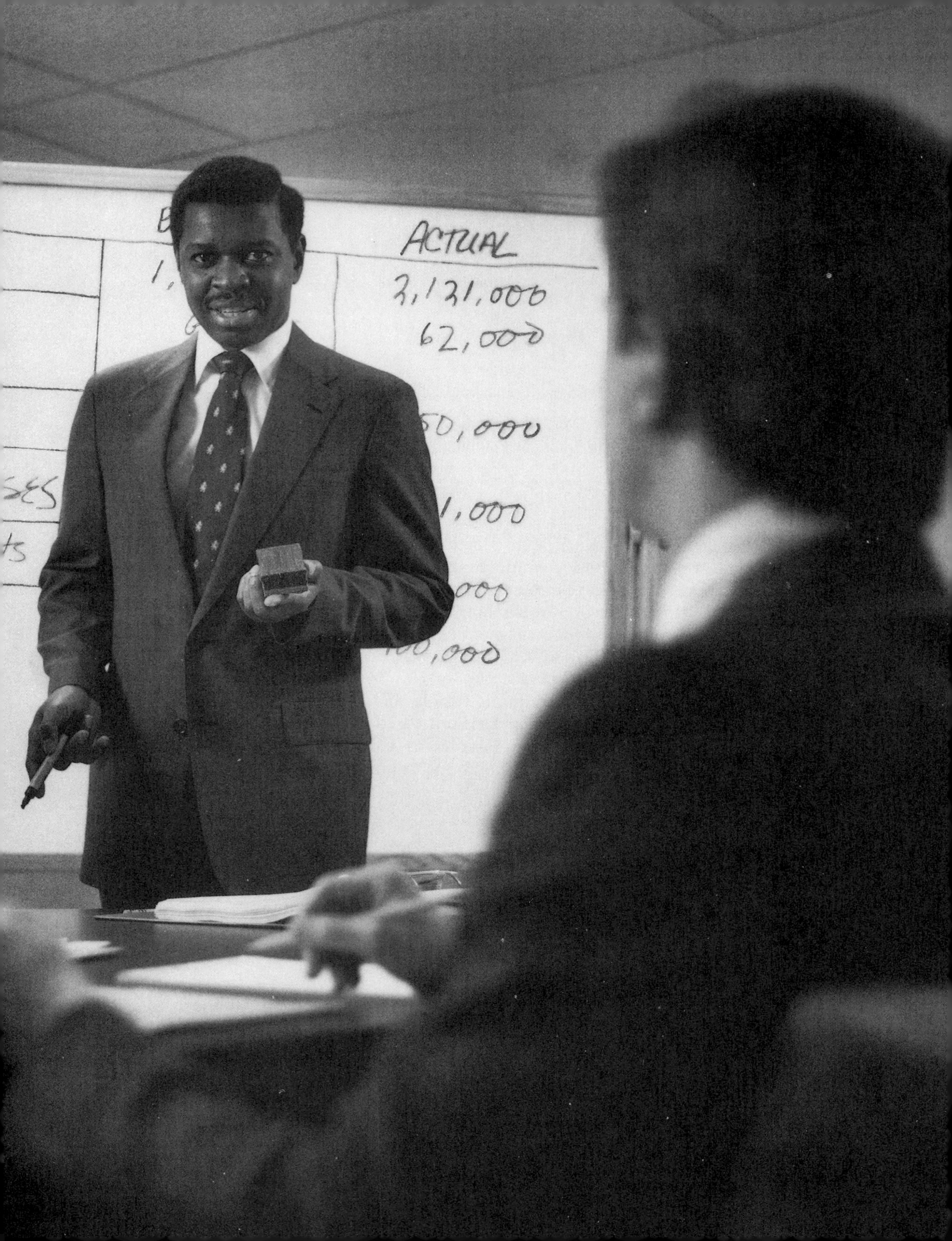
ACTUAL
62,000

3
Essentials of Planning

After studying the material in this chapter, you should be able to accomplish the following tasks:

1. Become a better planner.
2. Describe a generalized model for planning.
3. Understand the concept of a strategic plan and the related concepts of strategy, strategic decision, and strategic planning.
4. Explain what are operating plans, policies, procedures, and rules.
5. Outline how planning can be used for improving productivity.

Key Terms and Phrases

Planning
Goal
Objective
Action plan
Contingency plan
Strategic plan
Operational plan
Strategy
Strategic decision
Strategic planning

Mission
Policy
Judgmental forecast
Time-series analysis
Linear regression
Spreadsheet analysis
Operating plan
Procedure
Rule
Quality of work life (QWL)

Planning is the lifeblood of any intelligent organization. Lacking carefully drawn plans, the firm would bob and float much like a dingy placed upon the high seas (corporate planning executive).

Planning has been oversold in our business culture. Effective business people follow their hunches to figure out what to do next. If you solve today's problems, the future will take care of itself (owner of a wholesale meat-supply company).

These two contradictory viewpoints about the value of planning point out that, although not all executives agree on the importance of planning, it is a major management function. As explained in Chapter 1, **planning** is the process of establishing goals and objectives and figuring out how to achieve them.

A **goal** is a specific target that a person tries to achieve or a condition that the person wants to exist in the future. As the term is used in planning, an **objective** is a specific state or condition that contributes to a larger goal. An objective can thus be considered a subgoal. The terms *goals* and *objectives* often are used interchangeably. Technically, however, a goal is a high-level target and an objective is a subgoal.

Planning is an attempt to manage the future. Although Ralph Taylor (the owner of the wholesale meat-supply company) dismisses the importance of planning, he has a grand plan for running his business. He believes that the way to create a favorable future for the firm is to do a good job today—much like building a good reputation.

The purpose of this chapter is to describe the planning function in such a way that you can use this information to plan more effectively as a manager or as an individual contributor. First we look at the value of planning and at a framework for its application. After that we describe the major types of plans used in organizations. Then we describe an application of planning to productivity improvement. Finally, we look at some of the potential problems with planning.

WHY PLANNING IS NEEDED IN ORGANIZATIONS

The primary justification for planning is that it leads to improvements in organizational performance and productivity. A number of research studies with corporations support the idea that careful attention to planning leads to improved financial standing. A review of eighteen studies about the impact of planning indicated that formal planning by top executives frequently leads to improved financial performance.[1]

One study looked at the results of long-range planning over a seven-year cycle.[2] The researchers matched eighteen sets of companies for size, type of industry, and other important characteristics. Neither company in each pair engaged in formal planning at the outset. Then one firm in each pair began to plan. The differences in results were impressive. Companies that planned outperformed their own past performance and the performance of the nonplanning companies on every measure of success, including return on investment and growth in earnings per share. An extension of this study tracked company performance for an additional four years for three pairs of companies in the chemical industry.

Over the duration of the study, the formal planners continued to significantly outperform the nonplanners in dollar sales growth and pretax profit growth. In addition, the companies that planned also extended their margin of difference.[3]

One of the problems in evaluating the contribution of planning is that it is embedded in other managerial functions. For example, in the process of controlling performance, the manager has engaged in such planning activities as establishing performance standards.[4] To fully evaluate the merits of planning, it would also be necessary to evaluate how it contributes to other managerial activities.

A FRAMEWORK FOR PLANNING

Planning is a complex and comprehensive process involving a series of overlapping and interrelated elements, or stages. The framework presented in Figure 3-1 is a summary of the elements of planning: establish goals and objectives, define the present situation, forecast aids and barriers to goals and objectives, develop action plans to reach goals and objectives, develop budgets, implement the plans, and control the plans. We will examine each element separately, although in practice several of these elements often overlap. For example, a manager might be implementing and controlling the same plan simultaneously.

The steps in planning presented here are not always followed in order. Planners frequently start in the middle of the process, proceed forward, and then return to an earlier step. This change of sequencing frequently happens because the planner discovers new information or because objectives change.

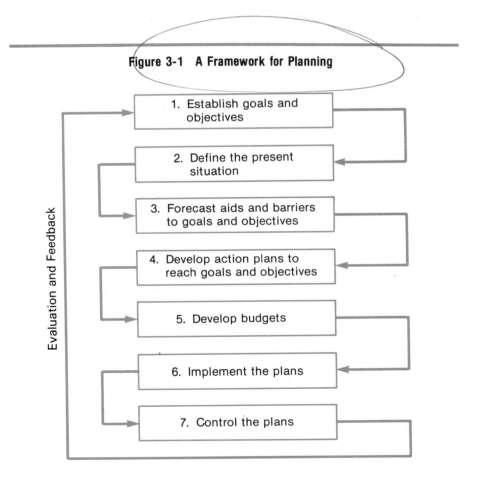

Figure 3-1   A Framework for Planning

Evaluation and Feedback

1. Establish goals and objectives

2. Define the present situation

3. Forecast aids and barriers to goals and objectives

4. Develop action plans to reach goals and objectives

5. Develop budgets

6. Implement the plans

7. Control the plans

Elements of Planning

Assume that Ralph Taylor, the meat-supply company owner, enrolls in a management course at a local community college and becomes a convert to planning. He observes that his sales of beef, pork, veal, and poultry have decreased in volume over the last several years. Concerned about the future, he now decides to engage in planning.

Establish Goals and Objectives.   The initial step in planning is to establish goals and to identify objectives that contribute to the attainment of these goals. For example, Taylor might establish the goal of diversifying Taylor Meats to compensate for what he perceives to be a declining demand for meat products. An objective might be to offer a line of health foods or meat substitutes (such as tofu or soybean-based food products). Specifically, Taylor's goal is to derive, within two years, 20 percent of gross revenues from the sale of nonmeat products. His objective is to sell, by next year, $8,500 worth of soybean-based food patties.

Define the Present Situation.   Taylor has already given some serious thought to the present—he was prompted to start planning because he noticed a decline in sales volume. His gross revenues, however, have not yet declined because his prices have increased enough to compensate for the decrease in sales volume. To define the present situation more clearly, Taylor works with his bookkeeper. She reports that the decrease in sales volume is most pronounced for beef, pork, and veal; poultry sales have declined to a lesser extent. Taylor concludes that he does not have to worry about a decline in poultry sales for the foreseeable future. In addition to checking the figures, Taylor talks to several of his long-term customers about the decline in orders. He is reassured that his firm is doing nothing wrong. The problem is that individual consumers are purchasing less red meat.

According to planning theory, defining the present situation includes measuring success and examining internal capabilities and external threats.[5] Taylor thus must engage in two more activities to complete this second step. *Success* here would mean that sales volume of new products equals or exceeds the decline in sales volume of meat.

Internal capabilities refer to the strengths and weaknesses of the firm, or organizational unit, that is engaging in planning. The capabilities of Taylor Meats include a solid core of reliable employees who provide timely and accurate deliveries to customers, a good record of complying with health regulations relating to the sale of meat, and excellent facilities for packing and storing food received from suppliers (such as farmers who supply chickens).

External threats and opportunities include competition, business conditions, customer loyalty, and government regulations. Taylor recognizes that other companies (the primary businesses of which are health foods and meat substitutes) have a competitive edge in selling these products because of their experience. On the other hand, he is convinced that his fine reputation in the community for providing high-quality products and good service has earned his firm a high degree of customer loyalty.

Forecast Aids and Barriers to Goals and Objectives. As an extension to defining the present situation, the manager attempts to predict which internal and external factors will foster or hinder attaining the desired ends. (Details about forecasting techniques are presented in "Strategic Plans and Strategy".) Taylor relies on his intuition and that of other business associates about the future demand for meat substitutes. One of Taylor's butchers, for example, says to him, "This health-food craze will end soon. If we get into it too heavily, we'll be stuck when the demand drops off." Nevertheless, Taylor is not dissuaded; he and the rest of his staff are convinced that the new generation of homemakers will continue to demand replacements for meat.

One barrier Taylor and his sales manager foresee is the image of the firm. Will his customers be prompted to purchase nonmeat products from a wholesale butcher? Can the firm change its image fast enough to make a profit selling products such as soybean patties and tofu? Taylor also wonders how much productive time the diversification into other lines will take away from his traditional business. The sales manager presents an alternative to Taylor. Why not simply increase the sales force as a straightforward way to increase sales? Taylor, however, does not think this is a good solution.

Develop Action Plans for Reaching Goals and Objectives. Goals and objectives are only wishful thinking until **action plans** (specific steps) are drawn for their attainment. Usually, alternative action plans can be developed to reach the same goal or objective. For example, you might think of several good action plans for earning a promotion. In this element of planning, Taylor and his associates have to figure out specifically how they are going to diversify. Taylor's logical action plans include matters such as the following:

- Personally visiting suppliers of health foods and meat substitutes (mills and farms) in the area, speaking to principals about costs and deliveries.

- Taking an informal survey of present customers to evaluate their potential interest in purchasing nonmeat products from Taylor.

- Speaking to the company lawyer about what must be done from a legal standpoint to change the name of the firm from Taylor Meats to Taylor Foods.

Develop Budgets. Planning often results in action plans that require money to implement. For instance, Taylor would have to allocate funds to purchase an inventory of soybean patties and to change the name of the firm. A formal budget would indicate how much money he can afford to spend on each action plan. Some action plans require almost no cash outlay, such as speaking to present customers about their potential interest in purchasing nonmeat items from Taylor. Purchasing soybean products and tofu from suppliers, however, involves considerable expense. The amount of inventory Taylor purchases is contingent in part on the sales forecast, if it appears that present customers are poised to make large purchases of nonmeat products, Taylor will budget more money for purchase of the nonmeat inventory.

Other plausible items to budget for would be advertising, converting to the name change (including items such as purchasing new stationery and having the name repainted on delivery trucks), and hiring one new salesperson to push the nonmeat product line.

Implement the Plans.   If the plans developed in the previous five steps are to benefit the firm, they must be put into use. A criticism frequently made of planners is that they develop elaborate plans and then abandon them in favor of conducting business as usual. If Taylor was suddenly deluged with an increase in meat orders, he might be tempted to neglect his strategy of diversifying into nonmeat products. We assume, however, that Taylor does proceed with diversification and attempts to sell the nonmeat line as planned. The firm changes its name to Taylor Foods, offers a new line of nonmeat products, and hires an additional sales representative to spearhead the line.

Control the Plans.   Planning does not end with implementation because plans may not always proceed as planned. The purpose of the control process is to measure progress toward goal attainment and to take corrective action if too much deviation is detected. The deviations from expected performance can be negative or positive. Assume that Taylor Foods planned for $3,000 per month in nonmeat sales. If the actual sales prove to be $600 per month, Ralph Taylor must take corrective action. Among the possible corrective actions would be (1) increasing the advertising budget, (2) working more closely with the sales representative, (3) calling on more prospective customers personally, or (4) lowering the original sales estimate because it appears unrealistic.

If actual sales were $5,000 per month, the corrective actions Taylor might take would be (1) increasing the regular orders from nonmeat suppliers, (2) increasing the advertising budget to capitalize on a good trend, (3) hiring an additional salesperson, or (4) increasing the sales forecast.

The notation "Evaluation and Feedback" on the left side of Figure 3-1 indicates that the control process allows fine-tuning of plans after they are implemented. One common example is setting a budget too high or too low in the first attempt at implementing a plan. A manager controls by making the right adjustment.

Contingency Planning.   Many planners develop a set of backup plans to be used in case things do not proceed as they hoped. A **contingency plan** is thus an alternative plan to be used if the original plan cannot be implemented. If Taylor's diversification efforts fail, he might establish an objective in his contingency plan to reduce his staff to an appropriate size for the decrease in sales volume associated with a decline in the demand for meat.

Contingency plans are often developed from objectives in earlier steps in planning. The plans are triggered into action when deviations are detected from these objectives, however early in the planning process.

A creative example of contingency planning is the *"completion bond"* offered by Film Finances, Ltd. The bond functions as an insurance policy that pays the extra costs when movie films exceed budget or are not completed on time. The demand for such guarantees has increased proportionately with the number of films being made by independent producers, most of whom receive money from outside investors.[6] The contingency covered by these bonds is the additional expense incurred when a movie exceeds its time or financial budget.

STRATEGIC PLANS AND STRATEGY

The framework for planning can be used to develop and implement both strategic and operational plans. **Strategic plans** are master plans that shape the destiny of the firm. When Ralph Taylor decided to supply customers with food rather than with meat only, he was beginning to develop a strategic plan for his firm. **Operational plans** are those that relate to running the organization on a day-to-day, short-term basis. In this section, we examine strategic plans and closely related concepts. In the next section, operational plans are described.

Determining Strategy

Strategic decisions are concerned with organizational strategy. A **strategy** is a comprehensive program for achieving an organization's goals and objectives and thus achieving its mission (or unique purpose). Simply stated, a strategy is an overall plan.[7] An organization that has a strategy has a purpose as it pursues its daily activities. The strategy also guides the use of resources that help to move the organization toward reaching its objectives. As used here, the terms *strategy* and *strategic plan* are synonymous. The accompanying ''Manager in Action'' illustrates organizational strategy at a lofty level.

A planner selects organizational strategy from among alternatives as the best way to obtain major objectives, paying serious attention to the relative capabilities, major functions, policies, and resources available.

MANAGER IN ACTION:

The High-Flying Trump

Financier Donald J. Trump was flying above Manhattan in one of his five helicopters. There in midtown was Trump Tower, his luxury condominium and commercial complex. Several blocks away was another posh development, Trump Plaza. Off in the distance was his latest condominium creation, Trump Parc.

As the helicopter moved swiftly south along the Hudson River, Trump told his pilot to circle back for one more look at the dilapidated Penn Central railroad yard and a few decaying docks sitting amidst the buildings below. Pointing downward, the 41-year-old real estate tycoon and casino baron said "There's where I'm going to build the world's tallest skyscraper."

In a ten-year period, Trump has transformed himself from a local landlord to one of the eminent real-estate moguls of his generation. The total value of his holdings is more than $3 billion. Upon completion of his $101 million purchase of 93 percent of Resorts International Inc.'s Class B stock, he will also become the largest casino operator in the United States.

His goals include becoming a businessperson of international stature who can make deals with heads of states as well as with heads of business corporations. He has already met with Soviet leader Mikhail Gorbachev to discuss the possible development by Trump of luxury hotels in Russia.

Source: As reported in "Donald Trump: What's Behind the Hype?" *Business Week* (20 July 1987): 93; "Flashy Symbol of an Acquisitive Age," *Time* (16 January 1989): 48–54.

Making Strategic Decisions

A **strategic decision** is one that deals with such matters as the mission of the firm and its relationship with the outside world; it covers a long period of time. A good example of a strategic decision was made years ago by Kenneth H. Olsen, the president of Digital Equipment Corp. (DEC). His goal was to radically transform his engineering-oriented company into a tough, market-conscious competitor. Olsen's strategic decision is contained in this statement: "The issues that led to this overhaul are not technical, but have to do with products and marketing. The key strategy of the corporation is making the new desktop products work together with DEC's bread-and-butter minicomputer line, then selling them together." (A five-year follow-up suggests that Olsen's strategic decision was highly effective.)[8] We will use this business decision to illustrate the five distinguishing characteristics of a strategic decision.[9]

1. *Relationship to environment*. The decision must be directed toward defining the organization's relationship to its environment. For a decision to be considered strategic, it must be externally oriented and concerned with specifying the nature of the interaction between an organization and its total environment. Strategic decisions focus fundamentally on what business the company is in or will be in and on the kind of company it is or is to be. Note that the president of DEC spoke of the firm responding to the market. He stated that his company would now be in the business of satisfying the needs of other firms for an integrated line of computer equipment.

2. *Unit of analysis*. The decision must take the organization as a whole as the unit of analysis. This criterion emphasizes the organization-wide character of the strategy concept. In a single-product firm, the term *organization* refers to the entire company. In a multiproduct firm, each large division could make its own strategic decision. DEC's decision to become more market- and consumer-oriented has affected the entire firm, particularly in manufacturing, marketing, and engineering. In other

words, a strategic decision is made outside of one functional area, such as human resources or accounting.

3. *Multifunctional input.* The decision must depend on input from a variety of functional areas. This criterion flows logically from the second one. For DEC to achieve its new marketing orientation, considerable coordinated activity had to take place among the major functional areas of the business. For example, the marketing division adopted aggressive tactics for selling office automation and personal computers to small businesses. Engineering and manufacturing, in turn, had to do their part in developing and making new products. Specifically, DEC developed a broad range of computers—from small desktop machines to large office minicomputers—that can communicate readily with one another.

4. *Scope of decision.* The decision must provide direction for, and place constraints on, administrative and operational activities throughout the enterprise. Although strategic decisions focus on the outside world, they have internal consequences. Olsen's decision to decrease the engineering orientation of the firm means that new-product developers have to change their emphasis. Instead of developing highly sophisticated computers, which are of interest primarily to scientists, they now have to develop products of more interest to small businesses.

5. *Importance of decision.* The decision must be important to the success of the enterprise; however, not all important decisions are necessarily strategic. A decision to grant each employee in the firm a one-time $5,000 bonus would not be a strategic decision. Obviously, Olsen's decision to embark upon a corporate overhaul was not only important but also strategic.

Undertaking Strategic Planning

Strategic planning encompasses those activities leading to the statement of goals and objectives for the firm and the choice of appropriate strategies to achieve those goals and objectives. Under ideal circumstances, an organization arrives at its strategy after completing strategic planning. In practice, many firms choose a strategy prior to strategic planning. Once the firm has the strategy, a plan is developed to implement that strategy. In this section, we describe the strategic planning model and how values shape strategy.

The Strategic Planning Model.   Although the general planning model can be applied to strategic planning, it is more beneficial to use a model exclusively designed for strategic planning. The model consists of the following five steps:[10]

1.   Analyze the environment to understand such factors as the characteristics of the industry, product demand, prevailing technology, and any government regulations. This analysis requires substantial time and effort. Some of this information is available in computer databases.

2. Analyze the organization to understand its position in the market, financial status, technical skills, organizational structure, and work force. A well-managed company will have much of this information on hand.

3. Analyze the key skills necessary for success, such as the ability to reach customers readily in order to sell a new product or service. For example, when Sears, Roebuck and Co. decided to enter the financial-services and real-estate businesses, top managers realized they had a critical skill in their favor. They knew how to reach the public through monthly charge-account mailings and through personal contact with customers in thousands of existing retail stores.

4. Assess the problems and opportunities of the organization that could influence the strategic decisions. When International Harvester made the mammoth decision to leave the farm-equipment business, it faced the problem of shrinkage in the farm-equipment market. When Sears Roebuck decided to diversify into financial services and real-estate sales, their opportunity was the office space available in their network of stores.

5. Develop, evaluate, and select alternative strategies to take advantage of opportunities. Because organizations have limited resources, they are forced to select one or two strategies to implement. Sears Roebuck had a number of alternative strategies open to them. One alternative strategy, for example, would be to revert to emphasizing its basic retail business more than pushing further into financial services. Sears Roebuck chose this alternative in the early 1980s.

As shown in Figure 3-2, the final outcomes of strategic planning are statements of mission, strategy, and policy. The **mission** of the organization is the general field in which the firm will operate. For example, "Standard Oil Company (Indiana) is in business to find and produce crude oil, natural gas and natural gas liquids; to manufacture high quality products useful to society from these raw materials; and to distribute and market these products and to provide dependable related services to the consuming public at reasonable prices."[11]

Specifying a mission answers the question, What business are we really in? A firm's mission may not be apparent to an outsider, as illustrated by the following anecdote:

> Andre Heiniger, the Chief Executive Managing Director of Rolex (the company that manufactures a line of expensive watches) was dining with another executive. A friend of Heiniger's dropped by the table and asked, "How's the watch business?" The chief executive replied, "I have no idea. We are not in the watch business. We are in the luxury business."[12]

As defined earlier, a strategy is a master plan to carry out an organizational mission. Rolex, for example, might introduce a line of sterling-silver fountain pens retailing for $400 each. As another example, the mission of the Depart-

Figure 3-2   The Strategic Planning Process

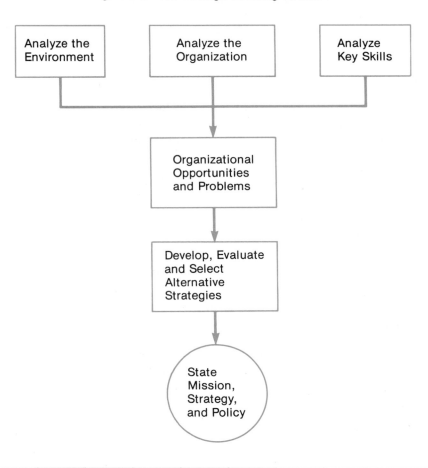

ment of Defense is to preserve peace, so part of its strategy might be to conduct peace-keeping conferences throughout the world.

After the mission and strategy have been established, it is necessary to develop policies that will guide employees toward reaching the organization's goals and objectives. A **policy** is a general guideline for making decisions and taking action. The relationship between mission and policy works in this manner: the mission leads to a strategy that leads to goals (broad purposes); the goals lead to objectives for achieving the goals; and policies help people attain these goals on a daily basis. For example, because Rolex is in the luxury business, a company policy might be that their watches will be made of the highest-quality parts and that service to their dealers also will be of the highest quality. A manufacturing specialist would then know to choose high-quality components when producing any watch made by the firm.

Values and Strategic Planning.   Strategic planning is heavily influenced by the values of the strategic planner. In practice this means that strategic planners will establish strategic goals that coincide with what they think is important. Planners who believe that human resources are important will develop strategies that protect, strengthen, and preserve human resources. Planners who are concerned primarily about finances will develop strategies that protect, strengthen, and preserve financial resources.

John Welch, the chairperson of General Electric Co. (GE), exemplifies a strategic planner whose most important value is profitability. Nicknamed Jumping Jack Flash because he leaps on a profitable deal when he sees one, Welch correspondingly places a low value on sentiment and tradition. Welch has pared away one quarter of GE's work force and made the company more profitable than at any time in recent history. An example of Welch's lack of concern for sentiment and tradition was his sale of GE's consumer electronics business to Thomson CSF, a multidivision company owned by the French government.[13] (Consumer electronics, of course, was the original foundation of GE's business.)

Using Forecasting

As shown in Figure 3-1, all planning includes making forecasts, or predicting future events. The forecasts used in strategic planning are especially difficult to make because they involve long-range trends. A number of unknown factors might crop up between the present and the time about which predictions are made. Here we will give an overview of forecasting by mentioning several of its approaches and types, and we will discuss how spreadsheet analysis is used in making forecasts.[14]

Qualitative and Quantitative Approaches.   Forecasts can be based on both qualitative and quantitative information, and most of the forecasting done for strategic planning relies on a combination of both. *Qualitative* methods of forecasting consist mainly of subjective hunches. For example, an experienced executive might predict that the high cost of housing will create a demand for small, less-expensive homes, even though this trend cannot be quantified. One qualitative method is a **judgmental forecast**, a prediction based on a collection of subjective opinions. It relies on analysis of subjective inputs from a variety of sources, including consumer surveys, sales representatives, managers, and panels of experts. For instance, a group of potential home buyers might be asked how they would react to the possibility of purchasing a compact, less-expensive home.

Quantitative forecasting methods involve either the extension of historical data or the development of models to identify the cause of a particular outcome. A widely used historical approach is **time-series analysis**. It is simply an analysis of a sequence of observations that have taken place at regular intervals over a period of time (hourly, weekly, monthly, and so forth). The underlying assumption of this approach is that the future will be much like the past. A basic example of a time-series analysis chart is shown in Figure 3-3.

This information might be used to make forecasts about when people would be willing to take vacations and would be important information for the resort and travel industry.

Linear regression is a quantitative method of predicting the relationship of changes in one variable to changes in another. For example, a resort industry economist might want to predict the influence of age on the number of vacations people take. Because the median age of the North American population is increasing, this could be useful information for business planning.

Types of Forecasts.   Three types of forecasts are used most widely: economic, sales, and technological. Each of these forecasts can be made by using both qualitative and quantitative methods.

Economic Forecasting.   No single factor is more important in managerial planning than predicting the level of future business activity.[15] Strategic planners in large organizations often rely on economic forecasts made by specialists they hire. Planners in smaller firms are more likely to rely on government forecasts. However, forecasts about the general economy do not necessarily correspond to the business activity related to a particular product or service offered by the firm.

A major factor influencing the accuracy of forecasts is their time span: shorter-range predictions are more accurate than are those made for the longer range. Strategic planning is long-range planning, and many strategic plans have to be revised frequently to match changes in business activity. For example, a sudden recession may abort plans for diversification into new products and services.

Figure 3-3   Time-Series Analysis (Hypothetical Data)

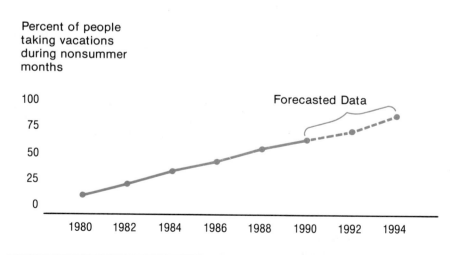

Sales Forecasting.   The sales forecast usually is the primary planning document for a business enterprise. Even if the general economy is robust, an organization needs a promising sales forecast before it can be aggressive about capitalizing on new opportunities. Strategic planners themselves may not be involved in making sales forecasts, but they rely on those made by the marketing unit to develop master plans. For instance, General Motors Corp. (GM) has embarked on a strategic plan of diversifying into a number of high-technology businesses. An important factor in the decision to implement this strategic plan was a forecast of sluggish sales for household appliances, which affected the Frigidaire Division of GM.

Sales forecasting is a risky business, even when conducted by the most astute planners. Marketing executives in large corporations generally prefer markets in which forecasts can be made accurately. Entrepreneurs in smaller businesses, however, are often willing to conduct business in markets where sales forecasts are less accurate, as illustrated in the accompanying "Manager in Action."

MANAGER IN ACTION:

Tom Corcoran, Ski Mogul

Tom Corcoran runs one of New England's largest ski resorts, Waterville Valley, in N.H. Outside his office, a visitor can hear the roar of compressed air and water showering human-made snow onto downhill trails, building a base for the new ski season. A sign over Corcoran's desk reads: "The ski business is an odd little segment of the industry that is better left to people who deeply care about it, and who are willing to have a less predictable bottom line than most big corporations will tolerate."

"I read that in *Fortune* magazine about twenty years ago and had it framed," said Corcoran, a 56-year-old Harvard MBA who was once on the U.S. Olympic ski team. "I can't say that the ski industry has changed much since. It's a business for entrepreneurs. Large corporations have tended not to do well in it."

Among the companies that have tried the ski business and then exited are Twentieth Century-Fox Film Corp. (Aspen and Breckenridge, Colorado), the Chrysler Corp. (Big Sky, Montana), and Scott Paper Co. (Squaw Mountain, Maine). Exceptions to this trend include the Keystone-Arapahoe resort owned by Ralston Purina Co., positioned just over the Colorado Divide.

"A ski area is not going to produce a stream of uninterrupted earnings that you can rely on for dividends," Corcoran said. "The business is seasonal. It's a weather-sensitive business, perhaps more so than farming. And it attracts managers who are individualistic and independent, not the kind of people who fit the corporate mold."

Source: As reported in John Fry, "Ski Business Works Best for Entrepreneurs," *New York Times* (20 December 1987).

Technological Forecasting.   Technological forecasting is predicting what types of technological changes will take place. Technological forecasts allow the firm to adapt to new technologies and thus stay competitive. For example, forecasts made in the late 1970s about the growth of robotics prompted many manufacturing firms to purchase robots to control manufacturing costs. The actual growth of robotics proved to be slower than predicted, because robots did not inevitably lead to productivity gains. A firm that delays shifting to a new technology until competitors have tried it may lose in the marketplace.

Spreadsheet Analysis.   Many managers and planning specialists use computer software that does spreadsheet analysis as a forecasting aid.[16] A **spreadsheet analysis** is a computerized method of simultaneously analyzing a large matrix (columns and rows) of values. Spreadsheets are also referred to as *"electronic worksheets,"* because they allow you to perform calculations on a large worksheet. In its basic form, a spreadsheet program is an electronic replacement for financial tools such as the accountant's pad, pencil, and electronic calculator. Spreadsheet analysis is used in forecasting to answer *"What if. . ."* questions such as the following: If the interest rate for consumer loans rises to 17.5 percent, what percent decrease in sales can we anticipate? The strategic planner in the human services branch of the government might ask a similar "What if. . ." question: If the unemployment rate increases to 10.5 percent, what percent increase in unemployment compensation will we face?

A key feature of the spreadsheet format is that it is a matrix of cells. If a value is changed in any one of the cells, the software recalculates the value of every other cell in the matrix that would be influenced by the changed value. The sales manager who did the spreadsheet analysis in Figure 3-4 wanted an answer to this question: What would happen to our net income and expenses if we increased sales in each quarter by a specified amount? The sales manager simply inserted hypothetical sales figures into the computer; the *Lotus® 1-2-3®* program produced the results shown in the bottom half of Figure 3-4.

Although spreadsheet analysis appears highly accurate and scientific, it can lead to substantial forecasting errors. An executive predicted that a computer soon to be introduced by his company would generate $55 million in sales in its first two years. He made his forecast using an electronic spreadsheet program on his desktop computer. Elated by that healthy projection, other managers began making bullish plans to add employees and inventory. Unfortunately, the executive erred. He neglected to include a price discount planned for one major component. When checking his figures later, he discovered that he had inflated the sales estimate by $8 million because his pricing formula was incorrect.[17]

The Line Manager's Role in Strategic Planning

Strategic planning is supposed to be the province of high-level managers because they have the overall perspective to make plans that affect the various functional areas of the firm. However, strategic planning is such a specialized activity and involves so many complex skills that top-level staff specialists do most of the formulations involved in strategic planning. Sometimes referred to as *"number-crunching professionals,"* strategic planners have gradually developed considerable power. They report to top managers in corporate

Figure 3-4 Spreadsheet Analysis of Hypothetical Sales Increases

```
Myco Distribution Company
Statement of Operations
Annual Forecast
```

	Qt. 1	Qt. 2	Qt. 3	Qt. 4
Sales	50000	52500	55125	57881
Cost	25000	26250	27563	28941
Margin	25000	26250	27563	28941
Expenses				
Salaries	17000	17000	17000	17000
Benefits	3400	3400	3400	3400
Trav & Ent	2000	850	850	850
Depreciation	3000	3000	3000	3000
Interest	3500	3500	3500	3500
Other	2500	2500	2500	2500
Total Expenses	31400	30250	30250	30250
Net Income	-6400	-4000	-2688	-1309

	Qt. 1	Qt. 2	Qt. 3	Qt. 4
Sales	121000	127050	133403	140073
Cost	60500	63525	66701	70036
Margin	60500	63525	66701	70036
Expenses				
Salaries	17000	17000	17000	17000
Benefits	3400	3400	3400	3400
Trav & Ent	2000	850	850	850
Depreciation	3000	3000	3000	3000
Interest	3500	3500	3500	3500
Other	2500	2500	2500	2500
Total Expenses	31400	30250	30250	30250
Net Income	29100	33275	36451	39786

Source: Prepared by James Biser, Rochester Institute of Technology, National Technical Institute for the Deaf.

headquarters, and they often develop strategic plans for division managers to implement.

The recent trend is for line (or operating) managers to become more involved in strategic planning and to use strategic planning specialists from corporate headquarters as advisors or support personnel. Daniel H. Gray says it has become fashionable to attack strategic planning as a source of American business's competitive problems. Excessively rational planning systems can be "time-consuming to complete, divorced from reality, and worst of all, conducive to a dangerous, short-term financial orientation in top managers." Nevertheless Gray believes that if strategic plans are carefully planned and implemented, they are beneficial.[18]

A major reason for the shift of strategic planning away from staff professionals and toward operating managers is that many planners are too far removed from the workplace and the marketplace to develop accurate intuition about future trends. Professional planners, however, have a number of tools and insights that can help operating managers make more useful strategic plans.

Middle- and first-level managers have an important contribution to make to strategic planning. A major reason is that lower-level managers are usually closer to available information about forces affecting the direction of the organization than are top-level managers. Middle- and first-level managers can provide top-level management with strategically useful information in such areas as product performance, customer reactions, competitive activity, and delivery problems.[19]

We have described a general framework for planning and examined the complicated subject of strategic plans. We will now look at several of the key ways in which strategic plans are translated into practice.

OPERATING PLANS, POLICIES, PROCEDURES, AND RULES

Strategic plans are formulated at the top of the organization. Four of the vehicles through which strategic plans are converted into action are operating plans, policies, procedures, and rules.

Operating Plans

Operating plans are the means through which strategic plans alter the destiny of the firm. Operating plans involve organizational efficiency (doing things right), whereas strategic plans involve effectiveness (doing the right things). Both the strategic and operational plans involve such things as exploring alternatives and evaluating the effectiveness of the plan. In a well-planned organization, all managers are responsible for making operating plans that mesh with the strategic plans of the business. Operational plans (a term used synonymously with operating plans) provide the details of how the strategic plans will be accomplished. In many organizations, suggestions to be incorporated into operating plans stem from employees at lower levels. As

Wal-Mart president David Glass says, "Most of the good ideas come from the bottom up. We keep changing a thousand little things."[20]

Operating plans focus more on the firm than on the external environment. To illustrate, the strategic plan of a local government might be to encourage the private sector to take over more governmental functions. One operating unit within the local government might then formulate a plan for subcontracting refuse removal to private contractors and phasing out the civil-service position of sanitation worker.

Operating plans tend to be drawn for a shorter period than are strategic plans. The plan for increasing the private sector's involvement in activities conducted by the local government might be a ten-year plan. In contrast, the phasing out of government sanitation workers might take two years.

The discussion of planning for productivity improvement presented later in the chapter provides examples of operational planning. The discussion deals with operating the organization in accordance with strategic plans.

Policies

Policies are general guidelines to follow in making decisions and taking action; as such, they are plans. Many policies are written; some are unwritten, or implied. Policies are designed to be consistent with strategic plans (in organizations that engage in strategic planning), yet to allow some room for interpretation by the individual manager. One important managerial role is interpreting policies to employees. Here is an example of a policy and an analysis of how it might require interpretation.

> Policy: When hiring employees from the outside, consider only those candidates who are technically competent or show promise of becoming technically competent and who show good personal character and motivation.

A manager attempting to implement this policy with respect to a given job candidate would have to make the following interpretations and ask the following questions:

* What do we mean by *"technical competence?"*

* How do I measure technical competence?

* What do we mean by *"show promise of becoming technically competent?"*

* How do I rate the promise of technical competence?

* What do we mean by *"good personal character and motivation?"*

* How do I assess good personal character and motivation?

Policies are not restricted to issues of managing human resources. They are developed to support strategic plans in every area of the organization, including purchasing, manufacturing, engineering, accounting, and information systems. For example, many firms have strict policies against employees accepting gifts and favors from vendors or potential vendors.

If policies are not so rigidly enforced that they become straitjackets, they offer many advantages to individuals and to the organization. Sound policies help people make decisions because they serve as a guide to action. They make it easier for employees to accept discipline, because people do not regard it as arbitrary when they are penalized for violating established policy. Another important advantage of policies is that they help guide the organization to reach its strategic goals. Assume, for example, that it is the strategic goal of a firm to create a high quality of work life for all employees. A policy of providing comfortable working conditions for employees will help the firm achieve its goal.

Procedures

Procedures are considered plans because they establish a customary method of handling future activities. They guide *action* rather than *thinking* in that they state the specific manner in which a certain activity must be accomplished.[21] Procedures exist at every level in the organization, but they tend to be more complex and specific at lower levels. For instance, store clerks may have quite strict procedures for handling checks, whereas managers may have less-strict procedures for handling any checks they might receive.

Consider the Rolex policy to offer high-quality goods to the public. To implement this policy, a number of procedures would need to be adopted, and they would be different at various organization levels. Managers might follow a procedure whereby no new product could be offered to the public unless it was approved for quality by a product-review committee at corporate headquarters. Operative employees might follow a procedure that specified the number of inspections a manufactured part would have to pass to be approved for quality. The procedure would specify the job titles of the employees performing the quality check and would explain the sequence of inspections.

Rules

A rule is a specific course of action or conduct that must be followed; it is the simplest type of plan. Ideally, each rule fits a strategic plan. In practice, however, many rules that are established are not related to organizational strategy. When rules are violated, corrective action should be taken. Two examples of rules are as follows:

Any employee engaged in an accident while in a company vehicle must report that accident immediately to his or her supervisor.

No employee is authorized to use company photocopying machines for personal use, even if he or she reimburses the company for the cost of the copies.

Rules are sometimes difficult to distinguish from policies or procedures. A policy is a much more general guide to action than is a rule. The rule about photocopying machines could be related to a policy that employees should not use company resources for personal purposes. A rule allows no room for discretion; nobody is authorized to use the office photocopying machine to make copies of income-tax forms or personal letters.

Procedures, like rules, are quite specific; however, they are broader than rules and may consist of a set of rules. With respect to handling of cash, the company may have certain procedures such as having one employee count another's cash at the end of the work day. A rule governing the handling of cash might be that all bills in denominations of fifty dollars or larger must be placed under the money tray.

We have described several major aspects of planning. Now we will show how planning is used to improve productivity.

PLANNING TO IMPROVE PRODUCTIVITY

Economist John W. Kendrick, in collaboration with the American Productivity Center, has developed an approach to productivity improvement based on his extensive industrial experience.[22] The major emphasis is that productivity is not "just another program." Instead, it is a continuous and orderly process requiring fine-tuning at various times. The core ingredient in the company-wide approach to productivity improvement is the sequence for productivity success:

1. Awareness and education

2. Strategic planning

3. Assessment

4. Implementation

5. Evaluation and refinement

These major phases are typically executed in sequence, although they may overlap.

Awareness and Education

The first step is for employees at all levels to believe that the productivity issue is real and important. Awareness and education start at the top of the organization and are continuous processes. The American Productivity Center believes that an improvement in the quality of work life should accompany gains in productivity. **Quality of work life (QWL)** is the degree to which employees find work meaningful and believe that it allows them to satisfy important needs, such as independence and self-fulfillment. One way to improve QWL is to create conditions that lead to high morale.

The messages and information communicated in the first phase are as follows:

1.   Improvements in productivity and QWL are both important.

2.   Both the organization and individuals will benefit from productivity gains.

3.   This is what is already being done about productivity in the organization.

4.   These are the specific procedures and techniques to use for achieving improvements in productivity QWL.

The roles played by people at various levels in the organization to achieve gains in productivity and QWL also should be explained. Every one in the organization must become aware of issues relating to productivity and QWL. Top-level managers are responsible for ensuring that other organization members understand the importance of QWL and for deciding how much priority productivity will receive. Middle managers have the prime responsibility for communicating and supporting the awareness messages about productivity and QWL. First-level managers provide the link between the organization's goals and the people who are creating the goods or services. Supervisors provide the day-by-day continuity for the productivity emphasis. Operative employees must communicate to management about productivity, make suggestions individually or as members of problem-solving groups, and understand that good job performance leads to gains in productivity.

Strategic Planning

The purpose of strategic planning is to make the productivity-improvement endeavor consistent with the mission, goals, and operating philosophies of the company. Strategic planning lends a productivity perspective to the philosophy and character of the organization. Frequently, an external productivity advisor works with top-level management in the early stages of the awareness and strategic-planning phases. Strategic planning for productivity entails answering these questions:

1.   Why do we need to improve productivity?

2.   How involved should top-level managers become in the process?

3.   How should we organize for improvement?

4.   How should we measure improvement?

5.   How should we reinforce improved performance?

6.   How productive do we want to be in twenty years?

Equipped with answers, an organization is in a good position to choose a course of action. Top-level managers can demonstrate their commitment by developing a written policy on productivity and QWL. In this way, the productivity perspective can become woven into the planning and budgeting process, leading to a long-term strategy.

Assessment

In the assessment phase, the organization considers its strengths and weaknesses and the barriers to improvement, and it evaluates its opportunities objectively. Assessment includes identifying relative potential for improvement in different areas, key individuals in the organization, manner of conducting the productivity effort, goals of the productivity effort, and plans for improvement.

The process of assessment leads to plans that capitalize on the most significant opportunities for productivity improvement. The plans should focus on seven elements:

1. *Assets*. How well does the firm use its human, material, capital, and technological resources? This includes systems, procedures, and practices that affect resource use.

2. *Goals*. What is the effect of organizational objectives, both official and unofficial, that set expectations for performance and channel the efforts of employees?

3. *Rewards*. How well do rewards, both financial and nonfinancial, encourage employees to be productive? For example, an effective reward must be given to employees only when they produce at the desired level.

4. *Communication*. What is the extent to which employees have the information necessary to perform their jobs well? Communication flows in three directions: top-down, bottom-up, and sideways.

5. *Measurement and analysis*. What is the accuracy of existing productivity measures and the hard data that assist managers in setting goals and making decisions?

6. *Employee participation*. How much opportunity do employees have to contribute to decisions made by managers? To what extent do managers seek ideas from employees?

7. *Organization and leadership*. What are the effects of various management practices? How well do various units of the organization interact?

Specific plans are drawn for each factor. Assume, for example, that one method of productivity improvement chosen by a firm is to install office automation. Point 6 would include a specific plan to request that office employees provide input on what aspects of their work needed to become more efficient and what type of equipment would be helpful. Managers, however, would have the final say on what equipment was purchased.

Implementation

The organization now is ready to implement the program for improving productivity and QWL. Productivity-improvement programs take many forms, many of which are described at various places in this text. The American Productivity Center lists a number of approaches to productivity improvement that can be accomplished as a joint labor-management effort (see Table 3-1).

A key part of implementation is to train thoroughly all individuals who will be involved in any aspect of the project. Separate training programs should be conducted for functional managers, first-level supervisors, union officers and stewards, and individual contributors. All groups must learn, for example, how the program will affect them and how they will be expected to contribute to the program.

Three broad activities are required for successful implementation of the program. One is enlisting the support and cooperation of others. Another is communicating effectively what needs to be done. Still another is initiating and controlling the effort.

Table 3-1   Joint Labor-Management Efforts for Productivity Improvement

- Quality improvements and zero-defect programs
- Recovery and salvage of materials
- Energy conservation
- Improved use, maintenance, and repair of equipment
- Job redesign, including simplifying jobs or making them more responsible and challenging
- Control of absenteeism, tardiness, overtime, and unproductive time
- Improved health and safety
- Planning of training programs
- Design of tools or products
- Organization of work and office or plant layout

Source: Based on information in John W. Kendrick, *Improving Company Productivity: Handbook with Case Studies* (Baltimore, MD: The Johns Hopkins University Press, 1984), 130.

Evaluation and Refinement

Kendrick explains that the evaluation-and-refinement phase is the time to measure, analyze, document, report, publicize, recognize, and reward results. Evaluations of the program generally take several forms. Actual results can be compared to planned results. New productivity figures can be compared to previous ones. The productivity of departments engaged in the program can be compared to the productivity of groups not so engaged.

During this phase, aspects of the program that are not working as well as planned can be fine-tuned. Assume that electronic mail is one of the productivity-improvement measures introduced. Some managers complain that reliance on electronic mail (messages sent on the computer) is not working well for sending messages about complex or sensitive issues. A potentially useful modification might be to use electronic mail mostly for routine messages.

POTENTIAL PROBLEMS WITH PLANNING

Although planning is highly valuable, it also has disadvantages. It can interfere with the spontaneity necessary for success. Many firms are launched with little formal planning. Entrepreneurs seize opportunities as they occur. For example, one study showed that the executives in some small, successful firms keep all strategic information in their heads.[23]

Another problem with planning is that managers can get so caught up in the process of planning (and its associated paperwork) that they neglect operating problems. Finally, plans are subject to misinterpretation; managers may waste energy carrying out the wrong plans.

A problem with strategic planning in particular is that it may lead firms into pursuing opportunities for which they are unsuited. To circumvent this problem, Robert H. Hayes recommends that firms first develop their internal capabilities and then look for opportunities that match those capabilities. His logic in short, is "Do not develop plans and then seek capabilities; instead build capabilities and then encourage the development of plans for exploiting them."[24]

Despite these reservations, planning should not be neglected. Anticipate potential problems, and design your plan to avoid them. Keep in mind that the purpose of planning is to create winning strategies, not thick planning books.[25]

SUMMARY OF KEY POINTS

Planning is concerned with anticipating the future. A general model of this complex and comprehensive process consists of seven related and sometimes overlapping elements: establish goals and objectives, define the present situation, forecast aids and barriers to goals and objectives, develop action plans, develop budgets, implement the plan, and control the plan.

Strategic plans are master plans that shape the destiny of the firm. They deal with strategic decisions that have five distinguishing characteristics: dealing with environment, taking the whole firm as the unit of analysis, using input from all the functional areas, giving direction to the enterprise, and being important to the firm's success. Strategic planning is composed of those activities leading to the statement of objectives for the organization and to the choosing of appropriate strategies for achieving those objectives. The outcomes of strategic planning are statements of mission, strategy, and policy. (Strategies and strategic plans refer to essentially the same concept.)

Forecasts, or predictions about future events, are an important aspect of planning. They can be made using qualitative or quantitative methods. Three types of forecasts are economic, sales, and technological. Many managers and specialists use spreadsheet analysis to assist them in forecasting. Line managers assume the major responsibility for making strategic plans; they are assisted by strategic-planning specialists. Line managers, however, devote more time to operational rather than strategic planning.

Operating plans provide the details of how strategic plans will be accomplished or implemented. They deal with a shorter time span than do strategic plans. Policies are plans set in the form of general statements that guide thinking and action in decision making. Procedures are plans that establish a customary method of handling future activities. A rule is the simplest type of plan; it sets a specific course of action or conduct.

A comprehensive plan has been developed to help organizations improve both productivity and the quality of work life (QWL). It follows the logic of other planning methods and consists of five key elements: awareness and education, strategic planning, assessment, implementation, and evaluation and refinement.

Planning has much to offer organizations; it leads to improved performance and productivity. At times, however, planning may inhibit spontaneity and result in wasted effort. Plans also may place too much emphasis on opportunities and may not fit them to internal capabilities.

QUESTIONS

1. Luck has been defined as what happens when preparation meets opportunity. How, therefore, can one plan to be lucky?
2. Some chief executive officers contend they want all their managers to think strategically. What do they mean?
3. How is a rule related to a strategic plan?
4. Write both a policy statement and a rule about energy use for any firm you choose.
5. How can you use planning to improve your personal life and family life?
6. How can you use strategic planning in career planning?
7. What similarities do you see between the framework for planning, shown in Figure 3-1, and the plan for productivity improvement, developed by the American Productivity Center?

ACTIVITIES

1. Several years ago, a barge loaded with 3,100 tons of refuse sailed for almost three months from port to port along the Atlantic Coast and into the Gulf of Mexico, only to be turned away at every port. The barge finally

returned home to find a landfill. Identify the planning errors in this famous odyssey.

2.   Speak to an executive from any firm you choose. Discover whether the firm has a strategic plan; if it does, what is it? Discuss your findings in class.

CASE PROBLEM 3-A: THE STRATEGY OF THE USAA GROUP

The USAA Group of San Antonio, Texas, is a large financial-services firm composed of the United Services Automobile Association and several subsidiaries, including a group of mutual funds, a life-insurance company, an investment firm, and a casualty-insurance company. Several years ago the president, Robert F. McDermott, delivered the following message to members of the association:

One of the central questions posed for business firms in the 1980s is, "What business are we really in?" More and more we are seeing that question addressed in boardrooms. This is particularly true in the financial-services marketplace. Retailers such as Sears Roebuck and J. C. Penney have entered the field by acquiring or establishing stock-brokerage firms, savings and loan associations, insurance companies, and so forth. Stockbrokers, insurance companies, banks and even manufacturing firms have entered, or attempted to enter, sectors of the financial services arena previously unknown to them.

What significance does this "financial revolution" have for a member-owned association such as the USAA Group? It is timely for us to ask ourselves, "What business are we really in?" The fact is that boards of directors and executives of the association have done just that on numerous occasions during the more than sixty years of our existence. They did so before we decided to enter the property-insurance field in the 1930s, before we offered our first life-insurance products in the 1960s, and before we established our first mutual funds in the early 1970s.

USAA long ago ceased to be "just an automobile insurer." It has evolved, in response to member needs, into a provider of a broad range of insurance and financial products. The best test of how well we have fared in these efforts lies in the response of our members. To determine this, let's take a look at the scorecard.

In 1960, no USAA member had a homeowners policy with the association. Today, USAA insures more than 700,000 homes owned by our members. In fact, more active-duty military officers insure their homes with USAA than with all other companies combined. Similarly, in 1960 no member had life insurance or mutual-fund investments with us. Today, more than a quarter of a million members have selected us for these products over the thousands of other providers in the marketplace, and that number is climbing steadily. I take a great deal of pride, and so do all of our employees, in this record of member acceptance.

Our mission in these changing times is what it has always been—to provide our exclusive group of members with the lowest cost and the highest quality of service available anywhere. That's our commitment. That's the business we are really in.

Case Questions

1. Identify the strategy statements made by McDermott.
2. Based on the information presented in the statement, what evidence can you present that the USAA Group is a well-planned organization?
3. What policy statement did McDermott make that would guide the behavior of company employees?
4. Specify two objectives implied in McDermott's statements about his firm.

Source: Adapted and paraphrased with permission from Robert F. McDermott, "What Business Are We Really In?" *Aide Magazine*, (Summer 1984): 3, USAA, San Antonio, Texas.

CASE PROBLEM 3-B: GOAL SETTING AT TAYLOR FOODS

Ralph Taylor is quite pleased with the results of planning in his newly renamed company, Taylor Foods. As he explained to the instructor who introduced him to planning, "I'm very impressed with what planning did for us at Taylor. There we were, an old company faced with a declining market. A few strategies and bang—we're now a multiproduct firm in an expanding market."

"Are you experiencing any problems with planning?" asked the management professor. Taylor replied, "I sure am. We are having problems in getting our people to personalize the planning process. They tend to regard planning as something that the owner should be doing rather than something they should be doing. Here are some notes I took from my planning meeting with Max Bloom, the sales manager for meats. He told me something to this effect: 'My plans are to beat out the competition and beat them good and to sell all the meat I can. Beyond that I have no plans. Each day I try to do my job the best I can. If I tell you anything else, I'm really stretching things.'"

Fascinated by what he heard, the professor asked for more evidence about planning problems within Taylor Meats. Taylor responded, "Okay, here are my notes from my planning conference with Georgia Anderson, my sales manager for nonmeat products. She said something of this nature: 'My plans are for my department to become the best it can be. But most of the things I would have to do to accomplish this are beyond my control. It's your job, Ralph, as the owner, to provide the budget so we can be tops in our area. Planning in a small company is really the owner's responsibility.'"

Taylor asked the professor, "Do you get my point about my sales managers not taking personal responsibility for planning?" The professor replied, "Maybe the situation isn't as hopeless as you think."

Case Questions

1. What deficiencies do you see in the planning statements made by the two sales managers?
2. What strengths do you see in the planning statements made by the two sales managers?
3. What might Ralph Taylor be doing wrong in his attempts to involve Bloom and Anderson in planning?

REFERENCES

1. John A. Pearce, II, Elizabeth B. Freeman, and Richard Robinson, Jr., "The Tenuous Link Between Formal Strategic Planning and Financial Performance," *Academy of Management Review* (October 1987): 658–675.
2. Stanley S. Thune and Robert J. House, "Where Long Range Planning Pays Off," *Business Horizons* (August 1970): 81–87.
3. D. M. Herold, "Long-Range Planning and Organizational Performance: A Cross-Validation Study," *Academy of Management Journal* (March 1972): 9–102.
4. John C. Camillus, Vasudevan Ramanujam, and N. Venkatraman, "Multi-Objective Assessment of Effectiveness of Strategic Planning: A Discriminant Analysis Approach," *Academy of Management Journal* (June 1986): 367.
5. Michael Mescon, Franklin Khedouri, and Michael Albert, *Management: Individual and Organizational Effectiveness*, 2d ed. (New York: Harper & Row, 1984), 229.
6. Ronald Grover, "Lights! Camera! Completion Bond!" *Business Week* (24 August 1987): 50.
7. Michael E. Porter, "From Competitive Advantage to Corporate Strategy," *Harvard Business Review* (May–June 1987): 43.
8. "A New Strategy for No. 2 in Computers," *Business Week* (2 May 1983): 66; "October's Crash Hasn't Crunched Demand So Far," *Business Week* (11 January 1988): 111.
9. Robert C. Shirley, "Limiting the Scope of Strategy: A Decision-Based Approach," *Academy of Management Review* (April 1982): 262–268.
10. Henry L. Tosi and Stephen J. Carroll, *Management*, 2d ed. (New York: John Wiley & Sons, 1982), 195.
11. John A. Pearce, II, and Fred David, "Corporate Mission Statements: The Bottom Line," *Academy of Management Executive* (May 1987): 110.
12. Mark H. McCormack, *What They Don't Teach You at Harvard Business School* (New York: Bantam Books, 1984); Quote from *Success* (October 1984): 53.
13. "Jumping Jack Strikes Again," *Time* (3 August 1987): 44.
14. For an excellent overview of forecasting methods see David M. Georgoff and Robert G. Murdick, "Manager's Guide to Forecasting," *Harvard Business Review* (January–February 1986): 110–120.
15. Arthur C. Laufer, *Production and Operations Management*, 3rd ed. (Cincinnati: South-Western Publishing Co., 1984), 383.
16. Bill Middleton, "Getting Up To Speed on Spreadsheet Software," *Supervisory Management* (April 1986): 12–18.
17. "How Personal Computers Can Trip Up Executives," *Business Week* (24 September 1984): 94.
18. Daniel H. Gray, "Uses and Misuses of Strategic Planning," *Harvard Business Review* (January–February 1986): 89.
19. Allan Brache, "Taking the Strategic Planning Initiative," *Management Solutions* (June 1986): 37.
20. "Make that Sale, Mr. Sam," *Time* (18 May 1987): 55.
21. Harold Koontz, Cyril O'Donnell, and Heinz Weihrich, *Management*, 7th ed. (New York: McGraw-Hill, 1980), 166.

22. Entire section based on John W. Kendrick, *Improving Company Productivity: Handbook with Case Studies* (Baltimore, MD: The Johns Hopkins University Press, 1984), 127–132.
23. Philip H. Thurston, "Should Smaller Companies Make Formal Plans?" *Harvard Business Review* (September–October 1983): 162.
24. Robert H. Hayes, "Strategic Planning—Forward in Reverse?" *Harvard Business Review* (November–December 1985): 118.
25. Richard G. Hamermesh, "Making Planning Strategic," *Harvard Business Review* (July–August 1986): 120.

4

Problem Solving and Decision Making

After studying the material in this chapter, you should be able to accomplish the following tasks:

1. Explain the steps involved in making a nonprogrammed decision.
2. Understand the major factors influencing decision making in organizations.
3. Describe organizational programs for improving creativity.
4. Implement several suggestions for becoming a more creative problem solver.
5. Appreciate the value and potential limitations of group decision making.

Key Terms and Phrases

Problem
Decision
Nonprogrammed decision
Programmed decision
Optimum decision
Satisficing decision
Suboptimum decision
Intuition
Values
Creativity

Creative problem solving
Ego permissiveness
Brainstorming
Synergy
Suggestion programs
Intrapreneurs
Group decision
Consensus decision making
Groupthink

Residents at a nursing home began to make repeated complaints about the quality of the food to both staff members and visitors, including the residents' children, relatives, and friends. As a result, new referrals to the home began to decrease.

Gwen Cotton, the executive director of the nursing home, thus faced **a problem**: a discrepancy between ideal and actual conditions. The ideal condition would be an absence of complaints about food quality; the actual condition is the continuing complaints about the food. To solve this problem, Cotton must make at least one **decision**: a choice among alternatives. Among Gwen Cotton's alternatives are these: change the menu, hire a new chef, consult a dietitian, spend more money on higher-quality food, or further investigate the complaints.

This chapter explores how managers and specialists solve problems and make decisions both individually and in groups. Decision making is an integral part of the planning process. Planning is making decisions about the goals of an organization and about alternative ways of achieving these goals.

Although problem solving and decision making are studied in conjunction with planning, decision making is required in carrying out all other management functions and roles.[1] For example, while managers are controlling, they must make a series of decisions about how to get performance back to standard.

TYPES OF DECISIONS

Some decisions faced by managers and specialists in organizations are difficult because they occur infrequently. These nonroutine decisions are **nonprogrammed decisions**. Many other decisions faced by managers are recurring, or routine, and therefore programmed (as a computer is programmed to make predetermined decisions). A **programmed decision** is repetitive and routine and a specific procedure has been developed for its handling. Simply stated, a programmed decision is governed by a procedure, as described in Chapter 3.

A manager's level influences the balance of programmed versus nonprogrammed decisions that he or she faces.

Nonprogrammed Decisions

When a problem has not taken the same form in the past or is extremely complex or significant, it calls for a nonprogrammed decision. A complex problem is one that contains many elements. Significant problems affect an important aspect of the organization. The food problem at the nursing home may be complex because there probably are many reasons why the residents do not like the food. It is significant because it affects the number of clients entering the nursing home. All strategic decisions (as described in Chapter 3) are nonprogrammed decisions.[2]

In an unusually well-planned and highly structured organization, there are few nonprogrammed decisions for managers to make. A company such as IBM Corp., for example, has hundreds of policies to help managers decide what they should do when faced with a given problem. In contrast, many small firms do not offer much guidance about decision making. A woman who joined a small clothing manufacturer as an assistant controller put it this way:

> At Rainbow Fashions we invent policy as we go along. Every decision of consequence we face gobbles up a lot of time because nobody knows how a similar problem was faced in the past. Just last week, I asked my boss how many more days we could extend credit to a good customer. He told me to do whatever seemed reasonable. The company had never given serious thought to that problem before and had no policy regarding it.

Nonprogrammed decisions involve a search for creative alternatives—imaginative and useful solutions. Handling a nonprogrammed problem properly requires original thinking. We will say more about creative decision making later in the chapter.

A person earns the reputation of being an effective decision maker when he or she makes sound nonprogrammed decisions. The skill required for decision making varies inversely with the extent to which it is programmed: highly programmed decisions require minimum decision-making skill, whereas highly nonprogrammed decisions require maximum skill. Here are two examples of nonprogrammed decisions faced by managers.

- *Plant manager in a food cannery:* During the height of the canning season, an out-of-control truck rams into the side of the plant, breaking through a section of a wall. Several supervisors ask the manager to shut down the plant for the afternoon because many employees are too upset to continue working. The plant manager must decide what to do, balancing concerns about production versus employee safety and morale.

- *Hospital administrator in a city hospital:* A quarterly report reveals a substantial decrease in average billings for privately insured patients, creating a shortfall in revenue. The administrator wants to discuss the problem with the medical staff but does not want to be accused of putting pressure on physicians to order more procedures and tests to generate revenue. Nevertheless, the administrator recognizes her performance will be measured by the financial condition of the hospital. The administrator must decide on a course of action soon.

Programmed Decisions

Managers and nonmanagers alike make many small, uncomplicated decisions for which the alternatives are specified in advance. Procedures specify how to handle these routine, programmed decisions. Here are two examples.

- *Rental manager in government-funded housing:* A person who earns $31,000 per year applies to rent a two-bedroom apartment. The manager refuses the application because there is a rule that families with annual incomes of $27,000 or more may not rent in this building.

- *Colonel in government facility:* A vendor offers to give the colonel two tickets to the Super Bowl in an attempt to establish better working relations with the officer. The colonel turns down the gift because military regulations prohibit accepting more than a token gift from a vendor or potential vendor.

Decision Making at Different Levels of Management

Who makes programmed decisions and who makes nonprogrammed ones? Under ideal circumstances, top-level management concerns itself almost exclusively with nonprogrammed decisions, whereas lower-level management handles all programmed decisions. In reality, executives do make many small, programmed decisions in addition to nonprogrammed ones. It is not unknown, for example, for top executives to sign expense account vouchers and answer routine correspondence. Middle managers and first-level managers generally make both programmed and nonprogrammed decisions, with first-level managers making a higher proportion of programmed decisions. A well-managed organization, however, encourages all managers to delegate as many small (programmed) decisions as possible.

The general trend of the relationship between management level and type of decision made is shown in Figure 4-1. The philosophy of top-level managers has a big influence on the extent to which lower-ranking managers make nonprogrammed decisions. A company that has a policy of passing much decision-making authority down the line encourages first-level managers to make nonprogrammed decisions. In contrast, a company whose policy has top-level managers controlling most of the authority attempts to have those managers make almost all the nonprogrammed decisions.

The accompanying "Manager in Action" illustrates the type of tough— and therefore nonprogrammed—decision often faced by top management.

MANAGER IN ACTION:

A Pharmaceutical Manager Chooses the Right Prescription for the Organization

When asked to name his toughest decision, Herbert J. Conrad, vice president of pharmaceuticals at Hoffmann-La Roche Inc., said: "The most difficult decision and one of the most important I've had to make was choosing the head of the marketing division of La Roche laboratory area. I had to decide where in the company the candidate should come from, taking into consideration what various reactions would be to that decision. Finally, I had to be extremely comfortable with the person I chose. I went within the company, but outside the existing administration to somebody who had been brought along by me, and in whom I had confidence (Pat Zenner). It turned out to be a very good decision."

Source: Ronald Schultz, *The Naked Hunch: Exposing the Inner Process of Today's High Pressure Decision Makers* (New York: John Muir, 1986). Used with permission of John Muir Publications, Santa Fe, NM.

STEPS IN PROBLEM SOLVING AND DECISION MAKING

Problem solving and decision making can be regarded as orderly processes, similar to the planning model described in Chapter 3 (review Figure 3-1). It would be naive, however, to think that every effective solution to a problem, or every effective decision, is the product of this orderly process. The key principle is that managers will find better solutions to complex problems—and therefore make better nonprogrammed decisions—when they follow an orderly

Figure 4-1   Decision Making at Different Management Levels

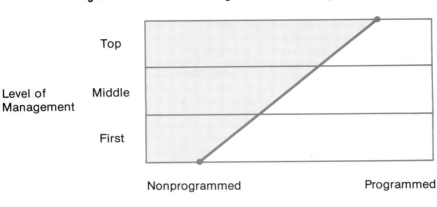

process. It is difficult to draw a consistent distinction between problem solving and decision making because they are part of the same process. The purpose of making a decision is to solve a problem, but you must analyze the problem prior to making the decision.

It is important to recognize that problem solving typically takes place in the context of an ongoing project or process and that decisions made early on will have profound influence as work progresses. In one financial-services firm, for example, the decision was made to relax credit standards when a branch first opened. The decision proved to be faulty because the firm later had to spend considerable time and effort trying to collect payments from loan delinquents.

As shown in Figure 4-2, problem solving and decision making can be subdivided into steps: (1) identify and diagnose the problem, (2) develop creative alternative solutions, (3) evaluate the alternative solutions, (4) choose one alternative solution, (5) implement the decision, and (6) evaluate and control. In addition, the process may be repeated if necessary.[3]

Identify and Diagnose the Problem

The process of problem solving and decision making begins with being aware that a problem exists. In other words, you must *identify* a problem before you can solve it. You become aware that a gap exists between desired and actual conditions. At times, the problem is imposed on a manager, such as when nursing home residents complain about food quality. At other times, he or she has to search actively for a worthwhile problem or opportunity. For example, a human-engineering manager proposed conducting an audit of office furniture to see if the furnishings were designed to minimize fatigue.

Figure 4-2   Steps in Problem Solving and Decision Making

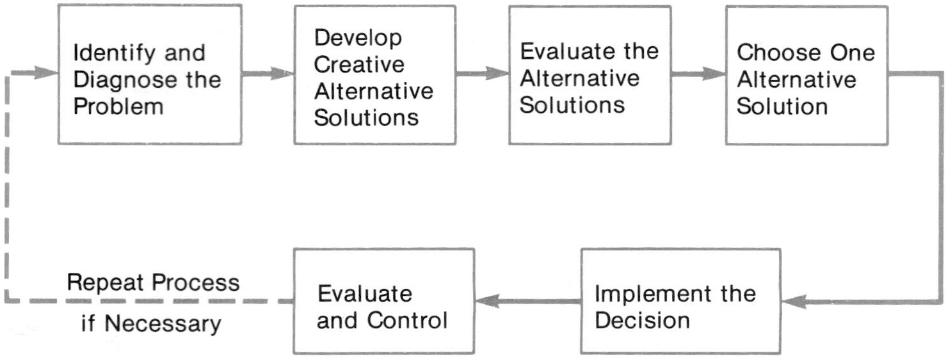

Methods of Problem Identification.   Identifying problems requires considerable skill. Researchers suggest several methods managers can use to locate problems.[4]

1. *Deviation from past performance.* If performance indicators are down, it strongly suggests that a problem exists. Among accepted problem indicators are declining sales, increased turnover, higher scrap rates, increased customer complaints, and increased number of bad checks cashed. Observing deviations from standard performance is part of the control function of management.

2. *Deviations from the plan.* When the results you hoped to attain with a plan are not forthcoming, you have a problem. This type of problem identification represents seeing a deviation from anticipated *future* performance. The possibility always exists that the established plan was unduly optimistic. It frequently happens in the movie industry, for example, that the anticipated box-office revenues for a film do not match planned revenues. As an escape hatch, movie producers often push overseas and television sales for the film.

3. *Criticism from outsiders.* Managers are sometimes made aware of problems by complaints from individuals and groups who are not employees of the firm. These sources of criticism include customers, governmental regulatory agencies, and stockholders. For example, during the last decade many stockholders have criticized firms that conduct business in South Africa despite that country's practice of apartheid (economic and social discrimination against the nonwhite majority).

4. *Competitive threats.* The presence of competition can create problems for an organization. For example, many small manufacturers of computers

compete with IBM. Their primary selling point is that their computers cost less than comparable IBM computers, yet are compatible with most IBM software. IBM has lowered its prices several times and introduced new, less "clonable" models to overcome the competitive advantage offered by the smaller firms. A few smaller firms had to cease competing with IBM; they entered different markets or went out of business.

Diagnosis. A thorough diagnosis of the problem is important because the real problem may be different from the one that a first look suggests. To diagnose a problem properly, you must clarify its true nature. An example of the importance of diagnosis took place in the nursing home mentioned at the beginning of the chapter.

Gwen Cotton, the executive director, took action to solve the problem of poor-quality food. The chief cook was empowered to spend more money on food and a consulting dietitian was hired to provide nutritious menu suggestions. Despite the objective improvement in the quality of food, the complaints about food quality did not diminish.

Perplexed, Cotton decided to interview a sample of the residents to learn more about their dissatisfaction with the food. Probing revealed that the food really was not bad. The true complaints focused on the abrupt way the residents were treated by several dining-room employees. Cotton gave these employees appropriate human-relations training. Complaints about food decreased substantially.

The extra money spent on food was not completely wasted; the residents enjoyed the new menu once the behavior of the dining-room staff changed. If the executive director had diagnosed the true problem earlier, however, the reputation of the nursing home might not have suffered.

Develop Creative Alternative Solutions

The second step in decision making is to generate alternative solutions. This is the intellectually freewheeling aspect of decision making. All kinds of possibilities are explored here, even if they seem unrealistic. Often the difference between good and mediocre decision makers is that the former do not accept the first alternative they think of. Instead, they keep digging until they find the best alternative solution.

Evaluate Alternative Solutions

Next, compare the relative value of the alternatives. Examine the pros and cons of each one. Consider the feasibility of each. Some alternatives may appear attractive, but implementing them would be impossible or counterproductive. For example, it would not be feasible for all the nursing home residents to prepare their own meals.

The cost of an alternative is closely related to its feasibility; alternatives that cost too much are not feasible. You must also consider the possible outcome of an alternative. If an unsatisfactory outcome is almost a certainty, you will reject that alternative. If a company is faced with low profits, one alternative would be to cut pay by 20 percent. The outcome of this alternative would be to lower morale drastically and create high turnover, so the company would not implement that alternative.

One approach to examining the pros and cons of each alternative is to list them. One of the alternatives Cotton considered was to fire the dining-room employees. The portion of her decision-making worksheet illustrating that particular alternative is shown in Table 4-1.

Choose One Alternative Solution

The process of weighing each alternative solution must stop at some point. You cannot solve a problem unless you choose one of the alternatives and therefore make a decision. Several factors influence the choice. A major factor is the goal the decision was intended to achieve. You should choose the alternative that appears to come closest to achieving it. Gwen Cotton would want to choose the alternative that held greatest promise of decreasing the complaints about food.

Another major consideration is the values of the decision maker. Choose the alternative solution that supports what you think is important. When Cotton chose to retrain rather than fire the discourteous employees, she was following the value of saving money; she realized that it probably would be less expensive to retrain current employees than to hire and train new ones. Her humanitarian values also may have influenced her choice, if she believed it is kinder to retrain than to fire poor performers.

Table 4-1   Portion of Decision-Making Worksheet, Pine Valley Nursing Home

Name: Gwen Cotton   Date: June 16, 1990

Alternative 3: Fire three dining-room workers about whom complaints have been received.

Advantages	Disadvantages
1. Swift solution to problem.	1. Could result in firing satisfactory workers based on hearsay.
2. Will give message to other employees: courtesy counts.	2. Could be bad for morale of other employees.
3. Can trim payroll costs by replacing with inexperienced workers, if replacements can be readily found and trained.	3. Hiring and training replacements could be costly.
	4. Could be sued for wrongful discharge.

Decision: Reject this alternative; disadvantages outweigh and outnumber advantages.

A third factor influencing the choice of an alternative is the degree of uncertainty with which it is associated. People who prefer not to take risks choose alternatives that appear to have the most certain outcomes; such people are uncomfortable with uncertainty. In contrast, risk takers are willing to choose alternatives with uncertain outcomes if the potential gains appear to be substantial. The payoff matrix described in Chapter 5, "Specialized Techniques for Planning and Decision Making," helps decision makers deal with uncertainty.

Despite a careful evaluation of alternatives, some ambiguity still exists in most decisions made by managers and specialists. The decisions faced by managers are often complex, unclear, and fuzzy.[5] Even when the alternative solutions are supported by quantitative evidence, the decision maker may be uncertain. Human-resource decisions often are the most ambiguous because of the difficulty in making precise predictions about human behavior. Deciding which person to hire among several good job candidates is always difficult. Although some personnel professionals claim to achieve 80 percent accuracy in hiring decisions, they must use a good deal of guesswork and intuition.

Implement the Decision

Converting the decision into action is the next major step. Until you implement a decision, it is really not a decision at all.[6] Many strategic decisions are wasted effort because nobody is held responsible for implementing them. The current emphasis on encouraging line managers to become involved in strategic decision making is a response to this problem. Line managers have always had the responsibility of implementing decisions made at the top of the organization.

Implementing decisions encompasses a substantial part of the organizing and leading functions of management. Much of a manager's job involves helping subordinates implement decisions. Parts Three and Four of this book, "Organizing" and "Leading," deal extensively with the implementation of decisions.

A fruitful way of evaluating the merit of a decision is to observe how well the decision was implemented. A decision cannot be a good one if people resist its implementation or if it is too cumbersome to implement. A company may try to boost productivity by decreasing the time allotted for lunch or coffee breaks. Employees resist the decision by eating while working and then taking the allotted lunch break. Productivity decreases as a result. The decision to boost productivity by decreasing the time for work breaks is a poor one.

Evaluate and Control

The final step in the decision making framework is to investigate how effectively the alternative you chose solved the problem. Controlling means ensuring that the results obtained with the decision are those you set forth when you first identified the problem. For example, Cotton hoped to achieve two objectives at the nursing home: decrease resident complaints about food and restore the number of referrals the home had been receiving. If educating her staff does not achieve her objectives, she must choose another alternative.

After gathering feedback, characterize the quality of the decision as optimum, satisficing, or suboptimum. **Optimum decisions** lead to favorable outcomes. **Satisficing decisions** meet a minimum standard of satisfaction; they are adequate, acceptable, passable, and OK. Most decision makers stop their search for alternatives when they find a satisficing one. Accepting the first reasonable alternative saves additional hard work—it is the easy way out. **Suboptimum decisions** lead to negative outcomes. Their consequences are disruptive to the employees and to the firm. When you obtain suboptimum results, you must repeat the problem-solving and decision-making process.

Evaluating and controlling your decisions will help you improve your decision-making skills. You can learn important lessons by comparing what actually happened with what you thought would happen. You can learn what you could have improved or done differently. Use this information the next time you face a similar decision.

According to the classical model of problem solving and decision making just presented, decision making is basically an orderly and rational process. In reality, decision making is seldom the logical, systematic process described above. One should strive to follow the orderly steps in problem solving and decision making. However, there is usually more than one problem in need of attention, and one may not have time to carefully evaluate each alternative.[7]

We have defined the two major types of decisions and examined the steps involved in effective decision making. Next, we examine the key factors that influence how smoothly the decision-making process proceeds and what quality decision you make.

INFLUENCES ON DECISION MAKING

Although most people can follow the decision-making steps we described, not everybody can arrive at the same quality of decision. People vary in their decision-making ability, and there are forces that can hamper anyone from finding the optimum solutions to problems. As shown in Figure 4-3, many key factors influence decision making.

Crisis Conditions

Under crisis or extremely high-pressure conditions, many decision makers panic. They become less rational and more emotional than they would in a calmer environment. Those decision makers adversely affected by crisis conditions exhibit symptoms of stress, including poor concentration, poor judgment, and impulsive thinking. Another problem with making decisions under crisis conditions is that some managers ignore differences of opinion. Decision makers facing a crisis may be aware of conflicting opinions but be too pressured to reach a solution to bother exploring these differences and incorporating them into their choices.[8]

Decision makers vary substantially in their abilities to make good decisions under crises such as pending bankruptcy or employee walkouts. Many managers rise to their peak of mental alertness when faced with the stiff challenge of a business crisis.

Intuition of the Decision Maker

Intuitive ability is a personal characteristic that influences the outcome of decision making. Effective decision makers do not rely on analytical and methodological techniques alone. They also use their hunches and intuition. **Intuition** can be described as an experience-based way of knowing or reasoning in which weighing and balancing of the evidence are done unconsciously and automatically. Intuition is also a way of arriving at a conclusion without using the step-by-step logical process.[9]

Herbert A. Simon, the renowned computer scientist and psychologist, says that every manager needs to be able to analyze problems systematically (and with the type of tools described in Chapter 5). Furthermore, every manager needs also to be able to respond to situations rapidly, a skill that requires cultivation over many years of experience and training.[10]

Studies conducted with executives in small businesses indicate that acting on hunches is a much-neglected but essential feature of successful problem solving. An expert on applied creativity comments: "Indeed, the shrewd insight, the fertile hunch, or the sudden leap to a decision can be the most valuable coin of the manager at work."[11] Mintzberg reached a similar conclusion about managers in larger organizations. He found that intuition played an important part in the decision making.[12] Intuition is particularly important in identifying problems and searching for creative alternative solutions.

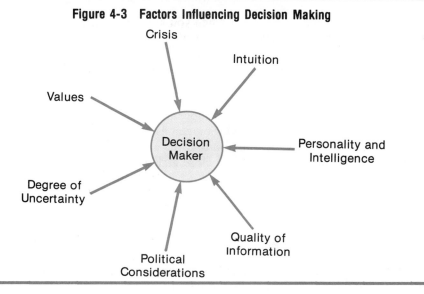

Figure 4-3   Factors Influencing Decision Making

Personality and Intelligence of the Decision Maker

The personality and intelligence of the decision maker influence his or her ability to find good solutions. One relevant personality dimension is a person's degree of cautiousness or conservatism. A cautious, conservative person will typically opt for a low-risk solution. If a person is extremely cautious, he or she may not want to make major decisions for fear of being proved wrong.

Perfectionism has a notable impact on decision making. People who seek the perfect solution to a problem are usually indecisive because they are hesitant to accept the fact that a particular alternative is good enough. As one writer notes, the real villain in most impossible decisions is perfectionism—thinking you have to arrive at the one flawless solution.[13]

Rigidity versus flexibility can influence decision making. Rigid people have difficulty identifying problems and generating alternative solutions, whereas flexible people perform well in these areas. Optimism versus pessimism is another relevant personality dimension. Optimistic people are more likely than are pessimistic ones to find solutions to problems; the former are less likely to perceive situations as being hopeless.

Intelligence has a profound influence on the effectiveness of decision making. In general, intelligent and well-educated people are more likely to identify problems and make good decisions than are those who have less intelligence and education. A notable exception is that some intelligent and well-educated people have such a fondness for collecting facts and analyzing them that they suffer from "analysis paralysis." One plant manager put it this way: "I'll never hire a genius again. They dazzle you with facts, figures, and computer graphics. But when they get through with their analysis, they still haven't solved the problem."

Quality and Accessibility of Information

You make more effective decisions when you use high-quality, valid information. One of the most important purposes of management information systems is to supply managers with high-quality information that they can use to make better decisions. A management information system collects, organizes, interprets, and disseminates information such that it meets the requirements of managers.

Accessibility may be even more important than quality in determining whether or not information is used. Sometimes it takes so much time and effort to search for quality information that the manager chooses rather to rely on lower-quality information that is close at hand.[14] Think of the decision-making process involved in purchasing a new automobile. Many people are more likely to use the opinion of friends than to search for more systematic information from reference sources.

Political Considerations

Under ideal circumstances, organizational decisions are made on the basis of the objective merits of competing alternatives. In reality, many decisions are based on political considerations, such as favoritism, alliances, or the desire of the decision maker to stay in favor with people who wield power.[15]

Political factors sometimes influence which data are given serious consideration in evaluating alternatives. The decision maker may select data supporting the position of the influential person whom he or she is trying to please. For instance, one financial analyst was asked to investigate the cost-effectiveness of the company purchasing its own corporate jet. She knew the president wanted a private jet for status purposes, so she gave considerable weight to the (probably biased) "facts" supplied to her by a manufacturer of corporate jets. This allowed her to justify the expense of purchasing the jet.

A person with high professional integrity should arrive at what he or she thinks is the best decision and then make a diligent attempt to convince management of the objective merits of that solution.

Degree of Uncertainty

We mentioned that the degree of uncertainty surrounding a decision influences the choice of an alternative. It can also influence other steps in the decision making process. For example, it may be more difficult to implement a risky decision because people are not confident the steps will lead to good results. Most nonprogrammed decisions have uncertain outcomes. Think of how many times large corporations buy smaller ones and then discover they have made a serious mistake. Frequently, the companies purchased are later sold at a loss.

Decision theorists divide degree of uncertainty into three categories: certainty, risk, and uncertainty.[16] A condition of certainty exists when the facts are well known and the decision outcome can be predicted accurately. A retail store manager might predict with certainty that more hours of operation will lead to more sales. It might be uncertain, however, whether the increased sales would cover the increased expenses.

A condition of risk means that a decision must be made based on incomplete, but accurate, factual information. Managers frequently use quantitative techniques to make decisions under conditions of risk. An example would be a promoter scheduling a tour for a popular singing group. Some statistical information about costs and past ticket sales would be available. The risk could be partially calculated on the basis of factual information about the past.

A condition of uncertainty occurs when a decision is based on limited or no factual information. When faced with a condition of uncertainty, managers rely on intuition. Gwen Cotton made a decision under a condition of uncertainty; she had no factual information to indicate that a human-relations program would solve her problem.

Values of the Decision Maker

A **value** in this context is something to which a person attaches importance, such as money, self-fulfillment, or quality of work life (QWL). Values influence decision making at every step, and all decisions ultimately are based on values.[17] A manager who placed a high value on the personal welfare of employees would try to avoid alternatives that create hardship for employees and would implement decisions in ways that did not create turmoil for employees.

Values can be classified in many ways. We will describe a standard method known as value orientations and provide examples of how these specific values could influence decision making.[18]

1.   *Theoretical values.* People who have theoretical values are strongly interested in the discovery of truth and the systematic arrangement of knowledge. Their interests are critical and rational. A manager with theoretical values favors diagnosing the underlying problem.

2.   *Economic values.* People with economic values are primarily interested in the best use of resources. They are interested in the practical affairs of the business world, including the production and marketing of goods and services, which lead to maximization of wealth. Managers with strong economic values try to make decisions with good potential financial return.

3.   *Aesthetic values.* People with aesthetic values are interested in the artistic aspects of life. They value form and harmony. These managers favor decisions that beautify the environment, such as constructing an appealing building.

4.   *Social values.* People with strong social values are altruists and philanthropists. They regard people as ends, not as means. They tend to be kind, sympathetic, and unselfish. Managers with strong social values choose alternatives that foster employee welfare and often are large contributors to charity.

5.   *Political values.* People with political values are strongly oriented toward acquiring power in the workplace. They favor decisions that bring them power, such as acquiring another department.

6.   *Religious values.* People who have religious values seek to relate to the universe in a meaningful way. They often have a mystical orientation. Strong religious values often direct managers to making decisions they think will be acceptable to their god(s).

Most people have a mixture of these six values. Top-level managers need well-rounded values to make good decisions.

CREATIVITY IN MANAGERIAL WORK

Creativity is an essential part of problem solving and decision making. To be creative is to see new relationships and produce imaginative solutions to problems. **Creativity** can be defined simply as the process of developing good ideas that can be put into action.[19] Stemming from creativity is **creative problem solving,** the ability to overcome obstacles by approaching them in novel ways.[20] The relevance of creativity to organizational effectiveness was aptly summarized by a panel of managers:

> Creative decision making and problem solving are two of the most important talents that employees can possess, talents that are necessary for the financial health and prosperity of any firm. Unless a firm can respond with unique products [or] services, innovative marketing strategies and creative responses to complex problems, it may find itself losing sales, shares of the market, and profits.[21]

Our discussion of creativity will focus on the creative aspects of the manager's job, the creative personality, managerial actions and organizational programs for creativity, and suggestions for becoming a more creative person.

The Creative Aspects of a Manager's Job

Managerial work requires a good deal of creativity, especially when it involves nonprogrammed decisions. A manager's workday is a miscellany of activities including holding scheduled meetings and impromptu conversations, writing memos, making presentations, dealing with emergencies and crises, and entertaining visitors. Managers jump from task to task and from person to person. To fashion order from this potential chaos requires creative problem solving.[22] Managers display creativity in the way they arrange and rearrange, juggle schedules, collect and disseminate information and ideas, make assignments, and lead people.[23]

Finding and defining problems is a creative act with similarities to artistic work. The manager shapes a problem in much the same way as a potter shapes a piece of clay. The difference is that managers practice their craft by using information rather than a tangible medium such as clay.

Effective managers regularly assign groups of people to work on specific tasks. These groups may include those that meet only once on an important issue or temporary task forces that exist for several weeks or months. They may also include the people a manager relies on to solve problems on a daily basis. Furthermore, a critical job of high-level managers is to create a network of people who will support them in carrying out their missions. Part of this involves thinking of creative ways to return favors. One manager who needed the support of other managers throughout the firm for his quality-improvement program told them that he would inform top-level managers when he discovered outstanding examples of quality improvement. In this way, he brought the good deeds of his colleagues to the attention of top-level management.

The Creative Personality

A distinguishing characteristic of creative people is that they are more emotionally open and flexible than their less creative counterparts. People who rarely exhibit creative behavior tend to be close minded and rigid. They suffer from "hardening of the categories"; they cannot overcome the traditional way of looking at things. Creative people are willing to be illogical for a moment and let their thoughts wander.

This ability to let go has been described as **ego permissiveness**. It is found in many creative artists and managers who allow themselves to relax the rules of logic for awhile to allow inspirational thoughts to take over. Salvatore Didato notes that it is akin to being carefree and childlike for the moment.[24] Ego-permissive people can relax enough to let their imaginative powers emerge.

To develop some preliminary insight into your degree of ego permissiveness, take the quiz presented in Table 4-2. All the questions on the quiz relate to dissociation, an alteration of consciousness. These states are influenced by our subconscious and allow us to disengage our thoughts from the demands of the moment. Although dissociation episodes may be puzzling or even upsetting, ego-permissive people seem to accept them without being flustered. Persons who can tolerate such unusual states of consciousness tend to score high on this test.

Ego permissiveness is important for managerial work because it promotes innovative thinking. Compared with those with average scores, people who score high on ego permissiveness tend to be imaginative, intuitive, impulsive, and willing to take sensible risks. They tend to display unconventional behavior and generally have a higher aptitude for intellectual work.

Managerial Actions and Organizational Programs for Improving Creativity

Creativity can be enhanced through a variety of managerial actions, techniques, and organizational programs. Those described in the next several pages are creativity-encouraging managerial actions, brainstorming, suggestions systems, and the creation of intrapreneurial units.

Creativity-Encouraging Managerial Actions. The most influential step management can take to bring about creative problem solving and decision making is to develop a permissive atmosphere that encourages people to think freely and does not penalize them for making honest mistakes. Employees are given positive feedback and an occasional tangible reward for making innovative suggestions. Additional creativity-encouraging actions on the part of managers include the following:[25]

1. *Acceptance of half-developed ideas.* Managers should hesitate to discourage the creative flow of ideas or nip innovation in the bud. Managers of productive research laboratories listen to and support half-formed proposals and encourage subordinates to develop their ideas. Of course, these managers do not encourage preposterous ideas.

2. *Willingness to stretch organizational policy.* Managers must know when to stretch company policy in order to launch an idea. One example would

Table 4-2   The Ego-Permissiveness Scale

Answer each statement "true" or "false," then score yourself and read the interpretation below and the explanation in the text.

                                                                      True   False

1. I would like to be hypnotized.
2. When I doze off, I often awaken with a jerking motion.
3. Several times in my life, I have had such unusual feelings about something that I probably could not put it into words to describe to someone else.
4. Several times, while asleep, I have carried on real conversations with another person who entered the room.
5. I have had the experience of doing some task in the middle of the night, such as jotting down a note, answering a telephone call, or getting a glass of water, and had no memory of it the next morning.
6. I have had the sensation of being hypnotized while driving or riding in a car ("highway hypnosis").
7. I have had the experience of seeming to watch myself from a distance as if in a dream.
8. Occasionally I have experienced deja vu—a feeling that I have been in the same place, done the same thing, or had the same conversation before.
9. I often become so deep in concentration that I do not hear others who call to me.
10. Some of my most interesting thoughts come to me when I am half or fully asleep.

What Your Score Means

To tally your score, give yourself one point for each true answer. This is an unofficial and unscientific test, but your score could indicate the following:

8–10 points: You are an ego-permissive person who is prone to innovative thinking.

5–7 points: You have about average ego permissiveness.

0–4 points: You have low ego permissiveness. Improve your ability by relaxing and allowing your thoughts to come and go freely.

Source: Adapted with permission from Salvatore Didato, "Willingness to Let Mind Wander: A Trait of 'Ego-Permissiveness'," *Democrat and Chronicle* (28 July 1984): 16B.

be spending unused travel money to help purchase special equipment to develop a prototype for a new product.

3. *Ability to make quick decisions.* Managers who foster creativity can spot a good idea and do not deliberate too long over whether to use organizational resources to develop the idea. This willingness to respond quickly to good ideas is important because creative people are eager to see their ideas translated into action.

Brainstorming.   The best-known method of improving creativity is **brainstorming,** a method of problem solving carried out by a group, in which people spontaneously generate numerous solutions to a problem without being discouraged or controlled. Brainstorming produces many ideas; it is not a technique for carefully working out details or plans. People typically use it when looking for tentative solutions to nontechnical problems. In recent years, however, many information systems specialists have used brainstorming to improve computer programs and systems. By brainstorming, people improve their ability to think creatively.

One of the key contributions of brainstorming is that it produces synergy. **Synergy** occurs when the actions of two or more people achieve an effect that none of the people could achieve individually. The many different viewpoints expressed in the group stimulates members to develop ideas they would not have thought of by themselves. To achieve the potential advantages of brainstorming, you must conduct the session properly. Rules for conducting a brainstorming session are shown in Table 4-3.

Examples of business problems well suited to brainstorming are as follows: coming up with a name for a new model sports car, developing an idea for a new corporate logo, identifying ways to attract new customers, and making concrete suggestions for cost cutting.

Suggestion Programs.   An estimated 6,000 companies use **suggestion programs** to stimulate employee creativity for purposes of developing cost-saving ideas. The typical arrangement is for the employee to receive a percentage of the savings resulting from his or her suggestion. In 1986, for example, Eastman Kodak Co. saved $26 million from adopted suggestions, and employees received $5 million in suggestion awards. The top winner, Edmund Q. Lewis, received $50,000 for a suggestion that helps paper from tearing in the sensitizing machine.

A committee is established to evaluate submissions to the suggestion program and to make awards. Creativity is fostered because of both the financial rewards and the prestige associated with having an idea accepted and implemented.[26]

Identification and Recognition of Intrapreneurs.   An important new trend in fostering creativity within the organization is to hire **intrapreneurs**—company employees who engage in entrepreneurial thinking and behavior for the good

Table 4-3   Rules for Conducting a Brainstorming Session

Rule 1   Enroll five to eight participants. If you have too few people, you lose the flood of ideas; if you have too many, members feel that their ideas are not important, and there can be too much chatter.

Rule 2   Give everybody the opportunity to generate alternative solutions to the problem. Have them call out these alternatives spontaneously. One useful modification of this procedure is for people to express their ideas in sequence (one after another) to decrease possible confusion.

Rule 3   Do not allow criticism or value judgments during the brainstorming session. Make all suggestions welcome. Above all, members should not laugh derisively or make sarcastic comments about other people's ideas.

Rule 4   Encourage freewheeling. Welcome bizarre ideas. It is easier to tone down an idea than it is to think one up.

Rule 5   Compliment people for their participation, not their specific ideas. If the leader compliments specific ideas, an atmosphere of approval-seeking develops and potentially inhibits freewheeling.

Rule 6   Strive for quantity rather than quality of ideas. The probability of discovering really good ideas increases in proportion to the number of ideas generated.

Rule 7   Encourage members to piggyback, or build, on the ideas of others.

Rule 8   Record each idea, or tape-record the session. Written notes should not identify the author of an idea because participants may worry about saying something foolish.

Rule 9   Do not take the preceding eight rules too literally. The essence of brainstorming is spontaneity.

Rule 10   After the brainstorming session, edit and refine the list of ideas and choose one or two for implementation.

of the firm. Companies are now making an effort to officially recognize employees with ideas for breakthrough products.[27] Once the potential intrapreneur is identified, he or she is officially encouraged by a top executive.

A growing number of consulting firms have developed in recent years to advise management on ways to encourage intrapreneurial thinking. These firms stress the implementation of ideas by empowering an intrapreneur to start a new business. According to these consultants, many big companies that wish to expand face a major problem: they have difficulty differentiating between a product that is simply an extension of their present product line and a product that warrants launching a new business. IBM, for example, did know the difference:

> For the PC (personal computer), IBM set up separate engineering, marketing, and distribution. The people in this group "were in line to succeed" as though they were an independent business and without such concerns as competing for engineering resources or fitting with the distribution networks of other IBM products. They just focused on "Let's beat Apple." They saw they had not just a new product but a whole new business.[28]

Intrapreneurs hone their intuitive skill so they can recognize when a new product or service is worthy of expansion into a new business. Even more fundamentally, they need to recognize when a creative idea is worthy of developing into a new product.

Self-Help Techniques for Improving Creativity

In addition to participating in organizational programs for creativity improvement, individuals can help themselves become more creative. The general goal of becoming a more creative problem solver and decision maker requires that you increase the flexibility of your thinking. Reading about creativity improvement or attending one or two brainstorming sessions is not sufficient. To develop habits of creative thinking, you must practice regularly the suggestions described next. You will need self-discipline to carry out these suggestions under the daily pressures of work or school.[29]

1. Keep track of your original ideas by maintaining an idea notebook. Few people have such uncluttered minds that they can recall all of their past flashes of insight when they need them.

2. Stay current in your field. Having current facts at hand gives you the raw material to link together information creatively. (In practice, creativity usually takes the form of associating ideas previously not associated, such as the idea of selling movie tickets by vending machines.)

3. Try to overcome approaches to problems that lock you into one way of doing things. Avoid becoming a prisoner of familiarity who cannot think about doing things more than one way. The accompanying "Manager in Action" presents an example of a person who overcame the traditional way of looking at a motel room.

4. Participate in creative hobbies, such as doing puzzles and exercises or pursuing arts and crafts.

5. Improve your sense of humor, including your ability to laugh at your own mistakes. Humor helps to reduce stress and tensions, and people are more creative when they are relaxed.

6. Adopt a risk-taking attitude when you try to find creative solutions to problems. You will inevitably fail a few times.

7. Allow the foolish side of you to emerge—develop a creative mental set. Creativity requires a degree of intellectual playfulness and immaturity. Many creative people are accomplished practical jokers.

8. Continually hunt for new ideas. A creativity expert says, "I've worked with creative people in many industries, disciplines, and professions, and the really good ones are hunters. These people look outside their areas for ideas, and when they find an idea, they bring it back to their own area and apply it."[30]

9. Identify the times when you are most creative and attempt to accomplish most of your creative work during that period. Most people are at their peak of creative productivity after ample rest, so try to work on your most vexing problems at the start of the workday. Schedule programmed decision making and routine paperwork for times when your energy level is lower than average.

10. Be curious about your environment. The person who routinely questions how things work (or why they do not work) is most likely to have an idea for improvement.

MANAGER IN ACTION:

The Motel Innovator

Most people walk into a motel room and see only a motel room. But Michael A. Leven, the president and chief operating officer of Days Inn Corp., perceives a motel room as a tub of margarine or even an airplane seat. "If you think of a room as a room you end up marketing it like everyone else," explains the cantankerous, fast-talking Leven. "Thinking of our rooms as consumer products opens up a whole world of new opportunities."

Leven's unusual vision has given Days Inn the largest economy motel company in the country. His innovations have included promotional campaigns with Blue Bonnet margarine and K Mart department stores. In one of his most successful moves, Leven applied airline-industry marketing tactics to the motel business and began offering "super-saver" discounts. Today, anyone who makes a reservation and leaves a deposit at least twenty-nine days in advance pays a rate discounted up to 70 percent off the standard rate.

Source: Mark B. Roman, "Five Who Broke the Rules: These Mavericks Defied Tradition and Did It Their Way," *Success* (December 1986): 30.

Despite all the positive things that have been said about creativity, there are times when being creative can work to a person's disadvantage because the organization does not want to disturb the status quo. Also, creativity for its own sake can result in discarding traditional, but useful ideas. Entrepreneur Henry M. Gottfried notes: "Creativity is wonderful, but creativity has its limits. You can create yourself into one gigantic hole and go out of business."[31]

GROUP PROBLEM SOLVING AND DECISION MAKING

We have described aspects of how individuals go about solving problems and making decisions. However, most major, nonprogrammed decisions in organizations are made by groups. **Group decisions** occur when several people contribute to a final decision. Since participative management has become popular, an increasing number of decisions have been made by groups rather than individuals.[32]

The group problem-solving and decision-making process is similar to the individual model in two important respects. First, as individuals contribute to group problem solving, they often follow the decision-making steps to arrive at their suggestions. Second, the group itself often follows the formal steps indicated in Figure 4-2. Many groups, however, tend to ignore this formal sequencing.[33]

We will examine when to use group decision making, how to conduct an effective meeting, and what are the advantages and disadvantages of group decision making.

When to Use Group Decision Making

Because group decision making takes more time and people than individual decision making, it should not be used indiscriminately. Group decision making should be reserved for nonprogrammed decisions of reasonable importance. Too many managers use the group method for making trivial decisions such as this: What should be the menu at the company picnic?

Aside from being used to enhance the quality of decisions, group decision making often is used to gain acceptance for a decision. If people contribute to a decision, they are more likely to be committed to its implementation. More details about when to use group decision making are presented in Chapter 5.

Conducting an Effective Meeting

Most group problem solving and decision making takes place within a meeting of several or more people. A practical way of improving the quality of group decision making therefore is to improve the effectiveness of meetings. Our concern here is primarily with suggestions for improving meetings that tie in directly with problem solving and decision making. Most of our suggestions are geared toward the meeting leader, but they also apply to participants. By following these suggestions, you increase the chances that a meeting will produce high-quality decisions.

1. *Meet only for valid reasons.* Many meetings lead to no decisions because there was no valid reason for calling them. Meetings are necessary only when there is a need for coordinated effort and group decision making. Memos can be substituted for meetings when factual information needs to be disseminated and no discussion seems important.

2. *Have a specific agenda and adhere to it.* Meetings are more productive when an agenda is planned and followed carefully. People should see the agenda in advance so they can give some careful thought to the issues—preliminary thinking helps people arrive at more realistic decisions. In addition, assign maximum discussion times to the agenda items; you might allot thirty minutes to a major agenda item.

3. *Rely on qualified members.* Groups often reach poor decisions because the contributors to those decisions are not qualified from the standpoint of knowledge and interest. An uninformed person typically is a poor decision maker. Also, a person who attends a meeting reluctantly sometimes will agree to any decision just to help bring the meeting to a close.

4. *Have the leader share decision-making authority.* A key attribute of an effective problem-solving meeting is authority sharing by the leader. Unless authority is shared, the members are likely to believe that the hidden agenda of the meeting is to seek approval for the meeting leader's tentative decision.

5. *Keep comments brief and to the point.* A major challenge facing the meeting leader is to keep conversation on track. As participants begin to ramble, the quality of problem solving and decision making deteriorates. An effective way for the leader to keep comments on target is to ask the contributor of a nonsequitur, "In what way does your comment relate to the agenda?"

6. *Strive for balanced contribution by members.* One justification for using group decision making is to gather the input of several people before making a decision. To accomplish this end, each member should participate equally in the problem-solving and decision-making process. A skillful leader may have to limit the contribution of domineering members and coax reticent members to voice their ideas.

7. *Provide summaries for each major point.* Decision-making quality improves when members clearly understand the arguments that have been advanced for and against each alternative; summarizing major points can help. Summaries also keep the meeting focused on major issues, because the minor issues are excluded from the summary.

8. *Congratulate members when they reach a decision.* Complimenting group members when they reach a decision reinforces (strengthens) decision-making behavior and increases the probability that consensus will be reached the next time the group faces a problem.

Advantages and Disadvantages of Group Decision Making

Group decision making often results in high-quality solutions to problems because many people contribute. It also makes people feel more committed to the decision. However, the group approach consumes considerable time and may result in compromise solutions that do not really solve the problem. These concerns are reflected in two stale jokes about group decision making: "A camel is a horse designed by a committee," and "In a group meeting, minutes are taken and hours are lost."

A more serious example of the potential disadvantages of group decision making took place in relation to the explosion of the space shuttle Challenger. According to several analyses of this incident, NASA managers were so committed to reaching space program objectives that they ignored safety warnings from people both inside and outside the agency. As reported in an internal NASA briefing paper dated 20 July 1986, both astronauts and engineers expressed concern that the agency's management has a groupthink mentality. (**Groupthink** is a psychological drive for consensus at any cost in which the group members lose their ability to evaluate bad ideas critically.) Furthermore, the management style of NASA managers is characterized by a tendency not to reverse decisions and not to heed the advice of people outside the management group. The analysis of their styles was conducted by a series of management-style tests several years prior to the Challenger explosion.[34]

The key advantages and disadvantages of group problem solving and decision making are summarized in Table 4-4.

Table 4-4   Advantages and Disadvantages of Group Problem Solving and Decision Making

Advantages

1. Groups provide a larger sum of knowledge than would be accessible to individual members, thus leading to more informed decisions.
2. Group members can help each other overcome blocks in their thinking, leading to more creative solutions to problems. Also, groups are less likely than individuals to get into ruts in their thinking.
3. Participation in problem solving and decision making increases the acceptance of decisions, leading to better motivation to implement the decision.
4. Groups are willing to take greater risks than individuals, leading to more aggressive solutions to problems. (This illustrates the point that some of these advantages to group decision making can readily become dis—advantages.)
5. Group members evaluate each other's thinking, so major errors are likely to be avoided.
6. Groups are more effective than individuals in establishing objectives, generating alternatives, and evaluating alternatives because of the increased knowledge and viewpoints available to them.

Disadvantages

1. Groups create pressures toward conformity in thinking and mediocrity in decision making. Group members sometimes engage in groupthink.
2. A group cannot be held responsible; group decision making may therefore result in buck passing.
3. When people make decisions in a group, there is a pronounced tendency to accept the first satisficing decision that comes along.

**Table 4-4   Advantages and Disadvantages of Group
Problem Solving and Decision Making (Continued)**

4. Dominant members of the group sometimes make the major decision in a group setting; thus, what appears to be a group decision may really be an individual decision.
5. Group decision making is time consuming. Time may be wasted as the group deliberates or even as the leader tries to get the group together.
6. Group decision making and problem solving may discourage highly intelligent and intuitive individuals who are too impatient to sit through meetings to deliberate over a problem they have already solved.

SUMMARY OF KEY POINTS

A problem is a discrepancy between ideal and actual conditions; a decision is a choice among alternative solutions to the problem. Both problem solving and decision making are an important part of planning. Higher-level managers tend to deal with more nonprogrammed (nonroutine) decisions than do lower-level managers, but they do make some programmed (routine) decisions.

The recommended steps for solving problems and making decisions are as follows: identify and diagnose the problem, develop creative alternative solutions, evaluate the alternative solutions, choose an alternative solution, implement the decision, evaluate and control, and repeat the process if necessary.

People vary in their decision-making ability, and forces in some situations can influence the quality of anyone's decisions. Seven such factors are as follows: crisis conditions, intuition of the decision maker, personality and intelligence of the decision maker, quality of information, political considerations, degree of uncertainty, and values of the decision maker.

Creativity is the ability to develop original, imaginative, and innovative perspectives on situations. Many aspects of managerial work require creativity, including giving shape to problems and creating working groups of people. Creative people are generally more open and flexible than are their less creative counterparts. Ego permissiveness, the ability to let the mind wander, is an important characteristic of creative thinkers.

Organizations can take steps to improve creativity. One strategy for improving creativity is for managers to create a permissive atmosphere. Group brainstorming is the best-known method of improving creativity. In a brainstorming session, a group of people spontaneously generate alternative solutions to a problem without being discouraged or controlled. Suggestion programs also encourage employee creativity. The creation of intrapreneurial programs (entrepreneurs within a corporation) is another way of stimulating organizational creativity. You can improve your own creativity by engaging in creative hobbies, taking risks, and hunting for new ideas.

Group decision making is used to handle most major, nonprogrammed decisions. Conducting meetings effectively leads to improved group decision making. Try to (1) meet only for valid reasons, (2) adhere to an agenda, (3) rely on qualified members, (4) share decision-making authority, (5) keep comments brief, (6) strive for balanced contributions, (7) provide summaries, and (8) congratulate members when they reach a decision.

Group decision making often results in high-quality solutions to problems because many people contribute. It also makes people feel more committed to the decision. However, the group approach consumes considerable time and may result in compromise solutions that do not really solve the problem and in groupthink. The latter occurs when consensus becomes so important that group members lose their ability to critically evaluate ideas.

QUESTIONS

1. Describe a problem a manager might face, and point out the actual and ideal conditions in relation to this problem.
2. Give three examples of decisions you have faced or will be facing that warrant completing the formal problem-solving and decision-making steps.
3. What personal factors about you are assets in making decisions?
4. Are line or staff managers more likely to face job crises? Explain your reasoning.
5. Given that creativity is so important in managerial work, should a company establish a formal department of creativity? Why or why not?
6. What can an organization do to reward innovation?
7. What do you think is the biggest error in problem solving and decision making made by most people?
8. What can managers and professional workers do to improve their decision-making skills?

ACTIVITIES

1. Interview a manager. Show that person Figure 4-2, and then ask the manager how well it matches the way he or she actually makes decisions. Be prepared to discuss your findings in class.
2. Attend any meeting you can in the next ten days. Provide a written critique of how well that meeting conformed to the guidelines for conducting an effective meeting as described in the text.

CASE PROBLEM 4: THE CORPORATE INNOVATORS

AMI is a $3 billion conglomerate, the primary businesses of which lie in the entertainment, cosmetics and beauty aids, and educational-services fields. The executive vice president, Brett Flagstone, is the manager most directly responsible for investigating new business opportunities for AMI. Typically, these are thriving business organizations taken over on a friendly basis. AMI begins by buying up much of the stock available for the firm they want to acquire; soon thereafter, AMI makes a formal bid to purchase a controlling interest in the company.

Recently, top managers of the firm decided to place more emphasis on investigating new opportunities. A problem AMI executives observed was that sales in their existing firms had begun to stabilize in many cases and decline in others. For example, one of their most recent acquisitions, a large pharmaceutical firm, lost $1 million during the previous year.

To generate new ideas for business expansion, Brett Flagstone assembled the Tiger Team. Members of this select group of eight employees were told they would have considerable latitude in investigating new business opportunities for AMI. Nina Morales was appointed project leader of the Tiger Team. She and her teammates were told they should not restrict their thinking to any one type of business expansion. Furthermore, they were encouraged to let their minds wander and to overcome any traditional ideas about how a conglomerate (a large firm that is really a collection of smaller firms) should conduct its business.

Morales and the other team members were ecstatic about being part of such an elite corporate group. Much to their delight, they were assigned a small office ten miles away from corporate headquarters. They were given the authority to hire two full-time secretaries and assigned a lavish budget for entertainment and any office equipment they needed.

Two months after the Tiger Team was launched, they made their first presentation to management about a new business they thought AMI should enter, a nationwide boat-rental company. The Tiger Team noted that leisure time was becoming increasingly important to people, and that interest in boating had become a permanent part of our culture. Brett Flagstone brought back to the Tiger Team the corporate verdict on this idea: "Your boat proposal has sunk. We think AMI would take a bath on this one. Back to dry land, and good luck."

Morales told the group not to be discouraged, that no new venture group can get all its ideas accepted. After a two-day brainstorming session, the Tiger Team developed a new idea for a business venture. They would form a company called Second Chance, the entire nonsupervisory work force of which would be composed of former prisoners. The firm would manufacture basic low-technology household furniture, such as kitchen tables, bookcases, and umbrella stands. Its advertising thrust would focus on the idea that AMI was helping society with one of its thorniest problems—giving former prisoners an opportunity to learn new skills and hold a useful job.

Fifteen minutes into the presentation about Second Chance, Flagstone stopped the Tiger Team. "Enough's enough," he said emphatically. "Our stockholders are neither social workers nor criminologists. They will not tolerate an idea this farfetched. I assume you would also have these ex-cons keeping the books of the firm. I, in no way, want to discourage your creativity, but please get back to your think tank."

Morales said to the group, "Only two of our ideas have been shot down so far. I still think Second Chance had good possibilities, but there's not much we can do. Top management has the final say."

Three weeks later, the Tiger Team received the following written memo from Flagstone:

TO: Nina Morales and the Tiger Team

FROM: Brett Flagstone, Executive Vice President

DATE: May 10, 19--

SUBJECT: Accountability for results

Soon you will be approaching the completion of the first quarter of your existence. As you know, your charter is to develop innovative ideas for expanding the business of AMI. By the time you have been in operation for six months, we would like to see a comprehensive report of your activities. We are giving you substantial advance notice to guide you in data collection for your status report. Please include the following items in your report:

1. How will the corporation benefit from your continued existence?
2. What will be the likely return on investment from the Tiger Team?
3. What are all the ideas you have developed? (including those you have rejected.)

I will be in touch with you in person to discuss this matter.

Several days later, Flagstone did get in touch with Morales. He told her, "Don't worry at all about the report. It's just a formality. The executive group and I just want to know what we're getting for our money. By the way, I'll be meeting with you every two weeks to discuss how the Tiger Team is progressing. We all have so much faith in you that we're eager to hear how you are doing."

Later that day, Morales relayed the substance of her meeting with Flagstone to the rest of the Tiger Team. Stan Golden, one of the team members, was the first to respond. Scratching his head, he said: "Now I know why they call us the Tiger Team. Brett Flagstone cracks his whip and we're supposed to stand up on our hind legs and perform stunts. Each week, I'm beginning to feel our team is a little less elite."

Claire Benson had a different reaction. "Brett Flagstone is just doing what has to be done. The entire AMI works under goals philosophy. Why should we be exempt just because we're a creative group?"

Case Questions

1. What is your evaluation of the Tiger Team concept as a way of encouraging corporate innovation?
2. How effective do you think Flagstone is in encouraging creativity?
3. How should Morales respond to Flagstone's memorandum and request for biweekly meetings?
4. What problems does the Tiger Team face, and what decisions must its members make?
5. Do you think the Tiger Team was given too many luxuries? What effect do you think the privileges had on the team members?

EXERCISE 4: CAN YOU MAKE BOLD DECISIONS?

Part of being a successful manager is the ability to make bold, or courageous, decisions. The following quiz may provide tentative insight into the extent of your decision-making boldness.

TEST YOUR BOLDNESS

To test your capacity for making bold decisions, mark the response that most closely matches your typical behavior.

1. Do you avoid ''yes'' decisions?
   Usually/Often . . Sometimes/Seldom

2. Do you avoid ''no'' decisions?
   Usually/Often . . Sometimes/Seldom

3. Do you avoid making ''that's gonna have to wait'' decisions?
   Usually/Often . . Sometimes/Seldom

4. Do you find that you make ''wait'' decisions *quickly*?
   Usually/Often . . Sometimes/Seldom

5. Boldness in saying ''no'' may well go against the grain at a given time, when there's a rush to do something, are you willing to take the heat?
   Usually/Often . . Sometimes/Seldom

6. Do you show discernment in decision-making by spotting and labelling ''groupthink,'' ''fashion,'' and ''wishful thinking'' among your subordinates who are jointly grappling with the problem?
   Usually/Often . . Sometimes/Seldom

7. Do you use your decision-making as a training and development opportunity for your subordinates? Do you explain your reasoning and indicate the tradeoffs you faced in reaching decisions?
   Usually/Often . . Sometimes/Seldom

8. Do you put off making decisions because you fear being wrong?
   Usually/Often . . Sometimes/Seldom

9. Are you annoyed that your subordinates want decisions from you on their recommendations too quickly?
   Usually/Often . . Sometimes/Seldom

10. Have you rebounded quickly from decisions you've made that in hindsight have proved to be wrong?
    Usually/Often . . Sometimes/Seldom

• • •

To determine your score on the quiz, check your answers below. For each correct answer, give yourself one point. Then mark the rating category that corresponds to your total score.

1. S/S	6. U/O	Superior . . 9–10
2. S/S	7. U/O	Good 8
3. S/S	8. S/S	Satisfactory . . . 7
4. U/O	9. S/S	Fair 6
5. U/O	10. U/O	Poor 0–5

Source: Allan Cox, *The Making of the Achiever: How to Win Distinction in Your Company* (New York: Dodd, Mead & Co., 1985).

REFERENCES

1. A general reference on the topic is George Wright, ed., *Behavioral Decision Making* (New York: Plenum Publishing Corp., 1985).

2. David J. Hickson and associates, *Top Decisions: Strategic Decision Making in Organizations* (San Francisco: Jossey-Bass, Inc., Pubs., 1986).

3. James L. Gibson, John M. Ivancevich, and James H. Donnelly, Jr., *Organizations: Behavior, Structure, Processes,* 6th ed. (Plano, Texas: Business Pubs., Inc., 1988), 580; Linda J. Segall and Carol Meyers, "Taking Aim at Problems," *Management Solutions* (February 1988): 5–15.

4. John M. Ivancevich, James H. Donnelly, Jr., and James L. Gibson, *Managing for Performance: An Introduction to the Process of Managing,* rev. ed. (Plano, TX: Business Pubs., Inc., 1983), 83–84.

5. This theme is developed in Morgan W. McCall, Jr., Robert E. Kaplan, and Michael L. Gerlach, *Caught in the Act: Decision Makers at Work* (Greensboro, NC: Center for Creative Leadership, 1982).

6. Edward C. Schleh, "How to Make Executive Decisions Work," *Management Review* (September 1987): 53.

7. Morgan W. McCall and Robert E. Kaplan, *Whatever It Takes* (Englewood Cliffs, NJ: Prentice Hall, 1985).

8. Dean Tjosvold, "Effects of Crisis Orientation on Managers' Approach to Controversy in Decision Making," *Academy of Management Journal* (March 1984): 137.

9. Eugene Raudsepp, "Can You Trust Your Hunches?" *Administrative Management* (October 1981): 35.

10. Herbert A. Simon, "Making Management Decisions: the Role of Intuition and Emotion," *The Academy of Management Executive* (February 1987): 63.

11. Raudsepp, "Can You Trust Your Hunches?" 34.

12. Henry Mintzberg, "The Manager's Job: Folklore and Fact," *Harvard Business Review* (July–August 1975): 54.

13. Theodore Issac Rubin, *Determining Indecisiveness: The Eight Steps of Effective Decision Making* (New York: Harper & Row, 1985), 1.

14. Charles A. O'Reilly, III, "Variations in Decision Makers' Use of Information Sources: The Impact of Quality and Accessibility of Information," *Academy of Management Journal* (December 1982): 769.

15. Bernard M. Bass, *Organizational Decision Making* (Homewood, IL: Richard D. Irwin, Inc., 1983), 9–11.

16. Robert Kreitner, *Management,* 3d ed. (Boston: Houghton Mifflin Co., 1987), 203–205.

17. Elizabeth C. Ravlin and Bruce M. Meglino, "Effect of Values on Perception and Decision Making: A Study of Alternative Work Values Measures," *Journal of Applied Psychology* (November 1987): 672.

18. William D. Guth and Renato Taguiri, "Personal Values and Corporate Strategy," *Harvard Business Review* (September–October 1965): 125–126.

19. Edward H. Meyer, "Creativity In Business," *Business Week's Guide to Careers* (September 1985): 27.

20. "Creativity: A Special Report," *Success* (March 1985): 54.

21. David R. Wheeler, "Creative Decision Making and the Organization," *Personnel Journal* (June 1979): 374.

22. Robert E. Kaplan, "Creativity in the Everyday Business of Managing," *Issues & Observations* (May 1983): 1.
23. Kaplan "Creativity in Managing," 2–5.
24. This section of the chapter is based on Salvatore Didato, "Willingness to Let Mind Wander: A Trait of 'Ego-permissiveness'," *Democrat and Chronicle* (28 July 1984): 16B.
25. David Campbell, *Take the Road to Creativity and Get Off Your Dead End* (Niles, IL: Argus Communications, 1977).
26. Robert H. Meehan, "Programs That Foster Creativity and Innovation," *Personnel* (February 1986): 32.
27. Franck A. de Chambeau and Fredericka Mackenzie, "Intrapreneurship," *Personnel Journal* (July 1986): 40–45.
28. "Here Comes the 'Intrapreneur'," *Business Week.* (18 July 1983): 188.
29. Some of the list is from Eugene Raudsepp, "Exercises for Creative Growth," *Success* (February 1981): 46–47.
30. Robert S. Wieder, "How to Get Great Ideas," *Success* (November 1983): 30.
31. Phil Ebersole, "Discuss Founder Moves on as Firm Stabilizes," *Democrat and Chronicle* (26 November 1987): 12D.
32. Ichak Adizes and Efraim Turban, "An Innovative Approach to Group Decision Making," *Personnel* (April 1985): 45.
33. John A. Seeger, "No Innate Phases in Group Problem Solving," *The Academy of Management Review* (October 1983): 683–689.
34. Kenneth A. Kovach and Barry Render, "NASA Managers and Challenger: A Profile of Possible Explanation," *Personnel* (April 1987): 40.

5

Specialized Techniques for Planning and Decision Making

After studying the material in this chapter, you should be able to accomplish the following tasks:

1. Explain the meaning and purpose of management science.
2. Describe how to use the Gantt charts, milestone charts, and PERT planning techniques.
3. Describe how to use break-even analysis, payoff matrices, and decision trees for problem solving and decision making.
4. Describe how to manage inventory by using the economic order quantity (EOQ) and just-in-time (JIT) techniques.
5. Describe how to use the nominal group technique.
6. Explain the basis of computer-assisted decision making.
7. Recognize when it is advisable to use any one of these techniques.

Key Terms and Phrases

Management science
Operations research
Decision sciences
Gantt chart
Milestone chart
Program evaluation and review
   technique (PERT)
Event
Activity
Expected time
Critical path
Break-even analysis

Payoff matrix
States of nature
Conditional value
Expected value
Economic order quantity (EOQ)
Just in time (JIT)
Decision tree
Nominal group technique (NGT)
Data-base management
Decision-making software
Expert systems

To make planning and decision making more accurate, a variety of techniques based on the scientific method, mathematics, and statistics have been developed. **Management science** is the field of study dealing with quantified planning and decision making. **Operations research** is another term denoting the same field. At present, professionals in the field refer to this discipline as

decision sciences. The central focus of the management-science approach is to provide managers with a scientific basis for solving problems and making planning and operating decisions.

Sufficient information is provided in this chapter for you to gain insight into several popular decision-support techniques. More detail about these methods and techniques can be found in books about production and operations management and managerial accounting. The other specialized technique for decision making described in this chapter fits more into the behavioral approach rather than the management-science approach. It is the nominal group technique for group decision making.

Management-science techniques are impressive because they use formulas and numbers and thus appear to offer precise answers to problems. Managers often rely on these quantitative tools for valuable assistance in making manufacturing and marketing decisions. Despite their scientific appearance, decision-support methods cannot replace careful managerial judgment. The numbers fed into the equations used in these methods usually are subjective estimates made by human beings, such as the shortest possible time it will take for an activity to be completed. If the subjective estimates are incorrect, no amount of quantified analysis will yield a valid guide for decision making.

Our message in this chapter is that the competent manager chooses the most appropriate technique to solve a particular problem.

GANTT CHARTS AND MILESTONE CHARTS

Two basic techniques for monitoring the progress of scheduled projects are Gantt charts and milestone charts. Closely related to each other, they both help the manager keep track of whether activities are completed on time.

Gantt Charts

A Gantt chart graphically depicts the planned and actual progress of work over the period of time encompassed by a project. Gantt charts are especially useful for scheduling one-time projects such as constructing buildings, making films, and launching satellites. Charts of this type also are referred to as time-and-activity charts, because these are the two key variables they take into consideration. Time is plotted on the horizontal axis, whereas activities are listed on the vertical axis.

A Gantt chart used to schedule the opening of a nightclub is shown in Figure 5-1. Gantt charts used for most other purposes would have a similar format. At the planning phase of the project, the manager lays out the schedule as shown by the rectangular boxes. As each activity is completed, the appropriate box is shaded in. At any given time, the manager can see which activities have been completed on time. For example, if a liquor license had not been obtained by 30 November, the activity would be declared behind schedule.

Figure 5-1   A Gantt Chart Used for Opening a Nightclub

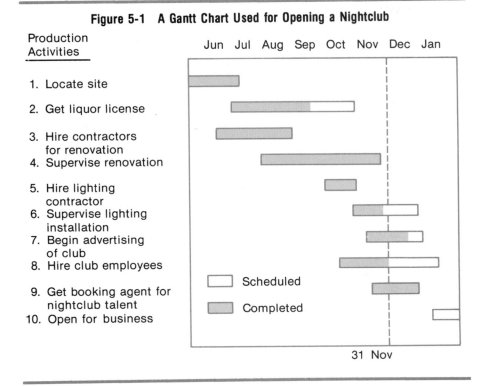

Because Gantt charts are used to monitor progress, they also are control devices. When the nightclub owner observes that obtaining a liquor license has fallen behind schedule, she can investigate the problem. Conceivably, the liquor commission needs more information that she can supply in order to facilitate getting the license.

The Gantt chart gives a convenient overall view of the progress made against the schedule. However, it does not furnish enough details about subactivities that need to be performed to accomplish each general item.

Milestone Chart

A **milestone chart** is an extension of the Gantt chart. It provides a listing of subactivities that must be completed to accomplish the major activities listed on the vertical axis. A milestone is the completion of one phase of an activity. The inclusion of milestones adds to the value of a Gantt chart as a scheduling and control technique. Each milestone serves as another checkpoint on progress. In Figure 5-2, the Gantt chart for opening a nightclub has been expanded into a milestone chart. The numbers in each rectangle represent milestones. A complete chart would list each of the thirty-three milestones. In Figure 5-2, only the milestones for hiring employees and the opening date are listed.

Figure 5-2   A Milestone Chart Used for Opening a Nightclub

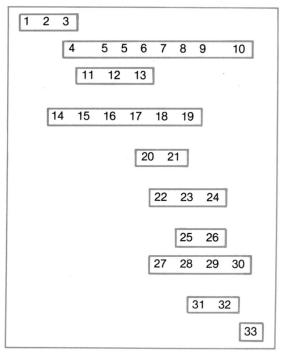

Production
Activities

	Jun	Jul	Aug	Sep	Oct	Nov	Dec	Jan

1. Locate site

2. Get liquor license

3. Hire contractors
   for renovation

4. Supervise renovation

5. Hire lighting
   contractor

6. Supervise lighting
   installation

7. Begin advertising
   of club

8. Hire club employees

9. Get booking agent for
   nightclub talent

10. Open for business

Milestones to Be Accomplished

-
-
-

27. Speak to friends and acquaintances about job openings
28. Put ad in local newspapers
29. Conduct interviews with applicants and check references
    of best candidates
30. Make job offers to best candidates
-
-
-
33. Have grand opening celebration 5 January

PROGRAM EVALUATION AND REVIEW TECHNIQUE (PERT)

Gantt and milestone charts are basic scheduling tools, exceeded in simplicity
only by a "to do" list. A more complicated method of scheduling activities
and events uses a network model; this model depicts all the interrelated events

that must take place for a project to be completed.[1] The most widely used network model is the **program evaluation and review technique (PERT)**. It is used for the planning activities required to complete a large-scale, nonrepetitive project.

An advanced-scheduling technique such as PERT is useful when certain tasks have to be completed before others if the total project is to be completed on time. In the nightclub example, the site of the club had to be specified and a lease drawn up before the owner could apply for a liquor license. The liquor commission will grant a license only after approving a specific location. The PERT diagram would indicate such a necessary sequencing of events.

PERT is used most often in engineering and construction projects. It also has been applied to such business problems as conducting marketing campaigns, relocating company headquarters, and coordinating and planning all the activities required when organizing a large convention.

Key PERT Concepts

Two concepts lie at the core of PERT: event and activity. An **event** is a point of decision or the accomplishment of a task. Events also are referred to as milestones. The events involved in the merger of two companies would include sending out announcements to shareholders, changing the company name, letting customers know of the merger, and having a banquet to celebrate the merger.

An **activity** is the physical and mental effort required to complete an event. In the merger example, an activity would be working with a public-relations firm to arrive at a suitable name for the new company. Activities that have to be accomplished in the nightclub example include supervising contractors and interviewing job applicants.

Steps Involved in Preparing a PERT Network

The events and activities included in a PERT network are shown in a PERT diagram. The essentials of preparing a PERT diagram can be divided into six steps:

1. Prepare a list of all the activities necessary to complete the project. In the nightclub example, the activities would include working with a realtor to study site locations, sending the appropriate forms to the liquor commission, searching for a talented lighting contractor, and preparing a list of positions that need to be filled.

2. Design the actual PERT network, relating all the activities to each other in the proper sequence. Considerable skill, experience, and judgment are called for in this step. It is generally difficult to anticipate all the activities that need to be done to complete a major project. Activities also must be sequenced—which activity must precede another? In the nightclub example, the owner must make sure that, before the lighting is put in place, the ceiling is painted.

3. The time required to complete each activity must be estimated carefully because the major output of the PERT method is a statement of the total time required by the project. Because the time estimate is so critical, several people should be asked to make three different estimates: optimistic time, pessimistic time, and probable time. The three estimates are then averaged to find the **expected time.**

   Optimistic time (O) is the shortest time it will take if everything goes well. In the construction industry, the optimistic time rarely is achieved.

   Pessimistic time (P) is the amount of time it will take if everything goes wrong (as it sometimes does with complicated projects such as installing a new subway system).

   Most probable time (M) is the most realistic estimate of how much time an activity will take to complete. The probable time for an activity can be an estimate of the time taken for similar activities on other projects. For instance, the time needed to build a cockpit for one aircraft might be based on the average time it took to build cockpits for comparable aircraft in the past.

   Using the following formula, compute the expected times for each activity and enter them in the appropriate place on the PERT network.

   $$\text{Expected time} = \frac{O + 4M + P}{6}$$

   These time estimates are established for choosing a site location for the nightclub: optimistic time *(O)* is 10 days; most probable time *(M)* is 30 days; and pessimistic time *(P)* is 50 days. Therefore,

   $$\text{Expected time} = \frac{10 + (4 \times 30) + 50}{6} = \frac{180}{6} = 30 \text{ days}$$

4. Calculate the **critical path**—the path through the PERT diagram that has the longest completion time. The length of the entire project is determined by the path with the longest elapsed time. The logic behind the critical path is this: a given project cannot be considered completed until its lengthiest component is completed. For example, if it takes one year to get the liquor permit, the nightclub project cannot be completed in less than one year, even if all other events are completed earlier than scheduled.

   In Figure 5-3, the PERT network's critical path requires a total elapsed time of sixteen weeks. It is calculated by adding the number of weeks scheduled to complete the activities between events A and B, B and C, C and D, D and E, and E and F. Notice that a path must follow the sequence of steps indicated by the direction of the arrows.

5. As a control measure, the project manager must pay careful attention to seeing that all critical events are completed on time. If activities in the critical path take too long to complete, the project will not be completed

Figure 5-3   A PERT Network

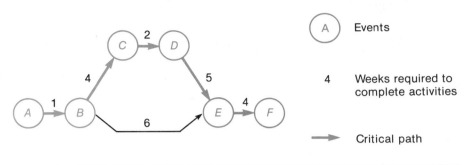

on time. The manager must take corrective action to move the activity along. Such actions might include hiring additional help, dismissing substandard help, or purchasing more productive equipment.

6.   The project manager can delay the start of activities that are not on the critical path. This will decrease the cost of the project because the organization will be able to delay payment for these activities, which in turn will save interest on outstanding loans or allow the organization to invest the money in short-term securities.

In practice, PERT networks often specify hundreds of events and activities. Each small event can have its own PERT diagram, similar to each department in an organization having its own organization chart.

BREAK-EVEN ANALYSIS

One of the more popular techniques used to provide information for making a specific kind of decision is **break-even analysis,** a relatively simple method of determining the relationship between total costs and total revenues at various levels of production or sales activity. The relationship expressed by the break-even analysis is static: both the cost and the revenue estimates are fixed at the time for which the analysis is being made.

The rationale behind break-even analysis is that, before adding new products, equipment, or personnel, it should be clear that the addition will make a financial contribution. Break-even analysis tells us at what point it is profitable to go ahead with a new venture.

Components of Break-Even Analysis

Break-even analysis is based on revenues and fixed and variable costs. Fixed costs are those that remain constant unless there is a dramatic expansion; they include rent and executive salaries. Variable costs are those that vary directly with the amount of units produced; they include the price of raw materials and overtime pay. If you know these two classifications of costs and the selling price, it is relatively simple to draw a break-even chart.

Figure 5-4 illustrates a typical break-even chart. It deals with a decision regarding adding a new product to an existing line of products. The point at which the total costs line and the total revenue line intersect is the break-even point. Sales beyond (to the right of) the break-even point represent a profit. Any sales below this point represent a loss.

Break-Even Formula

It is also possible to find the break-even point by mathematical formulas. One standard formula is as follows:

$$BE = \frac{FC}{P - VC}$$

where BE = Break-even point, a situation existing when total revenues equal fixed costs plus variable costs.
P = Selling price per unit.
VC = Variable cost per unit, the cost that varies with the amount produced.
FC = Fixed cost, the cost that remains constant no matter how many units are produced.

The chart in Figure 5-4 is based on the following data: the selling price *(P)* is $10 per unit; the variable cost *(VC)* is $5 per unit; and fixed costs *(FC)* are $300,000. By the formula, then, the break-even point is computed as follows:

$$BE = \frac{\$300,000}{\$10 - \$5} = \frac{\$300,000}{\$5} = 60,000 \text{ units}$$

Under the conditions assumed and for the period of time in which these cost and revenue figures are valid, a sales volume of 60,000 units would be required for the company to break even. Anything above that would be a profit and anything below that would result in a loss. If the sales forecast for this new product was above the 60,000 units, it would be a good decision to add it to the line. If the sales forecast was less than 60,000 units, the company would do well to abandon the plan.

Advantages and Limitations of Break-Even Analysis

Break-even analysis helps managers to keep their thinking focused on the volume of activity that will be necessary to justify a new expense. In addition to helping a manager decide whether to add a new product, break-even analysis can be applied to a number of common operations problems. It can help a manager decide whether to drop an existing product from the line, to

Figure 5-4   Break-Even Chart for Adding a New Product to an Existing Line

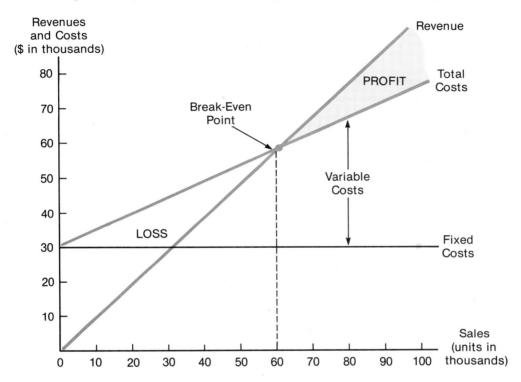

replace equipment, or to buy rather than make a part. (The problem facing the manager in the last point is this: how many units will be consumed before it is more profitable to make them rather than buy them? Generally, there are substantial start-up costs when manufacturing a new part.)

Another use of break-even analysis is to aid in pricing decisions. When the price of a product is altered the break-even volume of sales is changed. The new break-even point is compared to the market potential for that product or service at that specific price. It is a backwards way of generating a demand curve.

Despite its utility, break-even analysis does have some drawbacks. First, break-even analysis is only as valid as are the estimates of costs and revenues. Second, break-even analysis is static; it assumes there will be no changes in other variables. The dynamic nature of any business enterprise makes this a questionable assumption.

A third limitation of break-even analysis is potentially more serious. Figure 5-4 indicates that break-even analysis assumes a straight-line, total costs curve, meaning that variable costs and sales increase together in a direct relationship. In reality, unit costs may decrease with increased volume or they may increase because of such factors as increased production leading to higher turnover if employees prefer not to work so hard.

Break-even analysis is concerned with proceed-or-do-not-proceed decisions. Next we examine a more complicated decision-making aid that examines the desirability of several alternative solutions.

PAYOFF MATRIX

The **payoff matrix** is a technique for indicating possible payoffs, or returns, from pursuing different alternative solutions to a problem. These alternatives can be considered as possible courses of action. Each alternative is pursued under different **states of nature,** those circumstances beyond the control of the decision maker. Examples of states of nature affecting business decisions include the demand for a product, availability of qualified job applicants, and weather conditions.

To illustrate the use of a payoff matrix, assume that Funtime Products decides to manufacture and market a line of aboveground swimming pools. Jeff Rogers, the president, cannot really predict the demand for the swimming pools because he is uncertain about such critical factors as competitive products, the weather, interest rates, and the general state of the economy. Based on past experience with introducing expensive leisure products, he nevertheless assigns dollar-volume-of-sales values to the three possible levels of demand: low, medium, and high.

Funtime managers can choose how many pools to manufacture. Each quantity level represents a different alternative. Because the true level of demand is uncertain, Rogers can only guess what is the best number of pools to manufacture: a low, medium, or high number. A payoff matrix can help a manager reach the best decision in a problem of this nature. The managers use the best data available to show the possible revenue they can realize by pursuing each of the three alternatives under each of the three states of nature.

The possible payoffs to Funtime from pursuing each alternative under the three levels of demand are shown in Table 5-1. The possible payoffs often are called **conditional values,** because each depends on a particular condition. As indicated in the matrix, if Funtime produces a low quantity of pools under low

Table 5-1   Payoff Matrix Showing Conditional Values

Alternatives (Pools Produced)	States of Nature (Demand for Pools)		
	Low	Medium	High
	Conditional Values		
Low Quantity	$2,000,000	$2,000,000	$2,000,000
Medium Quantity	$2,000,000	$4,000,000	$4,000,000
High Quantity	$2,000,000	$4,000,000	$5,000,000

demand, anticipated revenues will be $2,000,000. A medium number of pools produced under medium demand will yield $4,000,000; a high number of pools under high demand will yield $5,000,000. Note that if Funtime produces only a low number of pools, its revenues will not exceed $2,000,000 under any of the demand conditions because it will have only the low quantity to sell.

To make a payoff matrix more accurate, probabilities usually are assigned to each of the various states of nature. The probabilities indicate the likelihood of each condition occurring. The sum of the probabilities must equal 1.0. As shown in Table 5-2, the probability of each state of nature is multiplied by each conditional value to arrive at an expected value. **An expected value** is the average value incurred if a particular decision is made a large number of times; it is the average return in the long run. The expected value for each state of nature is added to yield a total expected value for each alternative.

Table 5-3 presents the expected values for the three alternative quantities based on probabilities of 0.20 for low demand, 0.50 for medium demand, and 0.30 for high demand. The total expected value for the low alternative is $2,000,000; for the medium alternative it is $3,600,000; and for the high production alternative it is $3,900,000. Assuming the various estimates used in developing the payoff matrix are correct, manufacturing a large number of pools will have the biggest payoff. If Rogers believes the payoff matrix to be

Table 5-2 Calculating the Expected Value When a Low Quantity is Produced

Demand Level	Probability	×	Conditional Value	=	Expected Value
Low	0.20		$2,000,000		$ 400,000
Medium	0.50		$2,000,000		$1,000,000
High	0.30		$2,000,000		$ 600,000
			Total Expected Value	=	$2,000,000

Table 5-3 Payoff Matrix Showing Expected Values

Alternative (Pools Produced)	Probabilities of Each Demand Level			Total Expected Value
	Low (0.20)	Medium (0.50)	High (0.30)	
	Expected Values			
Low Quantity	$400,000	$1,000,000	$ 600,000	$2,000,000
Medium Quantity	$400,000	$2,000,000	$1,200,000	$3,600,000
High Quantity	$400,000	$2,000,000	$1,500,000	$3,900,000

accurate, he will manufacture a high number of aboveground pools—and hope for a warm, early summer.

The outstanding feature of the payoff matrix is that it forces managers to examine the probabilities of certain events taking place. As a result, managers tend to invest their resources in situations in which the expected payoff is highest. A major drawback of the payoff matrix is similar to that of other decision-making aids: it has an appearance of precision that may be unwarranted. Estimates are often based on historical information and the past is not inevitably a good predictor of the future.

INVENTORY CONTROL TECHNIQUES

A problem faced by virtually every manufacturing and sales organization is how much inventory to keep on hand. If a large inventory is kept on hand, goods can be made quickly or orders can be shipped rapidly. However, stocking inventory is expensive. The goods themselves are costly, and money tied up in inventory cannot be invested elsewhere. In this section we describe a decision support-technique used to manage inventory (economic order quantity) and a method of production inventory management (just-in-time inventory control). The latter method helps managers make decisions about inventory.

Economic Order Quantity

Economic order quantity (EOQ) is the inventory level that minimizes both ordering costs and carrying costs. (The latter include the cost of loans or the interest foregone because money is tied up in inventory and the cost of handling the inventory.) EOQ is expressed mathematically as follows:

$$EOQ = \sqrt{2DO/C}$$

where D = Annual demand in units
O = Ordering cost per unit
C = Annual carrying cost per unit

Assume the annual demand for the swimming pools is 100 units, and it costs $1,000 to order each unit. Furthermore, the carrying cost per unit is $200. We calculate the most economic number of pools to keep in inventory in this way:

$EOQ = \sqrt{2 \times 100 \times \$1,000/\$200}$

$EOQ = \sqrt{\$200,000/\$200}$

$EOQ = \sqrt{1,000}$

$EOQ = 32$ pools (rounded figure)

Funtime managers thus conclude that it is the most economical to keep 32 pools in inventory during the selling season. If you enter accurate figures into this formula, EOQ can vastly improve your inventory management.

Just-in-Time Inventory Control

Toyota Motor Corp. of Japan developed a system of production management to overcome losses from the oil crisis in 1973. At the heart of the system is **just-in-time (JIT)** inventory control, the procedure whereby inventory is minimized and moved into the plant exactly when needed. The JIT system of inventory control relies on **kanbans,** or cards, to communicate production requirements from the final point of assembly to the preceding operations that manufacture the components of the final product. The key principle underlying the JIT system is the elimination of excess inventory by producing or purchasing parts, subassemblies, and final products only when, and in the exact amounts they are needed.[2] JIT is generally used in a repetitive, single product, manufacturing environment.

Procedures and Philosophies.   Working within a JIT system, when an order is received for a product, a kanban is issued that directs employees to finish a product. The finishing department selects components and assembles the product. The kanban is then passed back to earlier stations in the process to resupply the components. This process continues all the way back to the material suppliers, who may even physically locate close to their major customers in order to make shipments promptly. At each stage, parts and other materials are delivered "just in time" for use.

As a result of JIT, inventories are kept quite low, thus reducing holding costs. JIT also requires a smooth working relationship between producer and supplier. For the system to work well, a stable, reciprocal relationship must be developed. Long-term contracts between producer and supplier reduce ordering costs and increase predictability. Because supplies are delivered only when needed, lot sizes are small and deliveries are frequent, often more than once daily. In some instances, the producer agrees to purchase the entire output of its supplier.[3]

There are three basic JIT philosophies:

1. *Setup time for assembly and cost must be reduced.* The goal is to make them so low that small batch sizes are economical, even to the point of manufacturing just one finished product. Many Japanese manufacturers have reduced the setup time of an eight-hundred-ton press to less than one minute. This remarkable efficiency has been achieved in part by the redesign of machinery and tooling.

2. *Safety stock is undesirable.* Stock held in reserve is expensive and hides problems such as inefficient production methods. The philosophy here is that "just in time" should replace "just in case."

3. *Productivity and quality are inseparable.* JIT is only possible when high-quality components are produced. The manufacturer will not be able to test, rework, and deliver products promptly. JIT therefore requires small batches, low inventories, rapid production, and a very high level of quality. The goal of the JIT system is 100 percent good items at each manufacturing step.

The accompanying "Organization In Action" provides more details and insights about the JIT system.

ORGANIZATION IN ACTION:

Whirlpool Converts to JIT

Approximately ten years ago, Whirlpool Corp. converted their Kitchen Products Division plant in Findlay, Ohio to JIT manufacturing. A JIT task force was formed of representatives from materials, procurement, quality control, and manufacturing. Within a few months, JIT delivery and production techniques were implemented.

The Findlay Plant manufactures 5,500 dryers, dishwashers, and ranges per day. Approximately 380 suppliers deliver to the plant. With JIT, Whirlpool maintains an average of a three-and-a-half-day supply of parts and materials from each of these suppliers. The JIT system depends upon inbound transportation, communications, and quality control.

All trucking arrangements needed to be modified for inbound shipping. The traffic supervisor worked out a new arrangement with the contract carrier, established "bid runs" whereby the carrier's drivers would essentially be on lease to the Findlay plant. Parts supplied from vendors are delivered by individual "bid drivers" who pick up shipments from vendors in their assigned areas and deliver them to Whirlpool.

Good internal communications is fostered by the Total Communications Program and a division-wide Work-in-Process Task Force. The Total Communications Program provides for an exchange of knowledge, experiences, and ideas on JIT, through such means as newsletters and meetings among managers and workers. The Work-in-Process Task Force is comprised of representatives from all manufacturing functions who meet monthly to discuss procedures in operation at the plant. Typical topics include ways to reduce inventories further and to quickly make mold and die changes.

Whirlpool instituted a Total Quality Assurance program with its suppliers. This program increased the likelihood of receiving parts that conform to acceptable quality standards, thus shortening inspection time.

Whirlpool's Source Assurance program has been quite effective in reducing inspection costs and quality control problems in production. A further bonus of the program is the new spirit of cooperation between Whirlpool and its vendors. Animosity between supplier and buyer seems to be dwindling as Whirlpool's vendors realize they will be rewarded with steady business if they live up to their part of the bargain.

Quality circles at the Findlay plant have also contributed considerably to the JIT program. Five circles made up of six to ten employees from the same department meet on a regular basis to solve problems they encounter in their work area.

Source: Adapted with permission from Harris Jack Shapiro and Teresa Cosenza, *Reviving Industry in America: Japanese Influences on Manufacturing and the Service Sector,* Copyright 1987 by Ballinger Publishing Company.

Advantages and Disadvantages of the JIT Inventory System.   Manufacturing companies have realized several benefits from adopting JIT. JIT can lead to organizational commitment to quality of design, materials, parts, employee-management relations, supplier-user relations, and quality of finished goods. With minimum levels of inventory on hand, finished products are more visible and defects are more readily detected. Quality problems can therefore be attacked before they escalate to an unsurmountable degree. Low levels of inventory also shorten production lead times, which enable a company to respond more readily to product and quantity changes.[4] A specific example of these benefits took place at Huffy Corp., the bicycle maker. Huffy cut its inventories almost in half, from $69 million to $36 million over a two year period.[5]

The primary disadvantage of JIT is that it must be placed in a supportive or compatible environment. Above all, JIT is applicable only to highly repetitive manufacturing operations such as automobiles and appliances. Also, JIT inventory management must be combined with JIT production. This leads to kanban's main vulnerability—work stoppages. Because no inventory is built up, interdependent parts of the manufacturing system must be shut down immediately. Specifically, the assembly operations will have to cease because they run out of component parts within a few hours.[6] Another cause for concern about JIT is that it leads to a captive relationship between manufacturer and supplier. For example, should a manufacturer cease dealing with a supplier for any reason, that supplier might have to close the facility it built just to be in physical proximity to the manufacturer.

DECISION TREES

Decision trees are another popular management-science technique for choosing the best alternative course of action, thereby improving the quality of decision making. A decision tree is a graphic illustration of the alternative solutions available to solve a problem. It is designed to estimate the outcome of a series of decisions. As the sequences of the major decision are chained out, the resulting diagram resembles a tree with branches.

To illustrate the essentials of a decision tree for making financial decisions, we return to the nightclub owner who used the Gantt and milestone charts. One major decision facing the owner is whether to open a nightclub only or to open a nightclub and dinner restaurant. According to the best data available to the owner, the probability of having a good first year is 0.6, whereas the probability of having a poor one is 0.4.

Discussion with a knowledgeable accountant indicates that the payout, or net cash flow, from a good season with the nightclub only would be $100,000.

The payout from a poor first year with the same alternative would be a loss of $10,000. Both these figures are conditional values because they depend on business conditions. It is also predicted that a good first year with the alternative of a nightclub and dinner restaurant would be $150,000; a poor first year would result in a loss of $30,000.

Using this information, the manager computes the expected values and adds them for the two alternatives:

$$\text{Expected value: Nightclub only} = \begin{array}{rcl} 0.6 \times \$100,000 &=& \$60,000 \\ 0.4 \times \$-10,000 &=& \underline{-4,000} \\ && \$56,000 \end{array}$$

$$\begin{array}{l} \text{Expected value: Nightclub and} \\ \qquad\qquad \text{dinner restaurant} \end{array} = \begin{array}{rcl} 0.6 \times \$150,000 &=& \$90,000 \\ 0.4 \times \$-30,000 &=& \underline{-12,000} \\ && \$78,000 \end{array}$$

As graphically portrayed in Figure 5-5, the decision tree suggests that the nightclub owner will probably show a first-year profit of $78,000 if she chooses the nightclub and dinner restaurant alternative. If a nightclub only is established, the owner is likely to show a profit of $56,000. Over the one-year period, running a nightclub and dinner restaurant would be $22,000 more profitable.

The advantage of a decision tree is that it can be used to help make sequences of decisions. After the nightclub owner has one year's experience in running a nightclub and dinner restaurant, she may think of expanding. One logical possibility for expansion would be to open the restaurant for lunch as well as dinner. A new branch would be added to the decision tree that would compare the conditional values for the nightclub and dinner restaurant with those of the nightclub and dinner plus lunch restaurant.

The new branch of the decision tree might take the form shown in Figure 5-6. The decision faced here is whether to add luncheon service. The nightclub owner would now have more accurate information about the conditional values for a nightclub and dinner restaurant—the choice the owner made when opening the establishment. We can assume that the owner had a good season if she is willing to think seriously about expansion. Because the owner has already had one year of success with the nightclub and dinner restaurant, the probability of having a second good season might be raised to 0.8. With each successive year, the owner would have increasingly accurate information about the conditional values.

NOMINAL GROUP TECHNIQUE (NGT)

Managers who must make a decision about an important issue sometimes need to know what alternatives are available and how people would react to these alternatives. The decision is sensitive enough for the manager to want to "test the water" before proceeding. Because of these considerations, the manager

Figure 5-5   First-Year Decision Tree for Nightclub Owner

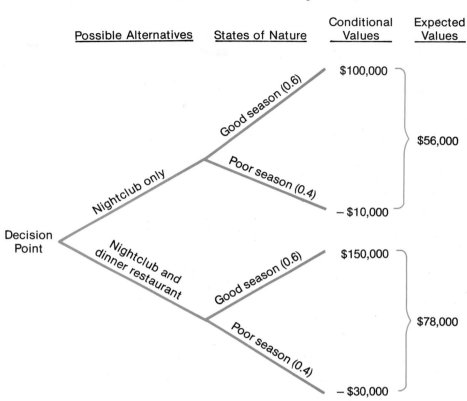

believes that group input would be helpful. Brainstorming would be of limited value because it is geared specifically to the generation of alternatives. Here the manager is looking for both alternatives to the problem and an evaluation of those alternatives. The problem facing the manager is still in the exploration phase.

A group problem-solving technique and decision-making aid called the **nominal group technique** (NGT) has been developed to fit this situation. NGT is a group decision-making technique that follows a highly structured format. Group members react to each other's suggestions individually and without interacting with each other. An example of the type of problem approached with the NGT is deciding which plants of a multiplant firm should be closed because of declining demand for a product. A decision of this type is highly sensitive and will elicit many different opinions.

A Step-by-Step Example of NGT

We will present a seven-step summary of NGT, developed by the originators of the technique.[7] The plant-closing problem is brought to the group by Sherry

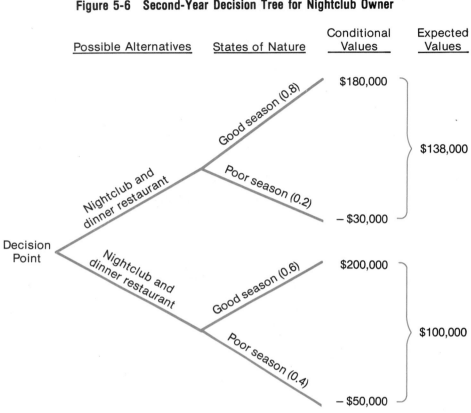

Figure 5-6   Second-Year Decision Tree for Nightclub Owner

McDivott, the company president. She has informed group members in advance of the topic.

1. Group members (called the target group) are selected and assembled. McDivott calls together her five top managers, each representing a key function of the business. Her administrative assistant also is asked to attend and to help organize the meeting and take care of administrative details.

2. Should the group be too large, it is broken down into subgroups of about eight members. McDivott decides to use the entire staff in a single group, because only five people are involved.

3. The group leader presents a specific question. McDivott tells the group, "Our board of directors say we have to consolidate our operations. Our output isn't high enough to justify keeping five plants open. I have to go along with the board's thinking. I foresee absolutely no increased demand for our products in the near future. We have excess capacity, so we have

to do something drastic, such as close a plant. Whatever we do, we must cut operating expenses by about 20 percent.

"Your assignment is to develop criteria for choosing which plant to close. However, if the group can think of another way of cutting operating costs by 20 percent, I'll give it some consideration. I also need to know how you feel about the alternative you choose and how our employees might feel."

4. Individual members write down their ideas independently and without speaking to other members. Using notepads, the five managers write down their ideas about reducing operating costs by 20 percent.

5. Each participant, in turn, presents one idea to the group without discussion. The ideas are summarized and written on a chalkboard or flip chart. The administrative assistant summarizes each idea on a flip chart. Here are some of the group's ideas:

a. Lay off about 35 percent of the work force throughout the company, including personnel at all plants and the home office. This should reduce costs about 25 percent. Our employees won't like it, but at least everybody's ox will be gored equally. No one plant will be closed.

b. Close the plant with the most obsolete equipment and facilities. We all know that the Harrisburg plant is running with equipment built at the turn of the century. Close the plant in sixty days. Give employees six months' severance pay and assist them to find new jobs. Transfer the most outstanding staff to our other plants.

c. Close the plant with the least flexible, most unproductive work force. Unproductive people give us more problems than outdated equipment. A lot of employees are likely to complain about this type of closing. But the rest of the work force will get the message that we value productive employees.

d. Forget about closing a plant. Instead, take our least productive plant and transfer all its manufacturing to our other four plants. Then, work like fury to get subcontracting business for the emptied-out plant. In other words, one of our plants will be in the business of handling the overload of other factories in its area. I think our employees and stockholders will be pleased if we take such a brave stance.

e. Replace as many production employees as we can with industrial robots. For every ten employees we replace with one robot, lay off one supervisor. We should be able to cut down on operating costs by 25 percent within three years. We'll have to make a big investment to realize this savings, but I think our customers will be pleased to know that we are moving into high-tech. Our employees will complain a little, but most of them know that automation is here to stay.

f. We need a careful financial analysis of which plant is producing the lowest return on investment of capital, all factors considered. We simply close that plant. This is the only sensible way of choosing a plant to close. It should be strictly a financial decision. Employees will accept this decision because they all know that business is based on financial considerations.

g. Closing one plant would be too much of a hardship on one group of people. Let's share the hardship evenly. Cut everybody's pay by 25 percent, eliminate dividends to stockholders, do not replace anybody who quits or retires for the next year, and ask all our suppliers to give us a 15 percent discount. These measures would be the starting point. We could then appoint a committee to look for other savings. If everybody pulls together, morale will be saved.

6. After each group member has presented his or her ideas, a discussion is held of the recorded ideas for purposes of clarification and evaluation. The length of the discussion for each of the ideas varies substantially. For example, the idea about closing the plant with the least productive people precipitated a thirty-minute discussion. The discussion about cutting salaries 25 percent and eliminating dividends lasted only three minutes. (Self-interest is always a powerful factor in any type of decision making.)

7. The meeting ends with a silent, independent rating of the alternatives generated by the group. The final group decision is the pooled outcome of the individual votes. The target group is instructed to rate each alternative on a one-to-ten scale, with ten being the most favorable rating. The ratings presented below are the pooled ratings (the sum of the individual ratings) received for each alternative. Here are the group preferences:

Alternative A, 35-percent layoff: 9.
Alternative B, close obsolete plant: 35.
Alternative C, close plant with unproductive work force: 41.
Alternative D, make one plant a subcontractor: 19.
Alternative E, replace employees with robots: 18.
Alternative F, close plant with poorest return on investment: 26.
Alternative G, cut everybody's pay by 25 percent: 4.

McDivott agrees with the group's preference for closing the plant with the least productive, most inflexible work force. Before presenting this idea to the board of directors, she and her administrative assistant do some research. They study personnel records and interview supervisors and managers to decide which plant has the least satisfactory work force. Ultimately, the alternative is accepted by the board. The best employees in the factory chosen for closing are offered an opportunity to relocate to another company plant.

Evaluation of NGT

We have presented considerable detail about NGT in operation because we believe it is a productive aid to making sound decisions about major issues. The evidence supports this optimistic position. Since its development about thirty years ago, NGT has gained substantial acceptance and recognition. It has been widely applied in many organizations. The NGT process does a good job of generating alternatives, keeping bloopers to a minimum, and satisfying group members.[8]

Much of the effectiveness of NGT can be attributed to the fact that it follows the logic of the problem-solving and decision-making method and allows for group participation. It also has a discipline and rigor often missing in brainstorming. From the standpoint of concept and method, NGT and quality circles have much in common.

COMPUTER-ASSISTED DECISION MAKING

An increasing number of managers are using computers to help them make higher quality decisions, aside from using computers to conduct statistical analyses. Three such applications are data-base management, decision-making software, and expert systems.

Data-Base Management

An important part of problem solving is to gather relevant data. Data gathering is greatly simplified by means of computerized files call data-bases. **A data-base** is a systematic way of storing files for future retrieval. An example of a data-base would be a list of all retail stores that sold sporting goods in a specific geographic region. **Data-base management** is a program designed to store and retrieve large quantities of data. A data-base management system thus allows you access to the data-base. Three widely used data-base management systems are dBASE III®, PC File III, and PFS:file.

A prime example of a data-base used to obtain job-relevant information is Dialog Information Services. It contains approximately 175 data-bases, which store information from more than 80 million journals, newspaper articles, reports, conference papers, and other documents. Part of this mammoth data-base is concentrated in the business area. The people who provide the basic input to this data-base enter high-quality information under the appropriate codes words (such as "export regulations, industrial pumps"). Thus, the use of the system benefits from the professional expertise of others, leading to higher quality decisions.

Decision-Making Software

A modern development in computer-assisted decision making is software that actually helps you reach valid alternative solutions to your problem. **Decision-making software** is any computer program that helps the decision maker work through the problem-solving and decision-making steps. In addition, they ask you questions about such things as your values, priorities, and the importance you attach to such factors as price and quality.

Three representative decision-making programs designed for use with personal computers are Trigger, Lightyear, and Expert Choice. The decision-making process used in these programs is referred to as "intuitive" because the programs rely more on human judgment than on heavy quantitative analysis.[9] The intent of these programs is to improve the quality of decisions rather than to just make computations or generate data. A decision-making program might help a traffic manager decide whether to make a large shipment by truck, railroad, or airplane.

Expert Systems (Artificial Intelligence)

A promising development in computer-assisted decision making is **expert systems,** computer programs that can "reason" and manipulate data in a manner similar to humans. Expert systems are a direct application of the more general field of artificial intelligence (the technology to make computers "think"). Expert systems are used to support decision making rather than to automate the decision-making process and replace managers.

Expert systems were developed originally to help physicians make medical diagnoses. The reasoning capability of these systems is based on rules of thumb used by human experts to make decisions in a wide range of business situations. Among these situations are inventory control, financial forecasting and investments, and credit analysis.[10] The rules of thumb are in the form of "if this, then that" statements. When asking advice from the system, the user provides known information or hunches. The expert system than draws conclusions that appear as computer output.

An example of a decision-assist that functions as an expert system is Digital Equipment Corp.'s XCON system. The system configures (selects a mix of) VAX minicomputers to fill sales orders by using a knowledge base of rules that indicates which components will work effectively together.[11] A manufacturing expert system under development is a diagnostic system that leads machine operators and mechanics through step-by-step analyses of equipment problems and provides repair instructions.[12]

An optimistic viewpoint of expert systems is that they will reduce the amount of human effort needed to do business tasks, making it possible for people to be much more productive and creative. Also, they may be able to mass merchandise human expertise at low cost. To date, expert systems have made modest progress in enabling computers to provide reliable assistance in making major decisions. On balance, the technology is making slow but steady progress; the aspects of expert systems are being incorporated into more conventional computer programs.[13]

SUMMARY OF KEY POINTS

Management science provides mathematical, statistical, and scientific methods for the solution of business problems. Although the field has an important contribution to make, most of the methods of management science are based on subjective estimates of figures and are only as accurate as the data you use.

Gantt and milestone charts are simple methods of monitoring schedules; they are particularly useful for one-time projects. Gantt charts graphically depict the planned and actual progress of work over the period of time encompassed by a project. A milestone chart, an extension of the Gantt chart, provides a listing of subactivities that must be completed in order to accomplish the major activities, which are listed on the vertical axis.

PERT networks are the method of choice when an estimate is needed of how long it will take to complete a complicated project and when the sequence of events must be planned carefully. In a PERT network, an event is a point of decision or accomplishment; an activity is the physical and mental effort required to complete an event. To complete a PERT diagram, all the events have to be sequenced and the time required for each activity has to be estimated. The expected time for each activity takes into account optimistic, pessimistic, and probable estimates of time. The critical path is the sequence of activities and events that must be followed to implement the project. The duration of the project is determined by the longest critical path.

Break-even analysis is used to estimate the point at which it is profitable to go ahead with a new venture. It is a method of determining the relationship between total costs and total revenues at various levels of sales activity or operation. Break-even analysis determines the ratio of fixed costs to the difference between the selling price and the variable cost for each unit. The results of break-even analysis are often depicted on a graph. Break-even analysis is based on an assumption of static costs.

A payoff matrix is used when a determination is needed of the returns or payoffs from pursuing different alternatives to a problem; it is expressed in financial terms. Each alternative is pursued under a different state of nature—a circumstance beyond the control of the decision maker. Possible payoffs are referred to as conditional values because each depends on a particular condition. To make the payoff matrix more accurate, probabilities are assigned to each state of nature. The probability of each state of nature is multiplied by each conditional value to arrive at the expected values—the estimated payoffs.

Economic order quantity (EOQ) is a decision-support technique widely used to manage inventory. The EOQ is the inventory level that minimizes both ordering and carrying costs. The technique helps a manufacturing or sales organization decide how much inventory to keep on hand.

Just-in-time (JIT) inventory is the procedure whereby inventory is minimized and moved into the plant exactly when needed. Although not specifically a decision-making technique, JIT helps shape decisions about inventory. The system relies on kanbans, or cards, to communicate production requirements. The key principle underlying the JIT systems is the elimination of excess inventory by producing or purchasing items only when and in the exact amounts they are needed. JIT inventory is best suited for repetitive manufacturing processes.

Decision trees provide a quantitative estimate of the best alternative course of action. A decision tree can be considered a graphic representation of a payoff matrix. It is a tool for estimating the outcome of a series of decisions. When the sequences of the major decisions are chained out, they resemble a tree with branches.

The nominal group technique (NGT) is recommended for the situation in which the manager must make a decision about an important issue and needs to know what alternatives are available and how people will react to these alternatives. In NGT, a group of seven to ten people contribute their written thoughts about the problem and then other members respond to their ideas. Members rate each other's ideas numerically, and the final group decision is the value of the pooled individual votes.

Many managerial decisions can be enhanced by computer-assisted decision making. A widely used approach is data-base management, whereby the manager accesses large amounts of information held in computer storage. Another tool is decision-making software, a program to help the decision maker work through the problem solving and decision-making steps in an intuitive fashion. The newest development, expert systems, are computer programs that simulate human reasoning. So far, they have been used in helping managers do such tasks as troubleshooting manufacturing problems.

QUESTIONS

1. In your opinion, is management science really a "science"? Explain your reasoning.
2. Explain how you might use a Gantt chart to help you do well at school this year.
3. Give three examples of work projects you think would benefit from the use of a milestone chart.
4. Why do you think PERT networks are used so frequently in the aerospace and defense industries?
5. Describe at least one possible application of PERT diagrams to home life.
6. How does break-even analysis contribute to decision making?
7. A community-college student who painted houses during the summer told a friend, "After I paint two houses during the summer, the rest is gravy." How does this statement relate to the concept of break-even analysis?
8. What applications might the just-in-time (JIT) inventory system have to operating a retail store?
9. Are you worried about being replaced by an expert system at some point in the future? Why or why not?

ACTIVITIES

1. Using hypothetical data, illustrate how a person might use a payoff matrix to help choose a career.
2. Using hypothetical data, illustrate how economic order quantity (EOQ) might be used to help run a restaurant efficiently.

CASE PROBLEM 5-A: PERT NETWORK

Assume you have been working as an assistant to the executive director of a large government agency. One day she meets with you and asks you to tackle the following assignment:

"We have been authorized to have a year-end party for the 458 people in our agency; we have been given a budget of $12,000 for the affair. This will be the first time anything like this has been tried in our agency, and I want you to organize the party. Your main goal is to see that this party is a real hit. Because this is a governmental agency, the party must be clearly planned before we can get the funds released. We must convince the higher authorities that we know what we are doing. Maybe you can use one of the scheduling techniques you learned in school. My knowledge may be a little rusty, but I think a PERT diagram would impress my boss."

Being a wise subordinate, you decide to prepare a PERT diagram. For each activity, calculate the expected time based on estimates of the optimistic, pessimistic, and probable times. You then calculate the critical paths so you can indicate how long the project will take. Here are the four major events you should be concerned with (not necessarily in the right sequence):

A.   Mail out invitations.
B.   Select an appropriate party site.
C.   Prepare an anticipated expense statement.
D.   Conduct an informal poll of employees to learn what kind of party they would prefer.

To save time, you can be your own panel of experts to estimate the values needed to compute the expected time.

CASE PROBLEM 5-B: BREAK-EVEN ANALYSIS

On recent vacation trips to New York City and Toronto, you noticed a large number of counter restaurants and street vendors selling souvlaki, a Greek dish consisting of spiced beef, vegetables, and sauce that is served on a roll. You have a flash of inspiration. Why not sell souvlaki from a van to the students back at your college? Your intention is to operate the souvlaki wagon from about five to nine o'clock, four nights per week. A substantial number of the students are working adults who take courses in the evening. If you could make enough money from your business, you could attend classes full-time during the day. You intend to sell the souvlakis for $1.49 each, and the beverages for $.75 each.

Based upon some preliminary analysis, you have discovered that your primary fixed costs per month would be: $500.00 for payments on a modified van, $75.00 for gas and maintenance, and $300.00 for a part-time assistant. Your variable costs would be: $.85 cents for each souvlaki (including condiments) and $.45 cents for each beverage (one size).

Case Questions

1.   How many souvlaki will you have to sell each month before you start to make a profit?
2.   How many beverages will you have to sell each month before you start to make a profit?
3.   The evening population of your school consists of 3000 students and 600 faculty, staff, and general employees. Should you go into this business venture? Explain the reasoning behind your decision. (You will have to forecast what percent of the population will purchase souvlaki and/or soft drinks.)

CASE PROBLEM 5-C: PAYOFF MATRIX

As the sales manager of Funtime Products, you have helped introduce a new line of pool tables. Compute the expected values for for low, medium, and high quantities of pool-table production. (The probability of low demand is 0.25; medium demand, 0.50, and high demand, 0.25.) Then decide which production volume represents the best bet for your firm. Exhibit 1 presents the conditional values you need for your computations. (Refer back to Tables 5-2 and 5-3 for assistance with the computations.)

Exhibit 1   Payoff Matrix Showing Conditional Values for Pool Tables

Alternatives (Pool Tables Produced)	States of Nature (Demand for Pool Tables)		
	Low	Medium	High
	(Conditional Values)		
Low Quantity	$200,000	$200,000	$200,000
Medium Quantity	$200,000	$400,000	$400,000
High Quantity	$200,000	$400,000	$500,000

CASE PROBLEM 5-D: ECONOMIC ORDER QUANTITY

You are the materials-handling manager in a home applicance manufacturing plant. Assume that the annual demand for microwave ovens is 5,000 units and it costs $75 to order the components for each unit. The carrying cost per unit is $15. How many component units should your plant maintain in inventory?

REFERENCES

1. Mark B. Roman, "The Critical Path," *Success* (September 1987): 56–57; a comprehensive reference on network models is Joseph J. Moder, Cecil R. Phillips, and Edward W. Davis, *Project Management with CPM, PERT and Precedence Diagramming* (New York: Van Nostrand Reinhold, 1983).
2. Harris Jack Shapiro and Teresa Cosenza, *Reviving Industry in America: Japanese Influences on Manufacturing and the Service Sector* (Cambridge, MA.: Ballinger Publishing Co., 1987), 40.
3. Adapted and paraphrased from Ramon J. Aldag and Timothy M. Stearns, *Management* (South-Western Publishing Co., 1987), 730–731.
4. Shapiro and Cosenza, *Reviving Industry in America*, 42.
5. Aldag and Stearns, *Management*, 731.
6. Robert Kreitner, *Management*, 3d ed. (Boston: Houghton Mifflin Co., 1986), 630.

7. Andrew H. Van de Ven and Andrew L. Delbecq, "The Effectiveness of Nominal, Delphi, and Interacting Group Decision Making Processes," *Academy of Management Journal*, December 1974, p. 606.

8. D. Scott Sink, "Using the Nominal Group Technique Effectively," *National Productivity Review* (Spring 1983): 181; Ramon J. Aldag and Arthur P. Brief, *Managing Organizational Behavior* (St. Paul, MN: West Publishing, Co., 1981), 281.

9. "Programs that Make Managers Face the Facts," *Business Week* (8 April 1985): 74.

10. Dorothy Leonard-Barton and John J. Sviokla, "Putting Expert Systems to Work," *Harvard Business Review* (March–April 1988): 91–98; Beau Sheil, "Thinking About Artificial Intelligence," *Harvard Business Review* (July–August 1987): 91–97.

11. Sheil, "Thinking About Artificial Intelligence," 96.

12. "The Chip Behind TI's Smart Weapons," *Business Week* (9 March 1987): 105.

13. Andrew Pollack, "Artifical Intelligence Firms Low on Savvy,"*New York Times* (5 March 1988); Sheil, "Thinking About Artificial Intelligence," 91.

PART THREE
Organizing

Chapter 6
Job Design and Organization Structure

Chapter 7
Delegation and Decentralization

Chapter 8
Staffing the Organization

Organizing is the process of dividing work into manageable sections and coordinating the results to serve a purpose. It follows planning as an essential management responsibility, and mobilizes organizational resources for action. Organizing ensures that there are the necessary human and physical resources to carry out the plans to achieve organizational goals.

Chapter 6 is about organizing at the level of the individual job, the small group, and the larger organization. These considerations are part of the organizing function because organizing includes assigning activities and dividing the work into specific jobs and tasks. Chapter 7 deals with delegation and decentralization, the two processes that make it possible for collective action to take place. The alternative is to have a few people carrying out all the tasks of an enterprise. Delegation and decentralization are part of organization because they break work down into manageable units.

Chapter 8 is about a special part of organizing: staffing. Staffing deals with finding the right people to carry out the work of the firm, training them, and then evaluating their performance. Staffing is considered part of organizing because it arranges human resources to achieve goals. Staffing is the topic in this book that is most directly tied in with the responsibilities of a personnel or human resources department.

6

Job Design and Organization Structure

After studying the material in this chapter, you should be able to accomplish the following tasks:

1. Identify several of the major dimensions of job design.
2. Describe the characteristics of an enriched job.
3. Describe the bureaucratic form of organization, including its advantages and disadvantages.
4. Explain the major ways in which organizations are departmentalized.
5. Describe the major forms of nonbureaucratic organization structures: project, matrix, System 4, and flat.
6. Explain the role of the informal organization structure.

Key Terms and Phrases

Organization structure	Territorial departmentalization
Job design	Product departmentalization
Operatives	Customer departmentalization
Task generalization	Process departmentalization
Task specialization	Project organization
Robot	Task force
Job enrichment	Matrix organization
Bureaucracy	Adhocracy
Organization chart	Flat organization structure
Functional specialization	Informal organization structure
Machine bureaucracy	Informal Group
Functional departmentalization	

To accomplish large tasks, such as building ships or providing insurance payments, you must divide work among individuals and groups. There are two primary ways of subdividing the overall tasks of the enterprise. One way is to design specific jobs for individuals to accomplish. The shipbuilding company must design jobs for welders, metal workers, engineers, purchasing agents, and contract administrators. The other primary way of subdividing work is to design an **organization structure**—a framework of task and authority relationships among different units of the firm. An organization structure is similar to the framework of a building or the skeleton of a body.

Our purpose in this chapter is to explain some of the ways in which work is organized among people engaged in collective effort. We will discuss how jobs are purposely made easy or complex, the nature of bureaucracy and organizing by departments, and the alternatives to the traditional organization structure.

BASIC CONCEPTS OF JOB DESIGN

The starting point in understanding how tasks are subdivided in the organization is to discuss job design. **Job design** is laying out job responsibilities and duties and describing how they are to be performed. The purpose of job design is to achieve the organization's goals or business plan.[1] Each position in the organization is supposed to serve an important purpose. We will discuss three important concepts in job design: defining the scope of individual jobs, automation, and enriching jobs to increase productivity and satisfaction.

The Scope of Individual Jobs

A major challenge facing the job designer is to estimate how many different tasks the individual employee can perform well. Generalists are supposed to be able to handle a large number of tasks relatively well, whereas specialists are supposed to be able to handle a narrow range of tasks very well. An extreme example of a top-level generalist is the owner of a small business who performs such varied tasks as helping make the product, selling, negotiating with banks for loans, and hiring new employees. An extreme example of a generalist at the first (or entry) occupational level is the maintenance worker who packs boxes, sweeps, shovels snow in season, mows the lawn, and cleans the lavatories.

Specialists also are found at different occupational levels. High occupational level specialists include the stock analyst who researches companies in one or two industries and the surgeon who concentrates on liver transplants. Specialists at the first occupational level usually are referred to as **operatives**. An example is an assembly-line worker who fastens two wires to one terminal. Table 6-1 presents a few more examples of generalists and specialists found at both the top and the first occupational levels. As you can see, jobs can be designed for generalists and specialists at all occupational levels.

The job designer must decide how much task specialization is desirable for a given job. **Task generalization** gives the employee a wide range of tasks to perform, whereas **task specialization** provides a limited number of tasks. The job of administrative assistant helps illustrate this issue. As generally conceived, the administrative assistant performs a wide range of tasks, such as keeping track of appointments, editing and word processing letters and reports, helping prepare department budgets, making travel arrangements, and providing administrative support to the chief and other members of the department.

From time to time, job designers have attempted to simplify the administrative assistant's job in order to improve office efficiency. These attempts include centralized word-processing facilities, travel specialists who handle all travel arrangements for company employees, and centralized

Table 6-1   Examples of Generalists and Specialists at High and First Occupational Levels

Type of Worker

Occupational Level	Generalist	Specialist or Operative
High	Business executive Family medicine physician College president	Business forecaster Neurosurgeon Professor
First	Maintenance worker Nurse's aide Groundskeeper	Restroom attendant Ambulance driver Floor waxer

photocopy centers. At times these centralized functions eliminate burdensome tasks for the administrative assistant and lower total costs of operating the office; at other times, however, these arrangements result in serious delays in getting work accomplished. Also, duplicate facilities may be created if some departments resist centralization.

Advantages and Disadvantages of Task Generalization.   Task generalization offers several important advantages to both the employee and the firm. Employees' job satisfaction and morale tend to be enhanced when their job comprises varied responsibilities. The majority of employees experience boredom when their work activity is limited to one or two repetitive tasks. Task generalization also enhances the quality of work life because greater job diversity leads to more challenge and personal growth. Employee growth in this context means two things: learning new job skills and satisfying the desire to acquire new knowledge and skills. When a large number of employees are assigned varied responsibilities, the organization benefits because its work force becomes better-trained. Employees who perform diverse tasks can readily shift from one job to another, as dictated by the needs of the organization.

Task generalization also has several notable disadvantages. When too much of the work force is composed of generalists, the organization loses the advantage of the expertise that derives from specialization. At the production-worker level, task generalization has an important disadvantage. It is much easier to replace highly specialized employees than it is to replace generalists. If a task is narrow enough, it can be taught to new employees relatively quickly. For example, high-technology companies have discovered they can readily train new work forces in foreign countries to assemble intricate equipment by breaking each job down into small subcomponents.

Advantages and Disadvantages of Task Specialization.   Task specialization has the opposite advantages and disadvantages of task generalization. The most important advantage of task specialization is that it allows for the development of work force expertise at all occupational levels. When employees perform the same task repeatedly, they become highly knowledgeable. Many employees derive status and self-esteem from being experts at some task.

Task specialization also has disadvantages. One problem is that coordination is difficult when several employees do small parts of one job. Somebody has to be responsible for pulling together the small pieces of the total task. Although some employees may prefer narrowly specialized jobs, the majority of workers prefer to engage in broad tasks that give them a feeling of control over what they are doing. Although they join the work force as specialists, many technical and professional workers become bored with performing a narrow range of tasks.

From the organization's standpoint, task specialization often can result in low productivity because there is not enough work to keep the specialist fully occupied. The volume of work thus places a limit on the specialization of labor.[2] Many organizations attempt to solve this problem by hiring highly trained specialists on a temporary basis when they need certain services.

Automation and Task Specialization

Ever since the Industrial Revolution, automation has been used to replace some aspects of human endeavor in the office and the factory. The replacement of human endeavor typically involves a machine performing a specialized task previously performed by people. Automation is widely used in factories and offices and, to some extent, in stores (for example, keeping track of purchases to decide upon inventory levels). Managers rely upon automated equipment to perform many of the clerical chores previously performed by people, such as typing correspondence and mailing out photocopies. In many offices managers now use facsimile machines to quickly send photocopies of documents to other locations.

A prime example of task specialization through automation is the use of industrial robots. A **robot** is defined technically as a "reprogrammable, multifunctional manipulator."[3] Industrial robots are, more accurately, mechanical arms that are controlled by a computer rather than the humanoids that are often depicted. Robots perform many specialized human tasks.

Two types of robots predominate in manufacturing, a flex-arm robot and the gantry-style robot. The flex-arm robot is stationed at an assembly line and performs a variety of tasks with a movable arm. The gantry-style robot is an overhead device that operates along a steel frame. The frames often run about four hundred feet, and some are long enough to span an automobile production line. The actual robot has five independent movements that can be programmed on a computer or directed by a hand-held unit. Both types of robots are used for such specialized tasks as welding, bolting, and spray painting.

Robots have been used widely in the automobile industry. Other applications include food processing, furnace construction, and the inspection of computer chips. Robots are highly flexible and can work under conditions that would be unsafe for humans. Although robots do occasionally malfunction and create some waste, they can work continuously and have high reliability. A robotics consultant expressed the following opinion, so often heard about industrial robots:

> The advantage of the robot is that it works around the clock, with no coffee breaks or vacations, and always does precisely what it's programmed to do. A robot isn't bothered by noxious fumes and it's less likely than a human to get its fingers squashed.[4]

Job Enrichment

Job enrichment is an approach to making jobs more challenging and responsible so they will be more appealing to most employees. At its best, job enrichment gives workers a sense of ownership, responsibility, and accountability. The process therefore provides task generalization rather than specialization. Because job enrichment leads to a more exciting job, it often increases employee job satisfaction and motivation. People usually are willing to work harder at tasks they find enjoyable and rewarding, just as they will put effort into a favorite hobby. The general approach to enriching a job is to build into it more planning and decision making, controlling, and responsibility.[5] For example, most managers have enriched jobs, whereas data-entry specialists usually do not have enriched jobs.

Enriching the Jobs of Individuals.   According to Frederick Herzberg, the way to design an enriched job is to include as many of the following eight characteristics as possible.[6] The characteristics and consequences of an enriched job are summarized in Figure 6-1.

1. *Direct feedback.* Employees should receive immediate evaluation of the results of their work. This feedback can be built into the job (such as a sales representative closing a sale) or provided by the supervisor.

2. *Client relationships.* A job is automatically enriched when an employee has a client or customer to serve, whether that client is inside or outside the firm. Serving a client is more satisfying to most people than performing work for only a supervisor.

3. *New learning.* An enriched job allows its holder to acquire new knowledge. The learning can stem from job experiences themselves or from training programs associated with the job.

4. *Scheduling.* Being able to schedule your own work contributes to job enrichment. Scheduling includes the authority to decide when to tackle which assignment.

5. *Unique experience.* An enriched job has some unique qualities or features, such as a public-relations assistant having the opportunity to interact with visiting celebrities.

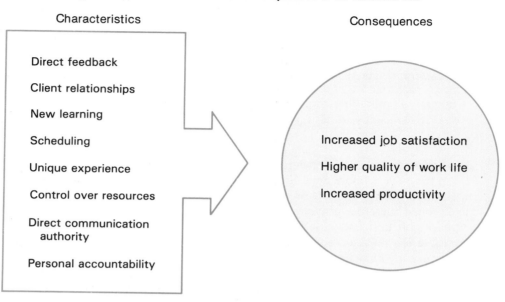

Figure 6-1   Characteristics and Consequences of an Enriched Job

6. *Control over resources.* Another contributor to enrichment is having some control over resources such as money, material, or people.

7. *Direct communication authority.* An enriched job provides workers the opportunity to communicate directly with other people who use their output, such as a software specialist handling complaints about problems with the software he or she developed. This dimension of an enriched job is quite similar to that of client relationships.

8. *Personal accountability.* In an enriched job, workers are responsible for their results. They accept credit for a job done well and blame for a job done poorly.

   A highly enriched job would have all eight of these characteristics; an impoverished job would have none. The more of these characteristics a job has, the more enriched it is. For example, administrative assistants usually have an enriched job. At times, their jobs are too enriched; they have too much responsibility and too many tasks.

The Team Approach to Job Enrichment.   One approach to job enrichment is to make jobs more interesting and responsible by organizing workers into small teams that have total responsibility for making a product or major component. An example would be building an entire television console (or everything but the cabinet). Today production work teams are used in several hundred offices and plants, especially, new, highly automated plants with work forces of twenty-five to five hundred employees.[7] In many instances, job enrichment through organizing workers into production teams has resulted in increased productivity.[8] The accompanying "Organization in Action" describes an example of the application of group job enrichment to an office environment.

We have discussed the design of work at the individual and team level. Next, we look at the design of a total organization.

ORGANIZATION IN ACTION:

Shenandoah Life Converts to Work Teams

About a decade ago, Shenandoah Life Insurance Co. installed a $2 million system to automate processing claims operations in its Roanoke, Virginia headquarters. The result from computerization was disappointing. It still required twenty-seven working days and handling by thirty-two clerks in three departments to process a representative claim. The delays stemmed from the elaborate maze of regulations, not from defects in the technology.

To speed up claims processing and capitalize upon automation, the company groups clerks into semiautonomus teams (another label for production work teams) of five to seven members. Each team now performs all the functions previously distributed over three departments. Team members learned new skills that brought increased job satisfaction and increased pay.

As a result of organization by teams, the typical case-handling time decreased to two days, and customer complaints about service were virtually eliminated. Within six years of installing production work teams, Shenandoah was processing 50 percent more applications and queries, with 10 percent fewer employees.

Source: As reported in "Management Discovers the Human Side of Automation," *Business Week* (29 September 1986): 70.

BUREAUCRACY AS A FORM OF ORGANIZATION

By far the most prevalent model of organization is the bureaucracy. A **bureaucracy** is a rational, systematic, and precise form of organization in which rules, regulations, and techniques of control are precisely defined. In everyday language, a bureaucracy is a form of organization characterized by a maze of rules, regulations, delays, and pettiness by officials at all levels. The popular definition of a bureaucracy is not untrue, but it is one-sided. It focuses on all that is wrong with bureaucracies and ignores their potential benefits.

In this section, we will describe the key features of the bureaucratic form of organization, and we will examine its advantages and disadvantages. Our description of departmentalization, presented later in the chapter, also deals with the various uses of bureaucracy.

Principles of Organization in a Bureaucracy

A convenient way of explaining the nature of the bureaucratic form of organization is to list its identifying characteristics and principles, which have evolved over time. Although Max Weber is most often associated with the development of ideas about bureaucracy, the entire traditional, or classical, school of management thought also contributes to our understanding of bureaucracy.[9]

Hierarchy of Authority.   The dominant characteristic of a bureaucracy is that each lower organizational unit is controlled and supervised by a higher one. The person granted the most formal authority is placed at the top of the hierarchy. Figure 6-2 graphically presents the bureaucracy as a pyramid. The number of employees increases substantially as you move down each successive level. Most of the power is concentrated at the top; the amount of power decreases as you move down the pyramid.

The principle of a well-defined hierarchy is also called the "chain of command." When someone skips his or her boss to speak to a higher-ranking official, that person is said to be violating the chain of command. The chain of command is illustrated by an **organization chart**, a diagram of the organization usually laid out in rectangles.

Task Specialization.   Division of labor should be based on task specialization, which means that each unit of the organization and each employee concentrates on one function. A pure bureaucracy is based on the concept of specialization of effort. To achieve task specialization, organizations have separate departments, such as manufacturing, accounts payable, and ophthalmology. Employees assigned to these organizational units have specialized knowledge and skills that contribute to the overall effectiveness of the firm.

Task specialization also is referred to as **functional specialization** because each unit performs a specialized function. Task specialization does not mean that a bureaucracy hires only specialists. It means that each employee is hired to carry out one primary function in which he or she is proficient.

Duties and Rights of Employees.   Rules to cover the rights and duties of employees should be established. In a highly bureaucratic organization, each employee has a precise job description, and policy and procedure manuals are kept current and accessible. Employees know what is expected of them and what they can expect from the organization in return.

Specific Policies and Procedures.   Procedures for dealing with work situations should be specified. According to bureaucratic theory, specifying procedures in advance helps ensure that work problems will be handled in approximately the same manner by different managers on different occasions. For example, managers in different divisions of the firm should handle work-related accidents in the same manner.

Figure 6-2   The Bureaucratic Pyramid

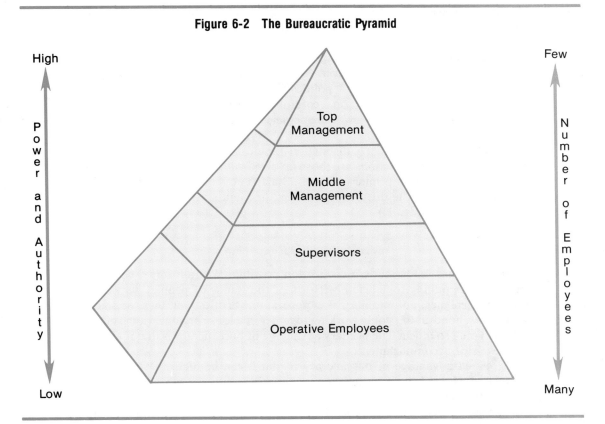

Definition of Managerial Responsibilty.   The responsibility and authority of each manager should be defined clearly in writing. When responsibility is defined in writing, managers know what is expected of them and what limits are set to their authority. This approach minimizes overlapping of authority and the accompanying confusion. Written responsibilities also make the transition easier when a manager leaves the firm. The new manager quickly knows what functions were carried out by his or her predecessor.

Managerial Authority.   Responsibility should be accompanied by sufficient authority to get the job accomplished. This is the best known, yet most frequently violated, principle of bureaucratic organization design. One application of this principle is that if you are responsible for doing a job, you should be given the authority to borrow or purchase the necessary tools and equipment and be able to influence the choice of new employees for the assignment.

Responsibility for Subordinates.   Higher authority has absolute authority for the actions of subordinates. Although a manager delegates a task to a subordinate, that manager is still responsible for seeing that the job gets done.

Managers receive some credit for the accomplishments of their subordinates, and some blame for the subordinates' mistakes.

Rational Decision Making.   Managerial decisions should be made rationally in every aspect of the organization. The ideal form of bureaucracy applies reason rather than emotion and politics to the solution of every problem. Every decision should be based on a carefully developed strategy, policy, procedure, or rule. In practice, few bureaucracies have achieved this ideal.

Line and Staff Functions.   A distinction should be drawn between line and staff functions. Line functions are those involved with the primary purpose of the organization, or its primary outputs. Staff functions are those that assist the line functions. (The differences between line and staff were explained in some detail in Chapter 1.)

Advantages of Bureaucracy

Bureaucracy has made modern civilization possible. Without large, complex organizations pulling together the efforts of thousands of people, we would not have airplanes, automobiles, skyscrapers, universities, vaccines, or space satellites. A handful of people working together in a loose organization can accomplish only so much. The primary advantage of bureaucracy is that it allows high levels of accomplishment.

A related advantage of bureaucracy is that it can be highly efficient and productive. Henry Mintzberg uses the term **machine bureaucracy** to refer to an organization structure fine-tuned to run as an integrated, regulated machine.[10] It is especially well suited to repetitive, recurring tasks such as the processing of social security claims or the manufacturing of television receivers. Bureaucracy can also be efficient in controlling the behavior of people, because employees are required to adhere to rules and regulations. When a manager brings a rules infraction to the attention of an employee, the manager cannot be accused of acting arbitrarily.

In general, the principles and characteristics of this bureaucratic model would all be advantages if they worked as intended. For instance, it would enhance organizational productivity if all employees knew what was expected of them.

Disadvantages of Bureaucracy

Despite the value of bureaucracy in efficiently carrying out mass-production, large-scale activities, it has several key disadvantages. Above all, the bureaucracy is subject to rigidity in handling people and problems. Its well-intended rules and regulations sometimes create inconvenience and inefficiency, as illustrated by the following incident.

A small-business owner invested in a bank Keogh plan. The plan allows people to invest up to 15 percent of their self-employment income in a retirement fund, with all contributions being tax-free until the income is withdrawn after retirement. In the system used by this bank, each deposit was assigned a new account number. In a period of five years, the owner made fifty-five separate deposits into his retirement account. At one point, the owner changed locations; he routinely filed a change of address notice with the bank. As each account matured, he was sent a notice giving him several redeposit options. Strangely, some of his mail from the bank continued to be sent to his old address. When he asked the bank why some of the notices about mature accounts were sent to his old address, the answer he received was: "You must file a change of address notice for each of your fifty-five accounts. We are not authorized to use information from one account for another."

After seventeen contacts (phone calls and letters) and a personal visit, a bank official finally rectified this problem.

High frustration accompanied by low job satisfaction is another key problem frequently found in the bureaucratic form of organization. The sources of these negative feelings include dealing with red tape, slow decision making, and limited chance to influence how well the organization performs. The bureaucratic form of organization is thought to be particularly frustrating to salaried professionals who prefer more autonomy than is typically allowed in a bureaucracy.[11]

Bureaucracy can be frustrating for other reasons as well. One analysis contends that what matters in the bureaucratic world is (1) not what a person is, but how well he or she matches the organizational ideal, (2) not a willingness to stand by decisions, but skill in avoiding blame, and (3) not what the person stands for, but with whom he or she has formed an alliance.[12]

DEPARTMENTALIZATION

In bureaucratic and other forms of organization, the work usually is subdivided into departments to prevent total confusion. Can you imagine an organization of 300,000 people, or even 300, in which all employees worked in one large department? The process of subdividing work into departments is called departmentalization (or departmentation). Bureaucracies pay such strict attention to departmentalization that the concept is sometimes used synonymously with bureaucracy.

Here we describe and illustrate by basic diagrams, the five most frequent approaches to departmentalization: function, territory, product, customer, and process. The most appropriate form of departmentalization is the one that provides the best chance of achieving the organization's objectives. The organization's environment weighs heavily in this decision. Assume that a company needed to use radically different approaches to serve different customers. It would organize part of the firm according to the customer served. A typical arrangement of this nature is to have one department serve commercial accounts and another department serve the government.

Functional Departmentalization

Functional departmentalization is arranging departments according to the function performed by each one. Departmentalizing work according to the function or activity performed is the traditional way of organizing the efforts of people. In a functional organization, each department carries out a specialized activity such as information processing, purchasing, sales, accounting, or building maintenance. It is the type of organization the developers of bureaucracy had in mind, because it allows for specialization. An organization chart showing functional departmentalization is illustrated in Figure 6-3. Sole reliance on a functional organization structure is becoming rare in large organizations, yet at least some part of every large firm is organized according to function.

Figure 6-3   An Organization Chart Showing Functional Departmentalization

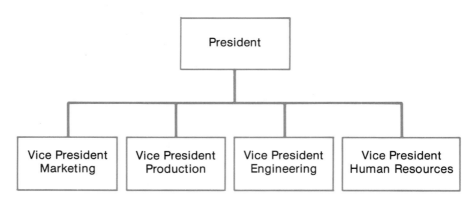

Advantages of Functional Departmentalization.   The advantages of this traditional form of organization are virtually the same as those of the bureaucracy. Functional departmentalization works particularly well when large batches of work have to be processed on a recurring basis and when the expertise of specialists is required. Also of note, the functional organization is a logical and time-proven method. At the same time, it helps ensure that the power and prestige of the basic activities of the organization will be defended by top executives.[13]

Disadvantages of Functional Departmentalization.   The problems encountered by a functional organization are similar to the problems of bureaucracy. Often, the disadvantages of a functional organization are partially due to its large size and complexity. A case in point is the delay in decision making. A problem might have to pass up the chain of command through many layers of management before a decision finally is reached.

A key disadvantage of the functional organization, or any other rigidly departmentalized structure, is that it leads to a narrow viewpoint, or tunnel vision. Department members often develop the false belief that their discipline and viewpoint is right, whereas those of other units of the firm are wrong. For example, the marketing executive might say, "If we don't sell the product, all manufacturing can do is make scrap." The manufacturing point of view is, "If we don't make something worthwhile, marketing will have nothing to sell. Besides, a well-manufactured product sells itself."

Delays in accomplishing major tasks are another potential disadvantage of departmentalization by function. Poor coordination of effort is typical of the functional organization. No one individual, except the company or division head, has complete responsibility for costs and profits. A related problem occurs when two people from different departments cannot resolve a dispute by themselves. In order to speak to a common boss about the problem, they have to go to the top of the organization; the two people in conflict have no boss between them at a lower organizational level.

Territorial Departmentalization

Territorial departmentalization is arranging departments according to the geographic area served. In this organization structure, all the activities for a firm in a given geographic area report to one manager. Territorial departmentalization is necessary for organizations conducting business in geographic areas far distant from each other. Marketing divisions often use territorial departmentalization, dividing the sales force into regions such as the northeastern, southeastern, midwestern, northwestern, and southwestern. Large insurance companies organize on the basis of territories, and so do the Internal Revenue Service and the U.S. Postal Service.

It is important to recognize that territorial departmentalization is typically used in addition to functional departmentalization. One such arrangement would be for the central headquarters to departmentalize by function while the field forces are organized by territory. Figure 6-4 illustrates this extension of the functional structure.

Advantages of Territorial Departmentalization.   The popularity of the territorial structure is well founded. A key advantage is that it allows for decision making at a local level, where the personnel are most familiar with the problems. The arrangement also overcomes the potentially awkward situation of the home office trying to coordinate activities at geographically distant places. Territorial departmentalization makes an important contribution to management development. Those people assigned as territorial managers obtain valuable experience in managing a total enterprise; they act as general managers or minicompany presidents. Another plus of the territorial arrangement is that it fosters identity with the company. As one regional manager put it, "In Montreal, we are Hewlett-Packard."

Figure 6-4 An Organization Chart Showing Functional and Territorial Departmentalization

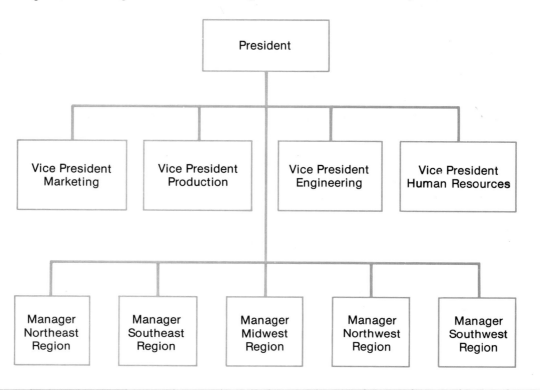

Disadvantages of Territorial Departmentalization. Territorial departmentalization also has some potential disadvantages. For the structure to work effectively, highly capable field managers are needed. The arrangement also can be quite expensive because of duplication of costs and effort. For instance, each region may build service departments (such as for purchasing) that duplicate functions already being carried out at headquarters. A bigger problem is that top-level management may have difficulty controlling the performance of field units.

Product Departmentalization

Product departmentalization is the arrangement of departments according to the products or services they provide. When the products or services provided by an organization are so important that they almost become independent companies, product departmentalization makes sense. Siemens USA is a representative example of product departmentalization. The company's forty-seven manufacturing and assembly plants and ten thousand manufacturing employees are divided into five product groups: communication systems, electronic components, energy and automation, information systems, and medical systems.

Product departmentalization makes the most sense when the product or service offered by the organizational unit has its own unique demands, as with the IBM PC. It would not make sense, however, for the Pontiac and Chevrolet divisions of General Motors Corp. (GM) to be organized into separate, independent units; they use quite similar manufacturing processes and have many virtually identical parts. However, the Saturn, an automobile now being made by GM, is unique enough to be the basis for a new company.

A version of product departmentalization is presented in Figure 6-5. If the product departments are sufficiently large, the functional departments at

Figure 6-5   An Organization Chart Showing Product Departmentalization

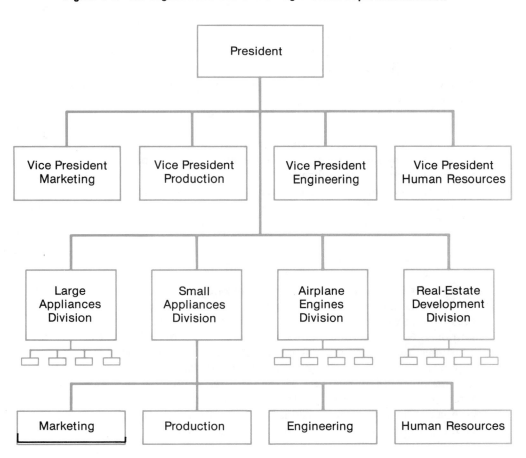

headquarters may be quite small. In a pure form of product departmentalization, the functional departments in the home office consist of only the top executive and a small staff.

Notice that the organization depicted in Figure 6-5 offers products and services with unique demands of their own. For example, the manufacture and sale of airplane engines is an entirely different business from the development of real estate. An important difference exists between a product manager and the division head of a major product unit of the organization. A product manager is responsible for seeing that his or her product gets the attention it needs from company personnel in order to prosper. However, the product manager does not have separate manufacturing and marketing facilities under his or her control.

Advantages of Product Departmentalization.   The overriding advantage of organizing by product line is that the arrangement gives major attention to the product or service, allowing it the maximum opportunity to grow and prosper. As aptly expressed by one manager, "Once they gave our group our own 800 number, I knew we were on our way to the big time." A good example is the attention Citibank pays to the home mortgages division, Citicorp's Homeowner Services. Equipped with its own headquarters in St. Louis, it handles mortgages throughout the United States. Similar to territorial departmentalization, grouping by product helps train general managers, foster high morale, and allow decisions to be made at the local level.

Disadvantages of Product Departmentalization.   Departmentalization by product has the same potential problems as territorial departmentalization or any other form of decentralization. It can be expensive because of duplication of effort, and top-level management may find it difficult to control the separate organization units. Another potential problem is that talented managers are needed to head the divisions.

Customer Departmentalization

Customer departmentalization is an organization structure based on customer needs. When the demands of one group of customers are quite different from the demands of other customers, customer departmentalization is often called into play. Many insurance companies, for example, organize their efforts into consumer and business departments. Similarly, many hotels have separate departments for dealing with individual guests or for handling conventions and banquets. Manufacturers of sophisticated equipment typically have different groups for processing government and commercial accounts. Aerospace companies have separate divisions for manufacturing and selling military and civilian aircraft. Commercial banks generally make use of customer departmentalization, as illustrated in Figure 6-6.

Customer departmentalization is similar to product departmentalization, and sometimes the distinction between these two forms of organization is blurred.

Figure 6-6   Customer Departmentalization in a Commercial Bank

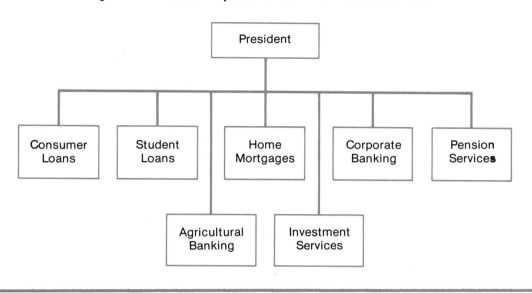

For example, is a bank department that sells home mortgages catering to homeowners, offering a special service, or both?

Advantages of Customer Departmentalization.   The outstanding advantage of this basis for structuring an organization is that it allows the company to pay careful attention to the needs of specialized customers. Those employees who specialize in serving a particular customer group are able to offer expert service. This special service in turn encourages customer loyalty.

Disadvantages of Customer Departmentalization.   Drawbacks to customer departmentalization also exist. If the demands for serving a particular customer group decrease, employees serving those customers will be underutilized. Another problem is the difficulty of coordinating units of the firm organized on a different basis with those departmentalized by customer. The customer groups may demand special treatment and remain somewhat aloof from the rest of the firm.[14]

Process Departmentalization

Process Departmentalization is the structuring of an organization on the basis of technical activities carried out by the organizational unit. Visualize a furniture-manufacturing company in which the following processes are carried out in sequence: department A cultivates a forest, chops down trees, and brings the trees to the plant; department B cuts the lumber and treats the wood;

department C assembles the furniture; department D finishes the furniture; and department E ships it to customers. This arrangement would not preclude the presence of functional departments, such as the marketing and accounting departments. Process departmentalization is described here only in relation to manufacturing (in a furniture factory), as illustrated in Figure 6-7.

People, as well as products, can be processed.[15] College registration procedures typically process students by having the student select courses in one department and then move on to another for tuition payment. Similarly, some discount department stores process customers by asking them to (1) check their bags at the front door, (2) ask for check verification in advance of making purchases, (3) select their purchases, and (4) go through the cashier's line.

Closely related to process departmentalization is equipment departmentalization, in which specified departments have specialized equipment. An illustration would be a quality-control department in a motor-manufacturing plant that houses an ultrasound machine to scan for minor defects in the motors.

Organizing work by processes or equipment makes the most sense when it is costly and technologically unfeasible to do otherwise. It is costly, for example, for a furniture factory to have more than one lumber-processing department. One potential disadvantage of process departmentalization is that it leads to job impoverishment rather than enrichment. Only employees in the last department get their hands on the finished product.

NONBUREAUCRATIC FORMS OF ORGANIZATION

To overcome some of the problems encountered in the bureaucratic form of organization, several other organization structures have been developed. Two of these structures, the project and matrix organizations, are essentially supplements to the traditional hierarchy. Two others, flat organizations and the System 4 model, are more clearly alternatives to the bureaucratic structure.

Figure 6-7   Process Departmentalization in a Furniture Factory

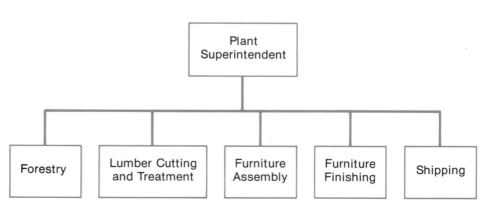

The Project Form of Organization

Departmentalization usually is poorly suited to performing special tasks that differ substantially from the normal activities of the firm. One widely-used solution to this problem is the **project organization**, a temporary group of specialists working under one manager to accomplish a fixed objective.[16] Projects are therefore viewed as a vital structure for bringing about change.[17] The project organization is used most extensively in the military, aerospace, construction, and motion-picture industries. Project management has four distinguishing characteristics:[18]

1. Project managers operate independently of the normal chain of command; they usually report directly to a member of top-level management, often an executive in charge of projects.

2. Project managers negotiate directly for resources with the heads of the line and staff departments whose members are assigned to a given project. For example, a project manager might borrow three architectural technicians from the building-design department.

3. Project managers act as coordinators of the people and material needed to complete the project's mission. They are therefore accountable for the project's success or failure, but they are not always accountable for the performance of the personnel assigned to the project.

4. The life of the project ends when its objectives are accomplished. In contrast, most departments usually are considered permanent.

Some form of project organization is found in almost every large company. Whenever a special project arises, either a formal project group is organized to accomplish the work or a task force is appointed. Project group members usually are relieved from their regular assignments for the life of the project. A **task force** is a group of people who are called on to solve a problem but who usually do not give up their regular assignments for the life of the project. Task forces are expected to arrive at solutions for a specific problem, such as developing a public-utility policy for dealing with people who cannot afford to pay their utility bills.

Amount of Authority Held by a Project Manager.   Project managers vary considerably in their level of formal authority. At one extreme, a project group may operate basically as a coordinating body for the major departments. In this situation, the project manager exerts minimum influence in obtaining the resources needed to accomplish the project's mission. In addition, the project manager may have difficulty commanding project members. At the other extreme, top-level management may announce that the project manager has been granted full authority to get the mission accomplished. He or she then can readily obtain resources from departments and can command project members.

Advantages of Project Organization.   The overall advantage of the project organization is that it overcomes most of the disadvantages of the departmentalized form of organization. Project organizations help overcome tunnel vision, allow project group members to have broad experience, speed up the decision-making process, and help reduce the problem of overspecialization.

Project organizations also offer other advantages.[19] First, the project structure encourages identification with the project, which often leads to high morale and productivity. A frequently observed attitude is "We can outperform the competition." Second, project organizations are well suited to dealing with unpredictable situations. They are flexible because so few employees are permanently attached to a project. If the project proves to be not worthwhile for whatever reason, the project group can be quickly disbanded. Third, project organization is ideally suited for such special assignments as relocating company headquarters, launching a new product, or developing a new program of studies at a school. If the new product or program becomes a big success, the project can become the nucleus for a new division of the company or school. Should the project fail, the blow is softened because vast resources have not been committed to it.

Disadvantages of Project Organization.   Despite their advantages, project organizations also have some notable disadvantages. One problem is that people assigned to the project may be underutilized once the project is completed. Unless there is another project that requires staffing, some of the project members may be laid off. Another problem is that project managers often are not given the authority they need to accomplish their mission. Unless the project manager has been granted substantial authority by top-level management, he or she has to rely on personal influence in obtaining needed support from other managers.

MATRIX ORGANIZATION

A form of organization has evolved to capitalize on the advantages of both the functional and project forms of organization, while minimizing their disadvantages. Called a **matrix organization,** it consists of a project structure imposed on top of a functional structure.[20] The project groups act as minicompanies within the larger firm. However, the project typically folds when its mission is completed. In some instances, the project is so successful that it becomes a new and separate division of the company. For example, a frozen-food project could become the frozen-food division. A distinguishing feature of the matrix is that the project managers borrow resources from the functional departments. In some firms, the project managers are referred to as program or product managers.

An important aspect of the matrix structure is that each person working on the project has two superiors—the project manager and the functional manager. The project manager, however, usually has one supervisor—a member of top-level management. At one time, matrix management was thought to be applicable to only technically oriented industries, such as aerospace. The matrix organization is now used in other industries that need the advantages of both the functional form and the project form of organization. Users of the matrix structure include banks, insurance companies, chemical manufacturers, and colleges.[21]

Colleges often use the matrix structure for setting up special-interest programs such as industry seminars, women's studies, black studies, and adult education. Each of these programs is headed by a director who uses resources from the traditional departments.

A popular version of the matrix structure is shown in Figure 6-8. The term *functional authority* means that the functional (or departmental) managers offer some guidance and supervision to their employees on the projects. In the diagram shown, the quality manager would occasionally meet with the quality specialists assigned to the projects to discuss their professional activities.

Advantages of Matrix Structure.   The matrix structure offers so many advantages; it would be difficult to find a large, complex organization that did not make some use of matrix management.

Figure 6-8   A Matrix Organization Structure

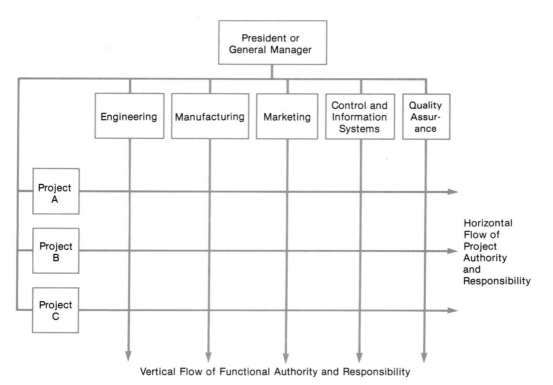

Above all, the matrix form of organization combines the best features of the project and functional structures. It is flexible, yet it offers the advantages of task specialization. The key advantages of the matrix organization include:[22]

1. *Efficient use of resources.* The project managers use only the specialized staff they need to get the job done, rather than building large groups of underutilized specialists. Staff specialists and other resources are shared by the various program managers.

2. *Flexibility in conditions of change and uncertainty.* As described, the project structure is flexible, and the group can be disbanded quickly if it is no longer needed.

3. *Technical excellence.* Matrix structures are known for their ability to facilitate high-quality and innovative solutions to difficult technical problems.

4. *Ability to balance conflicting objectives.* The matrix balances the customer's requirement for project completion and control of costs with the organization's need for high profit and the development of technical capability for the future.

5. *Improved motivation and commitment.* The majority of employees enjoy the excitement of working on a specific project, and they are therefore more motivated and committed than they would be if assigned to a stable department.

6. *Opportunities for personal development.* The project structure gives people a degree of freedom that enhances their development as managers. Also of note, there is ample opportunity for job rotation on many projects.

Disadvantages of Matrix Organization.   In addition to all the benefits, matrix management does create some problems. A frequent difficulty is conflict between project managers and functional managers over the control of resources. Functional managers usually have fewer resources available than are desired by project managers. How those resources are distributed is often determined by the persuasive ability of the various project managers. The project managers try to convince the functional manager that it would benefit him or her to give some resources to a particular project. Often, this means that resources are allocated on the basis of the interpersonal skills of the project managers rather than being put to the best use for the organization.

Another disadvantage of the matrix structure is that it can be difficult to find managers with the right talents. They must be able to operate effectively in a climate of ambiguity and conflict, and they may have to please more than one master at a time. There are few training experiences that adequately prepare a person for project management. Yet the success of the matrix structure depends a great deal on the skills and personality of the project manager.

Finally, a recent experiment with engineers and drafting technicians in a work setting suggests that the matrix structure does increase the quantity of communications, but the quality may suffer. Because of this occasional poor quality, coordination of effort may suffer.[23]

The System 4 Model

The System 4 model was developed by Rensis Likert to describe a highly participative, project-oriented organization.[24] It stands in contrast to the classical organization model. System 4 emphasizes shared decision making and easy communication among people at all organizational levels. System 4 is also referred to as an **adhocracy**, an organization structure characterized by temporary teams of workers who move from project to project. The term *ad hoc* means for a specific purpose; thus the term *adhocracy*.

Table 6-2 summarizes the differences between a bureaucracy and a System

---

Table 6-2 Differences in Management Practices and Philosophy Between a Bureaucracy and a System 4 Organization

Bureaucracy	System 4 Organization
Leadership involves no perceived confidence and trust between superiors and subordinates.	Leadership involves perceived confidence and trust between superiors and subordinates.
Motivational methods emphasize the use of fear and threats; result is unfavorable employee attitudes.	Motivational methods appeal to pride and self-fulfillment; result is favorable attitudes.
Communication method is to send messages down the chain of command; messages are often distorted and met with suspicion.	Communication method leads to free flow of information in all directions; information is undistorted and accepted.
Interaction among people is closed and restricted; subordinates have little influence on key activities in department.	Interaction is open and extensive; subordinates have great influence on key activities in department.
Decision making is highly centralized; top executives make all the big decisions.	Decision making occurs throughout the organization and is relatively decentralized.
Goals are set at the top of the organization, and group participation is discouraged.	Group participation in goal setting is encouraged, and higher goals are typically set.
Controls are centralized and emphasize fixing blame for mistakes.	Controls are dispersed, self-imposed controls are emphasized, and solving problems is more important than blaming people.

Source: Based on information in Rensis Likert, *The Human Side of Enterprise* (New York: McGraw-Hill, 1967), 13-46, 97–112.

4 organization. In comparing these organization models, remember that bureaucracy is not necessarily evil and that System 4 is not necessarily good. Rather, they serve different purposes. Bureaucracies are more effective in stable environments, whereas System 4 organizations can respond better to dynamic environments.

Flat Organization Structures

A long-standing problem with the traditional form of organization is that it accumulates too many layers of management. An antidote to this problem is to create a **flat organization structure**—a form of organization with relatively few layers. A flat organization structure is nonbureaucratic for two reasons. First, few managers are available to review the decisions of other people. Second, because the chain of command is shorter, there is less concern about authority differences between people.

Flat structures are used for several important purposes. One reason is to practice participative management; with fewer layers of management, people at lower levels in the organization have more say in decision making. The accompanying "Organization In Action" illustrates the use of flat structures to foster participative decision making.

ORGANIZATION IN ACTION:

Rohm & Haas Encourages Decision Making Down the Line

At Rohm & Haas Bayport Inc., a six-year-old specialty chemical plant near Houston, Texas, all sixty-seven employees play an active role in managing the plant. Technicians routinely perform a variety of tasks without supervision; workers even evaluate one another and interview job applicants. "The idea is to push responsibility and know-how farther and farther down into the organization, so that every person is a manager. We're trying to transfer ownership for decision making to the people who are going to get the work done," says plant manager Bob Gilbert.

At Bayport, the management team numbers a meager four executives. A finance director shares the front office with Gilbert. Out in the plant, two manufacturing managers head up the two different operating units. Only those two managers separate the plant manager from the forty-six process technicians and fifteen technical people (engineers and chemists) who keep the operation running. Unlike plants that are operated more traditionally, Bayport has no shift supervisors.

One piece of evidence about the effectiveness of this flat structure is that a customer's inspectors visited the plant to make a quality audit. They had never given a supplier's plant a higher grade than 83 percent, but Bayport scored 96 percent. Another time, when representatives of a potential customer made a visit, they decided to buy all of their company's needed supply of a particular product from the plant. The Bayport staff would have been satisfied with an order half that size.

Source: Adapted from Don Nichols, "Taking Participative Management to the Limit," *Management Review* (August 1987): 28–32.

Another reason for creating flat structures is to reduce personnel costs by eliminating some managerial positions. Reducing the number of managerial layers also speeds up decision making. With more layers of management, more approvals are required, thus increasing the amount of time required to make a decision. A related reason for creating flat structures is to reduce staffing because of other negative consequences of overstaffing. Charles Ames, chairman and chief executive officer of Acme-Cleveland Corp., says, "Many companies still have fat staffs, lots of layers and overcentralized control. People don't even know all the products their company makes anymore." Finally, flat structures are used by some organizations simply because a streamlined organization fits the spirit of the times. As Ames expounds:

> We are in turbulent times, and we must begin managing for survival in turbulent times. We must be geared to a more competitive environment, breaking apart overloaded organization structures and streamlining, emphasizing producer people over support staff, getting our cost/profit ratio more in line, taking the bull by the horns and doing what we have to do to survive.[25]

THE INFORMAL ORGANIZATION STRUCTURE

The preceding discussion about how organizations are structured describes the official pattern of reporting and the authority relationships. Although this information is vital in understanding how organizations work, it is incomplete. To understand how work gets accomplished, one must also understand the **informal organization structure**—the pattern of working relationships used to supplement and complement the formal structure. The informal organization thus fills in the gaps not anticipated by the formal structure.

One example of the informal organization is how Maggie Asano, a department administrative assistant, helps managers and professionals outside her department get work accomplished. She is officially assigned to the accounting department, yet managers and professionals outside her area routinely request her assistance in learning how to use their personal computers. Following the formal organization structure, these managers and professionals should ask the information-systems department for assistance. However, they have found it easier and quicker to be tutored by Asano. If Asano were transferred to the information-systems department as an "internal consultant for personal computers," asking for help would become part of the formal structure.

An important component of the informal organization is the **informal group,** a group that arises out of individual needs and the attraction of workers to one another. Membership is voluntary and is based on common interests and values.[26] These groups evolve naturally to take care of people's desire for friendship and companionship. Informal groups appear at all levels in the organization. These groups often carry out activities unrelated to the job, such as dining together or participating in sports. At other times the informal group conducts job-related activities. For example, three managers from different parts of the company might commute to work together every business day when they are in town. Often they discuss current events and the stock market, but they also discuss company business while commuting to work.

SUMMARY OF KEY POINTS

The two primary ways of subdividing the tasks of the overall enterprise are through job design and organization structure. Job design is the laying out of job responsibilities and duties and of how they are to be performed. One important consideration in job design is job scope—the number of different tasks performed by the job holder. A specialist handles few tasks, but performs them in depth. Task generalization enhances satisfaction and morale for many employees. However, it sacrifices some expertise. Automation, including robotics, contributes to task specialization. Robots perform many specialized tasks, including those that would be unsafe for humans.

Job enrichment is a method of making jobs more challenging and responsible so they will be more appealing to most employees. The characteristics of an enriched job include the following: direct feedback, client relationship, new learning, scheduling by the employee, unique experience, control over resources, direct communication authority, and personal accountability. Job enrichment also can be carried out on a group level by organizing teams of workers who are granted substantial responsibility in accomplishing their work.

The most widely used organization model is the bureaucracy, a multilevel organization in which authority flows downward, and rules and regulations are carefully specified. The principles of organization followed in a bureaucracy include the following: *(a)* well-defined hierarchy, *(b)* task specialization, *(c)* rules to cover the rights and duties of employees, *(d)* specified work procedures, *(e)* written responsibility and authority, *(f)* authority that matches responsibility, *(g)* ultimate responsibility at the top, and *(h)* division of authority into line and staff.

Bureaucracies can be highly efficient organizations, well-suited to handling repetitive, recurring tasks. However, they do create rigidity in interpreting rules, delays in decision making, high frustration, and low job satisfaction.

The usual way of subdividing effort in all organizations is to create departments. Bureaucracies place particularly heavy emphasis on departmentalization. Five commonly used bases for departmentalization are function, territory, product, customer, and process. All have their own advantages and disadvantages.

Several types of organization structures are used to either replace or supplement the traditional bureaucratic structure. The project form of organization has emerged from departmentalized organizations to accomplish new tasks and special-purpose missions. A project group is a temporary team of specialists working under one manager to accomplish a fixed objective. At its best, the project organization helps overcome tunnel vision, allows project members to achieve broad experience, speeds up decision making, and avoids overspecialization. However, the project structure also creates some human-relations problems such as job insecurity and conflicts between project and functional managers.

The matrix organization consists of a project structure superimposed on a functional structure. It represents a balanced compromise between the functional and project organizations. Personnel assigned to the projects within the matrix report to a project manager, yet they simultaneously report to a functional manager. Matrix organizations are widely used today, and their advantages seem to outweigh their disadvantages.

The System 4 organization is a prime example of an adhocracy, an organization structure characterized by temporary teams of workers who move from project to project. It emphasizes shared decision making and easy communication among people at all organizational levels.

Flat organization structures have fewer layers than the traditional hierarchy. They are created for such purposes as the following: increasing the extent of participative management; reducing personnel costs; speeding up decision making; and reducing other problems associated with overstaffing.

The informal organization structure encompasses the unofficial working relationships that supplement and complement the formal structure. The informal structure fills in the gaps not anticipated by the formal structure. Informal groups are a major component of the informal structure.

QUESTIONS

1. Is an executive a specialist or a generalist? Explain your reasoning.
2. Using the characteristics of an enriched job presented in this chapter, analyze whether or not the "job" of a student is enriched.
3. Why do some people particularly enjoy working in a bureaucracy?
4. In what way is it easier to control people in a bureaucracy rather than in a participative organization model?
5. It has been said that the complete opposite of bureaucracy is anarchy. Explain why this might be true.
6. What is the basis for departmentalization used in most department stores?
7. Why do social isolates ("loners") find it more comfortable to work in a functional structure rather than in a project structure?
8. Why does the movie industry make such extensive use of the project structure?
9. What would you guess to be an important disadvantage of a very flat organization structure?

ACTIVITIES

1. Obtain an organization chart from an organization of your choice. Then analyze the type of structure or structures displayed on the chart, using labels and concepts presented in this chapter.
2. Design a matrix organization for the development of either a new candy bar or a new automobile model.

CASE PROBLEM 6-A: THE AIRPORT SECURITY GUARD BLUES

Patti Freeman, supervisor of airport security at an international airport, met with her boss, Jack Indino, to discuss the job performance of her staff. "Jack," said Patti, "we're developing a group performance problem with my security staff. I want to lay out the problem with you and then suggest a solution."

"Go ahead," said Jack. "What's one more problem in the life of an airport operations manager?"

"As I see it," said Freeman, "our security guards are bored stiff. Each one of them has told me so either directly or indirectly. The general complaint is that they get bored checking through one passenger after another. They tell me that after awhile each face is the same, and every attache case or handbag looks the same.

"I think the job boredom is also creating performance problems. Some of the guards have become so lethargic that they don't pay serious attention to any potential security violation. Thank goodness, no terrorist or hijacker has gotten through."

"What are you proposing to do about this problem?" said Indino.

"My tentative solution is to enrich the jobs of the guards in some way. We could work out some way to give them more responsibility and challenge. Perhaps we can allow them to interview passengers to get their thoughts about airline safety."

"I don't see that as a solution," said Indino. "FAA regulations require that the guards be on duty all the time, checking passengers. The guards may be bored, but if the airport wants to stay in business, we need security guards doing exactly what they are doing. If our present crew of guards find their jobs boring, we may have to replace them with people who can concentrate on their jobs for a full shift."

"I'll get back to you again with this problem," said Freeman. "I understand your viewpoint, but I've got to find some way to get the security guards more wrapped up in their jobs."

Case Questions

1. How effective might task generalization or job enrichment be for purposes of curing the inattention problem observed by Freeman?
2. What is your evaluation of the tactic of replacing the security guards with others who might be more attentive?
3. What is your evaluation of Freeman's contention that job boredom might be adversely affecting the security guards' job performance?

CASE PROBLEM 6-B: THE DINOSAUR CORPORATION

Ram Gupta, president of Biotronics, was addressing his management team during a company gathering at a hotel. As he rested his hands on the podium, he made these comments: "Unfortunately, we are becoming victims of our own success. Several years ago, our firm of less than fifty employees pioneered its way into the field of electronic equipment for the medical field. We were young, aggressive, and freewheeling. We looked to the outside world and were not so concerned about our internal problems. If somebody had an idea that cost a few dollars to implement, that person could get immediate authorization to spend the money. Now we have five hundred employees, and it is hard to buy a pencil sharpener without approval from above.

"As our company grew, we became more bureaucratic. We began to give fancy names to our departments and fancy job titles to ourselves. I'm a little guilty of that myself. In place of 'owner,' I became 'chief executive officer,' and Ken over here became 'chief operating executive' in place of 'operations manager.'

"Ever since we let that team of consultants help us become a more systematized, more orderly, and more controlled corporation, we have lost something. What happened to our courageous spirit? What happened to our innovation? Our sales are up, but our capacity for future growth is limited. We are only as good as our capacity to respond to our changing environment.

"I'm afraid we have become a dinosaur corporation. Our brain is a long way from our operating parts. We now look to the top of the firm for inspiration and direction. Worse, our people in the field are not getting the information they need to do the job properly. Some of our field representatives deny requests from customers that would easily be granted by us in the home office. Just last week, one of our reps told a hospital we could not special order an electronic gauge to monitor a dialysis machine. Our prominence was built on responding innovatively to unusual requests.

"I think our firm has taken the form of a large corporation. And I don't think it serves our best interests or those of our customers. Our tail is too far from our brain. It takes us too long to know when something has gone wrong at the bottom of the corporation.

"We are going to start working on this problem today. We will be giving it careful thought over the next six months. My strategic plan is to prevent Biotronics from going the way of the dinosaur."

Case Questions

1. In terms of concepts of organization structure, to what problem is Ram Gupta referring?
2. Make a few specific recommendations to Biotronics for dealing with their problems.
3. In what way do you think Gupta might be part of the problem himself?
4. How realistic is Gupta's thinking? Might he just be a sentimentalist?

REFERENCES

1. Walter L. Polsky and Loretta D. Foxman, "Job Design and Job Evaluation; Surveying New Horizons," *Personnel Journal* (July 1987): 36.
2. William H. Newman, E. Kirby Warren, and Jerome E. Schnee, *The Process of Management*, 5th ed. (Englewood Cliffs, NJ: Prentice Hall, 1982), 207.
3. Fred K. Foulkes and Jeffrey L. Hirsch, "People Make Robots Work," *Harvard Business Review* (January–February 1984): 28.
4. "Forget Computers—Are You Trained to Fix Robots?" *Democrat and Chronicle* (29 August 1984): 28.

5. Bernard J. Reilly and Jospeh A. DiAngelo, Jr., "A Look at Job Redesign," *Personnel* (February 1988): 65.

6. Frederick Herzberg, "The Wise Old Turk," *Harvard Business Review* (September-October 1974): 70–80.

7. "Managment Discovers the Human Side of Automation," *Business Week* (29 September 1986): 71.

8. Several of these programs are described in Paul Bernstein, "Using the Soft Approach for Hard Results," *Business* (April-June 1983): 13–21.

9. Sources are Max Weber, *Essays in Sociology* (Oxford, England: Oxford University Press, 1946) and S. Avery Raube, "Principles of Organization," *Company Organization Charts* (New York: National Industrial Conference Board, 1954), 7–13.

10. Henry Mintzberg, *Structure in Fives: Designing Effective Organizations* (Englewood Cliffs, NJ: Prentice Hall, 1983), 163.

11. Guy Benveniste, *Professionalizing the Organization: Reducing Bureaucracy to Enhance Effectiveness* (San Francisco: Jossey-Bass, Inc., Pubs., 1987).

12. Robert Jackall, "Moral Mazes: Bureaucracy and Managerial Work," *Harvard Business Review* (September–October 1983): 130.

13. Harold Koontz, Cyril O'Donnell, and Heinz Weihrich, *Management*, 7th ed. (New York: McGraw-Hill, 1980), 362. Our basic discussion of departmentalization is based on this source.

14. Koontz, *Management*, 372.

15. Stephen P. Robbins, *Management: Concepts and Practices* (Englewood Cliffs, NJ: Prentice Hall, 1984), 172.

16. Per Jonason, "Project Management, Swedish Style," *Harvard Business Review* (November–December 1971): 106.

17. Leonard H. Aptman, "Project Management: Criteria for Good Planning," *Management Solutions* (November 1986): 30.

18. Jonason, "Project Management, Swedish Style," 106.

19. A reference on the advantages and disadvantages of project management is Harold Kerzner and Has Thamhain, *Project Management for Small and Medium Sized Businesses* (New York: Van Nostrand Reinhold, 1983).

20. William F. Joyce, "Matrix Organization: A Social Experiment," *Academy of Management Journal* (September 1986): 536.

21. Norman H. Wright, "Matrix Management—Fortifying the Organization Structure," *Management World* (May 1980): 24.

22. Kenneth Knight, "Matrix Organization: A Review," *Dimensions in Management* (Boston: Houghton Mifflin Co., 1982), 183–187.

23. Joyce, "Matrix Organization," 552.

24. Rensis Likert, *The Human Side of Enterprise* (New York: McGraw-Hill, 1967), 13–46.

25. "Why Image Counts: A Tale of Two Industries," *Business Week* (8 June 1987): 139.

26. Henry L. Tosi, John R. Rizzo, and Stephen J. Carroll, *Managing Organizational Behavior* (Marshfield, MA: Pittman Pub., 1986), 684.

7

Delegation and Decentralization

After studying the material in this chapter, you should be able to accomplish the following tasks:

1. Explain the meaning of delegation and decentralization and the difference between them.
2. Understand how the span of control influences delegation and decentralization.
3. Develop a tentative plan for becoming an effective delegator.
4. Recognize the advantages of both decentralization and centralization.
5. Recognize the conditions and factors favoring delegation and decentralization.

Key Terms and Phrases

Delegation

Delegatee

Authority

Decentralization

Centralization

Recentralization

Horizontal Decentralization

Span of Control

Obligation

Balanced Decision

Collective effort would not be possible, and organizations could not grow and prosper, if a handful of managers attempted to do all of the work themselves. In recognition of this fact, managers divide up their work with others in two directions. Subdividing work in a horizontal direction through the process of departmentalization was described in Chapter 6. This chapter is about subdivision of work along the vertical direction (the chain of command) through the closely related processes of delegation and decentralization.

DELEGATION AND DECENTRALIZATION

Delegation is the assignment to another person of the formal authority and responsibility for accomplishing a specific task. If managers do not delegate any of their work, they are not acting as managers. Instead, they are individual contributors. However, if managers delegate everything, they will have no work of their own to perform. Delegation allows for the subdivision of work and grants autonomy to the **delegatee**—the person receiving the delegated task. Delegation therefore goes beyond having group members participate or collaborate in making decisions.[1]

Delegation also can be regarded as the passing down of authority at the individual level. **Authority** is simply the formal right, granted by the organization, to carry out an activity. A manager may have the authority to make a job offer to a candidate, and a police officer has the authority to issue tickets for speeding.

Decentralization comes about as a consequence of managers delegating work to lower levels in the organization. It is the extent to which authority has been passed down to lower levels. In a completely decentralized firm, the top executives would have no formal authority—a situation that never exists. **Centralization** is the extent to which authority is retained at the top of the organization. In a completely centralized organization, one chief executive would retain all the formal authority. Complete centralization can exist only in a one-person firm. Decentralization and centralization are thus ends of a continuum. No firm is completely centralized or decentralized.

It is also important to spotlight a common misperception of the meaning of decentralization.[2] A multidivision firm departmentalized on the basis of territory has a flat organizational structure. (See the flat structure in Figure 7-2 page 194.) An organizational structure of this shape is often referred to as decentralized, which may or may not be true. If top-level management within the flat structure still retains most of the decision-making authority, the organization is centralized even though it is flat. However, if top-level management grants considerable authority and responsibility to the subunits, the firm is decentralized.

Recentralization

The typical sequence of events in building an organization is to begin with a concentrated, centralized structure and move toward a dispersed, decentralized structure as the firm grows. The bigger the company, the more difficult it is to have a handful of people making all the decisions. Once the organization is decentralized, managers may decide that decentralization has gone too far. Decentralization may result in too much duplication of support activities, overstaffing, too much expense, and loss of control by top-level management.

The solution is to recentralize, or to reverse the process of decentralization. **Recentralization** often leads to lowered costs because facilities are consolidated. The automobile divisions of General Motors Corp. (GM) went through such a process several years back. A marketing problem confronted GM: distinctions among the makes of automobiles had begun to blur in the minds of consumers. Prices of some models of Chevrolets, Pontiacs, Buicks, and Oldsmobiles were quite comparable. Even more confusing, at one time, the small J-car was made by all five divisions. The recentralization was designed to overcome the resulting marketing problem. GM's five car divisions (Chevrolet, Pontiac, Oldsmobile, Buick, and Cadillac) were reorganized into two sales groups. The small-car group sells Chevrolets and Pontiacs, while the large-car group sells Buicks, Oldsmobiles, and Cadillacs. This recentralization of GM's automotive sales divisions is depicted in Figure 7-1. A more recent development is the addition of a new, separate organization for the Saturn automobile.

Horizontal Decentralization

Another important way of subdividing the work of managers is to grant authority and responsibility for some of the work to staff groups. This process is called **horizontal decentralization**. It shifts authority from line managers to staff managers and various specialists.[3] Horizontal decentralization has become more widely practiced as managerial responsibilities have increased in complexity. Managers are often relieved to turn over a portion of their job to

Figure 7-1   Recentralization of GM'S Automotive Sales Divisions

Before Recentralization

Automotive Group

Chevrolet · Pontiac · Buick · Oldsmobile · Cadillac

After Recentralization

Automotive Group · Saturn

Small Cars · Large Cars

Chevrolet · Pontiac · Buick · Oldsmobile · Cadillac

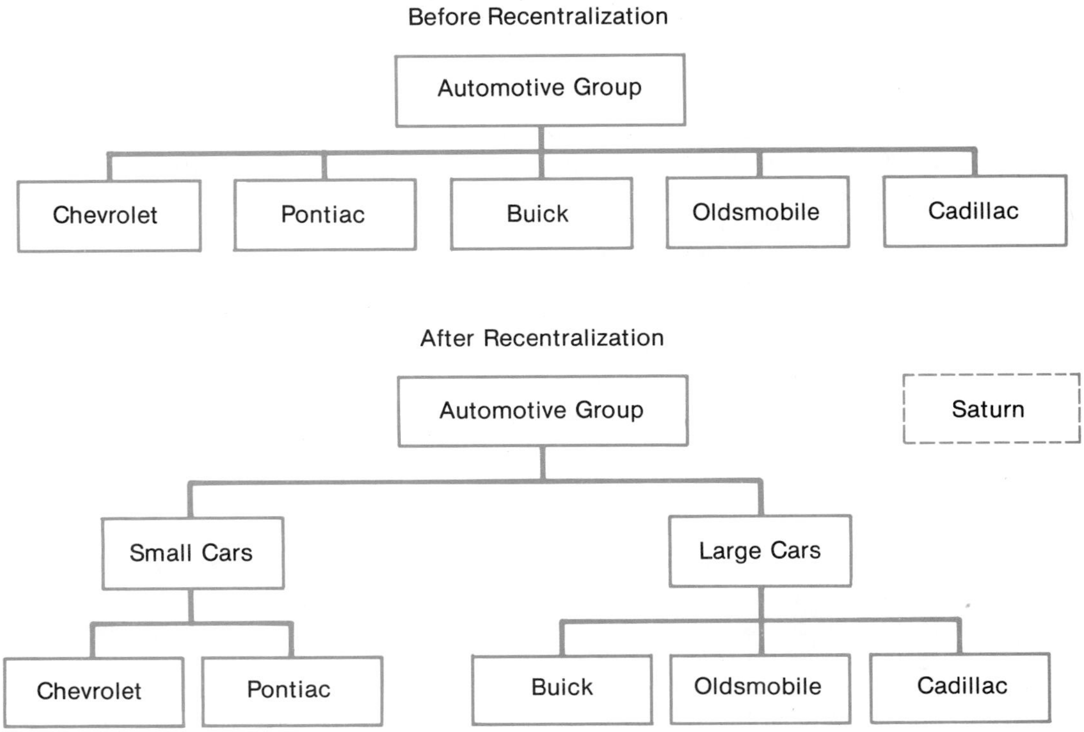

an appropriate specialist. An information-systems specialist explains how one manager delegated responsibility through horizontal decentralization:

> The head of the food-services department came to me one day and said, "We're so far behind the other departments in office automation. I feel like we're in the Middle Ages. But I don't know an Apple® Computer from an apple pie. Tell us what needs to be done to automate our office, and we'll buy your recommendations." I jumped at the opportunity for this much responsibility.

As does the traditional form of vertical decentralization, horizontal decentralization exists in different degrees. The food-service manager just described engaged in extensive horizontal decentralization. If he had merely asked for advice from the information-systems specialist, the degree of decentralization would have been modest.

So far, we have described delegation and decentralization. Our attention turns next to a major factor influencing how much delegation and decentralization takes place within an organization.

SPAN OF CONTROL

The number of subordinates reporting directly to a manager is referred to as the **span of control**. When managers have a large span of control, delegation is fostered because there are more subordinates available to share the managers' work. A wider span of control also generally leads to more decentralization because it is difficult to supervise closely many different groups. Figure 7-2 illustrates the difference between a wide and narrow span of control.

At one time, management researchers tried to identify the ideal number of subordinates that should report to a manager. Six was often thought to be the best span of control for most situations. Current wisdom suggests that the optimum span of control depends on many factors, as described below. According to the span-of-control principle, there is a limit to the number of subordinates a manager can supervise efficiently. Care should be exercised to hold the span of control within manageable limits.[4] Nine factors are of particular significance in determining whether the span of control should be wide (many subordinates) or narrow (few subordinates) in a given situation. These factors are summarized in Table 7-1.

At this point, it is worthwhile to review several key ideas. Span of control is closely linked to both delegation and decentralization. When managers have wide spans of control, there are more direct subordinates available to receive delegated responsibilities. When spans of control are wide throughout the organization, the structure is flatter than when spans are narrow. Refer back to the diagrams in Figure 7-2. Wide spans of control decrease the number of layers of management because fewer managerial positions are created. Flat organization structures, in turn, lead to decentralization of authority because it is logistically difficult to control the activities of so many subordinates.

Figure 7-2 How Span of Control Influences the Height of the Organizational Structure

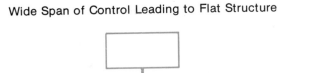

Wide Span of Control Leading to Flat Structure

Narrow Span of Control Leading to Tall Structure

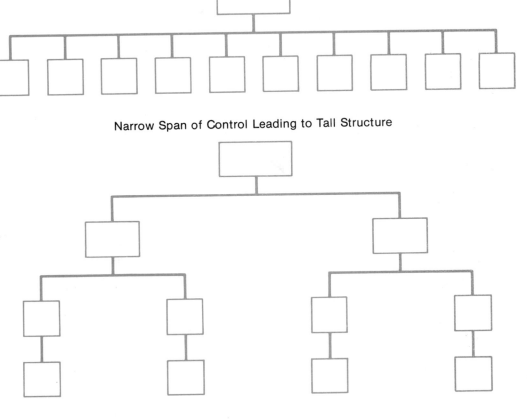

Also, many of the organizational units may be physically distant from top-level management.

THE THREE COMPONENTS OF DELEGATION

Delegation is a major building block of organized effort, and it is the starting point for decentralization. The process consists of three interdependent components: duties, authority, and obligation (or accountability).[5] The interdependence of the three components is illustrated in Figure 7-3. The three-legged stool indicates that the delegation process will be severely weakened if any one of the three components is missing.

Table 7-1 Factors Influencing Span of Control

1. *Capabilities of the manager.* An experienced, well-trained, and knowledgeable manager can supervise more subordinates than can a less capable manager.

2. *Capabilities of the subordinates.* Capable subordinates consume much less managerial time than do their less capable counterparts. Employees of low capability require more instruction, guidance, discipline, and follow-up.

3. *Outside help available to the manager.* If managers can readily obtain help from staff groups to get their work accomplished, they can direct the activities of a larger number of subordinates.

4. *Amount of flux within the work setting.* Frequent changes in the nature and scope of work assignments make it more difficult for the manager to carry a wide span of control. Conversely, if the work is relatively stable, the manager can supervise a larger number of employees.

5. *Similarities of work activities supervised.* When direct subordinates are all performing similar work, the manager can effectively handle a wide span of control. One basic reason is that the manager need be familiar with fewer work activities.

6. *Amount of planning required in the managerial job.* When managers have to invest considerable time in planning, or any other analytical work, they have less time to deal with human problems. A narrow span of control is therefore indicated if the manager must do a lot of planning.

7. *Amount of coordination among work activities required.* A narrow span of control is called for when considerable coordination among members of the work group is required. Integrating tasks and assignments among different people or departments is time-consuming.

8. *External pressures facing the manager.* In addition to interacting with subordinates, managers have contact with their own superiors, various staff groups, managers in other departments, and sometimes with outside groups. If these contacts are extensive, the manager will have less time available for supervisory work within the department. The number of subordinates such a manager can effectively handle is therefore restricted.

9. *Physical dispersion of employees.* When employees are physically dispersed, the manager has to spend more time traveling to meet with them, and can handle only a narrow span of control. When employees are in close proximity to each other, the span of control can be wider.

Source: Several of the ideas contained in this list are based on Ramon J. Aldag and Timothy M. Stearns, *Management* (Cincinnati: South-Western Publishing Co., 1987), 290–291.

To illustrate the delegation process, we take the example of Murph Ponti, the owner and operator of a new motorcycle dealership. After six months of operation, Murph realizes he cannot manage the entire business by himself. He asks Peter O'Neill, the more experienced of his two mechanics, to become the manager of the service department. O'Neill accepts the promotion, and Ponti now has the opportunity to delegate some of his managerial tasks.

Figure 7-3 The Three Components of Delegation

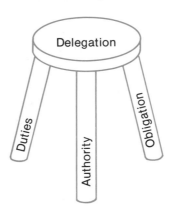

Duties

The first step in the delegation process is for the manager to assign duties to somebody else. The delegatee is told what work he or she is to perform. In this case, Ponti provides O'Neill with a careful list of what the manager of the service department at Murph's Cycle Shop is supposed to do. It includes writing up service orders for customers, pricing the repairs, collecting money when service jobs are completed, supervising the work of any other mechanics, hiring new mechanics and helpers as needed, keeping the service department clean, and informing Murph of any instances of customer discontent.

Authority

To accomplish tasks or duties, the subordinate must have the right or authority to do certain things without constantly checking with the boss. These rights center around using organizational resources such as money, material, time, and human effort. If O'Neill is to accomplish his job, Ponti must grant him the authority to do such things as establishing a price for each repair job; buying necessary tools and parts for inventory; telling the other shop help when they can go for lunch; and refusing to take on certain repair jobs that would be unprofitable.

Granting authority is more complex than it seems on the surface. In any large organization, the authority granted must be in keeping with organizational policy and strategy. For example, a middle manager may have the authority to hire and promote people within his or her chain of command. However, the manager does not have the right to practice any form of discrimination in the process of hiring and promoting.

The authority of any manager has its limits. Even the chief executive officer of a business corporation does not have the authority to enter into a merger agreement with another corporation. The board of directors must approve such a major decision. In the case of Murph's Cycle Shop, Murph Ponti limits Peter O'Neill's authority in a general way by saying, "Check with me about any unusual situation." O'Neill must use good judgment in interpreting the meaning of "unusual." On O'Neill's fifth day as a supervisor, a customer requested a new horn and headlamp for her cycle. She offered to paint three decorative posters for the store in exchange for the repairs. O'Neill thought he did not have the authority to grant this request. After consulting with Ponti, O'Neill told the woman, "Yes, the boss thinks it's a good barter."

Obligation

The third key ingredient to delegation is **obligation**, the assumption of responsibility by the subordinate to perform the assigned duty. Obligation can also be considered a process of holding the subordinate accountable for the delegated work. If a project fails, it is partially the subordinate's fault. The delegatee must assume responsibility for getting the work accomplished.

An implication of the obligation principle is that subordinates must have a strong work ethic for delegation to work effectively. If it does not bother them that assigned duties are neglected, delegation will sometimes fail. Fortunately, employees do get work accomplished for reasons other than obligation and responsibility. These reasons include a fear of the consequences of performing poorly and a desire to achieve the rewards from performing well.

The fact that delegation has only three major components does not mean that it is easy to become a skillful delegator. Effective delegation is an art requiring considerable practice.

HOW TO BECOME AN EFFECTIVE DELEGATOR

Becoming an effective delegator requires a knowledge of the appropriate concepts and techniques. To introduce you to both, the discussion here is divided into four sections: steps in the continuum, deciding what to delegate, steps in the delegation process, and suggestions for effective delegation.

The Delegation Continuum

Delegation is not an either-or proposition. Instead, it is a process that can take place in large or small amounts. When a manager decides to delegate, he or she should explain to the delegatee the extent of the delegation. Delegation can take place in at least five different degrees, as shown in Table 7-2.

Deciding What to Delegate

Early in the delegation process, the manager must decide what to delegate. Andrew E. Schwartz recommends that, in general, work to be delegated should adhere to these guidelines:

Table 7-2 The Delegation Continuum

Degree of Delegation		Behavior Required of Subordinate
Low	Investigate and report back	Delegatee gathers relevant facts; delegator uses those facts to select decision alternatives, makes a decision, and takes action.
	Investigate and recommend action	Delegatee gathers relevant facts and recommends alternative courses of action; delegator makes decision and takes action.
Medium	Investigate and advise on action planned	Delegatee gathers relevant facts and recommends a course of action; delegator accepts or rejects action.
	Investigate and take action; advise on action	Delegatee gathers relevant facts, makes decisions, takes action, and advises delegator about what action took place.
High	Investigate and take action	Delegatee gathers relevant facts, makes decision, and takes action without reporting back to delegator.

Source: Adapted from Marion E. Haynes, "Delegation: There's More To It Than Letting Someone Else Do It!" *Supervisory Management* (January 1980): 9–15.

- It can be handled adequately by subordinates.
- The information necessary for decision making is available to the delegatee.
- The work involves operational detail rather than strategic planning.
- The work does not require skills only possessed by the manager.
- An employee other than the manager can have direct control over the task.[6]

Steps in the Delegation Process

In learning to be a more effective delegator, it is helpful to regard delegation as an orderly, three-step process.[7] The delegation process begins when the manager decides to delegate. Next comes communication with the delegatee about the work delegated. Then the manager evaluates how well delegation has worked. The process can be summarized in this manner:

1. Manager makes decision to delegate and asks

    a. "What are the objectives of delegating this task?"

    b. "What are the resources available to the delegatee?"

    c. "Who should be the delegatee?"

2. Manager communicates with delegatee about

    a. Objectives of task to be accomplished.

    b. Resources available for getting the task accomplished.

    c. Checkpoints that will be used to measure progress.

3. Manager evaluates the delegation process, taking into account such factors as

    a. Have the objectives been achieved?

    b. Has the delegatee made efficient use of resources?

    c. Was delegation effective?

Why Some Managers Are Reluctant to Delegate

Every manager has heard of delegation, and most extol its advantages. Nevertheless, there are many reasons that managers fail to take constructive action about delegating responsibility. Knowing the reasons that many other managers are hesitant to delegate may help a manager overcome these problems.[8]

1. *"I can handle it better than you."* Managers often believe they can perform the delegated assignment better than the employee. As a result of this attitude, they do not project confidence in the employee's ability to perform the delegated task.

2. *The manager is a perfectionist.* Managers who are perfectionists are uncomfortable with delegation because control over how the job is performed is taken out of their hands. Perfectionists who do delegate tend to carefully monitor the work of delegatees and pester them to conform to their mode of operation.

3. *Poor skill in delegation.* Some managers have not developed the proper skills for delegation. To delegate effectively, a manager must be able to plan, organize, and communicate effectively to subordinates. Delegation involves much more than dropping an assignment on somebody's lap.

4. *Too much time consumed by delegation.* When a manager delegates a complicated assignment to an employee, the employee might need substan-

tial information to do the job. So much information might need to be transmitted that delegation hardly seems worth the effort.

5. *Subordinates lack the ability to take on greater responsibility.* Some managers are hesitant to delegate because their subordinates are not capable of taking on more responsibility. Unless the manager creates opportunities for delegation, the subordinates will remain incapable of taking on more responsibility because employees learn through assuming delegated tasks.

6. *Worry about the subordinate looking better than the manager.* The manager may worry that the delegatee will perform well and thus pose a threat to the manager's advancement. Or worse, the manager may worry about being replaced by the subordinate.

Suggestions for Effective Delegation

A number of suggestions and principles for effective delegation have been developed. The manager who follows them carefully improves his or her chances of getting more work accomplished through others. Thirteen suggestions and principles worth keeping in mind when delegating responsibility are summarized in the following list.[9]

1. *Assign duties to the right people.* Delegation proceeds more swiftly and effectively when capable, responsible, and well-motivated subordinates receive the delegated tasks. High-output tasks should not be assigned to incompetent subordinates.

2. *Grant people sufficient authority to accomplish delegated tasks.* To accomplish tasks or duties, the subordinate must have the authority to do certain things without constantly checking with the superior.

3. *Retain some important tasks for yourself.* Managers need to retain some high-output, or sensitive, tasks to perform by themselves. In general, any task that involves the survival of the unit should be handled by the manager. However, which important tasks you should retain always depends on the circumstances at hand. A list of tasks and items that should generally not be delegated is presented in Table 7-3.

4. *Recognize that managers cannot delegate final accountability.* Although responsibility for assignments can be delegated to subordinates, the manager is held accountable for whether the assignment gets accomplished. A case in point is the poison-gas leak that killed over 2200 residents of Bhopal, India in 1984. Although responsibility for ensuring that the storage tanks were safe had been delegated to technicians, top company officials had to accept the blame for the fatal accident. Several plant officials were arrested by the Indian government, which held them responsible for the mistakes of subordinates.

Table 7-3   Tasks and Items that Should Not Be Delegated

Resolving interdepartmental conflict
Formulating strategic planning
Development and coaching of subordinates
Resolving morale problems
Handling tasks assigned to the manager by his or her manager
Firing a subordinate
Handling confidential information
Formulating department budget or policies
Making capital and other large expenditures
Allocating travel expenses
Handling major new programs and services
Establishing sales prices and quotations
Preparing proposals and contracts
Establishing salary increase for unit members
Creating new staff positions
Disciplining and counseling subordinates
Handling a crisis

Source: William R. Tracey, "Deft Delegation: Multiplying Your Effectiveness," *Personnel* (February 1988): 40; Andrew E. Schwartz, "The Why, What, and to Whom of Delegation," *Management Solutions* (June 1987): 33.

5. *Measure progress on a delegated task*. It is insufficient to delegate a complex assignment to a subordinate and then wait until the assignment is completed before discussing it again. Instead, checkpoints and milestones should be established to measure progress.

6. *Delegate to the lowest level at which the task can be successfully accomplished*. One justification for this principle is that it frees up the highest-paid employees for working on more important tasks. Another is that this principle allows those people closest to the source of information to perform the task.

7. *Provide the necessary support to those receiving the delegated task*. The manager has the responsibility for helping subordinates perform their delegated tasks. This could include providing extra staff support, equipment, or training.

8. *Allow delegatees to participate in the delegation process*. To enhance enthusiasm and commitment, subordinates should help plan how the delegated task will be accomplished. They also should be given leeway in choosing how to get the job done.

9. *Delegate both pleasant and unpleasant tasks to subordinates*. A natural tendency is for a manager to delegate unpleasant assignments and retain pleasant ones. So doing leads to a reputation of delegating only "dirty

jobs'' and adversely affects morale. Subordinates consider it fairer when they are assigned a mixture of pleasant and unpleasant responsibilities. Few subordinates expect the manager to handle all the undesirable jobs.

10. *Be willing to let others make mistakes.* If people do not make occasional mistakes, it is because they are not taking risks. When a manager delegates freely, people will make some mistakes as they learn their new assignments.

11. *Trust others.* Delegation will be severely hampered or will not take place at all if the manager does not trust subordinates. Frequent checking destroys delegation. Subordinates lose initiative and begin to guess what the delegator would do in this particular situation. If this happens, innovation may be limited.

12. *Step back from the details.* This is the major delegation hurdle. Many managers are poor delegators because they have a tendency to get too involved with technical details. If a manager cannot let go of details, he or she never will be an effective delegator.

13. *Recognize that a manager is a coach, not a player.* Effective delegation requires that the manager understand the true role of a manager. Suzanne Savary says that effective supervisors must get their highs from coaching, not playing. The supervisor, or higher-level manager, can still do some of the tasks, but the emphasis is on showing other people how to proceed, motivating them, and measuring their performance.[10]

The suggestions for effective delegation just described lead to effective decentralization. A combination of effective delegation and decentralization leads to many important advantages for the manager and the organization.

CENTRALIZATION AND DECENTRALIZATION

One of the key issues in understanding an organization's structure is whether the firm is more centralized or decentralized. This section examines several topics with respect to centralization and decentralization.

Characteristics of a Decentralized Firm

A decentralized firm is best described in terms of key characteristics. According to Ernest Dale, the degree of decentralization is greater under certain conditions.[11] First, a large number of decisions must be made at low levels in the organization. Second, important decisions are made low in the management hierarchy. Third, several functions are affected by decisions made at lower levels. Some companies permit only operational decisions at the plant or branch level. These companies are less decentralized than companies that permit operational, financial, and personnel decisions at the plant or branch level.

Fourth, decentralized firms engage in less checking on decisions. Decentralization is greatest when no check at all must be made. Similarly, the fewer the people consulted and the lower their position in the firm, the greater the degree of decentralization.

Another important point is that many firms are centralized and decentralized simultaneously. Certain aspects of their operation are centralized, whereas others are decentralized. Fast-food franchise restaurants such as McDonald's, Long John Silver's, and Wendy's illustrate this trend. Central headquarters exercises tight control over such matters as the menu selection, food quality, and advertising. Individual franchise operators, however, make personnel decisions on their own. In this way, the franchise operators benefit from both centralization and decentralization.

Influence of Life Stage of the Firm

When a firm is first begun, all authority is centralized. As it grows and prospers, decentralization is necessary so the firm can quickly take advantage of opportunities. A minimum of restrictions for spending money and hiring people is advisable. As the growth slows and stabilizes, it becomes necessary to move toward centralization again in order to pare down expenses and minimize duplication of effort. The phrase "move toward centralization" points to a significant aspect of centralization versus decentralization. A firm is never fully centralized except when it is owned and operated by one person. Nor is it ever fully decentralized. Rather, the organization moves back and forth between the opposite poles of centralization and decentralization.

Figure 7-4 depicts how movement toward centralization and decentralization are related to milestones in the history of the firm. Both private and public firms have periods of growth and retrenchment. A state university serves as one illustration of this concept. Faced with a growing population, it may develop a number of satellite locations to serve students. Some of these satellite locations may be granted autonomy to develop some of their own programs. As the population growth slows down, it may become necessary to close some of the locations. Also, to control costs, the centralized authority may impose budget and program restrictions on the satellite locations.

Advantages of Decentralization

In this section of the chapter, we describe the major advantages of high delegation and decentralization. By reversing each advantage, the same discussion could be considered an analysis of the disadvantages of limited delegation and high centralization. For example, high delegation and decentralization offer the advantage of helping managers develop. Conversely, limited delegation and high centralization suffer the disadvantage of limited opportunities for development of managers. The following are some of the major benefits to be derived from delegation and decentralization.

Figure 7-4   The Centralization and Decentralization Cycle in the History of a Firm

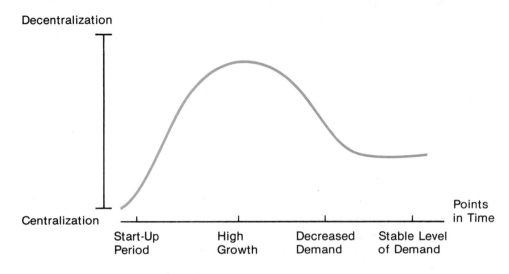

1. *Assists in the development of managers.* A person who is delegated significant responsibilities learns how to make decisions independently. The most direct way of gaining managerial skill is through job experience. Education and training in management are an important part of on-the-job experience. However, they are not a complete substitute.

2. *Encourages competition.* The managers in a decentralized organization are prompted to compete with each other because top management compares their performance. Delegation can create competition within a department in two ways. First, subordinates tend to compete to get choice assignments. Second, subordinates often try to outperform each other on the assignments they do receive.

3. *Enhances morale and creativity.* Because the managers in a decentralized firm are given more freedom, they perceive the problems they solve as their own. They are therefore motivated to put more effort and ingenuity into solving problems. The result is more creativity.

4. *Reduces workload.* Managers who are poor delegators assume a tremendous burden for themselves because their work load keeps increasing. Old responsibilities are retained and new ones added. When managers learn to delegate effectively, they have more time for planning and other analytical work.

5. *Leads to quicker decisions at lower organizational levels.* When managers in decentralized units are empowered with the right to make important decisions, they do not have to check with top-level management so frequently. Delegation also can lead to more rapid decision making. Those subordinates delegated ample responsibility do not need their supervisor's approval before making everyday decisions.

6. *Leads to higher-quality decisions.* Decisions made at lower levels in the organization often are of higher quality because people immediately associated with the details of the problem make the decisions. The accompanying "Organization in Action" illustrates how decentralized decision making is used to produce high-quality decisions about local conditions.

7. *Encourages more trusting working relationships between superiors and subordinates.* A potent way of communicating trust to a subordinate is to delegate important responsibilities to that person. Similarly, when managers at lower levels in the firm are empowered to make important decisions, they feel trusted. Trust also works in the other direction. When lower-ranking managers carry out delegated assignments well, higher-ranking managers develop trust in these people.

ORGANIZATION IN ACTION:

Campbell Soup Gets Closer to the Consumer

When R. Gordon McGovern became chief executive of Campbell Soup Co. Ltd., he began immediately to shift the company's marketing approach by pushing decision making down to levels that were closer to the consumer. He divided the company into about fifty divisions, each with responsibility for its own profits and losses. The first result was an outpouring of new products, many aimed at the blossoming convenience, premium, and health-conscious market segments. During a four-year period, Campbell introduced more than four hundred new products and varieties of products.

Campbell's regionalization plan divided the United States into twenty-two regions. Every regional staff studies marketing strategies and media buying and gets its own ad and trade-promotion budget. McGovern's stance is, "Here's the money, now you do what you want for your customers." Examples of Campbell's effort to respond to local tastes is that the company has experimented with a creole soup for southern markets and a red-bean soup for Hispanic areas in northern California.

Source: As reported in "Marketing's New Look," *Business Week* (26 January 1987): 64–65.

Advantages of Centralization

Despite the genuine advantages of delegation and decentralization, limited delegation and centralization also have merit. There are many times when managers should minimize delegation and maximize centralization. Here we will review the major advantages of centralization.

1. *Minimizes conflict and duplication of effort.* Although competition between subunits can be healthy, it can also lead to disruptive conflict. Two or more units may spend so much time trying to outperform each other that they act as rival companies. It would be better for the overall firm if they each did what they can do best. Similarly, centralization helps minimize duplication of functions within the subunits.

2. *Alleviates the problem of the shortage of executive talent.* Top executive talent is in short supply, and centralization concentrates the talent. Since there are so few talented executives available, why try to decentralize? Instead, place your star performers where they can do the most good. The same argument can be extended to delegation. Why should a talented manager bother delegating important decisions to less talented people? Democracy has its limitations.

3. *Facilitates coordination, integration, and conformity.* If all the major decisions are made at one place in the firm, it is easier to integrate the activities of subunits or individuals.[12] It also is easier to establish coordinated programs such as quality improvement or affirmative action. Different parts of organizations lacking centralization of programs often run off in different directions.

    Similarly, limited delegation means managers have less leeway in conducting their work. This prevents managers handling problems inconsistently across different units.

4. *Allows broader perspective and balance.* Based on their vantage point in the organization, high-level managers have a broader perspective of what is taking place. This helps them arrive at **balanced decisions**, giving consideration to the needs of the entire firm.

5. *Allows specialization of talent.* Functional departmentalization and bureaucratic structures make good use of specialized talent because both are usually centralized. Most decentralized subunits do not require the services of highly specialized workers on a full-time basis. If a decentralized unit needs the services of a specialist, one can be assigned from the functional department. The specialist becomes a consultant whose client is the subunit.

    Limiting delegation also capitalizes on specialization. When a manager is highly skilled in one area, it may be wasteful for him or her to delegate an assignment requiring the use of that skill. Instead, the manager might perform the task and give the subordinate an assignment not requiring that skill.

6. *Protects confidentiality.* A major problem faced by both private organizations and public organizations is the leaking of confidential information. It is difficult to keep information about strategic plans and product manufacturing secret even when tight precautions are exercised. The security problem multiplies geometrically when many people are involved in making decisions about sensitive topics. Centralization helps

because only a small number of trusted people at the top of the organization are involved in making a decision.[13]

7. *Gives strong leaders the opportunity to wield power.* Centralization gives strong leaders an opportunity to play a powerful role in shaping the organization. Instead of so many decisions being made by committees—as it is done in decentralized organizations—the top executives make many far-reaching decisions. One dominant motive for becoming an executive is to exercise power over others. In a decentralized organization, there is less opportunity to do so.

Conditions Favoring Decentralization

An implicit theme in this chapter is that delegation and decentralization often contribute to individual and organizational effectiveness. However, for these benefits to be forthcoming, existing conditions or factors have to be appropriate. We will summarize thirteen contingency factors and conditions favoring passing authority from higher to lower levels. It would be unusual for all of these conditions to be present at the same time. Top-level managers usually will make a decision to decentralize on the basis of the presence of conditions they think are of paramount importance.[14]

1. *Capable subordinates.* Delegation and decentralization make the most sense when there are capable people available to receive important assignments. In one of the author's early experiences as a consultant, he urged an overburdened manager at a potash mine to delegate more. The manager replied, "Young man, to whom do you suggest I delegate? Those in my command are barely capable of carrying out their own jobs."

2. *Large organization.* Decentralization is more urgent in large organizations because it becomes difficult for a handful of top-level managers to make all the firm's key decisions. A firm cannot grow substantially without a reasonable degree of delegation and decentralization. Some entrepreneurs attempt to centralize decision making for as long as possible. Often they are forced to hire professional managers who decentralize decision making enough to allow the firm to keep growing.

3. *Geographical dispersion.* As a firm spreads out geographically, it becomes more necessary to pass authority down the line. This principle is so fundamental that geographically dispersed organizations are frequently referred to as decentralized. Unless authority is passed down to the dispersed units, making important decisions takes an enormous amount of time. Divisional managers have to consult with home-office executives regularly, either in person or electronically. (Electronic communication includes telephones, voice mail, teleconferencing, electronic mail, and facsimile machines.)

4. *Technically complex tasks.* One factor forcing organizations to become more decentralized has been the technical complexity of many projects.

As tasks become more specialized and sophisticated, it becomes increasingly important for specialists to be granted substantial authority. The manager may not know much about the nature of the specialist's work.

5. *Need for rapid decision making.* Decisions can be made more rapidly when authority for decision making is set at lower levels. Instead of having to wait for clearance from central headquarters, the person on the spot can make the decision. Therefore, when decisions have to be made rapidly, it pays to delegate and decentralize. Rapid decisions are most needed in the face of competition or crisis. An example is an automobile sales representative who must be able to strike a deal quickly when customers are comparison shopping.

6. *Decision of below-average significance.* The single most important factor in deciding whether to decentralize decision making is the importance of the decision. The bigger the decision, the greater the tendency to centralize decision making. If the decision has a modest effect on finances and other resources, it is more suitable for delegation. A study with claims supervisors, for example, demonstrated that the supervisors were more likely to delegate routine rather than important decisions. An important decision in this context required evaluating a claim more on the basis of judgment than on an established procedure.[15]

7. *High importance attached to acceptance of the decision.* A proven principle is that people accept decisions better when they have been involved in making the decision. It is therefore advisable to delegate and decentralize decision making when acceptance by the group is important.

8. *High incidence of independent tasks.* When organizational subunits perform tasks that are not dependent on one another, decentralization can be more complete. For instance, if the different divisions of a company are in different businesses, the divisions can run with great autonomy. However, when the work of lower-level units or people is interdependent, more centralization is needed. Centralization helps coordinate and integrate the tasks performed by different people. The reporting of financial information is one aspect of business that usually requires coordination and integration by headquarters.

9. *Advanced control system.* Decentralization should be accompanied by a sophisticated control system to monitor the progress of those receiving delegated authority. Without an effective control system, top-level managers may become aware of serious mistakes too late to help correct the problem. The characteristics of an effective control system are described in Chapter 12, "Essentials of Control."

10. *Top-level managers already working at capacity.* It is time to delegate and decentralize when top-level managers are overloaded with work. A major purpose of delegation is to make collective effort possible. If a few people could accomplish all the work of an organization, there would be no need for delegation.

11. *Uniform policies not urgently needed.* When uniformity is needed, it is necessary to centralize policy. If uniformity in conducting business is not a requirement for organizational success, decentralization is indicated. As described previously, Campbell Soup believed that some degree of nonuniformity would help them achieve more success in regional and local markets.

12. *Need for organizational flexibility.* Small, decentralized units are favored when flexibility is required in solving problems and capitalizing on opportunities. For similar reasons, small, autonomous units are formed when creative problem solving is required. Large, centralized firms are notoriously inflexible. However, units within the firm can respond quickly. Have you ever noticed how quickly congressional committees can mobilize to bring about changes in tax proposals?

13. *Management philosophy favoring delegation and decentralization.* A final criterion is that top-level managers fundamentally believe in the value of passing authority down and across to others. As expressed by a team of management experts, "Some people find decentralization a means to make big business work. In those cases, top managers may see decentralization as a way of organizational life that takes advantage of the innate desire of people to create, to be free, and to have status."[16]

Current Trends in Decentralization and Centralization

Work organizations of all types are currently experiencing a movement toward decentralization and centralization. This movement in two opposite directions is due to several social, economic, and technological forces. The modern manager must therefore learn to cope in both centralized and decentralized operations.

The Trend toward Decentralization. The movement toward participative decision making and a high quality of work life has encouraged the growth of delegation and decentralization. Few managers today would admit they do not believe in participative decision making. Similarly, most organizations tell the outside world they rely on the input of workers at all levels. Automotive companies, for example, regularly advertise that production workers are involved in making decisions about product quality.

The rising expectations of the work force also call for more delegation and decentralization. Many polls have documented that many workers today seek self-fulfillment on the job. Decentralization contributes to self-fulfillment because it allows many employees more freedom and flexibility.

The formal education received by contemporary managers is another force encouraging delegation and decentralization. Virtually all courses in management, supervision, and human relations emphasize the potential value of participative management. It is not surprising that most formally educated managers are predisposed to participative decision making.

The Trend toward Centralization. At the same time that certain aspects of organizations are moving toward decentralization, other aspects are becoming more centralized. Many organizations move toward centralization to adapt to change and face current problems in a coordinated manner. Among these problems are dealing adequately with pollution, safety and health, fluctuations in the value of currency, and equal opportunity employment.[17]

The need to decrease operating expenses is another key force favoring centralization. Numerous banks have merged in order to save costs by combining functions such as human-resource management and data processing. Many large-scale organizations have moved toward centralized purchasing in order to save money by buying in large quantities. A number of firms in the telecommunications and financial-services fields have faced competitive pressures because of governmental deregulation. One response has been to lay off many managers to trim operating costs.

The development of information systems is another major force propelling large organizations toward centralized decision making. Fewer middle managers are needed today than in the past to provide input for top-level decisions. Instead, a relatively small number of information-systems specialists help provide computerized information to top-level management. The outlook is not altogether pessimistic. Although there are fewer middle managers today, the nature of their work is more exciting. The information-gathering aspects of their jobs is vanishing, and they are left with more creative, demanding tasks.

SUMMARY OF KEY POINTS

Delegation is the assignment to another person of the formal authority and responsibility for accomplishing a task. Decentralization stems from delegation. It is the extent to which authority has been passed down to low levels in the organization. Decentralized is not the same as geographically dispersed. Recentralization refers to moving a decentralized organization back toward centralization. Horizontal decentralization refers to the shift of power away from line managers to staff managers and various specialists.

The span of control is the number of subordinates reporting directly to a manager. Its appropriate size is influenced by such factors as capabilities of the manager and subordinates, help available to the manager, amount of change, similarity of the work activities supervised, amount of coordination required, and external pressures facing the manager. When the span of control is wide, delegation is easier. When spans of control are wide throughout the firm, the organization has a flat structure.

Delegation consists of three interdependent components: duties, authority, and obligation. The delegation process suffers if any one of these components is missing. The person to whom an assignment is delegated must have the necessary authority to get it done.

Becoming an effective delegator requires a knowledge of the appropriate concepts and techniques. Delegation is a matter of degrees on a continuum.

At one extreme, the delegatee investigates and reports back. At the other extreme, the delegatee investigates and takes action without consulting the delegator. Before delegating, the manager must decide which tasks should be delegated. There are three major steps in the delegation process: the manager decides to delegate, then communicates with the delegatee, and, finally, evaluates the delegation process.

Many managers are reluctant to delegate because they think they are more able than subordinates or they worry about being shown up by the subordinate. Suggestions for effective delegation include assigning duties to the right people, retaining some important tasks, recognizing you cannot delegate accountability, measuring progress on a delegated task, delegating both pleasant and unpleasant tasks, stepping back from the details, and recognizing that the manager is a coach, not a player.

A decentralized firm has certain characteristics: a large number of decisions are made at lower levels; important decisions are made at lower levels; these decisions affect several functions; and less checking on decisions is done. A balance must be chosen between centralization and decentralization at any given point in the life cycle of a firm. As the firm grows and prospers, decentralization is necessary so the firm can quickly respond to opportunities. As the firm becomes more stable, centralization may be necessary to reduce expenses.

Appropriate delegation and decentralization offer many advantages. Both processes develop managers, encourage competition among people and subunits, enhance morale and creativity, reduce managerial work loads, lead to quicker decisions, lead to higher quality decisions, and promote trust. Centralization and limited delegation also offer advantages. They minimize conflict and duplication of effort, relieve the shortage of executive talent, facilitate coordination and integration, allow a broader perspective for decision makers, allow specialization of talent, protect confidentiality, and provide opportunities for strong leadership.

Among the many conditions and factors favoring delegation and decentralization are capable subordinates, large organization, geographical dispersion, technically complex tasks, need for quick decisions, decision of below-average significance, need for decision acceptance, independent tasks, presence of advanced control system, need for organizational flexibility, and management philosophy in tune with delegation and decentralization.

Organizations of all types are currently experiencing a movement toward decentralization and centralization. Both movements are due to several social, economic, and technological forces. An example of a force for decentralization is the widespread faith in and demand for participative management. An example of a force for centralization is the need to reduce operating expenses.

QUESTIONS

1. Describe the difference between delegation and decentralization.
2. Visualize the photo-finishing kiosks (booths) in your town that are operated by a large photo-finishing firm. Explain whether these locations are most likely centralized or decentralized.
3. Which requires more managerial skill, working in a centralized or a decentralized organization? Explain your reasoning.

4. Give an example of how a company president might engage in horizontal decentralization.
5. Visualize yourself as a manager (if you are not presently one). All things being equal, would you prefer a span of control of two or ten? Why?
6. Why is the span of control of first-level supervisors typically much wider than that of executives?
7. Why do you think managers in large firms tend to delegate more than their counterparts in small firms?
8. Highly skilled technical specialists frequently are poor delegators when they first become managers. What do you think is the underlying reason for this problem?
9. At what stage in the history of a business organization is it likely to begin a movement toward recentralization?

ACTIVITIES

1. Interview an experienced manager, and ask that person how he or she gets around the problem of delegating tasks to people who are not yet carefully trained or capable of handling the delegated task.
2. Study any organization of your choosing, either through its annual report or through a printed story about the organization. Determine if the firm is more centralized or decentralized, based on any evidence you can gather from your information. Explain the basis for your conclusion.

CASE PROBLEM 7-A: THE PERFECTIONIST RETAILER

Kelly's is a group of three "deep-discount" drug stores. Each store sells brand merchandise at an average of 45 percent below list price. Although called drug stores, the chain sells hundreds of items in addition to pharmaceuticals, including stationery, watches, laundry materials, garden supplies, and beauty aids. In comparison to some discount stores, Kelly's sells only high-quality merchandise. The founder and owner of the chain is Kelly Gillen, a retail store professional who worked for a large department-store chain for fifteen years before opening the first Kelly's store.

Gillen explains why and how she started her own business: "I had a wonderful career with the big chain. They hired me as a store manager trainee right after I completed my degree in business administration. At age nineteen I saw no limits to my potential as a retailing executive. My career dreams were coming true. At age thirty-three I was promoted to a merchandising vice-president. One year later, I faced a career setback. My company was bought by a larger chain and they decided to cut most of our home-office staff. I was given six-months' severance pay.

"I couldn't find the job I wanted in my town, and I didn't want to relocate because of my husband and two children. Then it hit me that our city lacked a quality deep-discounter. So I founded Kelly's with some of my own cash, a home-equity loan, and money borrowed from a commercial bank. Getting started, I did everything that needed doing in the store, often working seventy hours per week. I merchandised; I unjammed cash registers; I hired employees; I even helped unload a truck when two of our warehouse employees were out sick. The business was an immediate success, and I was able to expand to two more locations."

Asked what challenges were facing her business these days, Kelly answered: "I'm having some problems with my three store managers. Each one has some problem accepting guidance and supervision from me. I like all three of my managers, but they seem to resist taking advice from a more experienced person. At times they seem to forget who calls the shots. They forget that they are employees and that I am the employer. I think this problem will take some time to resolve."

The three store managers were asked about the challenges they were facing. Each manager included comments about Ms. Gillen in his or her answer.

Luke Griffith, the most senior manager, raised this point. "God bless Kelly. She's one of the most successful deep-discounters in this region. But she runs the ship with the shortest leash you could imagine. One day she literally offered to fill my fountain pen for me because she can't stand to see a dry pen. When she visits my store, it's not unusual for her to straighten out merchandise in the aisles. She even sent one of my floor managers home because his shirt needed ironing."

Bridget Patton, the manager of the newest location, also commented on Gillen's approach to managing. "Our boss knows every detail about retailing, and she never lets you forget it. Kelly expects me to do things exactly the way she does. She appreciates my contribution, but she would rate my performance higher if I were her clone. At least once a week she says something to the effect, 'This is the proper way of handling this matter at Kelly's.' I like Kelly, but I wish she would give me more space."

Milt Bradley, the other store manager, said, "I'm happy to be working at Kelly's. Our profits are tremendous, and I think we have the potential for more growth. But to realize that growth, Kelly has got to realize she's a band leader, not the entire band. Her attitude is that the store managers are the pupils and that she's the master. Kelly tells me she offers so much advice because she wants everything to be perfect at Kelly's. It's hard for her to understand that people besides herself can properly manage one of her stores."

Case Questions

1. How does this case relate to the problem of delegation of authority?
2. What do you recommend the three store managers do to deal with the problems they are experiencing?
3. Whose perceptions about the issue of taking advice do you think is probably the most valid, Gillen's or the store managers'? What evidence does the case offer?

CASE PROBLEM 7-B: DECENTRALIZATION AT IBM

John F. Akers, chairman of IBM, decided several years ago that the sales improvements and cost-cutting measures taking place in his company were not good enough. In his evaluation, the measures taken were only temporary fixes. IBM therefore needed a major overhaul. On 28 January, 1988, a reorganization of IBM was announced that Akers described as the most significant restructuring of the company in thirty years.

Frustrated for many years by what he perceived to be a slow-moving headquarters bureaucracy, Akers delegated responsibility to a half-dozen general managers. With IBM's product lines and markets expanding continuously, Akers believed that "there's no way that one small set of managers at the top should think they are close enough to the action to make the decisions in all these areas." The relatively young managers were handed more power and asked to bring an entrepreneurial spirit to their lines of business.

A major reason for wanting to improve the efficiency of IBM is that the company is now being forced to compete on all fronts at once: minicomputers, PCs, software, and systems integration consulting. Even with the mainframe business, the company has worthy rivals, including Japanese computer manufacturers. Some analysts believe that IBM began to lose some of its competitive edge in the 1970s. For example, it has been charged that IBM salespeople lost sight of the problems customers wanted solved—concentrating more on just selling machines.

Improving products is the primary goal of the reorganization. By forming five autonomous product groups and pushing much of the decision-making down to general managers in these units, Akers hoped to overcome some of the delays in decision-making that had slowed product introductions. In the new structure, general managers in personal computer systems, midrange systems, mainframes, and communications will be given latitude to develop the products they need for their particular markets. The fifth new unit will be responsible for delivering state-of-the art building-block technology such as memory chips.

Source: As reported in "Big Changes at Big Blue," *Business Week* (15 February 1988): 92–93.

Case Questions

1. To what extent do you think the reorganization at IBM will achieve its aims of making IBM less bureaucratic and of improving its products?
2. How can one justify an executive tampering with the structure of an organization that has been so successful for so many years?
3. To what extent can an organization restructuring overcome the traditional ways of thinking at IBM?

REFERENCES

1. Carrie R. Leana, "Power Relinquishment Versus Power Sharing: Theoretical Clarification and Empirical Comparison of Delegation and Participation," *Journal of Applied Psychology* (May 1987): 229.
2. Henry Mintzberg, *Structure in Fives: Designing Effective Organizations* (Englewood Cliffs, NJ: Prentice Hall, 1983), 99.
3. Mintzberg, *Structure in Fives,* 105.
4. John R. Schermerhorn, Jr., *Management for Productivity,* 2nd ed. (New York: John Wiley & Sons, 1988).
5. William R. Tracey, "Deft Delegation: Multiplying Your Effectiveness," *Personnel* (February 1988): 36.

6. Andrew E. Schwartz, "The Why, What, and to Whom of Delegation," *Management Solutions* (June 1987): 33.

7. Personal communication from Bernard W. Weinrich, St. Louis Community College, St. Louis, MO.

8. Charles D. Pringle, "Seven Reasons Why Managers Don't Delegate," *Management Solutions* (November 1986): 26–30; Thomas J. Atchison and Winston W. Hill, *Management Today: Managing Work in Organizations* (New York: Harcourt Brace Jovanovich Inc., 1978), 102–104; Ricky W. Griffin, *Management,* 2nd ed. (Boston: Houghton Mifflin Co., 1988).

9. Some of the ideas in this list are based on David A. Whetton and Kim S. Cameron, *Developing Management Skills* (Glenview, IL: Scott, Foresman & Co., 1984), 363–369; and Tracey, "Deft Delegation," 36–38.

10. Suzanne Savary, "Ineffective Delegation—Symptom or Problem?" *Supervisory Management* (June 1985) 29.

11. Ernest Dale, *Planning and Developing the Company Organization Structure,* Research Report No. 20 (New York: American Management Assns., 1952), 107.

12. Howard M. Carlisle, *Management: Concepts and Situations* (Chicago: Science Research Assocs., Inc., 1976), 397–399.

13. Ross A. Webber, *Management: Basic Elements of Managing Organizations,* rev. ed. (Homewood, IL: Richard D. Irwin, Inc., 1979), 380.

14. Several of the items in this list are based on Carlisle, *Management: Concepts and Situations,* 401–402.

15. Carrie R. Leana, "Predictors and Consequences of Delegation," *Academy of Management Journal* (December 1986): 763.

16. Harold Koontz, Cyril O'Donnell, and Heinz Wiehrich, *Management,* 7th ed. (New York: McGraw-Hill, 1980), 435–436.

17. Robert L. Trewatha and M. Gene Newport, *Management,* 3d. ed, (Plano, TX: Business Pubs., Inc., 1982), 279.

8
Staffing the Organization

After studying the material in this chapter, you should be able to accomplish the following tasks:

1. Present an overview of the components of organizational staffing.
2. Be aware of the legal aspects of staffing.
3. Explain the importance of human-resource planning.
4. Summarize the basics of employee compensation and benefits.
5. Present an overview of recruitment selection and placement.
6. Present an overview of employee orientation, training, and development.
7. Describe a fair and reliable method of evaluating employee performance.

Key Terms and Phrases

Staffing	Job description
Affirmative action	Job specification
Affirmative action programs	Validity study
Comparable worth	Reference check
Human-Resource Planning (HRP)	Placement
Job evaluation	Employee orientation program
Job analysis	Training
Employee benefit	Development
Flexible benefit package	Performance appraisal
Recruitment	Traits
Contingent workers	Behavior
Realistic job preview	Results

This final chapter about organizing deals with the heart of human-resource management—staffing the organization. **Staffing** is the process of making sure there are the necessary human resources to achieve organizational goals.[1] Staffing the organization requires many subactivities. Among them are forecasting personnel requirements, recruiting and selecting employees, and evaluating employees' performance. The comprehensiveness of staffing is depicted in Figure 8-1, the organizational staffing model. Chapter 8 is organized around the components of this model.

Figure 8-1   The Organizational Staffing Model

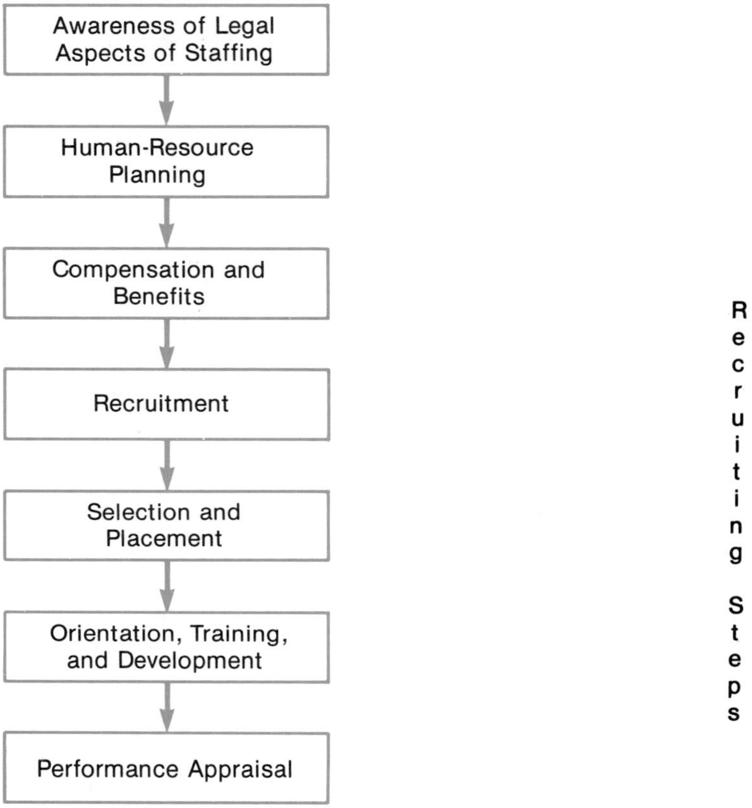

```
        ┌─────────────────────────┐
        │   Awareness of Legal    │
        │   Aspects of Staffing   │
        └─────────────────────────┘
                     │
                     ▼
        ┌─────────────────────────┐
        │    Human-Resource       │
        │       Planning          │
        └─────────────────────────┘
                     │
                     ▼
        ┌─────────────────────────┐
        │   Compensation and      │
        │       Benefits          │
        └─────────────────────────┘
                     │
                     ▼
        ┌─────────────────────────┐
        │      Recruitment        │
        └─────────────────────────┘
                     │
                     ▼
        ┌─────────────────────────┐
        │     Selection and       │
        │       Placement         │
        └─────────────────────────┘
                     │
                     ▼
        ┌─────────────────────────┐
        │  Orientation, Training, │
        │    and Development      │
        └─────────────────────────┘
                     │
                     ▼
        ┌─────────────────────────┐
        │  Performance Appraisal  │
        └─────────────────────────┘
```

Recruiting Steps

THE STAFFING MODEL

The staffing model communicates the important message that the process flows in a logical sequence. Although not every organization follows the same steps in the same sequence, we can outline how staffing ordinarily proceeds.

First, the major legal aspects of all phases of staffing are studied. Second, an attempt is made to predict the number and type of people who will be needed at various points in the future of the firm. Third, wages and salaries and employee benefits are established for the jobs to be filled. Fourth, recruitment is undertaken—a search for people to fill the jobs. Overlapping with recruitment is the fifth step, choosing from among the job candidates and assigning them to actual jobs. Sixth, the employees selected are oriented to the company, trained, and developed. Training and development is a continuing process that takes place at various points in the employee's tenure with the firm. Seventh, employees receive a performance appraisal; a manager evaluates how well employees are meeting their job responsibilities. Performance appraisals also include suggesting to employees the steps necessary to improve their performance and personal growth.

Human-resource (or personnel) specialists are heavily engaged in the staffing function. Their staffing activities include providing tools for making human-resource forecasts, setting up selection procedures, and conducting training programs. Line managers, however, still carry ultimate responsibility for staffing their own departments. The typical working relationship is for personnel specialists to work with managers to help make better staffing decisions. For example, an employment specialist in addition to your prospective boss may interview you for a job. The two will pool their thinking to reach an accurate evaluation of your suitability for employment.

Many of the components of staffing described in this chapter are more likely to be carried out by large rather than small organizations. Because many small firms may not have a full-fledged personnel department, they take shortcuts in staffing. For example, a small business is unlikely to conduct its own job evaluation in order to establish a salary level for a given job. Instead, management relies on an estimate of the going rate for the job. Despite these exceptions, most of the principles and procedures described in this chapter have some applicability for organizations of all sizes.

LEGAL ASPECTS OF STAFFING

Federal, state, provincial, and local laws influence every aspect of organizational staffing. Managers and human-resource specialists must keep the major provisions of these laws in mind whenever they make decisions about any phase of employment. For example, it is illegal to advertise "Young woman wanted for secretarial position." This ad would discriminate against three groups: older women, young men, and older men! To make matters worse, many readers would complain that the ad is sexist because it implies that women are more suited than men for secretarial work.

In this section, we summarize five key pieces of legislation that influence various aspects of staffing—not just employee selection. Later, as we examine the different components of staffing, we will describe relevant legislation again.

Civil Rights Act of 1964, Title VII

Title VII of the Civil Rights Act of 1964 prohibits discrimination, in all employment decisions, on the basis of race, sex, religion, color, or national origin. The Equal Employment Opportunity Act of 1972 extends this legislation to include discrimination against people with physical disabilities. All employers, including labor unions, with fifteen or more employees are covered by these two acts. Five groups of people are specifically protected under Title VII: blacks, Hispanics, Native Americans, Asian-Pacific Islanders, and women. However, the specification of five groups does not mean that it is legal to discriminate against other groups.

Because of the law's complexity, a special agency was created to administer Title VII. The Equal Employment Opportunity Commission (EEOC) both administers the law and investigates complaints about violations. It also has the power to issue guidelines for interpretation of the act.

Executive Orders and Amendments. Several executive orders provide specific guidelines on how employers must comply with the Civil Rights Act of 1964. Employers with federal contracts or subcontracts must develop affirmative action programs to help end discrimination. **Affirmative action** is a process of complying with antidiscrimination law *and* of correcting past discriminatory practices. An **affirmative action program** is a specific program implemented by an employer to eliminate job discrimination in all phases of employment. Under the plan, employers actively recruit, employ, train, and promote minorities and women who may have been discriminated against by the employer in the past and hence are underrepresented in certain positions. Part of an affirmative action plan might include a career development program for women to help them qualify for management positions.

The major intent of affirmative action programs is to overcome past injustices against minorities and women. To achieve this goal, there have been times when white males have been denied equal access to jobs. A 1987 Supreme Court decision ruled that an employer may sometimes favor women and minority-group employees to remedy a "conspicuous imbalance" in the employer's work force. Critics contend that this amounts to "reverse discrimination." The current status of affirmative action programs is that the seniority rights of white males *can* be protected. Nevertheless, the employer must proceed with an affirmative action program for women and minorities at the same time.

By the late 1980s, the U.S. government was playing a less active role in investigating complaints of employment discrimination. This was reflected in changed tactics by the EEOC. The EEOC began to concentrate on individual cases of alleged discrimination. In the past, the EEOC tried to identify company-wide or industry-wide employment biases. Also, federal agencies associated with EEOC are giving less weight to the number of minority employees hired and promoted. Instead, they emphasize making sure that personnel policies are fair.

The U.S. Commission on Civil Rights has acted in opposition to many of the initiatives of the EEOC. In recent years, the commission has criticized preferences for women, blacks, and Hispanics. In addition, the commission has challenged the Supreme Court's legal reasoning and its ability to understand the constitutional limits on affirmative action.[2]

Age Discrimination, Equal Pay, and the Handicapped

Several major acts have focused on specific aspects of staffing. These include the Age Discrimination Act, the Equal Pay Act, and the Vocational Rehabilitation Act. Their provisions are less comprehensive than those of Title VII, but these major legislative acts do influence organizational staffing.

Age Discrimination in Employment Act.   This 1967 act applies to employers with at least twenty-five employees. As amended in 1978, it prohibits discrimination against people between the ages of forty and seventy years in any area of employment because of age. Under this act, mandatory retirement ended in 1987 for most employees covered by its provisions. There is, however, a seven-year exemption for certain law enforcement and fire fighting personnel and tenured college faculty.[3] The median age of the work force is increasing, so the influence of this act will also increase. So far, this act has been enforced primarily with respect to pay and retirement policies and practices. Despite the emphasis on retirement policies, very few early-retirement programs or layoffs have been challenged by the courts.

Equal Pay Act.   According to this 1963 act, employers are prohibited from paying unequal wages on the basis of sex. It states, "When male and female workers perform work requiring equal skills, effort, and responsibility, and perform under similar working conditions, they must receive equal pay." This act still allows for paying women and men different wages if the difference is based on ability or seniority.

Current thinking is more concerned with **comparable worth** than with equal pay. This concept means that people performing jobs with different titles should receive equal pay if their jobs are of comparable value to the organization.[4] Based on this doctrine, an administrative assistant who is female should receive the same pay as an assistant to the manager who is male if the two positions are of comparable value to the organization. The challenge is to find a standard for measuring comparable worth. Job evaluation, to be described later in this chapter, is the best-known method of assigning equal pay to comparable jobs.

Vocational Rehabilitation Act.   Discrimination against people with physical or mental handicaps is prohibited by this law, which was passed in 1973. An important implication of the Vocational Rehabilitation Act is that employers are forced to make accommodations so that physically challenged people can perform jobs. This could include ramps for people in wheelchairs and telephones adapted to the requirements of the hearing impaired. Courts and governmental agencies have had a busy time interpreting who is "handicapped." One controversial interpretation is that an employer is obliged to pay for the rehabilitation of a drug abuser. A government agency has reasoned that a drug abuser is mentally handicapped. Therefore, rehabilitation is necessary to help this person attain satisfactory job performance.

HUMAN-RESOURCE PLANNING

Staffing begins with a prediction about how many and what types of people will be needed to conduct the work of the firm. Activity of this nature is referred to as **human-resource planning (HRP)**—the process of anticipating and providing for the movement of people into, within, and out of the organization.[5] HRP is one application of the planning model described in Chapter 3, and it uses similar tools.

Steps in HRP

According to James A. F. Stoner and Charles Wankel, there are four basic steps in human-resource planning.[6]

1. *Planning for future needs.* An estimate is made of how many people, and with what abilities, the firm will need to operate in the foreseeable future.

2. *Planning for future turnover.* A prediction is made of how many current employees are likely to remain with the organization. The difference between this number and the number of employees needed leads to the next step.

3. *Planning for recruitment, selection, and layoffs.* The organization must engage in these activities to attain the required number of employees.

4. *Planning for training and development.* An organization will always need a supply of experienced and competent workers. This step involves planning for training and development programs so the supply of people with the right skills meets the demand.

A major consideration in accomplishing these steps is to tie HRP to strategic planning. If the firm intends to expand, HRP must be geared toward such expansion. If retrenchment is on the horizon, HRP must find an effective way of paring down the size of the organization. Perfect predictions are rarely achieved through HRP. When the organization finds itself over- or understaffed, decisive action must be taken. Although planning of this type has much to offer an organization, relatively few firms yet carefully develop long-range human-resource plans.[7]

COMPENSATION AND BENEFITS

Compensation and benefits are a key part of staffing for obvious reasons. One is that almost every employee demands compensation in the form of money and company-paid benefits such as medical insurance and pensions. Another is that compensation and benefits represent the single biggest expense for most organizations. We discuss compensation and benefits before recruitment because it is difficult to recruit prior to setting wage levels.

External Forces on Compensation Levels

Pay levels are influenced by many factors outside the firm. One example is that certain occupations command relatively high pay. If a firm wants to hire employees in that occupation they have to pay them approximately what other firms pay.

Supply and Demand.   Wages are the price paid for the services of a person. Those people whose skills are needed and who are in short supply will receive relatively higher pay. Air-traffic controllers would fit into this category at present. Those people in large supply who have skills in low demand usually receive low pay. Farm workers fit into this category at present.

Government Influences.   Compensation levels are carefully monitored by all levels of government, particularly with respect to minimum wage. Unemployment compensation laws are a prime example of how the government influences an important employee benefit. According to these laws, employers must purchase unemployment insurance. Employees who are laid off or fired—not those who quit—are then eligible to receive unemployment compensation. Typically, these benefits extend to about one year.

The Fair Labor Standards Act (FLSA) exerts a strong influence on employee compensation. Private employers with revenues greater than $325,000 per year who are involved in interstate commerce are covered by this act. These employers are required to pay time-and-one-half for work over forty hours per week, and a minimum hourly wage for covered employees. Certain managerial, technical, and professional employees are exempt from these provisions.

Union Influences.   Unions directly influence the wages of employees in unionized firms by negotiating with employers to set wage levels. Union rates are often used to set minimum rates for nonunion jobs. Less obvious is the fact that unions also indirectly influence wages. To discourage employees from joining a union, companies often pay union-level wages. Well-established nonunion firms tend to pay wages that are quite competitive with union firms. Firms that dip below these wage levels may have difficulty attracting and retaining well-qualified employees. Union-employee salaries also tend to elevate the salaries of nonunion employees within the same firm.

Compensation Surveys.   A convenient method of setting pay rates is to obtain data from wage surveys. These are conducted by special-purpose firms and by trade magazines. State employment agencies also help in the wage survey. Knowledgeable employees often seek out these surveys to find out if they are being compensated fairly. If valid, the information contained in these surveys can help a firm prevent costly overpayments to employees or turnover due to underpayments. Wage surveys, nevertheless, have been criticized for providing irrelevant guidelines for salary decisions about individuals. Information about median salaries, for example, does not indicate how much a highly talented individual may be worth.[8]

Cost-of-Living Raises.   Many firms give employees an annual cost-of-living adjustment (COLA) based on the previous year's inflation rate. If the inflation rate is high, COLAs tend to perpetuate inflation. It works this way: first, assume last year's inflation rate was 6 percent; then, this year, everybody on a COLA system receives a 10-percent increase. This helps bolster inflation for the next year because wages, and therefore prices, are high for another year.

Establishing Pay Levels through Job Evaluation

The five external forces we mentioned provide information for establishing the pay rates for specific jobs. However, internal methods of setting wage rates are also important. The most widely used internal method is **job evaluation**, a systematic method of measuring the financial worth of a job. Job evaluations can be accomplished through several different methods.[9] We will describe the basics of the most widely used form of job evaluation, the point system.

A **job analysis** is a method of determining what tasks make up the job and what skills, abilities, and responsibilities are required of an individual in order to successfully accomplish the job.[10] For instance, the job of restaurant manager would require considerable skill in working with people and working under pressure. A job analysis is needed prior to conducting the job evaluation. Some factors included in a job analysis are contained in the left column of Table 8-1. A job evaluation measures how much of each dimension is required by the job.

Table 8-1 The Point System of Job Evaluation

Job Factor	Evaluation Points				
	Very Low	Low	Moderate	High	Very High
Education	20	40	60	80	100
Experience	25	50	75	100	125
Job complexity	35	70	105	140	175
Human relations	15	30	45	60	75
Physical demands	5	10	15	20	25
Totals	100	200	300	400	500

Establishing Point Values. An important step in the point system of job evaluation is to establish point values for the demands made on a job holder. The degree to which certain job factors are required determines how many points a job receives. For example, if education is a very high requirement, the job would receive 100 points for that factor alone. The five factors shown in Table 8-1 are education, experience, job complexity, human-relations skills, and physical demands. These are merely five representative factors. Another job evaluation is likely to use different factors.

A determination is made by a job-evaluation committee as to how much each factor is worth if it exists in certain degrees. In Table 8-1, very high job complexity is worth 175 points; very low human-relations skill is worth 15 points. Note that the total of the lowest points for all the factors is 100. This happens because the point value for the lowest degree of each factor is the percentage value assigned each factor. In Table 8-1, education is worth 20 percent; experience, 25 percent; job complexity, 35 percent; human-relations skill, 15 percent; and physical demands, 5 percent. All the higher degree points increase in an arithmetic progression. Observe that the factor of experience follows the progression: 25, 50, 75, 100 and 125.

Conversion to Pay Grades.   Point scores for specific jobs are converted into pay grades by establishing point range categories that correspond to salary grades. Once the points for a specific job are computed, these points are translated into a salary range. The more points, the higher the salary grade, and the higher the pay. The point range and corresponding salary grade for Table 8-1 are shown in Table 8-2.

Comparing Jobs.   Point values have now been established for the amount of each of five factors present in the job. Also, a chart has been prepared for converting the total points in a job to salary grades 1 through 13. We are now ready to evaluate jobs and compare their relative salaries. To illustrate, we will compare the jobs of robotics technician and office supervisor. To arrive at an accurate job evaluation, two key people are needed: a job-evaluation specialist and a knowledgeable supervisor.

The comparative evaluations of the two jobs are shown in Table 8-3. Observe that a judgment is made for how much of each job factor is contained

Table 8-2   Pay Grade Conversions

Point Range	Salary Grade	Point Range	Salary Grade
Below 145	1	295–315	8
145–165	2	320–340	9
170–190	3	345–365	10
195–215	4	370–390	11
220–240	5	395–415	12
245–265	6	420–500	13
270–290	7		

Table 8-3   Job Evaluation Comparison of Two Different Jobs

Job Factors	Robotics Technician	Office Supervisor
Education	Moderate = 60	High = 80
Experience	Low = 50	High = 100
Job complexity	High = 140	Moderate = 105
Human relations	Low = 30	Very High = 75
Physical demands	High = 20	Very Low = 5
Total Points	300	365

in the jobs of robotics technician and office supervisor. These judgments are made in reference to specific jobs in a specific setting. They may not necessarily reflect industry standards. According to this analysis, the job of robotics technician receives 300 points, whereas that of office supervisor receives 365. A robotics technician falls into salary grade 8, whereas the office supervisor falls into grade 10. The company assigns to these grades dollar values that are changed periodically to reflect inflation.

Not every person in the same salary grade receives identical pay. Each grade has a range, such as $21,500 to $26,750. Differences within each range are related to performance, seniority, and even favoritism.

Linking Compensation to Strategy and Performance. Under ideal circumstances, compensation should be closely tied in with organizational strategy and individual performance. The purpose of linking compensation programs to strategy is to help the organization attain its strategic goals. Assume that an organization has established the strategic goal of becoming more entrepreneurial and growth-minded. Executive compensation could then be geared to give managers high incentives for ideas that help the firm grow. If the organizational strategy were to increase earnings, the compensation strategy would be different. It would pay executives small incentives for holding down costs.[11]

The purpose of linking compensation to performance is to stimulate people to work harder. The technique of linking pay to performance has long been used with production workers. A dominant current trend is to relate the compensation of managers and many other workers to performance.[12] Table 8-4 presents a typical example of how organizations attempt to adjust pay to performance (or grant merit increases).

Employee Benefits

An **employee benefit** is any noncash payment given to workers as a condition of their employment. These payments were formerly referred to as "fringe" benefits because they were a trimming that made the compensation more attractive. Virtually all full-time employees today receive these benefits; they are no longer perceived as fringes. Employee benefits cost employers about 35 percent of cash salaries![13] This means an employee earning $30,000 per year in salary therefore receives a combined salary and benefit package of $40,500.

The fastest-growing trend in benefits is to offer employees **flexible benefit packages**. A benefit plan of this nature allows employees to select a group of benefits tailored to their preferences. Flexible benefits are also referred to as "cafeteria plans" because employees pick and choose benefits according to their tastes. Flexible compensation plans generally provide employees with one category of fixed benefits—minimum standards such as medical and disability insurance. The second category is flexible with a menu of benefits from which each employee chooses according to individual preferences. Each employee is allowed to select benefits up to a certain total cost. An employee who prefers less vacation time, for instance, might choose more life insurance. In some in-

Table 8-4   Linking Pay to Performance through Merit Increases

Performance Level	Merit Increase
1. **Excellent to Outstanding Performance** Employees in this category meet all and substantially exceed some performance expectations and exemplify outstanding commitment, dedication, and excellence.	8 percent or more
2. **Performance Fully Meeting All Expectations** These employees meet all performance expectations, are characterized by their full commitment to their job responsibilities, and are viewed as highly productive.	6 to 7 percent
3. **Performance That Needs Improvement** Employees in this category demonstrate performance that is uneven and not fully satisfactory, even though some performance standards may be met or even exceeded. Further development in certain areas of responsibility is required so that full potential for satisfactory performance may be achieved.	4 percent
4. **Unsatisfactory Performance** Employees in this category generally fail to meet key performance criteria and expectations. Substantial improvement is essential.	0 percent

stances, employees can choose between taxable and nontaxable benefits—a bonus that has stirred new interest in the flexible benefits concept.[14]

A comprehensive list of employee benefits is shown in Table 8-5. Organizations vary considerably in the benefits and services they offer employees.[15] No one firm is likely to offer all of these benefits. Large, older firms tend to offer the most benefits.

RECRUITMENT

Recruitment is the process of attracting job candidates with the right characteristics and skills to fill job openings. Generally, we think of recruiting people outside the firm, but job openings can also be filled with present employees. A major advantage of outside recruiting is that a wider range of candidates is attracted. A disadvantage is that the process of screening all these candidates is time-consuming and expensive.

A major advantage of internal recruitment is that current employees often refer only candidates they know will make a contribution to the company. A disadvantage is that current employees may restrict their referrals to people of

Table 8-5   Employee Benefits

Usually Mandatory

Social Security
Worker's Compensation
Unemployment Compensation

Group life insurance
Disability insurance
Retirement pensions
Paid vacations

Optional but Frequently Offered

Group life insurance
Retirement pensions
Disability insurance
Accidental health insurance
Paid lunch breaks
Paid sick leave
Health insurance
Relocation allowance, moving costs

Tuition assistance
Paid rest or refreshment breaks
Paid vacations

Company-subsidized cafeteria
Employee training
Personal time off
Paid maternity leaves

Optional and Less Frequently Offered

Paid travel time to work
Physical-fitness and
    wellness programs
Stress-management programs
Credit unions
Cash payments for unused vacation time
Discount-purchasing programs
Funeral pay

Carpooling services
Retirement counseling
Outplacement counseling
Child-care centers
Payment of adoption fees
Paid paternity leave
Parental leave
Vision-care plans

similar tastes, interests, and cultural backgrounds. This may prevent the firm from capitalizing on diverse thinking. It may also lead to the exclusion of some ethnic and racial group members as candidates.

Recruitment applies to searching for full-time employees, part-time employees, and temporary workers. The last two groups are referred to as **contingent workers**—people who perform work for the firm but are not members of the permanent work force. About one fourth of all employees are contingent workers. Some of these employees are temporary workers hired through temporary service agencies. Others are part-timers, employees of subcontractors, people who do piecework at home, and leased workers. Leasing occurs when an organization's work force is transferred to a leasing firm who hires the employees, pays their salaries and benefits, and then leases them back to the original employer. Leasing can provide cost advantages to small firms because the leasing firm can provide benefits more inexpensively when it takes over the work force of many firms.[16]

Recruitment also has a big influence on employee turnover and retention. When job candidates are given a realistic job preview, they are less likely to quit when they encounter job frustration.[17] **A realistic job preview** is a frank discussion of all aspects of the job, both positive and negative.

The two key aspects of recruitment discussed here are job descriptions and specifications, and sources of job candidates.

Job Descriptions and Job Specifications

A **job description** is a written statement outlining the key features of the job along with the activities required to perform the job effectively. The job description explains in detail what the job holder is supposed to do. It is therefore a vital document for several aspects of staffing, including HRP, job evaluation, and performance appraisal.

The **job specification** stems directly from the job description. It is a statement of the personal characteristics needed to perform the job. A job specification usually includes the education, experience, knowledge, and skills required to perform the job successfully. Both the job description and the job specifications should be based on a careful job analysis. A job analysis is a gathering of basic facts about the job. Job evaluations also rely on job descriptions.

Recruiting Sources

The term *recruitment* connotes newspaper advertisements and campus recruiters. Yet about 85 percent of jobs are filled by word of mouth. The remaining 15 percent are filled through external means such as classified advertisements, employment agencies, and recruiting trips.[19] Recruiting sources can be classified into three categories.

1. *Present employees.* A standard recruiting method is to post job openings so that current employees may apply. Another way to recruit current employees is for managers to recommend them for transfer or promotion. One potential problem with internal recruiting is that unqualified employees have to be turned down without creating morale problems. A computerized human-resource information system is helpful in identifying current employees with the right skills. This minimizes having to reject unqualified internal applicants.

2. *Referrals by present employees.* If a firm is already established, present employees can be the primary recruiting source. Satisfied employees may be willing to nominate relatives, friends, acquaintances, and neighbors for job openings.

3. *External sources.* There are a number of ways to reach potential employees outside the organization. The best known of these methods is a recruiting advertisement as illustrated in Figure 8-2. Other external sources include the following:

   - Placement offices at educational institutions
   - Private employment agencies

Figure 8-2   A Local Recruiting Advertisement for a Famous Company.

MANAGEMENT CAREER OPPORTUNITIES

At McDonald's We Give it to You Straight.

Affirmative Action Is Fair Business. In Fact, It's Good Business.

Call it Affirmative Action if you wish ... we call it fair business and good business. Fair because long before most others, we were hiring people by ability. Good business because of the special knowledge each person has about their friends and neighbors and the right way to treat them.

Your knowledge will help us ... and you ... achieve success. You'll learn virtually every aspect of management from the world's largest restaurant organization. This is a serious career with a Fortune 100 corporation which will provide you with:

- Valuable training.
- Salary increases and promotions based solely on performance—not seniority.
- An excellent starting salary.
- Excellent company-paid benefits.
- Advancement potential that's as strong as your desire to succeed.

If you have management experience and/or some college and are interested in a great career at McDonald's, send your resume to: Rich Dowd, McDonald's Corporation of East Henrietta, 2121 East Henrietta Road, Dept. RD1216, Rochester, NY 14623.

Always, An Equal Opportunity/Affirmative Action Employer.

Powered By People With Pride.

Source: Courtesy of McDonald's Corporation.

- Public employment agencies (those operated by the state or province)
- Labor union hiring hall
- Walk-ins (people who show up at the firm without invitation)
- Write-ins (people who write unsolicited job-seeking letters)

The matching of employers with job candidates is becoming increasingly computerized. Job seekers can now register with a computerized recruitment service at low or no cost. Employers, in turn, can decrease by 75 percent the cost of locating, screening, and hiring job applicants when the system works properly.[20]

SELECTION AND PLACEMENT

Selecting the right candidate for the job is part of a continuous process that includes recruitment and placement. Our summary of the steps in selection and placement follows the model presented in Figure 8-3. A hiring decision is based on a combination of information gathered in two or more of these steps. For instance, a person might receive a job offer if he or she was impressive in the interview, scored well on the tests, and had good references. Another important feature of this selection model is that an applicant can be rejected at any point. An applicant who is abusive to the employment specialist might not be asked to fill out an application form.

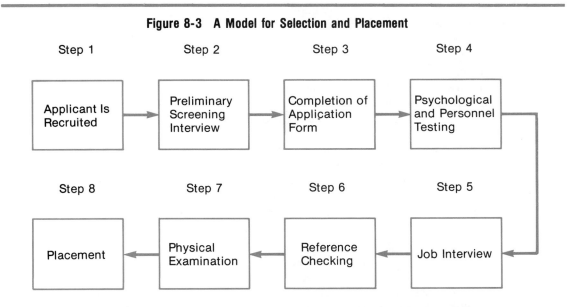

Figure 8-3   A Model for Selection and Placement

Preliminary Screening Interview

Selection begins as soon as candidates come to the attention of the recruiter. If candidates appear to come close to fitting the job specifications, a brief screening interview is conducted. The purpose of the screening interview is to determine if the candidate should be given further consideration. "Knockout" questions are sometimes used for this purpose. Should the candidate give an unacceptable answer to a key question, he or she is knocked out of further consideration. For example, assume a person is applying for a supervisory position in a nursing home. The interviewer asks, "How well do you get along with senior citizens?" A candidate who responds, "Very poorly," is immediately disqualified.

Candidates who pass the screening interview are asked to fill out a job application form. Sometimes this process is reversed, and a screening interview is conducted after the candidate successfully completes the application form.

Job Application Forms

Job application forms are a standard part of any selection procedure. They serve two important purposes. One is to furnish basic biographical data about the candidate, including his or her education, work experience, and citizenship. The other is to provide information that could be related to success on the job. Assume the job called for an individual with careful work habits. A sloppily completed application form *could* indicate that the candidate has poor work habits. In contrast, a carefully completed form *could* indicate that the candidate has the careful work habits needed for the job.

Job application forms and employment interviews no longer ask direct or indirect questions about race, religion, ethnic background, marital status, sexual preference, or handicap. All of these questions are considered discriminatory and thus are illegal if they are not job related.[21] Yet there are unusual circumstances in which it is acceptable to ask questions about race or ethnic background. If Air India wanted to hire an Indian to manage its New York office, it would be acceptable to ask a candidate, "Are you an Asiatic Indian?" It makes good business sense for the public to see an Indian working in the Air India office. It lends credibility to the fact that the airline is Indian.

In many firms, psychological and personnel tests are given before the interview. Some firms use the interview before the tests, and some firms skip testing altogether. It is helpful for testing to precede interviewing because the test results may provide some clues about topics to pursue in the interview. If a candidate scored very low on a scale measuring "energy," the candidate might be asked, "Do you find it difficult to get started working in the morning?"

Psychological and Personnel Testing

Hundreds of different tests are used in employment testing. All tests are really psychological tests in that measuring human ability is an important part of psychology. We also use the term *personnel testing* because many people think psychological tests deal with personality, whereas personnel tests deal directly with job skills. Three aspects of testing will be mentioned here: the different types of tests, EEOC requirements, and a comment about the validity of tesing in making staffing decisions.

Types of Psychological and Personnel Tests. Four principal types of psychological and personnel tests are in current use: achievement, aptitude, personality, and interest tests. A fifth category, honesty tests, is gaining in use.

1. *Achievement tests* sample and measure the applicant's knowledge and skills.[22] They require applicants to demonstrate their competency on job tasks or related subjects. A person applying for a position as a paralegal assistant might be given a test about real-estate and matrimonial law.

2. *Aptitude tests* measure an applicant's capacity or potential for performing satisfactorily on the job, given sufficient training. Mental-ability tests are the best-known variety of aptitude test. They measure ability to solve problems and learn new material. Mental-ability tests measure such specific aptitudes as verbal reasoning, numerical reasoning, and spatial relations (visualizing three dimensions). Scores on mental-ability tests are related to success in most jobs in which intelligence is important. An example of a specialized aptitude test is the Programming Aptitude Test, used to measure aptitude for computer programming.

3. *Personality tests* measure personal traits and characteristics that could be related to job performance. Among the many personal characteristics measured by these tests are dominance, self-confidence, energy, and impulsive thinking. Personality tests have been the subject of considerable controversy for many years. Critics are concerned that these tests invade privacy and are too imprecise to be useful. Nevertheless, personality factors have a profound influence on job performance.

4. *Interest tests* measure preferences for engaging in certain activities such as mechanical, clerical, literary, or managerial work. They also measure a person's interest in specific occupations such as accountant, veterinarian, or sales representative. Interest tests are designed to indicate whether a person would enjoy a particular activity or occupation. They do not attempt, however, to measure a person's aptitude for that activity or occupation.

5. *Honesty tests* are of two types: paper-and-pencil tests and polygraph tests (often referred to as lie-detector tests). Paper-and-pencil honesty tests ask people questions that directly or indirectly measure their tendency not to tell the truth. A direct question would be, "Should a person be fired for stealing ten dollars from the employer?" (A dishonest person would answer "no.") An indirect question would be, "Do you read the editorial page of the local newspaper every day?" (Only a dishonest person would answer Yes. Almost nobody can claim a perfect record in this regard.)[23]

Polygraphs record a person's blood pressure, heart rate, breathing rate, and galvanic skin response (a change in electrical resistance that can be triggered by stress). The tests last only a few minutes. Key questions in a job-screening test might include the following: Have you ever withheld information about a theft from a former or present employer? Have you ever omitted or falsified information on an application?

Polygraphs also take measures of a person's response to relatively neutral questions such as, "Do you have any hobbies or interests?" The level of emotional responses to neutral questions are then compared to the responses to key questions. According to the logic of polygraph testing, people experience surges of emotion when lying. These are measured by the physiological signs, such as increased breathing rate.

Polygraph tests are the subject of bitter controversy. Polygraph experts contend that, in the hands of a trained examiner, the test is reliable. Critics say the tests are intrusive, unreliable, detect nothing of value, and insult the people taking them.[24] William Safire says "The best polygraph operators often fail because honest people do get nervous and liars can be trained to beat the system."[25] The federal Employee Polygraph Protection Act virtually eliminates the use of polygraph for pre-employment screening. Pre-employment polygraphs can still be administered by federal, state, and local governments, and federal contractors engaged in national security activities. Job applicants for security firms hired to protect business activities involving health and safety can also be tested. Also, drug companies can test applicants for positions with direct access to drugs. The act provides penalties of up to $10,000 a day for violations.

Despite these restrictions on polygraph testing for job applicants, companies can still use polygraphs to investigate specific thefts. However, workers asked to take the test must be given at least forty-eight hours notice and a statement of their rights. Refusal to take the test cannot be used as the basis for dismissal.[26]

Equal Employment Opportunity and Testing.   The EEOC insists that selection tests should be scientifically accurate, job related, and not discriminatory against any group. These rules also apply to other selection instruments including application forms and interviews. A specific provision requires a validity study when a selection procedure has adverse impact on any race, sex, or ethnic group. A **validity study** is a statistical and scientific method of seeing if the selection device does predict job performance. Do high scorers perform well on the job? Do low scorers prove to be poor performers?

Validity of Psychological and Personnel Tests.   Thousands of studies have been conducted about the ability of tests to predict job performance. Some studies explore how well groups of tests used in combination predict job performance. These studies are considered the most valuable because, in practice, employment tests are often used in combinations referred to as test batteries. There is considerable disagreement about the contribution of employment tests to the selection process. Nevertheless, it appears that, used as intended, employment testing does improve the accuracy of selection decisions.

For example, long-term research conducted at the United States Employment Service concluded that standardized ability tests are fair and valid predictors of performance for all jobs. Furthermore, such tests provide employers and the country with a powerful tool for improving work force productivity.[27]

The Job Interview

The interview that follows testing is more thorough and comprehensive than the screening interview. Most job interviews are semistructured—they follow a format, yet allow the interviewer room for additional questioning. The unlawful inquiries mentioned in relation to job application forms apply equally well to the interview. The topics covered in a job interview include education, work experience, special skills and abilities, hobbies, and interests. Interviewers frequently use the candidate's resume as a source of topics. For example, ''I notice you have worked for four employers in three years. Why is that?''

Although the accuracy of the interview is frequently challenged by personnel psychologists, it is an indispensable tool. Interviews tend to be the most valid when they are carefully structured (tightly organized) and all applicants are asked the same standard questions.[28] (However, unique questions can also be asked of each candidate.) Selection interviews have a dual purpose. The interviewer is trying to decide whether the interviewee is appropriate for the organization. At the same time, the interviewee is trying to decide if this job and this organization are appropriate for him or her. Guidelines for conducting a productive job interview are presented in Table 8-6. Considerable practice is required to become a skillful interviewer. You must practice during both real and simulated job interviews.

Table 8-6 Guidelines for Conducting an Effective Selection Interview

1. *Prepare in advance.* Review carefully the applicant's job application form and resume prior to the interview. Keep in mind several questions worthy of exploration during the interview, such as ''I notice you have done no previous selling. Why do you want a sales job now?''
2. *Find a quiet place free from interruptions.* Effective interviewing requires careful concentration. Also, the candidate deserves the courtesy of an uninterrupted interview.
3. *Ask only lawful questions.* A general guideline is to ask only job-related questions. Also, ask no questions directly or indirectly related to race, age, nationality, marital status, sex, sexual orientation, or physical or mental handicaps.
4. *Take notes during the interview.* It is essential to take notes on the content of what is said during the interview. Also, record your observations about the person's statements and behavior. For example, ''Candidate gets very nervous when we talk about previous work history.''
5. *Use a brief warm-up period.* A standard way of relaxing a job candidate is to spend about five minutes talking about neutral topics such as the

Table 8-6   Guidelines for Conducting an Effective Selection Interview (Continued)

weather. This brief period can be extended by asking about basic facts such as the person's address and social security number.

6. *Avoid keeping in mind a stereotype of the ideal candidate for the job.* Stereotyped thinking may close your mind to the potential value of many candidates.

7. *Ask open-ended questions.* To encourage the employee to talk, ask questions that call for more than a one- or two-word answer. Sometimes a request for information works like an open-ended question. To illustrate, "Tell me about your days at business school."

8. *Follow an interview format.* Effective interviewers carefully follow a predetermined interview format. Additional questions can be asked based on responses to the structured questions.

9. *Give the job candidate encouragement.* The easiest way to keep an interviewee talking is to give that person encouragement. Standard encouragements include: "That's very good," "How interesting," "I like your answer," and "Excellent."

10. *Dig for additional details.* When the interviewee brings up a topic worthy of exploration, keep digging for additional facts. Assume the interviewee says, "I used to work as a private chauffeur, but then I lost my driver's license." Noticing a red flag, the interviewer might respond: "Why did you lose your license?"

11. *Make very limited use of a stress interview.* The purpose of a stress interview is to see how well the interviewee responds to pressure. Among the "stress tactics" are to insult the interviewee, to ignore him or her, or to stare at the interviewee and say nothing. These tactics create so much ill will that they are hardly worth pursuing. Besides, a job interview is stressful enough.

12. *Spend most of the interview time listening.* An experienced job interviewer spends little time talking. It is the interviewee who should be doing the talking.

13. *Provide the candidate ample information about the organization.* Answer any relevant questions.

14. *Have a wrap-up.* As the interview moves to a close, the interviewer should summarize the key issues brought up in the interview. It is also important to thank the interviewee and to provide truthful information about when you will write to or call him or her.

Reference Checking

A **reference check** is an inquiry to a second party about a job candidate's suitability for employment. Reference checks are now given less weight in making selection decisions than they were in the past. The major problem is that the providers of references are less candid today. Several factors help explain this hesitancy to provide frank references. First, job applicants have legal access to written references unless they specifically waive this right in writing (Privacy Act of 1974). Second, reference checks are subject to the same legal restrictions as are other selection devices. Many employers are therefore hesitant to make potentially unlawful statements about people.

Third, people who provide negative references worry about being sued for libel. Some major employers have a policy of not allowing anyone other than the personnel department to respond to reference checks, including telephone requests. The personnel department will give only the following information: dates of employment, job title, and whether or not the employee is eligible for rehire.

Reference checks overlap with background investigations. The latter usually are conducted by a firm that authenticates background facts. The investigation might also uncover facts not mentioned during the interview, such as a criminal record or bankruptcy.

The Physical Examination and Drug Testing

The physical examination is often the last hurdle a candidate faces before being hired and placed in the appropriate job, and it is important for at least two reasons. First, it gives some indication as to the person's physical ability to handle the requirements of a particular job. For instance, a candidate with a severe back problem would have difficulty handling a job that required constant sitting. High absenteeism would be the result. Second, the physical exam provides a basis for later comparisons. This lessens the threat that an employee may claim the job caused a particular injury or disease.

Testing job applicants for use of illegal drugs has increased substantially in recent years. Testing for substance abuse includes blood analysis, urinalysis, and observation of eyes and possible skin punctures. Although employers have a legal right to screen applicants for substance abuse, some people are concerned that inaccurate drug testing may unfairly deny employment to worthy candidates. A strong argument in favor of drug testing is that employee drug abusers may create such problems as lowered productivity, lost time from work, and misappropriation of funds to pay for drugs.[29]

Another controversial aspect of the physical examination is testing job candidates for human immunodeficiency virus (HIV) antibodies, which are linked to AIDS. Most HIV-antibody testing is voluntary, and it is practiced by approximately 6 percent of employers. Applicants who test positive for the HIV virus are frequently not hired.[30]

Placement

Placement refers to assigning the newly hired employee to the right job. When the employee is hired for a specific job and clear job specifications are drawn, placement is straightforward. However, when a firm is expanding, employees are sometimes hired for one of several possible jobs. It is important in these situations for the employee's first assignment to match his or her capabilities. Careful placement gives the new employee the best chance for job success. In turn, this leads to a positive reputation for the employer.

Interest in proper placement has strengthened in relation to hiring physically challenged (or disabled) people. With proper placement, the job performance of physically challenged people tends to equal or surpass that of non-physically challenged people.[31] An analysis of the physical abilities required for a job might reveal, for example, that sightedness is not necessary. A visually impaired person would therefore have an equal opportunity to perform well in that position.

ORIENTATION, TRAINING, AND DEVELOPMENT

Most firms no longer operate under a "sink or swim" philosophy of employee learning. Instead, employees are given ample opportunity to become oriented to the firm and then later are trained and developed.

Employee Orientation

Training new employees usually begins with an orientation program. An **employee orientation program** is designed to acquaint new employees with the company. Part of the orientation may deal with small but important matters, such as telling the employee how to get a parking sticker. Large firms often have elaborate orientation programs conducted by human-resource specialists. The program may include tours of the buildings, talks by department heads, videotape presentations, and generous supplies of printed information. Orientation, however, is still a major responsibility of the newly hired employee's boss. A boss can be especially helpful in reassuring employees that "everything will fall into place soon."

Employee orientation also includes telling the new employees specifically what their job is and what is expected in terms of performance. It is also valuable to hold periodic discussions of this same topic during the employee's time with the firm. Another aspect of orientation is informal. It consists of a socialization process, sometimes referred to as "hazing." New employees are introduced by co-workers to certain aspects of the organizational culture such as how well-motivated a new employee should be. Often newcomers are given co-worker perceptions of the competence level of key people in the organization. The informal orientation process can be disadvantageous because it may furnish the new employee with misinformation.

Training and Development

Training and development deal with systematic approaches to improving employee skills and performance. **Training** is any procedure intended to foster and enhance learning among employees. It is particularly directed at acquiring job skills. Training programs exist to teach hundreds of different skills such as repairing equipment, conducting performance appraisals, or preparing a department budget.

Development is a form of personal improvement generally consisting of enhancing knowledge and skills of a complex and unstructured nature. An example would be a program to help managers become better leaders. Leadership skills are not nearly as precise as preparing a budget.

Most of this text and its accompanying course could be considered an experience in management training and development. Here we describe two vital aspects of training and development for either employees or managers: needs assessment and selecting an appropriate program.

Needs Assessment. Before embarking upon a training program, it is important to determine what type of training is needed. Donald L. Kirkpatrick has developed a method of assessing the need for supervisory training and development.[32] It can also be used with individual contributors and higher-level managers. His approach provides good insight into the nature of effective training and development. It involves such steps as conducting a job analysis and asking managers themselves and their bosses and subordinates about the manager's needs for training. Also, the trainer observes the managers performing their regular duties to identify needs for improvement.

Despite the importance of matching training and development programs to specific needs, there are still some universal training needs. These include such topics as communication, motivation, decision making, counseling and coaching, and time management.

Selecting an Appropriate Training Program. After needs are assessed, they must be carefully matched to training and development programs. These programs are offered by colleges and universities, company training and development centers, consulting organizations, and training centers such as the Life Management Institute and the American Institute for Banking. A program will often have to be tailored to fit company requirements. The person assigning people to training and development programs must be familiar with people's needs for training and development and the content of the programs that match those needs. Table 8-7 presents an illustrative group of training and development programs. Thousands of different training and development programs are offered at one time or another.

PERFORMANCE APPRAISAL

Up to this point in the staffing model, employees have been recruited, selected, oriented, and trained. The next step is to evaluate performance. A performance appraisal is a formal system for measuring, evaluating, and reviewing performance. It is a useful device for discovering if the previous steps in the staffing model have been effective. For example, if most employees are performing well, it can be assumed that recruitment and selection have been adequate. Here we will mention the uses of performance appraisal and present a sample appraisal system.

Purposes of Performance Appraisal

Performance appraisals serve a number of important administrative purposes. They are also helpful in carrying out various aspects of the leadership func-

Table 8-7 An Illustrative Listing of Training and Development Programs

Training	Management Development
Interviewing candidates	Effective leadership
Listening to employees	Becoming a mentor
Motivating subordinates	International management
Coaching and counseling	Becoming a strategic thinker
Writing better reports	Business ethics
Improving communication skills	Policy making
Using spreadsheet analysis	Developing quality awareness
Preventing and controlling sexual harassment	Crisis management
Preventing accidents	Downsizing the organization
Negotiating skills for managers	

Note: Any of the training programs mentioned in the left column are often included in a program of management development. The programs in the right, however, are rarely considered to be specific training programs.

tion. The administrative purposes served by performance appraisals include the following:

1. Deciding who should receive merit increases and deciding the relative size of these increases.

2. Identifying employees with potential for promotion.

3. Assisting in HRP by identifying areas of weaknesses in the organization.

4. Providing documentation for discharging and demoting employees who are not meeting performance standards.

Performance appraisals help managers carry out the leadership function by such means as the following:

1. Increasing productivity by suggesting areas for work improvement to employees.[33]

2. Serving as a natural setting for communicating compliments and concerns to employees.

3. Helping employees identify their needs for self-improvement and self-development.

4. Motivating employees by providing feedback on performance—telling them how they are doing.

5. Giving employees a chance to express their ambitions, hopes, and concerns; simultaneously, this helps employees develop their careers.

These potential benefits are forthcoming only when the performance-appraisal system is carefully designed and properly conducted. Being properly conducted includes managers taking the time to do a careful job, being fair in their judgments, and listening carefully to employees. An effective manager, however, discusses regularly many of the topics listed above, rather than waiting for the performance appraisal.

Design of the Performance-Appraisal System

A number of different formats and methods of performance appraisal are in current use. They are designed to measure traits, behaviors, or results. Often the same appraisal system measures a combination of the three. **Traits** are stable aspects of people, closely related to personality. Job-related traits include enthusiasm, dependability, and honesty. **Behavior**, or activity, is what people do on the job. Behavior is often a consequence of one or more traits. Job-related behavior includes communicating with co-workers, working hard, keeping the work area clean, and maintaining a good appearance.

Results are what people accomplish, or the objectives they attain. A careful job analysis has to be conducted to measure people by results. However, if work objectives are clearly specified, they can serve as a substitute for a lengthy job analysis.

At first glance, measuring performance on the basis of results seems ideal and fair. Critics of the results method of appraisal, however, contend that personal qualities of people are important. A performance-appraisal system that measures only results ignores such important traits and behaviors as honesty, loyalty, and creativity. The Japanese system of management emphasizes traits much more than results. The Japanese managers believe that good results will be achieved in the long run by people with good inner qualities.[34]

Most American and Canadian companies still take traits and behavior into account when measuring performance. This does not mean that results are ignored. Many performance-appraisal systems attempt to measure both results and behaviors or traits. A portion of a performance-appraisal system of this type is shown in Table 8-8. The productivity factor measures results, whereas the other two factors deal more with behaviors.

Legal Requirements of Performance-Appraisal Systems

Performance-appraisal systems must meet the same stringent legal requirements faced by selection methods. The courts are more closely examining these systems to ensure that they are nondiscriminatory. One area of investiga-

Table 8-8   Portion of a Performance-Appraisal Form
that Measures Results and Behavior

IV. *Productivity* refers to what was accomplished and
how well the work was completed in the current
appraisal period. Particular emphasis is placed on
the tangible results of the employee's work. This
includes quality and quantity of work produced,
utilization of resources (savings) and consistency
of results.

    Comments

_____ Productivity level fails to meet minimum
requirements of the position.
_____ Productivity level usually meets minimum standards
of performance.
_____ Productivity at normal, reasonable level.
_____ Consistently exceeds expected levels of performance
in quality and quantity of work. Consistently shows
savings and excellent utilization of resources.

V. *Interpersonal skills and human relations* consider
the ability to work harmoniously and cooperatively
with subordinates, peers, and supervisors.

    Comments

_____ Shows some difficulty in getting along with people;
may be somewhat inconsiderate of others.
_____ Works well with subordinates, but is uncooperative
with peers and supervisors.
_____ Works effectively with subordinates and relates to
supervisors, but is uncooperative with peers.
_____ Works effectively with all levels.

tion is whether performance-appraisal systems have a disproportionately
negative impact on classes of people specifically protected under civil rights
legislation. For example, a performance-appraisal system might be considered
to have a disparate impact on older people if employees over age fifty have
lower average ratings than people under age fifty. An employer using this
system would then have the burden of demonstrating the following issues:

1. The performance-appraisal system is valid; it measures the aspects of job
    performance that it is designed to measure.

2. Those aspects in dispute of performance actually distinguish levels of job
    performance from one another.

3. There is no less discriminatory way to measure performance.[35]

SUMMARY OF KEY POINTS

Staffing is the process of making sure there are the necessary human resources to achieve organizational goals and objectives. The staffing model proposed here consists of seven phases: awareness of the legal aspects of staffing; human-resource planning; establishment of employee compensation; recruitment; selection and placement; orientation, training, and development; and performance appraisal.

Legislation influences all aspects of staffing, not just selection. Title VII of the Civil Rights Act of 1964 prohibits discrimination in all employment decisions on the basis of sex, religion, color, or national origin. Its provisions are enforced by the EEOC.

Human-resource planning is the process of anticipating and providing for the movement of people into, within, and out of the organization. It involves planning for future needs, turnover, recruitment, selection, layoffs, training, and development. Forecasts are made both by judgmental and statistical methods.

Compensation levels are influenced by forces outside and within the firm. External forces include laws, supply and demand, and union wage rates. Job evaluation is the primary internal method of setting compensation levels. It involves establishing point values for the components of a job. These points are then converted into pay grades. Compensation should be linked to both the strategy of the firm and the performance of individuals.

Employee benefits are noncash payments given to workers as a compensation for their employment. Flexible benefit packages allow employees to select a group of benefits tailored to their preferences. Benefits include such items as insurance, unemployment compensation, tuition assistance, credit unions, and child-care centers.

Recruitment is the process of attracting job candidates with the right characteristics and skills to fit job openings. The process requires both job descriptions and job specifications. A job description is a written statement outlining the key features of the job along with the activities required to perform the job effectively. A job specification is a statement of the personal characteristics needed to perform the job. Both external and internal sources are used in recruiting.

Selecting the right candidate from among those recruited involves a preliminary screening interview, completion of an application form, psychological and personnel testing, job interview, reference checking, and physical examination (including drug testing). The five types of psychological and personnel tests used most frequently in employee selection are achievement, aptitude, personality, interest, and honesty tests. The latter include both paper-and-pencil and polygraph tests. The use of tests is carefully regulated by the EEOC.

Most job interviews are semistructured. They follow a standard format, yet they give the interviewer a chance to ask additional questions. Reference checks are now given less weight in making selection decisions than they were in the past. The major reason is that many employers fear the legal consequences of being entirely candid about a person's weaknesses.

Placement is the process of assigning candidates to the right job after they are hired. An employee orientation program helps acquaint the newly hired employee with the firm. Training includes any procedure intended to foster and enhance employee skills. Development is a form of personal improvement that generally enhances knowledge and skills of a complex and unstructured nature. A careful assessment of needs should be conducted prior to selecting, training, and development programs.

A performance appraisal is a formal method of measuring, evaluating, and reviewing performance. It helps indicate whether the previous steps in the staffing model have been effective. Performance appraisals serve important administrative purposes, such as deciding on pay increases and promoting people. They also help managers carry out the leadership function. Performance appraisals measure traits, behaviors, or results. Many appraisal systems take into account more than one of these three aspects of job performance. Performance-appraisal systems must meet approximately the same legal requirements as selection systems.

QUESTIONS

1. In your own words, what is employment (or job) discrimination?
2. Identify at least one job for which you think it would be legally justifiable to hire only a male. Do the same for a female.
3. What is your forecast of the demand for people in your field? On what information did you base your forecast?
4. What influences on compensation levels have led to professional basketball players earning an average annual salary of about $350,000?
5. A person joins a firm right after graduation from business school. During the first ten years of employment, he or she receives only COLAs. After ten years, how would this person's pay compare to new hires from business schools?
6. In what way is "compensation" linked to the performance of students?
7. What benefits listed in Table 8-5 do you think should be mandatory for every employee?
8. How could you use your job description to help you do a better job?
9. Many job seekers carry around with them "To whom it may concern" letters of recommendation. How valid do you think these letters are as selection devices?
10. Why are performance appraisals considered part of organizational staffing?
11. Some people argue that promotions should be based on seniority to avoid charges of favoritism. What is your position on this issue?

ACTIVITIES

1. Evaluate the job of a sales representative of business equipment according to Table 8-1, and arrive at a salary grade for the job by using Table 8-2.

Make whatever assumptions you want about the job in order to do the evaluation.

2. Keep in mind the sales representative position mentioned in the first activity. Assume the role of a sales manager or employment interviewer, and then conduct about a twenty-minute interview of a classmate for the sales position. Before conducting the interview, review the guidelines in Table 8-6.

CASE PROBLEM 8-A: GIVE US OLDSTERS A CHANCE

Wright & Hauser, a financial services firm, was founded five years ago. Although a full-service brokerage house, its primary business is to issue low-priced stocks (referred to as penny stocks) for upstart firms in its geographic area. Wright & Hauser has a main office and a branch located in an adjacent city. The firm's primary method of obtaining new clients is through telemarketing. A staff of about ten financial consultants conducts the telephone solicitations. Wright & Hauser management insists that each telemarketer spend at least five hours per working day, including nights, calling potential clients.

A benchmark established by the firm is that every 100 telephone calls should result in five people interested in receiving a follow-up phone call and in two actual new customers. Telephone solicitation is therefore characterized by a large number of refusals and rejections in comparison to the number of new clients obtained. However, those financial consultants who attain the benchmark can earn a living almost as good as their counterparts in better established brokerage firms.

The turnover is high among newly hired financial consultants. Many of them complain that Wright & Hauser furnishes them no leads, which results in telephoning many people who have no interest in purchasing speculative stocks. Because of the high turnover, the firm is recruiting continuously.

Steve Wright, one of the owners, was conducting screening interviews for several financial consultant positions. Jeff Muldoon, a recently retired bank accountant, was one of the applicants. At the end of the interview, Muldoon said, "Let me be candid, Mr. Wright. I would like this job. My background in accounting is a good professional base for being a financial consultant. I'm eager to find a job that will supplement my modest retirement pay. What are my chances of getting this job?"

"I agree that your background is fine," said Wright, "but I'm not sure if you would be a good fit for the job. We are definitely an equal opportunity employer, and we want to hire people of all races, ages, sexes, and ethnic backgrounds. Yet, most people who would be successful in this job are age thirty or under for two reasons. First, making cold telephone calls five hours a day is a terrible grind for a middle-age person. Another problem is that most people who purchase penny stocks are young people. A young salesperson is therefore better able to establish rapport with our most likely customers. "But, I would like to give you first consideration should we need an accountant or controller for the firm."

"I can't accept your reasoning entirely, Mr. Wright," said Muldoon. "A person my age could handle this job just fine. I wish you would give us oldsters a chance."

Case Questions

1. Is Wright & Hauser practicing job discrimination, or are their points about the age factor valid?
2. If you were Muldoon, what steps would you take to be given more consideration as an applicant?
3. Did Wright make a mistake in telling Muldoon the reasons for his concerns about hiring him?

CASE PROBLEM 8-B: WOULD YOU HIRE THIS MAN?

Consider the following employment situation:

Job Description: Ms. Ann Druhan of Druhan Enterprises, Fort Lauderdale, Florida, wants to hire a combination administrative assistant and field investigator. The successful candidate would work with Druhan on a variety of administrative tasks such as budgeting, correspondence, and updating the company data bases. The main responsibility of the job holder, however, would be to conduct informal field audits of the twenty nightclubs and singles bars in the Druhan chain.

The assistant would also be required to investigate established clubs and singles bars for possible purchase by Druhan. The job would involve about 50 percent travel throughout the eastern half of the United States and Canada. Starting salary is $30,000 plus unlimited use of a company-furnished Corvette.

Description of the Candidate: Earl Green, age twenty-two years, has an associate's degree in Business Administration from Bryant and Stratton Business Institute and has a 3.56 grade point average. He is 5 feet, 11 inches tall, and weighs 159 pounds. Aside from mowing lawns and babysitting as a teenager, his work experience consists of one year as part-time bookkeeper in a department store and two years as the assistant manager of the appliances department of the same store. Green says he will be promoted to manager of his department store within one year.

Excerpts from Earl Green's interview with Ann Druhan:

Question: Earl, why are you applying for this job?

Answer: I'm looking for action and excitement. My present job is okay, but it's not the big time. I want to be somebody. And honestly, I can see myself buzzing around in a Corvette.

Question: What are some of your interests? What do you like to do when you're not working?

Answer: Lots of things, I guess. I read mysteries. I'm a big video watcher. I hike. I lift weights. I read a news magazine at least once a week. And every Saturday night is dance time for me. My partner and I once placed third in a dance contest held at Club 747. I've tried some ice skating, but cold-weather sports are not my style.

Question: Would you ever marry a woman you met in a singles bar?

Answer: First of all, I don't know if I'll ever get married. I'm having too much fun being single. But I wouldn't put down a woman I met at a singles bar, if that's what you mean. You can meet a nice woman anywhere. It's no disgrace if a woman looks for her Prince Charming in a bar. A buddy of mine met his wife at a singles bar.

Question: Why do you think you would be better qualified for this job than most of the applicants?

Answer: I haven't met the other applicants, so I don't know for sure. But I think I'm the man for this job. I like the details of business. I'm a first-rate book-keeper. And I like the glamour side of your business. I would fit right into the nightclub scene when I made those audits. I could also relate to the heart of your operation.

Question: What would you like to be doing in five years from now?

Answer: Something big, like an assistant vice president at Druhan Enterprises.

Question: If that's your goal, you and I would have to work well together. Do you think we could?

Answer: From what I see, the vibes are good. I admire what you've built, and I like your candid questions. You seem like a straight shooter to me, and that's important. I could fit right in here.

Case Questions

1. What strengths does Earl Green have for this position?
2. What weaknesses might he have?
3. How honest does he appear?
4. What do you think of the effectiveness of Druhan's questions?
5. Would you hire Green for this position?

REFERENCES

1. R. Wayne Mondy, Robert M. Noe, and Robert E. Edwards, "What the Staffing Function Entails," *Personnel* (April 1986): 55.
2. "Rights Group Lashes Court on Job Ruling," *The New York Times* (syndicated story), 14 May 1987.
3. Buck Consultants, Inc., "Changes in Mandatory Retirement and Benefit Accruals Take Effect," *Personnel Journal* (January 1987): 24.
4. Carl C. Hoffman and Kathleen P. Hoffman, "Does Comparable Worth Obscure the Real Issues?" *Personnel Journal* (January 1987): 83–95.
5. James A. F. Stoner and Charles Wankel, *Management,* 3d ed. (Englewood Cliffs, NJ: Prentice Hall, 1986), 322.
6. Stoner and Wankel, *Management,* 322.
7. Stella M. Nkomo, "The Theory and Practice of HR Planning: The Gap Still Remains," *Personnel Administrator* (August 1986): 76.
8. Herbert Z. Halbrecht, "Compensation Surveys: Misleading Guideposts," *Personnel Journal* (March 1987): 122–124.
9. Edward E. Lawler, III, "What's Wrong with Point-Factor Job Evaluation?" *Personnel* (January 1987): 38–45.
10. John M. Ivancevich, James H. Donnelly, Jr., and James L. Gibson, *Managing for Performance: An Introduction to the Process of Managing*, rev. ed. (Plano, TX: Business Pubs., Inc., 1983), 631.

11. Robert J. Greene and Russell G. Roberts, "Strategic Integration of Compensation and Benefits," *Personnel Administrator* (May 1983): 82.

12. William E. Lissy, "Outlook on Compensation and Benefits: Developments and Trends for 1986," *Personnel* (March 1986): 71.

13. Thomas J. Bergmann and Marilyn A. Bergmann, "Outlook on Compensation and Benefits: How Important Are Fringe Benefits to Employees?" *Personnel* (December 1987): 59.

14. Don Oldenburgh, "New Tax Rules on Perks May Be Aimed at Ordinary Worker," *Washington Post*, 27 January 1985.

15. Martha B. Sherwood, "Benefits: Justifying Health Promotion in Dollars-and-Cents Terms," *Personnel Journal* (November 1986): 98–104.

16. Michael Pollock and Aaron Bernstein, "The Disposable Employee Is Becoming a Fact of Corporate Life," *Business Week* (15 December 1986): 53.

17. James A. Breaugh, "Realistic Job Previews: A Critical Appraisal and Future Research Directions," *Academy of Management Review* (October 1983): 612–619.

18. Mark A. Jones, "Job Descriptions Made Easy," *Personnel Journal* (May 1984): 32.

19. Tom Jackson, "Unlocking the Hidden Job Market," *Business Week's Guide to Careers* (February–March 1985): 65.

20. Louis Rukeyser, "Computers Can Systematically, Cheaply Match Job Seekers, Employers," (syndicated column), 5 January 1985.

21. Carl Camden and Bill Wallace, "Job Application Forms: A Hazardous Employment Practice," *Personnel Administrator* (March 1983): 32.

22. Eric Rolfe Greenberg, "Workplace Testing: Results of a New AMA Survey," *Personnel* (April 1988): 36.

23. Paul R. Sackett and Michael M. Harris, "Honesty Testing for Personnel Selection: A Review and Critique," *Personnel Psychology* (Summer 1984): 221–245.

24. John A. Belt, "The Polygraph: A Questionable Personnel Tool," *Personnel Administrator* (August 1983): 91.

25. William Safire, "Use of Lie Detectors a Form of Mental Rape," *New York Times* (syndicated column), 2 March 1988.

26. Mike Boyer, "The Lie Detector is Supplanted by Written Tests," Gannett News Service, December 27, 1988.

27. Robert M. Madigan, K. Dow Scott, Diana L. Deadrick, and Jil A. Stoddard, "Employment Testing: The U.S. Job Service is Spearheading a Revolution," *Personnel Administrator* (September 1986): 102.

28. Michael A. Campion, Elliott D. Pursell, and Barbara K. Brown, "Structured Interviewing: Raising the Psychometric Properties of the Employment Interview," *Personnel Psychology* (Spring 1988): 25–42.

29. Rusch O. Dees, "Testing for Drugs and Alcohol: Proceed with Caution," *Personnel* (September 1986): 53.

30. Eric Rolfe Greenberg, "Workplace Testing: Results of a New AMA Survey," *Personnel*, April 1988, 42.

31. Gopal Pati and John I. Adkins, Jr., "Hire the Handicapped—Compliance Is Good Business," *Harvard Business Review* (January–February 1980): 14–15, 18, 20, 22.

32. Donald L. Kirkpatrick, "Effective Supervisory Training and Development, Part 1: Responsibility, Needs, and Objectives," *Personnel* (November–December 1984): 27-28.

33. William Weitzel, "How to Improve Performance Through Successful Appraisals," *Personnel* (October 1987): 18.
34. Nina Hatvany and Vladimir Pucik, "An Integrated Management System: Lessons from the Japanese Experience," *Academy of Management Review* (July 1981): 472.
35. Roberta B. Romberg, "Performance Appraisal, 1: Risks and Rewards," *Personnel* (August 1986): 20–21.

PART FOUR
Leading

Chapter 9
Leadership of Employees

Chapter 10
Motivating for Results

Chapter 11
Communicating with Other People

Part Four deals with the leadership function of management—those activities directed toward influencing subordinates to achieve organizational objectives. Managers do many things besides lead, yet it can be argued that providing leadership is a manager's biggest contribution. Leadership allows the manager to get things accomplished through others, and getting things accomplished through others is the major purpose of management.

Leadership is studied here from three perspectives. Chapter 9 emphasizes the traits, behaviors, and styles of leaders themselves. Chapter 10 explains the complicated process of motivation—getting people to spring into action. Chapter 11 focuses on person-to-person communication, one process by which leaders influence other people.

9
Leadership of Employees

After studying the material in this chapter, you should be able to accomplish the following tasks:

1. Describe how leaders are able to influence subordinates.
2. Be aware of several important leadership characteristics and behaviors.
3. Describe the autocratic, participative, free-rein, managerial grid, and Japanese styles of leadership.
4. Describe the entrepreneurial and intrapreneurial leadership styles.
5. Describe the essence of the path-goal theory of leadership.
6. Explain what a leader can do to help manage conflict and change.

Key Terms and Phrases

Leadership	Achievement need
Power	Power need
Authority	Sensitivity to people
Position power	Leadership style
Personal power	Autocratic leader
Legitimate power	Free-rein leader
Reward power	Participative leader
Coercive power	Democratic leader
Expert power	Consensual leader
Referent Power	Consultative leader
Charisma	Employee-involvement programs
Leading by example	Managerial Grid
Assertiveness	Transformational leader
Rationality	Path-goal theory
Ingratiation	Conflict
Exchange	Authoritative command

Leadership is the process of influencing the activities of an individual or group to achieve certain objectives in a given situation.[1] Coercive tactics, however, are not considered to be part of leadership. If they were, then robbing someone at gunpoint would be an act of leadership. An example of leadership would be a supervisor influencing an employee by giving him or her ample encouragement.

Leadership can be exercised in many settings. Our concern here is the leadership carried out by managers in organizational settings. Leadership is important to the organization because effective leaders can make a major contribution to organizational performance. Similarly, ineffective leaders can impair organizational performance.

The importance of leadership is underscored by the comments of Harvard Business School professor John P. Kotter. He contends that today's managers must know how to *lead* as well as manage, or their companies will become extinct. Kotter makes this distinction between management and leadership:

- Management is more formal and scientific than leadership. It relies on universal skills, such as planning, budgeting, and controlling. Management is a set of explicit tools and techniques, based on reasoning and testing, that can be used in a variety of situations.

- Leadership, by contrast, involves having a vision of what the organization can become.

- Leadership requires eliciting cooperation and teamwork from a large network of people and keeping the key people in that network motivated, using every manner of persuasion.[2]

Figure 9-1 presents an overview of the link between leadership and management. It also highlights several of the major topics presented in this chapter.

Figure 9-1   The Links Between Management and Leadership

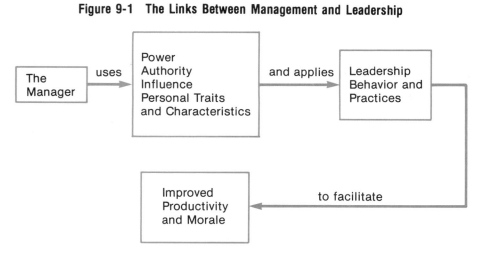

Source: Adapted from John R. Schermerhorn, Jr., *Management for Productivity*, 2d ed., (New York: John Wiley & Sons, 1988).

The concept underlying Figure 9-1 is that, to bring about improved productivity and morale, managers do two things. First, they use power, authority, influence, and personal traits and characteristics. Second, they apply leadership behaviors and practices.[3]

LEADERS USE POWER AND AUTHORITY TO INFLUENCE OTHERS

Leaders influence people to do things through the use of power and authority. **Power** is the ability to get others to do things or the ability to control resources. **Authority** is the formal right to get people to do things or the formal right to control resources. Factors within a person, such as talent or charm, help them achieve power. Only the organization, however, can grant a person authority. Authority is often referred to as **position power** because the power comes from the position. **Personal power** stems from the individual's characteristics and behaviors.

Leaders influence others through the use of position power, personal power, and specific tactics. Each of these has subcategories. Understanding these different approaches to exerting influence can help a manager become a more effective leader.

Position Power

Position power is divided into three subtypes. Each is a form of authority granted by the organization.[4] **Legitimate power** is the authentic right of the leader to make certain types of requests. It is the easiest type of influence for most subordinates to accept. For example, virtually all employees accept the manager's authority to conduct a performance appraisal. Nevertheless, there are always unspoken limits to legitimate authority. Employees would probably refuse to attend weekly staff meetings conducted at 6:00 A.M. on Saturday.

Reward power refers to the leader's control over rewards of value to the subordinate. Exercising this power includes giving salary increases and recommending employees for promotion. **Coercive power** refers to the leader's control over punishments. Organizational punishments include assignment to undesirable working hours, demotion, and firing. Effective leaders generally avoid heavy reliance on coercive power because it creates resentment and sometimes retaliation.

Personal Power

Personal power has two subcategories. **Expert power** is the leader's job-related knowledge as perceived by subordinates. This type of power stems from having specialized skills, knowledge, or talent. Expert power can be exercised even when a person does not occupy a formal leadership position. An advertising copywriter with a proven record of writing winning ad slogans would carry expert power. **Referent power** is based on personal characteristics others find desirable. To say a leader has **charisma** means that the leader has unusual charm, or referent power.[5]

Both position power and personal power are important to the leader. However, effective leaders rely more heavily on personal power to get things accomplished.[6] Instead of "pulling rank," they influence group members in other ways.

Specific Influence Tactics

In addition to using position and personal power, leaders use many other influence tactics to get things done. Five of the most frequently used influence tactics are leading by example, assertiveness, rationality, ingratiation, and exchange.[7]

Leading by example means that the leader influences group members by serving as a positive model of desirable behavior. A manager who leads by example shows consistency between actions and words. Also, actions and words confirm, support, and often clarify each other. For example, if a firm has a strict punctuality policy and the manager explains the policy and is punctual, a model has been provided that is consistent in words and actions. The action of following the punctuality policy provides an example that supports and clarifies the words used to describe the policy.[8]

Assertiveness refers to being forthright in your demands. It involves expressing both what you want done and the feelings you have. A leader might say, for example, "Your report is late, and that makes me angry. I want you to get it done within twenty-four hours."

Rationality means appealing to reason and logic. Strong leaders frequently use this influence tactic. Pointing out the facts of a situation to subordinates to get them to do something is an example of rationality. A middle-level manager might tell a supervisor, for example, "If our department goes over budget this year, the department is likely to be closed down." Knowing this, the supervisor probably will become more cost conscious.

Ingratiation refers to getting somebody else to like you, often through the use of political skill. A typical ingratiating tactic would be to act in a friendly manner just before making a demand. Can you think of any ingratiating tactics students use to help them gain concessions from instructors?

Exchange is a method of influencing others by offering to reciprocate if they meet your demands. Leaders with limited personal and position power are likely to use exchange and make a bargain with a subordinate. A manager might say to a subordinate, "If you can help me out this time, I'll go out of my way to return the favor." Exchange resembles using reward power. The emphasis in exchange, however, is that the subordinate goes out of his or her way to please the boss in order to receive a future favor.

Which Influence Tactic to Choose?

Leaders are unlikely to use all of the above influence tactics in a given situation. Instead, they tend to choose an influence tactic that fits the demand of the circumstances. Support for this conclusion was found in a study with 125 leaders employed by a bank. The influence tactics used by these leaders was determined by having both their superiors and subordinates complete a questionnaire. A major finding of the study was that in crisis situations, as opposed to noncrisis situations, the leaders used more expert power, formal power, referent power, and upward influence. Simultaneously, the leaders were less likely to consult with subordinates in a crisis situation.[9]

CHARACTERISTICS AND BEHAVIORS OF EFFECTIVE LEADERS

Although the situation is important in understanding leadership, leaders themselves must also be studied. In this section, we highlight some of the more consistent findings about the characteristics and behaviors of effective managerial leaders. Effective means that the leader achieves both high productivity and morale, as illustrated in Figure 9-1. You should not infer that the same characteristics and behaviors work equally well in all situations. Nevertheless, many leadership situations do require similar characteristics and behaviors. For instance, self-confidence helps a leader to be effective in any leadership assignment.

Personal Characteristics and Traits

One justification for studying leadership traits is that the traits of leaders are related closely to the degree to which they are perceived to be leaders. For example, managers who are perceived to be good problem solvers are more likely to be accepted as leaders.[10] All the characteristics and traits of leaders described here are important. However, the list is not all-inclusive. There are hundreds of human qualities that can enhance leadership effectiveness in some situations. The list of traits and characteristics cited here is based on several research studies.[11] In reviewing these studies, we have selected those factors we believe are most relevant to the largest number of situations.

Strong Need for Achievement and Power.   Successful leaders have strong needs both to accomplish things and to control other people.[12] The **achievement need** is a desire to get things accomplished for accomplishment's sake. This need is satisfied by such activities as building things from the ground up or by completing a major project. The **power need** is a desire to control others or get them to do things on your behalf. A leader with a strong power need enjoys exercising power and using influence tactics.

Self-Confidence.   Self-confidence contributes to effective leadership in several ways. Above all, self-confident leaders project an image that encourages subordinates to have faith in them.

Strong Work Motivation.   Most leadership positions demand considerable effort and self-starting ability. Effective leaders therefore must have strong motivation to work hard and long. They also have high standards for their own work, a high energy level, and an interest in career advancement.

Sensitivity to People.   **Sensitivity to people** means taking people's needs and feelings into account when dealing with them. It implies that the leader minimizes hurting the feelings of people and frustrating their needs. A sensitive leader gives encouragement to subordinates who need it, and does not belittle or insult poor performers.

A study of business leaders has demonstrated the important role sensitivity plays in career advancement. Executives who were held back in their careers were compared with those who had advanced to senior executive positions. A major reason for being held back was insensitivity to people as characterized by a bullying, intimidating, and abrasive style.[13]

Good Intellectual Ability.   Intelligence makes a contribution to leadership effectiveness. Intelligence, or problem-solving ability, is becoming increasingly important because managerial jobs are becoming more complex. The problem-solving and planning tools described in Chapter 5 illustrate that managers need to be intelligent. As Fred E. Fielder and Joseph E. Garcia observe: "Intelligent and competent leaders make more effective plans, decisions, and action strategies than do leaders will less intelligence and competence."[14]

Sense of Humor.   The effective use of humor is now regarded as an important part of a leader's job. Humor serves such functions in the workplace as relieving tension and boredom and defusing hostility.[15] A recent report on organizational humor contends:

> The interest in humor is a sign of the times. With restructurings, takeovers and layoffs sweeping the corporate world, employee insecurity and hostility are approaching flood level, and companies see humor as a remedy to reduce tensions and motivate workers. We are going from a climate where humor was belittled, or considered subversive, to a situation where it is highly prized.[16]

Because humor helps the leader dissolve tension and defuse conflict, it helps him or her exert power over the group. Psychologist Barbara Mackoff contends that "Humor is the ultimate power tool on the job."[17]

Vision.   Top-level managerial leaders need a visual image of where they see the organization headed and how it can get there. Organizational progress is dependent upon the top executive having this sense of vision.[18] "The role of the CEO," says John E. Pearson, chairperson and chief executive officer of Northwestern National Life Insurance, "is to sell a vision—a vision not only of what we are today, but of what we will be tomorrow."[19]

Behaviors and Skills of Effective Leaders

As described in Chapter 1, managers must possess good conceptual, human, technical, and political skills. Here we mention administrative skills and several behaviors linked to leadership effectiveness.

Good Administrative Skills. Administrative skills in this sense are skills necessary to carry out managerial functions other than leadership. Specifically, an effective leader is expected to do a good job of organizing, planning, decision making, and being creative.[20] Good work habits and time-management practices are part of having good administrative skills. Leaders who emphasize only working with people are neglecting important parts of their job.

Adaptability to the Situation.   Effective leaders adapt to the situation. This is the contingency viewpoint; a strategy is chosen based on the unique circumstances at hand. For instance, if a leader were dealing with psychologically immature subordinates, he or she would have to supervise them closely. If the subordinates were mature and self-reliant, they would require less supervision. Also, the adaptive leader selects an organization structure best suited to the situation at hand such as choosing between a brainstorming group or a committee.[21]

The ability to size up people and situations, and adapt tactics accordingly, is a vital leadership behavior. It stems from an inner quality called insight or intuition, both of which are a direct perception of a situation that seems unrelated to any specific reasoning process. Being sensitive to people helps give the leader insight. A manager who lacks insight, intuition, and sensitivity schedules a critically important department meeting on a day that is a religious holiday for a few of the participants.

Stability of Performance.   Effective leaders perform in a stable manner, even under heavy work loads and uncertain conditions. Remaining steady under conditions of uncertainty helps subordinates cope with the situation. Most people become anxious when the outcome of what they are doing is uncertain. When the leader remains calm, employees are reassured that things will work out satisfactorily. Stability also helps the leader meet the expectation that a manager should be cool under pressure.

High Standards of Performance for Subordinates.   Effective leaders consistently hold subordinates to high standards of performance, which raises productivity. Setting high expectations for subordinates becomes a self-fulfilling prophecy. People tend to live up to the expectations set for them by their superiors. Setting high expectations might take the form of encouraging subordinates to establish difficult objectives.

Emotional Support to Subordinates.   Supportive behavior toward subordinates usually increases leadership effectiveness. A supportive leader is one who gives frequent encouragement and praise. The emotional support generally improves morale and sometimes improves productivity. Being emotionally supportive comes naturally to the leader who has empathy for people and who is a warm person.

Frequent Feedback.   Giving subordinates frequent feedback on their performance is another vital leadership behavior. The manager rarely can influence the behavior of subordinates without appropriate performance feedback.

Feedback helps in two ways. First, employees are informed how well they are doing, so they can take corrective action if needed. Second, when the feedback is positive, it encourages subordinates to keep up the good work.

Recover Quickly from Setbacks.   Effective managerial leaders are resilient; they bounce back quickly from setbacks such as budget cuts, demotions, and being fired. An intensive study of executives revealed that they don't even think about failure and don't even use the word. Instead, they rely on synonyms such as "mistake," "glitch," "bungle," and "setback."[22]

LEADERSHIP STYLES

Another important part of the leadership function is **leadership style**. It is the typical pattern of behavior that a leader uses to influence his or her employees to achieve organizational goals.[23] Several different approaches to describing leadership styles have developed over the years. Most of these involve how much authority and control the leader turns over to the group.

We will first describe the classical approach for classifying leadership styles. Then we will discuss the managerial-grid styles of leadership, followed by the Japanese style of leadership. Finally, we describe two other types of leaders: entrepreneurial and intrapreneurial leaders and the transformational leader.

The Leadership Continuum

The leadership continuum, or classical approach, classifies leaders according to how much authority they retain for themselves versus how much is turned over to the group. Three key points on the continuum represent autocratic, participative, and free-rein styles of leadership. Figure 9-2 illustrates the leadership continuum.

Figure 9-2   The Leadership Continuum

AMOUNT OF AUTHORITY HELD BY THE LEADER

Autocratic Style   Participative Style   Free-Rein Style

Consultative   Consensus   Democratic

AMOUNT OF AUTHORITY HELD BY GROUP MEMBERS

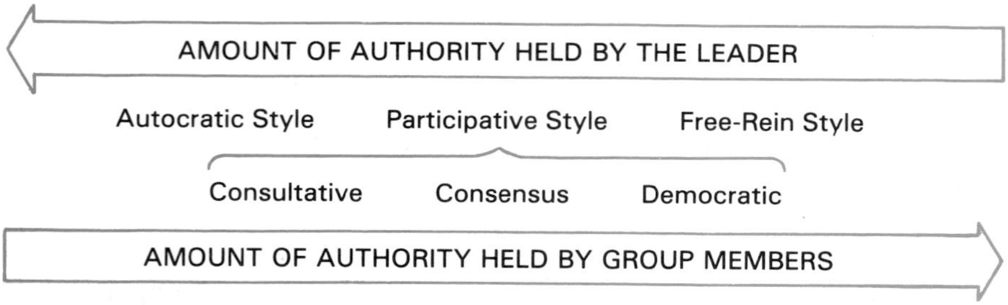

Autocratic Leadership Style.   **Autocratic leaders** retain most of the authority for themselves. They typically make a decision and then announce it to the group. Autocratic leaders are also referred to as *authoritative* because they act as authorities. The autocratic leader makes a decision in a confident manner and assumes that subordinates will comply. He or she usually is not concerned with the subordinates' attitudes toward the decision. Autocratic leaders are often considered highly task oriented because they place heavy emphasis on getting tasks accomplished. Typical autocratic behaviors including telling people what to do, asserting themselves, and serving as a model for group members.[24]

When autocratic leaders are liked and respected, they are perceived as being knowledgeable and decisive. Many successful managerial leaders are autocrats. A case in point is Donald Trump, the real estate developer and financial deal maker. He is perceived by many as decisive, directive, and charismatic (in addition to being a world-class egomaniac!). When autocrats are disliked, they are perceived as being heavy handed. Despite its occasional successes, the autocratic leadership style is losing ground in most organizations. Most of the new breed of leaders are willing to share authority with the group.

Participative Leadership Style.   A **participative leader** is one who shares decision making with group members. There are three closely related subtypes of participative leaders: democratic, consensual, and consultative. **Democratic leaders** confer final authority on the group. They function as collectors of opinion and take a vote before making a decision. **Consensual leaders** encourage group discussion about an issue and then make a decision that reflects the general agreement (consensus) of group members. Japanese managers in large Japanese firms typically use the consensus style of decision making. All workers who will be involved in the consequences of a decision have an opportunity to provide input. A decision is not considered final until all parties involved agree with the decision. **Consultative leaders** confer with subordinates before making a decision. However, they retain the final authority to make decisions.

The participative style is considered to be the teamwork approach. Predominant behaviors of the participative leader include coaching subordinates, negotiating their demands, and collaborating with others.[25]

Participative Style versus Autocratic Style.   Autocratic and participative leaders see people differently. This difference in perception has been termed Theory X and Theory Y in a famous statement by Douglas McGregor.[26] One reason McGregor developed this distinction was to help managers critically examine their assumptions about employees.

The Theory X, or autocratic, manager makes these assumptions about workers: people dislike work and must be coerced, controlled, and directed toward organizational goals; most people like to be treated this way so they can avoid responsibility.

The Theory Y, or participative, manager makes the opposite assumptions about workers. Most people genuinely enjoy the nature of their work. Furthermore, they want to be self-directing and they seek responsibility. If given a chance, they will be creative in solving business problems.

Autocratic and participative managers also differ in how they perceive their own role in getting the job done. The autocrat thinks mostly of the task itself. The participative manager thinks of the task and the people simultaneously. He or she tries to fit people to the task. The accompanying "Manager in Action" also contrasts the participative and autocratic leader.

MANAGER IN ACTION:

The Hard-Hitting Consultative Manager

Joseph T. Gorman played point guard for Kent State University. By the time this corporate lawyer was playing corporate-league ball, he no longer specialized in directing teammates from one position. "He was like the 2,000-pound canary—we put him wherever we needed him," recalls a former teammate. "He was good at any position." Gorman had been president and chief operating officer of TRW for three years, before being slated to become chairman and chief executive.

When the time came for cost-cutting at TRW, Gorman was mentally prepared for the task. Watching the bottom line is something of an obsession with Gorman. Several times in the past he has returned annual budget proposals to division heads, telling them to arrive at a "more realistic plan."

Still, Gorman is hardly regarded as an autocrat. A former TRW executive recalls that Gorman often solicited his input and that of other TRW executives. Gorman would take plentiful notes, no matter where he was—at a conference, in the office, and even at dinner. His former colleague says, "Joe asks questions until he is sure that he has enough information to make a well-rounded decision." When you're heading a company that manufactures everything from integrated circuits to truck axles, it is important to do your homework.

Source: As reported in, "The Legal Eagle Who Will Rule the Roost at TRW," *Business Week* (21 March 1988): 100–104.

Evaluation of Participative Leadership Style.   The participative leadership style is well suited to managing competent people who are eager to assume responsibility. These people want to get involved in making decisions and to give feedback to management. The majority of graduates from business and professional programs expect to be involved in decision making. Participative leadership would therefore work well with the new breed of managers and professionals. Furthermore, most successful profit and nonprofit firms do practice participative leadership.

Participative leadership, nevertheless, does have some problems. It often results in extensive and time-consuming committee work. Sometimes participative management is carried to extremes. Subordinates are consulted about trivial things the manager could easily handle independently. Another problem is that many first-level supervisors resist one form of participative management.

A survey was made of supervisors' attitudes toward **employee involvement programs**—formal programs in which employees contribute to decision making.[27] These include quality circles and quality-of-work-life (QWL) programs. Seventy-two percent of the supervisors polled said the programs are good for the company. Sixty percent said they were good for employees. Yet only 31 percent said the employee involvement programs were good for supervisors. Problems were uncovered that would also apply to participative leadership by higher-level managers: Supervisors were concerned about becoming redundant if workers participated in so many decisions, and they did not appreciate the extra work required by the programs.

Free-Rein Leadership Style. The free-rein leader turns over virtually all authority and control to the group. Leadership is provided to the group indirectly rather than directly. Group members are presented a task to perform and are given free rein to figure out how best to perform the task. The leader does not get involved unless requested. Subordinates are allowed all the freedom they want as long as they do not violate company policy. In short, the free-rein leader delegates excessively.

The free-rein leadership style sometimes works effectively with well-motivated and experienced employees. These people are self-sufficient and may not need help or emotional support from the boss. A problem with free-rein leadership, however, is that it often frustrates subordinates. They perceive the free-rein leader as being uninvolved in department matters and indifferent to what is happening. Free-rein leaders run the risk of being replaced because they appear to contribute so little to running the department. In their defense, free-rein leaders believe they are helping subordinates develop self-sufficiency.

Managerial Grid® Leadership Styles

The study of leadership styles presented so far has emphasized the leadership continuum—the authoritarian, participative, and free-rein styles. Other approaches to understanding leadership styles focus on two dimensions of leadership: tasks and relationships. The best-known of these approaches is the Managerial Grid.[28] It is based on different combinations of the leader's concern for production (tasks) and people (relationships). The Managerial Grid is a comprehensive program of leadership training and organizational improvement. The grid philosophy encourages the leader to size up each situation by making good use of knowledge of human behavior.

As shown in Figure 9-3, concern for production is rated on a one-to-nine scale on the horizontal axis. Concern for production includes results, bottom line, performance, profits, and mission. Concern for people is rated on a similar scale on the vertical axis, and includes concern for subordinates and co-workers. Both concerns are leadership attitudes or ways of thinking about

Figure 9-3 The Managerial Grid

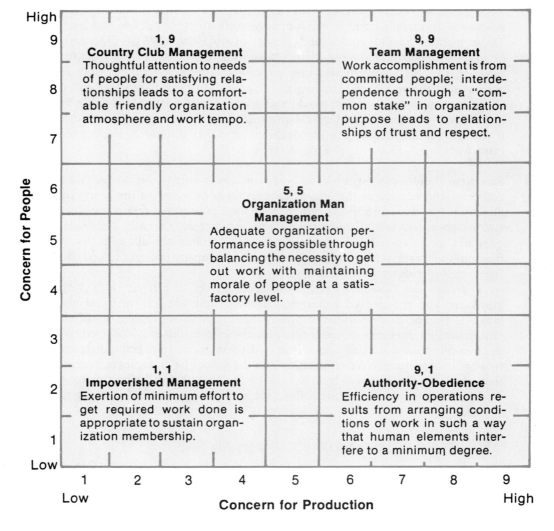

Source: The Managerial Grid figure from the *The Managerial Grid III: The Key to Leadership Excellence* by Robert R. Blake and Jane Srygley Mouton (Houston: Gulf Publishing Co., 1985), 12. Reproduced by permission.

leadership. The grid identifies five stereotypes, yet a leader could fall into any of eighty-one different positions on the grid.

The originators of the grid, Blake and Mouton, argue strongly for the value of team management (9,9). According to their research, the team-management approach pays off. It results in improved performance, low absenteeism and turnover, and high morale. Team management relies on trust and respect, which help bring about good results.

The Japanese Style of Leadership

In response to Japan's impressive performance over the last two decades, many other countries have become interested in Japanese management methods. Researchers and visiting executives have uncovered a wide range of human resource management methods and manufacturing techniques used by large Japanese companies. Our specific concern is with the Japanese style of leadership. First we present a summary of these leadership practices, followed by an evaluation of their effectiveness.

Japanese Leadership Practices.   Five aspects of Japanese management provide insight into the style of leadership used by many Japanese managers.[29] Of course, not every Japanese manager uses the same style of leadership. Some presidents and owners of Japanese companies are known to be strongly authoritarian.[30]

1. *Consensus decision making.* The consensus process of decision making used by Japanese managers goes beyond the conventional participative method. In the Japanese approach, an important decision, such as changing a production process would involve all who would likely be affected. This could include perhaps sixty to eighty people. The Japanese word to describe decision making is *nemawashi.* Literally, it means the process of implanting the roots of a tree into the soil so it can grow.[31] It refers to the unofficial understanding that is needed before a final decision is reached.

    Although consensus decision making is cumbersome and time-consuming, it improves implementation of the decision. Employees support the decision, they understand it better, and they are committed to its execution.

2. *Maximization of human-resource development.* Dozens of Japanese leadership practices stem from the Japanese interest in the development of people. Employees are offered long-term, and sometimes lifetime, employment. This prompts managers to value each employee and to offer each one ample coaching and training. Because subordinates will be employed for a long time, short-term results are not given top priority. Instead, employees who are cooperative and loyal generally receive high performance appraisal ratings. Managers offer employees company-sponsored cultural, athletic, and recreational facilities. In short, Japanese managers use a people-oriented style of leadership. They do so because it is the best way of accomplishing long-term results.

3. *Recognition of employees as experts.* Japanese managers assume that employees are intelligent enough to perform their jobs without extensive supervision and rules. The initial step taken to improve productivity is to get the worker's opinion on how this might be achieved. Quality circles

are a widely used technique based on the concept of employees as experts. Many observers believe quality circles are the most typical reflection of Japanese management and philosophy.

4. *Management by wandering around.* Japanese managers have brought attention to the importance of "management by wandering around." The manager intermingles freely among workers on the shop floor, in the office, and at informal social events. The managers who wander around include both first-level superiors and higher-ranking executives. By spending so much time in personal contact with employees, they enhance open communication.

5. *Focus on long-term results.* The Japanese leadership style emphasizes patience for results. Japanese executives are willing to listen to ideas that are likely to pay off in the long run. Short-term results are less important. Also of note, the long-term employment philosophy creates less worry about job security. This being true, Japanese workers are less likely to resist technological improvements.

Evaluation of Japanese Leadership Practices.   On the positive side, Japanese management has led to good business results. Japanese companies have been very successful in competing with American and European companies. Outstanding examples include electronic products, automobiles, and cameras. Furthermore, when Japanese firms take over American and Canadian firms, productivity increases have been observed. By the late 1980s there were over 550 Japanese manufacturing and/or parts-assembly companies located in these two countries, and the number is rapidly increasing.[32] Among these prospering firms are Toyota Motor Corp. in partnership with General Motors Corp. in Fremont, California, Anne Klein (high-fashion women's clothing), and the Japanese-owned Bridgestone Corp. tire plant in Tennessee.

After an initial enthusiasm for Japanese management, a more tempered viewpoint has developed in North America. Careful analysis has revealed that some of the successes of Japanese management have been exaggerated. One fact is that U.S. productivity still exceeds that of the Japanese. Data compiled by the Japanese Productivity Center indicate that Japanese industry is more productive than is U.S. industry in iron and steel and about the same in the production of automobiles. U.S. productivity is better in all other categories, including printing and publishing, foods, apparel, and total manufacturing.[33]

A controversial argument against the Japanese style of leadership is that it encourages conformity in thinking and behavior. Creativity suffers because of the emphasis on work group harmony, obedience, and consensus decision making. The basis for this argument is that Japan remains a net importer of foreign technology. Japanese industry typically copies, and further develops, the product ideas and technology of others.[34] The counterargument is that many Japanese companies choose not to be innovators. Part of the business strategy of these companies is to enter a market after the major costly risks have been taken. Most of their research budget is spent on product engineering.

Another reservation about Japanese management is that it is not readily transportable to other cultures. The Japanese mode of management is designed for a culturally homogeneous work force. When you have cultural diversity—many different ethnic and social groups—harmony is much more difficult to achieve. As the Japanese culture is becoming more Westernized, some Japanese management practices are beginning to lose their effectiveness.

Japanese young people are less enamored with the notion of lifetime employment at one company. Japanese workers are becoming more concerned about their own careers and are less interested in being submerged into a group. The traditional Japanese system of management will have to be modified to adapt to its young managers and professionals. For example, the new breed will want more individual recognition.

ENTREPRENEURIAL AND INTRAPRENEURIAL LEADERSHIP

An entrepreneur was described in Chapter 1 as a manager who initiates an innovative business enterprise. Intrapreneurs were described in Chapter 4 as managers who function as entrepreneurs within a corporation. Here, our focus is on the type of leadership practiced by entrepreneurs and intrapreneurs.[36] A general picture emerges of task-oriented and charismatic leaders. Entrepreneurs drive themselves and others relentlessly, yet their personalities inspire others.

Entrepreneurial leadership is closely related to the personal characteristics of the entrepreneur. (This is true of most leadership styles because personal characteristics influence which leadership style is the most comfortable for the manager to use.) Peter F. Drucker observes, however, that entrepreneurship is also a set of management practices or behaviors.[37] Entrepreneurs often possess the following personal characteristics and behaviors.

1. *A strong achievement need.* Entrepreneurs have stronger achievement needs than most managers. They enjoy accomplishment for its own sake. Building a business is an excellent vehicle for accomplishment. The high achiever shows three consistent behaviors and attitudes.

    a. Taking personal responsibility to solve problems.

    b. Attempting to achieve moderate goals at moderate risks.

    c. Prefering situations that provide frequent feedback on results (readily found in starting a new enterprise).[38]

2. *High enthusiasm and creativity.* Related to the achievement need, entrepreneurs are typically enthusiastic and creative. Their enthusiasm in turn makes them persuasive. As a result, entrepreneurs are often perceived as charismatic by their employees and customers. Some entrepreneurs are frequently so emotional that they are regarded as eccentric.

3. *Always in a hurry.* Entrepreneurs and intrapreneurs are always in a hurry. When engaged in one meeting, their minds typically begin to focus on the

next meeting. Their flurry of activity rubs off on subordinates and others around them. Entrepreneurs often adopt a simple dress style in order to save time. "He wears slip-on shoes so he doesn't have to bother with laces in the morning; he grows a beard; she cuts her hair short. Everything is hurry, hurry."[39]

4. *Visionary perspective.* Entrepreneurs, at their best, are visionaries. They see opportunities others fail to observe. Specifically, they have the ability to identify a problem and come up with the solution. Entrepreneurial insights have led to such popular consumer products as zippers, fiberglass skis, Velcro adhesive strips, and Big Mac hamburgers.[40]

5. *Uncomfortable with hierarchy and bureaucracy.* Entrepreneurs are not ideally suited by temperament to working within the mainstream of a bureaucracy. Many successful entrepreneurs are people who were frustrated by the constraints of a bureaucratic system (see the accompanying "Manager in Action"). Once an entrepreneur launches a successful business, he or she would be wise to hire a professional manager to take over the internal workings of the firm. The entrepreneur would then be free to concentrate on making sales, raising capital, and pursuing other external contacts. Intrapreneurs, by definition, fit reasonably well into a bureaucracy, yet they do not like to be restrained by tight regulations.

6. *A much stronger interest in dealing with customers than employees.* One of the reasons entrepreneurs and intrapreneurs have difficulty with bureaucracy is that they focus their energies on products, services, and customers. Some entrepreneurs are gracious to customers and money lenders but brusque with company insiders.

MANAGER IN ACTION:

The New Entrepreneurial Woman

Judy E. Meador graduated at the top of her class in an MBA program at Washington University in St. Louis, Missouri. She then joined the corporate finance department at A. G. Edwards & Sons, Inc., an investment banking and securities firm. Her starting annual salary was $6,000 in 1966, about half what male MBAs were earning at the time. In 1972 Meador became the first—and the youngest—female vice president in the history of A.G. Edwards. Yet when the firm's partners refused to appoint her manager of the corporate finance department in 1973, she left to start her own company.

Today she operates her own consulting firm in St. Louis, assisting closely held firms (those whose stock is not widely held) to make strategic planning and investment decisions. She earns a six-figure income, with one half derived from the firm and the other half derived from her own stock and real estate investments. Meador, now in her midforties, has no regrets about leaving what she perceived to be the corporate rate race. "I like to be my own boss," she explains.

Source: As reported in Rita Stollman, "The New Entrepreneurial Woman," *Business Week Careers* (October 1987): 84.

WOMEN AS MANAGERIAL LEADERS

An important new development in organizational leadership is that more women hold managerial positions today than in the past. The trend is noticeable at all levels of management. For example, women have become chief executive officers of several major firms including Northwestern Bell Telephone Co. and the Grocery Division of Nabisco Brands, Inc. Two aspects of women as managerial leaders are dealt with here: leadership characteristics and leadership style.

Leadership Characteristics

The traits and characteristics that make for effective leadership are about the same for men and women. Research suggests that there is little difference in the personal characteristics of men and women who become organizational leaders. A long-term study was conducted at AT&T to compare the characteristics of people of both sexes who advanced rapidly into managerial positions. Men and women who made rapid progress in the organization showed similar characteristics and behaviors. Factors aiding success for both males and females included oral communication skills, wide range of interests, and organizing and planning ability.[41]

Despite the "no difference" conclusion reached by the AT&T and similar studies, one controversial finding is worth noting. A study conducted by two psychologists suggests that physical attractiveness has a different effect on the careers of males and females.[42] "Attractiveness" in this study was measured by ratings given to photographs. Male and female students in a business administration class received resume packages for equally qualified candidates. Each resume included a photograph of either an attractive or an unattractive man or woman.

One conclusion reached was that being physically attractive was always an advantage for men. Attractive men received stronger recommendations for being hired. They were also judged to have better qualifications, and they were given higher suggested starting salaries than were unattractive men. The opposite findings were noted for women. Women who were judged to be less attractive were given more favorable recommendations for managerial positions. Physical attractiveness was an advantage only when women applied for individual-contributor positions.

A recent study by DuBrin of 350 managers, business owners, and professionals supported these findings. His research showed that men are more likely than women to use their personal appearance and charm to gain advantage in a work setting.[43] The results of both studies are consistent with the oft-repeated advice that women who aspire toward managerial work should not wear overly feminine clothing to work.

Leadership Style

Some people argue that women have certain acquired traits and behaviors that suit them for people-oriented leadership. Among these are the abilities to resolve conflict among subordinates, listen to people and counsel them, and size up people. It is also argued that women's natural sensitivity to people gives them an edge over men in being participative leaders.[44] This point of view implies at the same time that men are natural authoritarians! What is your opinion about the relative suitability of men and women for being people-oriented leaders?

THE TRANSFORMATIONAL LEADER

A relatively new concept in organizational leadership is the transformational leader—one who helps organizations and people make positive changes in the way they do things.[45] The transformational leader is contrasted to the transactional leader who mostly conducts transactions with other people rather than bringing about major changes. The transformational leader therefore exerts more influence than the transactional leader.

Transformational leadership has been viewed as the key to revitalizing large business corporations. The transformational leader can develop new visions for the organization and mobilize employees to accept and work toward attaining these visions. To bring about these changes, the transformational leader overhauls the organizational culture. Bernard Bass views the transformational leader as one who motivates employees to do more than we expected. Such transformations take place in one or more of three ways:

1. Raising people's level of consciousness about the importance and value of designated rewards and the ways to achieve them.

2. Getting people to transcend their self-interests for the sake of the work group and the firm.

3. Raising people's focus on minor satisfactions to a quest for self-fulfillment.[46]

Which particular manager classifies as a transformational leader is to some extent a matter of subjective interpretation. One person who might classify as a transformational leader is Tom Monaghan, the owner of Domino's Pizza and the Detroit Tigers. He was able to build a local pizzeria into one of the two largest pizza chains, to some extent by getting employees to believe in his high standards of on-time delivery. As implied from this example, transformational leaders are charismatic; their personal characteristics arouse positive emotion in others.

THE PATH-GOAL THEORY OF LEADERSHIP

The path-goal theory of leadership describes what a leader must do to be effective. The effective leader clarifies the paths to attaining goals, helps subordinates progress along these paths, and removes barriers on the path that may block goal attainment.[47] In general, the path-goal theory provides managers with specific guidelines for bringing about high productivity and morale in a given situation.

   The path-goal theory is a contingency explanation of leadership because it describes how a leader should behave in a given situation to bring about productivity and morale. The path-goal theory is complex and has several different versions. Its key features are in Figure 9-4. The major point illustrated is that the manager should choose a leadership style that takes into account the characteristics of the subordinates and the demands of the task.

Figure 9-4   The Path-Goal Theory of Leadership

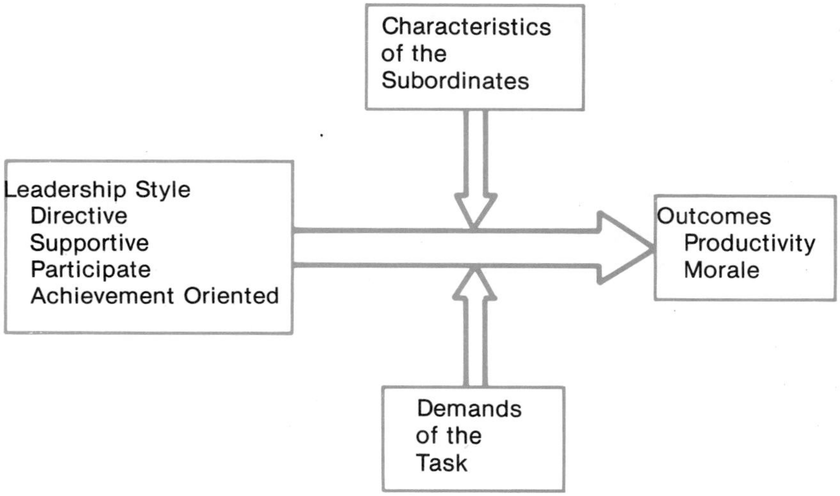

Matching the Leadership Style to the Situation

A cornerstone of path-goal theory is that the leader should choose among four different leadership styles to get the best results in a given situation. Two important aspects of the situation are the type of subordinates and the type of work they perform. For example, if the manager is leading capable subordinates who perform a nonrepetitive task, he or she should choose the participative style. Described next are the four leadership styles and the situation best suited for each one.

Directive Leadership Style.   The directive leader emphasizes formal activities such as planning, organizing, and controlling. Subordinates are told carefully what is expected of them. They are given specific guidelines on rules and regulations. The directive style of leadership improves morale when the task is unclear. However, the same style may lower job satisfaction when the task is clearly defined. Recent evidence confirms the idea that new employees may need a high degree of task structuring.[48]

Supportive Leadership Style.   The supportive leader displays concern for subordinates' well-being and tries to create an emotionally supportive climate. The leader also emphasizes developing mutually satisfying relationships among group members. The supportive leader aids morale when subordinates work on dissatisfying, stressful, or frustrating tasks. Workers who are unsure of themselves prefer the supportive leadership style.

Participative Leadership Style.   The participative leader consults with subordinates to gather their suggestions and then takes these suggestions seriously when making a decision. The participative leadership style improves the morale of well-motivated and capable subordinates who perform nonrepetitive tasks.

Achievement-Oriented Leadership Style.   The achievement-oriented leader sets challenging goals, pushes for work improvement, and sets high expectations for subordinates. Subordinates are also expected to assume responsibility. The achievement-oriented leadership style works well with achievement-oriented subordinates. When subordinates work on ambiguous and nonrepetitive tasks, this style of leadership works well. The subordinates become more confident that their efforts will lead to good performance.

How the Leader Influences Performance

In addition to suggesting leadership styles to fit the situation, path-goal theory offers many other suggestions to leaders. Most of these suggestions relate to motivating subordinates. The path-goal theory is based on the expectancy theory of motivation, described in Chapter 10, "Motivating for Results." There are a number of things the leader can do to improve the chances of subordinates following his or her wishes.[49]

1.   Recognize or activate subordinates' needs for rewards over which the leader has some control. An application of this principle would be for the leader to explain to employees how they can qualify for overtime pay.

2.   Increase the personal payoffs to subordinates for attaining work goals. The leader might give high-performing employees additional recognition.

3.   Make the path to payoffs (rewards) easier by coaching and direction. Here a manager might help a subordinate develop a skill that is valued by the organization.

4.   Help subordinates clarify their expectations of how effort will lead to good performance and how good performance will lead to a reward. The leader might say, "Five out of the last six sales reps who did well in this territory were later promoted."

5. Reduce frustrating barriers to reaching goals. For example, the leader might replace the employee's faulty equipment.

6. Increase the opportunities for personal satisfaction if the subordinate performs effectively. In this way, the path-goal theory is a contingency theory.

We have examined leaders themselves, leadership styles, entrepreneurial and intrapreneurial leaders, women as leaders, transformational leaders, and the path-goal theory of leadership. The next two sections of the chapter deal with a recurring demand of the leader's role: managing conflict and change.

THE LEADER'S ROLE IN MANAGING CONFLICT

Conflict is the simultaneous arousal of two or more incompatible motives, often accompanied by tension and frustration. In practice, this means that whenever two or more people in the workplace compete for the same resource, conflict occurs. For instance, two employees might want a telephone-answering machine, but there is money available for only one machine. Conflict can also be considered a hostile or antagonistic relationship between people. However, the hostility and antagonism stem from the incompatibility of motives. The two people in conflict over the answering machine may develop an antagonistic relationship.

Because resources in any organization are limited, not everybody's motives and desires can be satisfied. The manager must help people deal with conflict in order to keep the organizational unit running smoothly. An important role for the manager is therefore to act as a mediator in settling disputes among subordinates.[50] Two aspects of conflict of particular interest to the leader are its consequences and the methods for its resolution.

Consequences of Conflict

Conflict is a source of stress. The right amount of conflict may enhance job performance, whereas too much or too little stress lowers job performance. These relationships are shown in Figure 9-5. If the manager observes that job performance is suffering because of too much conflict, he or she should reduce conflict. If job performance is too low because employees are too placid, the manager might profitably increase conflict. For example, the manager might establish a prize for top performance in the group.

Positive Consequences of Conflict.   When the right amount of conflict is present in the workplace, one or more of the following outcomes can be anticipated.

1. *Increased creativity*. Talents and abilities surface in response to conflict. People become inventive when they are placed in intense competition with others.

Figure 9-5   The Relationship Between Conflict and Job Performance

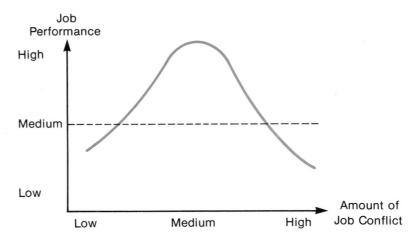

2. *Increased effort.* Constructive amounts of conflict spur people on to new heights of performance. People become so motivated to win the conflict that they may surprise themselves and their superiors with their work output.

3. *Increased diagnostic information.* Conflict can provide valuable information about problem areas in the department or organization. When leaders learn of conflict, they may conduct investigations that will lead to the prevention of similar problems. Frequent conflicts about expense accounts led one firm to switch to fixed travel allowances for meals, with some differentials for large metropolitan areas.

4. *Increased group cohesion.* Group cohesiveness is the tendency of a group to stick together and to work more closely with each other. When one group in the firm is in conflict with another, group members may become more cohesive. They perceive themselves to be facing a common enemy.

Negative Consequences of Conflict.   When the wrong amount or type of conflict exists, job performance may suffer. Some types of conflict have worse consequences than others. A particularly bad form of conflict is one that forces a person to choose between two undesirable alternatives. Negative consequences of conflict include the following.

1. *Poor physical and mental health.* Intense conflict is a source of stress, so the person under prolonged and intense conflict may suffer stress-related disorders.

2. *Wasted resources.* Employees and groups in conflict frequently waste

time, money, and other resources while fighting their battles. One executive took a personal dislike to one of his managers. The latter was given a special assignment that involved performing trivial tasks. At the same time, another manager was hired to replace the disliked manager. The wasted resources included the original manager's talents and the compensation given to the new manager.

3. *Important goals are sidetracked.* In extreme forms of conflict, the parties involved may neglect pursuing important goals. Instead, they are intent on winning their conflicts. A goal displacement of this type took place within an information-systems group. The rival factions spent so much time squabbling over which new hardware and software to purchase that they neglected some of their tasks.

4. *Self-interest becomes heightened.* Conflict often results in extreme demonstrations of self-interest at the expense of the larger organization. Individuals or departments place their personal interests over those of the rest of the firm or customers. A frequently observed example is when managers expend considerable effort to increase the size of their organizational units, whether or not this expansion serves the interests of the firm. Such behavior is referred to as "empire building."

Methods of Conflict Resolution

Managers spend as much as 20 percent of their work time dealing with conflict.[51] A leader who learns to manage conflict effectively thus can increase his or her productivity. In addition, being able to resolve conflict enhances one's stature as a leader. Employees expect their boss to be able to resolve conflicts. Here we describe five frequently used methods of resolving conflict: confrontation and problem solving, negotiation and bargaining, authoritative command, exchange of members between units, and modifying the organization structure.

Confrontation and Problem Solving.   This is the method of problem solving preferred by most behavioral scientists and management experts. Its purpose is to identify the real problem and then arrive at a solution that genuinely solves the problem. First the parties are brought together and the real problem is confronted. An accounting supervisor was in frequent conflict with the sales manager over money spent by sales representatives on meals. Sometimes the sales manager agreed with the accounting manager. When the sales manager did not agree with the accounting supervisor, conflict ensued. The two managers talked candidly to each other about the problem. They even admitted that the expense-account disagreement was leading to distrust between them. Jointly, they suggested the per-diem (fixed daily) rate used by some firms. The fixed rate would end suspicions about nonauthentic expense reports. The suggestion, including a geographic differential, was accepted and became company policy.

Negotiation and Bargaining.   The conventional way of resolving conflict is for both sides to negotiate or bargain until a compromise solution is reached. One side agrees to make a concession if the other side will do likewise.

Although negotiation leads to a compromise that may not solve the real problem, it remains a popular technique of conflict resolution. Managers and nonmanagers alike perceive negotiation to be the natural method of conflict resolution. Therefore, two employees in conflict often will accept a manager's request to reach a compromise.

Authoritative Command.   Managers frequently resolve conflict by the use of authoritative command—the use of formal authority to get subordinates to accept the manager's solution to the conflict. When using authoritative command, the manager acts as a judge. "I have heard both your sides of the story, and here is my verdict." Most people in a bureaucracy accept formal authority, so this approach to resolving conflict has merit. Its main drawback is that, like compromise, it does not get at the underlying problem. Suppose the common boss of the supervisor and manager said, "I don't want to hear any more about this problem from either of you. Here is what you must do." Conflict might be suppressed, but the problem would not be solved.

Exchange of Members between Units.   Empathy and understanding help reduce conflict. One way to acquire empathy and understanding for the other side is to work in their organizational unit. Exchanging members between groups in conflict, or potential conflict, is thus another helpful approach to conflict resolution. Reassigning people in this way can achieve the benefit of introducing different viewpoints in the affected groups. As the group members get to know each other better, they tend to reduce some of their distorted perceptions.

An important precaution in using exchange of members to resolve conflict is that the people involved must be technically competent to handle their new assignments. A positive example is that, in order to reduce intergroup conflict, a bank exchanged members between the consumer and commercial loan groups. The employees involved quickly learned their new assignments.

Changing the Organization Structure.   A widely used approach to conflict resolution is to change the structure of an organization in such a way that the sources of conflict are minimized. Changing the structure is particularly helpful in reducing conflict that stems from natural conflict between two groups. In one insurance company the programmers were in frequent conflict with end users. Among the conflict issues was that the programmers believed that the end users lacked sufficient technical knowledge to understand what computers could do for them. The end users believed that the programmers were more interested in computers than in solving their problems. A liaison position was then created whereby a buffer person would communicate between the programmers and end users. Labeled as computer-services coordinator, the person spoke the language and understood the demands of both groups. As a result of this new position, conflict between the programmers and end users was substantially reduced.

THE LEADER'S ROLE IN MANAGING CHANGE

Another leadership challenge is to help employees cope with change. Change can act as a stressor. The more profound the change, the greater the stress. Most people resist changes they think will have negative consequences for them. The perceived negative consequences might include low income, loss of friendships, need to learn difficult skills, or more physical exertion. Another major reason for resistance to change is fear of the unknown. People resist change when they are not clear about the effects of change on them.

Strategies for Managing Change

A sampling of strategies managers might keep in mind in overcoming resistance to change by subordinates, and by themselves, is presented here. It usually is more effective to use a combination of several of these approaches to managing change.

Understand the Change Process.   The most comprehensive method of overcoming resistance to change is to use the change model proposed by Lewin.[52] As shown in Figure 9-6, it involves three steps. First, unfreeze the status quo. This involves reducing or eliminating resistance. (The strategies described in the balance of this section can be applied here.) Second, change to a new state; the employees' attitudes and behavior shift in the desired direction. A typical desired shift would be to use enthusiastically a new piece of automated equipment. Third, refreeze, or permanently adopt, the new attitudes or behaviors.

Discuss the Changes.   One standard tactic for reducing or eliminating resistance to change is to discuss the changes with the people involved. As people talk about the changes and ask questions, many of their worries and concerns are lessened.

Figure 9-6   The Change Process

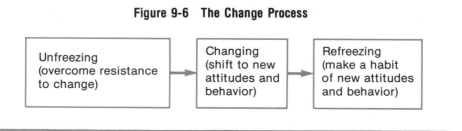

Encourage Participation.   Even more helpful than discussion alone is to encourage employees to participate in decisions about the change. When people contribute to a decision, they are unlikely to later call the decision foolish.

Allow for Negotiation.   Resistance to change can be lowered by negotiating some of the more controversial aspects of the change.[53] This tactic is often necessary when working with labor unions because of union interest in preserving jobs. A newspaper and its labor union faced a conflict over computerized typesetting, which would mean the loss of many jobs. The company and union reached a constructive agreement. The new machinery was installed, but no typesetters were laid off. However, when typesetters left the company voluntarily, they were not replaced.

Talk about Financial Benefits.   The prospect of earning more money helps overcome resistance to change. In the example just mentioned, management could reduce resistance to change by pointing out how the new machinery could lead to higher productivity bonuses for workers. Nonfinancial benefits can also be effective in overcoming resistance to change.

Place Adaptable People in Key Spots.   A tactic for implementing change is to put adaptable people into jobs most directly associated with the change. An enthusiastic pressroom technician might be made the internal expert on the new equipment. That worker's enthusiasm and adaptability would encourage other workers to accept the changes.

SUMMARY OF KEY POINTS

Leadership is the process of influencing people to achieve certain objectives without using unduly coercive tactics. The quality of leadership is known to influence organizational performance. Power is the ability to get other people to do things or the ability to control resources. Authority is the formal right to wield power.

Position power is the authority granted by the organization. It includes legitimate power, reward power, and coercive power. Personal power stems from the leader's personal characteristics. It includes expert power and referent power, or charisma. Leaders also use tactics such as leading by example, assertiveness, rationality, ingratiation, and exchange, to get other people to act.

Certain personal characteristics are associated with successful managerial leadership in many situations. These characteristics include a strong need for achievement and power, self-confidence, strong work motivation, sensitivity to people, good intellectual ability, sense of humor, and vision. Effective leaders also need good administrative skills, adaptability to the situation, stable performance, high standards of performance for subordinates, and the ability to give emotional support to subordinates. They should provide frequent feedback to subordinates and recover quickly from setbacks.

Leadership style is the typical pattern of behavior that a leader uses to influence employees to achieve organizational goals. Autocratic leaders attempt to retain most of the authority. Participative leaders share decision making with the group. One subtype of participative leader is the democratic leader who confers final authority on the group. Another is the consultative leader, who involves subordinates in decision making but retains final authority. A consensus leader also involves subordinates in decision making. The final decision reflects group consensus.

Autocratic managers make Theory X assumptions about people. They believe people basically dislike work and need to be controlled. Participative managers make Theory Y assumptions about people. They believe that people enjoy their work and want to be self-directing.

Participative leadership works well with competent and self-motivated employees. It is often good for the company and employees. However, first-level managers have some concerns about worker-participation programs. They worry about job security, job definitions, and the amount of extra work participation programs can create for them. Free-rein leaders turn over virtually all authority and control to the group. The free-rein style thus works best with self-sufficient and talented workers.

The managerial grid classifies leaders according to how much concern they have for both production and people. Team management, with its high emphasis on production and people, is considered the ideal.

The Japanese style of managerial leadership has five key components: consensus decision making, human resource development, recognition of employees as experts, management by wandering around, and focus on long-term results. Although the Japanese style of management has produced some excellent results, it is not well-suited to encouraging innovation or to employees who seek individual recognitiion.

Entrepreneurial and intrapreneurial leaders are generally task oriented and charismatic. They have a strong achievement need, high enthusiasm and creativity, and a visionary perspective. They are uncomfortable with hierarchy and bureaucracy and are always in a hurry.

Today, more women are managerial leaders, at all levels, than in the past. Effective male and female leaders have similar personal characteristics and display similar behaviors. There is some evidence, however, that physical attractiveness is more helpful to males in being selected as leaders. It is possible that women have certain acquired traits and behaviors that suit them for people-oriented leadership.

The path-goal leadership theory offers a comprehensive explanation of how leaders can bring about high productivity and morale. Effective leaders clarify the paths to attaining goals, help subordinates progress along these paths, and remove barriers to attaining goals. Leaders must choose a style that best fits the characteristics of the subordinates and the task. The four possible leadership styles are the directive, supportive, participative, and achievement-oriented styles.

An important part of a leader's role is to manage conflict. Conflict has both positive and negative consequences. Methods used by leaders to resolve conflict include confrontation and problem solving, negotiation and bargaining, authoritative command, exchange of members between organizational units, and changing the organization structure.

The leader is also called on to help manage change. To accomplish this, the leader should understand the change process (unfreezing, changing, and refreezing), discuss the changes with employees, encourage participation, allow for negotiation, talk about the financial benefits, and place adaptable people in key spots.

QUESTIONS

1. Is brainwashing a form of leadership? Why or why not?
2. What kinds of power does a CEO exercise both inside the office and outside the office?
3. What kinds of power does your instructor use for this course exercise?
4. What evidence would lead you to conclude that a person had a strong power need?
5. Describe how a leader might make use of a self-fulfilling prophecy in getting subordinates to perform.
6. What is your leadership style? Or, what do you think your style of leadership will be when you become a manager?
7. Why do so many people use the term *autocrat* in a derogatory manner?
8. For what type of leadership situation might a transformational leader not be appropriate?
9. Why is the path-goal theory of leadership considered to be a contingency theory?
10. Why would a manager want to increase the level of conflict in his or her organizational unit?

ACTIVITIES

1. Interview any practicing manager. Find out what that person thinks of participative management, and report your findings in class.
2. Two departments in your organization are in frequent conflict over whose demands should receive higher priority from the computer-services group. Suggest a new organizational structure (or arrangement) to alleviate this conflict.

CASE PROBLEM 9-A: TADUSCHI KAMATO PRACTICES PARTICIPATIVE MANAGEMENT

Home Electronics is a Japanese company that sells its products worldwide. Recently, it built a plant in Wisconsin to manufacture its successful line of telephone receivers. In addition to the standard telephone, Home Electronics offers many decorative ones. The biggest selling item among these is a telephone fashioned after one from the 1920 era. Taduschi Kamato was recently hired as manager of the Wisconsin plant for several reasons. Above all, his education and experience were appropriate for this high-level assignment. The company also thought that Kamato's first-hand knowledge of

Japanese management techniques would be useful. Few of the predominantly American work force at the Wisconsin plant had worked under the Japanese system of management. Part of Kamato's assignment would be to move the managers and supervisors toward the Japanese management model (a high degree of employee participation).

Several months after Kamato had been installed as plant manager, a consultant was hired to conduct an employee attitude survey. The survey was designed to measure how much employees enjoyed their work and to identify problem areas requiring remedial action by management. The team of consultants administered questionnaires to every employee. In addition, a sample of employees was interviewed about their job attitudes. (Individual employees were not identified in reports given to the company.) Following is an excerpt from two employee attitude interviews:

Consultant: What do you think of the leadership at this plant?

Plant Financial Manager: That's a loaded question. Since I report to the plant manager, "leadership at the plant" means Kamato. I assume this is a confidential report. Kamato is a fine fellow, but he's a weak manager. So I don't think much of the leadership at the plant.

Consultant: What do you mean "weak manager"?

Plant financial manager: I mean the guy just won't make decisions. He expects his staff to make all the tough decisions. Right now he's asking my advice on developing a strategic plan for Home's manufacturing activities in this country. He loves to pass assignments down the line. He's always pestering me and others for our opinions on everything. I think he should allow us more time to do our own work. I sometimes think he uses Japanese-style management as a cop-out. Instead of his doing any demanding work, he gets us to do it.

Consultant: Do others share your opinion about the leadership at the plant?

Plant financial manager: I think you'll find the answer to that question is affirmative. See for yourself when your survey is completed.

Following is an excerpt from the consultant's interview with the plant engineering manager:

Consultant: What do you think of the leadership at this plant?

Plant engineering manager: So far, so good. It's a big improvement over my experiences in working for American-owned companies. Our boss is trying his hardest to create a democratic climate around here. Instead of making all the big decisions on his own, Kamato carefully consults with us. He will not make any major decision until we have reached consensus. This makes me feel that I'm helping to run the plant.

I'm consulted not just on engineering decisions. Kamato consults me and the other managers reporting to him on all decisions. He encourages us to do the same with the people reporting to us. In this way, every worker in the plant provides some input to decision making.

Consultant: Anything else you would like to say about the leadership at this plant?

Plant Engineering Manager: Good thing you asked. I forgot to mention how much emphasis there is on the human element. Kamato has helped us learn by example that assisting our employees to achieve a good life is the most important thing we do. It is more important than making telephones.

Consultant: Would others agree with your assessment of leadership at the plant?

Plant Engineering Manager: Certainly not 100 percent. Not everybody wants to shoulder the responsibility of contributing to key decisions. Here and there you may find some manager or employee who just doesn't want to get involved.

Consultant: Thanks for your time. You've been very helpful.

Case Questions

1. What do these interviews tell you about participative management?
2. What do these interviews tell you about contingency management?
3. Based on these interviews, what advice can you offer Taduschi Kamato?
4. What advice can you offer the plant financial manager?

EXERCISE 9-A: THE ENTREPRENEUR'S QUIZ

The following questionnaire will provide some tentative insight into your entrepreneurial traits and characteristics. If your traits and characteristics are similar to those of entrepreneurs, you may be suited for entrepreneurial leadership. The questionnaire is based on extensive research conducted by the Center for Entrepreneurial Management.

1. How were your parents employed?
   a. Both worked and were self-employed for most of their working lives.
   b. Both worked and were self-employed for some part of their working lives.
   c. One parent was self-employed for most of his or her working life.
   d. One parent was self-employed at some point in his or her working life.
   e. Neither parent was ever self-employed.
2. Have you ever been fired from a job?
   a. Yes, more than once.
   b. Yes, once.
   c. No.
3. Are you an immigrant, or were your parents or grandparents immigrants?
   a. I was born outside of the United States.
   b. One or both of my parents were born outside of the United States.
   c. At least one of my grandparents was born outside of the United States.
   d. Does not apply.
4. Your career has been:
   a. Primarily in small business (under 100 employees).
   b. Primarily in medium-

sized business (101 to 500 employees).

c. Primarily in big business (over 500 employees).

5. How many businesses did you operate before you were 20?
   a. Many.
   b. A few.
   c. None.

6. What is you present age?
   a. 21-30.
   b. 31-40.
   c. 41-50.
   d. 51 or over.

7. You are __ child in the family.
   a. Oldest
   b. Middle.
   c. Youngest.
   d. Other.

8. What is your marital status?
   a. Married.
   b. Divorced.
   c. Single.

9. Your highest level of formal education is:
   a. Some high school.
   b. High school diploma.
   c. Bachelor's degree.
   d. Master's degree.
   e. Doctorate.

10. What is your primary motivation in starting a business?
    a. To make money.
    b. I don't like working for someone else.
    c. To be famous.
    d. To have an outlet for excess energy.

11. Your relationship with the parent who provided most of the family's income was:
    a. Strained.
    b. Comfortable.
    c. Competitive.
    d. Non-existent.

12. If you could choose between working hard and working smart, you would:
    a. Work hard.
    b. Work smart.

c. Both.

13. On whom do you rely for critical management advice?
    a. Internal management teams.
    b. External management professionals.
    c. External financial professionals.
    d. No one except myself.

14. If you were at the racetrack, which of these would you bet on?
    a. The daily double—a chance to make a killing.
    b. A ten-to-one shot.
    c. A three-to-one shot.
    d. The two-to-one favorite.

15. The only ingredient that is both necessary and sufficient for starting a business is:
    a. Money.
    b. Customers.
    c. An idea or product.
    d. Motivation and hard work.

16. If you were an advanced tennis player and had a chance to play a top pro like Jimmy Connors, you would:
    a. Turn it down because he could easily beat you.
    b. Accept the challenge, but not bet any money on it.
    c. Bet a week's pay that you would win.
    d. Get odds, bet a fortune and try for an upset.

17. You tend to "fall in love" too quickly with:
    a. New product ideas.
    b. New employees.
    c. Manufacturing ideas.
    d. New financial plans.
    e. All of the above.

18. Which of the following personality types is best suited to be your right-hand person?
    a. Bright and energetic.

b. Bright and lazy.
c. Dumb and energetic.
19. You accomplish tasks better because:
a. You are always on time.
b. You are super organized.
c. You keep good records.
20. You hate to discuss:
a. Problems involving employees.
b. Signing expense accounts.
c. New management practices.
d. The future of the business.
21. Given a choice, you would prefer:
a. Rolling dice with a one-in-three chance of winning.
b. Working on a problem with a one-in-three chance of solving it in the allotted time.
22. If you could choose between the following competitive professions, your choice would be:
a. Professional golf.
b. Sales.
c. Personal counseling.

d. Teaching.
23. If you had to choose between working with a partner who is a close friend and working with a stranger who is an expert in your field, your choice would be:
a. The close friend.
b. The expert.
24. You enjoy being with people:
a. When you have something meaningful to do.
b. When you can do something new and different.
c. Even when you have nothing planned.
25. In business situations that demand action, will clarifying who is in charge help produce results?
a. Yes.
b. Yes, with reservations.
c. No.
26. In playing a competitive game, you are concerned with:
a. How well you play.
b. Winning or losing.
c. Both of the above.
d. Neither of the above.

SCORING

1)	$a = 10, b = 5, c = 5, d = 2, e = 0$	14) $a = 0, b = 2, c = 10, d = 3$
2)	$a = 10, b = 7, c = 0$	15) $a = 0, b = 10, c = 0, d = 0$
3)	$a = 5, b = 4, c = 3, d = 0$	16) $a = 0, b = 10, c = 3, d = 0$
4)	$a = 10, b = 5, c = 0$	17) $a = 5, b = 5, c = 5, d = 5, e = 15$
5)	$a = 10, b = 7, c = 0$	18) $a = 2, b = 10, c = 0$
6)	$a = 8, b = 10, c = 5, d = 2$	19) $a = 5, b = 15, c = 5$
7)	$a = 15, b = 2, c = 0, d = 0$	20) $a = 8, b = 10, c = 0, d = 0$
8)	$a = 10, b = 2, c = 2$	21) $a = 0, b = 15$
9)	$a = 2, b = 3, c = 10, d = 8, e = 4$	22) $a = 3, b = 10, c = 0, d = 0$
10)	$a = 0, b = 15, c = 0, d = 0$	23) $a = 0, b = 10$
11)	$a = 10, b = 5, c = 10, d = 5$	24) $a = 3, b = 3, c = 10$
12)	$a = 0, b = 5, c = 10$	25) $a = 10, b = 2, c = 0$
13)	$a = 0, b = 10, c = 0, d = 5$	26) $a = 8, b = 10, c = 15, d = 0$

The scoring is weighted to determine your Entrepreneurial Profile.

235–285 . . . Successful entrepreneur*   170–184 . . . Potential entrepreneur
200–234 . . . Entrepreneur   155–169 . . . Borderline entrepreneur
185–199 . . . Latent entrepreneur   Below 154 . . . Hired hand

*The Center for Entrepreneurial Management member profile is 239.

Source: Reprinted with permission. J.R. Mancuso, Center for Entrepreneurial Management, Inc., 180
        Varick Street, New York, NY 10014.

REFERENCES

1. Paul Hersey and Kenneth H. Blanchard, *Management of Organizational Behavior: Utilizing Human Resources,* 5th ed. (Englewood Cliffs, NJ: Prentice Hall, 1988), 86.
2. As quoted in Scott DeGarmo, "The Leadership Factor," *Success* (April 1988): 2.
3. John R. Schermerhorn, Jr., *Management for Productivity,* 2nd ed. (New York: John Wiley & Sons, 1988).
4. John R. P. French, Jr., and Bertram Raven, "The Bases of Social Power," Dorwin Cartwright and Alvin F. Zander (eds.), *Group Dynamics: Research and Theory* (New York: Harper & Row, 1960), 607–623; an updating of this material is found in Timothy R. Hinkin and Chester A. Schriesheim, "Power and Influence: The View from Below," *Personnel* (May 1988): 47–50.
5. Jay A. Conger and Rabindra N. Kanungo, "Toward a Behavioral Theory of Charismatic Leadership in Organizational Settings," *Academy of Management Review* (October 1987): 637.
6. Gary Yukl and Tom Taber, "The Effective Use of Managerial Power," *Personnel* (March–April 1983): 42.
7. David Kipnis, Stuart M. Schmidt, and Ian Wilkinson, "Intraorganizational Influence Tactics: Exploration in Getting One's Way," *Journal of Applied Psychology* (August 1980): 440–452.
8. R. Bruce McAfee and Betty J. Ricks, "Leadership by Example: 'Do as I Do!'" *Management Solutions* (August 1986): 15.
9. Mauk Mulder and assocs., "Power, Situation, and Leaders' Effectiveness: An Organizational Field Study," *Journal of Applied Psychology* (November 1986): 566–570.
10. Robert G. Lord and assocs., "A Meta-Analysis of the Relationship Between Personality Traits and Leadership Perceptions: An Application of Validity Generalization Procedures," *Journal of Applied Psychology* (August 1986): 402–410.
11. Three classic references here are Edwin E. Ghiselli, *Explorations in Managerial Talent* (Santa Monica, CA: Goodyear, 1971); Jay Hall, "What Makes a Manager Good, Bad, or Average?" *Psychology Today* (August 1976): 52–53, 55; Burt K. Scanlon, "Managerial Leadership in Perspective: Getting Back to Basics," *Personnel Journal* (March 1979): 168–171, 183.

12. Michael J. Stahl, "Achievement, Power and Managerial Motivation: Selecting Managerial Talent with the Job Choice Exercise," *Personnel Psychology* (Winter 1983): 776.

13. Morgan W. McCall, Jr., and Michael M. Lombardo, *Off the Track: How and Why Successful Executives Get Derailed* (Greensboro, NC: Center for Creative Leadership, 1983), 14.

14. Fred E. Fiedler and Joseph E. Garcia, *New Approaches to Effective Leadership: Cognitive Resources and Organizational Performance.* (New York: John Wiley & Sons, 1987) [As quoted in book review, *The Academy of Management Review* (April 1988): 328.]

15. W. Jack Duncan, "Humor in Management: Prospects for Administrative Practice and Research," *Academy of Management Review* (January 1982): 136–140.

16. Glenn Collins, "Humor Is Newest Tool to Lessen Stress, Motivate Workers," *New York Times,* 2 May 1988.

17. Collins, "Humor Is Newest Tool."

18. Richard L. Lester, "Leadership: Some Principles and Concepts," *Personnel Journal* (November 1981): 870.

19. Sherry Siegel, "Selling Your Way to the Top," *Success* (January–February 1987): 41.

20. "Committee Seeks 'Value Added' Exam for Students, Added Value for B Schools," American Assembly of Collegiate Schools of Business, *Newsline* (October 1982): 1.

21. Joan Detz, "The Adaptive Leader," *Success* (June 1987): 44–47.

22. Warren Bennis and Burt Nanus, "The Leadership Tightrope," *Success* (March 1985): 62; Manuel London, *Developing Managers* (San Francisco: Jossey-Bass, Inc., Pubs., 1985).

23. Edward Glassman, "Leadership Style's Effect on the Creativity of Employees," *Management Solutions* (November 1986): 18.

24. Glassman, "Leadership Style's Effect," 24.

25. Glassman, "Leadership Style's Effect," 24.

26. Douglas McGregor, *The Human Side of Enterprise* (New York: McGraw-Hill, 1960), 33–48.

27. Janice A. Klein, "Why Supervisors Resist Employee Involvement," *Harvard Business Review* (September–October 1984): 88–89.

28. Robert R. Blake and Jane S. Mouton, *The Managerial Grid III: The Key to Leadership Excellence* (Houston: Gulf Publishing Co., 1985), 10–15.

29. Bernard J. Keys and Thomas R. Miller, "The Japanese Management Theory Jungle," *Academy of Management Review* (April 1984): 342–353.

30. Mari Taketa, "World's Richest Person is Stingy," *Associated Press,* 22 August 1987.

31. Keys and Miller, "The Japanese Management Theory Jungle," 345.

32. Harris Jack Shapiro and Teresa Cosenza, *Reviving Industry in America: Japanese Influences on Manufacturing and the Service Sector* (Cambridge, MA: Ballinger Publishing Co., 1987), 24.

33. Frank Swoboda, "Ohio Plant Beats Japanese in Quality, Productivity," *Washington Post* (syndicated story), 27 December 1987; *Japan 1983: An International Comparison* (Tokyo: Keizai Koho Center, 1983), 65.

34. Nicholas Valery, "The Fabled Giant's Might is Dwindling," *Economist,* 9 July 1983.

35. Steve Lohr, "Shadows of the Rising Sun," *New York Times,* 17 June 1984.
36. Gifford Pinchot, III, *Intrapreneuring* (New York: Harper & Row, 1985); Walter L. Polsky and Loretta D. Foxman, "Intrapreneurship: Charting New Courses," *Personnel Journal* (August 1987): 116–118.
37. Peter F. Drucker, *Innovation and Entrepreneurship* (New York: Harper & Row, 1985).
38. David C. McClelland, *The Achieving Society* (New York: Van Nostrand Reinhold, 1961).
39. Priscilla Petty, "The Budding Entrepreneur is Dissatisfied, Energetic, and a Visionary," *Democrat and Chronicle* (24 April 1984).
40. "The Comeback of Risk Takers: They're Reshaping Business," *U.S. News & World Report* (24 September 1984): 60.
41. Richard J. Ritchie and Joseph L. Moses, "Assessment Center Correlates of Women's Advancement into Middle Management: A Seven-Year Longitudinal Study," *Journal of Applied Psychology* (May 1983): 229.
42. Thomas F. Cash and Louis H. Janda, "The Eye of the Beholder," *Psychology Today* (December 1984): 48.
43. Andrew J. DuBrin, "Sex Differences in the Endorsement of Influence Tactics and Political Behavior Tendencies," *Journal of Business and Psychology* (scheduled for publication, 1989).
44. Judith D. Schwartz, "Are Women Better Managers?" *Success* (March 1986): 16.
45. Noel M. Tichy and May Ann DeVanna, "The Transformational Leader," *Training and Development Journal* (July 1986): 27–32.
46. Bernard M. Bass, *Leadership and Performance Beyond Expectations* (New York: The Free Press, 1985).
47. Two key references for this theory are Robert J. House, "A Path-Goal Theory of Leadership Effectiveness," *Administrative Science Quarterly* (September 1971): 321–339; and Robert J. House and Terence R. Mitchell, "Path-Goal Theory of Leadership," *Journal of Contemporary Business* (autumn 1974): 81–98.
48. Robert P. Vecchio, "Situational Leadership Theory: An Examination of a Prescriptive Theory," *Journal of Applied Psychology* (August 1987): 444.
49. House and Mitchell, "Path-Goal Theory of Leadership," 84.
50. Dan DeStephen, "Mediating Those Office Conflicts," *Management Solutions* (March 1988): 5.
51. Robert A. Baron, "Reducing Organizational Conflict: The Role of Attributions," *Journal of Applied Psychology* (August 1985): 434.
52. Kurt Lewin, *Field Theory and Social Science* (New York: Harper & Row, 1964), Chs. 9 and 10.
53. Wayne R. Mondy, Robert E. Holmes, and Edwin B. Flippo, *Management Concepts and Practices,* 2nd ed. (Boston: Allyn & Bacon, Inc., 1983), 433.

10
Motivating for Results

After studying the material in this chapter, you should be able to accomplish the following tasks:

1. Understand the limits to how much motivation can contribute to performance and productivity.
2. Apply the need-satisfaction approach to motivation.
3. Describe in detail how behavior modification is used to motivate employees.
4. Pinpoint how gainsharing often leads to increased worker motivation.
5. Explain the conditions under which a person will be motivated according to expectancy theory.
6. Describe the contribution of employee control over working hours to motivation.
7. Recognize the influence of corporate culture on employee motivation.

Key Terms and Phrases

Motivation
Productivity
Performance
$P = M \times A$
Role clarity
Need theory
Maslow's need hierarchy
Physiological needs
Safety needs
Social needs
Esteem needs
Self-actualization needs
Two-factor theory
Satisfier
Motivator
Dissatisfier
Value
Goal
Feedback
Behavior modification

Reward
Law of effect
External (extrinsic) reward
Internal (intrinsic) reward
Positive reinforcement
Negative reinforcement
Extinction
Punishment
Antecedent
Behavior
Consequences
Contingent reinforcement
Intermittent schedule
Gainsharing
Expectancy theory
Instrumentality
Valence
Flexible working hours
Telecommuting
Organizational culture

The term *motivation* refers to two different, but related, ideas. From the standpoint of the individual, motivation is an internal state that leads to the pursuit of objectives. From the standpoint of the manager, motivation is an activity to get people to pursue objectives. Both concepts have an important meaning in common; **motivation** is the expenditure of effort to accomplish results. The effort stems from a force to perform that stems from one or more of three sources: the individual, the manager, or the group. The purpose of motivating subordinates is to get them to achieve objectives (or results) that help the organization.

How to motivate employees is a perennial challenge faced by managers. One current countertrend, however, is that the work ethic of the American work force appears to be higher than in previous decades. For example, employee absenteeism has declined steadily.[1] Economic factors underlie this surge in employee motivation: the restructuring of so many firms has made workers fear losing their jobs; most families need more than one income to meet their expenses; and wages in general have not kept up with inflation.

In this chapter, several theories or explanations of work motivation are presented. In addition, a description is provided of specific approaches to motivating employees, such as allowing them to profit from their contribution to gains in productivity. All of the ideas presented in this chapter can be applied to motivating oneself as well as others. For instance, when you read about motivation through need satisfaction, ask yourself this question: "What unsatisfied needs of mine will compel me to work harder?"

THE RELATIONSHIP OF MOTIVATION TO PRODUCTIVITY AND PERFORMANCE

A common misperception is that strong motivation almost always leads to high productivity and performance. **Productivity** is the ratio of input to output, with attention paid to quality. **Performance** is a more general term, and it refers to the quality and quantity of work produced. Many people believe the statement, "You can accomplish anything you want," or "Think positively and you will achieve all your goals."

In truth, motivation is but one important contributor to productivity and performance. Abilities, skills, and the right equipment are also indispensable. Sam Killam, an office supervisor at a bank, desperately wanted to become chairperson of the board within three years. Despite the intensity of his motivation, Sam did not reach his goal. The factors against Sam included his lack of formal business education, limited conceptual skills, underdeveloped political skills, and inadequate knowledge of high finance. To make matters worse, the bank's chairperson had no intention of leaving his post.

The relationship between motivation and performance is shown in Figure 10-1. It can also be expressed by the relationship, $P = M \times A$, where P refers to performance; M, to motivation; and A, to ability. Note that skill, technology, and role clarity contribute to ability.[2] For instance, if you are skilled at using a computer and you have the right hardware and software, you can perform a spreadsheet analysis.

Figure 10-1 Motivation and Ability Contribute to Performance

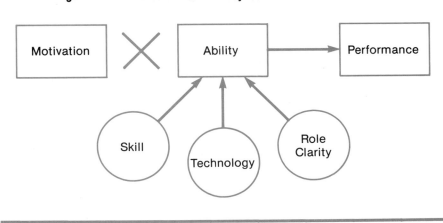

Role clarity is knowledge about what performance is required of the employee. It is the clearness of one's role in the organization. Information about role clarity must come from the organization. Role clarity contributes to performance directly. It is difficult to perform well if you are not sure what you should be doing.

The manager contributes to performance by motivating group members, improving their ability, and increasing role clarity. Has a manager ever contributed to your performance?

MOTIVATION THROUGH NEED SATISFACTION

The **need theory** of work motivation states that people work to satisfy needs. A need is a deficit within an individual, such as a craving for water or power. People are motivated to fulfill needs that are not currently satisfied. Need theory is covered here from three different perspectives. First, we describe a general model of need satisfaction. This is followed by a description of two cornerstone theories of work motivation: Maslow's need hierarchy and Herzberg's two-factor theory.

A General Model of Need Satisfaction

The central idea behind need theory is that needs that are unsatisfied motivate us until they become satisfied. When people are dissatisifed or anxious about their present status or performance, they will try to reduce this anxiety.[3] This need cycle is shown in Figure 10-2. Assume that a twenty-five-year-old man has a strong need for recognition. As a result, he experiences tension that drives him to find some way of being recognized on the job. The action he takes is to apply for a position as the assistant manager of a new restaurant.

Figure 10-2   The Need Theory of Motivation

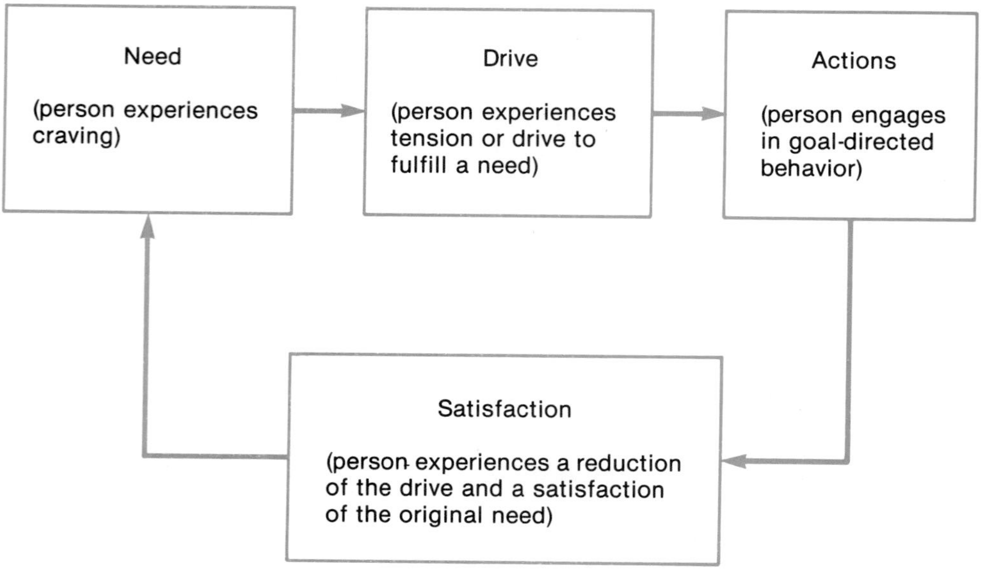

```
┌────────────────────┐     ┌────────────────────┐     ┌────────────────────┐
│       Need         │     │       Drive        │     │      Actions       │
│                    │ ──▶ │                    │ ──▶ │                    │
│ (person experiences│     │ (person experiences│     │ (person engages    │
│  craving)          │     │  tension or drive to│    │  in goal-directed  │
│                    │     │  fulfill a need)   │     │  behavior)         │
└────────────────────┘     └────────────────────┘     └────────────────────┘
         ▲                                                        │
         │            ┌──────────────────────────────────┐       │
         │            │           Satisfaction            │       │
         └─────────── │                                    │ ◀─────┘
                      │ (person experiences a reduction    │
                      │  of the drive and a satisfaction   │
                      │  of the original need)             │
                      └──────────────────────────────────┘
```

He realizes that helping run a new restaurant would provide ample opportunity for recognition, particularly if the restaurant becomes successful.

He is appointed to the position, and for now his need for recognition is at least partially satisfied as he receives compliments from the boss and customers. Once he receives this partial satisfaction, two things typically happen. Either he will soon require a stronger dose of recognition, or he will begin to concentrate on another need, such as autonomy. In either case, the need cycle will repeat itself. The man may seek another form of recognition, or satisfaction of his need for dominance. For example, he might decide to open his own restaurant. Ideally, his boss will give him more responsibility. This could lead to more satisfaction of his recognition need and to some satisfaction of his need to dominate others.

Needs People Try to Satisfy.   The work setting offers the opportunity to satisfy dozens of psychological needs. In the discussion of leadership and entrepreneurship, mention was made of the needs for achievement and power. Maslow's need hierarchy mentions five groups of well-known needs. Other important needs that can be satisfied on the job include the following:[4]

- *Autonomy.* The need to act independently and to be free of constraints.

- *Affiliation.* The need to seek close relationships with others and to be a loyal employee or friend.

- *Dominance.* The need to influence others toward your way of thinking, often by forceful methods.

- *Order.* The need to put things in order and to achieve balance, neatness, and precision.

- *Recognition.* The need to be acknowledged for one's contributions and efforts. The need for recognition is so pervasive that it has led to a large number of recognition programs, as illustrated in the accompanying "Organization in Action."

ORGANIZATION IN ACTION:

The Recognition People

According to the O. C. Tanner Co., a successful recognition program contains five key elements: a recognition symbol, an attractive means of display, a meaningful presentation, an effective promotion, and a review and updating.

Recognition Symbol. The first step is to develop an attractive symbol of service, which usually involves the company logo.

Display Option. Whether it's jewelry, pocket knives, pens, key chains, or desk accessories, it's important to get the service symbol out where it will be used and recognized by other employees.

Meaningful Presentation. By carefully deciding who presents the award and when and how it is presented, management can make the award worth many times its financial value.

Program Promotion. The company must show the employees that the recognition program is important by such means as descriptions presented on company bulletin boards and personal letters.

Review and Updating. In order to maintain excitement, recognition programs must be updated to meet shifting tastes. New accessories and gifts, new promotions, and new ways of presenting awards all sustain excitement.

Source: As reported in Abby Brown, "Today's Employees Choose Their Own Recognition Award," *Personnel Administrator* (August 1986): 52.

Using Needs to Motivate Employees. An important implication of need theory is that there are two key steps in motivating subordinates. First, you must know what people want—what needs they are trying to satisfy. This can be accomplished by directly asking or observing the person. Knowledge can also be obtained in a more indirect way by getting to know employees better. To obtain insight into employee needs, you must know something about the employee's personal life, education, work history, outside interests, and career goals.

Second, give each person a chance to satisfy the need in question on the job. To illustrate, one way to motivate a person with a strong need for autonomy is to allow that person to work independently.

A fundamental reason that need theories are so useful is that most people are strongly motivated by self-interest ("looking out for number one"). As Stephen P. Robbins notes, every person, consciously or unconsciously, asks himself "What's in it for me?" before engaging in any behavior.[5]

Maslow's Need Hierarchy

The most widely quoted explanation of human motivation was developed by psychologist Abraham Maslow.[6] His theory has been incorporated into new and more complex explanations of work motivation. According to **Maslow's need hierarchy**, people have an internal need pushing them toward self-actualization (self-fulfillment) and personal superiority. However, before these higher-level needs are activated, certain lower-level needs must be satisfied.

When a person's needs are satisfied at one level, he or she looks toward satisfaction at a higher level. The need cycle described in Figure 10-2 is based on the same principle. It is difficult for people ever to be fully satisfied for long. Maslow arranged human needs into a five-level pyramid, as shown in Figure 10-3. The groups of needs in ascending order are as follows:

1. **Physiological needs** refer to basic bodily needs such as the requirements for nutrition, water, shelter, moderate temperatures, rest, and sleep. Most office jobs allow us to satisfy physiological needs. Fire-fighting represents an occupation that can potentially frustrate some physiological needs. Smoke inhalation can block need satisfaction.

2. **Safety needs** include the desire to be safe from both physical and emotional injury. Many operatives who work at dangerous jobs—such as miners—would be motivated by the prospects of obtaining safety. Any highly stressful job can frustrate the need for emotional safety.

3. **Social needs** refer to needs for love, belonging to a group, and affiliation with people. Managers can contribute to the satisfaction of these needs by promoting teamwork and allowing people to chat with each other about work problems. Many employees regard their jobs as a major source of satisfaction of social needs.

4. **Esteem needs** reflect people's desire to be seen by themselves and others as a person of worth. Occupations with high status are a primary source for the satisfaction of esteem needs. Managers can help employees satisfy their esteem needs by praising the quality of their work.

5. **Self-actualization needs** refer to the desire to reach one's potential, and they include needs for self-fulfillment and personal development. True self-actualization is an ideal to strive for, rather than something that automatically stems from occupying a challenging position. Self-actualized people are those who are becoming all they are capable of becoming. Managers can help subordinates move toward self-

Figure 10-3   Maslow's Need Hierarchy

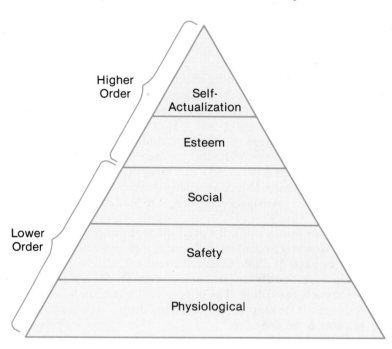

actualization by giving them challenging assignments and the chance for advancement and new learning.

Evaluation of the Need Hierarchy.   A major contribution of Maslow's need hierarchy is that it has prompted managers to take human needs seriously. It has dramatized the importance of satisfying needs in order to motivate employees. The need hierarchy has also helped managers realize that it is difficult to motivate people by appealing to satisfied needs. For example, offering overtime pay to an employee who is not concerned about money would not be motivational. Furthermore, Maslow has dramatized the fact that people are difficult to satisfy.

Despite its contribution, Maslow's need hierarchy should not be taken too literally. Not everybody wants to satisfy needs in a stepwise fashion. Some people will attempt to achieve esteem before satisfying their social needs. Another problem with the need hierarchy is that it overly simplifies motivation. It implies that people strive to satisfy one group of needs at a time. In reality, people usually try to satisfy more than one group of needs simultaneously.

Herzberg's Two-Factor Theory

The study of the need hierarchy led to the **two-factor theory** of work motivation. The key point to the theory is that there are two different sets of job factors. One set of factors can satisfy and motivate people. The other can only prevent dissatisfaction. The "two" in "two-factor" refers to these two sets of factors with different effects.

Psychologist Frederick Herzberg and his associates interviewed hundreds of professionals about their work. They discovered that some factors of the job give people a chance to satisfy higher-level needs.[7] Such elements of the job are called satisfiers or motivators. A **satisfier** is a job factor that, if present, leads to job satisfaction. Similarly, a **motivator** is a job factor that, if present, leads to motivation. Herzberg's theory originally dealt with job satisfaction, but now it is also considered a theory of job motivation. The two-factor theory implies that satisfaction leads to motivation and productivity. As described in Chapter 1, satisfaction is thought to lead *sometimes* to motivation and productivity.

Individuals vary somewhat in the particular job factors they find satisfying or motivating. However, satisfiers and motivators generally refer to the content (the heart or guts) of a job. These elements are achievement, recognition, challenging work, responsibility, and the opportunity for advancement. All of these factors are self-rewarding. The important implication here for managers is that they can motivate most people by giving them the opportunity to do interesting work or to be promoted.

Herzberg also discovered that some job elements appeal more to lower-level needs. Referred to as dissatisfiers, or hygiene factors, they are noticed primarily by their absence. A **dissatisfier** is a job element that, when present, prevents dissatisfaction—but does not create satisfaction. People will not be satisfied with their jobs just because hygiene factors are present. For example, not having a handy place to park your car would create dissatisfaction. But having a place to park would not make you happier about your job.

Dissatisfiers relate mostly to the context (the job setting or external elements). These include relationships with co-workers, company policy and administration, job security, and money. All of these factors deal with external rewards. Money, however, does work as a satisfier for many people. Some people want or need money so much that high pay contributes to their job satisfaction.

Also, financial incentives are now regarded as a powerful motivational tool (see the later discussion of gainsharing). One underlying reason that money can be a motivator is that high pay is often associated with high status and high esteem.

The major aspects of the two-factor theory of job motivation are summarized in Table 10-1. An important implication of this table is that the opposite of satisfaction is no satisfaction—not dissatisfaction. Similarly, the opposite of dissatisfaction is no dissatisfaction—not satisfaction.

Table 10-1 The Two-Factor Theory of Work Motivation

Satisfiers or Motivators
{ Presence   Positive effect on motivation and satisfaction
{ Absence   No negative effect on motivation or satisfaction

1. Achievement   4. Responsibility
2. Recognition   5. Advancement
3. Work itself   6. Growth

Dissatisfiers
{ Presence   No positive effect on motivation or satisfaction
{ Absence   Negative effect on motivation and satisfaction

1. Company policy   6. Relationships with peers
2. Supervision   7. Personal life
3. Relationship with supervisor   8. Relationships with subordinates
4. Work conditions   9. Status
5. Salary   10. Job security

Evaluation of the Two-Factor Theory. Herzberg's theory has had considerable influence on the practice of management. Job enrichment is a direct application of this theory, and Herzberg has prompted managers to ask "What really motivates our employees?" Another positive feature of the two-factor theory is that it is supported by many studies.[8] Despite this support, conflicting results have also been found. One mistake Herzberg may have made was assuming that virtually all workers seek more responsibility and challenge on the job. It is more likely that people in higher-level occupations strive for more responsibility and challenge. But even in a given occupational group, such as managers or production workers, not everybody has the same motivational pattern. One executive admitted to this author that she works as a company president because "The job pays well enough for me to maintain my yacht."

Another problem with the two-factor theory is that it goes too far in concluding that hygiene factors cannot contribute to satisfaction and motivation. Many people do experience high job satisfaction and motivation because of job elements such as job security and pleasant working conditions. What are your key motivators?

MOTIVATION THROUGH GOAL SETTING

Goal setting is a pervasive managerial activity, including being a core ingredient in planning. Here we are concerned with the psychology behind goal setting: why and how it leads to improved performance.

Goal-Setting Concepts and Theory

Goal setting is an important part of most formal motivational programs and managerial methods of motivating employees. The premise underlying goal theory is that behavior is regulated by values and goals. A **value** is a strongly held personal standard or conviction. It is therefore a belief about something very important to the individual, such as dignity of work or honesty. Our values create within us a desire to behave consistently with them. If an executive values honesty, the executive will establish a goal of trying to hire only honest employees. He or she would therefore make extensive use of reference checks and honesty testing.

With respect to planning, a goal has been defined as an overall condition one is trying to achieve. Its psychological meaning is about the same. A **goal** is what the person is trying to accomplish, or a conscious intention to act.

A substantial amount of research has been conducted in recent years about the contribution of goal setting to work performance.[9] Fortunately, there is enough consistency in these findings to provide some firm guidelines for managerial action. The basic facts about goal setting are summarized in Figure 10-4. These facts are presented in detail in the following list.

1. *Specific goals lead to higher performance than do generalized goals.* Telling someone to "do your best" is a generalized goal. A specific goal would be, "Decrease the turnaround time on customer inquiries to an average of two working days."

2. *Performance generally increases in direct proportion to goal difficulty.* The harder one's goal, the more one accomplishes. There is an important exception, however. When goals are too difficult, they may lower performance. The difficulty in reaching the goal leads to frustration, which in turn leads to lowered performance.

3. *For goals to improve performance, they have to be accepted by the employee.* If you reject a goal, you will not incorporate it into your planning. This is why it is often helpful to discuss goals with employees, rather than just imposing the goals on them.

4. *Employee participation in goal setting makes a minor, and only indirect, contribution to performance.* Participating in setting goals has no major effect on the level of job performance. A recent experiment even concluded that individuals who were assigned goals showed higher motivation than those who participated in setting goals.[10] However, participation can improve performance in the following cases:

    a.   Participation leads to the setting of a specific goal.

    b.   The specific goal is more difficult than the one set by a supervisor.

    c.   Participation improves the acceptance of the goal.

    These findings—about the relatively small improvement that participative decision making contributes to goal setting—require elaboration. The

Figure 10-4   Goal-Setting Theory

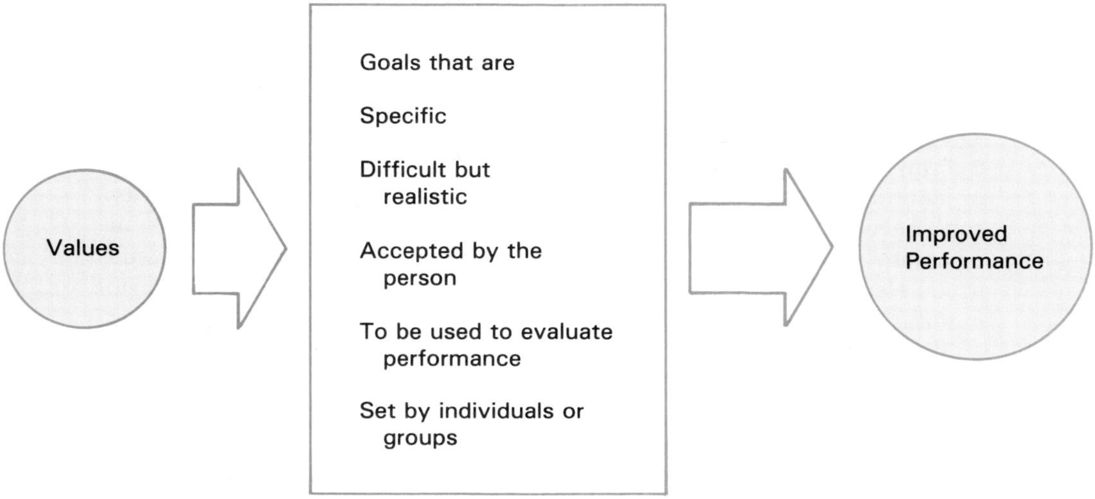

```
                    ┌─────────────────────────────┐
                    │                             │
                    │   Goals that are            │
  ╭────────╮        │                             │        ╭────────────╮
  │        │  ══▷   │   Specific                  │  ══▷   │            │
  │ Values │        │                             │        │ Improved   │
  │        │        │   Difficult but             │        │ Performance│
  ╰────────╯        │      realistic              │        ╰────────────╯
                    │                             │
                    │   Accepted by the           │
                    │      person                 │
                    │                             │
                    │   To be used to evaluate    │
                    │      performance            │
                    │                             │
                    │   Set by individuals or     │
                    │      groups                 │
                    │                             │
                    └─────────────────────────────┘
```

issue of participative decision making should be regarded as a practical rather than a moral one.[11] Too often management is told that participative leadership is "good" and authoritarian leadership is "bad." An authoritarian style of leadership does not emphasize participative decision making. Yet it does not mean that an authoritarian leader necessarily ignores goal setting or giving support to employees. The goals imposed by authoritarian leaders may be just as effective as those jointly established by participative leaders.

5. *Group goal setting is as important as individual goal setting.* Having employees work as teams with a specific team goal rather than as individuals with only individual goals increases productivity.[12] Furthermore, the combination of compatible group and individual goals is more effective than either individual or group goals.[13]

What a Manager Does After Goals Are Established

Goal-setting theory makes the manager's job sound simple. It could imply that, once goals are set, the results take care of themselves. In contrast, Kenneth Blanchard believes that the manager's biggest job begins after goals are set. He also notes one reason many goal-setting programs fail—managers do not follow up on progress after goal setting.[14]

When employees do make progress toward reaching goals, this fact should be brought to their attention. Correspondingly, employees must be reminded when they are not making progress toward goals. Both types of feedback help motivate employees. **Feedback** means giving information to people about how well they are doing.

BEHAVIOR MODIFICATION

The most systematic method of motivating people is **behavior modification**. It is a way of changing behavior by rewarding the right responses, and punishing or ignoring the wrong responses. **A reward** is something of value received as a consequence of having attained a goal. So much information has been accumulated about behavior modification that it has become a field of study itself. Here we will describe several key concepts and strategies of behavior modification (also referred to as "behavior mod" or "organizational behavior modification" [OB Mod]).

Key Concepts of Behavior Modification

The **law of effect** is the foundation principle of behavior modification. According to this principle, behavior that leads to positive consequences tends to be repeated. Similarly, behavior that leads to negative consequences tends not to be repeated. Perceptive managers rely on the law of effect virtually every day in managing people. Assume that a supervisor of a paint shop wanted her employees to put on a face mask every time they used a paint spray gun. When she observed an employee using the mask properly she might comment, "Good to see that you're wearing the safety mask today." If the supervisor noticed that an employee was not wearing a mask, she might say: "Please put down the spray gun, and go get your mask. If this happens again, I will be forced to suspend you for one day."

Behavior modification offers a different explanation of human motivation than do need theories. According to need theories, people are driven to engage in certain behaviors by internal forces, such as the need for self-fulfillment. According to behavior modification theorists, people engage in certain behaviors because they have been conditioned by past rewards and punishments. Note the fine line between *learning* and *motivation*. Learning is a relatively permanent change in behavior, based on experience. We learn to do something the first time based on rewards and punishments. In the future, we must be motivated to repeat that behavior.

Rewards can be external or internal. An **external**, or **extrinsic**, reward is one received from outside the person, such as money or praise. An **internal**, or **intrinsic**, reward stems from inside the person, such as a sense of satisfaction for having done something right. People may need external rewards the first several times they undertake a behavioral response, but, ideally, the right responses become self-rewarding.[15] The first time you did a break-even analysis, you may have done so to get rewarded with a good grade. In the process of studying, you may have derived some internal satisfaction. In the future, doing a break-even analysis correctly on your own may become its own reward.

Behavior-Modification Strategies

There are four behavior-modification strategies used either individually or in combination: positive reinforcement, negative reinforcement, extinction, and punishment.

Positive Reinforcement.   **Positive reinforcement** increases the probability that behavior will be repeated by rewarding people for making the right response. The phrase "increases the probability" is noteworthy. No behavior-modification strategy guarantees that people will always make the right response in the future. However, the chance is increased that the desired behavior will be repeated. The term **reinforcement** means that the behavior (or response) is reinforced in the sense of being strengthened.

Positive reinforcement is the most effective behavior-modification strategy. People respond much better to being rewarded for the right response than to being punished for the wrong response. Incentive pay programs are a widely used application of positive reinforcement.[16]

Negative Reinforcement.   **Negative reinforcement** is a process of rewarding people by taking away an uncomfortable consequence. It is a method of strengthening a desired response by making the removal of discomfort contingent on the right response. Assume that an employee is placed on probation because of excessive absenteeism. After twenty consecutive days of coming to work, the employee is rewarded by removing the probation. Because the opportunity for removing punishments is limited, negative reinforcement is not a widely used behavior-modification strategy.

Observe that negative reinforcement is often confused with punishment. Negative reinforcement is the *opposite* of punishment. It is rewarding someone by removing a punishment.

Extinction.   Extinction is the process of weakening or decreasing the frequency of undesirable behavior by removing the reward for such behavior. It is the absence of reinforcement. Extinction often takes the form of ignoring undesirable behavior. It works this way. An employee engages in undesirable behavior, such as creating a disturbance, just to get a reaction from co-workers. If the co-workers ignore the disturbance, the perpetrator no longer receives the reward of getting attention and stops the disturbing behavior. The behavior is said to be extinguished.

Extinction must be used with great care because there are many times when it does not work. An employee may habitually come to work late. If the boss does not reprimand the employee, the employee's lateness behavior may strengthen. The employee may interpret the boss's attempt at extinction as a form of approval.

Punishment.   **Punishment** is the presentation of an undesirable consequence for a specific behavior. Yelling at an employee for making a mistake is a direct form of punishment. Another form of punishment would be to take away a privilege, such as working on an interesting project, because of some undesirable behavior. When used appropriately, punishment can be a motivator for those punished and those observing the punishment. Using punishment appropriately means delivering it in a manner that is clearly impersonal, corrective, focuses on a specific act, and relatively intense and quick.[17]

Punishment also has many adverse consequences. Employees who are punished often become defensive, angry, and eager to seek revenge. Punishment can also be ineffective because it tells people what not to do, but it does not teach the right behavior.

ORGANIZATIONAL BEHAVIOR MODIFICATION

Most organizational behavior modification (OB Mod) programs in the workplace rely on a positive reinforcement strategy. It is important to follow an accepted set of procedures whether or not you use positive reinforcement as part of an OB Mod program.

Steps for Implementing an OB Mod Program

The OB Mod program described here is used in a number of firms.[18] Five steps are necessary for its implementation.

1. *Identify the desired performance behavior.* Specifying the desired performance-related behavior is the first step. The desired behaviors vary with the organization and the job. Some possibilities include finding quality defects, smiling at customers, locking prescription drugs in a cabinet, and making deliveries on time.

2. *Measure the behavior identified in the first step.* Obtain precise measures of good performance to avoid argument over what behavior is eligible for a reward. Company records often have useful information about the quality and quantity of production or service. For example, an airline might have information about the number of incoming calls versus the number of passengers who actually make reservations. Good performance behavior here would be a relatively high ratio of bookings to telephone inquiries.

    Obtaining precise measures of good performance is a difficult challenge. If accurate company records about performance behavior are not available, they must be developed for the OB Mod program. This step is time-consuming, but well worth the investment.

3. *Analyze the antecedents, behavior, and consequences (ABCs).* An essential part of behavior modification is to examine these three aspects of how

the employee functions. An **antecedent** is a signal from the environment that prompts a person to behave in a certain manner. A customer walking into the store would be an antecedent for an employee to stand up straight and smile.

Behavior in the ABC sequence is the observable behavior engaged in by the employee. Instead of the employee's intentions or promises being taken into account, only overt behavior is measured. The behaviors mentioned in the first step are all examples of the B factor in the ABC sequence. In behavior modification, the supervisor wants to see results, such as closing a sale.

Consequences are subsequent events that either encourage or discourage future behavior. Observations must be made of what is currently happening when the employee behaves in a particular way. Perhaps when a telephone sales representative says, "May I take your order" the boss nods in approval. Or maybe this constructive behavior is ignored.

This ABC analysis is important in developing a strategy for giving rewards. Often, the desired behavior does not occur because the antecedent is faulty. The employee may be unaware of the goals or may lack the training or information to behave properly. However, the problem usually stems from the consequences. It is likely that employees are not receiving appropriate rewards for constructive behavior. This is why a behavior modification program is necessary.

4.   *Take action to increase the desirable performance behaviors and decrease the undesirable ones.* The major action strategy is to provide feedback on the performance behaviors and positive reinforcement for attaining goals. To achieve the best results, feedback should be immediate, objective, accurate, and positive. It is much better to emphasize the positive rather than the negative when giving feedback.

Positive reinforcement can take many forms, as shown in Table 10-2. The key is that reinforcement must be administered when goals are attained. This is known as **contingent reinforcement**, meaning that getting the reward depends on giving a certain performance.

Positive reinforcement can be administered under different types of schedules. The most effective and sensible type is an **intermittent schedule**, in which rewards are administered often, but not always, when the appropriate behavior occurs. Intermittent rewards sustain desired behavior for a long time. In addition, they help to prevent the behavior from fading away when it is not rewarded.

Intermittent rewards are generally more practical than continuous rewards. Few managers have enough time to dispense rewards every time subordinates attain performance goals. Also, a reward loses its effect if given every time the employee makes the right response. Would you become tired of receiving praise everytime you did something right?

Table 10-2   Rewards Suitable for Use
in Positive Reinforcement

Monetary	Social and Pride-Related
Salary increases or bonuses	Compliments
Trading stamps	Encouragement
Discount coupons	Comradeship with boss
Company stock	Access to confidential information
Time off from work with pay	Pat on the back
Profit sharing	Expression of appreciation in front of others
Paid personal holiday (such as birthday)	Note of thanks
Movie or athletic-event passes	

Job and Career-Related	Status Symbols
Challenging work assignments	Bigger desk
Job security	Bigger office
Favorable performance appraisal	Exclusive use of personal computer
Freedom to choose own work activity	Freedom to personalize work area
Promotion	Private office
Improved working conditions	Wall plaque indicating accomplishment
More of preferred tasks	Special commendation (e.g., employee of the month)
Boss's stand-in when he or she is away	Company recognition plan
Presentations to top-level management	
Job rotation	

Food and Dining	
Business luncheon paid by company	
Company picnics	
Department parties	
Holiday turkeys and fruit baskets	

Source: Based on information in Robert Kreitner, *Management,* 3d ed. (Boston: Houghton Mifflin Co., 1986), 482–483; Andrew J. DuBrin, *Human Relations: A Job-Oriented Approach,* 4th ed. (Englewood Cliffs, NJ: Prentice Hall, 1988), 44.

5. *Evaluate the action to ensure that performance is really improving.* The purpose of OB Mod is to increase motivation and productivity. It is important to measure whether this is really being achieved. The evaluation is made by comparing results with the level of performance measured in the

second step. If the program is not improving performance, it may have to
be redesigned.

Suggestions for the Informal Use of Positive Reinforcement

Behavior modification may take the form of a large program, as described in
the previous section. However, managers and professionals use positive reinforcement more frequently on an informal, daily basis. Some of the points
made so far can be applied in this manner. Several additional suggestions
should also be kept in mind.

1. *Focus on the positive aspects of job performance.* Most negative job
   behaviors have a positive counterpart. To improve performance, reward
   the employee for engaging in positive behavior. Assume a drafting
   technician typically turns in sketches with distracting smudges. When the
   technician turns in a smudge-free drawing, the manager should offer a
   compliment. The typical managerial approach is to complain about the
   smudges, but ignore the clean drawings.

2. *State clearly what behavior will lead to a reward.* The nature of good performance, or the goals, must be agreed to by both superior and subordinate. Clarification could take this form: "What I need are high-quality,
   no-smudge drawings. When you achieve this, you'll be credited with good
   performance."

3. *Use appropriate rewards.* An appropriate reward is an effective one
   because it is valued by the person being motivated. As you examine the
   lists of rewards in Table 10-2, note that some have more appeal to you
   than do others. The best way to motivate people is to offer them their
   preferred rewards for good performance. It is helpful to discuss with
   employees what they are interested in attaining.

4. *Vary the size of the reward with the size of accomplishment.* Big accomplishments deserve big rewards; small accomplishments deserve small
   rewards. Rewards of the wrong magnitude erode their motivational
   power. An important corollary of this principle is that people become embarrassed when overlavished with praise.

5. *Avoid "jelly bean" motivation.* Closely related to the above rule is an ad-
   monition against "jelly bean" motivation, the heaping of undeserved
   rewards upon another person.[19] It is an acknowledgement of performance
   that has never materialized. A typical example is a manager saying "Keep
   up the good work," to an employee who has accomplished virtually
   nothing all day.

6. *Administer rewards shortly after they are deserved.* The proper timing of
   rewards will often be difficult because the manager is not present at the
   time of good performance. In this case, a telephone call or a note of

appreciation within several days of the good performance would be appropriate.

7. *Change rewards periodically.* Rewards grow stale quickly, making it necessary to change them periodically. A related problem is that a repetitive reward can even become an annoyance. How many times can one be motivated by the phrase, "nice job"? How many clock radios can one wish to receive for making quota?

The accompanying "Organization in Action" describes an incentive program in a bank that incorporates many of the ideas presented about both OB Mod programs and informal use of positive reinforcement.

ORGANIZATION IN ACTION:

Positive Reinforcement at Union Bank

Currently, Union National Bank of Little Rock, Arkansas has seventy-five individualized incentive programs designed for 70 percent of its 485 employees, from entry-level clerks to senior vice presidents. In a recent year, $1 million out of a $9 million payroll was composed of incentive payments. The bank estimates that using behavior modification principles has increased productivity 200–300 percent. Union National Bank's net profit per employee is $11,100 per year while other Little Rock banks show approximately $5,000 profit per employee.

One of the incentive programs involved tellers. The goals of the program were to increase the number of customers who open new accounts, increase transactions, and improve daily cash discrepancies. During the baseline period (a period in which productivity was measured before the program began), the tellers averaged 32 points. Currently the average is 71 points. Prior to the incentive program, the tellers obtained 102 new accounts. Four years later, the tellers obtained 4,300 new accounts. Daily cash discrepancies have improved from a yearly outage of $15,961 to $13,772, and the average hourly transaction count increased from 17.9 to 29.5.

The bank has benefited from the incentive program in several ways. While customer volume has increased 67 percent, teller staffing has decreased. Daily difference savings are translated directly into profit, and 17,750 new accounts have been obtained since the teller incentive began. Tellers now request transfers to busy branches and have a stake in keeping the staff lean, because tellers at the busy branches have the most opportunity to earn incentives. Benefits to tellers include increased compensation, recognition for outstanding work, and specific work goals.

A bank official notes, "With Union National Bank's incentive program, we make entrepreneurs out of our employees; we provide the resources and they provide the outputs." The main disadvantage to the employee is that there is no guaranteed income above the base salary; if they don't work, they don't receive incentive; and they are not rewarded for busyness that doesn't produce anything."

Source: As reported in Wayne Dierks and Kathleen A. McNally, "Incentives You Can Bank On," *Personnel Administrator* (March 1987): 61–65.

Arguments For and Against Behavior Modification

Behavior modification offers more concrete evidence of improving productivity than does any other motivational program.[20] Nevertheless, behavior modification has been the subject of constant controversy. The most vehement concern is that behavior modification manipulates employees against their will. A counterargument is that behavior modification cannot work if people are offered rewards they do not value. Thus, people do exert some control over the motivational process. It is also worth noting that managers control people anyway. Behavior modification at least makes explicit the behaviors that will be rewarded.

Some critics argue that the impressive gains of positive reinforcement can be attributed to goal setting, not to the dispensing of rewards. If this argument is valid, it means that people will improve their performance without receiving external rewards. Behavior modification is therefore a more equitable motivation system. People are given the opportunity to earn both tangible and intangible rewards for achieving goals.

Another antibehavior modification argument is that the system is too mechanistic. It works well with only simple aspects of job performance, such as spotting quality defects. This argument is based on an incomplete understanding of the use of positive reinforcement on the job. Workers at all levels respond well to appropriate rewards. For example, senior vice presidents were included in the behavior modification program at the Union National Bank.

MOTIVATION THROUGH GAINSHARING

Many organizations attempt to increase motivation and productivity through a company-wide plan of linking incentive pay to increases in performance. **Gainsharing** is thus a formal program of allowing employees to participate financially in the productivity gains they have achieved. Gainsharing is based on principles of positive reinforcement, and it also recognizes the motivational impact of money. Here we examine the goals and typical results of gainsharing plans.

Purposes of Gainsharing Plans

The ultimate goal of any gainsharing plan is to improve productivity. This is usually accomplished by using financial incentives to improve performance. Other goals and objectives of gainsharing plans include the following:

- Increasing employee motivation and job satisfaction.

- Increasing employee involvement in the improvement of company performance.

- Improving the quality of work life within an organization.

- Improving communications and cooperation between departments.

- Giving recognition for good work at the individual, departmental, and organizational level.

- Providing employees with an understanding of the problems and opportunities of the company, industry, and country.

- Encouraging employees at all levels to identify and help solve problems.[21]

Typical Bonus Measures and Results of Gainsharing Plans

Gainsharing plans have a forty-five-year history of turning unproductive companies around and making successful companies even more productive. Major companies with gainsharing plans include Dana Corp., General Electric Co., Honeywell Inc., Johnson & Johnson, 3M Corp., Motorola, Inc., TRW Inc., and Xerox Corp. The gainsharing bonus in these plans can be relatively uncomplicated such as awarding employees a bonus for exceeding a targeted level of productivity. Productivity is often defined as a ratio of labor costs to output. For example, the earnings of workers on a particular project would be divided by the number of acceptable units produced to obtain a productivity index. (One such index would be $100 per unit.) The size of the bonus varies according to the amount of improvement.[22] At the other extreme, the bonus can be as complicated as calculating a profit-sharing bonus.

Productivity can be interpreted to include quality levels, costs, and the quality of customer service. Plans can be designed around the goal of beating a target, earning a specified return on investment, or bettering past performance (the most frequently used alternative).

Based on their personal involvement with gainsharing plans, Larry L. Hatcher and Timothy L. Ross have reported on some of the potential results of gainsharing.[23]

Identity. When gainsharing is successful, an organization develops *identity*— most of the employees are familiar with its history and plans, and they share the same image of the firm. Employees at middle and lower levels perceive a meshing of organizational and individual goals. At the same time, executives develop a recognition of and sensitivity to the goals of employees.

Employee Involvement. Employee involvement is the underlying mechanism of most gain-sharing plans. All of these plans capitalize upon the knowledge of nonmanagement personnel, including operative employees. Employee involvement is so important for the success of gainsharing that most plans provide a formal system for obtaining the input of employees. Typically a two-tier system of committees reviews improvement ideas and facilitates communication across departments and between management and employees.

Improved Financial Results. Gainsharing plans often lead to increased profits and decreased costs. The U.S. General Accounting Office (GAO) investigated thirty-six manufacturing facilities that had implemented gainsharing. It was found that companies with sales of less than $100 million averaged annual work-force savings (through fewer employees required to accomplish the same amount of work) of 17.3 percent. Companies with sales in excess of $100 million averaged annual work force savings of 16.4 percent. Substantial decreases were also found in grievances, absenteeism, and turnover, while 81 percent of the companies reported improved labor-management relations.[24]

EXPECTANCY THEORY OF MOTIVATION

The **expectancy theory** of motivation centers around the idea that people will expend effort if they expect the effort to lead to performance and the performance to lead to a reward. A key advantage expectancy theory has over need theories is that it takes into account individual differences and perceptions. Expectancy theory often is preferred to behavior modification because it emphasizes the rational, thinking side of people.

A Basic Model of Expectancy Theory

Expectancy theory integrates important ideas found in the other generally accepted motivation theories. There are several different versions of expectancy theory. The version of expectancy theory presented in Table 10-3 captures the key ideas, yet minimizes most of the technical detail. According to expectancy theory, four conditions must exist for motivated behavior to occur.[25]

Condition A is based on the hypothesis that people will expend effort when they believe that their effort will lead to performance. This is referred to as the $E \longrightarrow P$ expectancy. Subjective probabilities range between 0.0 and 1.0. Rational people ask themselves, "If I work hard, will I really get the job done?" If they evaluate the probability as being high, they probably will invest the effort to achieve the goal. People tend to have higher $E \longrightarrow P$ expectancies when they have the appropriate skills, training, and self-confidence.

Table 10-3   Basic Version of Expectancy Theory of Motivation

Person Will Be Motivated under the Following Conditions:

A. Person believes effort will lead to favorable performance ($E \longrightarrow P$; also referred to as **expectancy**).
B. Person believes performance will lead to favorable outcome ($P \longrightarrow O$; also referred to as **instrumentality**).
C. Outcome or reward satisfies an important need (**valence** is strong).
D. Need satisfaction is intense enough to make effort seem worthwhile.

Condition B is based on the idea that people are more willing to expend effort if they think that good performance will lead to a reward. This is referred to as a $P \longrightarrow O$ instrumentality, and it too ranges between 0.0 and 1.0. (The term *instrumentality* refers to the idea that the behavior is instrumental in achieving an important end.) The rational person says, "I am much more willing to perform well if I am assured that I will receive the reward I deserve." To strengthen a subordinate's $P \longrightarrow O$ instrumentality, the manager should give reassurance that the reward will be forthcoming. A cautious employee might take such steps as asking other employees if they received their promised rewards for exceptional performance.

Condition C refers to valence, the value a person attaches to certain outcomes. The greater the valence attached to an outcome, the greater the effort. Valences can be either positive or negative. If a student believes that receiving an *A* is very important, he or she will work very hard. Also, if a student believes that avoiding an *F* is very important, he or she will work hard. Valences range from -1 to $+1$ in most versions of expectancy theory, with a positive valence indicating a preference for a particular reward. A truer picture of individual differences in human motivation would spread valences out over a range of -1000 to $+1000$.

In most work situations, there are several possible outcomes with different valences attached to each outcome. Assume Nicole Blackwell is pondering whether or not obtaining certification as a certified purchasing manager (CPM) will be worth the effort. Possible outcomes or rewards from achieving certification, along with their valences to her, include the following:

- Status from being a CPM, 0.75

- Promotion to purchasing manager, 0.95

- Plaque to hang on office wall, 0.25

- Bigger salary increase next year, 0.90

- Letters of congratulations from friends and relatives, 0.50

- Expressions of envy from one or two co-workers, -0.25

Valences are useful in explaining why some people will put forth the effort to do things with very low expectancies. For example, most people know there is only one chance in a million of winning a lottery, becoming a rock star, or writing a best-selling novel. Nevertheless, a number of people vigorously pursue these goals. They do so because they attach an extraordinary positive valence to these outcomes (perhaps 1000!).

Condition D indicates that the need satisfaction stemming from each outcome must be intense enough to make the effort seem worthwhile. Would you walk two miles on a very hot day for one glass of ice water? The water would undoubtedly satisfy your thirst need, but the magnitude of the satisfaction would probably not be worth the effort. Similarly, an operative employee turned down a promotion to an inspector position because the raise offered was only twenty-five cents per hour. The worker told his supervisor, "I need more money. But I'm not willing to take on added responsibility for ten dollars a week."

Implications for Managers

One reason expectancy theory is popular is that it has several important implications for the effective management of people. Expectancy theory helps pinpoint what you must do to motivate subordinates. Several major implications of the theory are:[26]

1. *Individual differences among employees must be taken into account.* Different people attach different valences to different rewards, so an attempt should be made to match rewards with individual preferences. OB Mod carries this same implication.

2. *Rewards should be closely tied to those actions the organization sees as worthwhile.* For example, if the organization values quality, people should be rewarded for producing high-quality work.

3. *Employees should be given the appropriate training and encouragement.* This will strengthen their subjective hunches that effort will lead to good performance.

4. *Employees should be presented with credible evidence that good performance does lead to anticipated rewards.* Similarly, you should reassure employees that good work will be both noticed and rewarded.

5. *The meaning and implications of second-level outcomes should be explained.* It can be motivational for employees to know of the values of certain outcomes such as receiving an assignment to a select task force (a first-level outcome). Some employees are not aware that favorable performance on a task force can have a positive impact upon their careers (a second-level outcome).

MOTIVATION THROUGH EMPLOYEE CONTROL OVER WORKING HOURS

For many office employees, the standard eight-hour day with fixed starting and stopping times has ended. Instead, these employees exert some control over their work schedules through a system of **flexible working hours**. The hours of work are organized to allow employees flexibility in choosing their own hours. Flexible working hours are also referred to as flextime, flexitime, and modified work schedules. Furthermore, a growing number of employees are not even required to spend much time at the office. Instead, they work out of their homes.

Flexible Working Hours and Motivation

Employees on flexible working hours are required to work certain core hours such as 10:00 A.M. to 3:30 P.M. However, they are able to choose which hours they work during the workday period from 7:00 A.M. to 10:00 A.M. and from 3:30 P.M. to 6:30 P.M. A basic model of flexible working hours is presented in Figure 10-5. Time recording devices are frequently used to monitor whether employees have put in their fair share of work for the week.

Flexible working hours are sometimes used as a method of motivating employees. It is assumed that if workers participate in making decisions about working hours, their satisfaction and motivation will increase. Sometimes motivation and productivity do increase because employees feel they have more control over their work.[27] The underlying psychology is that being in control satisfies higher-level needs.

Although flexible working hours can be used to increase motivation, the method is much more likely to increase job satisfaction. Several studies have found that employees are more satisfied, but not necessarily more productive, under flexible working hours. One study conducted in two government agencies observed the conditions under which flexible working hours do contribute to productivity. It was found that when busy workers had to share physical resources, flexible working hours did contribute to productivity. Specifically, it was found that computer programmers who shared a mainframe computer became more productive under flexible working hours. Data-entry operators who did not share resources were about equally productive when working under flexible and fixed hours.[28]

Figure 10-5   A Typical Flexible-Working-Hours Schedule

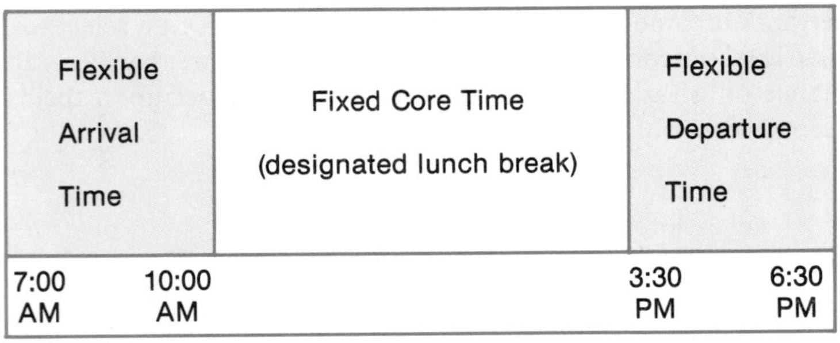

Flexible Arrival Time	Fixed Core Time (designated lunch break)	Flexible Departure Time
7:00 AM 10:00 AM		3:30 PM 6:30 PM

Telecommuting and Employee Motivation

Another deviation from the traditional work schedule is **telecommuting**, an arrangement in which employees perform their regular work duties from home or in another location (such as a yacht). Usually the employees use a computer tied into the company's main office, telephones, and fax machines. In addition to electronic communication with the office, telecommuters also attend meetings on company premises and work in the office occasionally.[29]

Telecommuting is an indirect motivational program. Telecommuters are often highly motivated because they have more control over their work lives. Also, many employees are willing to work hard to hold a job that allows them to cut down on commuting and take care of home responsibilities more readily. The preliminary evidence is that telecommuting does increase productivity and therefore may be enhancing motivation. Where direct measurements have been possible, productivity increases have averaged about 20 percent.[30]

MOTIVATION THROUGH THE RIGHT CORPORATE CULTURE

The approaches and programs described so far are aimed at motivating people by working with them individually. A more strategic way of motivating employees is to establish an environment or corporate culture that encourages hard work. **Organizational culture** is the overall set of values shared by members of the organization. The concept of organizational, or corporate, culture was popularized by the famous book, *In Search of Excellence: Lessons from America's Best Run Companies.*[31] The management consultants who wrote the book believed that the right corporate culture can drive employees to be productive. At the same time, the wrong culture can lead to low productivity.

Organizational culture can also be regarded as the employee's perceptions of the organization's "personality." For instance, many Hewlett-Packard employees perceive their company to be dynamic, exciting, demanding, and powerful. One of the Hewlett-Packard values that contribute to this perception is that winning requires hard work.

It takes a long time to develop an organizational culture that fosters strong motivation. A corporate culture that leads to high employee motivation would have many of these characteristics:

1. *An atmosphere that rewards creative thought by giving tangible rewards to innovators.* At the same time, very few penalties are imposed on people whose creative ideas lead to failure. Risk taking needs to be encouraged to foster high motivation.

2. *An atmosphere that rewards excellence by giving big rewards to top performers.* Employees promoted to responsible jobs are those whose performance has been excellent. Conversely, poor performers are not elevated into top jobs because of favoritism. Employees thus can see a relation between hard work and rewards.

3. *A pervasive belief that the organization is a winner.* If employees think that they have been chosen to join a winning team, they are likely to be well motivated. Proud companies like Procter & Gamble Co., Marriott, and Sears, Roebuck and Co. capitalize on this aspect of culture.

4. *A spirit of helpfulness that encourages employees to believe they can overcome setbacks.* Employees believe that when they experience work dif-

ficulties, the company will do everything in its power to help them.[32] Many companies today, for example, provide child-care facilities so that working parents can better concentrate on their job without having to worry about their children's welfare.

SUMMARY OF KEY POINTS

From the standpoint of the individual, motivation is an internal state that leads to the pursuit of objectives. From the standpoint of the manager, motivation is an activity carried on to get subordinates to pursue objectives. The purpose of motivating employees is to get them to achieve results. Motivation is but one important contributor to productivity and performance. Other important contributors are abilities, skills, and technology.

According to need theory, unsatisfied needs motivate people. People engage in goal-directed behavior until the need is satisfied. People try to satisfy a wide range of needs through work. These include autonomy, affiliation, dominance, order, and recognition.

Maslow's need hierarchy states that people strive to become self-actualized. However, before higher-level needs are activated, certain lower-level needs must be satisfied. When a person's needs are satisfied at one level, he or she looks toward satisfaction at a higher level.

The two-factor theory of work motivation contends there are two different sets of job-motivation factors, or elements. One set gives people a chance to satisfy higher-level needs. These are satisfiers or motivators. Satisfiers and motivators generally relate to the content of the job. They include achievement, recognition, and opportunity for advancement. Dissatisfiers are job elements that appeal more to lower-level needs. When they are present they prevent dissatisfaction, but they do not create satisfaction or motivation. Dissatisfiers relate mostly to the context of a job. They include company policy and administration, job security, and money.

Goal setting is an important part of most motivational programs, and it is a managerial method of motivating subordinates. It is based on these ideas: specific goals are better than generalized goals; the more difficult the goal, the better the performance; only goals that are accepted improve performance; participation makes a minor and indirect contribution to goal setting; and, group goal setting is important.

Behavior modification is the most systematic method of motivating people. It changes behavior by rewarding the right responses and punishing or ignoring the wrong ones. Behavior modification is based on the law of effect: behavior that leads to positive consequences tends to be repeated, and behavior that leads to negative consequences tends not to be repeated.

There are four behavior-modification strategies. Positive reinforcement rewards people for making the right response. Negative reinforcement rewards people by taking away an uncomfortable consequence. Extinction is the process of weakening undesirable behavior by removing the reward for such behavior. Punishment is the presentation of an undesirable consequence for a specific behavior. Punishment is often counterproductive, but if used appropriately, it can be motivational.

One approach to implementing organizational behavior modification consists of five major steps: identify the desired performance behavior; measure that behavior; analyze the antecedents, behavior, and consequences (ABCs); take action to increase the right behaviors and decrease the wrong ones; and evaluate the effectiveness of the action.

Suggestions for the informal use of positive reinforcement in a work setting include the following: focus on the positive, state clearly what behavior leads to a reward, use appropriate rewards, administer the rewards shortly after the good behavior, avoid "jelly bean" motivation, and change rewards periodically.

Gainsharing is a formal program of allowing employees to participate financially in the productivity gains they have achieved, and it is thus a motivational program. Gainsharing plans are credited with improving organizational identity, employee involvement, and financial results.

Expectancy theory contends that people will expend effort if they expect the effort to lead to performance and the performance to lead to a reward. According to the expectancy model presented here, a person will be motivated under these conditions: the person believes effort will lead to performance, the person believes performance will lead to a reward, the reward satisfies an important need, and the need satisfaction is intense enough to make the effort seem worthwhile.

Flexible working hours allow employees to exert some control over their actual hours of work. The aspect of control is said to lead to increased motivation. Telecommuting (or working from the home) is gaining momentum, and can also be used as motivational strategy. Both types of flexible work arrangements usually increase job satisfaction, and under some conditions, they improve productivity.

A strategic way of motivating people is to establish a corporate culture that encourages hard work. It is particularly important for employees to see excellence rewarded, to not fear making mistakes, to work in an atmosphere of helpfulness, and to see a relationship between hard work and rewards.

QUESTIONS

1. Based on information in this chapter, what can managers do to motivate "lazy" employees?
2. Give an example of a job in which motivation would have a strong influence on performance and productivity.
3. What needs are likely to be satisfied by operating a successful small business?
4. How can goal theory be used to explain the fact that students with a specific major tend to be more motivated than students with a more general major?
5. What evidence can you present from your own life that goal setting leads to improved performance?
6. In what way does an instructor use behavior modification to influence student performance?

7. Why is gainsharing more likely to lead to cooperation than competition among employees?
8. Why do some employees object to their managers using positive reinforcement?
9. What personal characteristics and traits should employees possess before they are assigned as telecommuters?
10. Describe the type of corporate culture you think would appeal to a person who has strong needs for achievement.

ACTIVITIES

1. Ask a manager what techniques he or she uses to motivate subordinates. Discuss the information in class.
2. Design a program to motivate entry-level office workers who are performing repetitive operations and who receive close to the minimum wage.

CASE PROBLEM 10-A: THE STALE REINFORCERS

Charlie Adamski is the postmaster of a large mail-processing facility. One factor in his annual performance appraisal is the number of accidents occurring during the work year. Most accidents typically occur either on the workroom floor, where the mail is processed, or on the street, during mail delivery. On occasion, a postal employee in a more sedentary job will incur an accident.

Adamski remains on the alert of ways to reduce work-related accidents without incurring costs that will adversely affect other measures of his performance. Several years ago he instituted a program of providing coffee and doughnuts to any unit that did not have a chargeable accident within the previous quarter. Adamski would arrive in the conference room with the coffee and doughnuts, and a plaque commemorating that quarter's achievement. Usually, he would then give a brief speech congratulating the unit before hurrying off to his next appointment. This motivational program has been place for about three years.

The employees in the accounting section had only one accident in all the time Barbara Catrett was their manager. Connie Raven broke her wrist upon slipping and falling in the parking lot one winter day when it had not been adequately cleared of snow. As a result of this generally good record, the walls of the accounting section were cluttered with plaques. Relevant facts about the department employees include the following:

Barbara Catrett, manager. Mid-thirties, health and fitness conscious, a casual dieter.

John Valvano, supervisor. Mid-thirties, has a mild diabetic condition, generally passes on sweets.

Connie Raven, technician. Early forties, very overweight, not on a serious diet.

Ed Small, technician. Late fifties, still relatively trim, will eat one of anything.

Linda Wang, technician. Early twenties, just discovering that she can no longer eat everything, constantly dieting.

Frieda Fromholtz, technician. Late forties, hates sweets.

Cheryl Friedman, technician. Early forties, watches her weight, but will not refuse sweets.

Bob Gambrelli, technician. Late forties, has a medical problem that prevents him from eating most sweets.

One day Charlie arrived with the usual fanfare in the accounting section to deliver his quarterly rewards. About halfway through his typical speech, he stopped and said: "I'm getting pretty tired of these things. Aren't you? Hasn't everybody really had enough doughnuts? These aren't even that good. I wish someone would come up with another way to reward the areas that have done a good job of avoiding accidents."

Barbara looked around the room and observed everybody looking pensive. Each employee was jotting down ideas waiting for Charlie to give the cue to speak. Charlie then said, "If you think of anything, let me know," and walked out of the conference room.

Case Questions

1. What concerns do you think the department members are likely to have about Adamski's program of behavior modification.
2. What rules for applying behavior was Adamski violating?
3. How can Adamski revitalize his motivational program?

Source: Case researched by Barbara P. Catrett, Rochester Institute of Technology.

CASE PROBLEM 10-B: PRODUCTIVITY IN THE CLAIMS DEPARTMENT

Mandi Wilson is a medical-claims supervisor at Cosmopolitan Life Insurance Co. Her department is responsible for processing dental-insurance claims in the company's northwestern region. The claims are filed by dentists throughout the area for services rendered to their patients. After the claims are processed, reimbursement checks are sent to patients or dentists as appropriate. This aspect of the business has grown rapidly in recent years for two primary reasons. One is that an increasing number of firms are offering dental-insurance benefits to employees. Another reason is that Cosmopolitan Life offers an efficient and quick claims system.

Wilson's boss, Janice Altman, has been prodding Wilson lately to boost productivity in the dental claims department. Altman has observed that Wilson's unit processes approximately 10 percent fewer claims per worker than does the other dental claims unit. Wilson has explained to Altman that her unit may produce a slightly smaller volume of work, but that it is probably of higher quality. Altman's rebuttal is that the company has no official way of knowing whether this assertion is true. Altman has also informed Wilson that even if the quality is high, the company still wants more productivity.

Back in her department, Wilson began to give serious consideration to the company's demand for increased productivity. Wilson then sent out a memo informing the claims processors of a department meeting about office efficiency.

After a few introductory remarks, Wilson moved to the central issue: "The main reason I've called this meeting is to figure out how to motivate you folks to work faster. The company is on my back to raise productivity by 10 percent. I thought I'd share the problem with you in order to get some of your thinking."

"Give us all 10-percent raises, that will do the trick," said one of the claims processors. The other department members cheered in agreement. Nellie Cryme, one of the older women in the department, then offered these comments:

"All kidding aside, I doubt 10 percent more money will have much effect around here. Mandi, I suspect you may have some problems appreciating our point of view, perhaps because you are young. Most of us really don't care that much about earning a few extra bucks—especially if it means working faster than we feel is comfortable.

"I think I can speak for most of us, when I say we're old enough to be looking toward retirement. We've learned to live with our salaries. The previous regional manager had something in mind when he set up this department. It was staffed with people who were conscientious, but who weren't bucking for promotion. We all expect to do a fair day's work, but we don't want work to be a hassle."

Before Wilson could respond to Cryme, the rest of the department clapped in appreciation. When the excitement subsided, Wilson said to the group:

"Thank you, Nellie, for being so candid. Even though I am young enough to be your daughter, I'm still the boss. Therefore, it's still my responsibility to carry out management's desires. I think we've gone far enough for today, but I want you folks to think about how we can all work harder. I'll be thinking about the same problem also, and we will meet again next week."

Case Questions

1. What approach would you recommend for boosting department productivity?
2. What do you think of Wilson's candid approach of asking her subordinates how to motivate them?
3. Should Wilson's age be an issue in her ability to motivate the workers in her department?
4. Can you offer any criticism of Altman's handling of this problem?

REFERENCES

1. "The Work Ethic Lives!" *Time* (7 September 1987): 40–42.
2. Henry L. Tosi and Stephen J. Carroll, *Management,* 2d ed. (New York: John Wiley & Sons, 1982), 398.
3. Bill G. Gooch and Betty J. McDowell, "Use Anxiety to Motivate," *Personnel Journal* (April 1988): 54.
4. For a current analysis of needs and their measurement, see Michael J. Stahl, *Managerial and Technical Motivation: Assessing Needs for Achievement, Power, and Affiliation* (New York: Praeger Pubs., 1986).
5. Stephen P. Robbins, *Organizational Behavior: Concepts, Controversies, and Applications,* 2d ed. (Englewood Cliffs, NJ: Prentice Hall, 1983), 133.
6. Two original sources of information on this topic are: Abraham H. Maslow, "A Theory of Human Motivation," *Psychological Review* (July

1943): 370–396; Maslow, *Motivation and Personality* (New York: Harper & Row, 1954), ch. 5.

7. An original source here is Frederick Herzberg, *Work and the Nature of Man* (Cleveland: World, 1966).

8. A synthesis of positive and negative evidence for the two-factor theory is John B. Miner, *Theories of Organizational Behavior* (Hinsdale, IL: Dryden Press, 1980), 76–100.

9. Mark E. Tubbs, "Goal Setting: A Meta-Analytic Examination of Empirical Evidence," *Journal of Applied Psychology* (August 1986): 474–475.

10. Christina E. Shalley, Greg R. Oldham, and Joseph F. Porac, "Effects of Goal Difficulty, Goal-Setting Method, and Expected External Evaluation on Intrinsic Motivation," *Academy of Management Journal* (September 1987): 559.

11. Edwin A. Locke and D. M. Schweiger, "Participation in Decision Making: One More Look," Barry M. Staw (ed.), *Research in Organizational Behavior,* vol. 1 (Greenwich, CN: JAI Press, 1979), 265–340.

12. Tamao Matsui, Takashi Kakuyama, and Mary Lou Uy Onglatco, "Effects of Goals and Feedback on Performance in Groups," *Journal of Applied Psychology* (August 1987): 414.

13. Charles R. Gowen III, "Managing Work Group Performance by Individual Goals and Group Goals for an Interdependent Group Task," *Journal of Organizational Behavior Management* (Fall 1985): 5–27.

14. Kenneth Blanchard, "Getting the Results You Want," *Success* (January 1985): 16.

15. "Conversation with B. F. Skinner," *Organizational Dynamics* (Winter 1973): 39.

16. Thomas Rollins, "Pay for Performance: Is It Worth the Trouble?" *Personnel Administrator* (May 1988): 42–46.

17. Mel E. Schnake, "Vicarious Punishment in a Work Setting," *Journal of Applied Psychology* (May 1986): 343.

18. Fred Luthans, Walter S. Maciag, and Stuart A. Rosenkrantz, "OB Mod: Meeting the Productivity Challenge with Human Resources Management," *Personnel* (March–April 1983): 28–36.

19. Kenneth Blanchard, "Jelly Bean Motivation: Know When to Applaud Your Workers and When to Leave Them Alone," *Success* (February 1986): 8.

20. W. E. Scott, Jr., and P. M. Podsakoff, *Behavioral Principles in the Practice of Management* (New York: John Wiley & Sons, 1985).

21. Larry L. Hatcher and Timothy L. Ross, "Organization Development through Productivity Gainsharing," *Personnel* (October 1985): 44.

22. Larry L. Hatcher, Timothy L. Ross, and Ruth Ann Ross, "Gainsharing: Living Up To Its Name," *Personnel Administrator* (June 1987): 153–162; Timothy L. Ross, Ruth Ann Ross, and Larry Hatcher, "The Multiple Benefits of Gainsharing," *Personnel Journal* (October 1986): 14–25.

23. Ross, "Multiple Benefits of Gainsharing," 19.

24. Reported in Hatcher, "Development Through Productivity Gainsharing," 49. The GAO study has been updated in 1988, with similar results.

25. The original explanation of expectancy theory as applied to work motivation is Victor H. Vroom, *Work and Motivation* (New York: John Wiley & Sons, 1964). A recent synthesis is Henry L. Tosi, John R. Rizzo, and Stephen J. Carroll, *Managing Organizational Behavior* (Marshfield, MA: Pitman Pub., 1986), 240–246.

26. Terence R. Mitchell, "Motivational Strategies," Kendrith M. Rowland and Gerald R. Ferris (eds.), *Personnel Management* (Boston: Allyn & Bacon, Inc., 1982), 286; Ramon J. Aldag and Timothy W. Stearns, *Management* (Cincinnati: South-Western Publishing Co., 1987), 450.

27. John R. Turney and Stanley L. Cohen, "Alternative Work Schedules Increase Employee Satisfaction," *Personnel Journal* (March 1983): 202.

28. David A. Ralston, William P. Anthony, and David J. Gustafson, "Employees May Love Flextime, But What Does It Do to the Organization's Productivity?" *Journal of Applied Psychology* (May 1985): 272–279.

29. Carol-Ann Hamilton, "Telecommuting," *Personnel Journal* (April 1987): 91–101.

30. "Telecommuting: Is Your Operation Ready?" *Research Institute Personal Report for the Executive* (14 May 1985): 8.

31. Thomas J. Peters and Robert H. Waterman, Jr., *In Search of Excellence: Lessons from America's Best Run Companies* (New York: Harper & Row, 1982).

32. Michael E. Cavanagh, "In Search of Motivation," *Personnel Journal* (March 1984): 81.

11
Communicating with Other People

After studying the material in this chapter, you should be able to accomplish the following tasks:

1. Summarize the steps in the communication process.
2. Explain and illustrate the difference between formal and informal communication channels.
3. Understand the role of nonverbal communication in the workplace.
4. Overcome many of the communication barriers you may encounter.
5. Develop an action plan for sending your messages more persuasively.
6. Become more effective at receiving messages.

Key Terms and Phrases

Communication
Sender
Ideation
Encoding
Transmission
Communication channel
Receiver
Decoding
Understanding
Action
Feedback
Formal communication channel
Informal communication channel
Grapevine
Communication network
Downward communication
Upward communication

Horizontal communication
Diagonal communication
Nonverbal communication
Throughput
Semantics
Difficulty level of language
Biased language
Defensive communication
Denial
Filtering
Hostile organizational culture
Communication information
    overload
Flaming
Empathy
Informational skills
Frontloaded writing

Communication is the process of exchanging information by use of words, letters, symbols, or nonverbal behavior. So vital is communication that it has been described as the glue that holds organizations together. Most foul-ups in the workplace are considered to be communications problems. Furthermore, communication is more important than ever because the network of contacts people have on the job is multiplying. For example, you can belong to several different work groups at once, such as your department and a task force.

Any time people send information back and forth to each other they are communicating. Communication is an important aspect of leadership. Unless leaders transmit messages to others and receive messages in return, they cannot exert influence. Communication is also an integral part of other managerial functions. Unless managers communicate with others, they cannot plan, organize, or control. Person-to-person communication is as much a part of management as running is a part of basketball and tennis.

Communication is also vitally important to specialists and many operatives. All but the most routine jobs involve communicating with other people. Furthermore, the ability to communicate effectively is closely related to career advancement.[1] If an employee is a poor communicator, he or she often will be bypassed for promotion. This is particularly true if the new position involves much contact with people.

The information in this chapter is designed to improve communication among people in the workplace. Two approaches are used to achieve this end. First is a description of key aspects of organizational communication, including communication channels and barriers. Second, many suggestions are presented for improving communication among people. The accompanying "Manager in Action" provides an illustration of the challenges of trying to be an effective communicator in business. In addition to overcoming communication barriers, it may be necessary to become familiar with novel words, phrases, and language use.

MANAGER IN ACTION:

The Colorful Language of Business

Managers and specialists in organizations are usually well-educated people with good communication skills. Nevertheless, they often depart from traditional vocabulary and grammar. The newcomer to an organization may choose to become conversant with company jargon. Knowing these "buzz words" can improve your communication with others. It can also improve your acceptance by the group. However, you have to draw the line somewhere. For instance, many people will choose to avoid language uses that are grossly incorrect. Following is a sampling of the colorful—and sometimes incorrect—language of work organizations.

Input me about your problem. This means, "I would like to receive information from you about your problem." Observe that a noun is converted into a verb. However, so many people in organizations use the word *input* as a verb that it may soon be considered correct usage.

I could care less. This means just the opposite—"I could not care less." It appears that this language reversal was brought into business from the military.

Trust me. Although this is an accurate and grammatically correct phrase, its true meaning requires clarification. It usually means, "Please take my word for it, even though I have no hard data to support what I'm saying."

Copy me. "Send me a photocopy of that document."

Greenmail. A bonus paid for a company's stock over the market price. It is paid by the company management to the raiders to get them to go away.

Golden Parachute. An agreement in which an executive is guaranteed substantial salary and benefits for several years should that executive be fired after an acquisition or merger. The executive with the golden parachute would be more objective about the merits of a group of sharks taking over the company. If fired, he or she will have a happy landing.

Marketing (or the mention of any other organizational function). Terms such as marketing, manufacturing, and purchasing are often used correctly to identify an organizational function or process. At least half the time, however, the terms are used to indicate a department or division. Instead of saying, "Send this to marketing." Government managers make extensive use of this shortened phrase—"Send this to human services," or "Find out what CIA wants to do with this."

Hatchet man. This ancient term refers to an organization official delegated such uncomfortable jobs as firing high-level managers. The hatchet man is delegated this assignment by a senior executive, who does not want to be perceived as nasty.

When using the terms just defined, make sure that your receiver understands your terminology. Unfamiliar terms lead to communications breakdowns.

THE COMMUNICATION PROCESS

Sending messages to other people, and having the messages interpreted as intended, is both complex and difficult. You could no doubt furnish an example of garbled communication. A typical communication snafu took place in a repair shop. A mechanic said to her boss, "I'm behind schedule. Can I work Sunday so I can get caught up?" The boss replied, "Sorry, I don't want you to work any longer." Angered, the mechanic replied, "You mean I'm being fired just because work has backed up in the shop?" She then ran out the door without waiting for an explanation. The supervisor was able to reach the mechanic at home and explain that "work any longer" meant working more than forty hours that week.

Steps in the Communication Process

The complexity of the communication process is illustrated in Figure 11-1. This diagram is still a simplification of the baffling process of sending and receiving messages. The theme of the model is that two-way communication involves many steps, and that each step is subject to interference or noise. Our discussion is organized around the elements in Figure 11-1.

Figure 11-1   The Communication Process

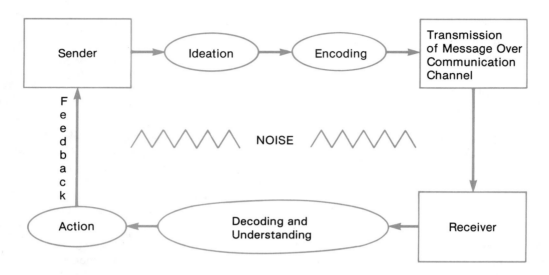

Sender.   The **sender** is the person who initiates the message. Without a sender there can be no communication. In the repair-shop example, the mechanic was the first sender. When the boss replied to the sender's message, he became the sender. People generally become senders when they have a purpose for communicating. At other times a person may send a message unintentionally, such as through a frown of disbelief.

Ideation.   **Ideation** is the organization of one's thoughts in order to send a message. This stage is both the origin and framing of an idea or message. The boss said to himself, "I know work has backed up in the shop, but we cannot afford to pay overtime this week."

Encoding.   **Encoding** is the process of organizing ideas into a series of symbols, such as words and gestures, designed to communicate with the receiver. One's choice of words has a strong influence on communication effectiveness. The better a person's grasp of language, the easier it is for him or her to encode. If the choice of words or any other symbol is appropriate, communication will proceed more smoothly. In the example at hand, the boss chose to use the phrase, "I don't want you to work any longer." A more effective message would have been, "We don't have overtime pay in this week's budget."

Transmission.   **Transmission** is the actual sending of a message over a communication channel. The channel is the medium carrying the message, such as voice, telephone, memo paper, or electronic bulletin board. It is important to select a channel that fits the message. It would be appropriate to use the spoken word to inform a co-worker that his shirt was torn. It would be inappropriate to send the same message over an electronic bulletin board. Many messages in organizations are sent nonverbally, using gestures and facial expressions. For example, a smile from a superior in a meeting is an effective way of communicating the message, "I agree with your comment."

Receiver. The **receiver** is the person who interprets the message. He or she is the target of the communication process. In its simplest form, communication is sending a message to a receiver. To be an effective sender, it is necessary to understand the receiver. The repair-shop supervisor knew from past experience that his mechanic was somewhat literal-minded. He therefore should have offered a few words of explanation rather than using an ambiguous message such as "I don't want you to work any longer." Many receivers require considerable explanation both oral and written.

Decoding and understanding. **Decoding** involves the receiver interpreting the message and translating it into meaningful information. Barriers to communication are the most likely to surface at the decoding step. People often interpret messages according to their psychological needs and motives. The mechanic in this situation many have been fearful of losing her job because she was behind schedule. Therefore when she heard the message, "work no longer," she interpreted it as a termination notice. Decoding can therefore be regarded as **understanding.**

Action. After understanding comes **action**—the receiver does something about the message. If the receiver acts in the manner the sender wants, the communication has been totally successful. From the manager's perspective, the success of a message is measured in terms of the action taken by a subordinate. Understanding alone is not sufficient. Many people understand messages but take no constructive action.

Action is a form of feedback because it results in a message being sent back to the original sender from the receiver. A small-business owner may receive a message from a supplier, "Please send us $350 within ten days to cover your overdue account." The owner understands the message but decides not to comply because the $350 owed is for defective parts. His noncompliance is not due to a lack of understanding.

Feedback. **Feedback** occurs when the receiver sends a message back to the sender. It restarts the communication process. The receiver becomes the sender by beginning with ideation, followed by encoding, and so forth. If sending the original message results in a two-way conversation, the communication process often goes through many cycles.

ORGANIZATIONAL CHANNELS OF COMMUNICATION

Messages in organizations travel over many different channels or paths. One key aspect of communication channels is whether they are formal or informal.

Another is their direction: downward, upward, horizontal, or diagonal. The situation of the shop supervisor sending a message to his mechanic illustrates a formal communication channel in a downward direction.

Formal Communication Channels

The **formal communication channels** are the official pathways for sending information inside and outside the organization. The primary source of information about formal channels is the organization chart. It indicates the channels messages are supposed to follow. By carefully following the organization chart, a maintenance worker would know how to transmit a message to the chief executive officer. In many large organizations (such as the one in Figure 11-2), the worker would have to go through eight management or organiza-

Figure 11-2   Formal Communication Pathway for Message Sent From the Bottom to the Top of a Large Company

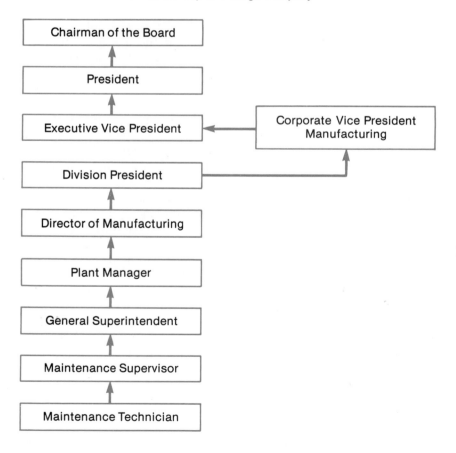

tional levels. Figure 11-2 illustrates the passage of a message concerning a manufacturing problem up the organization from the bottom to the top.

At times, the formal chain of command is broken by the communication channels used to take care of work. At one construction site, a steeplejack (a worker who climbs high structures) told his boss: "I want you to get those rivets reinspected. They don't look sturdy enough to hold the weight they are supposed to." The safety-conscious boss accepted this upward delegation. He did so even though the upward delegation reversed the normal downward flow of work assignments.

Formal communication channels are closely related to formal methods of communicating messages in organizations. These formal methods are primarily publications such as newsletters and newspapers, meetings, written memos, bulletin boards on walls, and electronic bulletin boards.[2]

Informal Communication Channels

Organizations could not function by formal communication channels alone. Another system of communication, called an **informal communication channel,** is also needed. Informal communication channels are the unofficial network used to supplement the formal channels. Most of these informal channels arise out of work necessity. People will sometimes depart from the official communication channels to consult with a person with specialized knowledge. For example, the manager of pension services in a bank became knowledgeable about calculating exchange rates between the U.S. dollar and other currencies. Bank employees from other departments regularly consulted this manager when they faced an exchange-rate problem.

Hundreds of possibilities for using informal communication channels exist in any organization. Any time two or more employees consult each other outside of formal communication channels, an informal communication channel has been used. Two other major aspects of informal communication channels are the grapevine and the rumors it carries.

Grapevine. The **grapevine** is the informal means by which information is transmitted in organizations. As such, it is the major informal communication channel. The term *grapevine* refers to tangled pathways that can distort information. Grapevines are often thought to be used primarily for passing along negative rumors and gossip. This perception is an over-simplification. The grapevine is sometimes used purposely to disseminate information along informal lines. For example, management might want to hint to employees that the plant will be closed unless the employees become more productive. Although the plans are still tentative, feeding them into the grapevine may result in improved motivation and productivity. Some important characteristics of the grapevine are as follows:[3]

● A substantial number of employees consider the grapevine to be their primary source of information about company events. The grapevine often has a bigger effect on employees than do messages sent over formal channels. Messages sent over formal communication channels are often perceived to be stale news.

- Information is transmitted along the grapevine with considerable speed. The more important the information, the greater the speed. For example, information about the firing or sudden resignation of an executive can pass through the company in thirty minutes.

- Approximately three-fourths of messages transmitted along the grapevine are true. Because so many grapevine messages are essentially correct, employees believe most of them. They have received intermittent reinforcement for having believed them in the past. Nevertheless, these messages frequently become distorted and misunderstood. By the time a rumor reaches the majority of employees it is likely to contain false elements.

A representative distortion of this type is as follows:

A company president gave a personal donation to a gay rights group. The funds were to be used to promote local legislation in favor of equal employment opportunities for gay people. These facts traveled over the grapevine. The last version of the story took this form: "The president has finally come out of the closet. He's hiring three gay managers and is giving some year-end bonus money to the Gay Alliance."

- Grapevine messages are usually communicated orally rather than in writing or nonverbally. Yet there are instances of written transmission of rumors. Envelopes marked "personal and confidential" are sometimes used to transmit written rumors.

- Only about 10 percent of employees who receive rumors pass along the information to others. Those who do, however, usually communicate the information to several other employees, rather than only to one.

- Managers sometimes use the grapevine to gauge employee reaction to a controversial issue before making a formal announcement. If the reaction is too negative, managers can modify their plans.

Rumor Control.   False rumors can be disruptive to morale and productivity. Some employees will take action that hurts the company and themselves in response to a rumor. It is not unknown for a few valuable employees to leave a firm in response to rumors about an impending layoff. The reason valuable employees are often first to leave is that they have skills in demand at other firms. To cut rumors short, managers are advised to communicate the information people want. The communication should be prompt, clear, accurate, and factual. At the same time, formal channels of communication should be kept open, and employees should be encouraged to use them.[4]

As a manager, you need to accept informal channels and try to use them to your advantage. Ignoring these channels could result in the loss of important information.

Communication Directions

Messages in organizations travel in four directions: downward, upward, horizontally, and diagonally. Over time, an organization develops communication networks corresponding to these directions. A **communication network** is a pattern or flow of messages that traces the communication from start to finish.[5] An example of a conventional communication network was shown in Figure 11-2.

Downward communication is the flow of messages from one level to a lower level. It is typified by a boss giving orders to a subordinate or by top-level management sending announcements to employees. Downward communication enables managers to carry out the basic functions of planning, organizing, controlling, and leading. A major problem with downward communication is that it is often overemphasized at the expense of receiving upward communication. Information is sometimes transmitted from a higher level to a lower one without inviting a response.

Two-way communication allows immediate feedback. If the action the receiver takes is the intended one, it indicates that the message has been received and accepted. If no action—or the wrong action—is taken, the manager knows that either the message was not received as intended or it is being resisted. Two-way communication about an event helps clarify what is happening.

Upward communication is the transmission of messages from lower to higher levels in the organization. As just stated, upward communication tells management how well messages have been received. Upward communication is also the most important network for keeping management informed about problems within the organization. A well-known electronics company came close to bankruptcy because of a failure in upward communication. Top-level management was unaware that their major product was accumulating rapidly on dealer shelves. The company persisted in building products for an already saturated market. By the time complaints from dealers reached top-level management, the company was in deep financial trouble. Dealers were eventually given rebates on the products, enabling them to hold discount sales. Middle managers were aware of the inventory buildup, but never bothered to inform top-level management.

Upward communication is more widely practiced in nonbureaucratic than bureaucratic organizations. Employees in strongly bureaucratic organizations tend to shy away from upward communication. They perceive it to be somewhat in violation of the chain of command. Employee fear is another factor limiting upward communication. The workers may fear that managers will object to them speaking up. Another fear is that they will be chastised for being bearers of bad news. An example of an upward communication vehicle used in many bureaucracies is a complaint program. Complaints sent up through channels include those about supervisors, working conditions, personality conflicts, sexual harassment, and inefficient work methods.[6]

Horizontal communication is sending messages among people at the same organizational level. Horizontal communication frequently takes the form of co-workers from the same department talking to each other. Another type of horizontal communication takes place when managers communicate with other managers at the same level. Horizontal communication is the basis for cooperation. People need to communicate with each other in order to work effectively in joint effort. For example, they have to advise each other of work problems and ask each other for help when needed.

Departmentalization tends to impede horizontal communication among employees in different departments. Informal communication channels are frequently used to circumvent this barrier. Workers from different departments decide by themselves to discuss work problems. If formal communication channels were strictly followed, workers from different departments could communicate with each other only by going through their bosses.

Diagonal communication is the transmission of messages to higher or lower organizational levels in different departments. Zigzag patterns are also included in diagonal communication. A typical diagonal communication event occurs when the head of the marketing department needs some pricing information. She telephones a supervisor in the finance department to get his input. The supervisor, in turn, telephones a specialist in the data-processing department to get the necessary information. The marketing person has thus started a chain of communication that goes down and across the organization.

NONVERBAL COMMUNICATION IN ORGANIZATIONS

Nonverbal communication is sending messages by means other than language or symbols. The subject is of interest to managers because it is difficult to understand employees by observing spoken and written communication alone. Instead the manager must pay attention to how things are said and to the facial expressions of the person who is communicating. (How something is said can be more meaningful than what is said.) Similarly, individual contributors must understand nonverbal communication to communicate with their superiors and co-workers.

Another important perspective about nonverbal communication is that messages include both the content of the message and a relationship between the sender and the receiver.[7] A message sent with a smile and a reassuring look often enhances communication and fosters a warm personal relationship. The same message sent with a grimace may make the receiver defensive.

Summarized here are the major modes of transmitting nonverbal messages.[8] Be aware, however, that nonverbal communication messages cannot yet be contained in an accurate dictionary. The same nonverbal indicator may mean different things to different people; a given nonverbal action may therefore be misinterpreted. For example, a nod by a person might be interpreted as a "Yes" signal. In reality, the person was using the nod to communicate the message, "I understand."

Head, Face, and Eye Behavior

The most reliable nonverbal guide to peoples' attitudes toward others is revealed by head movements, facial expressions, and eye movements. Combinations of head, face, and eye behaviors are more reliable than any one of them alone. Assume that a person makes what he thinks is a creative suggestion to his boss. The boss responds, "Sounds okay," but also shakes her head from side to side, frowns, and moves her eyes upward. The subordinate can rightfully conclude that the boss is not sold on this idea. How would you interpret the boss's response?

Eye contact provides significant communication. People who look directly at others tend to be perceived as self-confident. Looking away from another person while talking to that person is often an indicator of low self-confidence. Messages accompanied by eye contact are more favorably interpreted by observers than are messages without eye contact.[9]

Posture

Posture is another widely used clue to a person's true attitude. Leaning toward another person suggests that you have a favorable attitude toward the message that person is trying to communicate. Leaning backward communicates the opposite. Standing up straight is generally interpreted as an indication of self-confidence. Slouching is generally interpreted as a sign of low self-confidence.

Physical Distance from People

The closeness of one's body to another person communicates an important message. Standing close to another person suggests positive attitudes toward that person. Standing far away suggests neutral or negative attitudes. It is particularly significant when one person makes an obvious attempt to move toward or away from another individual. Visualize the following scenario. One person enters a conference room and takes a seat. The person next to her immediately shuffles his chair away. What do you think would be the reaction of the first person?

How close should one person stand to another person in a typical business situation? An approximate answer is to use personal distance or social-consultative distance. In our culture, personal distance ranges from about one-and-one-half to four feet. Social-consultative distance is about four to eight feet and is usually reserved for impersonal interaction.[10] Cultural traditions are important in selecting the right physical distance. For example, French males stand much closer to business associates than do British males.

Gestures

Gestures, especially hand movements, are a fundamental aspect of nonverbal communication. Gestures include such varied behaviors as hand waving, finger pointing, head scratching, and holding out palms. Some negative hand gestures are so well recognized that they can lead to disciplinary action if displayed on the job. Positive attitudes are generally shown by frequent hand movements. An exception is that some people wave their hands furiously while arguing. Dislike or disinterest usually produces few gestures.

Gestures can also serve as clues to a person's dominance or submissiveness. Gestures of the dominant (or very assertive) person are usually directed outward toward the other person. These would include touching the other person and palm-down gestures. Submissive gestures are usually protective, such as shrugging one's shoulders or touching oneself.

Voice Quality

More significance is often attached to the way something is said than to what is said. A high-quality voice is characterized by a varied tone, moderate pitch, and moderate rate. A low-quality voice is characterized by a monotone, high or low pitch, and a fast or slow rate. Table 11-1 provides some suggestions for developing an impressive voice quality.

Table 11-1   How to Speak with an Authoritative Voice

A good voice alone will not make a businessperson successful. Yet, like clothing, voice quality should always add to a person's image, not subtract from it. Here are several practical suggestions, developed by voice coaches, for improving voice quality.

- *Avoid most nasal sounds.* The only noise that should come through the nose are *m*'s, *n*'s, and *ng*'s. The rest of speech should be sounded in the mouth. Follow this advice: "There's an easy test to see if you talk through your nose. Say "that." Now, pinch your nose and say "that" again. There should be no difference. If you sound like a duck when you pinch your nose and say "that," then you have a nasal voice. To solve this problem, throw open your mouth and repeat "that" as you yawn. This will bring the vowel down into your mouth. With practice, you will sound the vowels in your mouth and lose the nasal tone.

- *Vary your voice tone.* If you speak in a monotone, your voice will sound mechanical. One way to overcome a monotone is to practice singing several of your typical presentations. This will help you develop skill in using vocal variety.

- *Decrease voice hesitations.* Vocal hesitations are a nonverbal clue to weakness and insecurity. When you hesitate between words, people may think you have not thought through your comments. This problem can be solved by slowing down your speech.

- *Avoid breathiness.* People who take a breath after almost every word appear anxious. To remedy breathiness, take the time to fill your lungs with air before speaking. Practice until you can speak two sentences without taking a breath.

- *Practice conveying commitment in the sound of your voice.* Tape yourself as you talk extemporaneously about a topic you care about, such as describing your fantasy goals in life. Replaying the tape, you will hear your voice move up and down the musical scale.

Source: Based on information in Charles Livingston McCain, "Say It in the Voice of Authority," *Success* (May 1984): 48, 51; Roger Ailes and Jon Kraushar, "Are You A Communications Wimp?" *Business Week Careers* (June 1988): 76.

Physical Setting

The physical setting in which a message is transmitted can influence how well it is received. The physical setting is tied to status, which also influences the perception of a message. People are more likely to respond to a message sent to them in an attractive setting rather than in an unattractive setting. It is advisable to organize your work area neatly before communicating an important message to a visitor. Business entertaining capitalizes on this principle. When important messages have to be communicated, senders often invite potential receivers to an impressive restaurant. Less important messages are more likely to be communicated in the office environment.

Clothing, Dress, and Appearance

A person's external appearance influences his or her communication effectiveness. People listen more carefully to messages of senders they perceive to be well dressed and neatly groomed. Job seekers pay heed to this principle when they dress their best for job interviews. However, dressing well in order to communicate more effectively with others can reach a point of diminishing returns. Overdressing for the occasion may result in self-consciousness. This leads to a temporary decrease in self-confidence, which may detract from one's communication effectiveness.

BARRIERS TO COMMUNICATION

Messages sent from one person to another rarely are received exactly as intended. Barriers exist at every step in the communication process. Figure 11-3 is a diagram showing how barriers to communication influence the receiving of messages. The input is the message sent by the receiver. Ordinarily, the message is spoken or written, but it could be nonverbal.

Barriers to communication, or noise, are shown as **throughput,** the processing of input. The barriers may be related to the receiver, the sender, or the environment. For example, the receiver may be so overloaded with information at the time that he or she is unable to receive the message. The sender might use language that is too difficult for the receiver to understand. The

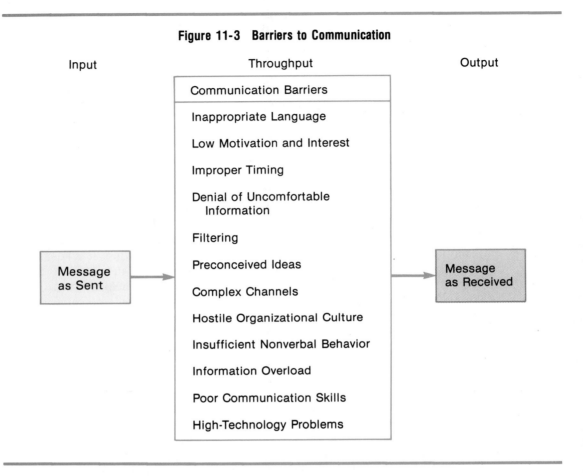

Figure 11-3   Barriers to Communication

Input   Throughput   Output

Communication Barriers

Inappropriate Language

Low Motivation and Interest

Improper Timing

Denial of Uncomfortable
Information

Filtering

Preconceived Ideas

Complex Channels

Hostile Organizational Culture

Insufficient Nonverbal Behavior

Information Overload

Poor Communication Skills

High-Technology Problems

Message as Sent

Message as Received

organization culture may be so hostile that most messages are distrusted. The output in this model is the message as received.

Which messages are the most likely to encounter the most barriers? Interference is the most likely to occur when a message is complex, emotionally arousing, or clashing with a receiver's mental set. An emotionally arousing message deals with such topics as money or personal inconvenience (e.g., being assigned a more remote parking space). A message that clashes with a receiver's usual way of viewing things requires the person to change his or her typical pattern of receiving messages. To illustrate this problem, try this experiment. The next time you order food at a restaurant, order the dessert first and the entree second. The waiter or waitress will probably not hear your dessert order.

Routine or neutral messages are the easiest to communicate. An exception is that sometimes trivial messages are ignored.

Inappropriate Language

The language used to frame a message must be suited to the intended receivers. Language can be inappropriate for a host of reasons. Three factors of particular significance in a work setting are semantics, difficulty level, and use of biased terms.

Semantics is the study of meaning in language forms. The message sender should give careful thought to what certain terms will mean to receivers. A good example is the term *productive*. To prevent erecting communication barriers, you may have to clarify this term. Assume a manager says to his subordinates, "Our department must become more productive." Most employees will correctly interpret the term to mean something like "more efficient," but some employees will interpret it to mean "work harder and longer at the same rate of pay." Consequently, these latter employees may resist the message.

The **difficulty level of language** is its ease of comprehension. Communicators are typically urged to speak and write at a low difficulty level. There are times, however, when a low difficulty level is inappropriate. For instance, when a manager is communicating with technically sophisticated employees, using a low difficulty level can create barriers. The employees may perceive the manager to be patronizing and thus may tune out him or her. The use of jargon, or insider language, is closely related to difficulty level. When dealing with outsiders, jargon may be inappropriate, whereas with insiders (people who share a common technical language), it may be appropriate. Jargon can help the sender establish a good relationship with the receivers.

Another implication of semantics is that certain words are interpreted by some people as a sign of bias. **Biased language** contains a prejudgment toward another person or group based on something other than fact.[11] The recipient of the biased language may become defensive and distort the important part of the message. For example, referring to a woman assistant as a girl in front of others may lead to an immediate communication barrier. Table 11-2 presents a list of biased terms and their bias-free equivalent. All of these terms are subject

Table 11-2 Biased Terms and Their Bias-Free Substitutes

Category	Biased	Bias-Free
Gender-Related	Girl	Woman
	Boy	Man
	Salesman, Saleswoman	Sales representative
	Chairman, Chairwoman	Chairperson, Chair
	Lady engineer	Engineer
	Male nurse	Nurse
Disabilities	Handicapped	Physically challenged
	Deaf	Hearing impaired
	Blind	Visually impaired
	Confined to a wheelchair	Wheelchair user

Table 11-2   Biased Terms and Their Bias-Free Substitutes (Continued)

Race	Nonwhite	Black, Afro-American, Afro-Canadian, Asian
	Indian (American)	Native American
	Whitey	White, White person, Caucasian
Nationality	Jewish person	Jew
Ethnic Background	"Scottish in you"	"Your frugality"
	Ethnic jokes	Jokes with nationality specified
Occupational	Sales clerk	Sales associate
Status	Floor sweeper	Custodian
	Help, Helper	Employees, Assistant

Source: Several of the pairs of terms are from Judy E. Pickens, "Terms of Equality: A Guide to Bias-Free Language," *Personnel Journal* (August 1985): 24–48; Andrew J. DuBrin, *Human Relations: A Job Oriented Approach,* 4th ed. (Englewood Cliffs, NJ: Prentice Hall, 1988), 256.

to change over time, and not everybody agrees on which term is biased. The safest approach is to avoid terms that refer to race, sex, ethnic background, and occupational status unless absolutely necessary.

Low Motivation and Interest

Many messages never get through because the intended receiver is either not motivated to hear the message or is not interested. The challenge to the sender is to frame the message in such a way that it appeals to the needs and interests of the receiver. This principle can be applied to conducting a job campaign. When sending a message, the job seeker should emphasize the needs of the prospective employer. An example would be, "If I were hired, what problem would you like me to tackle first?" Many job seekers send low-interest messages of this type: "Would this job give me good experience?"

Improper Timing

Knowing when to send a message is an important part of communicating effectively. Messages should be sent at a time when they are the most likely to meet with a good reception. The reverse is also true; messages should not be sent at a time when they are the most likely to meet with a poor reception. Following this principle, a good time to talk over a problem with your boss is when he or she is in a good mood. Also, try to avoid sending messages to people when they are heavily fatigued, stressed, or already flooded with information. Fatigue, stress, and information overload interfere with giving careful attention to messages.

Defensive Communication

An important general communication barrier is **defensive communication**—the tendency to receive messages in such a way that our self-esteem is protected. Defensive communication is also responsible for people sending messages to make themselves look good.[12] People communicate defensively through the process of **denial**, the suppression of information one finds to be uncomfortable. It serves as a major barrier to communication because so many messages sent in organizations are potentially uncomfortable. When an anxiety-provoking message is sent, sometimes just part of it is denied. A long-term employee was told that he would be asked to move from his window office to one without windows (a loss of perceived status). He nodded in agreement. When moving day came, the employee discovered that he was being moved to an inside office. He protested to the president, saying that he was never told that the move would mean giving up his window office.

Filtering

Filtering is the coloring and altering of information in order to make it more acceptable to the receiver.[13] It is another variation of defensive communication. For example, an employee becomes aware of information that should be communicated to management. However, the employee realizes that management would be upset if the full controversial story were known. The solution chosen by the employee is to filter the truth, rather than deal with the wrath of management.

Preconceived Ideas

People tend to hear what they want to hear. Clearly, this acts as a major communication barrier. Hearing what you want to hear means that you have already made up your mind on an issue. An employee might believe that the organization cares more about budgets than people. When top-level management initiates a drastic cost-cutting procedure, the employee concludes: "This is more proof that my beliefs are correct." In reality, following orders to balance a budget does not indicate a lack of concern for people.

Complex Channels

The more people a message must pass through, the greater the chance for misunderstanding. This is a major reason why rumors become so distorted—they pass through so many communication channels. In multilayered organizations, the chances for distortion of messages increases. As was shown in Figure 11-2, a message must travel through many organizational layers to get from the bottom to the top of a large organization. Diagonal communication patterns also create complex channels. The message often becomes distorted as it zigzags through the organization.

Some organizations are so complex that it takes considerable time for an outsider to reach the right person. Assume a person called the home office of the Social Security Administration with an inquiry about a deceased relative's social security account. It could take up to an hour to reach the right official. Thus organization structure may create a communication barrier.

Hostile Organization Culture

A **hostile organization culture** is one in which people tend to be defensive, suspicious, angry, and distrustful of each other. Under these conditions, receivers regard many messages with skepticism. People are not sure when they are being told the truth. Lack of trust serves as a formidable communication barrier because people will not take action on messages they think may be false. For example, one manager might truthfully say to another, "The vice president told me to tell you to go ahead and hire that candidate." The recipient of the first message might distrust the source and therefore take no action. By the time the manager contacts the vice president to verify the message, the candidate may have taken another job.

Insufficient Nonverbal Behavior

Effective communicators rely on both verbal and nonverbal communication. If verbal communication is not supplemented by nonverbal communication, messages may not be convincing, as illustrated by this situation:

> A supervisor asked an employee to get rid of two large boxes that were blocking the aisle. Later that day, the supervisor discovered that the boxes had not been removed. He asked the employee if she had heard his request. The employee responded, "Oh, I heard you. But since you didn't wave your hands, I didn't think you wanted it done today."

Communication Overload

Communication, or **information, overload** is a condition in which the individual receives so much information to process that he or she becomes overwhelmed. As a result, the person does a poor job of processing information and receiving new messages. Communication overload also works as a stressor. Many managers suffer from information overload because of the blitz of memos, reports, advertisements, and telephone calls they receive. The explosive growth in the use of photocopying machines and computers is a major contributor to information overload. It is easier than ever to send written material and electronic messages to other people.

Many managers are trying to prevent information overload. They may require that each report be accompanied by a brief summary. Also, many managers subscribe to various abstract services, including tape cassettes, which summarize current articles and books of interest to managers. The tapes can be played while driving a car or doing personal chores.

Poor Communication Skills

Many messages fail to register because the sender lacks effective communication skills. The written or spoken message may be so garbled that the receiver cannot understand it, or it may be so poorly delivered that the receiver refuses to take it seriously. Communication barriers can also be erected because of deficiencies within the receiver. A common one is that the receiver is a poor listener. A later section of this chapter deals with improving communication skills, both in sending and receiving messages.

High-Technology Problems

High technology in the office has created several new communication barriers. The problems associated with electronic mail are representative of these barriers. One communication barrier associated with electronic mail relates to its impersonality. A video display terminal (VDT) is a poor substitute for person-to-person interaction. Much like any printed document, an electronic message can seem much harsher than a spoken message. A manager can smile and express sympathy through a nod of the head. These messages are difficult to communicate via a computer screen. Electronic mail is thus better suited to communicating routine rather than complex or sensitive messages. As an example, it would be insensitive to criticize someone by leaving a message on his or her VDT.

Another potential communication barrier created by electronic mail is flaming. **Flaming** is rudeness, profanity, and other emotional outbursts made by people when they carry on conversations via computer. One problem with flaming is that it becomes an end in itself. Computer buffs become so involved in entertaining each other with shocking messages that work-related messages are forgotten. Flaming inhibits communication in another important way. Some people find the flamed messages unbusinesslike and offensive. Consequently they do not receive the important information accompanying the flamed message. Here is a sample of flaming:

> Big Brother in Department 45 has zapped you this time baby. I caught the fantasy in your cost estimates. So bite the dust, you ———.

OVERCOMING BARRIERS TO COMMUNICATION

Most of these barriers to communication are surmountable. The general strategy for overcoming them has two parts. First, you must be aware that these potential barriers exist. Second, you should develop a tactic to deal with each one.

We will describe a variety of methods for overcoming communication barriers. Table 11-3 lists these methods and shows how they can help overcome the communication barriers already described. Barriers are listed in the left-hand column. Methods for overcoming barriers are listed by letter in the right-

Table 11-3   Methods for Overcoming Communication Barriers

Barriers	Methods
Inappropriate language (A, B, C, F)	A. Understand the receiver
Low motivation and interest (A, B, D)	B. Use empathy
Improper timing (A, B, D)	C. Use appropriate language
Defensive communication (A, B, D, I)	D. Repeat messages and use multiple channels
Filtering (A, B, H)	E. Increase the opportunity for informal interaction
Preconceived ideas (A, B)	F. Engage in two-way communication
Complex channels (A, F, G)	G. Decrease the physical barriers
Hostile organizational culture (A, E, H)	H. Create right communication channel
Insufficient nonverbal behavior (A, I)	I. Use verbal and nonverbal feedback
Information overload (A, F, J)	J. Avoid communication overload
Poor communication skills (A, K)	K. Improve communication skills
High-technology problems (A, B, E)	

hand column. The letters to the right of or below each barrier indicate the method that can help overcome the communication barrier. To illustrate, the communication barrier "communication overload" can be reduced with use of methods A, F, and J in Table 11-3.

Understand the Receiver

To be an effective communicator, you must understand the receiver. Understanding the receiver is a strategy that can assist in overcoming every communication barrier. For example, part of understanding the receiver is to be aware that he or she may be overloaded with information, or be poorly motivated. Understanding the receiver is one of the most important success factors in conducting international business. Ways of communicating effectively in one culture may not be appropriate in another. For example, western businesspeople communicate agreement with a handshake. Arab businesspeople both resent and resist shaking hands. North Americans might create a communication barrier by offering to shake hands in an Arab country.

Use Appropriate Language

Overcoming the communication barrier of inappropriate language requires the sender to use appropriate language. Appropriateness here refers to choosing the right key words and difficulty level and using bias-free terms. Although this antidote is straightforward, it is not always easy to implement. The sender must assess carefully the language of the receiver. Casual conversation with others will give the sender a chance to make these observations. Before negotiating a deal with out-of-town customers, a loan officer listened carefully to their language. He discovered the term *under air* meant that a property was air conditioned. The loan officer then used that jargon to help establish rapport with customers and potential customers from that geographic region.

Use Empathy

Empathy is the ability to see things as seen by the other person, or to "put oneself in the other person's shoes." Empathy is closely tied to the proper decoding of messages. Empathy leads to improved communication because people are more willing to engage in a dialogue when they feel understood. Managers need empathy to communicate with employees who do not share their values. A typical situation would be when an employee does not identify with company goals and is therefore poorly motivated.

Empathy is not sympathy. A manager might understand why an employee does not identify with company goals. Yet, the manager does not have to agree that the company goals are not in the employee's best interests.

Repeat Messages and Use Multiple Channels

Several communication barriers may prevent messages from getting through the first time they are sent. These barriers include the receiver not wanting to hear or see the information; they also include information overload. An important message should be repeated when it is first delivered. Repeat the message one or two days later. Experienced communicators often repeat a message during their next contact with the receiver. The sender of a message might say, "Why don't we review briefly what we agreed on Tuesday?"

Repetition of the message becomes even more effective when more than one communication channel is used. Effective communicators follow up spoken agreements with written documentation. The use of multiple channels helps overcome the problem that some people respond better to one communication mode than another. For example, a supervisor asked an employee why she did not follow through with the supervisor's request that she wear safety shoes. The employee replied, "I didn't think you were serious. You didn't put it in writing."

Increase the Opportunity for Informal Interaction

An important way of decreasing physical barriers to communication is to provide employees with ample opportunity to chat with each other about work. Informal interaction also overcomes the problem of messages being misinterpreted. Furthermore, informal conversations among employees helps reduce the problem of mutual distrust. People become more open with each other as informal interaction increases.

Increased opportunity for informal interaction can be provided through seating employees in close proximity to each other. Committee work also increases the opportunity for informal interaction. Company-sponsored social events are another vehicle for encouraging informal interaction on the job.

Engage in Two-Way Communication

Many communication barriers can be overcome if senders engage receivers in conversation. A dialogue helps reduce misunderstanding by communicating feelings as well as facts. Both receiver and sender can ask questions of each other. Here is an example:

> Manager: I want you here early tomorrow. We have a big meeting planned with our regional manager.
>
> Employee: I'll certainly be here early. But are you implying that I'm usually late?
>
> Manager: Not at all. I know you come to work on time. It's just that we need you here tomorrow about thirty minutes earlier than usual.
>
> Employee: I'm glad you asked. I'm proud of my punctuality.

Decrease the Physical Barriers to Communication

Interpersonal communication can be enhanced by removing specific physical barriers. One method of accomplishing this would be to use a flat organizational structure. Flat structures decrease the number of channels that messages have to pass through when moving up and down the organization. Another important way of reducing physical barriers to communication is to use round tables in conference rooms. Rectangular tables tend to encourage communication with the leader and not with other members.

Develop the Right Communication Climate

A strategic way of improving interpersonal communication is to establish a communication climate that encourages openness and mutual trust.[14] An approach to establishing mutual trust is for people to be honest with each other. This would include less filtering of information, less deception, and more honest feedback. For example, group members might be told the reason an executive resigned. A statement such as, "So and so resigned to pursue personal interests," tends to arouse suspicion.

Openness, however, does have some drawbacks. According to Eric M. Eisenberg and Marsha G. Witten, there are some situations in which openness may be inappropriate.[15] Among these exceptions are when individuals prefer not to reveal their career plans to superiors and when management wants to keep secret plans about a pending merger.

Use Verbal and Nonverbal Feedback

To be sure that one's message has been understood, it is helpful to ask for verbal feedback. A recommended managerial practice is to conclude a meeting with a question such as, "To what have we agreed this morning?" The receiver of a message should also take the responsibility to offer feedback to the sender. The expression "This is what I heard you say," is an effective feedback device. Feedback can also be used to facilitate communication in a group meeting. After the meeting, provide everyone in attendance with a written follow-up to make sure they all left with the same understanding.

It is also important to observe and send nonverbal feedback. Nonverbal indicators of comprehension or acceptance can be more important than verbal indicators. For example, the manner in which somebody says "Sure, sure," can indicate if that person is truly in agreement. If the "Sure, sure," is a brush-off, the message may need more selling. The expression on the receiver's face can also be a tip-off to message acceptance or rejection.

Avoid Communication Overload

Avoiding communication overload involves several aspects. First, many wasted communication events will be prevented if messages are not sent to an already overloaded person. Second, management should minimize flooding employees with information. Both managers and individual contributors often receive so many memos, that they lose track of some top-priority ones. Third, it is important to avoid communication overload for oneself. For example, many people can learn to do a better job of assigning priorities to paperwork.

IMPROVING YOUR COMMUNICATION SKILLS

Another pervasive strategy for overcoming communication barriers is for organization members to develop better communication skills. Fewer barriers to communication occur when people speak well, listen carefully, write crisply, and transmit clear nonverbal messages. Effective communication skills are also a success factor in organizational life. Few people are nominated for advancement who cannot communicate effectively with workers.[16] Four sets of communication skills are necessary for overcoming barriers and advancing one's career: face-to-face speaking skills, listening skills, nonverbal skills, and writing skills.

Face-to-Face Speaking Skills

Few workers other than executives are required to give public presentations. What most managers and specialists do require is improvement in person-to-person speaking skills, including becoming more persuasive. Skills of this type are called for in such varied situations as conferences with other workers, interviews, and meetings. Table 11-4 provides several tips on how to improve your face-to-face speaking skills.

Table 11-4   How to Improve Your Face-to-Face Speaking Skills

1. *Speak in a meeting whenever the opportunity arises.* Volunteer appropriate comments in class and committee meetings. Remember, however, that "hogging" time detracts from communication effectiveness.

2. *Obtain feedback by listening to tape or video recordings of your voice.* Attempt to eliminate pauses and phrases such as "okay," "you know," or "all right." Ask an instructor or knowledgeable friend for his or her opinion about your voice and speech.

3. *Pattern yourself after appropriate models.* A television or radio newscaster may have the type of voice and speech behavior that fits your personality. The goal is not to imitate your model but to use him or her as a guide to generally acceptable speech.

4. *Practice interviewing and being interviewed.* Take turns with a friend conducting a simulated job interview. Interview each other about a controversial current topic or about your hobbies.

5. *When trying to sell an idea, first capture your audience's attention, then isolate a need for your idea and show how your proposal satisfies that need.* A standard formula for persuading others is to convince them that your plan will work to their benefit.

6. *Practice expressing the feelings behind your factual statements.* A statement that combines facts and feelings is more persuasive than a statement that is only fact-oriented.

Source: Adapted from Andrew J. DuBrin, *Human Relations: A Job Oriented Approach,* 4th ed. (Englewood Cliffs, NJ: Prentice Hall, 1988), 258; point 5 is from D. Keith Denton, "If You want Your Ideas Approved," *Management Solutions* (September 1986): 11.

A special case of improving face-to-face speaking skills is to improve one's ability to sell ideas, or to be persuasive. Selling ideas to others enters into any form of negotiation, including buying and selling and asking for a salary increase. Managers also need to sell ideas when motivating or disciplining subordinates. To sell ideas to others, you must first establish credibility. If a person frequently presents half-thought-out or untruthful ideas to others, that person will develop a poor reputation. The poor reputation becomes a communication barrier. Once credibility is established, four rules for selling ideas can be used to advantage:[17]

First, never suggest an action without telling its end benefit. In asking for a raise, one might say, "If I get this raise, I'll be able to afford to stay with this job as long as the company likes."

Second, explore the reasons for people's objections. Assume a potential customer says, "I like this model but I don't want it in my living room." An effective response would be, "What is it that you don't like about it?" Another response would be, "What features do you like in this product?"

Third, explain why you are asking whenever you ask a question. The sales representative above might say, "The reason I asked you about features is that maybe we have another model with the same features."

Fourth, say why you think it is so when you assert something. The raise seeker might say, "I think my request for a salary increase is justifiable because of the contribution I am making."

Listening Skills

Listening is a basic part of communication. Unless a person receives messages as intended, he or she cannot get work done properly. It has been estimated that 45 percent of the time people spend on communicating is devoted to listening.[18] Managers need to be good listeners because so much of their work involves eliciting information from others in order to solve problems. Consultant Tom Peters believes that careful listening is behind many marketing triumphs in difficult circumstances. He cites as evidence the success of Indiana-based Weaver Popcorn in penetrating the Japanese market:

> The key to Weaver's triumph is listening to Japanese distributors—about local customs [for instance, patient learning of the intricacies of the Japanese distribution system], local beliefs [Japan's obsession with quality] and local tastes [they wanted orange, not yellow popcorn].[19]

Listening is also important because of the cost of not listening. Countless numbers of costly mistakes are made because one worker did not listen carefully to another. Listening mistakes led to rescheduling of appointments, reshipping of orders, retyping of letters, and needlessly repeated work in general. Suggestions for effective listening are presented in Table 11-5.

Table 11-5 Keys to Effective Listening

If you practice these suggestions regularly and are patient, you can become an effective listener. Coaching and feedback by an observer could also be helpful. Learning to be an effective listener may also require breaking habits that conflict with these suggestions.

- *Limit distractions.* Hold telephone calls, close the door, and find a quiet place away from work responsibilities.
- *Discipline yourself to concentrate.* Take notes, maintain eye contact with the speaker, and ask questions to make sure that you understand the message. Such signals assure the speaker that you are actively listening.
- *Stop interrupting.* A poor listener waits for the chance to jump in with his or opinion or argument. To be a good listener, one has to adopt a passive mode sometimes.
- *Capitalize on the fact that thought is faster than speech.* A poor listener tends to daydream with slow or average speakers. A good listener uses the

Table 11-5   Keys to Effective Listening (Continued)

time to evaluate carefully what the speaker is saying. He or she also listens to voice tone and observes nonverbal signs, thus reading between the lines.

Source: Diane Cole, "Now Hear This: Paying Attention Can Pay Off," *USA Weekend* (18 April 1986): 20.

Nonverbal Communication

Nonverbal communication skills also can be improved with practice. However, the guidelines for improvement in other modes of communication are better established. Following are several suggestions to follow when trying to improve your ability to communicate nonverbally.

As a starting point, obtain feedback on your current methods of nonverbal expression. Ask friends for their impression of how you express yourself other than in words. A particularly useful technique is to have a videotape prepared of you conversing with another individual. After studying your nonverbal behavior, attempt to eliminate mannerisms and gestures that you think detract from your effectiveness. Among these would be overuse of gestures, frowning too frequently, and moving your knee from side to side.

Make a conscious effort to relax when talking to people. Take a deep breath, exhale, and concentrate on loosening your muscles. Relaxation improves nonverbal communication because external indicators of tension make one appear unsure and unconvincing. Another advantage of being relaxed when conversing is that it helps others relax. When others are relaxed, it is easier for them to talk freely.

Nonverbal behavior can also be improved through modeling. Observe carefully the nonverbal behavior of people you consider to appear cool and confident. Many of their gestures, facial expressions, and body movements can be incorporated into your nonverbal behavior. Modeling is widely used in the acting profession. To improve their nonverbal skills, actors and actresses typically observe the behavior of more accomplished actors and actresses.

Use facial expressions and gestures to supplement your speech. A good starting point is to use a variety of nonverbal behaviors to express enthusiasm. Among them would be firmly shaking hands, smiling, moving toward another person, and touching the receiver on the arm or shoulder.

Use role playing to practice nonverbal communication. A good starting point would be for one person to play the role of a buyer and another person, the role of a seller. The two of you engage in serious negotiation about the price of an item. During the interchange, make use of as many nonverbal behaviors as seem appropriate. After the role-playing session, discuss each other's communication effectiveness.

Writing Skills

An ever increasing number of employees are expected to possess **informational skills**. They must be able to send, process, and receive information. The ability to write clear, concise, and well-organized prose is a critically important informational skill.[20] Poor writing creates many business problems. As observed by the coordinator of a business-writing program, "Customer relations may be suffering because of a generally negative tone in correspondence. Quality control may be hampered by incomprehensible reports. Mistakes in use of equipment may occur because of confusing instructions."[21]

Our purpose here is not to present a minicourse in effective business writing. Instead, the accompanying "Manager in Action" suggests several important techniques to improve business writing. All of these suggestions can be used with word processors and memory typewriters as well as with writing by hand.

MANAGER IN ACTION:

Edward T. Thompson, Writing Expert of *Reader's Digest*

Editor-in-chief Thompson encourages people not to be afraid to write. Most writing assignments require only that the writer get across ideas simply and clearly. Effective writing has three basic requirements. First, you must want to write clearly. Second, you must be willing to work hard. Since writing is a form of thinking, it is hard work. Third, you must know and follow some basic guidelines that cover the most common problems.

1. *Outline what you want to say.* A convenient method of outlining is to put separate points of information on index cards. Sort and re-sort the cards until they form a sensible and logical outline. Cards containing similar points should be grouped together with a paper clip. Then, within each group, arrange the points in logical, understandable order.

2. *Start where your readers are.* Avoid writing at a level higher than your readers' knowledge of the subject. Remember that your prime purpose is to explain something, not to prove that you are smarter than your readers. Yet, do not insult readers by writing at too low a level.

3. *Minimize jargon.* Minimize the use of words, expressions, and phrases known only to people with specific knowledge or interests. When jargon is used, it should be translated.

4. *Use familiar combinations of words.* One way to accomplish this is to sprinkle your writing with everyday phrases and expressions.

5. *Use "first-degree" words.* These are words that immediately bring an image to mind. Second- and third-degree words have to be translated back to first-degree words. For example, *book* is a first-degree word. *Volume, tome,* or *publication* are third-degree words.

6. *Stick to the point.* All sentences in your report should relate to your outline. Sentences that do not relate to the outline usually should be discarded. However, new points of merit can be added to the outline.

7. *Be as brief as possible.* Condensing your writing almost always makes it tighter, straighter, and easier to read and understand. One approach to brevity is not to waste words telling people what they already know. Excess evidence and unnecessary anecdotes should be eliminated. Usually, one or two facts or examples will support a point. It is also important to delete "word wasters" such as saying "in the event of" instead of "if." Using active verbs instead of passive verbs can also save words. Instead of writing "Our company was founded by Jason Wentworth," write "Jason Wentworth founded our company."

Source: Abridged and paraphrased with permission from an International Paper Co. Advertisement. Copyright © 1982, International Paper Co.

SUMMARY OF KEY POINTS

Communication is the process of exchanging information via words, letters, symbols, or nonverbal behavior. Managers carry out their functions through the process of communication.

The communication process involves many elements, all of which are subject to interference, or noise. The process begins with a sender. The sender ideates the message, encodes it, and then transmits it over a channel to a receiver. In successful communication, the receiver decodes the message and understands it and then acts on it. Feedback occurs when the receiver sends a message back to the sender.

Messages in organizations travel over many different channels. Formal channels are revealed by the organizational chart. Informal channels are the unofficial network of communications that supplement the formal pathways. The grapevine is the major informal communication pathway. Messages are transmitted in four directions: upward, downward, sideways, and diagonally.

Nonverbal communication is the transmission of messages by means other than language or symbols. The major modes of transmitting nonverbal messages are as follows: head, face, and eye behaviors; posture; interpersonal distance; gestures; voice quality; physical setting; and clothing, dress, and appearance.

Barriers exist at every step in the communication process. These barriers must be identified and an appropriate remedial strategy selected. Effective communication skills help overcome communication barriers and can enhance a person's career. Communication skills comprise four modes: face-to-face, listening, nonverbal, and writing.

QUESTIONS

1. Some education officials have objected to businesses conducting remedial reading programs for employees. The officials claim this activity

should be left to professional educators. What is your opinion on this issue?

2. How can you guard against overcommunicating information to other people?
3. Why might some people find it easier to communicate facts than feelings?
4. If deficient communication skills are such a deterrent to career success, should people with communication deficits be covered under the Vocational Rehabilitation Act and similar legislation? Defend your answer.
5. Assume you have an urgent message for top-level management. What would be the best way to get the message up through the organization?
6. Suppose a person believes strongly in using long, flowing sentences in writing. Should that person sacrifice his or her beliefs in order to write conventional business memos?
7. A business student said, "I'm not worried about improving my report-writing skills. In almost any place I might work, administrative assistants are paid to correct your reports." What do you think of her reasoning?
8. How effective is the phrase, "trust me," when you want someone's trust?
9. Xerox Corp. has spent time, money, and effort trying to stop the public from using the term *Xerox copy* in reference to any photocopy. (There are legal reasons for this concern.) What communication barrier is Xerox facing?
10. Should a company have a formal policy about *flaming*? Why or why not?

ACTIVITIES

1. Ask a manager what is the biggest communication problem faced by his or her organization. What communication barrier described in this chapter does the problem most nearly resemble?
2. Assume that all employees in your company now receive all their pay in salary, including merit increases. Your company then decides to divide pay in this manner: 65 percent straight salary and 35 percent based on a company-wide incentive program similar to gainsharing (see Chapter 10). Develop a strategy for communicating to employees information about the new pay plan; do this in such a way that distortions are minimized.

CASE PROBLEM 11-A: THE OFFICE SCHMOOZERS

Joe Murphy, a regional vice president of a financial-services firm, was concerned about the limited interaction he observed among key employees. He analyzed the problem in these words:

"Our regional headquarters is a good example of the problem I have in mind. Our professional-level employees all work in private offices or enclosed cubicles with doors. They get together at lunch and coffee breaks, but beyond that they have very little contact. Each person seems to work in his or her own little world.

"Consequently, we are not getting the cross-fertilization of ideas that we should be getting. The result is limited creativity. Hardly any new ideas surface about important things such as how to improve loan collections or how to find qualified borrowers. We get too many loan applicants who have been turned down by banks because of shaky credit."

One month later, Joe Murphy had implemented a solution to the problem. He said, "After wrestling with this problem, I decided that the solution was straightforward. We were missing out on the interaction we needed because we had set up too many physical barriers to communication. My solution was to get rid of almost all the private offices and cubicles. In their place, we installed office landscaping. This took the form of carpeted partitions to set off each work area. Now if somebody wants to talk over an idea with another worker, it is easy. There is no door to knock on. Managers and professionals now have easy access to each other."

Three months later, Joe Murphy was asked how well his new office design was working. He reported, "I still think I'm on the right track, but the office landscaping seems to be working too well. We are getting a few more creative ideas. Yet, on balance, we're losing too much productivity. Our professional help is 'schmoozing' too much. They drop by each others' work areas and chat about many things not strictly related to our business. While walking down the aisles, I have overheard some of them chatting about industry trends and the stock market. It seems like they are partying on the job.

"I told people in advance why I was modifying the office. Most agreed that they did need to exchange more ideas on a regular basis. I have also shared my observations with them about the schmoozing problem. They smile in agreement, but the problem persists.

"I'm now thinking about getting rid of the office landscaping, and putting up some offices without doors. However, I don't want to create turmoil or low morale."

Case Questions

1. What is your opinion of Murphy's assumption that office landscaping would lead to improved communications?
2. What is your opinion of Murphy's assumption that informal conversation would improve the creativity of professional-level workers?
3. What is your evaluation of Murphy's new idea of erecting offices without doors?
4. Advise Murphy on a sensible course of action that will help him achieve his goal of improved communication and creativity.

EXERCISE 11-A: RATE YOUR COMMUNICATION SKILLS

The following questionnaire is designed to help you evaluate the effectiveness of your communication skills. Give yourself 3 for excellent, 2 for good, and 1 for fair. The developer of the questionnaire advises you to be fair in making your ratings: "You are probably a better communicator than you think."

COMMUNICATION

Rate Your Communication Skills

In speaking:
_____ My attitude is positive.   _____ I plan my purpose related to
_____ I analyze the situation and   listener interest and attitude.
   listener and adapt to these.   _____ I try to get on common ground.

_____ My prejudices are submerged.

My message:
_____ Is organized clearly.
_____ Has a definite and clear purpose.
_____ Adapts opening remarks to listener(s).
_____ Presents points (not too many) in clear order.
_____ Goes clearly from one point to another (transitions).
_____ Has sufficient proof and support
_____ Holds interest and attention
_____ Uses appropriate language
_____ Shows clear thinking.

In presenting the message:
_____ My manner is enthusiastic.
_____ I look directly at listener(s).
_____ My posture and gestures are appropriate.
_____ I project my voice with emphasis and variety.
_____ I speak clearly and distinctly.
_____ I adapt to listener reactions.

As a listener:
_____ I pay full attention to the speaker.
_____ I look at the speaker.

_____ I am openminded and empathetic.
_____ I help establish a pleasant climate.
_____ I try to understand the speaker's purpose.
_____ I separate facts from opinion.
_____ I evaluate, not jumping to conclusions.
_____ I avoid daydreaming.
_____ I listen fully before trying to talk back or refute the speaker.
_____ I apply the message to my needs.

_____ **Total score**

Evaluating your communication rating:

80–90 — Excellent
70–80 — Good
60–70 — Fair

Harold P. Zelko *is a communication and training consultant and author of "Better Seminars and Workshops for Both Sponsor and Participant,"* Personnel Journal, *February 1986.*

Exercise Questions

1. What are the possible sources of distortion in the above evaluation of your communication skills?
2. Which questions in the test relate to nonverbal aspects of communication?

REFERENCES

1. Roger Ailes and Jon Kraushar, "Are You a Communications Wimp?" *Business Week Careers* (June 1988): 75.
2. Paul L. Blocklyn, "Consensus on Employee Communications," *Personnel* (May 1987): 62–63.
3. Walter St. John, "In-House Communication Guidelines," *Personnel Journal* (November 1981): 877; James L. Gibson, John M. Ivancevich, and

James H. Donnelly, Jr., *Organizations: Behavior, Structure, Processes*, 6th ed. (Plano, TX: Business Pubs., Inc., 1988), 564–565.

4. St. John, "In-House Communication," p. 877.

5. Michael L. Peters, "How Important is Interpersonal Communication?" *Personnel Journal* (July 1983): 555.

6. James T. Zigenfuss, Jr., "Communication: Corporate Complaints Programs Make Gains from Gripes," *Personnel Journal* (April 1987): 40–41.

7. Larry E. Penley and Brian Hawkins, "Studying Interpersonal Communication in Organizations: A Leadership Application," *Academy of Management Journal* (June 1985): 324.

8. Andrew J. DuBrin, *Contemporary Applied Management: Behavioral Science Techniques for Managers and Professionals*, 3d ed. (Plano, TX: Business Pubs., Inc., 1989.), 97–107.

9. John E. Baird, Jr. and Gretchen K. Wieting, "Nonverbal Communication Can Be a Motivational Tool," *Personnel Journal* (September 1979): 610.

10. Barry L. Reece and Rhonda Brandt, *Effective Human Relations in Organizations*, 2d ed. (Boston: Houghton Mifflin Co., 1984), 45.

11. Judy E. Pickens, "Terms of Equality: A Guide to Bias-Free Language," *Personnel Journal* (August 1985): 24.

12. Robert A. Giacalone and Stephen B. Knouse, "Reducing the Need for Defensive Communication," *Management Solutions* (September 1987): 20–25.

13. R. Wayne Mondy, Robert E. Holmes, and Edwin R. Flippo, *Management: Concepts and Practices*, 2d ed. (Boston: Allyn & Bacon, Inc., 1983), 396.

14. Corwin P. King, "Crummy Communication Climate (and How to Create It)," *Management Solutions* (July 1986): 30–31.

15. Eric M. Eisenberg and Marsha G. Witten, "Reconsidering Openness in Organizational Communication," *Academy of Management Review* (July 1987): 418.

16. Harold P. Zelco, "Communication: Rate Your Communication Skills," *Personnel Journal* (November 1987): 133.

17. Jesse Nirenberg, *How to Sell Your Ideas* (New York: McGraw-Hill, 1984).

18. Dave Lewis, "Listening: The Forgotten Skill," *BNAC Communicator* (Winter 1987): 15.

19. Thomas Peters, "Respectful Listening is Key to Success," *Democrat and Chronicle* (syndicated column) 17 January 1988.

20. Steven S. Ross, "Technical Skills You Need to Succeed," *Business Week's Guide to Careers* (Fall–Winter 1983): 25.

21. Diana C. Reep, "Stop Writing the Wrongs," *Personnel Journal* (September 1984): 68.

PART FIVE
Controlling

Chapter 12
Essentials of Control

Chapter 13
Managing Ineffective Performers

Chapter 14
Managing for Quality

Controlling is the managerial function of ensuring that performance conforms to plans. It involves comparing actual performance to a predetermined standard. Controlling is studied from three perspectives in this part of the book. Chapter 12 presents an overview of the control process. Included in the overview is a description of the use of budgets in control and the human element in the use of controls.

Chapter 13 describes the application of the control process to managing ineffective performers. Dealing with substandard performance is not typically included in a discussion of controlling. However, using a control model to manage poor performance can lead to gains in organizational productivity.

Chapter 14 describes various managerial strategies and methods for improving the quality of products and services. Managing for quality is chosen as a capstone topic in the study of management because of the current emphasis on quality awareness and improvement.

12
Essentials Of Control

After studying the material in this chapter, you should be able to accomplish the following tasks:

1. Explain how control relates to the other management functions.
2. Describe the steps in the control process.
3. Give examples of several nonbudgetary control techniques.
4. Summarize the major types of budgets.
5. Explain how budgets are used for control.
6. Outline the basics of a management information system.
7. Explain the workings of a computerized supervisory system.
8. Name several characteristics of effective controls.

Key Terms and Phrases

Control function of management
Precontrol
Concurrent control
Postcontrol
External control strategy
Internal control strategy
Deviation
Exception principle
Qualitative control technique
Quantitative control technique
Budget
Fixed budget
Flexible budget

Revenue-and-expense budget
Time, space, material and product budgets
Capital-expenditure budget
Cash budget
Gross profit margin
Management information system (MIS)
Decision support system (DSS)
Traditional MIS
On-line MIS
Computerized supervisory system (CSS)

The **control function of management** involves measuring performance and then taking corrective action if goals are not being achieved. One purpose of control is to ensure productive behaviors of all organization members.[1] Without the control function, it is difficult to know if people are carrying out their jobs properly. Organizational control has another major purpose. Controls enable managers to gauge whether or not the organization is attaining its goals.

Much of controlling involves measuring performance. After accurate measurements are made, a corrective course of action often suggests itself. A case in point is the measurement of inventory levels. If an audit indicates that inventory levels are too high, the manager knows it is time to stop accumulating inventory. When the inventory level is adjusted to a desirable condition, the performance of the inventory manager is improved.

In this chapter we emphasize the types and strategies of controls, the control process, how budgets relate to controls, and the use of management information systems in control. Finally, we examine the characteristics of effective controls.

CONTROLLING AND THE OTHER MANAGEMENT FUNCTIONS

Control has been referred to as the terminal management function because it takes place after the other functions have been completed. Control is used to evaluate whether or not the manager has done a good job of planning and decision making, organizing, and leading. Controlling is most closely associated with planning and decision making. Planning and decision making are used to establish goals and methods of achieving the goals. Controlling investigates the extent to which planning has been successful.

The links between controlling and other major management functions are illustrated in Figure 12-1. Controlling helps measure how well planning and decision making, organizing, and leading have been performed. The control function is also used to measure the effectiveness of the control system. On occasion, it will be discovered that the control measure used is inappropriate. For example, one measure of sales performance might be the number of sales calls made. Such a measure might encourage calling on a large number of poor prospects just to meet the performance standard. It would be more effective to spend more time with better prospects. More will be said about effective control measures later.

The planning and decision making tools and techniques described in Chapter 5 also are considered tools and techniques of control. For example, a

Figure 12-1   The Links Between Control and the Other Management Functions

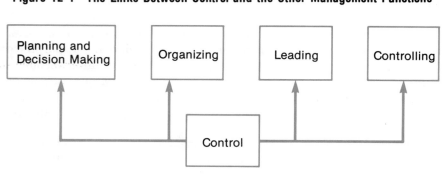

Gantt chart is used to keep track of how well target dates for a project are being met. ''Keeping track'' is a control device. If an event is behind schedule, the project manager will often take corrective action.

Controlling at the Three Management Levels

Controlling is an important part of any manager's job. However, the amount of time spent controlling and the type of control activity, vary with management level. The type of control used is significantly influenced by the level of management. Supervisors use short-range controls. These first-level managers are typically concerned with daily and weekly production reports. In some instances, the supervisor might make hourly judgments of how well performance is meeting the standard. Visualize a retail store in which the checkout lines are getting too long. The length of the line serves as a trigger for the supervisor to open up an additional checkout line.

Middle managers tend to be more concerned with weekly, monthly, and quarterly performance. They are less directly involved in monitoring day-to-day work performance. Middle managers also tend to rely more on written reports than do first-level managers. In fact, middle-level managers are often deluged with control reports. They are responsible for summarizing and integrating these reports in a form useful to top-level management.

Top-level managers use a longer-range perspective in controlling. The control reports read by top-level management typically deal with monthly, quarterly, semiannual, and annual performance. Top-level managers also rely much more on written control reports than on direct observations of performance. There are always exceptions. Some chief executive officers mingle with employees, first-level supervisors, and customers in order to develop a firsthand understanding of organizational performance. Top-level managers may take this approach to help overcome the filtering of control information by subordinates. The people doing the filtering are concerned that they will be penalized if they report unfavorable performance to top-level management.

Figure 12-2 presents a diagram of the current status of controls at the three levels of management. However, these relationships are in a state of flux. Advances in information systems continue to influence the nature and type of controls used by top-level management. A growing number of executives now use personal computers to access the company's mainframe computer. In this way, top-level managers have access to computerized control information collected anywhere in the firm. Another trend is that middle-level managers are shifting toward computerized controls and away from direct observation of performance.

TYPES AND STRATEGIES OF CONTROL

Many types of controls are used in organizations. As already mentioned, controls can be described according to their overall perspective: short range, intermediate range, and long range. Controls can also be classified according to

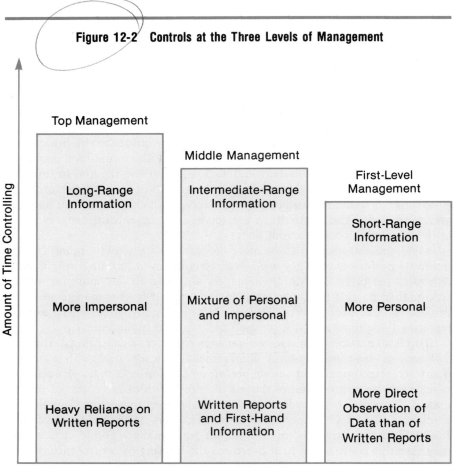

Figure 12-2   Controls at the Three Levels of Management

the time at which the control is applied to the activity. Another important way of describing controls relates to the source of the control: external versus internal.

Time Element in Controls

Precontrols take place prior to the performance of activities. The purpose of precontrols is to prevent problems that result from deviation from standard. Precontrols are generally the most cost effective. A manufacturing company that specifies quality standards for purchased parts has established precontrols. By purchasing high-quality parts, the manufacturer prevents many instances of machine failure. Precontrols are also used in the management of human resources. Standards for hiring employees are precontrols. For example, an airline may require that any pilot hired must have 20/20 vision. This precontrol helps to prevent accidents stemming from poor vision.

Concurrent controls monitor activities while the activities are being carried out. A typical concurrent control takes place when a supervisor observes performance, spots a deviation from standard, and immediately makes a constructive suggestion. For example, a sales manager might overhear a telemarketing specialist fail to ask a customer for an order. The telemarketer would then be coached on the spot about how to close an order.

Postcontrols evaluate an activity after it has been performed. Postcontrols measure history; they point out what went wrong in the past. In the process, guidelines for future corrective action may be provided. Financial statements and production reports are forms of postcontrols. To illustrate, a quarterly financial report might indicate that one division of a company had lost money. Top-level management would then confer with division management to see what could be done to improve the situation.

Figure 12-3 summarizes the three types of controls based on a time perspective. Most organizations use a combination of precontrols, concurrent controls,

Figure 12-3   Three Types of Controls Based on the Time Element

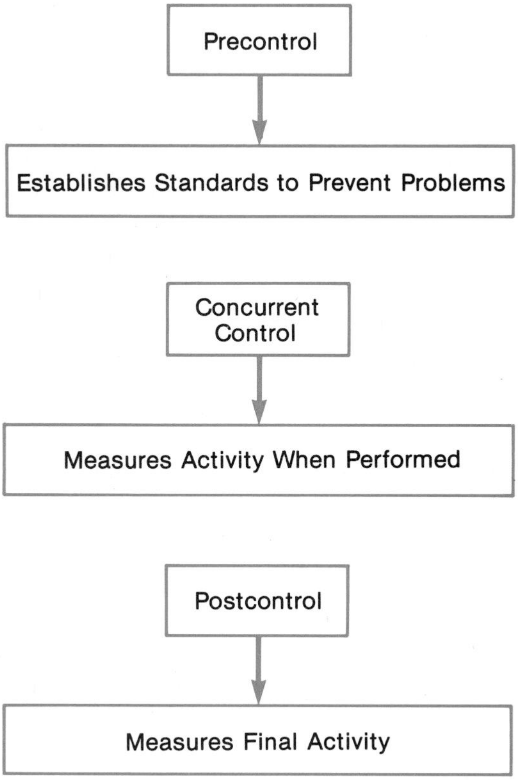

and postcontrols. An important part of a manager's job is choosing controls appropriate to the situation.

External versus Internal Controls

Controls can also be classified according to their underlying strategy. Most controls are based on the assumption that individuals have to be controlled by external forces. Other controls place more reliance on the motivation and ability of people to set their own controls.

The **external control strategy** assumes that employees are motivated primarily by external rewards and need to be controlled by their managers. Autocratic management and Theory Y use an external control strategy. Three steps are required to use an effective external control system. First, the objectives and standards need to be made relatively difficult in order to stretch subordinates and leave little leeway in performance. Second, the objectives and standards must be set in such a way that people cannot manipulate or distort the measures. For instance, top-level management might make its own investigation of customer satisfaction rather than taking the word of field personnel. Third, rewards need to be directly and openly tied to performance.

The external strategy has several different effects.[2] On the positive side, employees may channel considerable energy into achieving objectives. Employees do so because they know that good performance leads to a reward. If the control system is tightly structured, the result will be a high degree of control over employee behavior.

On the negative side, external control creates some problems. Employees may work toward achieving standards, but they may not develop a commitment to the organization. As a result, they may reach standards, but they may not be truly more productive. Reaching standards without being productive is sometimes referred to as "looking good on paper." The top-level managers of an outpatient clinic might establish a very high number of patients processed as a performance standard. To achieve this standard, the business manager in the clinic instructs the telephone receptionist, "When anybody calls with even a minor complaint, tell that person to come in for a visit." As a result, the medical staff spends brief amounts of time with many people who do not require medical attention. A more effective strategy would be to spend more time with fewer patients who truly need medical care.

A problem related to lack of commitment is that morale sometimes suffers under an external control strategy. Employees may perceive the external standards as being arbitary and therefore may resent them. How would your morale be affected by controls imposed by management?

Another problem is that an external strategy may result in misdirected effort. People may put too much effort into achieving standards and, as a result, neglect other important aspects of the job. High sales quotas may result in neglect of customer service. Externally imposed standards may also result in filtering, or hiding, poor performance results.

The **internal control strategy** assumes that employees can be motivated by building their commitment to organizational goals. Participative and Theory

Y management use an internal control strategy. Three steps are required to build an effective internal control system. First, goals must be set participatively. These goals are later used as performance standards for control purposes. Second, the performance standards (control measures) are used for problem solving rather than for punishment or blame. When deviations from performance are noted, superiors and subordinates get together to solve the underlying problem. Third, although rewards are tied to performance, they are not tied to only one or two measures. The total contribution of an employee is evaluated, rather than one or two quantitative measures of performance.

A positive consequence of internal controls is that they usually lead to a higher commitment to attain goals. Thus, they may direct greater energy toward task performance. Another good result is that the system encourages the upward and horizontal flow of valid information about problems.

Self-imposed controls also have some negative effects. Employees may be motivated to establish easy performance standards for themselves. Another problem is that the supervisor loses control over subordinates and thus may feel powerless. Finally, an internal control system creates some problems in giving out equitable rewards. Because performance standards may be loose, it is difficult to measure good performance.

An internal control system is not necessarily good, and an external control system is not necessarily bad. Internal controls work satisfactorily when a high-caliber, well-motivated work force is available. External controls compensate for the fact that not everybody is capable of controlling their own performance. If applied with good judgment and sensitivity, external control systems work quite well. The effective use of controls thus follows a contingency, or "if . . . then", approach to management.

STEPS IN THE CONTROL PROCESS

The steps in the control process follow the logic of planning and decision making. The control process follows these steps: standards are set, performance is measured, performance is compared to standards, and corrective action is taken if needed.[3] The following discussion describes these steps, and highlights the potential problems associated with each step.[4]

Setting Standards

A control system begins with a set of standards that are realistic and acceptable to the people involved. The characteristics of effective objectives described in Chapter 3 are applicable here. Historical information about comparable situations is often used when standards are set for the first time. Assume a manufacturer wants to establish a standard for the percent of machines returned for repairs to the dealer. If the return rate was 3 percent for other machines with similar components, the new standard might be a dealer return rate of no more than 3 percent.

At times it is necessary to set standards that are dictated by profit-and-loss consideration. A case in point is the establishment of an occupancy-rate standard for a hotel. Assume break-even analysis reveals that, unless the hotel has an average occupancy rate of 75 percent or higher, costs will not be covered. Hotel management must then accept a higher-than 75 percent occupancy rate as a standard.

Should every activity have a standard? A strong advocate of control would insist that every activity be measured against a jointly agreed standard. Another view is that not all organizational activities require standards. According to this view, standards are necessary for only those activities that are critical to achieving organizational objectives. If standards are not set for every activity, top-level management must identify those key activities that merit standards. Key activities in a store might be sales levels, inventory turnover, inventory slippage (theft), and employee turnover.

Measuring Actual Performance

To implement the control system, performance must be measured. Performance appraisals are but one major way of measuring performance. Supervisors often make direct observations of performance to implement a control system. A simple example would be observing a sales associate ask a customer, "Is there anything else you would like?" A more elaborate performance measure would be a ten-page report submitted to top-level management on the status of a major project.

Measurement of performance is much more complex than it would seem on the surface. Three important conditions for effective measurement are as follows:[5]

1. *Agree on the specific aspects of performance to be measured.* Top-level managers in a hotel chain might think that occupancy rate is the best measure of performance. Middle-level managers might disagree in these words: "Don't place so much emphasis on occupancy rate. If we try to give good customer service, the occupancy rate will take care of itself. Therefore, let's try to measure customer service."

2. *Agree on the accuracy of measurement needed.* In some instances, precise measurements of performance are possible. In deciding whether to retain or replace a coach, his or her record of wins and losses can be measured precisely. In other instances, precise measurements of performance may not be possible. Assume top-level management of the hotel chain buys the idea of measuring customer service. Quantitative measures of customer service would be available. These would include the ratings by guests in response to brief questionnaires and the number of formal complaints. However, any measurements would have to be subjective, such as observing the behavior and comments of guests. Qualitative measures of performance, including spontaneous comments about service made by guests, might be more relevant than the quantitative measures.

3. *Agree on who will use the measurements.* In most organizations, managers at higher levels have the authority to review performance measures of people below them in their chain of command. Few people at lower levels object to this practice. Another issue here concerns how much access the staff has to control reports. Line managers sometimes believe that too many staff members make judgments about their performance.

Comparing Actual Performance to Standards

Once standards have been established and performance measurements taken, the next step is to compare actual performance to standards. Unless comparisons are made between performance and expectations, the control process will not be taken seriously. Key aspects of comparing performance to standards include measuring the deviation and communicating information about it.

Deviation in a control system is the size of the discrepancy between standards and actual results. It is important to agree beforehand how much deviation from the standard is a basis for corrective action. When using quantitative measures, statistical analysis can determine how big a deviation is significant. With the 75 percent occupancy-rate standard in the hotel example, it might be that plus or minus 3 percent is not meaningful. Deviations in this range are considered random events. Deviations of 4 percent or more would be considered significant. Taking corrective action on only significant deviations is called the **exception principle**. The discussion of quality control statistics in Chapter 14, ''Managing for Quality,'' has more to say about deviations from standard.

There are times when a deviation as small as 1 percent from standard can have a big influence on company welfare. If a division fails by 1 percent to reach $100 million in sales, the firm will have $1 million less money with which to work. At other times, deviations from standards as high as 10 percent might not be significant. A claims department might be 10 percent behind schedule in processing insurance claims. However, the claims manager might not be unduly upset because all the claims eventually would be settled.

When statistical limits are not available, wisdom and experience are needed to diagnose a random deviation. Sometimes random factors beyond a person's control lead to a one-time deviation from performance. If the manager believes this to be the case, the deviation can be ignored. For example, a person might turn in poor performance one month because he or she faced a family crisis.

For the control system to work, the results of the comparison between actual performance and standards must be communicated to the right people. These people would include the employees themselves and their immediate managers. At times, the results also should be communicated to top-level management and selected staff specialists. Exceptional deviations from safety and health standards would qualify here. For example, nuclear power plants are equipped with elaborate devices to measure radiation levels. When a specified radiation level is reached or exceeded, several key people are notified automatically.

Taking Corrective Action

After making an evaluation of the discrepancy between actual performance and standard, the manager has three courses of action: do nothing, solve the problem, or revise the standard.[6] Each of these alternatives may be appropriate, depending on the results of the evaluation.

Do Nothing. The purpose of the control system is to determine if the plans are working. If the evaluation reveals that things are proceeding according to plan, no corrective action is required. Doing nothing, however, does not mean abdicating, or giving up, responsibility. A manager might take the opportunity to compliment employees for having achieved their objectives, thus increasing employee motivation, but 'doing nothing' about the approach to reaching objectives.

Solve the Problem. The big payoff from the control process concerns the correction of deviations from substandard performance. If the manager decides that the deviation is significant (nonrandom), problem solving is initiated. Typically the manager meets with the subordinate to discuss the nature of the problem. Other knowledgeable parties might be brought into the problem-solving process. At times, the deviation from standard is so large that a drastic solution is required. J. C. Penney Co, Inc., faced this problem several years ago. Their costs for corporate office space and salaries in New York City were so unacceptably high that the company decided to relocate to Plano, Texas (near Dallas). Many top-level employees bitterly protested the move, and many refused to relocate. Nevertheless, top-level management believed that the relocation was justified from a cost standpoint.

At other times, the manager can correct the deviation from standard without being forced to overhaul current operations. An office manager in a group dental practice used a control model to measure the percent of professional time allotted to patient care. Her analysis revealed that nonbilled time had exceeded 10 percent—an unacceptable deviation. The corrective action involved two steps. First, dental records were scanned to find patients who were overdue for cleaning and checkups. Second, the office manager telephoned these people and asked them if they would like to schedule an appointment for cleaning and checkup. The telemarketing campaign was so successful that virtually all the slack time was filled within ten days.

Revise the Standard. Deviations from standard sometimes should be attributed to errors in planning rather than to performance problems. Corrective action is thus not warranted because the true problem is that the standard is unrealistic. An analogy to the classroom can be drawn. If 90 percent of the students fail a test, the real problem could be an unrealistically difficult test.

Standards are most frequently revised when the planning is for a relatively new task. Performance quotas may be based on "guesstimates" that prove to be unrealistically difficult or overly easy to reach. A performance standard would be deemed unrealistically difficult if virtually no employee met the standard. The standard would be deemed too easy if it was exceeded by virtually all employees. As shown in Figure 12-4, revising the standards means repeating the control cycle.

Figure 12-4   Steps in the Control Process

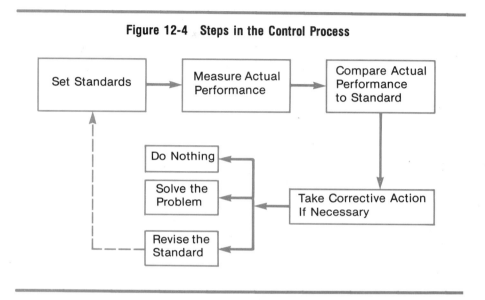

NONBUDGETARY CONTROL TECHNIQUES

Because control is one of the major functions of management, many specific techniques of control are in use. Several of them, including direct observation and financial reports, have already been mentioned. This section describes control techniques not related to budgeting. Table 12-1 describes qualitative control techniques, and Table 12-2 describes quantitative control techniques. **Qualitative control techniques** are methods based on human judgments about performance. **Quantitative control techniques** are methods based on numerical measures of performance. Although quantitative control techniques use numbers, they can be as subjective as qualitative techniques. For example, a numerical performance standard may be derived from somebody's hunch about what is good performance.

Our purpose in listing a sampling of control techniques is primarily to alert you to their existence. Chapter 5 provides more details about four of the quantitative control techniques described in Table 12-2.

Table 12-1   Qualitative Control Techniques

Technique	Definition	Key Features
Audit	Examination of activities or records to verify their accuracy or effectiveness	Usually conducted by someone from outside the area audited
External audit	Verification of financial records by external agency or individual	Conducted by outside agency such as CPA firm
Internal audit	Verification of financial records by internal group of personnel	Wide in scope, including evaluation of control system
Management audit	Use of auditing techniques to evaluate the overall effectiveness of management	Examines wide range of management practices, policies, and procedures
Personal observation	Managers' first-hand observations of how well plans are carried out	Natural part of manager's job
Performance appraisal	Formal method or system of measuring, evaluating, and reviewing employee performance	Points out areas of deficiency and areas for corrective action; superior and subordinate jointly solve the problem
Policy	General guideline to follow in making decisions and taking action	Indicates if manager is following organizational intentions.

Controls are widely used in organizations to keep costs at acceptable levels. Postcontrols often are used when costs have risen too high. In response, the organization begins to cut costs; as many variable costs as possible are reduced. Major areas of cost reduction include trimming payroll, selling off an unprofitable portion of the business, and reducing travel by company personnel. Typical minor areas of cost cutting include restricting the use of photocopiers, canceling magazine subscriptions, and eliminating the purchase of fresh flowers for reception areas.

Precontrols are used by some firms to guard against the need to trim costs. Some firms use temporary employees as a precontrol. By hiring temporaries, the firm prevents a portion of payroll costs from reaching an unacceptable level. When a temporary worker's assignment is completed, he or she is removed from the payroll. In contrast, permanent workers often are kept on the payroll when they are between assignments because the company anticipates that constructive work soon will be found for them.

Table 12-2   Quantitative Control Techniques Used in Production and Operations Control

Technique	Definition	Purpose
Gantt chart	Chart depicting planned and actual progress of work on a project	Describes progress on a project
PERT	Method of scheduling activities and events using time estimates	Measures how well project is meeting schedule
Break-even analysis	Ratio of fixed costs to price minus variable costs	Measures organization's performance and gives basis for corrective action
Economic order quantity (EOQ)	Inventory level that minimizes ordering and carrying costs	Helps control having too much or too little inventory
ABC analysis	Method of assigning value to inventory; A items are worth more than B or C items	Indicates where emphasis should be placed to control money
Variance analysis	Major control device in manufacturing	Establishes standard costs for materials, labor, and overhead, then measures deviations from these costs

BUDGETS AND BUDGETARY CONTROL

When people hear the term *budget*, they typically think of tight restrictions placed on the use of money. You have probably heard a statement of this kind: "The only way I can afford to take an airplane trip is on a budget plan." In management, a budget does place restrictions on the use of money, but the allotted amounts can be quite generous. A **budget** is a spending plan for a future period of time expressed in numerical terms. These numerical terms typically refer to money, but they could also refer to such things as amount of energy or printer ribbons consumed.

Virtually every manager has some budget responsibility, because a budget is a plan for allocating resources. Without budgets, there would be no way of keeping track of how much money is spent in comparison to how much money is available. Two aspects of budgets of particular interest to managers are the different types of budgets and how budgets are used for control. We will also give you suggestions for preparing a budget.

 Types of Budgets

Budgets can be classified in many ways. For example, budgets are sometimes described as either fixed or flexible. A **fixed budget** allows for expenditures based on a one-time allocation of resources. The organizational unit is given a fixed sum of money that must last for the budget period. A **flexible budget** allows for variation in the use of resources based on activity. Under a flexible budget, a sales department would receive an increased telephone budget if the department increased its telemarketing program. Any type of budget can be classified as fixed or flexible. The four basic types of budgets are as follows:[7]

1.   Revenue-and-expenses budgets

2.   Time, space, material, and product budgets

3.   Capital-expenditure budgets

4.   Cash budgets

A **revenue-and-expense budget** describes plans for revenues and operating expenses in dollar amounts. It is the most widely used, and most readily understood, type of budget. The sales budget used by business firms is a revenue-and-expense budget. It forecasts sales and estimates expenses for a given period of time. Many organizations use a monthly budget. The monthly budgets are later converted into quarterly, semiannual, and annual budgets.

Most revenue-and-expense budgets divide expenses into a reasonable number of categories. Operating-expense budgets contain hundreds of entries reflecting the many costs of operating an organization. Major operating expenses include salaries, benefits, rent, utilities, business travel, building maintenance, and equipment. Minor operating expenses include business entertainment, gifts to employees and vendors, office supplies, charitable contributions, and relocation allowances to executives. Care must be exercised to obtain accurate measures of these expenses, because many organizations lack accurate information about costs.[8]

Time, space, material, and product budgets express expenditures in physical rather than monetary terms. At some point, these expenditures may be translated into monetary units. For example, the number of photocopies used can be converted into the cost of these photocopies. Expressing expenditures in physical quantities is likely to make more sense for control purposes. It is often easier for an employee to be concerned about the amount of material consumed than about the cost of the material consumed.

Time, space, material, and product budgets are used for such items as labor hours, machine hours, square feet allocated, amount of lumber consumed, and units produced. The units-produced category is different from the others. It refers to an output that will be sold. Time, space, and materials are all expenses.

Capital-expenditure budgets are plans for spending money on things used to produce goods or services. Capital expenditures are usually regarded as major expenditures and are tied to long-range plans. Capital expenditures include money spent for buildings, machinery, equipment, and major inventories. In a typical budgeting system, the purchase of a mailing machine would be included in the capital budget. The monthly payment to the U.S. Postal Service for postage would be an operating expense.

Cash budgets are forecasts of cash receipts and payments. They are compared against actual expenditures. The cash budget is an important control measure because it reflects the firm's ability to meet cash obligations. Many firms that are working to capacity—such as an overflowing restaurant—can still go bankrupt. Their expenses are so high that even full production cannot generate enough revenue to meet expenses. A typical problem is that the firm has borrowed so much money that having a cash surplus becomes almost impossible. Principal and interest payments on the loans consume most of the cash receipts.

Cash budgeting also serves another important function. It shows the amount of cash available to invest in revenue-producing ventures. In the short range, businesses typically invest cash surpluses in stocks, bonds, and money-market funds. For the long range, the cash is likely to be invested in real estate or in the acquisition of another company. Another long-range alternative is to use surplus cash to expand the business.

Budgets and the Control Process

Budgets fit naturally into the control process. Planned expenditures are compared to actual expenditures and corrective action is taken if the deviation is significant. A budget as a control device is illustrated in Table 12-3. The nightclub and restaurant owner described in Chapter 5 operates with a monthly budget. The owner planned for revenues of $40,000 in March. Actual revenues were $42,500, a positive deviation. The discrepancy is not large enough, however, for the owner to change the anticipated revenues for April. Expenses were $100 under budget, a positive deviation the owner regards as insignificant. In short, the performance against budget looks good. No corrective action will be taken on the basis of March performance.

Table 12-3   March Revenue-and-Expense Budget for Nightclub and Restaurant

Item	Budget	Actual	Over	Under
Revenues	$40,000	$42,500	$2,500	—
Salaries	18,500	18,500	—	—
Food	10,500	10,000	—	$500
Liquor	8,750	9,000	250	—
Rent and utilities	1,500	1,500	—	—
Renovation debt	650	650	—	—
Miscellaneous	100	250	150	—
Total	$40,000	$39,900	$ 400	$500

Budget summary: Revenues exceed budget by $2,500; expenses are $100 under budget.

The nightclub and restaurant owner, however, may be making a budgeting error that will need to be corrected in the future. Two of the expense items, food and liquor, should be placed on a flexible budget. Both expenses will vary in direct proportion to sales.

A more advanced method using budgets for control is to use financial ratios as guidelines to performance. One such commonly used ratio is **gross profit margin**, expressed as sales, minus the cost of goods sold, divided by sales, or

$$\frac{\text{Sales} - \text{Cost of Goods Sold}}{\text{Sales}}$$

The purpose of this ratio is to measure the total money available to cover operating expenses and to make a profit. If performance deviates significantly from a predetermined standard, corrective action must be taken.

Assume the nightclub owner decides that she should be earning a 10 percent gross profit margin. For March, the figures are as follows:

$$\text{Gross Profit Margin} = \frac{\$42,500 - \$39,900}{\$42,500} = \frac{\$2,600}{\$42,500} = .06$$

Based on the gross-profit-margin financial ratio, the business is not performing as well as planned. One could argue that the owner is being unrealistic: a 6 percent gross profit margin in the nightclub business is fine. If the owner finds this margin unacceptable, she must find ways to increase sales, decrease costs, or both. The owner may choose to advertise a special promotion on the radio. This step might bring in additional revenues that exceed the additional costs incurred by the promotion.

Advantages of Using Budgets.   Above all, budgets can be a sensible method of controlling the expenditures of an organization. This is particularly important because cost control receives top priority today in both profit and non-profit organizations.[9] Without budgets, an organization can get out of financial control quickly. Some people will squander funds, leaving little money for important purposes. Even worse, there will be no systematic way of knowing if funds are available to cover legitimate expenses.

Another contribution of budgets is that they communicate the objectives of the organization in terms of what activities are important enough to receive adequate funding. Similarly, budgets help organizational units understand where they fit into the whole. A manager might conclude after reviewing her budget, "I guess our activities acccount for 1 percent of the company's annual expenditures."

Budgets are also a good way of measuring performance. Meeting revenue forecasts and keeping expenses within budget are both indicators of good performance. The accompanying "Organization in Action" illustrates how a budget can be used to document poor financial performance in the construction business. Budgets are also motivational assists because they act as goals. People will strive to meet realistic budgets.

ORGANIZATION IN ACTION:

The Escalating Costs of a High-Rise Hotel

In July 1983, a developer announced plans to build a twenty-seven-story Hyatt Regency hotel in Rochester, New York. Actual construction began New Year's Eve, 1986. Two years later, construction was still significantly delayed due in part to disputes between the developer and the hotel's general contractor. The following budget summarizes the cost overruns on the project:

The Rising Cost of the Hyatt

Hyatt costs	Original budget	New budget	Variance
General construction	$24,128,000	$27,500,000	+ $3,372,000
General construction contingency	500,000	1,000,000	+ 500,000
Furniture, fixtures & equipment contingency	385,000	525,000	+ 140,000
Design and construction consultants	2,100,000	2,850,000	+ 750,000
Project management	500,000	700,000	+ 200,000
Legal, accounting, appraisal & insurance	1,400,000	1,850,000	+ 450,000
Construction loan fees	270,000	710,000	+ 440,000
Permanent loan fees	412,000	450,000	+ 38,000
Interest on loans during construction	1,500,000	910,000	− (590,000)
Taxes during construction	178,000	730,000	+ 552,000
COMIDA bond fee	10,000	10,000	− 0 −
Bank fees (CD float & interim equity)	289,000	588,000	+ 299,000
Investment advice	345,000	870,000	+ 525,000
Technical assistance fee	230,000	230,000	− 0 −
Initial business budget	900,000	1,100,000	+ 200,000
Working capital reserve	627,000	627,000	− 0 −
Operating deficit	541,000	541,000	− 0 −
Non-construction contingency	− 0 −	209,000	+ 209,000
Total budget	$39,500,000	46,800,000	+ $7,300,000

Source: Data furnished by city of Rochester, New York. Reprinted in "Hyatt Revived in New Bailout Plan," *Democrat and Chronicle*, 2 June 1988.

Disadvantages of Using Budgets. A major problem with budgets is that they can be so rigid that constructive behavior is inhibited. For example, labor-saving machinery is sometimes left unused because there is no money left in the budget to make necessary repairs. Budget reporting also can be so time-consuming that time is diverted away from revenue-producing activity. For instance, sales representatives often complain that filling out detailed expense reports takes time away from dealing with customers.

A current concern about budgets, particularly in manufacturing, is that they are based on outmoded accounting concepts. The traditional way of evaluating capital expenditures is to determine how much money they save in labor. If the cost of the equipment cannot be justified in labor savings, the equipment may not be purchased.[10] A broader viewpoint is needed for true productivity increases. Other cost-justification measures include how useful the new equipment is in cutting lead times, boosting quality, increasing customer satisfaction, and surviving in the marketplace. As one small-business owner put it, "I don't care if my accountant says the new labeling machine will not provide a satisfactory return on investment. If we don't supply our customers with computerized mailing list, we won't have any more customers."

Suggestions for Preparing a Budget

Under a philosophy of participative management, managers at all levels provide some input into preparation of their budgets. Some items in the budget are fixed, such as costs of benefits for department employees. Other items, such as money for travel and supplies, are much more negotiable. Part of preparing a budget is making accurate estimates of how much money will be needed to cover expenses. How much each item will cost is estimated on the basis of both past experience and anticipated changes for the upcoming budget period.

Another part of budget preparation is convincing others that these expenses are both legitimate and important. An experienced manager offers the following suggestions for preparing a budget.[11]

1. *Identify needs for your service or product.* This is particularly applicable to staff departments. Find out what other departments in the organization would like your department to accomplish. It is easier to obtain funds for "popular" than for "unpopular" causes.

2. *Locate internal competition for funds.* Be prepared to outdocument and outsell the competition at budget time. It may also be necessary to outperform them all year long.

3. *Establish a realistic budget expectation.* Suppose your department was allocated 5 percent of the total company budget last year. During the year, your department did not increase its productivity and sales were stable. Asking for 5 percent of budget again this year would be realistic.

4. *Start the budget process early.* Why wait until you receive a letter stating, 'All budget input is due in two weeks'? About thirty days before this letter normally arrives, begin figuring out what you hope to accomplish for the next year and how much it will cost. In many instances, it is helpful to start the budget process an entire year beforehand.

5. *Offer proof of your budget requirements.* It is important to be detailed and concrete. You should provide a substantial rationale to support your proposed budget. Proof could include (1) a list of operating improvements within your department, (2) a list of the important duties and functions performed by your department, (3) the trend data showing the increasing work load of your department over the years, and (4) the documentation of long-range commitments from top-level management for the programs in your department.

6. *Offer proof of how new programs in the company will affect your expenses.* For example, the implementation of a nine-digit ZIP Code could mean that your computer files would have to be upgraded.

MANAGEMENT INFORMATION SYSTEMS AND CONTROL

A **management information system (MIS)** is a formal system for providing management with information useful or necessary for making decisions. Most MISs are computerized, but the system can be based on manually collected and collated information. The MIS is usually based on a mainframe computer, but recent advances allow for some of these systems to be based on personal computers.[12] A **decision support system** refers to any MIS that provides backup information for making sound decisions. Managerial control is based on valid information, so an MIS is an indispensable part of any control system. MISs are based on two types of information: historical and on-line.[13]

A **traditional MIS** is based on historical information contained in scheduled reports and word-of-mouth communication. A monthly budget report could provide data for the official part of the traditional MIS. It takes some time for this information to be generated, so it may lose some of its value by the time it is reported. To help overcome this problem, the traditional MIS also includes an unofficial aspect. Data can be communicated informally by telephone messages, handwritten notes, and conversations. A drawback of using historical data is that inefficiencies may be concealed in past performance.

An **on-line MIS** is designed to supply information at the time it is generated. A computerized cash register that automatically records changes in inventory based on purchases is an on-line MIS. The main advantage of the on-line MIS is its timeliness. Management can react immediately to brewing problems. A practical problem with the use of an on-line MIS is that few managers are inclined to monitor a display terminal continuously. They are more likely to read control information when it is convenient for them.

Typically, the MIS is regarded as an overhead, either paid for out of a central budget or shared among users of the service. An important new development, however, is to make the MIS a profit center rather than a cost center. The MIS earns a profit by charging other departments for its services. For example a user might be charged $4.25 for a report, $11.50 for a payroll check, or $32.50 per employee.[14] If the revenues exceed the expenses of operating the information system, the MIS has earned a profit.

Elements of an MIS

There are many differences of opinion about the key elements contained in an MIS. Nevertheless, there are four basic elements contained in most of them. As shown in Figure 12-5, these elements are: to analyze the information requirements, to develop an information base, to design an information-processing system, and to build controls into the system.

Figure 12-5   Basic Elements of an MIS

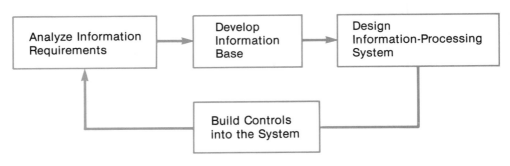

Analyze Information Requirements. The first step in designing an MIS is to research what kinds of decisions managers and specialists need help to make. A related step is to decide what type of information is needed to provide that help. For example, research might show that managers need help in making decisions about which employees are qualified for overseas assignments. The MIS designed to help them would include data about employees' preferences for travel, foreign-language skills, and ability to work without close supervision.

The people who are going to use the data from the MIS should decide on the information requirements. This involves managers giving the MIS specialists a clear picture of their information requirements. Too often, other people, such as systems analysts, guess what the users want. Or the systems analyst may purchase software that is able to produce only limited information. Frequently, the systems analyst makes a wrong guess about requirements and the user is left with an inadequate system. Also, users are more committed to a system that they help select.

Develop Information Base. A base of valid information is the heart of any MIS, and ingenuity is required to develop relevant information. Sometimes, much of the information already exists in company records and simply must be coded and stored. At other times, information must be collected. In the overseas assignment example, it may be necessary to develop a questionnaire for candidates for the job. The questionnaire could be answered both in writing and during interviews. The results could be combined with company information about work performance.

Design Information Processing System.   In this step, a system is designed for collecting, storing, transmitting, and retrieving information. Specialized knowledge about computer systems is required to design the system successfully. Many firms use outside assistance. The total MIS is a composite of a number of specific information systems. The same system that is designed to select candidates for overseas assignments cannot keep track of spare parts.

Build Controls into the System.   At the beginning of this chapter, we mentioned that controls are necessary to evaluate the control function. Building controls into the MIS is a special case of this general principle. Most MISs are impressive on the surface because they involve modern electronic equipment. However, an MIS can generate invalid or outdated information. The information system for foreign assignments might generate a list of employee names at the press of a few buttons. If inaccurate performance-appraisal data were used, however, many of these people could be unqualified for overseas work.

Another type of control built into an MIS is a control against misappropriation, or unauthorized use, of information. Controls against such computer theft include an elaborate system of passwords and other security devices.

A good set of controls enables management to pinpoint the deficiencies in the system. Effective controls also are useful in updating the system as information requirements change. In many organizations, numerous reports are generated but are not read by anyone.

Control Information Supplied by an MIS

The information-systems field is expanding rapidly. This can be partly attributed to the growing requirements for useful control information. The control information that can be generated by an information system is virtually unlimited. A sampling of what MISs keep track of is shown in Table 12-4. The potential contribution of such information is illustrated in the accompanying "Manager in Action."

MANAGER IN ACTION:

King of One Price Women's Clothing

Cut-rate bargains are the mainstay of One Price Clothing Stores, Inc., founded several years ago by Henry D. Jacobs, Jr. For a uniform price of six dollars, the shopper can purchase women's sportswear, blouses, and skirts intended to sell for three to four times as much. Jacobs and his staff stay in touch with more than six-hundred apparel makers and brokers for surplus production, canceled orders, and odd lots. One Price often purchases unsold inventories below manufacturer's costs.

An important part of Jacob's operation is an MIS that allows One Price to poll cash registers in all its stores nightly for sales information, down to size and color. The information system helps One Price turn its inventories 12.7 times a year versus 5 turns at The Gap and 7.1 at Clothesline, according to a retail analyst.

Source: As reported in Dean Foust, "One Word for One Price: Success," *Business Week*, (May 23, 1988): 123.

Table 12-4 Examples of Control Information Supplied by an MIS

- Sales of products by territory, sales representative, and customer categories.
- Inventory levels by region, plant, and department.
- Magazine subscribers by age, income, occupational level, and ZIP Code.
- Turnover rates by age, sex, job title, and salary level.
- Time, place, and frequency of telephone calls made by employees during working hours.
- Amount of money spent by players in a gambling casino (in order to identify the true big spenders).
- Budget deviations from expenses by location, department, and manager.
- Automatic compilation of financial ratios, comparing this information to industry trends.
- Automatic compilation of production and operation control indexes, comparing this information from plant to plant.
- Overdue accounts according to customer, and goods or services purchased.
- Hospital bed occupancy rates according to diagnosis, sex, and age of patient.
- Return on investment of cash surpluses by subsidiary.

Computerized Supervisory Systems

A rapidly growing, yet controversial, application of MIS is the **computerized supervisory system (CSS),** the use of a computer-based system to monitor the work habits and productivity of employees.[15] These systems capitalize upon the networking of computer terminals to monitor employees who use the computer terminals in their jobs or who operate complex machine tools. Once the supervisory software is installed, the central computer processes information from each terminal and records the employee's efficiency and effectiveness.

Office workers, including those who are in frequent telephone contact with the public, are the most likely to be monitored. Word-processing specialists are measured by such factors as words keyed per minute, the number of breaks taken, and the duration of each break. Specific examples of a CSS include the monitoring of taxpayer assistance operators by the Internal Revenue Service and the monitoring of AT&T operators who must complete calls within an average work time. Also, Safeway Stores, Inc., equips its trucks with small, computerized boxes that record the truck's speed, the gas mileage, the shifting of gears, and whether the truck strays from its route.

The major advantage of a CSS is the close monitoring of employee productivity that it allows management. Some employees welcome computerized monitoring of their work because it supplements arbitrary judgments by supervisors about their productivity. Computerized work-monitoring systems also have substantial disadvantages. It is argued that these systems invade employee privacy and violate their dignity, along with contributing to job stress. A case in point is Toni Watson, an airline reservation operator:

> During her eight-hour shift Toni is allowed 12 minutes away from her post; she must complete calls within 109 seconds and allow no more than 11 seconds between calls. The airline CSS allows her boss to listen to her conversations and chart her work by computer. Watson says: "One day I just cracked up. I got to where I couldn't function because the stress became so bad. I was crying every day."[16]

CHARACTERISTICS OF EFFECTIVE CONTROLS

An effective control system improves job performance and productivity by helping workers correct problems. For control systems to achieve these results, employees must cooperate with the system. If they are more intent on beating the system than on improving performance, controls will not achieve their ultimate purpose. For example, the true purpose of a time-recording system is to ensure that employees work a full day. If workers are intent on circumventing the system through such means as having friends punch in and out for them, the time-recording system will not increase productivity.

An effective control system has distinct characteristics. The greater the number of these characteristics a given control system contains, the better the system will be for providing management with useful information and improved performance.

1. *The control measure must be appropriate and meaningful.* People tend to resist control measures that they believe do not relate to performance in a meaningful way. Directory-assistance operators, for example, may object to a control measure based primarily on the amount of inquiries processed. Experienced operators contend that giving the right assistance to fewer callers would be a better measure of performance.

2. *An effective control measure provides diagnostic information.* If controls are to improve performance, they must help the people correct deviations from performance. A sales manager might be told that she was perform-

ing well in all categories except selling to small-business owners. This information might prompt the manager to determine what services the company sells that would have more appeal to small businesses.

3. *Control standards should motivate people to achieve high performance levels, but should be realistic.* Well-motivated people take pride in achieving performance standards that stretch their capability.

4. *Effective controls allow for self-feedback and self-control.* It saves considerable management time if the control system is self-administering. Employees can do much of their own controlling if the system permits them to obtain their own feedback. An example is a system whereby clients complain directly to the employee instead of going to management.

5. *Effective control systems provide timely information.* Controls are more likely to lead to positive changes in behavior when the control information is fed back quickly. It is more helpful to give workers daily rather than monthly estimates of their performance against quota. Given day-by-day feedback, the employee can make quick adjustments. If feedback is withheld until the end of a month or a quarter, the employee may be too discouraged to make improvements.

6. *Control measures are more effective when employees have control over the behavior measured.* People rebel against being responsible for performance deviations beyond their control. For example, a resort hotel manager might fall below profit expectations because of a factor beyond his or her control—for example, a sudden shift in weather that results in cancellations.

7. *Effective control measures do not contradict each other.* Employees are sometimes asked to achieve two contradictory sets of standards. As a result, the control system is resisted. If employees are told to increase both quantity and quality, the result can be confusion and chaos. A compromise approach is to improve quality with the aim of thereby increasing net quantity. It works in this manner: if care is taken in doing something right the first time, less rework is required, and eventually the quantity of goods produced increases.

8. *Effective controls allow for random variations from standard.* An ineffective way of implementing a control system is to jump quickly at the first deviation from acceptable performance. A one-time deviation from any control measure may not indicate a genuine problem. It could simply be a random variation that probably will not be repeated for years.

9. *Effective controls are cost-effective.* Control systems should result in satisfactory returns on investment. In many instances, this is not the case because the costs of control are too high. In recognition of this fact, some fast-food restaurants allow employees to eat all the food they want during working hours. (This same policy may be used to build morale as well as to decrease the cost of controls.)

Deciding whether a given control is cost-effective requires careful study. An electronics supplier decided it would not be cost-effective to rebill any customer whose payment was within $5.00 of the correct amount. Eventually, a large number of customers started trimming $4.99 from their invoices. It now became cost-effective either to rebill customers or to add the missing amount to the next bill. The message that full payments were expected had to be communicated.

SUMMARY OF KEY POINTS

The control function of management involves measuring performance and then taking corrective action if goals are not being achieved. Controlling is used to evaluate whether the manager has done a good job of planning and decision making, organizing, and leading. Controls are also used to evaluate control systems.

Controlling is an important part of any manager's job. First-level management uses short-range controls. Middle management tends to be concerned with weekly, monthly, and quarterly performance. Top-level management uses a longer-range perspective in controlling.

Controls can be classified by the time element involved. Precontrols take place prior to the performance and are thus preventive. Concurrent controls monitor activities while they are being carried out. Postcontrols evaluate and take corrective action after an activity has been performed. Controls also can be classified according to their underlying strategy. The external-control strategy assumes that employees are motivated primarily by external rewards and need to be controlled by their managers. The internal-control strategy assumes that managers can motivate employees by building commitment to organizational goals.

The steps in the control process are set standards, measure actual performance, compare actual performance to standards, and take corrective action if necessary. The three courses of action open to the manager are to do nothing, to solve the problem, or to revise the standard.

Nonbudgetary control techniques can be qualitative or quantitative. Qualitative techniques include audits, personal observation, and performance appraisal. Quantitative techniques include Gantt charts, PERT, and economic order quantity.

A budget is a spending plan for a future period of time, and it is expressed in numerical terms. A fixed budget allocates expenditures based on a one-time allocation of resources. A flexible budget allows variation in the use of resources based on activity. The four basic types of budgets are revenue-and-expense budgets; time, space, material, and product budgets; capital-expenditure budgets; and cash budgets. All businesses use revenue-and-expense budgets.

Budgets are a natural part of the control process. Planned expenditures are compared to actual expenditures, and corrective action is taken if the deviation is significant. Budgets are a sensible method of controlling the expenditures of an organization, and they are helpful in measuring performance. However, budgets can lead to rigidity in behavior, and they can be time-consuming to prepare.

A management information system (MIS) is a formal system for providing management with information useful or necessary for making decisions. An MIS can be based on historical or on-line information. To develop an MIS, you must analyze the information requirements, develop an information base, design an information processing system, and build controls into the system. An MIS can keep track of a wide range of facts that are used for control purposes. An important new application of an MIS is the computerized supervisory system (CSS), a method monitoring the work habits and productivity of employees. Although the method helps managers monitor employee performance, it has met with considerable criticism.

An effective control system results in improved job performance and productivity by helping people correct problems. An effective control measure is appropriate, provides diagnostic information, allows for self-feedback and self-control, provides timely information, allows for employee control over the behavior measured, does not have contradictory measures, allows for random variation, and is cost-effective.

QUESTIONS

1. Discuss whether a safe in which valuable papers are kept is a control device.
2. Which style of leader do you think would be the most likely to establish and implement controls? Refer to Chapter 9 for information about leadership styles.
3. Why is controlling sometimes referred to as the terminal function of management?
4. What corrective action do you typically take when you have exceeded your budget for a particular type of expenditure?
5. Many cost overruns on construction projects are blamed on the effects of inflation. Explain whether you think this is a justifiable excuse.
6. A supervisor was criticized for going over budget on paper towels for the washroom. Her response was, "People have to dry their hands, don't they? What can you do?" What is your reaction to this statement?
7. Identify one or two control techniques used in the classroom.
8. How might an MIS be used to detect expense account abuses?
9. Why are computerized supervisory systems often referred to as Big Brother?
10. Why do you think many employees find a computerized supervisory system (CSS) more bothersome than a manager directly observing their work?

ACTIVITIES

1. Ask a manager or specialist what three major control devices are used in his or her firm. Report back to the class with the information you collect.
2. A company that manages pension funds for college employees mails out

the following form letter after a policyholder requested an address change.

To Our Policyholder

Your address has been changed to the following in our records:

Jane S. Sidwell
5101 Madison Road
Cincinnati, Ohio 45227

This letter has been sent to your previous address so that it could be forwarded to you. If your new address is correct as shown above, no action on your part is needed. If your new address is not correct as shown above, please complete the section below and return this letter to us.

Analyze whether or not the above letter is a control device.

CASE PROBLEM 12-A: THE SHRINKING OFFICE SUPPLIES

Eric Jung, the purchasing manager at the headquarters mortgage department of a large bank, was reviewing the requisitions for office supplies one October morning. "Here we go again," said Jung to his assistant, Priscilla Danforth. "It's October and half the departments we serve have exceeded budget on office supplies. I'm not accusing any one person of stealing, but the drain on pencils, pens, yellow pads, paper clips, and diskettes is enormous this time of year. I've often thought that the local school system should reimburse our bank for all the school supplies we furnish the students of our employees."

"What happened to your last campaign to cut down the autumn drain in office supplies?" asked Danforth.

"You'll recall, Priscilla, that I also tried to cut down the overbudgets all year round. But I agree that the August and September drain is the worst. I sent confidential memos out to all the department heads and spoke to a few of them in person.

"The reaction I received was neutral at best. Most of the managers didn't think the problem was important enough for them to deal with. Two managers even took offense that I was indirectly accusing their employees of misappropriating company property. Two managers said they would discuss the issue with their groups, but both were hesitant to do anything that would lower morale. Mindi Cohen told me she would rather pay for the supplies out of her own pocket rather than alienate herself from her employees over such a trivial offense."

"How does our boss, Kerry (Perez), feel about the problem of shrinking office supplies?" asked Danforth.

"Kerry wants me to come up with a workable system to control this problem before the end of the fiscal year," said Jung.

Case Questions

1. What is your opinion of the relevance of the problem of employees taking home office supplies?

2. Develop an effective control system for taking care of the problem of budget overruns on office supplies.

CASE PROBLEM 12-B: MANAGERIAL CONTROLS AT ODYSSEY AIRLINES

Odyssey Airlines has experienced more financial troubles than its major competitors recently. The airline lost over $5 million for four consecutive years. An impatient board of directors replaced the Odyssey president with Skip Marston. The board thought that, with Marston at the helm, the airline's profits would once again soar. Shortly after taking over, Marston brought the top-ranking managers in the company together to discuss his managerial philosophy. Excerpts from Marston's talks are as follows.

"I have purposely waited several weeks before making a formal presentation to the key members of the Odyssey team. I needed that time to acquaint myself with the operations of the airlines and to study some figures. I have arrived at some conclusions that may surprise you. Odyssey Airlines has a good customer base. We get our share of customers calling in directly for reservations, and our relationships with travel agents are not all that bad. Our safety record slightly exceeds the industry average. Our ground service is at least as good as the other airlines. Our flight attendants are as courteous as are those of our competitors.

"I have been trying to discover why we are so financially troubled even though we have all these things in our favor. The answer, ladies and gentlemen, can be summed up in two words: poor controls. We hardly have any checkpoints to measure our progress. We know what constitutes good performance for only a small proportion of our jobs. We have a full package of budgets, but nobody seems to take them seriously.

"The major change I am making at Odyssey is a complete overhaul of our control system. With approval from the board of directors, we are hiring a prominent management-consulting firm to help us develop a modern control system. All of you, and the managers reporting to you, will be involved in implementing these controls. Just as in basketball, the name of the game in business is control."

Within six months, a new control system was installed at Odyssey. The controls included new sets of job standards for every position in the company and reformulated budgets at every level of management. In addition, the company MIS was updated to provide more timely and accurate information. For example, the controller's office was made aware of the occupancy rate of every Odyssey flight, just moments after takeoff. Measures were even made of the percentage of surplus meals aboard each flight.

Six months later, Marston and the controller, B. J. Weedsport, began an assessment of the new control system. Weedsport looked up from a thick computer printout on his desk, and he gave the president this preliminary analysis:

"So far, it looks like we are suffering from the same problem we have had for several years. Decent sales, but no profits. The advantage we have now is that we get a quicker and more accurate picture of how poorly we are doing. I still think our new control system will help us in the long run, but so far it is not cost-effective. In fact, a good chunk of our loss the last quarter can be attributed to the start-up costs of the new information system. It takes a lot of flight tickets to cover the monthly payments on a $2 million information system."

Marston replied, "So we now have a good control system, but so far it has not improved operating results. Let's get Gloria Perkins, our marketing director, in here. Maybe she can give us some insights as to why our profits are still hurting. She has an excellent grasp of things."

An hour later, the president and controller met with Perkins to get her view on why expenses were still out of line. She commented, "I have reached some conclusions about this problem. My guess is that a few other managers who have been at Odyssey for several years would share the same opinion.

"The new control system is fine. The information systems people are feeding managers timely, useful information. Most of the managers now spend some time each day tapping into the information system. However, the control systems we had before really weren't so bad. As in the past, managers who want to use the information can do so.

"The problem is that we are gathering a lot of information without making good use of it. Most managers are gathering data about things such as variances from budgets and below-average seat-occupancy rates. They enjoy logging onto the mainframe to get the information. The problem is that although managers read the information, they don't do much about it. It's like finding out that you have a high plasma cholesterol level but then making no changes in your diet or exercise habits. Our managers study the information and then often ignore it."

Weedsport commented, "You mean the control measures aren't motivating our managers to change things when they do spot a problem?"

Perkins replied, "That's exactly it. We have a modern information system giving us what we need. But the control system isn't spurring us into taking corrective action. Something is missing. Odyssey managers have a history of being more concerned about sales than profits."

Case Questions

1. What steps should Marston and Weedsport take to increase the effectiveness of the control system at Odyssey Airlines?
2. To what extent does Perkins's analysis seem plausible?
3. Explain what is meant by Perkins's statement that Odyssey managers are more concerned about sales than profits.
4. Does it seem to you that the consulting firm directed Odyssey to install a control system that was not right for the airline's needs?

REFERENCES

1. Kenneth A. Merchant, *Control in Business Organizations* (Marshfield, MA: Pitman Pub., 1984), 1.
2. Cortlandt Cammann and David A. Nadler, "Fit Control Systems to Your Managerial Style," *Harvard Business Review* (January–February 1976): 65.
3. For a current summary of this traditional topic see Waldon Berry, "The

Human Side of Control," *Supervisory Management* (June 1985): 34–39.

4.   The basic idea behind this version of the control process is from Robert L. Trewatha and M. Gene Newport, *Management*, 3d ed. (Plano, TX: Business Pubs., Inc., 1982), 434–439.

5.   Richard O. Mason and E. Burton Swanson, "Measurement for Management Decision: A Perspective," *California Management Review* (Spring 1979): 70–81.

6.   Leonard H. Aptman, "Project Management: Setting Controls," *Management Solutions*, (November 1986): 33.

7.   Harold Koontz, Cyril O'Donnell, and Heinz Weihrich, *Management*, 7th ed. (New York: McGraw-Hill, 1980), 745–746.

8.   Robert S. Kaplan, "One Cost System Isn't Enough," *Harvard Business Review* (January–February 1988): 61–66.

9.   Andrew Sherwood, "To Control Costs, Manage People Better," *Management Solutions* (July 1986): 41.

10.   Karren Pennar, "The Productivity Paradox," *Business Week* (6 June, 1988): 101.

11.   David K. Lindo, "How To Increase Your Budget," *Administrative Management* (October 1981): 28–30, 46.

12.   Stephen G. Perry, "The PC-based HRIS," *Personnel Administrator*, (February 1988): 60-63.

13.   Arthur C. Laufer, *Production and Operations Management*, 3d ed. (Cincinnati: South-Western Publishing Co., 1984), 64–65.

14.   Brandt Allen, "Make Information Services Pay Its Way," *Harvard Business Review* (January–February 1987): 59.

15.   Ravinda Nath and Barry Gilmore, "Managing Computerized Supervisory Systems," *Management Solutions* (July 1987): 5; much of the discussion here is based on Nath and Gilmore: 5-11.

16.   Kevin Ellis, "Big Brother Creeping Into Offices," *Gannett News Service*, 27 June 1987.

13
Managing Ineffective Performers

After studying the material in this chapter, you should be able to accomplish the following:

1. Identify factors contributing to poor job performance.
2. Describe in detail the control model for managing ineffective performers.
3. Counsel and constructively criticize employees.
4. Explain the purpose and operations of an employee assistance program.
5. Explain the recommended approach to terminating employees including the contribution of outplacement.

Key Terms and Phrases

Ineffective job performance	Progressive discipline
Confrontation	Positive discipline
Improvement goal	Decision-making leave
Technostress	Red-hot-stove rule
Ergonomics	Employee assistance program
Counseling	(EAP)
Constructive criticism	Recovery rate
Open-ended question	Termination
Discipline	Wrongful discharge
Summary discipline	Due process
Corrective discipline	Outplacement

An important aspect of managerial control is to deal constructively with **ineffective job performance.** Job performance is considered ineffective when it lowers productivity below a standard considered acceptable at a given time. Ineffective performers are also referred to as problem employees because they create problems for management.

The effect of ineffective performers on organizational productivity follows the 80/20 principle. Most of the poor job performance is attributed to a small proportion of the work force. One study showed, for example, that 28 percent of the company's employees were responsible for 100 percent of the grievances, 37 percent of the occupation-related hospital visits, 40 percent of the sick leaves, and 38 percent of the absenteeism.[1]

Poor performers lower organizational performance directly by not accomplishing their fair share of work. The same people also lower organizational productivity indirectly. Poor performers decrease the productivity of their superiors by consuming managerial time. Additionally, the productivity of co-workers is often decreased because they have to take over some of the ineffective performer's tasks. The relatively high turnover rate of poor performers also lowers productivity because of the time and expense involved in recruiting and training replacements.[2]

The general approach in this chapter is to regard ineffective performance as a control problem, with a special emphasis on taking corrective action. Information is presented both about informal approaches and about formal programs to improve poor performance.

FACTORS CONTRIBUTING TO INEFFECTIVE PERFORMANCE

Employees become ineffective performers for many different reasons. The cause of poor job performance can be rooted in the person, the job, the manager, or the company. At times, the employee's personal traits and behaviors create so much disturbance that he or she is perceived as ineffective. The accompanying "Managers in Action" presents some humorous yet valid insights into why some employees are considered ineffective.

MANAGERS IN ACTION:

What Executives Dislike About Employees

Liars, goof-offs, egomaniacs, laggards, rebels, whiners, airheads, and sloths. A survey of executives in 100 large companies revealed that people with these traits are those most disliked by executives. A marketing research firm asked, "What employee behavior disturbs you the most?" It found that annoying behaviors and characteristics can blind employers to employees' good qualities.

Dishonesty and lying topped the list. "If a company believes that an employee lacks integrity, all positive qualities—ranging from skills and experience to productivity and intelligence—become meaningless," said the survey director.

The other seven deadly sins, in order of irritation, are as follows:

1. Irresponsibility, goofing-off, and doing personal business on company time were first on the list. A particularly annoying behavior pattern was running a private business out of the office.

2. Arrogance, ego problems, and excessive aggressiveness were next. Employees who spent more time boasting about their accomplishments than actually getting their work done bothered their bosses.

3. Absenteeism and lateness also were considered annoying. One employer said, "It doesn't make any difference if we start at 9:00 A.M. or 10:00 A.M., some people always will be fifteen minutes late."

4. Not following instructions or ignoring company policies were the next most commonly cited behaviors. Then came whining and complaining. According to the survey director, there was a whiner in every office. "Do we have to do it by Thursday?" is a standard whining complaint.

5. Absence of commitment, concern, or dedication was the fifth problem. This behavior often was grounds for absence of raises and promotions.

6. Finally, the executives did not like laziness and lack of motivation. The survey director noted that both traits demonstrated to the managers that these people did not care about the company. So why should the company care about them?

7. Other behaviors that cause employees to be perceived as ineffective performers included lack of character, inability to get along with others, disrespect, displays of anger, or taking credit for the work of others.

Source: Adapted from Rick Hampson, "Boss Uptight? Quick, Take a Look at Your Behavior," Associated Press story reprinted in *Democrat and Chronicle,* 29 December 1984. Updated with information from Donald H. Weiss, "How to Handle Difficult People," *Management Solutions* (February 1988): 33–38.

Factors contributing to ineffective performance are summarized in Table 13-1. These factors are divided into four categories: person, job, manager, and company. Usually, the true cause of ineffective performance is a combination of several factors. Assume that a man is late for work so frequently that his performance becomes substandard. The contributing factors in this situation could be the following: the man's disrespect for work rules, an unchallenging job, and an unduly harsh supervisor. One factor may be more important than others, but they are all contributors.

Table 13-1   Factors Contributing to Ineffective Performance

Ineffective performance can be caused by any one or more of these factors. Factors not listed here also can contribute to ineffective performance.

Factors Within the Person

*   *Insufficient mental ability.* Employee lacks the problem-solving ability necessary to do the job. Poor communication skills are included here.
*   *Insufficient job knowledge.* Employee is a substandard performer because he or she has insufficient training or experience.
*   *Emotional problem or personality disorder.* Employee has emotional outbursts and periods of depression that interfere with human relationships and work concentration. Cynical behavior also lowers performance because the negative attitude may spread to other employees.[3]

- *Alcoholism and drug addiction.* Employee cannot think clearly because of temporarily or permanently impaired mental or physical condition attributed to alcohol or other drugs. Attendance is also likely to suffer.
- *Cigarette addiction.* Employee smokes so many cigarettes that the employee's work is disrupted, and he or she is often fatigued. The smoking may also annoy other employees and thus lower their productivity.
- *Job burnout.* Employee becomes apathetic, cynical, and impatient as a result of prolonged job stress. Employee can no longer generate the energy to perform effectively.
- *Technological obsolescence.* Employee does not keep up with the state of the art in his or her field. The employee becomes ineffective because he or she avoids using new ideas and techniques.
- *Excessive absenteeism and tardiness.* Employee often is not at work for a variety of personal or health reasons. The lost time leads to low productivity.
- *Conducting outside business on the job.* Employee may be an "office entrepreneur" who sells merchandise to co-workers or spends time on phone working on investments or other outside interests.[4] Time commitment to these activities is so extensive that it lowers productivity.
- *Chronic complainer.* Employee spends so much time complaining about working assignments, working conditions, and co-workers that the employee wastes his or her time and that of supervisors.
- *Family and personal problems.* Employee is unable to attend to work fully because of preoccupation with off-the-job problems such as marital dispute, conflict with children, or a broken romance.
- *Physical limitations.* Employee's job performance is lowered as a result of injury or illness.

Factors Within the Job

- *Ergonomics problems.* A poor fit between the human requirements of the job and the machinery or office furniture creates performance problems. For example, employee develops neckache and eye strain because of working at a poorly designed computer configuration. The physical problems become so distracting that performance suffers.
- *Repetitive, physically demanding job.* Employee becomes bored and fatigued from physically taxing job, leading to lowered performance.
- *Built-in conflict.* The nature of the job leads to so many conflicts that the employee experiences enough job stress to lower performance. A collection agent for a consumer-loan company might fit this category.
- *Night shift work assignments.* Employees assigned to night shifts (11:30 P.M. to 7:30 A.M.) suffer many more mental lapses and consequent productivity losses than those assigned to morning or evening shifts.[5]

Factors Within the Manager

- *Supervisor provides inadequate communication to employee about job demands.* Employee performs poorly because he or she lacks a clear picture of true job responsibilities.
- *Supervisor does not give employee adequate feedback about job performance.* Employee makes large number of errors because he or she is not given feedback early enough to prevent poor performance.

- *Supervisor uses inappropriate leadership style.* Employee performs poorly because the supervisor's leadership style does not fit what the employee needs. For example, an immature employee works for a manager who gives him or her too much freedom. This employee needs closer supervision and performs poorly as a result of the freedom.

Factors Within the Company

- *Organizational culture that tolerates poor performance.* The organization has a history of not imposing sanctions on employees who perform poorly. When the situation demands better performance, many employees may not respond to the new challenge.
- *Counterproductive work environment.* Employee lacks proper tools, support, budget, or authority to accomplish the job. An example would be a sales representative who does not have an entertainment budget sufficient to meet expectations of customers.
- *Negative work-group influences.* Group pressures restrain good performance or work group penalizes high-performing worker.

Source: Many of the above items are based on Andrew J. DuBrin, R. Duane Ireland, and J. Clifton Williams, *Management and Organization* (Cincinnati: South-Western Publishing Co., 1989), 418–419; and, information throughout John B. Miner, *People Problems: The Executive Answer Book* (New York: Random House, 1985).

THE CONTROL MODEL FOR MANAGING INEFFECTIVE PERFORMERS

The approach to improving ineffective performance presented here follows the logic of the control process, as shown in Figure 13-1. It is also based on the approach many experienced managers use in correcting unacceptable performance and behavior. The control model is divided into seven steps, which should be followed in sequence:

1. Define effective or acceptable performance.

2. Detect deviation from acceptable performance.

3. Confront the substandard performer.

4. Set improvement goals.

5. Select and implement action plan for improvement.

6. Reevaluate performance after time interval.

7. Continue or discontinue action plan for improvement.

We will describe each of these steps in detail. Two key methods of improving ineffective performance, discipline, and employee assistance programs are given separate attention later in the chapter.

Figure 13-1   The Control Model for Managing Ineffective Performers

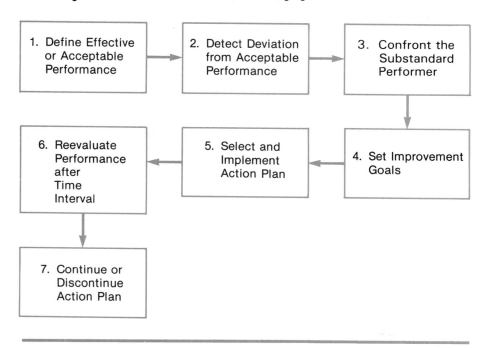

Define Effective or Acceptable Performance

The first step in the control model for managing ineffective performers is to define adequately what is expected of employees. (This step is identical to the step labeled "Set Standards" in the control model shown in Figure 12-4 on page 369.) Performance standards are commonly established by such means as job descriptions, work goals, production quotas, and formal discussions of what is to be accomplished in a position.

Whatever method of setting standards is chosen, these standards must be carefully communicated to the employee. Unless employees clearly understand performance standards, it is unfair to penalize them for not reaching standard.

Detect Deviation from Acceptable Performance

Detection is the process of noting when an employee's performance deviates from an acceptable standard. The various control measures described in Chapter 12 are used to detect substantial deviations from acceptable performance. For performance to be considered ineffective or poor, it must deviate substantially from the norm.

At times, quantitative measures can be used to define ineffective performance. For some jobs, ineffective performance might begin at 30 percent below standard. For other jobs, the cutoff point could be 20 or 50 percent or any other percent deviation that fits the situation. What percent deviation from standard do you think would be acceptable for a diamond cutter? For a nuclear-reactor technician?

Personal observation plays a key role in detecting ineffective performance. One reason that observation is so important is that it is a concurrent control. By the time quantitative indicators of poor performance have been collected, substantial damage may have been done. Assume a bank branch manager observes that one of the loan officers is taking unduly long lunch hours on Fridays. When the officer returns, he usually appears to be under the influence of alcohol. Eventually, this unacceptable behavior will show up in quantitative indicators of performance. However, it might take a year to collect these data.

Confront the Substandard Performer

The third step in the control model is a difficult one for most managers. It involves confronting the poor performer with his or her unacceptable behavior. At times, a simple discussion will suffice. **Confrontation** means dealing with a controversial or emotional topic directly. Confrontation is necessary whenever the employee does not readily admit he or she is experiencing a problem.

A survey of managers concluded that confrontation of ineffective performers is rare in large corporations. Instead, more reliance is placed on the tactics of transferring and "working around" problem employees.[6] One reason managers avoid that confrontation is that they have limited skill in criticizing employees. Another is that they prefer not to deal with the anger and resentment confrontation is likely to trigger. A third reason is that many managers realize how uncomfortable they are when confronted by somebody else.

A recommended confrontation technique is to communicate an attitude of concern about the confronted person's welfare. This approach has been called "carefrontation." The term implies that confronting another person means that you care about him or her. It is easier to ignore the problem or work around the person.[7]

Communicating that one cares can sometimes be done by confronting the person in a sincere and thoughtful manner. Using the words *care* and *concern* can be helpful. For instance, "The reason that I'm bringing up this problem is that I care about your work. You have a good record with the company. And I'm concerned that your performance has slipped way below its former level."

Set Improvement Goals

The fourth step in the control model is to set improvement goals or objectives. An **improvement goal** is one that, if attained, will correct an unacceptable deviation from standard performance. Improvement goals should have the same characteristics as other objectives (see Chapter 3). Above all, the improvement goals should specify the behavior that is required. Vague improvement goals are not likely to cause changes in performance.

An example of a specific improvement goal would be, "During this month, nine of your ten inventory reports must be in on time." This specific goal is likely to be more effective than a general improvement goal such as "Become more prompt in submitting inventory reports." Or, for a basketball coach, "Effective immediately, no throwing towels and no swearing at the referee or at your players during the game."

Should the improvement goals be set jointly by the superior and subordinate? If the ineffective performer expresses an interest in improvement, joint goal setting would be advisable. By providing input into goal setting, the substandard performer stands a good chance of being committed to improvement. There are times, however, when improvement goals have to be imposed on substandard performers. This is certainly the case where performance problems stem from low motivation. If the employee was interested in setting improvement goals, he or she would not have a motivation problem.

When improvement goals are imposed on the poor performer by the manager, it is still important to explain the reason for the goals. Returning to the example of the loan officer, the manager might explain how the officer's drinking was damaging the bank's image. An even more basic explanation might be that bank policy forbids employees to consume alcohol during lunch breaks.

Select and Implement Action Plan

The setting of improvement goals leads logically to the selection and implementation of action plans to attain those goals.[8] Much of the art of remedying ineffective performance is contained in this step. Unless appropriate action plans are developed, no real improvement is likely to take place. Many attempts at improving substandard performance fail because the problem is discussed and then dropped. The poor performer thus has no concrete method of making the necessary improvements.

Types of Action Plans   An action plan for improvement can include almost any sensible approach tailored to the specific problem. An action plan could be formulated to deal with every cause of ineffective performance listed in Table 13-1.

Action plans for improving ineffective performance can be divided into two types, or approaches. One type is within the power of the manager to develop and implement. This would include coaching the subordinate, giving him or her encouragement, and offering small incentives for improvement. Another type, or approach, is used in formal programs offered by the organization or purchased on the outside. These would include training programs, stress-management programs, and referral to an alcoholism-treatment center. Table 13-2 lists a selection of feasible corrective approaches and programs.

Table 13-2   Corrective Actions for Ineffective Performers

Managerial Actions and Techniques

- *Closer supervision.* The manager works more closely with the subordinate, offering frequent guidance and feedback.
- *Reassignment or transfer.* The ineffective performer is given a new assignment or transferred to a position that he or she can handle better.
- *Referral for personal counseling.* The manager refers the problem employee to the employee assistance program or other resource for personal counseling.
- *Use of motivational techniques.* The manager attempts to improve employee motivation by use of positive reinforcement or some other motivational technique.
- *Corrective discipline.* The manager informs employee that his or her behavior is unacceptable and that corrections must be made if the employee is to remain employed by the firm. Employee is counseled as part of corrective discipline.
- *Temporary leave.* The employee is offered the opportunity to take a leave of absence for a specified time in order to resolve problems causing the poor performance.
- *Lower performance standards.* The manager lowers expectations of subordinate because performance standards may have been too high. Consultation with higher management would probably be necessary to implement this step.
- *Job rotation.* If ineffective performance results from staleness or burnout, changing to a different job of comparable responsibility may prove helpful.

Organizational Programs

- *Employee assistance program (EAP).* The employee is referred to a counseling service that specializes in rehabilitating employees whose personal problems interfere with job performance.
- *Stress-management program.* The employee is referred to company-sponsored program designed specifically to help overcome the adverse effects of stress. The program might include advice on physical exercise, diet, and stress-reduction techniques.
- *Health-and-wellness programs.* Employees are encouraged to stay physically and mentally healthy through specialized programs. By doing so, employees may prevent and cope with health problems—such as heart disease and eating disorder—that interfere with job performance or lead to absenteeism.[9]
- *Career counseling and outplacement.* The employee is given professional assistance in solving his or her career problem. This includes being counseled on how to find a job outside the firm.
- *Job redesign.* Specialists in human-resource management and industrial engineering redesign elements within the job that could be causing poor performance. For example, the job is changed so that the employee has less direct contact with others, leading to reduced conflict.

- *Training and development program.* The employee is assigned to a training or development program directly linked to his or her performance deficiency. For example, an overly reserved sales representative is given assertiveness training.

Source: Several items are based on Robert H. White, "Corrective Action: A Treatment Plan for Problem Performers," *Personnel* (February 1985): 7.

One manager thought of an effective action plan. An employee was suffering from **"technostress"** (an adverse reaction to working many hours at a computer terminal). The employee complained specifically about becoming dizzy from watching the "little green trails" found on the screen. Her output fell significantly below average. The manager's solution was to purchase, on a trial basis, a computer terminal with an amber screen. The performance problem was eliminated through this insightful use of **ergonomics.** (adapting machines to human capabilities). The original terminal was then replaced permanently by the terminal with the amber monitor. (It is conceivable that in time the same employee will complain of "little amber trails.")

Implementation of the Action Plan.   After the action plan is chosen, it must be implemented. As shown in Figure 13-1, implementation begins in step 5 and continues through step 7. The manager has to implement the approaches listed under "Managerial Actions and Techniques" in Table 13-2. Organizational programs are implemented primarily by human-resource specialists outside the manager's department.

An important part of implementation is for the manager to continue the remedial program. Under the many pressures facing a manager, it is easy to forget the poor performer who needs close supervision or a motivational boost. Often, a brief conversation is all that is needed.

Reevaluate Performance After a Time Interval

Step 6 (in the control model for managing ineffective performers) helps ensure that the control process is working by measuring the employee's current performance. If the remedial process is working, the employee's performance will move up toward standard. The greater the performance problem, the shorter should be the interval between reevaluations of performance. In instances of behavior problems, such as alcoholism, weekly performance checks are advisable.

Formal and Informal Reviews.   Reevaluation of performance can be done formally or informally. A formal review of progress would take the form of a performance-appraisal session. It might include written documentation of the employee's progress and samples of his or her work. Formal reviews are particularly important when the employee has been advised that dismissal is impending unless improvements are made. Reviews are critical to avoid lawsuits over a dismissal.

The first level of informal review would be for the manager to check whether or not the employee has started the action plan. For example, the sales representative we mentioned might have agreed to attend an assertiveness training program. One week later, the manager could ask him, "Have you signed up for or started the training program yet?"

The next level of informal review is to discuss the employee's progress outside of a formal review session. The manager can ask casual questions such as, "How much progress have you made in accounting for the missing inventory?" and "Have you learned how to use the new diagnostic equipment yet?"

Positive Reinforcement and Punishment.   If the employee has made progress toward reaching the improvement goal, positive reinforcement is appropriate. Rewarding an employee for progress is the most effective way of sustaining that progress. The reward might be praise, encouragement, or even the prospects of longer intervals between review sessions. The longer time between reviews may be rewarding because the employee will feel that he or she is "back to normal."

Giving rewards for making improvements is generally more effective than giving punishments for not making improvements. An exception is that a small minority of employees respond better to punishment than to reward. In either case, if the problem employee does not respond to positive motivators, some form of organizational punishment is necessary. More will be said about punishment in our discussion about employee discipline.

Continue or Discontinue Action Plan for Improvement

Step 7 in the control model for managing ineffective performers is a decision to continue or discontinue the action plan. This step can be considered the feedback component to the control process. If the performance review indicates that the improvement goals have not been met, the action plan is continued. If the performance review indicates goals have been met, the action plan is discontinued.

An important part of using the control model to manage ineffective performers is realizing that positive changes in behavior may not be permanent. Performance is most likely to revert to an unacceptable level when the employee is faced with heavy job pressures. For instance, a problem employee may have been counseled about unacceptably poor work habits. The employee and the manager may have formulated a useful action plan, and suitable improvements may have been made. When the employee is under pressure, his or her work may once again become badly disorganized. The cycle should then be repeated, beginning with confrontation.

COUNSELING AND CONSTRUCTIVE CRITICISM

Counseling is a formal discussion method for helping another person overcome a problem or develop his or her potential. As implied several times in this chapter, it is an essential method for improving employee performance. **Con-**

structive criticism is a form of criticism designed to help people improve. Most on-the-job counseling includes constructive criticism.

Giving counseling and constructive criticism requires considerable skill. The suggestions that follow will help you improve your skill if you practice them carefully. In addition, two other steps should be taken. First, observe carefully and model yourself after an effective counselor. Second, obtain feedback on your counseling and criticizing from a knowledgeable person. A workshop or training program may be necessary to fulfill both steps.

1. *Choose a suitable time and place for counseling.* You should pick a time for the counseling session when you and the person to be counseled are in a good mood and when you are not rushed. The meeting should be held in a quiet place where you can talk without interruptions. It is important that both the manager and the employee be able to relax.[10]

2. *Provide specific feedback to the employee about the problem.* Specific feedback improves understanding, whereas general comments may be interpreted as a total rejection of the employee. An example of specific feedback would be, "Four of the checks you made out last month resulted in large overpayments to suppliers." A general statement about the same issue would be, "You don't take your check-writing responsibilities seriously." When a general statement is made, it should be bolstered with specific examples of the problem behavior. To illustrate, a manager might tell an employee that the firm believes that the employee is dishonest. This assertion should be supported with a few examples of dishonest behavior, such as expense account cheating.

3. *Listen actively and make interpretations.* An essential component of counseling employees is to listen carefully to both their presentation of facts and their feelings. The suggestions for effective listening presented in Chapter 11 apply directly here. Listening during counseling encourages the employee to talk. As the employee talks about his or her problem, the manager may develop a better understanding of how to help improve performance.

    The technique of asking open-ended questions is well suited to counseling an employee about ineffective performance. An **open-ended question** requests that the person provide details rather than responding either "Yes" or "No." "How are your plans coming along?" is an open-ended question. "Have you made any progress in your plans for improvement?" is a closed question. The employee can readily respond "Yes" to the latter, thus providing little information about his or her progress. Listening enters the picture because the manager has more information to which to listen after asking an open-ended question.

    Another part of being an active listener is to interpret what you think is really happening to the employee. The interpretation involves a diagnosis of the problem situation that goes beyond the obvious. Suppose the employee says to the manager, "I'm trying to catch up on my work, but so many people keep interrupting me that it's impossible." The manager might reply, "It sounds like you cannot keep up with both the paperwork requirements and the people demands of your job at the same time." Relieved that he or she is understood, the employee may then present more details about the problem. As more details are revealed, it will be easier to develop an effective action plan.

4. *Face facts squarely*. A training program about constructive criticism states that the "sandwich technique" often is mistakenly advocated.[11] This is when you start with a compliment to make the employee feel good, then throw in a criticism, and end with more compliments. A more effective sequence is to discuss weaknesses first, strengths second, and the future third.

5. *Focus on what is wrong with the work*. A major principle of employee counseling and coaching is to focus on substandard behavior itself and not on the person. Tell subordinates what is wrong with their work, not what is wrong with them. When a person's self-image is attacked, he or she is likely to become hostile. The person's energy will then be focused more on getting even than on getting better.

6. *Criticize without making comparisons to co-workers*. Unfavorable comparisons to other employees tend to breed resentment within the work group. Another problem is likely to arise when the ineffective employee is compared to an effective employee. The supervisor and ineffective employee may wind up in a heated discussion of the merits of the employee being used as a standard of comparison.

7. *Engage in joint problem solving*. According to this suggestion, the superior and subordinate should work together to resolve the performance problem.[12] One reason joint problem solving is effective is that it conveys a helpful and constructive attitude on the part of the superior. The help required by an employee often involves assistance in overcoming work problems beyond his or her control. For example, the poor performer might need repair of equipment, more clerical support, or better heating or air conditioning. The manager is in a better position to get problems of this type resolved than is the employee. Nevertheless, the superior and subordinate jointly work on the problem.

8. *Establish realistic improvement goals*. Ineffective performers generally have to be brought along slowly. If improvement goals are set too high, the employee is likely to experience frustration stemming from failure. If improvement goals are set too low, the employee's performance may not turn around fast enough to suit the organization. A manager can help the employee set realistic goals by encouraging a discussion of each improvement goal.

9. *Offer constructive advice*. In the role of a counselor, a manager should do more listening than giving advice. Yet, some constructive advice can be useful to the employee in overcoming performance problems. A

recommended way of giving advice is first to ask an insightful question. The manager might ask the employee, "Could the real cause of your problem be poor work habits?" If the employee agrees, the manager can then offer some specific advice about improving work habits.

10. *Obtain a commitment to change.* Poor performers frequently agree to make improvements but are not really committed to change. At the end of a performance-review session, the manager should discuss the employee's true interest in changing. One clue that commitment may be lacking is when the employee readily accepts everything the manager says about the need for change. Another clue is when the employee agrees to the need for change but displays no emotion. In either case, further discussion is warranted.

11. *Give the poor performer an opportunity to observe and model someone who exhibits acceptable performance.* A simple example of modeling would be for the manager to show the employee how to operate a piece of equipment properly. A more complex example of modeling would be to have the employee observe another employee making a sale or conducting a job interview.

12. *Counter anger or hostility with objectivity and patience.* Employees who are being counseled about poor performance are likely to be frustrated and therefore may display anger and hostility. The recommended counterstrategy is to be objective about the need for improvement and to display some patience about the employee's stirred feelings.[13]

Table 13-3 provides a summary of our suggestions for giving constructive criticism.

Table 13-3   Suggestions for Counseling and Constructive Criticism

1. Choose a suitable time and place for counseling.
2. Provide specific feedback to the employee about the problem.
3. Listen actively.
4. Face facts squarely.
5. Focus on what is wrong with the work.
6. Criticize without comparison to co-workers.
7. Engage in joint problem solving.
8. Help establish realistic improvement goals.
9. Offer constructive advice.
10. Obtain a commitment to change.
11. Give the poor performer opportunity to observe and model acceptable performance.
12. Counter anger or hostility with objectivity and patience.

EMPLOYEE DISCIPLINE

The positive aspects of improving substandard performance have been emphasized so far. There are times, however, when the control model requires disciplining employees in an attempt to keep performance at an acceptable level. **Discipline**, in its general meaning, refers to punishment used to correct or to train. Discipline in organizations is divided into two types, summary and corrective.

Summary discipline refers to the immediate discharge of an employee because of a serious offense. The employee is fired on the spot because of rule violations such as stealing, fighting, or selling illegal drugs on company premises. In unionized firms, the company and the union have a written agreement specifying which offenses are subject to summary discipline.

Corrective discipline occurs when employees are given a chance to correct their behavior before punishment is applied. Employees are told that their behavior is unacceptable and that corrections must be made if they want to remain with the firm.[14] The manager and the employee share the responsibility for solving the performance problem. The control model for managing ineffective performers includes corrective discipline. Steps 3 through 6 in Figure 13-1 are based on corrective discipline.

We will examine two other aspects of discipline. First, we explain the two variations of corrective discipline (progressive discipline and positive discipline). Second, we describe the rules for applying discipline. Before following these suggestions for applying discipline, the manager in a unionized firm must carefully examine the clauses in the union agreement that cover employee discipline.

Progressive Discipline

Progressive discipline is the step-by-step application of corrective discipline, as shown in Figure 13-2. The manager confronts and then counsels the poor performer about the performance problem. If the employee's performance does not improve, the employee is informed in writing that improvements must be made. The written notice often includes a clear statement of what will happen if performance does not improve. The ''or else'' could be a disciplinary layoff or suspension. If the notice is ignored and the disciplinary action does not lead to improvements, the employee may be discharged.

Positive Discipline

Positive discipline is an approach to improving substandard behavior that emphasizes coaching, individual responsibility, and a mature problem-solving method.[15] Progressive discipline, in contrast, places more emphasis on punishment. Positive discipline focuses on motivating employees to improve perfor-

Figure 13-2   Steps in Progressive Discipline

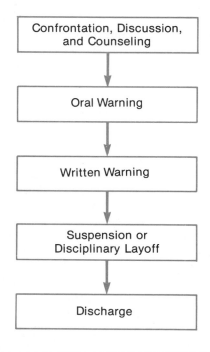

```
┌──────────────────────────┐
│  Confrontation, Discussion, │
│     and Counseling        │
└──────────────────────────┘
             │
             ▼
┌──────────────────────────┐
│       Oral Warning        │
└──────────────────────────┘
             │
             ▼
┌──────────────────────────┐
│      Written Warning      │
└──────────────────────────┘
             │
             ▼
┌──────────────────────────┐
│      Suspension or        │
│    Disciplinary Layoff    │
└──────────────────────────┘
             │
             ▼
┌──────────────────────────┐
│        Discharge          │
└──────────────────────────┘
```

mance rather than punishing them for poor performance. Written and spoken warnings are replaced with the following:

- Discussions and written reminders of employee responsibility.

- Use of the term *reminder* in preference to the term *warning*.

- The employee's agreement to maintain certain standards of performance and behavior.

- A paid day off as the final step in the disciplinary process.

The cornerstone of positive discipline is the **decision-making leave**, a paid one-day suspension to help the employee think through the disciplinary problem. If preliminary measures fail, the employee is given one day off with full pay. During the time off the employee is supposed to decide to remain on the job and meet performance standards or to resign. If the employee decides to remain with the firm, the manager helps that person develop improvement goals and action plans. The manager encourages the employee, but makes it clear that failure to reach goals will result in termination.[16]

Many managers are naturally skeptical about the merits of a paid suspension for ineffective performance or rule violations, yet the system appears to be working. A study conducted in the Tampa Electric Co. found that decision-making leaves reduce the need for employees to get even with the organization. Also, employees did not abuse the system in an attempt to gain a free day off. Tangible results of the positive discipline program included fewer terminations, less absenteeism, and virtually no grievances (formal complaints).[17]

Rules for Applying Discipline

Discipline has been discussed here as it relates to correcting ineffective performance. However, discipline is more frequently used to deal with infractions of policies and rules. The employee in these situations may not necessarily be a poor performer. Certain time-tested rules should be followed when administering discipline for poor performance or rule violations.

The red-hot-stove rule is an old-fashioned, but still valid, general rule for administering discipline. According to the **red-hot-stove rule**, employee discipline should parallel what would happen if an employee touched a very hot stove. The situation should contain a warning (the red metal), and the punishment should be immediate, consistent, and impersonal. When a manager disciplines an employee, these and other suggestions should be followed.[18]

1. *All employees should be warned of what punishments will be applied for what infractions.* For example, paralegal assistants might be told that discussing the details of client cases with outsiders, a violation of company policy, will result in suspension or discharge.

2. *Discipline should be applied immediately after the infraction is committed.* As soon as practical after learning of the rule violation, the manager should confront the employee.

3. *The punishment should fit the undesirable behavior.* If the punishment is too light it will not be taken seriously by the offender; if it is too heavy it may create anxiety and actually diminish performance.[19]

4. *Managers should be consistent in the application of discipline for each infraction.* Every employee violating a certain rule should receive the same punishment. Furthermore, managers throughout the organization should invoke the same punishment for the same rule violation. Few organizations have yet achieved such consistency in administering discipline.

5. *Disciplinary remedies should be applied impersonally to offenders.* "Impersonal" here implies that everybody who is known to violate the rules should be punished. No one should play favorites. As described in Chapter 6, impersonality is one of the advantages of a bureaucracy. It is important in matters of discipline.

6. *Documentation of the performance or behavior that led to punishment is
    essential.* A basic principle of discipline is that the justification for the
    discipline should be documented in substantial detail. Documentation is
    necessary to defend the company position in the event of an appeal by the
    employee or the union or in the case of a lawsuit.

We have described the many causes of ineffective performance and the
manager's role in helping the employee directly. Next we will consider a comprehensive program designed to rehabilitate troubled employees.

EMPLOYEE ASSISTANCE PROGRAMS

An **employee assistance program (EAP)** is an organizational unit or free-
standing agency designed to help employees deal with personal problems that
affect their job performance and morale. In many instances, the personal problems facing the employee are contributed to by job stress. Attempts by
organizations to control alcohol and drug abuse have been the major impetus
behind the growth of EAPs.[20] Financial, family, and medical problems,
however, are also treated by EAPs. Financial problems are rapidly increasing
as a reason for referral. Employee concerns about "eldercare" (caring for
older parents) is a long-standing problem that is recently being addressed by
some assistance programs. Our discussion of EAPs centers around a description of their key features and contribution to productivity.

Key Features of an EAP

EAPs are designed and operated differently in different companies. The major
similarity among them is that they offer confidential, professional help to
employees seeking assistance with their personal problems. The common
characteristics of EAPs are summarized in the following paragraphs.[21]

Overall Philosophy Emphasizes Rehabilitation.   EAPs are usually committed
to rehabilitating employees. An EAP assumes that personal problems spill
over to the job. Any problem can adversely affect individual and organizational productivity. Professional help is therefore warranted.

Programs Address Specific Problems.   The majority of EAPs have programs
to deal with specific problems, such as a financial-counseling program for people who have financial problems. These programs are usually quite formalized. A
representative approach is referral to a firm such as Personal Performance Consultants (PPC). Each company pays a flat rate to PPC for employee assistance
services. The accompanying "Organization in Action" presents information
about another treatment facility to which troubled employees can be referred.
A treatment program for gamblers is provided to illustrate the diversity of help

available to troubled employees. Problems relating to alcohol and drug abuse and to financial difficulties are more frequently treated in assistance programs.

Many large organizations now have their own self-contained EAPs. Another recent development is to use both an in-house EAP and outside agencies, depending on the particular problem. Many employees believe that anonymity is better protected by external facilities. However, an internal EAP communicates the message that top management is strongly committed to helping employees cope with personal problems.

ORGANIZATION IN ACTION:

Help for Gamblers

Drug and alcohol addictions have long been recognized and understood. But there is another addiction, equally strong, equally compelling, and equally destructive, that has only recently been recognized as a major emotional problem. It is the addiction to gambling.

Like those addicted to alcohol and drugs, the compulsive gambler soon loses sight of everything but his or her addiction. Home, family, friends, employment, respect, and self-esteem all become secondary to the next big bet, the next big chance, the next surge of excitement.

For compulsive gamblers caught in the vice of obsession, life is out of control. To regain that loss of control and return their lives to normalcy, they need the kind of specialized help available from the Taylor Manor Hospital Gambling Treatment Center. This unique program offers an intensive, highly individualized approach to the thorough rehabilitation of the compulsive gambler, with special focus on the needs of both the patient and the family.

The program's aim is to break the addiction's hold and to restore the patient to the normal worlds of family, work, and community.

Source: Brochure from Taylor Manor Hospital, Ellicott City, Maryland 21043.

Policies Recognize that Personal Problems Detract from Performance.   EAP policies recognize that employees' personal problems often influence job performance. The policies emphasize treatment and rehabilitation rather than punishment. (Traditional approaches to personal problems emphasize threats of punishment and discipline.) These policies are put in writing and they are formally communicated to employees.

Performance and Productivity Are Emphasized.   Assistance programs are aimed at improving job performance. Written records are kept, and employees are notified promptly of performance problems. These records are ordinarily part of the performance-appraisal system. However, when employee performance is well below standard, performance appraisals are supplemented with additional documentation. The documentation becomes a permanent record.

The EAP is intended to help the employee get job performance back to standard.

Managers Are the Major Source of Referral. The majority of referrals to EAPs are from managers who identify performance problems and then strongly suggest the employee seek such help. As EAPs have gained in acceptance, more self-referrals take place. Primary responsibility for administering the program usually rests with the human resources (personnel) department. The medical services department is the second most frequent location of the EAP. Employees are responsible for using the EAP as a method of improving job performance.

Treatment Rather Than Prevention Is Emphasized. EAPs are much more concerned with treatment than prevention. Upon detecting deviations from performance, the manager reacts by referring the employee to the EAP. Employees are rarely sent to an EAP to acquire skills and insights that might help them prevent future trouble.

Assistance Is Generally Given by Professionals. All EAP programs require professional assistance from specialists such as physicians, psychiatrists, clinical psychologists, psychiatric social workers, and financial planners. Some EAP counselors, however, are not licensed or certified professionals. Instead they are counselors who themselves have recovered from such problems as drug or gambling abuse. At Taylor Manor Hospital, for example, some members of the treatment team are addiction counselors who themselves are often recovering, compulsive gamblers.

Time Span of Treatment Is Relatively Short. The time framework for EAPs tends to be short (from one hour to one year). During this period, the employee can obtain professional assistance, become rehabilitated, and improve job performance. Several EAPs have achieved good results by using telephone consultations with troubled employees. The time span of these treatments is often as short as five minutes.

The Program Is Confidential. An essential feature of EAPs is that they are confidential. Publicity about the program emphasizes its confidentiality. Brochures, notices, and articles in company newspapers all state that the program is confidential and that records remain in EAP files only. The Eastman Kodak Co. EAP brochure includes this statement: "Information about your counseling or the assistance provided will not be revealed to anyone without your permission. No information will be entered into your personnel record unless you request it."[22]

Confidentiality is broken if the EAP specialist thinks that the employee is homicidal, suicidal, or a potential saboteur. Despite the confidentiality of EAPs, the organization is aware of which people they refer to the EAP. Yet most EAPs do not reveal the name of self-referrals.

Contribution of EAPs to Organizational Productivity

EAPs are routinely found in business organizations, hospitals, government agencies, and universities. One reason for the growth of EAPs is that they serve humanitarian purposes. It is a worthwhile endeavor in itself to help troubled people. The primary reason for the growth of EAPs, however, is that it has proven profitable to rehabilitate employees whose performance deficiencies stem from personal problems. When an employee's substandard performance is brought back to acceptable levels, his or her productivity is increased. If this happens to a large number of employees, organizational productivity also increases.

One method of measuring the cost-effectiveness of EAPs is through **recovery rates,** defined as the percent of employees who return to satisfactory performance after treatment. Some of the known recovery rates are as follows: The New York City Police Department, 75 percent; DuPont, 66 percent; Illinois Bell, 57 percent; Eastman Kodak Co., 75 percent; General Motors Corp., 80 percent; and Inland Steel Industries, Inc., 82 percent.[23] Richard M. Weiss, however, contends that the claims of such programs are often exaggerated and unsubstantiated by the people who administer them.[24]

The effectiveness of EAPs has also been measured by return on investment. One study showed that each dollar invested in the program brought a return of seven dollars in reduced benefits usage and absenteeism. Another study showed that a good assistance program returns $5 for each $1 invested.[25] Some of the return on investment from EAPs stems from the improved job performance of those employees who are treated successfully.

One concern with EAPs is that some employees feel coerced into attending them. They therefore make no commitment to change when being counseled by an EAP professional. Another concern about EAPs is that they allow to stay on the job some employees whose best interests would be served by employment elsewhere. For example, the employee may need the shock of being fired to overcome his or her ineffective behavior patterns. Finally, many supervisors tend to refer problem employees to the EAP rather than trying to discipline those employees themselves.

TERMINATION AND OUTPLACEMENT

When corrective actions fail to improve ineffective performance, only one alternative remains—to terminate the employee. The company may also assist the person in finding new employment. Termination is considered part of the control process because it is a corrective action. It can also be considered part of the organizing function because it involves placing people.

Termination

Termination is the process of firing an employee because of poor job performance, unacceptable behavior, or interpersonal problems. Termination is regarded as the last alternative. It represents a failure in staffing and in management of ineffective performers. Nevertheless, a firm often is forced to terminate nonproductive employees in order to maintain discipline and control costs. Firing a substandard performer can also be valuable because it may increase the productivity of employees who are not fired. When substandard performers are discharged, it communicates the message that adequate performance must be maintained.

Termination usually takes place only after the substandard performer has been offered the type of help described throughout this chapter. In general, every feasible alternative such as retraining and counseling should be attempted before termination, as diagrammed in Figure 13-3. It is also necessary to accumulate substantial written documentation of substandard performance. Appropriate documentation includes performance appraisals, special memos to the file about performance problems, and statements describing the help offered the employee.

If these steps are not documented, the employer can be accused of wrongful discharge. **Wrongful discharge** is the firing of an employee for arbitrary or unfair reasons. In recent years, many employers have been sued for wrongfully discharging employees. Many employees—acting alone or assisted by their unions—have been awarded damages in these cases. The increase in these suits has made employers more reluctant to dismiss workers and more thorough in documenting reasons for a firing. Also, employers have become more cautious in the reasons they give for termination, both to the worker and to future employers.[26]

Another way of looking at wrongful discharge is the idea that employees have certain rights in relation to preserving their jobs. According to the idea of **due process**, employees must be given a fair hearing before being dismissed. This includes progressive discipline and the right to present one's side of the story to management. Thirteen states recognize that there is an implied contract between employer and employee. If the employee performs satisfactorily, he or she cannot be discharged without just cause. The discussion in Chapter 2 about the legal rights of employees relates directly to the job security of employees.

Outplacement

Outplacement is helping laid off or terminated employees find new employment through the use of professional career counseling. The major goal of an outplacement program, according to the president of an outplacement firm, "should be to provide a compassionate transition for employees who no longer fit into the corporate picture—for whatever reason."[27]

Outplacement counselors provide the terminated employee with services such as assessment of skills, resume development, interview preparation, job-campaign training, and emotional support. The displaced employee also may be given the use of a desk, telephone, business mailing address, photocopying machine, and so forth.[28] An important point made by outplacement firms is that they do *not* find jobs for people; instead they help their clients find jobs for themselves.

Figure 13-3   Framework for Deciding Whether to Terminate or Provide Additional Counseling to an Employee

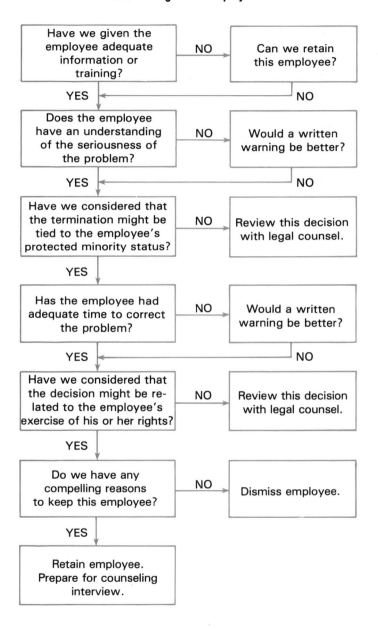

Source: Reprinted, by permission of the publisher, from Steve Buckman, "To Fire or Not to Fire?" *Supervisory Management* (February 1986): 31. Copyright © 1986 American Management Assns., New York. All rights reserved.

Outplacement services were first offered to executives whose jobs were eliminated because of poor business conditions or a merger of two companies. The growth of corporate restructuring has lead to a dramatic increase in outplacement activity.[29] These services are now offered to workers at all levels, whether they are displaced because of business conditions or poor performance. Outplacement services are usually subcontracted to a firm specializing in this work.

The major argument in favor of outplacement counseling is that it does help many employees find a new job or even a new career. By reducing unemployment, these programs help to reduce many negative conditions. Unemployed people have a high rate of stress disorders, suicide, homicide, spouse battering, and child battering. Outplacement services also help prevent the erosion of company goodwill and may sometimes increase goodwill. Helping laid off employees find new employment is looked on more favorably than is laying off employees and providing them with no help.

The major argument against outplacement counseling is that it often over-markets employees. So much effort is put into marketing the terminated employee that his or her problems are disguised. The employee may then find a new job for which he or she is underqualified. The result is another job failure for the employee.[30] Another argument against outplacement services is that they do little for job seekers that these people cannot do for themselves, including the reality that job seekers have to furnish their own leads.

SUMMARY OF KEY POINTS

Job performance is considered ineffective when productivity is below a standard considered acceptable at a given time. Most instances of poor job performance are attributable to a small proportion of the work force. Ineffective performers consume considerable managerial time. The causes of poor job performance can be rooted in the person, the job, the manager, or the company. Usually, ineffective performance is caused by a combination of several factors.

The approach to improving ineffective performance presented here is a control model. It is divided into seven steps that should be followed in sequence: (1) define effective or acceptable performance, (2) detect deviation from acceptable performance, (3) confront the substandard performer, (4) set improvement goals, (5) select and implement an action plan for improvement, (6) reevaluate performance after a time interval, and (7) continue or discontinue the action plan.

Corrective actions for ineffective performers are divided into managerial actions and techniques and organizational programs. Managerial actions include close supervision and corrective discipline. Organizational programs include career counseling and outplacement and job redesign.

Counseling and constructive criticism are useful approaches to managing poor performers. Counseling is a formal discussion method for helping a person overcome a problem or develop his or her potential. Most on-the-job counseling includes constructive criticism. Skill is required to counsel and constructively criticize poor performers.

The control model may also call for discipline. Summary discipline is the immediate discharge of an employee because of a serious offense. Corrective discipline gives employees a chance to correct their behavior before punishment is applied. Both the manager and the employee share the responsibility for solving the performance problem. Corrective discipline therefore involves counseling.

One type of corrective discipline is called progressive discipline, and it is really a step-by-step application of corrective discipline. The manager confronts and then counsels the poor performer about the problem. If the employee's performance does not improve, the employee is given a written warning. If this fails, the employee is suspended or given a disciplinary layoff. The next step is discharge. Another type of corrective discipline is positive discipline. It emphasizes coaching, individual responsibility, providing a mature problem-solving method, and motivating the employee to improve.

The red-hot-stove rule is recommended for administering discipline. The situation should include a warning, and the punishment should be administered consistently and impersonally immediately after the infraction is committed.

An employee assistance program (EAP) is an organizational unit, or separate firm, designed to help employees deal with personal problems that affect job performance and morale. These problems include alcoholism or other drug addiction, financial problems, and family problems. EAPs are committed to rehabilitation and offer specific programs and professional assistance for each type of problem. They emphasize improving job performance. EAPs are cost effective because they improve productivity.

When corrective actions taken by the manager or the organization fail to improve ineffective performance, terminating the employee is the only alternative. Careful documentation of poor performance is necessary to prevent charges of wrongful discharge. Employees who are terminated because of poor performance, as well as those laid off, can be offered the services of an outplacement program. Outplacement is designed to help the surplus employee find suitable employment for themselves, with the assistance of professional counseling.

QUESTIONS

1. Refer back to "Managers In Action; What Executives Dislike about Employees." Do you think the executives were being too harsh about employee behavior?
2. Now that smoking is banned in most working areas, to what extent do you think productivity will increase in most organizations?
3. In what way might rudeness toward customers by sales associates lead to losses in productivity?

4. How can a person prevent himself or herself from becoming a substandard performer?
5. What similarity is there between the control models in Figures 13-1 and 12-4?
6. Why do some managers actually enjoy confronting employees?
7. What type of nonverbal communication would be helpful in the process of "carefrontation"?
8. What can a manager do to ensure fairness in administering discipline?
9. Do you think it is fair to other employers to hide the true reason why an employee was fired from the organization?
10. If so many firms are attempting to "outplace" surplus employees at the same time, where will these people all find new jobs?

ACTIVITIES

1. Develop an action plan to improve the performance of a supervisor who is ineffective because he or she is a free-rein leader.
2. Ask an experienced manager what he or she thinks is the most frequent cause of ineffective performance. Relate the manager's answer to Table 13-1, and be prepared to discuss your findings in class.

CASE PROBLEM 13-A: THE CURT SALES ASSOCIATES

"Can you direct me toward the small vacuum cleaners used to clean autos?" asked the customer. "Sorry, I can't help you," answered the sales associate. "I just started working here last week. I don't know where nothing is. Just look around yourself."

"Good heavens, if you are not familiar with the merchandise, or even with the proper grammar, you do not belong on the floor," said the customer in a loud and angry tone. Before leaving the store, the customer demanded to see the manager, Scott McNiven. During the fifteen-minute interview with McNiven, the customer recounted her brief conversation with the sales associate. McNiven pleaded with the woman to forgive the store this once, and he assured her of courteous treatment in the future.

The next day McNiven telephoned the corporate training director, Katrina Rhodes, to schedule a meeting about the issue of customer courtesy. McNiven and Rhodes met in her office the next day.

"I hope what I'm going to tell you will not make me appear weak as a store manager. I suspect other branches are having the same problem. Some of our sales associates are so rude that they are driving our customers to use mail-order shopping services."

"Tell me more about the problem," said Rhodes. "I need some specifics."

"As the store manager, I receive a lot of complaints. To verify some of the customer complaints I asked my wife and children to shop in my store and then tell me what kind of treatment they received from the sales associates. They didn't bring back horror stories, but some of their observations were along the lines of those made by our customers.

"Many customers say our sales associates just ignore them. They carry on conversations with co-workers while the customer is trying to check out or ask for help. I've also received a few complaints about gum chewing. Another problem I've noticed is that some of our employees never look the customer in the eye or smile at them."

"What have you done so far about the problem?" asked Rhodes.

"Occasionally, I talk to the store employees about the problem. I've even brought a few of the ruder ones into my office for a little chat about customer courtesy.

"What do your employees say about the problem?" asked Rhodes.

"Most of them say it's the customer's fault. The customers show them very little respect. My sales associates say some of the customers treat them like servants. Furthermore, there is the problem of customers taking out their hostility on the store employees."

"What would you like me to do about this entire problem?" asked Rhodes.

"Fix it," replied McNiven, "You're the corporate training director."

Case Questions

1. Whose responsibility is it to fix this problem?
2. Describe a realistic plan to deal with the problems identified in this case.
3. How widespread are the problems identified in this case?

CASE PROBLEM 13-B: THE IRATE EAP COORDINATOR

Jacques Marchant, the EAP coordinator at his company, was discussing the status of his program with his boss, Elliot McFadden, the personnel director. McFadden said, "How are things going for you, Jacques? You've been on this assignment long enough to appreciate the good and bad sides of running the company EAP."

"I appreciate your interest, Elliot," responded Marchant. "I see some very good things in this job, and I also see some problems. Let me start with the good side. I think we are on an important mission. The program is helping a lot of employees with problems to get back on their feet. I have also accumulated some statistics to show that our EAP is a good financial investment for the company."

"Okay, I'm waiting for the punch line," said McFadden. "What is the bad side of the job?"

Marchant responded, "I was just getting to that. It's a sensitive issue that points a finger at a lot of our managers. Some of these people are misusing the program. They should be using the program as an aid to helping troubled employees restore their equilibrium."

"How are they using the EAP, then?"

"They are using the EAP as a club over the head of employees who are having any sort of performance problems. I'll give you an example that happened last week. An office supervisor discovered that one of her data-entry specialists had slipped 20 percent in productivity. The supervisor thought the problem was due to poor concentration. Furthermore, she thought that the poor concentration was probably due to personal problems. Having made this diagnosis of the problem, she told the employee she must either sign up for the EAP or risk being disciplined. When the employee did get to our office, she was defensive and angry. She looked at us as disciplinarians who were doing the dirty work for the manager.

"I'll give you another example of what I'm talking about. A custodian was late a few times. His supervisor told him that he should either resign or sign up for the EAP.

In general, some of our managers are acting like judges of twenty years ago. When young male offenders came up for sentencing, many judges offered the young men two alternatives: they could either go to jail or enlist in the Army. You can imagine how the men felt about the Army under these circumstances."

McFadden commented, "You're saying then, Jacques, that some of our managers are fostering negative attitudes toward the EAP."

"That's exactly what I'm saying. Our own managers are creating some negative misperceptions of the EAP. If things don't change within two years, the EAP won't function properly."

Case Questions

1. Do you think Jacques Marchant might be overreacting? Could it be that Marchant is wrong and that the managers are right?
2. What would be a legitimate way for the company managers to use the EAP as a method of improving employee performance?
3. Under what circumstances should problems of poor concentration and absenteeism be referred to an EAP?

REFERENCES

1. Edward N. Cole, *Factory Management* (August 1966): 173.
2. Glenn M. McEvoy and Wayne F. Cascio, "Do Good or Poor Performers Leave? A Meta-Analysis of the Relationship Between Performance and Turnover," *Academy of Management Journal* (December 1987): 744–762.
3. Shane R. Premeaux and R. Wayne Mondy, "Problem Employees: The Cynic," *Management Solutions* (October 1986): 14–16.
4. R. Wayne Mondy, Shane R. Premeaux, and Clyde Newmiller, "People Problems: The Office Entrepreneur," *Management Solutions* (December 1986): 17–19.
5. Lucy Young, "Night Workers Suffer More Mental Lapses," *Gannett News Service,* 20 July 1987.
6. Philipp A. Stoeberl and March J. Schniederjans, "The Ineffective Subordinate: A Management Survey," *Personnel Administrator* (February 1981): 76.
7. Quoted in Priscilla Petty, "Shortest Route to Good Communications is Often a Straight Question," *Gannett News Service,* 18 October 1983.
8. Donald H. Weiss, "How to Handle Difficult People," *Management Solutions* (February 1988): 38.
9. Richard P. Sloan, Jessie C. Gruman, and John A. Allegrante, *Investing in Employee Health* (San Francisco, CA: Jossey-Bass, Inc., Pubs., 1987).
10. "What to Do about the Marginal Employee," *Supervisory Sense* (New York: AMACOM, 1981), 16.

11. Guvenc G. Alpander, "Training First-Line Supervisors to Criticize Constructively," *Personnel Journal* (March 1980): 220.

12. T. J. Griffith, "Want Job Improvement? Try Counseling," *Management Solutions* (September 1987): 15.

13. J. Kenneth Matejka, D. Neil Ashworth, and Diane Dodd-McCue, "Managing Difficult Employees: Challenge or Curse?" *Personnel* (July 1986): 46.

14. Ira G. Asherman, "The Corrective Discipline Process," *Personnel Journal* (July 1982): 530.

15. Alan W. Bryant, Jr., "Replacing Punitive Discipline with a Positive Approach," *Personnel Administrator* (February 1984): 79.

16. "Positive Discipline: Motivating Employees to Improve Performance," *Business Update* (vol. 1, issue 9, 1985): 15.

17. David N. Campbell, R. L. Fleming, and Richard C. Grote, "Discipline without Punishment—At Last," *Harvard Business Review* (July–August 1985): 163.

18. James Belohlav, "Realities of Successful Employee Discipline," *Personnel Administrator* (March 1983): 75; L. Wade Humphreys and Neil J. Humphreys, "The Proper Use of Discipline," *Management Solutions* (May 1988): 5–10.

19. Humphreys and Humphreys, "The Proper Use of Discipline," 9.

20. Howard W. French, "Employee Drug Abuse Programs Spawn a New Industry," *New York Times,* 27 March 1987; James W. Schreier, "Survey Supports Perceptions: Work-Site Drug Use Is on the Rise," *Personnel Journal* (October 1987): 114.

21. Robert W. Hollman, "Beyond Contemporary Employee Assistance Programs," *Personnel Administrator* (September 1981): 37–38; William J. Sonnenstuhl and Harrison M. Trice, *Strategies for Employee Assistance Programs: The Crucial Balance* (Ithaca, NY: ILR Press, 1986).

22. "Employee Assistance Program for Kodak Employees and their Families," Eastman Kodak Co. brochure, June 1985): 3.

23. Gopal C. Pati and John L. Adkins, Jr., "The Employer's Role in Alcoholism Assistance," *Personnel Journal* (July 1983): 569.

24. Richard M. Weiss, "Writing Under the Influence: Science versus Fiction in the Analysis of Corporate Alcoholism Programs," *Personnel Psychology* (Summer 1987): 354.

25. John Hoerr, "The Drug Wars Will Be Won with Treatment, Not Tests," *Business Week* (13 October 1986): 114–119.

26. Roger Gillott, "More Fired Workers Suing Their Former Bosses," *Associated Press* (story), 23 November 1986.

27. "Outplacement Counseling Services," *Research Institute Personal Report for the Executive* (21 January 1986): 5.

28. Edmund B. Piccolino, "Outplacement: The View from HR," *Personnel* (March 1988): 24–27.

29. Don Lee Bohl, ed., *Responsible Reductions in Force: An American Management Association Research Report on Downsizing and Outplacement.* (New York: American Management Assns., 1987).

30. F. Leigh Branham, "How to Evaluate Executive Outplacement Services," *Personnel Journal* (April 1983): 323.

14
Managing For Quality

After studying the material in this chapter, you should be able to accomplish the following tasks:

1. Understand the meaning of quality and identify its contributing factors.
2. List and explain several key principles of quality management.
3. Explain the difference between quality assurance and quality control.
4. Describe the basics of a quality circle.
5. Understand how to develop quality awareness in your organizational unit.

Key Terms and Phrases

Quality
Quality assurance
Robust quality (robust design)
Taguchi method
Suggestion system
Quality control

Statistical process control
Acceptance inspection
In-process inspection
Statistical quality control
Lot
Zero defects

This chapter on quality has purposely been saved for a place near the end of the text. One reason is that managing for quality is traditionally considered part of the control function. Another is that managing for quality should be kept in mind in every action a manager takes. The quest for quality can be considered a strategic goal. Whether the manager is planning, organizing, leading, or controlling, quality awareness is important. If a company is planning to purchase another firm, the new firm should offer quality goods and services. If the maintenance supervisor is hiring a custodial worker, the new employee should take pride in cleanliness.

Quality is defined here as conformance to customer or user requirements.[1] If a product or service does what it is supposed to do, it is said to be of high quality. If the product or service fails its mission, it is said to be of low quality. The requirements conformed to can be objective or subjective. A high-quality automobile might contain certain parts that deviate less than 0.0005 from standard. This small deviation would be an example of meeting objective requirements. The same automobile might also generate a high-quality image, thus meeting a subjective requirement of quality. Figure 14-1 presents an advertisement for an automobile regarded by many as meeting objective and subjective quality requirements. As shown in Figure 14-2, a service can also provide high objective and subjective quality. In order to retain this high-quality reputation, both Jaguar Cars Inc.'s automobiles and United Van Lines' services must continue to satisfy customer requirements.

Figure 14-3 summarizes the relationship of quality to some topics previously described in this text. The thesis of the figure is that all managerial functions, activities, and techniques should include quality awareness. If this awareness is maintained, organization-wide quality is achieved. Quality awareness will also lead to the production of high-quality goods and services.

SIX DIMENSIONS OF QUALITY

Quality has been defined as conformance to customer or user requirements. To appreciate the full meaning of quality, it is also helpful to look at the dimensions or components that contribute to consumer satisfaction.[2] When using a product or service, consumers have many interests or concerns. Among them are how it appears, how it performs, how reliably it performs, how long it lasts, how easy it is to get serviced, and what are its features.

1. *Aesthetics.* A product or service that has a favorable appearance, sound, taste, or smell is perceived to be of good quality. A Jaguar automobile rates well on this dimension of quality. Hickory-flavored meat might have the right aesthetics for some, but not all, people. One of the challenges in choosing the right aesthetics is that aesthetics is mostly a matter of personal judgment and a reflection of individual preferences.

2. *Performance.* A product or service that performs its intended function scores high on this dimension of quality. A few years back, several luxury automobiles powered by diesel engines operated so poorly that owners gave a poor-quality reputation to the manufacturers. A temporary employment agency that provides customers with capable workers would score high on the operation dimension of quality.

3. *Reliability.* Reliability, or dependability, is such an important part of product quality that quality-control engineers are sometimes referred to as "reliability engineers." Many customer complaints about products are concerned with the product breaking down readily. How many times have you heard someone say, "My car has spent more time in the shop than on the road"? Service personnel, such as office temporaries, are also judged in terms of how long they provide high output. Many people are capable of starting with a flurry of activity but then fizzling down to ordinary productivity.

Figure 14-1 An Advertisement that Projects a Quality Image

The 1989 Jaguar XJ6—its elegance is refreshing. Unmistakably Jaguar, the XJ6 reflects the classic character of its forebears, while achieving a higher degree of aerodynamic efficiency and high-speed stability.

Beneath the low, tapering hood resides Jaguar's latest masterpiece in double overhead cam engine design. Jaguar's light-alloy 3.6-liter engine incorporates the added sophistication of four valves per cylinder for enhanced power and responsiveness. Revised torque converter specifications and a new final drive ratio for 1989 give the XJ6 even more vivid performance.

Jaguar's fully independent suspension provides smooth riding comfort and athletic handling agility. Patented pendulum isolation tunes out the annoying effects of minor road imperfections. The self-leveling rear suspension automatically compensates for changes in passenger or cargo loads. And Jaguar's four-wheel power disc brakes are complemented by one of the most advanced anti-lock (ABS) systems.

Spacious and serene, the XJ6 cabin is rich in Old World splendor and enlightened comfort and conveniences. It is trimmed with hand-finished and inlaid walnut veneers. The orthopedically contoured seats are faced with finely stitched leather. The automatic climate control system is regulated by computer. The 80-watt stereo system plays through six speakers. Infrared remote control lets you operate the central locking system without a key.

To appreciate all of the art and Jaguar traditions of the XJ6, see your dealer for a test drive. He can provide details on Jaguar's uniquely comprehensive three-year/36,000-mile limited warranty, applicable in the USA and Canada, and on Jaguar's Service-On-Site℠ Roadside Assistance Plan. For the name of the dealer nearest you, call toll-free: 1-800-4-JAGUAR.
Jaguar Cars Inc., Leonia, NJ 07605

ENJOY TOMORROW. BUCKLE UP TODAY.

The British have an affection for art and tradition and a motorcar that embodies both. The 1989 Jaguar XJ6.

STOW-ON-THE-WOLD, GLOUCESTERSHIRE, ENGLAND

JAGUAR
A BLENDING OF ART AND MACHINE

Source: Courtesy, Jaguar Cars Inc.

Figure 14-2   An Advertisement that Conveys Service Quality

"United Van Lines Ranks First in Overall Customer Satisfaction."

But you don't have to take our word for it.

Those were the findings of NFO Research, Inc.* in a recent nationwide survey of families who have moved. In category after category, United finished well ahead of the country's top seven van lines.

All the more reasons for entrusting your personnel relocations to America's Number One Family Mover. See the Yellow Pages for the name of your nearby United Agent.

*National Family Opinion Research, Inc.

the QUALITY SHOWS in every move we make.

For more survey information, write:
Robert M. Andersen
Vice president–Marketing Services
United Van Lines
1 United Drive, Fenton, MO 63026

Figure 14-3 How Quality Awareness Is Important in All Managerial Activities

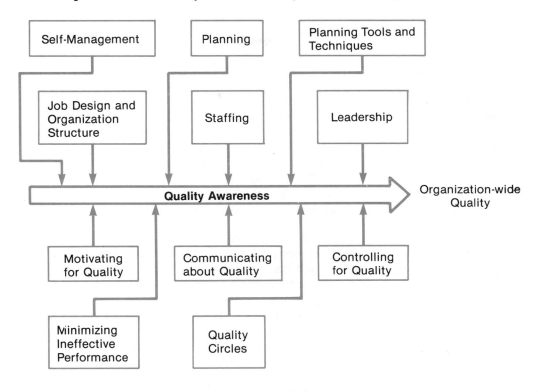

4. *Durability.* Durability can be defined as the amount of use one gets from a product before it no longer functions properly and replacement seems more feasible than constant repair.[3] Consumers generally prefer more durable products, but they are often unwilling to invest the money required for a long-lasting product. Also, some consumers tire of using the same product and therefore enjoy purchasing a replacement.

5. *Serviceability.* Speed, courtesy, competence, and ease of repair are all important quality factors. Serviceability has become especially important as many products have become more complex and quite difficult to repair by oneself. Personal computers, video cassette recorders (VCRs), and television sets are prime examples. Serviceability is also important in judging the quality of industrial products such as farm equipment, trucks, and photocopying machines.

6. *Features.* Features are characteristics about a product or service that supplement its basic functioning. Examples include a remote control dialing on a television set and an executive lounge open only to frequent travelers on an airline.

In some cases, one of these dimensions might be considered more important than another. The quality of light bulbs, for example, tends to be evaluated primarily in terms of durability.

The Monetary Value of Quality

A best-selling book about quality is titled *Quality Is Free*.[4] The implication of this title is that quality is so important that it more than pays for itself. The organization that provides low-quality goods and services incurs both measurable and hidden costs. Rework, such as repairing machine defects or rewriting reports, is expensive. Scrap and other forms of waste are another cost attributable to failing to do something right the first time. Orders are lost because former customers were dissatisfied with a previous order and are now buying from a competitor. Loss of potential new business, stemming from a reputation for poor quality, is perhaps the biggest cost of low quality.

The monetary value of quality includes both costs to the consumer and costs to the provider of the goods or services. The adage, "You get what you pay for," implies that there is a direct relationship between price and quality. Nevertheless, the relationship between price and quality is not perfect. In some instances, lower-priced goods and services are of better quality than their higher-priced counterparts. For example, Chrysler minivans require fewer repairs and are safer than many vehicles of twice the price. Can you furnish another example of a situation in which a lower-priced product or service is of higher quality than a higher-priced one?

Several attempts have been made to calculate the monetary value of quality. One survey indicated that companies with an inferior product have an average return on investment of 4.5 percent. Those with an average product have a 10.4 percent return; and those with a superior product 17.4 percent.[5]

The typical factory invests about one-fifth to one-fourth of its operating budget in finding and fixing mistakes. As many as one-fourth of factory employees spend their time reworking things that were done improperly the first time. When the costs of repairing or replacing products that do get into the hands of consumers are included, the total burden of quality problems can be about 30 percent of production costs.[6]

FACTORS CONTRIBUTING TO QUALITY

Slogans such as "Take pride in your work," and "Our most important product is quality," contribute to quality. However, there are underlying factors of greater significance in creating quality goods and services. Among these factors are policy, design, equipment and tools, consumer education, and service after delivery. Each of these factors is discussed separately here.[7]

Policy

Organizational policy is a major contributor to quality. If the strategy calls for offering the public high-quality goods or services, appropriate policies will follow. If organizational strategy neglects mention of quality, low-quality goods and services will probably result. If organizational policy states explicitly that poor quality is acceptable, poor quality is almost guaranteed.

The market aimed at by an organization helps shape its policy about quality. A law firm that catered only to wealthy individuals would have one set of policies about the depth of services offered to clients. A law firm with a broader appeal and lower fees would have another set of policies about quality. The second firm would offer briefer services to clients. In many states and provinces, these firms advertise specials such as "Bankruptcy, $225," or "Uncontested divorce, $400." The client purchasing these services would receive brief treatment. Brevity would be an indicator of low quality from one viewpoint. From another viewpoint, brevity is an indication that the firm handles only simple, straightforward cases.

Design

The design of a product or service is a key determinant of its quality. Design includes such factors as the shape, size, color, materials, and inner workings of a product or service. The engineering of a product is part of its design.

If a product is poorly designed, its quality may be lower because it is difficult to produce or service. For instance, if the parts are too close to each other, assemblers may have difficulty fastening the parts properly. When it comes time for repairs, technicians may not have sufficient room to maneuver. The result can be time-consuming and therefore can cause expensive repairs. J. M. Juran estimates that no more than 20 percent of quality defects can be traced to the production line. The other 80 percent is attributed to either design errors or purchase of low-quality components.[8]

A poorly designed service is one that creates problems for the consumer after the initial purchase. For instance, it is extremely cumbersome to make payments to some types of retirement plans because of inappropriate forms. Also, customers may be asked to complete extensive paperwork at the end of the year.

Stevenson cautions that high-quality design alone does not ensure high-quality products and services.[9] High-quality work is required to implement high-quality designs. Those people responsible for making the product or delivering the service must conform to the design specifications. Employees need to know how to perform good work, and they must be motivated to accomplish it.

Equipment and Tools

High-quality specifications cannot be achieved without high-quality equipment. A firm that lacks high-quality equipment is at a competitive disadvantage in producing high-quality products. Equipment can be faulty for a variety of technical reasons. A direct-sales firm provides an example. Many advertising letters contained errors because the computer sent random errors to the printer. The problem surfaced when a letter intended for Doug Ambers was sent to "Dog" Ambers. An inspection revealed that many other input errors were occurring. An electronics technician ultimately fixed the problem, but the firm's quality image suffered.

Employees also need high-quality tools to perform high-quality work. Often supervisors have to negotiate with management to obtain the right tools and equipment for their employees because management may want to defray the costs of purchasing new tools.

Consumer Education

The determination of quality does not end with producing high-quality goods and services. Consumer education is necessary to increase the chances that a product will be used for its intended purpose. Customers also have to be informed how to use the product so that it will function safely. A case in point is the hand injuries incurred by some owners of snow blowers. These injuries occur when the operator removes a clump of snow that is preventing the blades from rotating. When the clump is released, the blades return to normal speed and catch the person's hand. One could argue that these injuries are due to customer negligence, and are not a quality defect, but good consumer education would prevent the problem. Consumers also have to be educated about the proper use of services. For example, if consumers do not give travel agents enough advance notice, they may not be able to obtain the quality of service they desire.

Service After Delivery

A high-quality product or service must be backed by dependable after-the-sale service (as implied in the serviceability dimension of quality). Almost no equipment is immune to malfunctioning once it is on the customer's premises. A firm that offers efficient repair services can retain its high-quality image despite an occasional malfunction. Some of the best-known brands of office and factory equipment sometimes break down. However, the excellent service offered by these firms gives them a competitive advantage. The service technicians in the field stand ready to ensure that the equipment does conform to requirements. In some cases, the customer is lent a replacement while his or her machine is being repaired. The result is that product quality is enhanced.

Field service must also be used to support services as well as products. Financial services illustrate this point well. To retain a quality image, a financial services firm must be willing to accurately answer questions about investments. They must also be willing to adjust their service quickly to meet changing customer demands. A high-quality financial firm, for example, would make it relatively easy for a customer to shift from one type of investment to another.

We have explained the meaning of quality, along with its contributing factors. Described next are some of the most important principles of managing for quality.

KEY PRINCIPLES OF MANAGING FOR QUALITY

So much information is available about managing for quality that a set of principles can be established. These principles are shown in Figure 14-4. As with any other principles of management, the situation should be taken into account in applying those principles concerned with quality. For example, one principle states that slogans alone are not particularly effective in achieving quality. Some employees, however, rally behind slogans such as "Do it right the first time," or "Quality is Job 1."

The twelve key principles of managing for quality are as follows:[10]

1. *Include the desire for high-quality products and services in the organization's mission statement.* If a statement about quality is not contained in

Figure 14-4   Twelve Principles of Managing for Quality

Include
Quality in
Organizational
Strategy

Use Statistical
Methods

Get Top Management
Committed

Eliminate
Arbitrary
Work Quotas

Make Quality an
Objective of
Each Manager

Go Beyond
Slogans

**High-Quality Products
and
Services**

Conform to
Requirements

Control the
Manufacturing
Process

Prevent Defects

Use a Quality-Information
System

Use the
Zero-Defects
Performance Standard

Select and
Train Suppliers

the organization's strategy, quality will be subordinated to other goals. Some companies use quality as their strategy in gaining their desired market share. The accompanying "Organization in Action" illustrates an advertisement for a company that makes the quality of its services a key marketing strategy.

2. *Have top-level management carry out this commitment to quality.* One important way of demonstrating this commitment is for the director of the quality-control department to report to a member of top-level management. A study of quality in the air-conditioning industry illustrated this point. At plants with poor quality performance, the quality-control manager invariably reported to the director of manufacturing or engineering. At the plants with good quality performance, the quality-control manager had more visibility. Several companies had vice-presidents of quality control. At the factory level, the heads of quality control reported directly to the plant manager.

3. *Include the desire for quality products or services in the objectives of each manager.* The desire for quality should be as important as producing a high volume of goods. Managers should be held as responsible for achieving quality goals as they are for achieving quantity goals.

4. *Focus on customer needs.* Earlier, we mentioned that conformance to customer requirements can be a definition of quality. If management invests time in getting people to agree on customer requirements of a product or service, the end result will be good quality. In recent years, American industry has increased its emphasis on listening to customer requirements. The Black and Decker power tools are prime examples. Much of their success has been attributed to the fact that these home tools satisfy a broad range of customer preferences.

This same principle of meeting customer requirements has been stated in many ways, including "Quality means pleasing consumers, not just protecting them from annoyances," and "Unless you're striving for higher quality in order to deliver more value to your customer—and *only* to deliver more value to your customer—you will fail."[11]

5. *Prevent defects.* This strategy is superior to detecting defects. In many organizations, managing for quality focuses primarily on inspecting products to catch defects after the fact. It is much more effective to prevent them in the first place.

6. *Use the zero-defects performance standard.* This ideal principle lies at the heart of Crosby's system of managing for quality. He claims that if people are truly committed to error-free work, they will accomplish it. For instance, the payroll department virtually never mispays people (at least the payroll departments observed by Crosby do not). The concept of zero defects has not gone unchallenged. The point is expressed in Chapter 2 that absolute perfection may not be worth the cost in most situations. For example, if snow shovels sell for $7.98, the cost of pro-

ducing shovels with zero defects may well be higher than the price at which they can be sold.

7. *Select high-quality suppliers and train them properly.* A company needs high-quality components and materials to produce high-quality products. Careful selection of suppliers (or vendors) is therefore a major aspect of ensuring reliable and defect-free production. In addition to selecting the right suppliers, you must inform them about the company's quality requirements. Sharp Corp., the electronics firm, exemplifies this approach. The company teaches many of its suppliers how to produce high-quality components.

   Business should not necessarily be awarded to the lowest bidder. In an attempt to control costs, many companies award contracts to the lowest bidder. Such a policy often leads to the purchasing of materials and components of low quality. Choosing the lowest bidder is acceptable if bids are accepted only from suppliers who can produce satisfactory quality.

8. *Establish an accurate and responsive quality-information system.* Without accurate and timely information on defects and product failures, quality improvement is difficult to achieve. Companies with poor quality performance seldom have this type of information on hand. One study showed that air-conditioning manufacturers with reputations for high quality had accurate information about quality. They reported defect rates for each inspection point on the assembly line and failure rates in the field by individual model.[12]

9. *Control the manufacturing process.* An "in control" manufacturing process is one that is carefully managed. Machinery and equipment are well maintained, workplaces are clean and orderly, workers are well trained, and inspection procedures detect deviations rapidly.

10. *Reinforce slogans about quality with training.* Slogans about quality may have some benefit in encouraging teamwork and building morale. Yet they should not be a substitute for carefully training employees about quality-improvement techniques. Slogans such as "Do it right," do not explain how to do it right.

11. *Eliminate arbitrary work quotas.* Output quotas often result in employees pushing for quantity at the expense of quality. When work quotas are assigned, they should result from a careful analysis of how quantity affects quality. Quotas should take into account normal variations in the system. In addition, quotas should indicate what corrective action would be taken when deviations are detected.

12. *Establish training programs in statistics so that managers can understand how to manage quality.* Statistical methods are necessary aids for identifying causes of waste, low productivity, and poor quality. Statistical methods are the foundation of quality control, the process of inspecting goods and services to see if they meet standard. Purolator is one example

of a company that gives employees training in how to chart their own quality statistics.

QUALITY ASSURANCE

Quality assurance is the prevention of quality problems through the use of many different approaches.[13] Quality assurance is generally regarded as much broader in scope than quality control. The scope of quality assurance is usually limited to improving the quality of products and services. Yet, there really are no formal restrictions on what quality assurance can encompass. Recently, ideas about quality improvement have been applied to the human resources field. For example, an orientation program that confuses new employees reflects a quality defect in the design of the program.[14]

The twelve key principles of managing for quality can be considered part of quality assurance. If the organization practices these principles, many quality problems will be prevented. Quality circles, as described later in this chapter, can also be considered part of quality assurance. Circle members typically make suggestions for improving quality and preventing customer dissatisfaction. The aspects of quality assurance described here are the sources of ideas for quality improvement and a currently popular quality-assurance method.

Sources of Ideas for Quality Improvement

Good ideas for quality improvement stem from the research-and-development groups, competitors, customers and clients, employees, and management.[15]

Research and Development. The research-and-development (R&D) group has the formal responsibility of developing new technological ideas to move the firm forward. An R&D group in an automobile manufacturer might develop a new concept for an engine. At a bank, the R&D group might develop a new concept of delivering services to the consumer. R&D groups also investigate new materials and processes that have the potential for making quality improvements. An R&D group at a manufacturer of computer supplies might investigate methods of making disks less sensitive to magnetic fields. If the disks were able to retain information longer, their quality would be improved.

Competitors. Many good ideas for quality improvement stem from competitors. These improvements can usually be adopted without violating the patent rights of a competitor or stealing trade secrets. Stevenson expresses this viewpoint:[16]

> There is nothing inherently wrong with noting how a competitor is able to achieve higher reliability, or that the competitor uses special packaging to reduce damage during shipment, or that the competitor uses newer and more efficient methods, or offers free in-home repair services.[16]

The net effect to the consumer of the competition for quality improvement is usually favorable. The major disadvantage occurs when a race for quality improvements is in reality a race to add attractive, but unnecessary, features. In your opinion, are electronic door locks on an automobile a feature that adds quality to the product? Or are manually controlled doors of equal or better quality?

Customers and Clients.   Users are a potentially valuable source of ideas for quality improvement. These ideas can stem from either suggestions or complaints. Customers can be systematically interviewed to determine their perception of the need for quality improvement. Acting on these suggestions early can sometimes prevent quality problems from hurting the reputation of a product or the firm.

The brief consumer-survey cards used in many hotels and restaurants are a basic form of quality control and assurance. Specific complaints such as "The food was tasteless," are part of quality control. Suggestions such as "We would like to see more entertainment," can be considered quality assurance.

Employees.   Employees are a natural source of input for quality improvement. Quality circles represent one formal method of obtaining this input. Suggestion systems are widely used to solicit employee input about quality improvements. A suggestion system is a formal method of collecting and analyzing employee suggestions about processes, policies, products, and services. Many organizations give cash awards for money-saving suggestions. These suggestions about quality often deal more with control than assurance. For instance, an assembly worker might spot a recurring defect such as too wide a gap between two interfacing parts. At other times, suggestions deal with the prevention of quality problems. A basic quality-assurance idea would be to suggest that plastic nuts, and bolts, replace metal ones in order to prevent rusting under moist conditions.

Management.   Managers play a key role in making quality improvements. Part of this role is to make decisions about the necessity for quality improvement. Managers also decide which sources of quality improvement will be used and how much money will be invested in quality. Ensuring that managers set objectives of striving for quality also fosters quality improvement.

Another way management can contribute to quality improvement is by helping to develop an organizational culture favoring quality. A chief executive officer at a hospital took such an approach. She embarked on a hospital-wide quality-improvement campaign. Her initial efforts were aimed at making hospital personnel more quality conscious. The steps she took included the following:

- Hospital personnel were required to wear clean and freshly pressed uniforms or other clothing.

- All artificial flowers were removed from the hospital; where budget permitted, they were replaced with fresh flowers.

- All frayed and worn magazines were removed from waiting rooms.

- All patients were greeted with a smile by hospital personnel and addressed by name whenever feasible.

Although management has primary responsibility for improving quality, many of the ideas are derived from employees. One way this occurs is for managers to solicit ideas from subordinates. Another source of employee input is ideas that employees voluntarily give to management. Input of this type is more likely to occur when the manager encourages freedom of expression.

Robust Quality (The Taguchi Method)

Because quality is the business buzzword of the 1980s and 1990s, formal methods of quality improvement have proliferated. One of the most widely used of these methods is the principle of robust quality, developed by Genichi Taguchi. **Robust quality** (or robust design) means that engineers must build quality into the design of a part or process so that it can withstand fluctuations on the production line without a loss of quality.[17] The principle of robust quality is said to transcend quality assurance methods that concentrate on keeping the production lines stable through constant monitoring. It is vastly superior to traditional quality control methods of inspection, rejection, and rework.

The philosophy behind the Taguchi method is similar to some of the ideas proposed by W. Edwards Deming, the quality pioneer. One of his key points for achieving quality is: "Cease dependence on mass inspection to achieve quality. Eliminate the need for inspection on a mass basis by building quality into the product in the first place."[18]

The **Taguchi method** is based on the concept that in any process you have a number of factors that can be combined in an almost infinite number of ways. Finding the best way to run the process by experimenting with all the possible combinations could take years. Robust quality provides statistical methods to define a specific sample that reveals the trends toward the best conditions for the process. As a result, engineers can specify an optimal process by running just a small number of experiments.

Bell Labs applied robust design to improve the reliability of a nine-variable operation on a semiconductor production line. The Bell Lab engineers needed only eighteen experiments to identify a set of conditions that resulted in one-third as many defects and doubled output. Applying the Taguchi method took only several weeks.[19]

 QUALITY CONTROL

Quality control involves determining the extent to which goods or services match some specified quality standard. There are two primary ways to control quality. One way is to inspect all units of output (100-percent inspection).

Another way is to inspect samples of the total output, such as checking every two-hundredth can of tuna fish produced. Similarly, a random sample can be used instead of inspecting every predetermined sample of the product.

When a sample is used for quality control, you must decide how many units to inspect. You must also decide what to inspect. One strategy is **acceptance inspection**, the checking of finished goods. To many consumers, this type of inspection makes the most sense. Consumers are concerned about receiving a fully functioning, finished product. Here are several examples of products that did not receive adequate acceptance inspection:[20]

- A well-known cassette recorder was prone to accidental erasures.

- Nine brands of travel-model hair dryers sucked in long, straight hair through their intake openings and entangled the hair around their fans.

- A key-copying machine sold to hundreds of retail outlets produces only about 90 percent usable keys. The other 10 percent of copied keys varies so much from an exact copy that they cannot be used as replacements.

Numerous products do receive adequate acceptance inspection. A sampling of high-quality, American-made products include Levi's jeans, Hobart mixers, Polk loudspeakers, Rockwell International modem board, the North Face geodesic dome tent, and the Parker Jotter ballpoint pen.[21]

Another strategy is **in-process inspection**, in which products are checked during production. If flaws are detected, changes can be made before the product is assembled. Tearing down finished products is expensive and may result in considerable scrap. It would be much better to catch pieces of fish tail in a batch of tuna meat before it is canned. A refinement of in-process inspection was developed by W. Edwards Demming. Referred to as **statistical process control (SPC)**, it is a technique for spotting defects at the point at which they are made rather than after a part or product is completed. SPC gauges the effectiveness of the manufacturing process by carefully monitoring changes in whatever is being produced. Potential problems are detected before they result in poor quality products. The reasons for the deviation are diagnosed, and the process is rectified to overcome the problems. Part of the turnaround of the Harley-Davidson Motor Co, Inc., has been attributed to the application of SPC.[22]

A third strategy is to combine both acceptance and in-process inspection. Goods and services of the highest quality generally receive both types of inspection.

The 100-Percent Inspection

Under the 100-percent inspection technique, all units are inspected. Those that do not meet quality standards are rejected. A 100-percent inspection is impossible when the process of inspection ruins the product. For instance, after a can of tuna is inspected, it cannot be sold. In contrast, visually inspecting a baseball bat does no harm to the bat.

A 100-percent inspection technique is necessary when the cost of poor quality is enormous. The cost could be measured in terms of money, human lives, or human suffering. Suffering or loss of life would result if there were defects in products such as contact lenses, automobile brakes, airplane controls, and heart pacemakers. The cost of lawsuits would be significant also.

Inspecting every unit is quite expensive when humans perform the inspection. Robots are now used in some forms of inspection. An even more recent development in a nonhuman quality-control device is a machine-vision system. It has a sensing device that can perform such tasks as checking a stream of metal parts going along a conveyor belt to make sure that holes bored in the part are the right size and to reject parts with holes too big or too small.

Even a 100-percent inspection technique will not catch every defective product. The inspection device—whether human or electronic—is not perfect. The person or machine may have quality problems too.

Inspection by Sampling

Statistical quality control is the process of checking parts or products by using a sampling technique. A small number of samples are drawn from the **lot,** or the total number of units. Characteristics of the lot are inferred from those of the sample. Assume that a lot of ten-thousand cans of tennis balls is being manufactured. A quality-control inspector selects twenty of these cans at random. If one of these cans lacks the required air pressure, the inspector could assume that 5 percent of the lot is defective. It would therefore be concluded that approximately five-hundred cans in the lot have unacceptably low pressure.

In practice, sampling is much more complicated than the example just given. The inspector would have to pick a representative sample and would specify the probability of making errors in prediction. Using a sampling technique is less expensive and time-consuming than inspecting every unit. The technique also has disadvantages.[23] There is a risk that a greater number of low-quality products will be purchased by consumers. In any sampling technique, some defective parts will go undetected. There is thus an increased probability that customer goodwill may decline. Some customers will receive the defective parts that went undetected. Any method of quality control requires that you determine what constitutes an acceptable number of defects or poor-quality products. The accompanying "Organization in Action" describes an inspection sampling procedure that has worked very well.

ORGANIZATION IN ACTION:

Pepsi Accepts the Quality Challenge

The Springfield, Missouri facility of Pepsi-Cola General Bottlers, Inc., has the most superior quality of two-hundred Pepsi bottlers in the country. Pepsi USA evaluates each bottler's quality by taking samples of cola from production facilities and from various stores within each franchise area. Those with the highest quality receive the Caleb Bradham Award, named after the person who invented Pepsi-Cola.

A particularly impressive accolade is the 100-percent rating the Springfield bottling plant received from Pepsi USA—the first 100 percent rating ever given. The rating means that when samples were taken at the production plant and at local retail outlets, Pepsi USA found no deviation from the standards. In this regard, a state of perfection, or zero defects, was achieved.

One of the major reasons for the success of the Springfield facility is its adherence to quality standards that exceed national standards. The company performs the same tests as all Pepsi bottlers, but more frequently and with more seriousness. If any production employee notices something suspicious, production is halted until management is satisfied that the problem has been corrected.

Inspection is an almost continuous process and adhered to strictly. If tests are necessary, they are conducted, no matter how much time the inspection takes. The production manager notes, "Most plants run tests on the production line every hour. We run them every fifteen minutes, all day long, on both shifts. We want to know instantly if anything goes wrong."

Source: As reported in D. Keith Denton, "Quality Is Pepsi's Challenge," *Personnel Journal* (June 1988): 143.

QUALITY CIRCLES

An important part of the quality movement in business and industry is the application of quality circles to improve both quality and productivity. A **quality circle (QC)** is a small group of employees that meet regularly to solve problems affecting their work area and to sometimes implement their solutions. The circle usually consists of eight to ten members and meets once a week for about one hour during normal working hours.

The QC concept was brought to Japan in 1950 by W. Edwards Deming, an American quality-control expert. QCs received widespread attention in the United States during the late 1970s and early 1980s, based on the belief that they were a major contributor to Japan's growth in productivity. In recent years, much of the enthusiasm for QCs has waned, but they are still widely used.

QC meetings are essentially well-structured group problem-solving sessions. Although they have elements in common with brainstorming, they have a formal structure and make use of statistics, graphs, and charts. Meetings take place in a conference room or other suitable space furnished with the supplies and equipment needed to discuss and perform analytical tasks. The steps involved in a typical QC are shown in Figure 14-5. Although QCs originally were developed in manufacturing settings, they are now also used in office and store settings. The balance of our discussion of QCs describes evidence about their effectiveness and the key elements of a successful program.

Figure 14-5   The Quality Circle Process

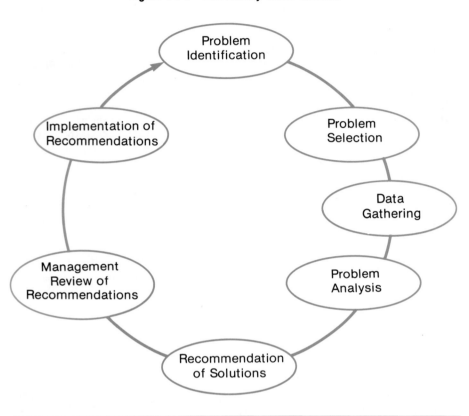

Evaluation of QC Effectiveness

QCs are used in at least seven-hundred U.S. firms. Many of these QC programs have been successful and therefore have endured; others have been unsuccessful and have been abandoned. One of the most comprehensive evaluations of QCs synthesized the results of studies in work settings. Fifteen of these studies showed uniformly positive results. The positive results were reported in terms of consequences both to individuals and to organizations. These consequences included higher job satisfaction, improved product quality, and increased productivity. Among the work settings included in the study were electronic-equipment makers, hospital employees, factory and shop employees; and nine manufacturing plants, in general, and Tektronix, Inc., Tenneco, Inc., the Department of Defense, and Martin Marietta Corp., in particular.

Eight of the thirty-two studies identified negative consequences (decreases in job satisfaction and productivity) to the individual and the organization.

One of these results was found at a division of Honeywell Inc., one, at a computer firm, one, among government employees; and five, at the Department of Defense. The researchers who synthesized the studies hypothesized that the organizational climate in the Department of Defense may not be appropriate for the conduct of QCs. Also, the QCs may not have been conducted long enough to obtain good results.[24]

A recent study, of seventy-three employees organized into eight QCs over a three-year period, indicates that positive results with QCs may not be long lasting. The purpose of the study was to assess the consequences of QCs to both individuals and organizations. Scores for individual consequences of job satisfaction, commitment to the organization, performance, and intentions to quit improved gradually for close to two years. After this time period, all the scores decreased back to their initial levels. During the same periods, management's perceptions of the effectiveness of the QC program followed the same pattern.[25] An optimistic interpretation of these results is that QCs are excellent short-range morale and productivity boosters.

Key Elements of Successful QC Programs

Whether a QC succeeds or fails depends heavily on the conditions under which it is implemented and on certain characteristics of the QC.[26] As with most management techniques, it is important to state explicitly the goals of the program, such as improving product quality, increasing productivity, or decreasing production costs. When good employee-management relations already exist, the QC is predisposed to success. One reason is that the employees are less likely to believe that management is using the QC merely to squeeze extra productivity from them.

It is important for QC leaders to use a participative style because the QC is a technique of participative management. The employees who volunteer for membership in the QC should be competent and interested in making an extra contribution, and they should receive ample training. A final consideration here is that QC members should receive some external rewards for outstanding suggestions. These external rewards can include recognition and money. Paying for suggestions, however, is controversial because it may create resentment among nonmembers of the QC.

DEVELOPING QUALITY AWARENESS

The strategic approach to managing for quality is to develop quality awareness on the part of every employee. As Robert Michna of Xerox Corp. states, "A really high-quality organization doesn't need a quality department. In the top-quality outfits, quality is everybody's job."[27] Most of the principles and techniques already mentioned in this chapter should make a contribution to quality awareness. Mentioned here are six additional ideas specifically aimed at enhancing quality awareness.

1. *Create a corporate culture of quality.* Improving quality may require an upheaval in corporate culture. Engineers, designers, marketers, administrators, production workers, and support staff all have to understand they are essential to bring about quality improvement.[28]

2. *Develop an organizational policy about quality.* Policies about quality stem directly from strategies about quality. Philip B. Crosby recommends that a policy about quality should include this statement: "We will deliver defect-free products and services to our customers and clients, on time."[29] It is important that the policy be clear enough to minimize misinterpretation.

3. *Communicate widely the concept of quality.* Key people in the organization should communicate information about quality at every appropriate opportunity. Specific communication vehicles include managers engaging in conversations about quality with group members at their workplaces, and top-level management giving speeches on the topic.

4. *Conduct five-minute quality updates.* According to Tom Peters, to keep quality awareness in the forefront of people's minds, begin meetings with a five-minute quality update. Also, every agenda item, no matter how indirectly related to quality, could begin with a brief discussion of the quality implications of the item.[30]

5. *Stress the importance of Kaizen.* Quality awareness can be regarded as a gradual process rather than a crash program. It therefore fits well the spirit of "Kaizen," a philosophy of continuing gradual improvement in one's personal and work life. Employees following the spirit of Kaizen will be constantly on the lookout for small improvements.[31]

6. *Emphasize meeting customer requirements.* To repeat, the essence of quality is satisfying customer needs. To be able to meet customer requirements, employees must first understand those requirements. Also, the requirements must be documented and reviewed regularly to plan for necessary changes and to avoid future misinterpretation.

SUMMARY OF KEY POINTS

Quality can be considered to be conformance to customer or user requirements. A high-quality product or service does what it is supposed to do. The requirements conformed to can be objective or subjective. All managerial functions, activities, and techniques should include quality awareness.

Six key dimensions of quality are aesthetics, performance, reliability, durability, serviceability, and features. Consumers are interested in how a product or service appears, how well it performs, how long it lasts, how easy it is to get serviced, and what are its features.

Quality is so important that it usually pays for itself. The monetary value of quality includes costs to the provider of the goods or service. It has been estimated that the total burden of quality problems are approximately one third of production costs.

Many factors contribute to producing high-quality goods and services. These include company policy about quality, proper design, good equipment, education of consumers about the proper use of the product or service, and service after delivery.

Key principles of managing for quality include the following: obtain top-level management's commitment to quality, focus on customer needs, prevent defects, strive for zero defects, use a quality-information system, control the manufacturing unit, and do not purchase parts and supplies by price alone.

Quality assurance is the prevention of quality problems. One aspect of quality assurance is collecting ideas for quality improvement. These ideas stem from the research-and-development (R&D) group, competitors, customers and clients, employees, and management. A recent development in quality assurance is robust quality, building quality into the design of a part or process so that it can withstand fluctuations on the production line without a loss of quality.

Quality control involves determining the extent to which goods or services match some specified quality standard. A 100-percent inspection involves checking every unit. Statistical quality control involves making inspections by using a sampling method. One type of inspection is called acceptance inspection, the checking of finished goods. Another strategy is in-process inspection, the checking of products during production. An important new refinement of this method is statistical process control (SPC), a technique for detecting potential problems before they result in poor-quality products. A third strategy combines both acceptance and in-process inspection.

Quality circles (QCs) are an important part of the quality movement. A QC is a small group of employees that meets regularly to solve problems affecting their work area and to sometimes implement their solutions. QCs have achieved positive and negative results, and some of the positive results may not be long-lasting. Positive results are more likely to occur under certain conditions such as top-level management's commitment to the program and participative leadership of the QC.

The strategic approach for managing quality is to develop quality awareness on the part of every employee. Specific approaches to developing quality awareness include the following: create a corporate culture of quality, develop the right policies, communicate about quality, conduct brief quality updates, emphasize Kaizen, and emphasize meeting customer requirements.

QUESTIONS

1. What quality defects have you spotted in a product lately? How might these defects have been prevented?
2. When you say a product is of high quality, what do you really mean?
3. How might a program of positive reinforcement be used to improve the quality of a product or service?

4. How does the problem of rudeness by sales associates (described in Chapter 13) fit into the idea of managing for quality?
5. Describe the difference between quality assurance and quality control.
6. Would you be willing to purchase a $600 stereo set that was inspected by a sampling technique? Why or why not?
7. How does pride in one's work relate to quality?
8. What is your opinion of the feasibility of achieving zero defects?
9. Give two examples of products and services for which consumers typically are ready to sacrifice quality for low price.
10. What can top-level management do to promote a culture favoring quality?

ACTIVITIES

1. Ask five people of different ages and occupations what the term *quality* means to them. What dimensions of quality are revealed by their answers?
2. Attempt to identify any service (nonmanufacturing) organization that has a formal quality-assurance or quality-control department. Be prepared to compare your findings with those of your classmates.

CASE PROBLEM 14-A: THE ZERO-DEFECTS DEBATE

Puritan Vacuum Cleaners has been in business for over fifty years. In addition to vacuum cleaners, the company also manufactures rug shampooers, vacuum-cleaner bags, and replacement parts for the cleaners and shampooers. Puritan has maintained a comfortable market share for many years. Recently, the company president, Warner Tasselman, has looked for ways to increase the company's share of market. His two-pronged effort involved increased attention to both marketing and quality improvement.

To aid in quality improvement, Tasselman appointed Heidi Gilmore as director of quality assurance. Gilmore had worked previously as the head of the quality-control department. Her responsibilities were expanded and she now reports directly to Tasselman. One of Gilmore's first initiatives was to begin a zero-defects program.

After she had been in her position for about one year, Gilmore received a telephone call from Matt Vinson, the marketing director. Vinson expressed a strong interest in getting together for lunch with her that week. Gilmore and Vinson agreed to meet at the Royal Palms.

"No drink for me," said Gilmore. "It's hard to push zero defects if I show up in the afternoon a little defective myself." Vinson laughed, and then responded. "Heidi, I'm glad you brought up the topic of zero defects first. It's just what I wanted to talk about."

"I take it you are beginning to see good sales results from zero defects," said Gilmore.

"I'm afraid the opposite is taking place. That's why I have to talk to you. My analysis is that the top-quality program you and Vincent are pushing may be hurting business."

"How could high-quality products be hurting business?" asked Gilmore.

"In some of the very ways I predicted before the program was implemented," responded Vinson angrily. "Of course, we in marketing want

Puritan to make a high-quality product, but the zero-defects program is pushing things too far.

"One major problem is that we now make such high-quality cleaners and shampooers that they are above average in price. Another problem is that it now takes longer to build these machines. We are having some shipping delays because of the amount of inspection we do."

"I still don't see that as a major problem," said Gilmore." In the long run, a high-quality product will generate more revenue."

"There's another problem. You folks in quality assurance don't understand the point of view of our Puritan retail centers. Our dealers want the customers to come back in with repairs. First of all, repairing machines is very profitable for our dealers. Besides that, when the customer is in the store, he or she may buy a new machine or rent a shampooer. Also, the customer might purchase vacuum-cleaner bags, belts, or shampoo for the rug cleaner.

"If customers never get back to the store for service, that's a lot of lost business for our dealers. We suffer too, because our dealers purchase most of their supplies from us."

"Matt, I think you're taking a short-range point of view. In the long range, high quality pays off for the company."

"Again, I'm not objecting to high quality. I just don't think we should go overboard. Maybe the two of us should sit down with Warner to talk about this problem some more."

Case Questions

1. How valid is Matt Vinson's view that high-quality vacuum cleaners, shampooers, repair services, and supplies may be hard to sell?
2. What do you think of the appropriateness of a zero-defect program for a vacuum-cleaner company?
3. Assume that Matt Vinson and Heidi Gilmore do meet with Warner Tasselman, the president. What point of view should Tasselman take?
4. To what extent do you think many marketing executives share Vinson's view that dealers may not really want top-quality products?

CASE PROBLEM 14-B: THE QC COMPLAINERS[32]

Kerry Industries formed a QC in its automatic bagging operations. The QC was formed because the level of machine bag failures was unacceptably high. Rebags and equipment failures were running at 20 percent and 10 percent, respectively. The goal set for the QC improvements were rebags at a 5 percent level in six months and equipment failures at 2 percent in three months.

Plant management moved quickly to give the QC the support it needed, including ample budgeting and hiring an outside consultant. The QC met ten hours in the first month, and five hours per month thereafter. After six months, the goal of 5 percent rebags was met. Equipment failures were reduced to 3 percent. QC members believed they could achieve the goal of 2 percent improvement within another month.

As the QC completed its first six months of operation, Diane Gonzalez, the QC leader, asked to speak with Chris Kantor, the plant manager. Four minutes into their meeting, Gonzalez said to Kantor: "Let me be candid. Our group has met with excellent success. We've made tremendous strides in overcoming the two key problems in the bagging operations. But I don't think the members are going to bring forth any more money-saving suggestions."

"Why not?" asked Kantor, "you've been doing beautifully so far."

"Because we're tired of being ripped off by management," said Gonzalez. "If one of you had submitted those great ideas to a suggestion system, he or she would have received approximately $4,000 in suggestion money. Because the suggestions have come out of the QC, all we will get is a recognition plaque to hang on the wall. None of us thinks that's very fair."

"Diane, I don't think you are taking this in the right spirit," said Kantor. "I will discuss your concerns with my staff and then get back to you soon."

Case Questions

1. What should Kantor do about the demands of the QC members for financial rewards for their efforts?
2. What should the company policy be about paying for the suggestions made through the suggestion system but not for those made through the QC?
3. What is your opinion about the ethics of how the QC members are behaving?

REFERENCES

1. Phillip B. Crosby, *Quality Without Tears: The Art of Hassle-Free Management* (New York: McGraw-Hill, 1984), 60; David A. Garvin, "Competing on the Eight Dimensions of Quality," *Harvard Business Review* (November–December 1987): 103.
2. William J. Stevenson, *Production/Operations Management*, 2d. ed. (Homewood, IL: Richard D. Irwin, Inc., 1986), 618; Garvin, "Eight Dimensions of Quality," 101–109.
3. Garvin, "Eight Dimensions of Quality," 103.
4. Phillip B. Crosby, *Quality Is Free* (New York: McGraw-Hill, 1979).
5. "Organizational Excellence: New American Goal," *BNAC Communicator* (Winter 1983): 6.
6. Otis Port, "The Push for Quality," *Business Week* (8 June 1987): 132.
7. Stevenson, *Production/Operations Management*, 620–622; James H. Donnelly, Jr., James L. Gibson, and John M. Ivancevich, *Fundamentals of Management*, 5th ed. (Plano, TX: Business Pubs., Inc., 1984), 552–553; Andre Nelson, "Who Really Controls Quality?" *Supervisory Management* (April 1986): 8–10.
8. Port, "Push for Quality," 135.
9. Stevenson, *Production/Operations Management*, 620.
10. These twelve principles are based on four sources: Crosby, *Quality Without Tears*, 59–96; Jack Reddy and Aber Berger, "Three Essentials of Product Quality," *Harvard Business Review* (July–August 1983): 153–159; David A. Garvin, "Quality on the Line," *Harvard Business Review* (September–October 1983): 65–75; John Guaspari, *Theory Why* (New York: AMACOM, 1986).
11. Garvin, "Eight Dimensions of Quality," 103; Guaspari, *Theory Why*, jacket.

12. Port, "Push for Quality," 132.

13. Garvin, "Quality on the Line," 65–75.

14. Clay Carr, "Injecting Quality Into Personnel Management," *Personnel Journal* (September 1987): 44.

15. Stevenson, *Production/Operations Management*, 622–624.

16. Stevenson, *Production/Operations Management*, 622.

17. Tom Barker, "Aussies Buy Taguchi Methods," *RIT News & Events* (20 August 1987): 3; Port, "Push for Quality," 142.

18. W. Edwards Deming, *Out of Crisis* (Cambridge, MA: MIT Press, 1986).

19. Port, "Push for Quality," 142–143.

20. The first two examples are from an advertising flyer for *Consumer Reports* (March 1985); the third example was researched by Shih-Jen Williams, 1988.

21. All but the Parker Jotter example are from "Some Things the U.S. Still Does Right," *Business Week* (8 June 1987): 133.

22. "Bulletins from the Quality Front," *Management Review* (February 1988): 8.

23. Donnelly, Gibson, and Ivancevich, *Fundamentals of Management*, 555.

24. Murray R. Barrick and Ralph A. Alexander, "A Review of Quality Circle Efficacy and the Existence of Positive-Finding Bias," *Personnel Psychology* (Autumn 1987): 579–592.

25. Ricky W. Griffin, "Consequences of Quality Circles in an Industrial Setting: A Longitudinal Assessment," *Academy of Management Journal* (June 1988): 338–358.

26. Sandy J. Wayne, Ricky W. Griffin, and Thomas S. Bateman, "Improving the Effectiveness of Quality Circles," *Personnel Administrator* (March 1986): 79–88.

27. Personal communication, June 1988.

28. Karen Pennar, "America's Quest Can't Be Half-Hearted," *Business Week* (8 June 1987): 136.

29. Crosby, *Quality Without Tears*, 101.

30. Thomas Peters, "Quality Starts with Zealous Supervisor," (syndicated column) 8 November 1987.

31. Scott DeGarmo, "Managing with Kaizen," *Success* (April 1987): 1; Massaki Imai, *Kaizen: The Key to Japan's Competitive Success* (New York: Random House, 1987).

32. The statistics in this case were researched by Roger H. Hinds, 1988.

PART SIX
Managing for Personal Effectiveness

Chapter 15
Managing Yourself

The final chapter of this text deals with a topic sometimes neglected in an introductory study of management—managing yourself. Effective career people are as concerned about managing their own resources as they are about managing organizational resources. Chapter 15 includes such topics as career planning, improving work habits and time management, and keeping job stress under control.

15
Managing Yourself

After studying the material in this chapter, you should be able to accomplish the following tasks:

1. Develop an overall strategy for managing yourself.
2. Understand and put into practice the basic elements of managing your career.
3. Establish a career plan and a career path.
4. Improve your chances of conducting an effective job search.
5. Implement a number of strategies, techniques, and methods for improving your personal productivity.

Key Terms and Phrases

Career	Mentor
Career plan	Networking
Career path	80/20 principle
Contingency plan	Job stress
Social maturity	Job burnout
Stress interview	Type E stress
Sponsor	Relaxation response

Most of this book is about the challenge of managing work and other people. To do this effectively, you must also manage yourself. To achieve organizational goals, managers need to achieve high levels of success in their own careers and extraordinary productivity in every aspect of their jobs. However, most managers who do a good job of managing people and work also do a good job of managing themselves.

Our discussion of self-management deals with three major aspects of work life: managing your career, increasing your personal productivity, and managing stress and burnout. As shown in Figure 15-1, these three components of self-management overlap, or are interrelated. Consider these three possibilities:

1. To do a good job of managing your career, it is important to maintain a high level of personal productivity and to keep stress and burnout under control.

Figure 15-1   Three Important Aspects of Managing Yourself

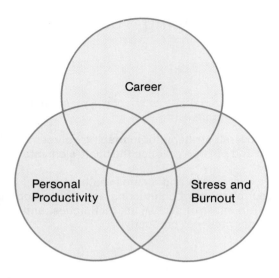

2. You are more likely to maintain a high level of personal productivity if you enjoy your career and keep stress and burnout under control.

3. Stress and burnout are easier to control when you enjoy your career, have good work habits, and manage time well (the two major aspects of personal productivity).

MANAGING YOUR CAREER

A **career** is a lifelong series of positions that form a relatively coherent pattern. An example of a career would be beginning employment as a sales associate in a retail store, moving up to department manager, and then eventually becoming a corporate executive for a large retailer. However, not every career has an upward growth pattern.[1] Some career people are more concerned about growth within their jobs than promotion. A person who does not have a career simply moves from one position to another or stagnates in a job, with no particular plan. Another distinguishing characteristic of a career is that it requires a seriousness of purpose.

Although many organizations assist employees to develop their careers, individuals still have the primary responsibility for managing their careers, particularly because their careers usually involve more than one employer. Sikula and McKenna offer this analysis:

Effective career management should no longer be viewed as the responsibility of the personnel department; rather, individuals now must assume authority and responsibility for their own careers as they chart out career paths on an interorganizational basis. What complicates this problem further is that only a few individuals are both technically prepared and willing to handle this new assignment.[2]

The major purpose of this section is to present information that will help you manage your own career. The discussion is organized into topics geared toward the perspective of people getting started in their careers: establishing a career path and a career plan; entry points into management careers; qualifications sought by employers; conducting a job campaign; and career advancement tactics and strategies.

Establishing a Career Plan and a Career Path

A vital part of managing your career is to establish both a career plan and a career path—two closely related approaches to career management. A **career plan** is an overall blueprint for achieving your career goals by specifying those goals and developing action plans to attain them. A **career path** is the sequence of jobs necessary to achieve personal and career goals. Setting a career path is this part of a career plan.

Is career planning really worthwhile? If upward mobility is restricted to people of certain backgrounds, career planning is a wasted exercise. A current study of 425 top business leaders paints an optimistic picture of career growth. The researchers concluded that "Success is not necessarily a function of cultural background, economic class, or influential contacts; it is the sum total of factors over which each individual has control by reasons of personal effort and ability."[3]

Steps in Career Planning.   A version of career planning developed by Archer provides a useful framework for managing one's career. Five steps are included in the plan.[4]

Step 1: Establish a Position Objective. The first set of career plans should state a position objective, or job goal, for four to five years in the future. If you are searching for a career objective and therefore cannot answer this question, you can evaluate your options. A review of your likes and dislikes in relation to past jobs and schooling may provide useful clues. For example, if you enjoy solving practical problems and having frequent contact with people, industrial sales might be a tentative position objective. Other ways of exploring position objectives include speaking to people experienced in occupations of potential interest; obtaining career information from libraries; obtaining career counseling and testing; and scanning the classified advertisements to look for jobs of potential interest.

Step 2: Describe the Position Content. Identify clearly the tasks carried out by a person who holds your goal position. The *Occupational Outlook Handbook* could prove useful.[5] Another tactic is to telephone a governmental agency or a large company in your area. Ask a representative of the human resource department to grant you an interview to review position descriptions of interest to you or to mail you a nonconfidential position description.

Step 3: Identify Needs for Personal Development. A candid self-assessment is required to specify what skills you need to learn to hold the work position you want. If you aspire to be a claims manager in an insurance company, you need to be able to describe an accident and deal with conflict. (The latter quality would be important in responding to insureds who believe the insurance company has underestimated their loss.)

Step 4: Set a Plan for Personal Development. Set a plan of action, including a timetable, for acquiring each needed skill you identified in step 3. Your development plan could include formal course work, specialized workshops, or coaching by a supervisor. For example, if you stated that you were too shy, you might attend a shyness workshop.

Step 5: Acquire the Necessary Credentials. These include both formal credentials, such as school, and informal credentials, such as good performance on a related task. Documenting the informal credentials is also important. One method of documentation is to prepare a personal portfolio that includes samples of important accomplishments, such as reducing costs for your employer.

Effective career planning is not a one-shot exercise. You will need to repeat these steps as your goals change or if your first plan proves to be unfeasible. Repeating the five career-planning steps also will be necessary if you choose to lay out a career path. As you attain each position on the career path, you usually will require a new plan.

Laying Out a Career Path.   The basics of a career path (in this case, for a manufacturing manager) are shown in Figure 15-2. Each rung on the ladder represents a position the individual would have to attain to reach his or her goal. Each step represents more formal authority and income.

An example of the career path of a specific manager is the route traveled by A. Barry Rand. In 1987, Rand was selected to head the U.S. marketing organization at Xerox Corp., making him one of the highest placed black men in corporate business. His career path from 1968 to date at Xerox is as follows: sales representative -- > sales manager -- > corporate director of major account marketing -- > vice president of field operations -- > corporate officer (while still retaining field operations position) -- > director of marketing.[6]

When you establish a career path, make provisions for possible deviations by making **contingency plans**. A contingency plan specifies what you might do if an unfavorable event takes place. In the current era, many middle-level managers must make contingency plans because many middle-management positions have been eliminated.[7] Two examples of contingency plans for the career path in Figure 15-2 are:

- If I am not considered promotable to first-level supervisor by the time I am twenty-six years old, I will join my in-laws in their family business.

Figure 15-2   Career Path for a Manufacturing Manager

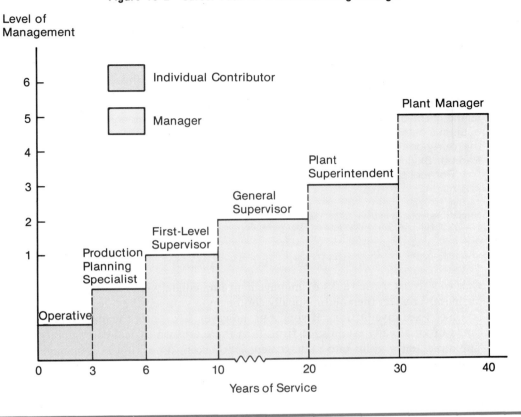

- If I am not promoted past general supervisor by the time I have fifteen years of experience, I will look for a job with a competitor.

A set of personal goals, with tentative time targets, can be superimposed on the career path shown in Figure 15-2. For instance, a person might include the following items on a career path:

- Nine years into my career, we will own our own triplex house.

- We will plan our family so that we have two children within the first four years of marriage.

- After thirty years of employment, we will have a retirement home in the Canadian Rockies.

An example of a frequently followed career path is described in the accompanying "Manager in Action." Many successful executives in fields such as publishing and banking have traveled this path.

MANAGER IN ACTION:

The Path from Secretary to Manager

When Teresa Bardwell completed her degree in English at Colorado State University in Fort Collins, Colorado, she faced the prospect having to earn an advanced degree or changing career paths. "My original plan in majoring in English was to enter library science. But I later realized that to get a job, I would need two master's degrees," she said.

Completing two degrees involved more time than Bardwell wanted to spend in the classroom. Instead, she became a secretary and enrolled in night business classes. Her eventual goal was to climb the corporate ladder. Today the thirty-one-year old Bardwell is a commercial banking officer at United Bank of Skyline in Denver.

"For me, being a secretary helped me make the contacts that I needed," she said.

Source: As reported in Mark Tatge, "More and More Secretaries Using the Job to Move Into Management," *LA Times-Washington Post News Service*, 20 April 1986.

Entry Points into Management

One way to enter the ranks of management immediately is to start your own business. You can then automatically confer upon yourself the title President, or Chief Executive Officer. If your aim, however, is to enter the management ranks of an already established firm, then there are two logical entry points. The direct entry point into management is to accept a position as a management trainee. The trainee is typically given an opportunity to work in several different departments briefly before being permanently assigned to one. In some cases, it is possible to be assigned the job title Supervisor or Manager upon being hired.

The indirect route into management is to join a firm as a technical specialist, and then later earn a promotion into management. Assuming that person is judged to be performing well and has displayed leadership qualities, a promotion into first-level management generally takes somewhere between one and six years. Among the dozens of individual-contributor positions open to business majors are purchasing agent, buyer, claims examiner, underwriter, inventory-control specialist, quality-control analyst, stock analyst, financial analyst, personnel assistant, and sales representative. Approximately one-half of entry-level jobs for business majors are in sales and marketing.

As illustrated in Figure 15-2, business graduates sometimes begin their careers as production workers to gain manufacturing experience. Often this experience is gained during summers and in part-time work before graduation. Whatever the entry point into management, it is important to understand what qualifications employers are seeking.

Qualifications Sought by Employers

The term *employer* encompasses many firms and many interviewers; all have their own perspectives, needs, stereotypes, and biases. Caution must therefore be exercised in placing too much faith in a general list of qualifications sought by all employers. The relevant issue usually is, "What qualifications are sought by one particular firm at this time?" Nonetheless, we can describe qualifications that a substantial number of employment interviewers and prospective bosses look for in job applicants.[8]

Appropriate Education.   Many jobs leading to a career in management offer substantial on-the-job training. Consequently, prospective employers often look for a broad education related to business rather than an intensive education in a subspeciality. Many other employers, however, do expect graduates to have specialized education and training. These employers want to hire people with special skills, such as statistical process control, so they can make an immediate contribution to productivity. In general, it is probably easier to find a job when you possess specific skills.

Good Communication Skills.   Employers look for solid communication skills in candidates, particularly for jobs involving people contact. Oral skills are judged during the employment interview. Your follow-up letter will provide an example of your written communication skills.

Good Interpersonal Skills.   The ability to get along with other people in a work setting is one of the most desirable qualities in a job candidate. Interpersonal skills are considered important because most jobs require interaction with people. Also, your willingness to accept individual differences and work with people you do not ordinarily choose to associate with is crucial in becoming a team player. Your interpersonal skills are often judged by how well you interact with the interviewer and, perhaps, with the receptionist.

Relevant Work Experience.   Work experience related to the job is helpful for two reasons: experienced applicants may require less training than inexperienced ones, and related job experience may reflect interest in the field. For example, any kind of sales experience is helpful in obtaining a professional-level sales job. It demonstrates to the prospective employer that you have the self-confidence to approach people and try to persuade them of the merits of your product or service. Many jobs in management, however, do not require comparable experience. Strength in several of the other qualifications described here can compensate for lack of relevant experience.

Good Problem-Solving Ability.   When hiring people for complex jobs, all employers seek people who have above-average intelligence. Indicators of intelligence used by employers include a candidate's grades, mental ability, test scores, ability to answer questions during the interview, and quality of outside interests. Many employers, however, prefer not to hire highly abstract thinkers for jobs in which they must deal with everyday problems.

Motivation and Enthusiasm.   High motivation and enthusiasm are important qualifications for virtually every job. The strength of a candidate's motivation often is inferred from the intensity with which he or she has pursued school, sports, and other interests. Having received a job promotion in the past also could be evidence of strong motivation. High grades are another potential indicator of strong motivation. As stated by an official from PPG Industries, Inc., ''Good grades indicate that the applicant is motivated and goal-oriented. The person who has earned high grades throughout college is particularly impressive.''[9]

Enthusiasm is usually inferred from the job candidate's comments and behavior during the interview. Enthusiastic candidates make many positive comments, express an interest in the company and the job, and research the company in preparation for the interview.

Adaptability.   A corporate recruitment manager observes that the work environment is typically fast-paced and technologically complex. It is constantly changing as new equipment, such as the FAX machine, invades the workplace. The newly hired employee must adapt to the work environment, juggle several assignments on a given workday, and be flexible in all aspects of work. The prospective employer therefore will want to know how well applicants can adapt as shown by their ability to deal with several situations simultaneously.[10] A student who attended school full-time, held a part-time job, and was an active parent would be considered adaptable.

Good Judgment and Common Sense.   Making decisions at any job level requires both technical skill and common sense. The recruiter or hiring manager will look for evidence that applicants have made practical decisions during their lives to show that they have common sense. For example, a person who earned part of her educational expenses by operating a word-processing service for student papers gives evidence of good judgment and common sense.

Social Maturity.   Closely related to judgment and common sense is **social maturity,** the ability to handle oneself properly in demanding situations. Indicators of immaturity during the interview include misplaced giggling, offensive jokes, profanity, crudeness, rudeness, and preoccupation with trivial topics.

Leadership Qualities.   Many entry-level positions for business graduates lead to managerial or staff positions that require leadership. Employers routinely look for evidence of some of the leadership qualities described in Chapter 9, such as initiative and good organizing ability. Previous work experience, and school, athletic, and religious activities can reflect leadership qualities. For example, a job candidate might have worked as a restaurant manager and a class president.

Evaluate yourself against the qualifications we have discussed. If you believe you are below standard in one or more of these areas, try to remedy the deficiency. For instance, if you have not made many practical decisions, seek out opportunities to do so in job, family, or community situations.

Conducting the Job Campaign

Any placement office, bookstore, or general library has ample information available on finding a job. We will summarize three parts of the job campaign: sources of job leads, the resume and cover letter, and conducting yourself well in a job interview.

Sources of Job Leads.   An important strategy for finding a job suited to your needs is to use multiple approaches. Many people who complain of poor luck in finding a job have relied on only one or two sources of job leads. Seven major sources of job leads are available to the job seeker.

Personal Contacts (Networking).   Employment professionals estimate that about 85 percent of jobs are filled through referrals from insiders. Therefore, the best way to find a position is to inform as many people as possible that you are looking for a job. It is also helpful to specify the type of job you are seeking. Persons in your network might include relatives, friends, acquaintances, acquaintances of acquaintances, former employers, and members of professional societies. The accompanying ''Job Seeker in Action'' illustrates a creative method of networking.

JOB SEEKER IN ACTION:

Bob Multiplies His Contacts

Bob's spouse had been transferred to another city. He only knew two people there, but he quickly scheduled appointments to meet with them. He told them the type of job he was seeking and what he thought he had to offer an employer. Next, he asked them for several names of the other people in town with whom he might have something in common. Each of the two people gave him three additional names. When visiting these six people, he requested still more names. Instead of exhausting all his leads early in the job-hunting process, the more people he visited, the more names he added to his network.

Eventually, by looking for leads and not for a job, Bob learned of an opening through a friend of a friend; he was interviewed and landed the job.

Source: As reported in Karen O. Dowd, ''Creative Job Search Strategies,'' *Business Week Careers How to Get a Job Guide* (1988 edition): 27–28.

School Placement Office.   Any thorough job search conducted by a student would include visiting the school placement office. As with any source of job leads, not all those given by the placement office prove to be promising. Employers sometimes register with the placement office even if they have few jobs available, or they may be searching for specific job skills possessed by a small proportion of graduates. Companies justify these listings as an attempt to maintain goodwill even during periods of low hiring.

Private and Public Employment Agencies. Newcomers to the job market may not find private agencies or those run by the government to be a valuable source of job leads. Agencies tend to be more valuable for applicants with several years of experience. A concern sometimes expressed about agencies is that they encourage the job seeker to take whatever position is available in order to collect their fee. Applicants are therefore sometimes encouraged to accept positions below their skill level and salary expectations. Despite these reservations, agencies are a legitimate source of jobs leads. Typically the employer pays the fee, or the job seeker pays the fee only after being hired.

Unsolicited Contacts. Another way of developing job leads is to write letters to officials of organizations for which you would like to work. The names of managers and their companies can be obtained from trade directories such as *Standard & Poors Register* or *Dun and Bradstreet*, both of which are available at most large libraries.[11] Also consult the annual issue of *Business Week Careers* that provides information about the one-thousand companies that hire the most college graduates.[12] Chamber of Commerce listings are also valid sources of unsolicited contacts. The success rate of these unsolicited direct contacts is about one in two-hundred for managerial positions—but finding a good job is well worth the effort.

Classified Advertisements. "Help Wanted" advertisements in local and national newspapers, as well as in trade magazines, should not be ignored. Many people do find the job they want through this source. Classified advertisements can be a disappointment, however. They generally list jobs that are hard to fill for reasons such as below-average wages. When attractive-sounding jobs are offered, the employer is flooded with resumes and applications.

Faculty and Administrators. Job seekers enrolled in school should not overlook a special category of personal contacts—faculty and administrators. These people frequently have contact with managers and employment specialists in local firms, and they may be able to personally recommend you for consideration as a prospective employee. Because faculty members and administrators represent the school, they usually prefer to endorse only those students they know to be of high caliber.

Internships and Work Study Programs. Working for an organization as part of a program of study can be an excellent path to full-time employment after graduation. Assuming the employer was impressed with your work, you would be given top consideration for a permanent position. A college relations representative at Adolph Coors Co. puts it this way: "We are constantly seeking people with practical experience. Interns and cooperative education students are a valuable resource for us."[13]

The Resume and Cover Letter. It is difficult to conduct an effective job campaign without a resume and an accompanying cover letter. Your resume should be patterned after one of the models readily available at your school placement office or in a standard source of information about job finding search.[14] Figure 15-3 presents the Chrysler-Plymouth resume input form that you can use as a resume format and worksheet.

Your resume must attract enough attention for an employer to invite you for an interview. Effective resumes are straightforward, factual presentations of a person's experiences and accomplishments. They are neither over-detailed nor too sketchy. For a recent graduate with limited work experience, a one-page resume may be acceptable. For more experienced people, one page would seem too short.

The most useful resumes contain both biographical information, such as education and work experience, and a list of accomplishments and skills. Accomplishments could include anything of merit done in a work setting, such as "reduced customer complaints 27 percent in one year," or "increased membership in our hang-gliding club from six to twenty-seven people in ten months." Skills could include such things as "proficient at spreadsheet analysis," "able to write hard-hitting sales promotion letters," or "can relate well to production workers."

Resume Mistakes to Avoid. You should avoid the following common mistakes when preparing your resume.[15] A frequent mistake is a poorly typed or word-processed resume, including leaving excessive space between words in order to achieve line justification. Excessive length stemming from including extraneous information (such as listing the product line of General Foods Corp.) is another common error. It is essential to avoid misspellings, input errors, errors corrected by pen, poor grammar, and frequent abbreviations.

Avoid disorganization, such as placing the same type of information under different headings. Watch out for skimpy or insufficient information, such as not specifying job title or address of employer. Many resume writers neglect to list accomplishments or skills, thus not giving clues to their capabilities.

Another mistake is starting sentences with phrases such as "I did," "I was," or "I am," instead of action verbs such as *initiated, adapted, created,* and *coordinated.* Avoid placing so much emphasis on designing a nontraditional resume that you omit basic facts (for example, work experience and addresses of schools attended). If the company official cannot verify facts or assess qualifications, he or she will discard the resume.

Finally, avoid inflating facts about yourself that will prove to be untrue when references are checked. This type of resume error usually leads to immediate disqualification. If the false information is discovered after you are hired, you are liable for dismissal and you have also jeopardized future employment.

Cover Letter. You can use the same resume to apply for a wide range of jobs, except that the job objective section may have to be changed for some positions. The cover letter accompanying the resume, however, should be specific to the position. It explains why you are applying for this particular job, and it

Figure 15-3 Chrysler-Plymouth Resume Input Form

Chrysler-Plymouth Resume Input Form

Be as neat as possible when filling this out.
Check all spelling and punctuation. Use another sheet of paper if necessary.
Remember, this is merely a suggested format, use it as a guide in creating your own resume!

Chrysler Plymouth

Name: ______________________

Home Address:
Street: ______________________
City: ______________________
State: ______________ Zip: ________
Phone: ( ) ______________________

School Address: (if you currently reside there)
School: ______________________
Street: ______________________
City: ______________________
State: ______________ Zip: ________
Phone: ( ) ______________________

JOB OBJECTIVE:

(Your work direction—not a necessity, but helpful if you can target enough to define)

EDUCATION:

DATE ATTENDED	SCHOOL	DEGREE or CERTIFICATE	SUBJECT AREA

CAPABILITIES:

(Describe what you can do here—use action words)

ACCOMPLISHMENTS:

(Things you've accomplished that are related to your target)

WORK EXPERIENCE:

PERIOD EMPLOYED	ACTIVITY AND EMPLOYER	TITLE

ACTIVITIES AND INTERESTS:

List and describe relevant activities and interests, include dates when appropriate)

Source: Reprinted with permission of The Chrysler Corporation

briefly summarizes your background and qualifications. Darlene C. Pibal says
the cover letter should address the following questions.[16]

1.   Why is the applicant writing?

2.   What would the applicant bring to the company as an employee?

3.   Why is the applicant looking for a job?

4.   What response does the applicant expect to obtain?

   Because employers receive so many inquiries about attractive job openings,
it may prove beneficial to begin the cover letter with an attention-getting statement of this type: "Is Journey's End looking for a management trainee who
believes so strongly in your motel concept that he has already stayed in your
motels fifteen times? If so, take my application seriously."

Handling Yourself in a Job Interview.   A successful job search almost always
requires at least one interview. Common sense provides a guide on how to conduct yourself. For example, we all know how to dress neatly, show up for the
interview on time, and smile frequently. In addition, here are five key suggestions for performing well in a job interview.

Research the Organization.   In advance of the interview, search for relevant
information about the prospective employer. Useful sources include annual
reports, magazine articles about the firm, and company brochures. It is very
helpful to speak to present or former employees and to customers or clients of
the organization. When you research the firm, look for a natural link between
you and the firm that can be used to establish rapport during the interview. A
successful applicant for a position with the Federal Bureau of Investigation
made this comment during the interview: "One of the reasons I'm applying to
the FBI is that a neighbor of mine is an FBI agent. He told me it's a high-
spirited unit of the government, and that you're always kept on your toes."

Rehearse Answers to Likely Questions.   Both managers and professional interviewers tend to ask similar questions. A list of these questions is shown in
Table 15-1. It is worth rehearsing, but not necessarily memorizing, answers to
these questions. Of particular note, almost every interview conducted by an
employment specialist will include at least one question about your
weaknesses, limitations, or needs for improvement. Although no one should lie
during an employment interview, it may prove helpful to describe job-related
weaknesses that could be converted into strengths. For example, "I get so involved in my work that I've been told I don't spend enough time socializing
with my co-workers." Or, "I'm too impatient with goldbrickers."

Table 15-1   Typical Interview Questions

1. What special preparation do you have that relates to the qualifications required for this position?
2. Tell me about your current and previous employers.
3. What would be an ideal job for you?
4. What is your greatest strength? Your greatest weakness?
5. What are your career goals?
6. What have you learned from your mistakes?
7. What have you done that shows initiative?
8. What do you know about our company?
9. What can you do for our company?
10. Why do you want to leave your present job?
11. What difficulties have you had in your relations with co-workers at any previous place of employment?
12. How effective are you in working with other people?
13. How do you spend your leisure time?

Source: Most of the questions are adapted from Darlene C. Pibal, "How to Apply for the Job and Get It," *The Balance Sheet* (March–April 1984): 15; questions 3 and 4 are from James E. Challenger, "10 Tough Interview Questions," *Business Week Careers* (April–May 1988): 24–26.

Ask Perceptive Questions.   An experienced interviewer will expect the applicant to show initiative in asking perceptive questions about the job and the organization. It is generally helpful to ask about important matters such as the nature of the work, the goals of the firm, or the organization structure of the unit. Here are samples of questions that should be well received in a job interview.

- What would you expect an outstanding performer to accomplish on this job?

- If I were successful on the job, what others jobs would I be eligible for in your firm?

In addition to asking perceptive questions, avoid asking imperceptive questions such as: "How many holidays will I get?" "How many sick days?" "At what age can an employee retire from your firm?" You can ask about benefits when you receive a job offer, and answers to these types of questions are usually found in a company handbook.

Take a Stress Interview in Stride.   A **stress interview** is a deliberate method of placing a job applicant under pressure and then observing his or her reaction. The purpose of the stress interview is to see how well the applicant handles pressure. It is difficult not to become defensive, distraught, or angry when the interviewer does such things as the following:

- Sits across from you and says nothing, waiting for you to begin talking about yourself.

- Says, "I have the impression that others see you as kind of an airhead."

The best way to handle a stress interview is to try to relax, perhaps by exhaling or saying to yourself, "I won't let this get to me." Remember, there is really no one best answer to any of these upsetting questions and comments. Sandra Davis also recommends that you keep in mind anecdotes to illustrate your strengths.[17] In this way, if an interviewer tries to create stress for you by challenging your positive points, you can back up what you say.

Write a Follow-Up Letter.   The job-campaign cycle is not complete until the applicant writes a follow-up letter to the interviewer. A brief thank-you note is due, saying that you appreciate the time the interviewer spent with you. Include a statement of your current thinking about the position. You should specify whether you (1) hope to receive a job offer, (2) have decided to accept another offer, or (3) are looking forward to learning the outcome of the interview. Even if you do not wish to join the firm, it is important to write. In this dynamic work society, you never know whether you will apply to the same company again in the future.

Tactics and Strategies for Career Advancement

Once the job applicant becomes an employee, it is time to use tactics and strategies for advancing one's career. The career planning process described earlier is the bedrock for career advancement. The tactics and strategies described here are designed to supplement career planning.

Develop Expertise.   The logical way to launch a career and gain power for yourself is to become highly knowledgeable in a relevant job skill. This tactic is obvious if you are working in a specialist job, such as a production planner or an employee trainer. It is also important for managers. For example, it helps your status as a manager if you become a good planner, memorandum writer, budget preparer, or expert at helping other managers learn how to make good use of the computer.

Display Good Job Performance.   In any organizational promotion plan based on merit, above-average job performance is required in your present job before you can advance. All other tactics and strategies are supplements to being competent. Organizations often tolerate the idiosyncrasies of an extremely competent person, whereas they condemn the same behavior in an average performer. As one executive said, "We tolerate arrogant people around here, as long as they are very talented." In addition to displaying good job performance, it is wise to obtain written documentation of your achievements. Such reports are useful when your credentials are being reviewed for possible promotion.

Be Honest about How Much Responsibility You Want.   A career person can save a lot of needless frustration by admitting early how much responsibility he or she really wants. Many people would not aspire to become executives if they were familiar with the lifestyles of these managers. A study of chief executive officers in sixty large corporations revealed that nearly 60 percent had not taken a vacation in the past three years. "Those who tried [vacations] didn't enjoy them much; they carried with them the same psychological baggage they have year around and used the vacation as time to catch up on work, often bringing along briefcases and even calling the office every few hours."[18]

Be Visible.   To get ahead in your career, it helps immensely to bring favorable attention to yourself and your accomplishments. Ways of gaining visibility include performing well on committee assignments, performing well in company recreational activities (such as winning a racquet-ball tournament), getting an article published in a trade magazine, getting your name in the firm's newspaper, or distinguishing yourself in community activity.

Find a Sponsor.   One of the key positive consequences of being visible is that it brings you to the attention of higher-up managers who can assist you in your career. A **sponsor** is any high-ranking person in the organization who recommends you for promotion and other choice assignments. Your sponsor might be a relative by blood or marriage.

Find a Mentor.   Being visible may also help one find a **mentor**—a superior who takes a personal interest in a subordinate, and guides, teaches, and coaches that person. An emotional tie usually develops between the mentor and the protege. Effective mentors are said to perform these functions for their proteges: providing resources, supplying information, showing an interest in the apprentice's work, being a role model, setting high standards, building the apprentice's confidence, coaching him or her, and protecting the apprentice when the latter makes poor decisions.[19]
People can have several sponsors and mentors during their careers. However, being too closely identified with one sponsor or mentor may backfire; if the person loses a power struggle, you may be demoted or even lose your job.

Do What You Do Best.   One of the best pathways to success is to identify your strongest talents and build your career around them. Achieving high levels of responsibility and income usually result. Talents around which you could build a career include unusually good ability to sell, solve problems, or motivate and influence others.

Identify Growth Fields and Growth Companies.   Seek positions that offer posibilities for growth. This means seeking growth industries or growth firms or migrating to a part of the country where job opportunities are plentiful. Information about growth opportunities can be found in government publications (such as the *Occupational Outlook Handbook*[20]), business magazines, and local and national newspapers. A representative list of predicted growth fields for the 1990s is shown in Table 15-2.

Find an Organization that Matches Your Personality.   If there is a good fit with the organizational culture and your personality, you are more likely to function at a high level. It is also important to find a firm in which the predominant approach to managing employees suits you. Some people feel most comfortable in a firm that encourages risk taking, creativity, and informality. Others feel more comfortable in a firm that emphasizes caution and formality.

Table 15-2   Predicted Business Growth Fields for the 1990s

General Field	Entry-Level Positions
Health-Care Management	Health administrator Budget analyst Records supervisor Supervisor, Geriatric technicians
Computers and Information Systems	Systems analyst Programmer
Telecommunications	Telecommunications marketing assistant Systems analyst
Finance	Accountant Auditor Broker trainee
Marketing	Sales representative Sales trainee, Telemarketer
Human-Resource Management	Human-resource specialist Job analyst Trainer
International Business	Administrative assistant Assistant manager
Travel (hotel, motel, and resort business)	Travel agent, Assistant manager

Source: Based on information from John Stodden, "Ten Best Careers for the '90s," *Business Week Careers How to Get a Job Guide* (1988 edition): 4–6; John Naisbitt, "Careers of the Future," *Success* (January–February 1987): 12.

Develop a Network of Contacts.   Networking is as important for getting ahead as is finding a job. Most successful people have established a large number of personal contacts who help them in such ways as recommending them for promotions, purchasing their goods and services (if they are in sales), recommending competent employees to work for them, and giving them technical advice when needed. Networking is based on the idea that you earn the trust of a number of people who know you personally.

To develop networking relationships, you must be willing to get involved and to participate in formal and informal activities.[21] Volunteer ideas and services that are helpful to your co-workers. Some people even develop contacts for their network while traveling or engaged in recreational activities.

Achieve Broad Experience.   You can strenghten your qualifications for advancement by broadening your experience. Broadening can come about by performing a variety of jobs within the same firm or by switching firms. At one time it was believed that job hopping (moving from firm to firm) led to more rapid advancement than being loyal to one employer. Evidence collected during the last decade, however, indicates that people who stay with one firm receive more promotions and higher pay in the long range.[22]

Look Successful.   "To ensure complete success on the job, you will need to pay as much attention to the various elements of style that make up your image as you will to your next report presentation."[23] Although this advice may be exaggerated, a basic career-advancement tactic is to project a successful image. Your clothing, speech, desk and work space, attache case or handbag, and car should project the image of a successful, but not artificial or affected, person. Physical fitness also is part of a success image. One difficulty in implementing this tactic is that what constitutes a "success image" involves some subjective interpretation. For instance, a number of top executives drive pickup trucks or battered station wagons to the office.

Develop a Good Relationship with Your Boss.   A key career-advancement tactic is to develop a positive relationship with your boss. This is essential for receiving favorable performance reviews, good salary increases, and promotions. Furthermore, not being liked by someone in authority has been identified as the single, most important reason why people are discharged.[24] Be supportive and loyal, and perform your job well. A subordinate who performs well makes the boss look good. To perform well, you may have to clarify what the boss considers to be good job performance. In some organizations, it is standard practice for each supervisor to clarify his or her expectations; however, you may have to ask.

Consider the Possibilities of Moonlighting.   Ideally, you should concentrate all your professional energy into your present job and self-improvement. Approximately 5 percent of the work force, however, also engages in other employment (moonlights). The reasons for moonlighting include meeting regular expenses, meeting additional expenses, enjoying the job, and gaining valuable experience.[25] A second job might also provide you with a new forward thrust to your career. For example, many people who begin selling real estate part time later become full-time realtors. It is important to recognize that moonlighting can retard one's career when management disapproves of such activity. (See the comprehensive case, "The Management-Minded Landlords" in the appendix to this book.)

We have looked at managing yourself from the standpoint of managing your career. In the next major section, we describe tactics for improving your personal productivity.

INCREASING YOUR PERSONAL PRODUCTIVITY

Productive people are efficient and effective. Efficiency refers to doing things right (not wasting resources); effectiveness refers to doing the right things (working on matters of consequence). Increased personal productivity leads to positive outcomes on the job such as higher income, more responsibility, and recognition. It also allows you to devote more worry-free time to your personal life. If you have things under control on the job, you can enjoy your leisure time. Finally, being productive helps reduce the stress you incur when your job is out of control. Our discussion of increasing personal productivity focuses on two related topics: improving work habits and time management and reducing procrastination.

Improving Work Habits and Time Management

A direct method of improving personal productivity is to improve your work habits and management of time. Work habits and time management overlap: if you have good work habits, you manage time well; if you manage time well, you have good work habits. These techniques can be helpful to a student who wishes to increase productivity. Here we will summarize some of the best-accepted principles of maintaining good work habits and developing time-management practices. The accompanying "Manager in Action" illustrates the importance successful business people attach to this topic.

MANAGER IN ACTION:

The Well-Organized Designer

Most days, designer Bill Blass has his work cut out for him: keeping track of a fashion empire that includes thirty-five domestic and seventy overseas manufacturing licensees. "I do about a half-dozen things at one time," says Blass in his New York office. "I thrive on a half-chaotic background while I'm working." He offers these tips on work habits and time management:

Figure out peak performance hours. A "morning person," he's at work by 8:30 A.M.

Schedule more work than you may complete. "The busier you are, the more you'll get done. In the morning I usually have an appointment every half hour. But my official day stops at lunchtime. I'm creative in the afternoon—designing, fitting, sketching, making notes."

Source: Adapted from Esther Shapiro, "Get Organized in '87," *USA Weekend* (26–28 December 1986): 13.

Clean Up Your Work Area and Sort Out Your Tasks.   To get started improving personal productivity, clean up your work area and sort out what tasks you need to accomplish. This is also an excellent technique to initiate a campaign of improving your grades if you are a student. People sometimes become inefficient because their work area is messy; they waste time looking for things and neglect important papers.

Schedule Planning Time Each Day.   To keep yourself on top of your job, and to set priorities, it is crucial to set aside at least five minutes each day for planning. No excuses allowed; every successful person spends some time thinking ahead about what he or she is doing or should be doing.

Prepare a List and Assign Priorities.   A "to do" list lies at the heart of every time-management system. In addition to writing down tasks you need to do, assign to them priorities. A simple categorization such as top priority versus low priority works well for most people. In general, top-priority items should be taken care of before low-priority ones. There are so many things to do on any job that some very-low-priority items will never get done.

Taking care of a small, easy-to-do item—such as getting a ballpoint pen refilled—has a hidden value. It tends to be relaxing because it gives you the psychological lift of having crossed at least one item off your list. A representative "to do" list for a manager is shown in Figure 15-4. This particular manager sorts priorities according to when they need doing: today, this week, or this month.

Work at a Steady Pace.   Although a dramatic show of energy (such as in "pulling an all-nighter") is impressive, the steady worker tends to be more productive in the long run. The spurt worker creates many problems for management; the spurt student is in turmoil at examination time or when papers are due. Managers and individual contributors who expend the same amount of effort day-by-day tend to stay in control of their jobs. When a sudden problem or a good opportunity comes to their attention, they can fit it into their schedule.

Avoid Perfectionism.   It helps the organization when each worker is interested in quality, but compulsive striving for unrealistic goals can impair creativity, cause tension between the perfectionist and others, and waste valuable time.[26] There is a point of diminishing returns on invested time in any

Figure 15-4   A Sample ''To Do'' List

From the Desk of Gabe Jackson

December 7

Today
Order telephone answering machine
Get rattling sound in disk drive checked
See Gloria about her transfer request
Set up an appointment with finance V.P. (budget)

This week
Speak to personnel dept. about hiring a new sup.
Make first estimate of department budget
Begin department strategic plan for next year
Talk to Jerry about his drinking problem

This Month
Visit St. Paul plant about inventory problem
Enroll in company Mgt. development prog.
Lunch with Operations manager to discuss
shipping delays.

PMC   **Precision Manufacturing Corporation
Houston, Texas**

activity. A case in point would be a bank branch manager who insists that each teller's draw be balanced out to within one dollar at the end of each work day. The tellers would have to spend so much time counting and recounting each customer's cash transaction that service would suffer markedly. In turn, the manager's branch would have below-average productivity.

Set Deadlines for Yourself and Others.   Deadlines help people manage time better. In addition, deadlines create the type of pressure many people need to accomplish their work. For example, when an instructor assigns a paper without a deadline, many students demand that one be clearly stated. Relatively few people are effective at setting their own deadlines. To be highly productive, however, you must set them regularly. Notice that Gabe Jackson, the manager mentioned in Figure 15-4, used deadlines for organizing his work.

Delegate Routine Tasks.   A major strategy for managing a heavy work load is to delegate to others as many routine tasks as is feasible. It is also desirable to delegate some nonroutine projects so that you can devote time to highly significant matters. If you are a manager, people are paid to accept your delegated tasks. If you are an individual contributor, you probably have to rely on administrative support staff to accept your delegated chores. Tasks that might be delegated to support staff include proofreading of memorandums, checking on computations, photocopying reports, and investigating customer complaints.

Get Sufficient Rest and Relaxation.   A highly productive manager tackles important tasks in a refreshed and relaxed state. Your work week must be long enough to allow you to achieve your personal and organizational objectives, yet short enough to allow you some leisure time. How you use your leisure time is also significant. Reading company reports while on vacation, for example, may not give you a recharged feeling when you return to work.

Concentrate on One Task at a Time.   Productive managers have a well-developed capacity to concentrate on the problem facing them at the moment, however surrounded they are with other obligations. Intense concentration leads to sharper judgment and analysis and also decreases the chances of making major bloopers. Another useful by-product of concentration is that it helps reduce absentmindedness. The person who concentrates on the task at hand has less chance of forgetting what he or she intended to do.

Concentrate on High-Output Tasks.   To become more productive on the job or in school, concentrate on tasks in which superior performance could have a large payoff. A high-output managerial task would be to develop a strategic plan for the department; a high-output student task would be to think of a creative idea for an independent study project. Looking for high-output items for your work effort is analogous to looking for a good return on investment for your money.[27]

Concentrating on high-output tasks is an application of the **80/20 principle**: 80 percent of the results in a given field are derived from 20 percent of the activity. Thus, 20 percent of a firm's customers yield 80 percent of the sales, and 20 percent of a manager's job produces 80 percent of the important results. A manager's high-output 20 percent often is concerned with planning or talking directly to subordinates about their work problems.

Stay in Control of Paperwork.   No organization today can accomplish its mission unless paperwork is given appropriate attention. If you handle paperwork improperly, your job may get out of control. Once your job is out of control, it may lead to heavy stress. Invest a small amount of time in paperwork every day. The best time to take care of routine paperwork is when you are at less than your peak of efficiency but are not overfatigued. Reserve your high-energy periods for high-output tasks.

Avoid becoming a paper shuffler. The ideal is to handle a piece of paper only once. When you pick up a piece of paper, take some action: throw it away, route it to someone else, write a short response to the sender, or put it in your briefcase. The next time someone makes you wait for an appointment or the start of a meeting, work on the papers in your briefcase. Of course, some memorandums are so important, or require so much work, that you must put them aside for later action. For instance, if your boss asks you to develop recommendations for improving department productivity, you will have to do more than file the request.

Schedule Yourself by Computer.   Software enables people to use a personal computer as an electronic calendar to help keep track of appointments and maintain "to do" lists. To implement these programs, you enter your appointments, tasks, and errands into the computer. Gabe Jackson's list in Figure 15-4 could provide the following input:

7 December	Order telephone answering machine.
	Set up appointment with VP of finance about budget.
10 December	Make first estimate of department budget.
	Begin department strategic plan for next year.
20 December	Visit St. Paul plant about inventory-shrinkage problem.
	Enroll in company management-development program.

Suppose Gabe could not remember when he was due to make his first estimate of the department budget. He could command the computer to find date of budget estimate. Another use of this type of software is to flag key appointments and tasks. An indicator such as "URGENT" might be used.

Reducing Procrastination

Procrastination is the number-one time waster for most people. Reducing procrastination therefore pays substantial dividends in increased productivity. Before describing remedial tactics, we will review the leading reasons why people procrastinate.[28]

First, some people fear failure or other negative consequences. As long as a person delays doing something of significance, he or she cannot be regarded as having performed poorly on the project. Other negative consequences include looking foolish in the eyes of others or developing a bad reputation. For instance, if a manager delays making a presentation, nobody will know how ineffective he or she is at giving oral presentations. Second, some people fear success. People sometimes believe unconsciously that, if they succeed at an important task, they will be asked to take on more responsibility in the future—which they dread. Similarly, success can raise others' expectations of you, demanding repeat performances in the future.

Third, some people fear being controlled. If the procrastinator does not do things on time, he or she has successfully rebelled against being controlled by another person's time schedule. Fourth, a large task may be overwhelming. People delay getting started because the job seems unmanageable. Fifth, people sometimes are assigned tasks they perceive to be useless and needless, such as rechecking someone else's work. Rather than proceed with the trivial task, the person rebels by procrastinating.

Break the Task Down into Smaller Units.   By splitting the larger task down into smaller units, you can make the job appear less overwhelming. Subdividing the task is referred to as the "Swiss-cheese method," because you keep biting little holes into the bigger tasks. This approach is useful, of course, only if the task can be done in small pieces.

Make a Commitment to Others.   Your tendency to procrastinate on an important assignment may be reduced if you publicly state that you will get the job done by a certain time. For example, a manager might say at a staff meeting, "Count on me to have those five office temporaries hired by this Friday." The manager might then feel embarrassed if the temporaries are not hired by Friday.

Reward Yourself for Any Progress.   A potent technique for overcoming any counterproductive behavior pattern is to give yourself a reward for progress toward overcoming the problem. If you did hire the office temporaries without procrastinating, you might buy yourself something special. The reward should be commensurate with the magnitude of the accomplishment.

Do the Trivial Task Immediately.   An individual may think an assigned task is trivial, whereas the organization has an opposite view. It is best to proceed with the task, get it done, and give it no further thought. It is self-defeating to refuse to do an assigned task because you think it trivial.

Calculate the Cost of Procrastination.   You can sometimes reduce the extent of your procrastination by calculating its cost.[29] One example is that you might lose out on obtaining a high-paying job you really want by not having your resume and cover letter ready on time. Your cost of procrastination would include the difference in the salary between the job you do find and the one you really wanted. Another cost would be the loss of potential job satisfaction.

Up to this point we have explored managing yourself from the standpoints of career management and improvement of personal productivity. We now shift our attention to our final major consideration: how to cope with potential negative side effects from job pressures.

MANAGING STRESS AND BURNOUT

Job stress and its related condition, job burnout, always have been potential sources of discomfort and poor physical and mental health of workers at all levels. Our discussion of stress and burnout focuses on a number of steps you can take to prevent and control these problems. However, let us first review the nature and causes of these conditions.

The Nature of Stress and Burnout

Stress, in general, is an internal response to a state of activation. Stress will ordinarily occur in a threatening or negative situation: an argument, a near accident, or being fired from a job. However, stress also can be caused by positive situations such as getting married or receiving a large cash bonus. **Job stress** has a more specific meaning; it is a condition in which job-related factors prompt the worker to change his or her physiological state, so that the worker is forced to deviate from normal functioning.[30] Notice that job stress is also a state of activation—the stressed person is physically and mentally aroused.

A person experiencing stress displays certain symptoms indicating that he or she is trying to cope with a stressor (any force creating the stress reaction). These symptoms can include a host of physiological, emotional, and behavioral reactions.

Physiological symptoms include an increase in heart rate, blood pressure, breathing rate, pupil size, and perspiration. If these physiological symptoms are severe or persist over a prolonged period, the result can be a stress-related disorder, such as a heart attack, hypertension, migraine headache, ulcer, colitis, or allergy. Stress also leads to a chemical imbalance which adversely affects the body's immune system. The person therefore becomes more susceptible to a wide variety of diseases and suffers more intense symptoms of health problems than he or she already is experiencing.[31]

Emotional symptoms of stress include anxiety, tension, depression, discouragement, boredom, prolonged fatigue, feelings of hopelessness, and various kinds of defensive thinking, including rationalization. Behavioral symptoms include nervous habits such as facial twitching, sudden decreases in job performance due to forgetfulness and errors in concentration and judgment in addition to increased use of cigarettes, alcohol, and other drugs. The questionnaire in Table 15-3 will help you assess the amount of stress you are currently experiencing.

Not all stress is bad. People require the right amount of stress to keep them mentally and physically alert. However, if the stress is particularly uncomfortable or distasteful, it will lower job performance—particularly on complex, demanding jobs. An example of a stressor that will lower job performance for most people is having a bullying, abrasive boss who wants to see them fail. It is usually a person's perception of something (or somebody) that determines whether it will be a positive or negative stressor. For example, one person might perceive a first parachute jump to be so frightening that he freezes up to the point of immobility just before the jump. The next person on the jumping mission, however, might delight at the prospect of her first jump, claiming it to be an exhilarating experience.

After prolonged exposure to job stress, a person runs the risk of feeling burned out—a drained-out, used-up feeling. **Job burnout** is a pattern of emo-

Table 15-3 The Stress Questionnaire

Here is a brief questionnaire to give a rough estimate of whether you are facing too much stress. Apply each question to the last six months of your life. Check the appropriate column.

	Mostly Yes	Mostly No
1. Have you been feeling uncomfortably tense lately?		
2. Are you engaged in frequent arguments with people close to you?		
3. Is your romantic life very unsatisfactory?		
4. Do you have trouble sleeping?		
5. Do you feel lethargic about life?		
6. Do many people annoy or irritate you?		
7. Do you have constant cravings for candy and other sweets?		
8. Is your cigarette consumption way up?		
9. Are you becoming addicted to soft drinks, coffee, or tea?		
10. Do you find it difficult to concentrate on your work?		
11. Do you frequently grind your teeth?		
12. Are you increasingly forgetful about little things like mailing a letter?		
13. Are you increasingly forgetful about big things like appointments and major errands?		
14. Are you making far too many trips to the lavatory?		
15. Have people commented lately that you do not look well?		
16. Do you get into verbal fights with other people too frequently?		
17. Have you been involved in more than one physical fight lately?		
18. Do you have more than your share of tension headaches?		
19. Do you feel nauseated much too often?		
20. Do you feel light-headed or dizzy almost every day?		
21. Do you have churning sensations in your stomach far too often?		
22. Are you in a big hurry all the time?		
23. Are far too many things bothering you these days?		

Scoring: The following guidelines are of value only if you answered the questions sincerely.

0–5 Mostly Yes answers: You seem to be experiencing a normal amount of stress.

6–15 Mostly Yes answers: Your stress level seems high. Become involved in some kind of stress-management activity, such as the activities described later in this chapter.

16–23 Mostly Yes answers: Your stress level appears much too high. Seek the help of a mental-health professional or visit your family doctor (or do both).

Source: Andrew J. DuBrin, *Human Relations for Career and Personal Success*, 2d. ed. (Englewood Cliffs, NJ: Prentice Hall, 1988), 82. Reprinted by permission of Prentice Hall.

tional, physical, and mental exhaustion in response to chronic job stressors.[32] Cynicism, apathy, and indifference are the major behavioral symptoms of the burned-out worker. Job burnout was first observed among people whose work centered around trying to help other people, such as social workers. Now all types of workers, including managers and office workers, are known to experience burnout.

Factors Contributing to Stress and Burnout

Factors within the person as well as adverse organizational conditions can cause or contribute to both stress and burnout. For instance, a worker may have a personality pattern that propels him or her to attack the job with such intensity that it leads to high stress. Or an organization can place such heavy demands on managers that most who work there suffer from stress disorders.

Factors within the Individual.   Hostile, aggressive, and impatient people find ways of turning almost any job into a stressful experience. Such individuals are labeled Type A, in contrast to their more easygoing Type B counterparts. In addition to being angry, the outstanding trait of Type A people is their strong sense of time urgency, known as "hurry sickness."[33] This sense of urgency compels them to achieve more and more in less and less time. Angry, aggressive (usually male) Type A people are more likely to experience cardiovascular disorders because they are under constant stress. It is important to recognize that not every hard-driving, impatient person is correctly classified as Type A. Those managers who love their work and enjoy other people are not particularly prone to heart disease.

Women who attempt to be outstanding career people, mothers, and homemakers often suffer from **Type E stress,** an overstressed condition characteristic of women who try to have and do it all. By spreading themselves too thin, women with a Type E behavior pattern eventually end up feeling exploited, resentful, frustrated, and burned out. Type E women differ from Type A men because instead of being angry toward others, these women tend to direct the anger inward and feel depressed and guilty.[34]

People who have high expectations are likely to experience job burnout at some point in their career because there will be times when they do not receive as many rewards as they are seeking. People who need constant excitement are also at high risk of job burnout because, "They bore easily and quickly. This constant need for change is fine so long as they can move to new situations. Frequently, however, this is not possible because of lack of work opportunities or family commitments, so they often experience high rates of burnout."[35]

Organizational Conditions.   Under ideal conditions, workers would experience just enough stress that they responded to their jobs creatively and energetically. Unfortunately, high stress levels created by adverse organizational conditions lead to many negative stress symptoms. A major contributor to job stress is work overload or underload—too much or too little to do. Deliberate understaffing, for example, places such heavy pressure on employees that it leads to high stress levels.

Job frustrations caused by such factors as part shortages, excessive politics, or insufficient funds can create job stress. Extreme conflict with other workers or with management is also a stressor. Heavy responsibility without the right amount of formal authority upsets many employees. Another annoyance is short lead times—too little notice to get complex assignments accomplished. Constant assignment changes or repetition of tasks day after day are other stressors.

Job stress can be created by ongoing contact with stress carriers: highly anxious, indecisive, or depressed people who create stress for others. At the other extreme, social isolation on the job can create stress. Finally, stress can be created by having to handle too many things related to office work, such as attending conferences, meeting daily deadlines, talking with the boss, writing memos, listening to complaints, making presentations to management, and being held up by people who are late for appointments.

Absence of ample positive feedback and other rewards is strongly associated with job burnout. As a consequence of not knowing how well they are doing and not receiving recognition, employees often become discouraged and emotionally exhausted. The result is often—but certainly not always—job burnout.

Methods of Prevention and Control

Organizations can and often do play a major role in preventing and remedying stress by correcting the kinds of conditions we have discussed and by offering stress-management programs. Our emphasis in this chapter, however, is on what individuals can do to prevent and treat stress and burnout. Techniques for managing job stress can be divided into three categories: control, escape, and symptom management.[36]

Control of Stressful Situations. Control techniques consist of both actions and mental evaluations of the situation that are "take charge" in tone. Several of these control techniques are as follows:

1. *Get social support*. Few people can go it alone when experiencing prolonged stress. Receiving social support—encouragement, understanding, and friendship—from other people is an important strategy for coping successfully with job stress. Nevertheless, as with most stress-reduction techniques, research shows that social support is not always effective.[37]

2. *Improve your work habits*. You can use techniques we described for improving your personal productivity to reduce stress. People typically experience stress when they feel they are losing or have lost control of their work assignments. Conscientious employees are especially prone to negative stress when they cannot get their work under control.

3. *Develop positive head talk*. Stress-resistant people have a basic orienta-

tion to optimism and cheerfulness. Robert A. Jud says this kind of positivism can be learned, by switching to "positive head talk" instead of thinking so many negative thoughts.[38]

4. *Hug the right people.* Hugging is now being seriously regarded as vital for physical and mental well-being. People who do not receive enough quality touching may suffer from low self-esteem, ill health, depression, and loneliness. Conversely, quality touching may help people cope better with job stress. The hugging, however, has to represent loving and caring.[39]

Symptom Management.   This category of stress management refers to tactics that manage the symptoms related to job stress in general. Dozens of symptom-management techniques have been developed, including the following:

1. *Make frequent use of relaxation techniques.* Learning to relax reduces the adverse effects of stress. The **relaxation response** is a general-purpose method of learning to relax by yourself. The key ingredient of this technique is to make yourself quiet and comfortable and think of the word one (or any simple chant or prayer) with every breath for about ten minutes.[40] The technique slows you down both physiologically and emotionally. An extremely easy relaxation method is to visualize yourself in an unusually pleasant situation, such as floating on a cloud, walking by a lake, or lying on a comfortable beach. Pick any fantasy that you find relaxing.

2. *Get appropriate physical exercise.* Physical exercise helps dissipate some of the tension created by job stress, and it also helps the body ward off future stress-related disorders. A physically fit, well-rested person usually can tolerate more frustration than can a physically run-down, tired person. One way in which exercise helps combat stress is that it reduces blood pressure; it also releases hormones that act as pain killers and antidepressants.

3. *Try to cure hurry sickness.* The basic strategy is for people with hurry sickness to learn how to relax and enjoy the present for its own sake. Specific tactics include having at least one idle period every day; learning how to savor food by taking time when eating; eating nutritious, not overly seasoned foods to help decrease nervousness; and finding enrichment in an area of life not related to work.

Escape Methods of Stress Management.   Escape methods refer to actions and reappraisals of situations that lead the stressed individual to get away from the stressor. Eliminating the stressor is the most effective escape technique. For example, if a manager is experiencing stress because of serious understaffing in his or her department, that manager should negotiate to receive authorization to hire additional help. Mentally blocking out a stressful thought is another escape technique, but it may not work in the long run.

SUMMARY OF KEY POINTS

To manage work and people effectively, you must manage yourself. Unless you have a satisfying, productive career and are mentally and physically fit, your effectiveness as a manager may be limited.

The version of career planning presented in this chapter involves five steps: establish a position objective, describe its content, identify needs for personal development, design a personal-development plan, and acquire the necessary credentials. A career path lays out the steps or positions leading to a long-range goal. It should include contingency plans and personal goals. Two logical entry points into management are management-training programs and working up from technical specialist to manager.

Another aspect of career management is understanding the qualifications sought by employers. These include appropriate education, good communication skills, some relevant work experience, good problem-solving ability, motivation and enthusiasm, adaptability, good judgment and common sense, social maturity, and leadership qualities.

Do not overlook certain steps when you conduct a job campaign. Develop several sources of job leads. Prepare a careful resume and cover letter. Learn how to handle yourself well in a job interview; ask perceptive questions and write a follow-up letter.

After you are hired, use career-advancement tactics such as the following: develop expertise, display good job performance, be honest about how much responsibility you want, be visible, find a sponsor, find a mentor, do what you do best, identify growth fields and growth companies, find an organization that matches your personality, develop a network of contacts, achieve broad experience, look successful, develop a good relationship with your boss, and consider moonlighting.

One way of increasing your personal productivity is to develop an array of techniques to improve your work habits and management of time. Clean up your work area and sort out your tasks, schedule planning time each day, prepare a "to do" list and assign priorities, work at a steady pace, set deadlines, delegate routine work, concentrate on one task at a time, and concentrate on high-output tasks. Avoid procrastinating, by understanding why you procrastinate, and take remedial action.

Learn to manage stress and burnout. Stress is an internal response to a state of arousal. Job burnout is a pattern of emotional, physical, and mental exhaustion in response to chronic job stressors. Key stress symptoms include tension, anxiety, and poor concentration and judgment. Job stress is caused by factors within the individual, such as Type A and Type E behaviors, and by adverse organizational conditions. People with high expectations are candidates for burnout. Limited rewards and lack of feedback from the organization also contribute to burnout.

Methods of preventing and controlling stress and burnout can be subdivided into attempting to control stressful situations, managing symptoms, and escaping the stressful situation. Specific tactics include eliminating stressors, getting sufficient physical exercise, using relaxation techniques, curing hurry sickness, getting emotional support from others, and improving your work habits.

QUESTIONS

1. What do you see as the major advantages of having a career plan rather than allowing fate and luck to play major roles in shaping your career?
2. What defense might a student with below-average grades offer a prospective employer who said that decent grades are important to his or her firm?
3. What type of businesses or other work organizations are likely to give you the most management responsibility early in your career?
4. If an interviewer asked you why you wanted to be a manager, what do you think would be an impressive answer?
5. What types of extracurricular activities are good experience for management jobs in business?
6. How can a person start developing a network of contacts while still in school?
7. How can a person be very well organized yet still be unproductive?
8. How could the 80/20 principle be used to help busy managers decrease the number of hours they work each week?
9. Based on information about managerial roles presented in Chapter 1, what do you think are several of the major sources of stress in the manager's job?
10. Explain why some students suffer from burnout.

ACTIVITIES

1. Interview a successful person in any field, and find out if that person used a career plan on the way to success. Bring your results back to class.
2. Conduct a group interview with about six students who contemplate looking for a job within the next six months. Find out what qualifications they are seeking in an employer. Bring your results back to class.

CASE PROBLEM 15-A: THE AMBITIOUS CAREER PLANNER

Hector Lopez, a twenty-one-year-old senior at a business school, prepared the following career plan and career path.

My Career Plan

Position Objective: Operations manager for a medium-size manufacturing company with sales of about $30 million. I intend to move into this position after spending three years as a manufacturing supervisor and plant manager.

Position Content: Total responsibility for the manufacturing and shipment of the product. I will take on a full range of management responsibilities, including planning, organizing, leading, and controlling. I will assist my boss, the division head, in contributing to the long-range plans of the division.

Needs for Development: I seem to have the right leadership qualities to become successful in management. I will need to learn more about the technical aspects of manufacturing. I need some specific knowledge about robotics and CAD/CAM, and maybe other new manufacturing techniques. I need more skill in making public presentations.

Plan for Personal Development: I will learn most of what I need through practical experience, but I will also take a few seminars in advanced manufacturing techniques. I intend to enroll in Toastmasters Club to improve my public speaking.

Acquire Necessary Credentials: Being a business-school graduate should give me the formal credentials I need. I will develop the reputation of a superstar shortly after landing my first job. I will be known for my dedication to work and for my creativity.

My Career Path

Work: First I will work two years as a first-line supervisor in a manufacturing plant. Then I will spend one or two years as an assistant plant manager, followed by one or two years as a plant manager. I will then reach my position objective: an operations manager. After three years as operations manager, I will become division head. After four years as division head, I will become executive vice-president, and hold that position for about four years. I will then become a company president at about age thirty-nine years. I will remain president for four years, then become chairman of the board of a medium-sized company. I will then shift to the presidency of a major business corporation. I will stay there until I am about fifty years old, when I will buy my own satellite business or some other high-technology firm.

My contingency plan concerns the presidency of a major corporation. If that does not materialize, I will buy my own firm sooner.

Personal Plans: I intend to remain single until I am thirty-five years old, when I will marry the right professional woman. We will have four children of our own or adopt two sets of twins. We will own a house in the country where I am employed, plus a vacation villa in Spain or France. I will stay in shape by doing exercises at my desk and weight lifting three times per week.

Case Questions

1. What criticisms do you have of Hector Lopez's career plan and career path?
2. What positive comments do you have about Lopez's documents?
3. What career-advancement strategies should Lopez use to increase his chances of reaching his goals?
4. Which personal productivity techniques should Lopez emphasize to reach his goals?

CASE PROBLEM 15-B: THE FORGETFUL SYSTEMS ANALYST

Jill Partridge looked apprehensively at the message her boss had sent via electronic mail: "Let's talk today about the meeting you missed yesterday. I'll expect you at four this afternoon." Partridge appeared promptly for her appointment. She said to her boss, Davina Chen, "You put something on my screen about missing a meeting yesterday. What is that all about?"

Chen answered, "Unfortunately Jill, that is just the answer I expected of you. You are not even aware that there was a meeting to discuss how the department can develop and implement the new executive information system. This is the hottest new project our department has had in years, and you didn't even remember the meeting."

"I apologize," said Partridge. I have no recollection of being told about the meeting. I'll speak to one of the other analysts to find out what I missed. I guarantee you nothing like this will happen again."

"I wish I could be confident that you won't have another memory lapse in the future. But your record over the last year suggests that you are becoming forgetful about things such as due dates on reports, meetings, and even the names of some our most important users."

"I didn't know things had gotten that bad," said Partridge. "I must admit I have been under considerable pressure lately. But I think things will eventually calm down."

"What kind of pressures are you facing?" asked Chen. "I want to know what kind of shape you're in before I assign you to the executive information-system project."

"Believe it or not," replied Partridge, "my biggest pressure is trying to get ahead in this company. I want to become a senior systems analyst for reasons of pride and money. My boyfriend and I plan to get married and purchase a condo. I need to save another $4,000 to hold up my end of the deal. The second biggest pressure I face is that I'm not sure I want to marry my boyfriend. I do get distracted sometimes thinking about that problem."

"What other problems are you facing?" asked Chen.

"This my be a shocker to you," said Partridge, "I'm beginning to wonder if I'm in the right field. I'm getting a little tired of the constant concentration my job requires. One of the reasons I want a promotion is that a senior analyst spends less time on computers and more time with people. But even beyond that, I'm beginning to wonder if I would be better off in sales than in information systems.

"I've also been active politically, which is taking up a good deal of my time. This past weekend I worked ten hours on the campaign. It was no easy matter concentrating on work Monday morning."

"I can see why you have been forgetful on the job," said Chen. "But excuses don't carry much weight with me. What I need is good performance. I expect you to be much more alert from now on."

"I'll do my best," said Partridge. "But I haven't intentionally forgotten anything. My mental lapses have been beyond my control."

Case Questions

1. How do Jill Partridge's problems relate to time management and stress management?
2. How can Partridge be helped?
3. What do you think of Davina Chen's approach to dealing with Partridge?
4. How might the company help Partridge?

REFERENCES

1. Anne Krueger, "Career Sourcebook for the '90s," *Business Week Careers*, (Spring–Summer 1988): 4.
2. Andrew F. Sikula and John F. McKenna, "Individuals Must Take Charge of Career Development," *Personnel Administrator* (October 1983): 90.
3. Joel E. Ross and Darab Unwalla, "Making it to the Top: A 30-Year Perspective," *Personnel* (April 1988): 78.
4. Frank W. Archer, "Charting a Career Course," *Personnel Journal* (April 1984): 62–63.
5. *Occupational Outlook Handbook* (Washington, DC: U.S. Government Printing Office, annually).
6. Jonathan P. Hicks, "An Unusual Climb to the Executive Suite at Xerox Corp.," *New York Times* (syndicated story), 24 May 1987.
7. Elizabeth M. Fowler, "Middle Mangers Seen as Expendable," *New York Times* (syndicated story) 6 June 1988.
8. Based in part on William T. Leonard, "What the Recruiter Looks For," *Business Week's Guide to Careers* (Fall–Winter 1983): 22–23; Bob Weinstein, "What Employers Look For," *Business Week's Guide to Careers How to Get a Job Guide* (1985 edition): 10–13.
9. Weinstein, "What Employers Look For," 10.
10. Leonard, "What the Recruiter Looks For," 23.
11. *Standard & Poor's Register of Corporations, Directors and Executives* (New York: Standard & Poor, current edition); *Dun and Bradstreet Million Dollar Directory* (Parsippany, NJ: Dun and Bradstreet, current edition).
12. "The Careers 1000," *Business Week Careers* (November 1987): 14–127. See also current edition.
13. Robert Wendover, "How to Land the Job You Want," *Business Week Careers How to Get a Job Guide* (1987 edition): 39.
14. Two such books are Richard N. Bolles, *What Color Is Your Parachute? A Practical Guide for Job Hunters and Career Changers* (Berkeley, CA: Ten Speed Press, published annually); and Robert D. Lock, *Job Search: Career Planning Guidebook, Book II* (Pacific Grove, CA: Brooks/Cole Publishing Co., 1988).
15. Much of this information is based on two sources: Tom Jackson, "Writing the Target Resume," *Business Week's Guide to Careers* (Spring 1983): 26–27; and Lock, *Job Search: Career Planning Guidebook, Book II*, 60–61.
16. Darlene C. Pibal, "How to Apply for a Job and Get It," *The Balance Sheet* (March–April 1984): 15; Julie Griffin Levitt, *Your Career: How to Make It Happen* (Cincinnati: South-Western Publishing Co., 1985), ch. 7.
17. Sandra L. Davis, "How to Handle the Stress Interview," *Business Week's Guide to Careers* (March–April 1985): 28.
18. "All Work Makes Jack an Executive," *Purdue University Perspective* (Summer 1984): 6.
19. Gene W. Dalton and Paul H. Thompson, *Novations: Strategies for Career Management* (Glenview, IL: Scott, Foresman and Co., 1986). (As cited in book review appearing in *The Academy of Management Review* (October 1986): 873.
20. *Occupational Outlook Handbook*.
21. Loretta D. Foxman, and Walter L. Polsky, "Learn to Play the Networking Game," *Personnel Journal* (July 1984): 30.

22. Cathy A. Grayson, "Inside Moves," *Success!* (November 1986): 65–69.

23. Alfred Fornay, "Image Investment Portfolio," *Business Week Careers* (September 1987): 23.

24. Elizabeth M. Fowler, "Layoffs Also Shake Up Those Who are Left on Corporate Work Force," *New York Times* (syndicated story), 24 June 1986.

25. Muhammad Jamal, "Is Moonlighting Mired in Myth?" *Personnel Journal* (May 1988): 50.

26. Peter A. Turla and Kathleen L. Hawkins, "The Flaws of Perfectionism," *Success* (December 1982): 23.

27. Andrew Grove, *High Output Management* (New York: Random House), 1983.

28. Some of this information is based on two sources: Jane Burka and Lenora Yuen, *Procrastination: Why You Do It, What to Do About It* (Reading, MA: Addison-Wesley Publishing Co., 1984); Henry C. Everett, "Conquering Procrastination," *Success* (June 1981): 26.

29. Alan Lakein, *How to Gain Control of Your Time and Your Life* (New York: Peter H. Wyden, Inc., 1973), 141–151.

30. Terry A. Beehr and John E. Newman, "Job Stress, Employee Health, and Organizational Effectiveness: A Facet Analysis, Model, and Literature Review," *Personnel Psychology* (Winter 1978): 668.

31. Deepak Chopra, *Creating Health: Beyond Prevention Toward Perfection* (Boston: Houghton Mifflin Co. 1987).

32. Phillip L. Rice, *Stress and Health: Principles and Practice of Coping and Wellness* (Pacific Grove, CA: Brooks/Cole Publishing Co., 1987), 223.

33. Salvatore Didato, "People with 'Hurry Sickness' Are More Likely to Have Heart Problems," *Democrat and Chronicle* 28 January 1984, 10C. This article is based partially on Meyer Friedman and Ray H. Rosenman, *Type A Behavior and Your Heart* (Greenwich, CT: Fawcett Crest, 1975).

34. Harriet B. Braiker, *The Type E Woman—How to Overcome the Stress of Being Everything to Everybody* (New York: Dodd, Mead & Co., 1986).

35. Morley D. Glicken, "A Counseling Approach to Employee Burnout," *Personnel Journal* (March 1983): 226.

36. Janina C. Latack, "Coping With Job Stress: Measures and Future Directions for Scale Development," *Journal of Applied Psychology* (August 1986): 378.

37. Gary K. Kaufmann and Terry A. Beehr, "Interactions Between Job Stressors and Social Support: Some Counterintuitive Results," *Journal of Applied Psychology* (August 1986): 522–526.

38. Robert A. Judd, "Making Stress Manageable," *Business Week Careers* (November 1986): 78.

39. Patricia Rodriguez, "Hugging for Health," *Gannett News Service* (syndicated story), 21 May 1988.

40. Herbert Benson, *The Relaxation Response* (New York: Wm. Morrow & Co., Inc., 1975). Updating of the technique reported in Joseph, "You Can't Fight or Flee," *USA Today*, 20 October 1983.

Comprehensive Cases

COMPREHENSIVE CASE A: SEARS FACES A TOUGH CHALLENGE

The heavy activity began in February 1988 when Chairman Edward A. Brennan of Sears, Roebuck & Co. invited some of the company's biggest investors to Chicago for a formal presentation. The purpose of the meeting was to describe management's progress in turning around the huge retailing and financial-services company. However, the result was a heated debate. The portfolio managers had become impatient with the progress of Sears. They made it clear that they thought Brennan's job was in jeopardy.

By late June, Wall Street analysts were preparing break-up analyses and saying that Sears stock was undervalued by as much as 50 percent. By fall, rumors elevated the stock up as high as forty-six dollars per share versus thirty-three dollars per share in May. Many people were beginning to wonder if the world's largest retailer was a potential takeover candidate.

Stalling for Time

Chairman Brennan is working hard to ensure that Sears is not taken over by another firm or group of investors. In late October, he unveiled a plan that reemphasizes Sears' current retail and financial-services strategy instead of pointing the company in a new direction. The message was unequivocal: despite widespread skepticism after seven years of mediocre results, Brennan will follow his strategic plan. He maintains, "I think the strategy is absolutely sound."

To pay for a 10 percent stock buyback, Brennan plans to sell the 110-story Sears Tower, located in Chicago. Also up for sale is the commercial real-estate division of Coldwell Banker & Co. and the group life and health business of Allstate Insurance Co. The Sears Tower alone could sell for $1 billion. Brennan has also pledged Sears to a new retail strategy that will replace frequent promotions in the 825 outlets with storewide "everyday low prices." These moves will cost more than $400 million in various write-offs. However, they buy Sears time to solidify its financial-services businesses and to transform its stores.

Because Sears's pension fund already owns approximately 15 percent of the stock, decreasing the number of shares outstanding by 10 percent will strengthen management's grip, in addition to elevating the price of the stock. Sears may be further insulated from a takeover by the very business that makes it appear most vulnerable: its $28 billion retailing empire. The problems facing Sears in its retail outlets are so formidable that analysts contend selling the unit would be exceedingly difficult, and turning it around would take too long to support the debt. "Anyone who thinks he or she can do any better or faster is absurd," contends a managing director with Shearson Lehman Hutton Inc.

Holding Steady

While Sears revenues increased consistently through the 1980s, earnings have been unstable. Since 1984, return on equity has fallen from 14.5 percent to 12.4 percent. Allstate was already a reliable growth business, but Dean Witter and Coldwell Banker, purchased in 1981 for a combined sum of $790 million, have yet to yield suitable returns.

Sears World Trade had a short existence, as did the Sears Savings Bank. Revenues at the retail group, despite many reorganizations and redirections, have grown at an annual average of only 2.9 percent over the last five years. During the same time, earnings have dropped an average of 2.6 percent. In the first nine months of 1988, corporate earnings dropped 17.9 percent, to $893.1 million, while revenues gained 11.9 percent, to $38.5 billion.

After reviewing all business units for possible sale, with the exception of retailing, management decided it was best to stay the course. Brennan points out that investors' returns will be higher if Sears remains in financial services instead of selling assets and reinvesting the proceeds in retailing. The tactic Sears will take is to eliminate any business that is not directly consumer-related and focus its effort on a retail rejuvenation plan that is creating shock waves throughout the company.

At Coldwell Banker, Sears opted to emphasize residential real estate, Coldwell Banker has experienced low profits as a result of an expansion program. But it divested the $400 million commercial leasing business. Individual lines of insurance will continue to be emphasized at Allstate, and the $1 billion group life and health insurance business will be eliminated.

At Dean Witter, Sears intends to add four-thousand retail sales representatives and direct them to sell managed investment products such as Allstate annuities and closed-end bond funds. A company insider said that Sears is pondering buying a regional retail brokerage. During this time, the company has cut back Dean Witter's weak capital-markets businesses, shaving bond trading and paring down securities inventories.

Analysts, pointing to a slow environment for both real-estate and retail-brokerage services, question whether the financial units can ever yield hefty profits—particularly because they turned in mediocre results during the mid-1980s boom. Yet some of Brennan's most severe critics say Sears could be ready for a payoff in financial services in the near future.

Stores with More Pizzazz

With its 11 percent share of home sales nationally, Coldwell Banker should do better as its costs for national expansion lessen. And while Dean Witter's retail brokers generally perform below the competition, analysts say their productivity has been partially hidden by $34 billion in sales of "backloaded" mutual funds. (A backloaded fund is one in which the selling fees are spread over four years instead of being charged up front.) Furthermore, while the Discover Card is not as widely used as its competitors, the unit has recently turned in a profit.

Sears' retail business is considered its biggest challenge. The company is implementing a plan to transform itself into a "Store of Superstores," featuring brand-name merchandise and more exciting stores. Furthermore, Brennan describes the introduction of everyday low pricing as "the most important thing we've done in twenty-five years."

The plan will demand substantial change throughout Sears. Sales and promotion have been the mainstay of Sears' marketing strategy. By permanently lowering prices on all merchandise, Sears will have to change its thrust to customers and cut costs enough to maintain profits. Brennan maintains that getting rid of constant promotions will cut administrative and inventory costs dramatically. Approximately eight-thousand merchandise group employees will move from Sears Tower to smaller, less expensive offices. It is likely that some of them will lose their jobs.

Observers think that this may be Brennan's last chance to prove he is capable of turning the retailing and financial services giant around. Many analysts are convinced that the restructuring will not boost the stock price substantially. This means that operations themselves will soon have to grow.

Case Questions

1. What is your evaluation of Brennan's strategy to improve the profitability of Sears?
2. In what way might the sale of the Sears Tower affect quality awareness throughout the organization?
3. Is Brennan paying too little attention to employee motivation in his attempted redirection of Sears?
4. What is your opinion of the financial health of Sears, using the formula for calculating gross profit margin?
5. To what extent do you think Mr. Brennan is resisting change?
6. How can sales associates at Sears be sold on the value of "everyday low prices"?
7. What hints about the Sears organization culture are revealed in this case?
8. Visit a Sears store, and form your own impressions about the company's prospects for the future.

Source: Based on facts reported in Michael Oneal, "Sears Faces a Tall Task," *Business Week* (14 November 1988): 54–55.

COMPREHENSIVE CASE B: THE MANAGEMENT-MINDED LANDLORDS

Shortly before graduating from Mississippi Vocational Technical Institute, Debra Randolph found the type of job she wanted. Randolph was offered a position as a junior financial analyst by the gas and electric company in a medium-size city. Her starting salary was less than she had hoped to earn. However, the prospects of obtaining excellent experience compensated for the low salary. Randolph's first assignment involved helping the investment manager keep track of the performance of the company's investments.

To help reduce costs, Randolph shared living quarters with an aunt who lived in town. She commuted about six miles to work in a compact car she purchased after three months of employment. At the end of her first six months on the job, Randolph received her first performance appraisal. Her manager informed Randolph that her performance was above average. He also said that if her good work continued she would be eligible for promotion to financial analyst within two years. When Randolph asked what her above average performance meant in terms of salary, she was told, "You can anticipate at least a 5-percent raise after twelve months."

Over dinner, Randolph and her aunt, Midge Jackson, discussed the day's events. Randolph told Jackson that her performance had been evaluated. "How did it go?" inquired Jackson.

"Not too bad and not too good," answered Randolph. "I'll be getting a raise next year that amounts to a cost-of-living adjustment. If I get the same raise every year, my real income will never increase. That's because a cost-of-living adjustment only keeps you even with inflation.

"Another concern flashed through my mind after I left the appraisal session. I really don't want my financial future dependent on somebody else's evaluation of how well I'm doing. I want to be my own woman. I don't want to have all my financial eggs in one basket."

"What do you have in mind?" asked Jackson, "Are you thinking of buying your own utility company?"

"Not quite," answered Randolph with a smile. "But I am thinking of the two of us going into the real-estate business. Here is my plan. When Dad died he left me about $10,000, which has been placed in a trust fund. I'm old enough to get that money now. If you had some money saved, the two of us could combine savings and purchase a rental property. I took a personal finance course at Vo Tech that covered income properties.

"There's a lot of money to be made in buying an old apartment building, fixing it up, and then renting out the units. If I recall correctly, the more units in the building, the better. There's almost no chance of getting any cash flow with a double house. With four units in the building, you can actually generate some cash. If you have six units, you might even clear four hundred dollars per month."

Jackson said, "You've really put my mind in gear. I've thought about owning income property for many years. But I've never taken action on my thoughts. Buzz Hawkins, an old friend of mine, specializes in older city properties. I'll give Buzz a call tomorrow."

One week later, the two women and Hawkins met to discuss opportunities in real estate. Hawkins explained that rehabilitating old buildings and then renting them could be very profitable. He also pointed to some potential pitfalls:

"Under the right circumstance, you can make money doing what we've talked about. I own fifteen buildings myself that I've accumulated over a ten-year period. However, you have to be willing to do two very important things. First of all, you must be able to put the time into maintaining these properties. You simply can't afford to hire people to make all the repairs. For example, it can cost eight-thousand dollars to paint the exterior of the building. That wipes away three years of profits. If you did the job yourself, your costs might be about eight-hundred dollars plus your time.

"Another point you have to understand is that income property is not a passive investment. I call owning real estate a business rather than an investment. It takes a lot of management time. If you just sit back and wait for your rent payments, you're in trouble. You have to make frequent checks on the property and keep close tabs on what your tenants are doing."

Randolph and Jackson thanked Hawkins for his candor. After several further discussions between themselves, they got back in touch with Hawkins. They told him to look for the best deal he could find for about $15,000 down. The two prospective landlords added these criteria:

1. The building must already contain four or more units. They reasoned that converting a building into additional units would be too much to tackle at this time.

2. The total closing costs involved in purchasing the building must not exceed $17,000 including the down payment, initial taxes, legal fees, and so forth.

3. The building must not be located in a high-crime neighborhood.

4. It must appear probable that the building would be able to pass city inspection after an investment of $7,000 in repairs. (Randolph and Jackson planned to use $3,000 in cash for the repairs, and borrow the other $4,000 with Jackson's bank credit card.)

Two months later, Hawkins found a building meeting these criteria, and Randolph and Jackson purchased the property for $130,000. A commercial bank gave them a $116,000 mortgage. The total startup cost of the income property was $24,000, including down payment, closing costs, and initial repairs. The money came from these sources:

Randolph's inheritance	$10,000
Jackson's cash	5,000
Jackson's credit-card loan	4,000
Second mortgage from owner	5,000
	$24,000

Randolph and Jackson prepared the following monthly revenue-and-expense budget for operating the building:

Revenues		
Rent from four apartments	$2,400	
Expenses		
Principal and interest on $116,000 first mortgage (20 years at 12.0 percent)	$1,278	
Principal and interest on $5,000 second mortgage (10 years at 14 percent)	78	
Principal and interest on $4,000 credit-card loan (4 years at 18 percent)	118	
Real-estate taxes	250	
Water	80	
Maintenance and repairs	250	
Miscellaneous	50	
Total expenses	$2,104	
Excess of revenues over expenses	$ 296	

Randolph and Jackson therefore predicted an average monthly cash flow of $296. In addition, there would be income-tax deductions resulting from depreciation and interest costs. However, Randolph and Jackson both wondered how they would handle a large, unanticipated expense, such as a new roof.

The first two months of operating the building were financially draining because it took over forty-five days to find tenants for all four units. Another problem occurred during the fifth month of operation. Although the tenth of the month had passed, two of the tenants still had not paid their rent. It took four trips to the units to collect all the rent. The next month, Randolph and Jackson faced the problem of late rent payments again.

Randolph approached Jackson with a possible solution to the problem of rent collection. "Why not offer the tenants a tangible reward for paying their rent on time for six consecutive months? It would work something like behavior mod in industry. We would offer each tenant a choice of prizes for good rent-paying performance. The prizes might include a headset radio, an alarm clock, or a set of kitchen knives. This might even set up a little competition among the tenants to be prompt with their rent."

Jackson responded, "Wait a minute, Debra. You are saying we should be rewarding people for doing something that is their legal obligation. That's farfetched. The bank doesn't pay us for making our mortgage payments on time. But I'll give your system a try for awhile."

Three of the tenants welcomed the idea. The fourth tenant countered with a suggestion of his own. He responded, "I'm starved for cash right now. How about giving me a six-dollar-per-month rent reduction if I pay on time? This would be about the equivalent of the gift." Randolph granted the concession.

The following month the tenant paid the rent late and took the reduction anyway. The owners discussed the problem. The tentative conclusion they reached was that they would overlook this problem for now. It didn't seem worth the hassle to go after the tenant for six dollars.

One Sunday afternoon, Jackson took her turn inspecting the property. She observed that considerable litter had accumulated on the front lawn. She also noticed that three garbage cans were overturned in the back yard. She asked one of the tenants what happened. The tenant replied, "My family and the family downstairs have declared war on each other. They won't do their share of cleaning up, so we won't do our share. If you want a clean place, evict those people."

Jackson then spoke to the downstairs tenants to get their side of the story. In response to Midge's inquiry, an elderly woman living downstairs responded in these words: "I'm glad you're here. If you didn't come soon, I was going to call the police. The people upstairs have been throwing their garbage in front of my apartment. They say they're doing it because I turned over their garbage can. It wasn't me. It was my dog. Please get them to cooperate, or I'll have to look for a new place."

Jackson decided to handle this conflict between the two tenants by writing them each a stem letter. She informed them that strewing garbage about was a violation of city codes. The letter also stated that if they didn't abide by her request to keep the property clean, their leases would not be renewed.

Several months later, Randolph was seated at her desk at the utility company. Her superior, Bruce Hodges, entered the office she shared with two other financial analysts. Hodges said, "I'm glad you're here, Debra. I need you to calculate the return to shareholders for the last three years. I want you to take into account both dividends and stock appreciation. I suspect you are familiar with this kind of financial analysis. I'll need this information this afternoon."

"Bruce, I'd like to take care of this matter. But I doubt that I can get it finished this afternoon. I'm taking one-half of a personal day this afternoon to go the County Clerk's office."

"Why are you going there?" asked Hodges.

Randolph replied hesitatingly, "I have to take care of a problem about the deed to my income property. It's a very important appointment. My lawyer is going to meet me there."

"Debra, to be honest with you, I think your priorities are distorted. This isn't the first time you have put aside your work with us in order to manage your property. It certainly doesn't sit well with the company."

"Bruce, don't be concerned about my priorities. My real estate is just a minor sideline."

Over dinner that evening, Randolph told Jackson about her conversation with Hodges. She explained, "I know the reason we started in real estate was to become more independent. Yet, Bruce's comments have started me thinking. I wonder if my primary career is really being held back by our real-estate business. If that's true, the little cash flow we're getting from the property may not be worth it."

"In what way could managing the real estate be hurting your career?" asked Jackson.

"First of all, Bruce thinks that I'm not giving my all to the company. That alone could block my progress. Also, every time a crisis comes up with the building, my concentration suffers. Remember last month when it was my turn to take care of the next crisis? The hot-water heater burst, and the basement was flooding. Two tenants got hold of me at the office. I had to make at least four phone calls to get the problem under control. I doubt I did much good for the company that morning.

"I also wonder how much money I would have to make in real estate to compensate for any career problems it might create. I guess I'm asking what is my break-even point."

"A lot depends on how much you enjoy being a landlord," commented Jackson.

Case Questions

1. What is your opinion of the completeness of the revenue-and-expense budget prepared by Randolph and Jackson?

2. What kind of financial returns (expressed in terms of gross profit margin) are these landlords receiving?

3. Are these two women entrepreneurs? Why or why not?

4. How might Randolph and Jackson make more systematic use of behavior modification to improve rent collections?

5. How would you evaluate the conflict-resolution technique that Jackson used with her tenants?

6. How might Randolph evaluate the effect of her real-estate business on her career?

7. Should these two women purchase another four-family apartment building as soon as they raise enough capital?

GLOSSARY

Acceptance inspection The inspection of finished goods in quality control. The finished goods are either accepted or rejected.

Achievement need The desire to get things accomplished for accomplishment's sake.

Action A step in the communication process in which the receiver does something about the message.

Action plan A series of steps indicating how each objective will be achieved. Action plans are a necessary part of *planning*.

Activity (in a PERT network) The physical and mental effort required to complete an event, such as with installing wiring.

Adhocracy An *organization structure* characterized by temporary teams of workers who move from project to project.

Administrator A manager who works in a government or nonprofit organization rather than in a business firm.

Affirmative action program A specific program implemented by an employer to eliminate job discrimination in all phases of employment.

Antecedent (of behavior) A signal from the environment that prompts a person to behave in a certain manner, such as a customer calling on the telephone.

Assertiveness Being forthright with one's demands and saying what one thinks and feels.

Authoritative command A method of *conflict resolution* in which the manager requires the subordinates to accept his or her solution to the conflict.

Authority The formal right granted by an organization to carry out an activity.

Autocratic leader A leader who attempts to retain most of the authority for himself or herself.

Balanced decision A decision that gives consideration to the needs of the entire firm.

Behavior What people actually do on the job, or their activity.

Behavior modification A way of changing behavior by rewarding the right responses and punishing or ignoring the wrong responses.

Behavioral school of management The school of management giving primary consideration to improving the management of people through understanding their psychological makeup.

Biased language Words that contain a prejudgment toward another person or group based on something other than fact.

Brainstorming A method of solving problems, gathering information, and stimulating creative thinking. The basic technique is to encourage unrestrained and spontaneous participation by group members.

Break-even analysis A technique of determining the relationship between total costs and total revenues at various levels of production or sales activity. At the *break-even point,* there is no profit or loss, and total revenues equal total costs.

Budget A spending plan, for a future period of time, that is expressed in numerical terms.

Bureaucracy A rational, systematic, and precise form of an *organization* in which rules, regulations, and techniques of control are precisely defined.

Burnout A pattern of emotional exhaustion and cynicism towards one's work in response to chronic job stressors.

Capital-expenditure budget A plan for spending money on things used to produce goods or services.

Career A lifelong series of positions that form a relatively coherent pattern.

Career path The sequence of jobs necessary to achieve personal and career goals.

Career plan An overall blueprint for achieving one's career goals by specifying those goals and developing action plans to attain them.

Cash budget Forecasts of cash receipts and payments used to compare against actual experience.

Centralization The extent to which authority is retained at the top of the organization.

Charisma The charm, or *referent power*, characteristic of some leaders, which helps them to influence others.

Classical school of management The original formal approach to studying management that searches for solid principles and concepts that can be used to manage people and work productively.

Coercive power A leader's ability to influence people by having control over punishments.

Communication The process of exchanging information by the use of words, letters, other symbols, or nonverbal behavior.

Communication channel The medium carrying the message, including voice, written memos, and electronic mail.

Communication network A pathway over which messages are sent in an organization.

Communication overload A condition in which the individual receives so much information to process that he or she becomes overwhelmed. Same as *information overload.*

Comparable worth The idea that people performing jobs with different titles, but of comparable value to the firm, should receive equal pay.

Conceptual skill In relation to managerial work, the ability to see the organization as a total entity.

Concurrent controls Devices that monitor activities while they are being car-

Concurrent controls (continued) ried out, such as a supervisor observing performance.

Condition of certainty The condition that exists when the facts are well known and the decision outcome can be predicted accurately.

Condition of risk The condition that exists when a decision must be made based on incomplete, but factual, information.

Condition of uncertainty The condition that exists when a decision is based on limited or no factual information.

Conditional value The possible payoff of pursuing an alternative solution to a problem under a particular level of demand.

Conflict The simultaneous arousal of two or more incompatible motives, often accompanied by tension and frustration.

Confrontation Bringing forth a controversial topic or contradictory material in which the other party is personally involved. To say, "Your performance is unsatisfactory," is a *confrontation technique.*

Consensual leader Leader who encourages group discussion about an issue and then makes a decision that reflects the general agreement *(consensus)* of group members.

Consensus decision making A situation in which the manager shares the problem with the group and they reach general agreement on a solution. Even though everyone may not agree entirely with the decision, they accept it.

Consequence (of behavior) Events taking place after behavior that either encourage or discourage future behavior. Receiving encouragement after making a sale would be a consequence of behavior.

Constructive criticism A form of criticism designed to help people improve. It usually involves making positive suggestions.

Consultative leader A leader who encourages a high degree of involvement from subordinates, yet retains final authority to make the decision.

Contingency approach A perspective on management emphasizing that there is no one

Contingency approach *(continued)*
best way to manage people or work. The situation must be studied to select the best method or approach.

Contingency plan An alternative plan to be used in case the original plan cannot be implemented.

Contingent reinforcement A method of rewarding people in which getting the reward depends on certain behavior. ***Contingent reinforcement*** is an essential part of ***behavior modification.***

Control function of management *See* ***controlling.***

Controlling The managerial function of ensuring that ***performance*** conforms to plans. It involves comparing actual performance to a predetermined standard.

Corporate culture *See* ***organizational culture.***

Corrective discipline A form of discipline in which employees are given a chance to correct their behavior before punishment is applied.

Counseling A formal discussion method for helping another person overcome a problem or develop his or her potential.

Creative alternative An alternative solution to a problem that is imaginative and useful.

Creative problem solving The ability to overcome obstacles by approaching them in novel ways.

Creativity The process of developing original, imaginative, and innovative perspectives on situations.

Critical path The path, through a ***PERT network***, with the longest completion time.

Cultural sensitivity Awareness of local and national customs and their importance in effective interpersonal relationships.

Customer departmentalization An ***organization structure*** based on customer needs.

Data base A systematic way of storing files for future retrieval.

Data-base management A program designed to store and retrieve large quantities of data.

Decentralization The extent to which authority has been passed down to lower levels in an organization.

Decision A choice among alternatives.

Decision-making leave A paid one-day suspension to help an employee think through a disciplinary problem.

Decision-making software Any computer program that helps the decision maker work through the problem-solving and decision-making steps.

Decision sciences The field of study dealing with quantified ***planning and decision making.*** A synonym for both ***management science*** and ***operations research.***

Decision support system (DSS) A ***management information system (MIS)*** that does an effective job of providing backup information for making sound decisions. More generally, a synonym for ***MIS.***

Decision tree A graphic illustration of the alternative solutions available to solve a problem, with estimates of the probable outcomes of these alternatives.

Decoding The step in communication that involves the receiver interpreting the message and translating it into meaningful information.

Defensive communication The tendency to receive messages in such a way that our self-esteem is protected.

Delegatee The person receiving the delegated task.

Delegation The assignment to another person of the formal authority and responsibility for accomplishing a specific task.

Democratic leader A ***participative leader*** who confers final authority to the group. The group makes the final decision.

Denial The suppression of information one finds to be uncomfortable. Denial can also be considered a defense mechanism for blocking out uncomfortable thoughts.

Departmentalization The process of dividing work into departments.

Development Form of personal improvement generally consisting of enhancing knowledge and skills of a complex and unstructured nature.

Deviation In a control system, the size of the discrepancy between standards and actual results.

Diagnostic skill The skill involved in investigating a problem situation and then deciding on and implementing a remedial course of action.

Diagonal communication The transmission of messages to higher or lower organizational levels in different departments.

Difficulty level of language The ease of comprehension of spoken or written messages.

Direct environmental force An external force that has a direct effect on the organization's goals, strategies, and tasks.

Discipline Punishment used to correct, train, or control employees.

Dissatisfier A job element that is noticed primarily by its absence. When not present, it creates dissatisfaction, but when present, it does not create satisfaction. Same as *hygiene factor.*

Downsizing Reducing the size of an organization by laying off workers in order to decrease costs.

Downward communication The flow of messages from one level to a lower level in an organization.

Due process In relation to employee rights, giving a worker a fair hearing before he or she is terminated or receives another type of disciplinary action.

Duties The tasks assigned to an employee by his or her superior.

Eclectic viewpoint The attitude that useful information should be taken from a variety of perspectives, depending on what information is needed. For example, a manager

Eclectic viewpoint (continued) with an *eclectic viewpoint* would use information from several schools of thought.

Economic forecasting The process of making predictions about economic events such as prices and inflation rates.

Economic order quantity (EOQ) The inventory level that minimizes both ordering costs and carrying costs.

Ego permissiveness The ability to let go mentally that is characteristic of creative people. The process involves relaxing the rules of logic.

Eighty/twenty (80/20) principle The principle stating that 80 percent of the results in most fields are derived from 20 percent of the activity.

Electronic mail A method of transmitting, storing, and receiving messages by computer.

Empathy The ability to see things as seen by the other person.

Employee assistance program (EAP) An organizational unit designed to help employees deal with personal problems that affect their job performance and *morale.*

Employee benefit Any noncash benefit given to employees as a compensation for their work.

Employee-involvement program Formal programs in which employees contribute to decision making. *Quality of work life (QWL)* programs are a representative example.

Employee orientation program Formal activity designed to acquaint new employees with the organization.

Encoding The process of organizing ideas into a series of *symbols,* such as words and hand gestures, designed to communicate with the receiver.

Entrepreneur An individual who establishes and manages a business in an innovative manner.

Entrepreneurial leadership A style of leadership characterized by *charisma* and a high task orientation.

Environmental determinism A belief that stems from the law of effect, contending that our environment determines our behavior. Specifically, our past history of reinforcement is responsible for making us what we are today.

Equipment departmentalization A form of *organization structure* based on specialized equipment existing in those departments. For example, one unit of the organization might be the "stamping-machine department."

Ergonomics The discipline that adapts machines to human needs and capabilities. Same as *human engineering.*

Esteem needs Psychological needs that reflect people's desire to be seen by themselves and others as a person of worth.

Ethics The study of moral obligation or separating right from wrong.

Exception principle An approach to control in which corrective action is taken only on significant deviations from standard.

Exchange A method of influencing others by offering to reciprocate if they meet one's demands.

Executive Managers at the top one or two levels in an *organization* who are empowered to make the major decisions affecting the present and future of the firm.

Expectancy In expectancy theory, the probability assigned by the individual that effort will lead to performing the task correctly.

Expectancy theory Explanation of motivation centering around the idea that people will expend effort if they expect the effort to lead to performance and the performance to lead to a reward.

Expected time An estimate of the time necessary to complete each activity in the *PERT network* method. The expected time takes into account estimates of the *optimistic, pessimistic,* and *most probable times* to complete the activity.

Expected value The average value one would incur if a particular decision were made a large number of times.

Expert power The ability to control others based on the leader's knowledge as perceived by subordinates.

External control strategy An approach to control that assumes employees are motivated primarily by external rewards and need to be controlled by their managers.

External reward A reward received from outside the person, such as money or praise.

Extinction The process of weakening or decreasing the frequency of undesirable behavior by removing the reward for such behavior.

Event (in a PERT network) A point of decision in, or accomplishment of, a task. Breaking ground in a construction project would be an event.

Expert system A computer program that can "reason" and manipulate data in a manner similar to humans.

Family leave A leave of absence from work to meet responsibilities at home.

Feedback Information given to people telling them how well they are doing. Also, the sending of a message by the receiver back to the sender.

Filtering The coloring or altering of information to make it more acceptable to the receiver.

Financial resources The money the manager and the organization use to pay for the steps necessary to reach organizational goals.

First-level manager Managers who supervise *operative* employees. Also referred to as *supervisors* or *first-line managers.*

Fixed budget A budget for expenditures based on a one-time allocation of resources. The budget does not change as circumstances change during its time period.

Flaming Rudeness, profanity, and emotional outbursts engaged in by people when they carry on conversations by electronic mail.

Flat organization structure A form of *organization* with relatively few layers.

Flexible benefit package A benefit plan that allows employees to select a group of benefits tailored to their preferences.

Flexible budget A budget allowing for variation in the use of resources based on activity.

Flexible working hours A method of organizing working hours so that employees can choose their own hours to some extent.

Formal communication channel The official pathway for sending information inside and outside the organization.

Free-rein leader A leader who turns over virtually all authority and control to the group.

Frontloaded writing A process of placing key ideas at the beginning of a memo, paragraph, or sentence.

Functional authority Right to act, within an area of expertise or knowledge, in guiding employees outside of one's chain of command. For example, the vice president of marketing can give advice to marketing personnel anywhere in the organization.

Functional departmentalization A form of *organization* based on the function performed by each department.

Functional manager A manager who supervises the work of employees engaged in specialized activities, such as *quality control* or engineering.

Functional specialization The same idea as *task specialization* (a job design that gives employees a narrow range of tasks to perform).

Gainsharing A formal program of allowing employees to participate financially in the productivity gains they have achieved.

Gantt chart A chart for the scheduling of activities, depicting the planned and actual progress of work during the life of the project.

General manager A manager responsible for the work activities of several different groups that perform a variety of functions.

Global sourcing The international division of labor in its most basic sense.

Goal What the person or the organization is trying to accomplish or consciously intends to do. Goals are often considered to be high-level objectives.

Grapevine The informal means by which information is transmitted in the organization.

Gross profit margin A measure of financial performance expressed as sales, minus the cost of goods sold, divided by sales.

Group decision A decision reached by the manager after obtaining input from several members of the group.

Groupthink An extreme form of *consensus* in which the members lose their ability to evaluate ideas critically.

Hawthorne effect A phenomenon whereby employees react positively to a program if they think it means that management cares about them.

Horizontal communication The transmission of messages between and among people at the same organizational level.

Horizontal decentralization The shift of authority from *line managers* to *staff managers* and various specialists.

Hostile organizational culture An organizational atmosphere in which people tend to be defensive, suspicious, angry, and distrustful of each other.

Human-resource planning Anticipating and providing for the movement of people into, within, and out of the organization.

Human resources The employees that are needed to get the job done.

Human skill In reference to a manager, the ability to work effectively as a team member and to build cooperative effort within the unit.

Hygiene factor See *dissatisfier*.

Ideation The organization of one's thoughts in order to send a message.

Improvement goal A goal that, if attained, will correct an unacceptable deviation from standard performance.

Indirect environmental force An external force that has an indirect effect on the organization's goals, strategies, and tasks.

Individual contributor Any employee who is not a manager, including the *operatives*, the *specialist*, and the professional.

Ineffective job performance Job performance that lowers productivity below a standard acceptable at a given time.

Informal communication channel The unofficial network of communications used to supplement the formal pathways.

Informal group A group that arises out of individual needs and the attraction of workers to one another.

Informal organizational structure The pattern of working relationships used to supplement and complement the formal structure.

Information overload See communication overload.

Information resources The forms of information the manager and organization use to get the job done.

Informational skills The ability to send, process, and receive information.

Ingratiation Exerting influence by getting somebody else to like you, often through the use of political skill.

In-process inspection A method of *quality control* in which products are checked during production.

Insight See intuition.

Instrumentality In expectancy theory, the probability assigned by the individual that performance will lead to certain outcomes or rewards.

Intermittent (reward) schedule Administering rewards often, but not always, when the appropriate behavior occurs.

Internal control strategy An approach to control that assumes employees can be motivated by building their commitment to organizational goals.

Internal reward A reward stemming from inside the person, such as a sense of satisfaction for having done something right.

Intrapreneur A company employee who engages in *entrepreneurial* thinking and behavior for the good of the firm.

Intuition A direct perception of truth or fact that seems unrelated to any specific reasoning process. Same as *insight.*

Japanese style of management An approach to management widely used by Japanese firms. It emphasizes the importance of *human resources, consensus decision making,* and loyalty to the work group and firm.

Job analysis A method of analyzing the components and human demands of a job.

Job burnout A pattern of emotional, physical, and mental exhaustion in response to chronic job stressors.

Job description A written statement outlining the key features of the job along with the activities required to perform the job effectively.

Job design Laying out job responsibilities and duties and describing how they are to be performed.

Job enrichment Making jobs more challenging and responsible so they will be more appealing to employees.

Job evaluation A systematic method of measuring the financial worth of a job.

Job specification A statement of the personal characteristics needed to perform the job.

Job stress A condition in which job-related factors prompt the worker to change his or her physiological state so that the worker is forced to deviate from normal functioning.

Judgmental forecast A prediction based on a collection of subjective opinions.

Just in time (JIT) The procedure whereby inventory is minimized and moved into the plant exactly when needed. *See also kanban.*

Kanbans The cards used in *just-in-time (JIT)* inventory in order to communicate production requirements from the final point of assembly to the preceding operation that manufactures the components of the final

Kanbans (continued)
product. Also, a synonym for *just in time (JIT)*.

Labor agreement A written contract between management and the union specifying a wide range of work issues.

Law of effect A principle asserting that behavior that the *behavior* leading to positive consequences tends to be repeated and leading to negative consequences tends not to be repeated.

Leading by example The leader influences group members by serving as a positive model of desirable behavior.

Leadership The process of influencing people to achieve certain objectives without using unduly coercive tactics.

Leadership style The typical pattern of behavior engaged in by a leader in dealing with subordinates.

Leading The *management function* of influencing others to achieve organizational objectives.

Lean and mean A restructured organization in which all the excess, or corporate "fat," has been removed. *See also restructuring.*

Learning A relatively permanent change in behavior based on experience.

Legitimate power The authentic right of the leader to make certain types of requests of subordinates. It is power granted by the organization.

Line manager Managers who are responsible for people involved with the primary purpose (output) of the firm.

Linear regression A quantitative method of predicting the effects of changes in one variable on another.

Lot The total number of units from which samples are drawn in *quality control.* More generally, the total number of units under consideration.

Machine bureaucracy An *organizational structure* fine-tuned to run as an integrated, regulated machine.

Management The process of using organizational resources to achieve organizational goals through the functions of *planning, organizing, leading,* and *controlling.*

Management by objectives (MBO) A system of management in which people are held accountable for reaching objectives that they usually set jointly with their superiors. Objectives set at lower levels in the organization contribute to the attainment of goals set at the top of the *organization.*

Management function A process, or series of actions, carried out by a manager to attain organizational objectives. Leading is an example of a management function. Same as *managerial function.*

Management information system (MIS) A formal system for providing management with information useful or necessary for making decisions.

Management science The field of study dealing with quantified approaches to *planning and decision making.*

Management-science school The school of management thought that concentrates on providing management with a scientific basis for solving problems and making decisions.

Manager A person who is responsible for the work performance of one or more other persons and who can commit organizational resources to get the job done.

Managerial grid Approach to analyzing leadership styles based on different combinations of the leader's concern for production and people. Also a comprehensive program of leadership training and organizational improvement.

Managerial role The expected set of activities or behavior stemming from the job of a manager.

Maslow's need hierarchy The theory of *motivation* contending that people have an internal need pushing them toward *self-actualization.* Before higher-level needs are activated, certain lower-level needs must be satisfied. Human needs are arranged into a five-step ladder, or *hierarchy of importance.*

Maslow's need hierarchy *(continued)*
From low to high level, these are ***physiological, safety, belongingness, esteem,*** and ***self-actualization needs.***

Matrix organization A form of ***organization*** consisting of a project structure imposed on top of a functional structure.

Mentor A superior who takes a personal interest in certain subordinates and guides, teaches, and coaches them. An emotional tie usually develops between the ***mentor*** and the learner. *See also* ***protege.***

Middle-level manager All managers who are neither ***executives*** nor ***first-level managers.***

Milestone chart A chart or graph used to monitor progress on a project. It provides a listing of subactivities that must be completed in order to accomplish the major activities listed on the vertical axis.

Mission The general field in which the firm operates. Also, a long-term view of the purpose of the ***organization.***

Mission statement A brief description of the general field in which the organization will operate.

Morale An employee's general satisfaction with and feeling of well being about, not only his or her job, but also the organization.

Moral laxity A slippage in moral behavior because other issues seem more important at the time.

Motivation An internal state that leads to the pursuit of objectives. Also, an activity carried on by managers to get people to pursue objectives.

Motivator A job element that gives people a chance to satisfy higher-level needs. If the ***motivator*** is present, it leads to job motivation.

Multinational corporation A firm that has units in two or more countries.

Need theory (of work motivation) The explanation of work motivation contending that people work to satisfy needs.

Negative reinforcement The process of rewarding people by taking away an uncomfortable consequence or punishment.

Network model A method of depicting all the interrelated events that must take place in order to complete a project.

Networking Establishing a large number of personal contacts who can help you in such ways as recommending you for a job, purchasing goods or services from you, or giving you advice.

Nominal group technique (NGT) A group decision-making technique that follows a highly structured format. Group members react to each others' suggestions individually and without interacting.

Nonprogrammed decision Nonroutine decision that requires careful thought or creativity. *See also* ***programmed decision.***

Nonverbal communication The transmission of messages by means other than language or symbols.

Objective A specific end state or condition that contributes to a larger goal. An ***objective*** can thus be considered to be a subgoal.

Obligation The assumption of responsibility by the subordinate to perform the assigned duty.

On-line management information system (MIS) A system of supplying management with information at the time it is generated.

Open-ended question A question requesting that the person provide details rather than responding "Yes," "No," "Agree," or "Disagree."

Operating plan *See operational plan.*

Operational plan A plan that relates to running an organization on a day-to-day, short-term basis. On occasion, however, ***operational plans*** can be intermediate or long range. Same as ***operating plan.***

Operations research The field of study dealing with quantified ***planning and decision making.***

Operative A bottom-ranking employee who reports to a *first-level manager.* *Operatives* perform the basic work of the *organization* but are not involved in planning or managing the work.

Optimum decision A decision leading to a favorable outcome for the organization or individual.

Organization A group of two or more people working together in an agreed fashion to attain goals.

Organization chart A diagram of the *organization,* usually laid out with rectangles representing organizational units and arrows showing the lines of authority.

Organization structure A framework of tasks and authority relationships among different units of the firm.

Organizational culture The shared values and beliefs of people in an *organization.*

Organizational politics An influence process for gaining advantage using tactics and strategies in addition to merit.

Organizational social performance The extent to which an *organization* responds to the demands of its *stakeholders* for behaving in a socially reponsible manner.

Organizational strategy The comprehensive program chosen by the *organization* for achieving its goals and objectives and thus achieving its *mission.*

Organizing The process of dividing work into manageable sections and coordinating the results to serve a purpose. Or, more simply, the process of making sure the necessary physical and human resources are available to carry out the plan.

Outplacement A method of helping terminated employees find new employment through the use of professional career counseling.

$P = (M \times A)$ Performance equals Motivation times Ability.

Participative leader A leader who shares decision making with the group. Both

Participative leader (continued) democratic **leaders** and *consultative* **leaders** are *participative leaders.*

Path-goal theory of leadership Contends that an effective *leader* clarifies paths to goal attainment, helps subordinates progress along these paths, and removes barriers to goal attainment.

Payoff matrix A technique for indicating possible payoffs, or returns, for pursuing different alternative solutions to a problem.

People-oriented style of leadership A management style that places more emphasis on working with people than on the tasks those people perform.

Performance The quality and quantity of work produced.

Performance appraisal A formal system for measuring, evaluating, and reviewing performance.

Personal power Power stemming from the individual's characteristics and behaviors.

PERT network The *program evaluation and review technique* network. A model designed for the planning activities required to complete a large-scale, nonrepetitive project.

Physical resources All the organization's tangible goods and real estate, including raw materials, office space, production facilities, office equipment, and vehicles.

Physiological needs Bodily needs such as the requirements for nutrition, water, shelter, moderate temperatures, rest, and sleep.

Placement Assigning the newly hired employee to the right job.

Planning The process of establishing goals and objectives and figuring out how to achieve them.

Planning and decision making The same as *planning*, except that the importance of decision making is highlighted.

Policy General guidelines to follow in making decisions and taking action.

Polygraph An instrument that records a person's blood pressure, heartbeat, breathing rate, and galvanic skin response. *Polygraphs*

Polygraph (continued)
are often used in honesty testing. Also called a *lie detector*.

Position objective A job candidate's statement concerning the type of work he or she is seeking. Also called a *job objective*.

Position power Formal authority to get people to do things or to control resources.

Positive discipline An approach to improving substandard behavior that emphasizes coaching, individual responsibility, and mature problem-solving methods.

Positive reinforcement In *behavior modification,* rewarding people for making the right response.

Postcontrol A device for evaluating and taking corrective action for an activity after it has been performed.

Power The ability to get others to do things or to control resources.

Power need The desire to control others or get them to do things on your behalf.

Precontrol A device for evaluating and taking corrective action for an activity before it is performed.

Problem A discrepancy between ideal and actual conditions.

Procedure A customary method for handling an activity, such as a procedure for cashing checks.

Process departmentalization The structuring of an *organization* based on technical activities carried out by the organizational unit.

Product departmentalization A form of *organization* based on the products or services provided by each department. An example is the baby food division of a food company.

Product manager The person responsible for seeing that his or her product gets the attention it needs from company personnel in order for the product to prosper.

Production work teams Groups of individuals who work somewhat independently to perform a large task, with each team member being a generalist rather than a *specialist*.

Productivity The amount of useful work accomplished in relation to the amount of resources consumed.

Program evaluation and review technique See *PERT network*.

Programmed decision A recurring or routine decision.

Progressive discipline The step-by-step application of *corrective discipline*.

Progressive relaxation A tension-reduction method in which one muscle group after another is induced to relax.

Project organization A temporary group of specialists working under one manager to accomplish a fixed objective.

Protégé Individual selected by *mentor* for guidance, teaching, and coaching. Also, one whose *career* is enhanced by an influential person.

Punishment The presentation of an undesirable consequence for a specific behavior. *Punishment* can also involve removing something desirable as a consequence of behavior.

Qualitative control technique A method of controlling performance based on human judgments about performance.

Quality The extent to which a product or service conforms to requirements.

Quality assurance The prevention of quality problems through the use of various approaches.

Quality circle (QC) A small group of employees who perform similar work and who meet periodically to discuss production, quality, and related problems.

Quality control Any method of determining the extent to which goods or services match some specified quality standard.

Quality of work life (QWL) The extent to which work is meaningful and contributes to one's self-fulfillment.

Quantitative control technique A method of controlling performance based on numerical measures of performance.

Rationality The influence tactic of appealing to reason and logic.

Realistic job preview A frank discussion held with a job candidate about the positive features and potential problems in a job.

Receiver In the communication process, the person who interprets the message.

Recentralization The process of moving *decentralization* back toward *centralization.*

Recovery rate The percent of employees who return to satisfactory performance after treatment for a problem that interfered with their work.

Recruitment The process of attracting job candidates with the right characteristics and skills to fill job openings.

Red-hot-stove rule A rule stating that employee discipline should parallel what would happen if an employee touched a very hot stove. There should be a warning, and the punishment should be immediate, consistent, and impersonal.

Reference check An inquiry to a second party about a job candidate's suitability for employment.

Referent power See charisma.

Relaxation response A tension-reduction technique in which a person learns to relax by sitting quietly and repeating a word such as *one* with every breath.

Reliability The dependability aspect of the quality of a product or service.

Restructuring The slimming down of operations in order to focus resources and boost profits or decrease expenses. *See also lean and mean.*

Results What people actually accomplish, or the objectives they attain.

Revenue-and-expense budget A document that describes plans and revenues for operating expenses in dollar amounts.

Reward Something of value received as a consequence of having attained a *goal.*

Reward power Power stemming from the leader's control over *rewards* of value to the subordinate.

Right-to-know law A law that requires the manufacturers, sellers, and users of hazardous chemicals and drugs to inform their employees and the public of the nature of their products and the dangers involved.

Robot A reprogrammable, multifunctional manipulator.

Robust quality A condition in which engineers build quality into the design of a part or process so that it can withstand fluctuations on the production line without a loss of quality. Same as *robust design.*

Role An expected set of activities or behaviors stemming from one's job.

Role clarity Knowledge about what performance is required of the employee.

Rule A specific course of action or conduct that must be followed. It is the simplest type of plan.

Safety needs Those needs reflecting the desire for physical safety as well as being safe from physical and emotional injury.

Sales forecast A prediction of sales that is usually the primary planning document for business enterprises.

Satisficing decision A decision that meets a minimum standard of satisfaction.

Satisfier A job element that leads to job satisfaction because it allows for the satisfaction of higher-level needs.

Scientific management The school of management that emphasizes the use of scientific procedures to discover the most efficient way to accomplish a job.

Self-actualization needs Those needs reflecting the desire to reach one's potential, including the needs for self-fulfillment and personal development.

Semantics The study of meaning in language forms.

Sender The person who initiates the message in communication.

Sensitivity to people Taking into account the needs and feelings of people when dealing with them.

Small-business owner An individual who establishes and manages a business for the principal purpose of furthering personal goals.

Social audit A systematic measure of an organization's social impact.

Social maturity The ability to handle oneself properly in demanding situations.

Social needs The needs related to attaining love, belonging to a group, and being affiliated with people.

Social responsibility The idea that *organizations* have an obligation to groups in society other than owners or stockholders beyond that prescribed by law or union contract. *See also stockholder viewpoint of social responsibility* and *stockholder viewpoints of social responsibility.*

Span of control The number of subordinates reporting directly to a manager.

Specialist A highly skilled individual contributor who performs narrow tasks.

Sponsor Any high-ranking person in an organization who recommends a lower-ranking individual for promotion or choice assignments.

Spreadsheet analysis A computerized method of analyzing a large grid of values at the same time. A change in one value leads automatically to changes in other related values.

Staff manager A manager responsible for the activity of employees who give advice or provide services to other departments.

Staffing The process of making sure there are the necessary *human resources* to achieve organizational *goals.*

State of nature A circumstance in the environment beyond the control of the decision maker.

Statistical process control A technique for spotting defects at the point they are made rather than after a part or product is completed.

Statistical quality control The process of checking parts or products by using a sampling technique.

Stakeholder viewpoint of social responsibility The perspective that an organization must hold itself responsible for the quality of life for the many groups affected by the actions of the organization.

Stockholder viewpoint of social responsibility The traditional perspective that a business organization is only responsible to its owners and stockholders.

Strategic decision A decision that deals with such matters as the *mission* of the firm and its relationship with the outside world and that covers a long-range time period.

Strategic plan A master plan that shapes the destiny of the firm.

Strategic planning Activities leading to a statement of the goals and objectives of the firm and to the appropriate strategies to achieve those goals and objectives.

Strategy A comprehensive program for achieving an organization's goals and objectives, thus achieving its mission.

Stress The body's internal response to a state of activation.

Stress interview A deliberate method of placing a job applicant under pressure and then observing his or her reaction.

Suboptimum decision A decision that leads to a negative outcome because its consequences are disruptive to employees and firm.

Suggestion programs A formal method of collecting and analyzing *employee suggestions* about processes, policies, products, and services. The suggestions are solicited by the firm.

Summary discipline The immediate discharge of an employee because of a serious offense.

Synergy The action of two or more people achieving an effect that none of the people could achieve individually.

System 4 organization A highly participative, *adhocratic organization.*

Systems approach (to management) A perspective on management, based on the

Systems approach (to management) (continued) concept that the *organization* is a system, or an entity, of interrelated parts.

Taguchi method See Robust design.

Task force A group of people who are called on to solve a problem but who usually do not give up their regular assignments for the life of the project.

Task generalization A job design that gives the employee a wide range of tasks to perform.

Task specialization A job design that gives the employee a narrow range of tasks to perform.

Team approach to job enrichment A method of making jobs more interesting and responsible by organizing workers into small teams that have total responsibility for production of a product or a major component.

Technical skill An understanding of, and proficiency in, a specific activity that involves methods, processes, procedures, or techniques.

Technological forecasting The process of predicting what type of technological change will take place in the future.

Technology The systematic application of scientific or other organized knowledge to practical tasks.

Technostress An adverse reaction to working many hours at a computer terminal.

Telecommuting Performing jobs at home and communicating with the office over a geographical distance. Same as *teleworking.*

Termination The process of discharging an employee because of poor job performance, unacceptable behavior, or interpersonal problems.

Termination at will The doctrine stating that employers are allowed to dismiss employees for good cause, or no cause, without being guilty of legal wrong.

Territorial departmentalization A form of *organization* based on the geographic area served by each department.

Throughput The processing of input in order to convert it to output.

Time, space, material, and production budgets Spending plans that express expenditures in physical rather than monetary terms.

Time-series analysis An analysis of a sequence of observations that have taken place at regular intervals over a period of time.

Top-level managers Executives, or people who give the organization general direction.

Traditional management information system (MIS) An information system based on historical data contained in scheduled reports and word-of-mouth communication.

Trailing spouse The spouse who has to follow the partner relocated by the employer.

Training Any procedure intended to foster and enhance learning among employees.

Transformational leader A person in charge who helps organizations and people make positive changes in the way they do things.

Traits Stable aspects of people, closely related to personality.

Transmission The sending of a message over a *channel.*

Two-factor theory (of work motivation) Herzberg's theory contending that there are two different sets of job elements. One set of elements can satisfy and motivate people *(motivator).* The other set can only prevent dissatisfaction *(dissatisfier,* or *hygiene factor).*

Type E stress An overstressed condition characteristic of women who try to "have and do it all."

Understanding In communication, the condition that exists when a message has been decoded as intended.

Upward communication The transmission of messages from lower to higher levels in an organization.

Valence In expectancy theory, the value, worth, or attractiveness of an outcome.

Validity study A study of how well a prediction device actually predicts what it is supposed to do.

Value The importance a person attaches to something such as money, self-fulfillment, or *quality of work life (QWL).*

Whistle blowing The disclosure of organizational wrongdoing to parties who can take action.

Wrongful discharge The *termination* of an employee for arbitrary or unfair reasons.

Zero defects The absence of any detectable quality flaws in a product or service.

Does this book have zero defects? If not, please bring any flaws to the attention of the publisher or author. We will try to correct any problems in the third edition. Thank you.

NAME INDEX

SUBJECT INDEX